Florence Nightingale Today: Healing Leadership Global Action

Barbara Montgomery Dossey, PhD, RN, HNC, FAAN
Director, Holistic Nursing Consultants, Santa Fe, New Mexico

Louise C. Selanders, EdD, RN
Associate Professor, College of Nursing , Michigan State University, East Lansing, Michigan

Deva-Marie Beck, PhD, RN
International Director, Nightingale Initiative for Global Health, Washington, D.C. & Ottawa, Canada

Alex Attewell, BA, AMA
Director, The Florence Nightingale Museum , London, England

American Nurses Association
Silver Spring, Maryland
2005

To all of our colleagues in nursing
who understand Florence Nightingale's tenets
of healing, leadership, and global action,
their relevance for contemporary nursing,
and the need to realize her future
in our present.

Library of Congress Cataloging-in-Publication data

Florence Nightingale today : healing, leadership, global action /
Barbara Montgomery Dossey ... [et al.].
p. ; cm.
Includes bibliographical references and index.
ISBN 1-55810-220-5
1. Nightingale, Florence, 1820-1910. 2. Nurses—Great Britain—Biography.
3. Nursing—Philosophy.
[DNLM: 1. Nightingale, Florence, 1820-1910. 2. Nursing—Biography.
3. Delivery of Health Care. 4. Nursing—trends. 5. Spirituality. WZ 100 N688F 2005]
I. Dossey, Barbara Montgomery.

RT37.N5F563 2005
610.73'092—dc22 2004020642

The opinions in this book reflect those of the authors and do not necessarily reflect positions or policies of the American Nurses Association. Furthermore, the information in this book should not be construed as legal or professional advice.

Photo Credits, front cover: Leftmost nurse, courtesy of World Health Organization; P. Virot, photograph of Florence Nightingale portrait, courtesy of Florence Nightingale Museum.

Published by nursesbooks.org
The Publishing Program of ANA
American Nurses Association
8515 Georgia Avenue, Suite 400, Silver Spring, MD 20910
1-800-274-4ANA • http://www.nursingworld.org/

ANA is the only full-service professional organization representing the nation's 2.7 million Registered Nurses through its 54 constituent member associations. ANA advances the nursing profession by fostering high standards of nursing practice, promoting the economic and general welfare of nurses in the workplace, projecting a positive and realistic view of nursing, and by lobbying the Congress and regulatory agencies on healthcare issues affecting nurses and the public.

ISBN 1-55810-220-5 04FNT 2M 11/04

Acknowledgments

Our book flows out of the larger questions related to healing, leading, and global action. We celebrate with our colleagues in nursing and others who understand Florence Nightingale's vision for contemporary nursing and global wellness. We honor the work of the numerous Nightingale scholars who have informed our work. We also thank the many transdisciplinary scholars with whom we have discussed Nightingale and related work, and to our numerous friends who have listened to us "think out loud" about Nightingale.

Few books are written in isolation, and we have received the assistance of many individuals, Nightingale scholars, institutions, and from archival documents during the development of book. Many of Florence Nightingale's original copies of her books, publications, and letters were an inspiring source of information. She left more than 14,000 letters that are in archival museums and in public and private collections. Many documents and books were consulted in the preparation of this book, and selected references are at the end of each book chapter.

Several of our fellow scholars assisted us early in the project by their review of the proposal manuscript we submitted to our publisher. Their review comments helped the author–publisher team develop our focus on issues and items large and small. For those insights, we thank: Nightingale scholar Janet Macrae, PhD, RN, and Adjunct Professor, New York University School of Nursing; Elaine Marshall, PhD, RN, Dean and Professor, Brigham Young University; and pioneer nurse-theorist Jean Watson, PhD, RN, HNC, FAAN, Murchuson-Scoville Chair in Caring Science, University of Colorado Health Science Center, School of Nursing, Denver, Colorado, where she is also Distinguished Professor of Nursing, and former dean.

In the preparation of the manuscript, we acknowledge with apprection the careful proofreading by Kathy Kelly and references checking by Jennifer D'Inzeo, both freelancers engaged by nursesbooks.org, our publisher. The lovely look and feel of both the inside and outside of our book we owe to Stacy Maguire, founder and lead designer of Eyedea Advertising and Design Studio. (The fact that Stacy's mother is a working nurse of many years in her native Nebraska motivated her all the more.)

Finally, at nursesbooks.org, ANA's book publishing program, we thank Rosanne O'Connor Roe, Publisher, and Eric Wurzbacher, Editor and Project Manager who truly understood our dream for this book. Writers always expect technical expertise from their editor; when they receive penetrating insight into their subject in addition, they are blessed. Eric, you have been a writer's dream.

We thank The Reverend Canon Ted Karpf, now working with the World Health Organization in its Partnerships Officer, Partnerships/External Relations/Communications Team, Department of HIV/AIDS, HIV/TB/Malaria Cluster, former HIV/AIDS Coordinator of the worldwide Anglican Communion and Provincial Canon for HIV/AIDS in the Anglican Church of the Diocese of Washington, former Canon of Washington National Cathedral, for his support to Barbara M. Dossey and Louise C. Selanders during 1997–2000. This support resulted in the formal proposal and successful re-consideration by the Episcopal Church General Conventions of Florence Nightingale name for inclusion in the Episcopal Church's Liturgical Calendar, which is now included in the *Book of Common Prayer* (2004) and Lesser Feasts and Fasts (2004).

We thank former Dean and Precentor, the Very Reverend Nathan D. Baxter, and the Reverend Canon Peter F. Grandell, Washington National Cathedral, Washington, D.C., for their support of the Inaugural Florence Nightingale Service, August 12, 2001.

We thank the Right Reverend John Chane, Bishop of Washington and Dean, Washington National Cathedral, and Mr. Bill Petersen, Cathedral Worship Department Manager, for their support and guidance with the Florence Nightingale Service on May 9, 2004. This will continue to be a bi-annual service. We also thank Lippincott Williams & Wilkins for the sponsorship of the Florence Nightingale Service Leaflet in 2001 and The Johnson & Johnson Campaign for Nursing's Future in 2004.

Barbara M. Dossey and Deva-Marie Beck wish to thank M. Willson Williams, PhD, their Core Faculty Advisor, Union Institute & University, Cincinnati, Ohio, for her ever-present kindness, enthusiasm, encouragement, and consistent mentoring in their dissertation process and doctoral programs. Barbara acknowledges the support of her doctoral committee members: Roshi Joan Halifax, PhD; JoEllen Koerner, PhD, RN, FAAN; H. Lea Gaydos, PhD, RN, CS, HNC; Margaret A. Jordan, PhD, RN; and Donald A. Klein, PhD. Deva-Marie acknowledges the support of her doctoral committee: Margaret A. Burkhardt, PhD, RN; Sharon G. Mijares, PhD; Margaret A. Jordan PhD, RN; and Marianne L. Matzo, PhD, RN.

Barbara extends a special thanks to celebrate with my holistic nursing colleagues in the American Holistic Nurses' Association and all nurses as we explore new meanings of healing in our work and lives. I thank my colleagues and dear friends, Cathie Guzzetta, PhD, RN, HNC, FAAN; Lynn Keegan, PhD, RN, HNC, FAAN; and Noreen Frisch, PhD, RN, HNC, FAAN, for their continued support and the joy within our collaboration and development of holistic nursing projects for over two decades.

And another special thanks from Barbara to my twin brother, Bo Montgomery, whose research, writing, and editorial assistance helped me shape many of the ideas in my initial research and in my illustrated biography, *Florence Nightingale: Mystic, Visionary, Healer* (Lippincott Williams & Wilkins, 2000). Most of all to my husband, Larry, with whom I continually weave the rich healing tapestry and bond of unity and oneness.

Louise C. Selanders extends her special thanks to those who understand the vitality, vision and wisdom of Florence Nightingale; to the nurses who daily keep the vision alive; to my academic colleagues who encourage and challenge; and most especially to my family — husband, Bill, our daughters and their husbands, Kate and Chris, Aimee and Ben, and my father, Rayl, who endure the long hours and the absences.

Deva-Marie Beck wishes to thank her housemates and friends, Eleanor Kibrick and Bill Rolph, who feel like my sister and brother, and to these special friends who also feel like family: Howard and Kathy Bertram, Beverley Britton, Peggy Burkhardt, Anne and Daryl Carlson, Jim Hawkins, Christina Jackson, Noreen Teoh, and Bernadette Zorio; to my sister, niece and nephew, Christine, Alessandra, and Javier Diaz de Leon; and to my cousin Janet Boettger McGurk. Thanks so much to each of you for understanding me so well and encouraging these endeavors.

Deva-Marie also extends special appreciation to James Beck and Jeremy Wright. Through the decades of discussions and collaborations with the two of you, I have honed the global vision I needed to see Nightingale's fuller legacy and to understand her tenets for the 21st century. I would also like to particularly thank you, Jeremy, for your major contributions to our related efforts at the United Nations Human Settlements Summit in Istanbul.

Much appreciation goes from Deva-Marie to Wayne Kines for the unique love and support you share with me, both personally and professionally. And finally, in appreciative remembrance of Jane Stuart Kines, a 1957 Nursing School graduate, Middlesex Hospital, London, an ardent, effective global citizen whose profound love for Florence directly started me on the journey of my own Nightingale research and authorship.

Alex Attwell extends his special thanks to the Curator, Dr. Sue Laurence, for her comments on an early chapter draft, and to all his curatorial colleagues and volunteers at the Florence Nightingale Museum whose work embodies so much of Florence Nightingale's spirit.

Contents

Chapter 9.
21st Century Citizenship for Health: "May a Better Way Be Opened!"
Deva-Marie Beck

Part Four: Writings

Part Five: Epilogue

Foreword

Caroline Cox

In my teenage days when I first learned about Florence Nightingale, I developed a profound respect for her. She was a role model for my generation in many ways: a person of global vision, deep commitment to fundamental principles, great moral and physical courage, and an ability to make her mark as a woman in a very male-dominated society.

During my days as a student nurse, I grew to appreciate her multifaceted professional contributions. These include her endeavors to transform nursing from a lowly and often discredited occupation to a profession with demanding standards of practice together with a vision of a healing ministry that combines respect for knowledge-based practice with holistic care of patients' spiritual, emotional, and physical needs.

Later, my admiration reached new levels when I visited the famous barracks at Scutari. I was visiting Turkey to work with colleagues developing nursing research. It seemed appropriate to request a visit to the rooms occupied by Florence Nightingale and I came away even more humbled and inspired by the courage and gritty determination of this amazing woman.

The "Golden Horn" and the Bosphorus may conjure up pictures of a beautiful blue sea lapping romantically at the shores of historic cities. The reality on the day of my visit was very different. A freezing wind was driving flurries of snow over rough, swirling water. Florence Nightingale's office on the corner of the building was buffeted by the storm. A little staircase led up to her equally bleak and comfortless bedroom. I was humbled and challenged to imagine the life she must have chosen: leaving the comforts of upper-class England to live in these harsh conditions to try to bring some comfort to countless wounded and dying men, with so little to offer by way of treatment compared with the resources available to us today.

Her care and compassion became legendary. "The Lady with the Lamp" became a symbol of the essence of nursing: the commitment to be with those who are suffering, in their darkest hours, and to minister to each person's spiritual, psychological, and clinical needs.

Nowadays, everybody knows the name Florence Nightingale and her role in the Crimean War. But this was one relatively brief episode in her life. Her professional and political contributions extend much further. Having taken charge of nursing at Scutari, she systematically set about overcoming the obstacles to improved health for her patients. She took on the cut-throat male-dominated world of military and medical politics and succeeded against the odds during a century with very few similar female role models.

The beneficiaries of her dedication included not only the soldiers of the Crimean War, but also the sick in the workhouses and the poverty-stricken slum dwellers in England; the lower caste peoples of India; the aborigines and Maoris whose numbers were declining as the empire advanced; and children in Sri Lanka, Natal, and West Africa.

Long before the advent of modern communications, Florence Nightingale had a truly global vision, combined with the motivation of a strong faith and an understanding of the complex relationships of politics, poverty, and ill health. Together with her fierce determination and indomitable courage, she became a formidable force for good.

My own work in the field of humanitarian aid has taken me to be with many of today's forgotten peoples in forgotten lands, many of whom are trapped behind closed borders, suffering at the hands of brutal regimes. They are often unreached by major aid organizations, and are left to suffer and die, unhelped and unheard. They include the people of Sudan, where well over 2 million have died and over 5 million been displaced by war since the present brutal military regime took power by military coup in 1989. On my last visit, children were dying of whooping cough because local health workers had no medicines; young mothers sat and wept as their infants died on their breasts, empty of milk as the mothers were themselves starving. Twice this year, I have visited the ethnic national groups suffering at the hands of another brutal regime in Burma. Peoples such as the Karen, Karenni, Shan, Chin, and Kachin are being subjected to ethnic cleansing or cultural genocide.

On my last visit, I talked to many victims. They included a young mother who had just lost five children to malaria in an area where aid organizations are denied access, and a young man who had been used as a human minesweeper by the regime's soldiers: his leg had been blown off and he had been left to die.

These are just two examples of places in today's world that are, in their own ways, as dark and hopeless as the wards of Scutari. Florence Nightingale's vision and inspiration are still needed as much now as they were in her own times.

Also still needed is her vision for the highest possible professional standards of nursing care in particular and health care in general. I therefore hope that her story will be more widely available in the education system, as an inspiration for children and students in this country and abroad.

I also hope that this book will be read by the leaders of our health professions and by policymakers whose decisions can enhance the quality of care for those who are vulnerable and in need. The contributions all shed light on Florence Nightingale's personality and vision. They challenge us to commit ourselves to involvement in campaigning for the causes which she advocated so forcefully nearly a century and a half ago: ensuring the highest possible standards of care for all in need, providing comfort for all who suffer, and bringing light to the darkest places of human misery in our world today.

Baroness (Caroline) Cox of Queensbury is a nurse and social scientist who has won international awards for her humanitarian campaigns. She became a Life Peer in 1982 and has been a deputy speaker of the House of Lords since 1985. She is president of HART (Humanitarian Aid Relief Trust) and a vice president of the Royal College of Nursing.

Preface

As Nightingale scholars, we have brought together our passion and dedication to historical research, and our recent scholarship on Florence Nightingale's legacy and relevance, for contemporary nursing. This book reconnects nurses with the fire and soul and their sense of calling in the nursing profession. Together, nurses can *relight the lamp* and carry Nightingale's tenets—healing, leadership, and global action—to a new generation of nurse healers and to the world.

History is one of the most important aspects of any profession. Contemporary nursing has a proud heritage through its philosophical founder, Florence Nightingale (1820–1910). She was a mystic, visionary, healer, reformer, activist, transdisciplinarian, environmentalist, feminist, practitioner, scientist, and politician. Nightingale's achievements and her contributions to nursing theory, research, statistics, public health, and healthcare reform are foundational and inspirational. As a bold and brave risk-taker, Nightingale possessed uncommon vision, dedication, and commitment. She referred to her work as her *must,* one that involved the personal, political, social, and scientific domains. Although Nightingale's work, letters, and books date to a century ago, today they are the roots of healing, leadership, and global action. They stimulate us to carry on her mission in shaping healthcare reform and enhancing our own personal and professional journeys.

This is a chaotic period for health care worldwide. Healthcare organizations are now attempting to reinvent themselves and to bring caring and healing into these environments. This restructuring and redesign has a direct impact on local, national, and international health issues. The world is in search of visionary leaders to assist with a new healthcare agenda, in order to bring peace and healing to the planet. Florence Nightingale's message can help us get there.

Nightingale's enduring legacy is socially relevant because the profession of nursing shows signs of losing its soul; it is in crisis. Two major causes of the problem are the current state of managed care and the nursing shortage. Another reason that this book is socially relevant is the continued appearance of trivialized and fictionalized accounts of Nightingale's life and work. Many authors have given and continue to give superficial interpretations, or have actually tried to discredit Nightingale's life and work.

Certainly, Nightingale can be criticized. She pushed hard—as a woman in 19th-century England, she had to push hard in order to get things done. This meant that she sometimes offended those in power and made enemies. As a practical mystic she was driven by social action and the inward tug to serve God and humanity. Her complementary conflicts as a genius with a vast vision, her reclusiveness and declaring herself an invalid at the age of 37, and her brusque style continue to irritate some people to this very day. Moreover, Nightingale was not perfect; she freely admitted that she made mistakes and recorded these in her diaries and letters; she was troubled that she did not completely attain all of her goals. And surely her repeated failure to take care of herself (as she admonished her students to do) must have chafed at her as well. Also, in her day as in ours, some people were irritated by her transcendent spiritual vision that went beyond specific religions to honor all the great traditions. The fact is, spiritually advanced people can indeed be hard to take. When we are around them, we may feel inadequate, as if we don't measure up. As the old saying goes, no priest wants a saint in his parish.

Once she is considered in a complete and balanced manner as befits scholars, however, Florence Nightingale can be clearly seen to be one of us as surely as she was extraordinary. And surely our own extraordinary aspects and achievements, large or small, do not need to remove us from our time and our kind.

Barbara Montgomery Dossey
Louise C. Selanders
Deva-Marie Beck
Alex Attewell

The Flame of Florence Nightingale's Legacy

Deva-Marie Beck

Today, our world needs healing and to be rekindled with Love.

Once, Florence Nightingale lit her beacon of lamplight to
comfort the wounded

And her Light has blazed a path of service across a century to us,

Through her example and through the countless nurses and
healers who have followed in her footsteps.

Today, we celebrate the flame of Florence Nightingale's legacy.

Let that same Light be rekindled to burn brightly in our hearts.

Let us take up our own lanterns of caring, each in our own ways.

To more brightly walk our own paths of service to the world.

To more clearly share our own noble purpose with each other.

May human caring become the lantern for the twenty-first century.

May we better learn to care for ourselves, for each other,
and for all creation.

Through our caring, may we be the keepers of that flame.

That our spirits may burn brightly

To kindle the hearts of our children and great-grandchildren

As they, too, follow in these footsteps.

Pentimento

Painter's term for the evidence in a work that the original composition has been changed. Often the opaque pigment with which the artist covered a mistake or unwanted beginnings will, with time or injudicious cleaning, become transparent, and a revelation of original intentions will become visible through the finished composition. A celebrated example is Caravaggio's *Lute Player* (Metropolitan Museum of Art) in which X-ray photography was used to uncover evidence of the painter's original intention.

from *Columbia Encyclopedia, Sixth Edition*, 2004.
http://www.encyclopedia.com/html/p1/pentimen.asp

Old paint on canvas, as it ages, sometimes becomes transparent. When that happens, it is possible, in some pictures, to see the original lines: a tree will show through a woman's dress, a child makes way for a dog, a large boat is no longer on an open sea. That is called pentimento because the painter "repented," changed his mind. Perhaps it would be as well to say that old conception, replaced by later choice, is a way of seeing and then seeing again. That is all I mean about the people in this book (in our case-exhibition). The paint has aged and I wanted to see what was there for me once, what is there for me now.

Lillian Hellman, in the preface to her
Pentimento: A Book of Portraits (1973)

Introduction

Barbara M. Dossey

Florence Nightingale (1820–1910) was one of the most important women of the 19th century. Nightingale was a giant in her time who achieved greatness against immense odds. She ranks among the most brilliant reformers in history for her pioneering contributions to the sanitary, medical, and nursing work of her time. Nightingale's sheer intellect and genius is why she is recognized as one of the most astonishing analytical minds of the 19th century. Her power of analysis and her amazing memory were remarked upon again and again by her contemporaries. Perhaps the most comprehensive view of her intellectual powers comes from Sir Edward Cook, her first biographer: "A man of affairs, who in the course of a long and varied life had come in contact with many of the greatest intellects and administrators of the time, said of Miss Nightingale that hers was the clearest brain he had ever known in man or woman" (Cook, 1913, Vol. 1, p. xix).

Florence Nightingale's messages, as uncovered in this book, provide a foundation on which nurses' beliefs and human potential can be enhanced in order to engage in the depth of the art and science of nursing. Nightingale's messages, as uncovered in this book, are at the core of healing, leadership, and global action, and are the foundation and roots for contemporary nursing.

Pentimentos: The Levels of Story in Our Work and Lives

Another aspect of this book is that it is about Nightingale's story, which is in turn a part of our story, the nurses' story. Denzin (1989) states: "Representing lives is like a pentimento, which is something painted out of a picture which later becomes visible again. When the paint is scraped off an old picture, something new becomes visible. What is new is what was previously covered up" (p. 81). In contrast to the often stereotypical, superficial, and surficial interpretation that is sometimes given to her work, by studying her major works, Nightingale's pentimentos—her underlying stories—become revealed. While this central concept (as well as a central methodology that is described in the next paragraph) has inspired and guided the creation of this book, it has also led to a series of pentimentos in the form of illustrated essays that appear at the end of each chapter.

To better achieve insights beneath the usual biographical surfaces, we have employed the form of scholarship known as *interpretive biography* in this book (see Appendix B for more details on this approach). It challenges the traditional approaches by, in effect, asking the biographer to recognize how studies are both read and written. The researcher studies collected documents and narratives—for instance, Nightingale's 13 formal letters to her nurses—to trace evidence of the personal experiences or self-stories contained within these documents. In these formal letters Nightingale not only told stories, but she also placed stories upon stories and stories within stories. She also wrote her own self-narrative as well as the external narrative to others.

Nightingale's life stories—her pentimentos—are the history and legacy for contemporary nursing (see the Pentimento in each chapter). Our challenge is to once again uncover and study her original messages and documents, and to find new vision in our work and lives. Trying to understand the roots of the art and science of nursing without a sense of history is like planting cut flowers and expecting them to grow. Nightingale used this analogy of roots in her 1878 letter to her nurses (called probationers) when she asked them to delve deeply into the philosophy and ethic of caring for and healing of self:

> There is a great temptation in a community of Probationers to be in a hurry [God is never in a hurry:] to scratch the ground & not dig deep: to do surface-work: like sticking in cut flowers, instead of sowing flowers & fruit too from the seed or root. Strike your roots deep, rather than spread your branches too far. (Nightingale, 1878, p. 12)

Her life stories, and the messages contained within the primary documents that are discussed in this book, along with other supporting primary and secondary sources, move out from her and inward to nurses and others. From this, we—authors and readers alike—can explore new meaning, structure, and richness that have significant implications and relevance for today.

About This Book

The book is divided into four parts. The first three parts are Nightingale's Tenets—Healing, Leadership, and Global Action. Each chapter concludes with a section Directions for Future Research, and Reflections on Florence Nightingale's Tenets, related to the specific book part on healing, leadership, and global action. One or more related topics can be found at the end of each chapter, in a Pentimento related to Nightingale's life, with photographs and tables on specific topics. These topics include an overview of Florence Nightingale's life; her work as a practical mystic; her writing on the medieval mystics; her personality type; her Crimean Fever and chronic illness; her thoughts on dirt and germs and her connections with leading sanitarians, physicians, and statisticians; her work as a passionate statistician; her health determinant lens; her global lens, and contemporary international health charters and a new global health language for nurses; the 1893 World's Columbian Exposition and her 1893 essay "Sick-Nursing and Health-Nursing"; nursing's lens to create better health-sustaining conditions; tributes to Nightingale's legacy; and remembrance of nursing's broad scopes of practice from micro to macro.

Part One, *Healing*, focuses on Florence Nightingale as healer and her impact on healing. Chapter 1 provides an overview of Nightingale's tenets and contains three areas: healing, leadership, and global action. Chapter 2 contains the synthesis of Florence Nightingale's 13 formal letters to her nurses (1872–1900). This synthesis gives us new insight into Nightingale's views of healing, her spirituality, her influences on nursing theory, the four fundamental patterns of knowing in nursing, and the timeless immediacy of a timeless tradition.

Part Two, *Leadership,* explores Nightingale's life as a leader in nursing and health care. Chapter 3 expands our understanding of Nightingale as the philosophical founder of contemporary nursing and the first nurse theorist. Chapter 4 discusses social change and Nightingale's leadership, the leadership paradigm, and the dynamic forces for nursing. Chapter 5 explores Nightingale's work as the first nurse theorist, and her theory of environmental adaptation. Chapter 6 discusses Nightingale as the reclusive campaigner, and her relevance and legacy for contemporary nursing.

Part Three, *Global Action*, is an in-depth discussion of Nightingale's far-reaching vision that can empower nurses and others today and beyond. Chapter 7 explores standing at the millennium crossroads and reigniting the flame of Nightingale's legacy. Chapter 8 is an analysis of her famous 1893 essay, "Sick-Nursing and Health-Nursing." Chapter 9 shows Nightingale's life as a visionary and calls for 21st-century citizenship for health and for a better way to be open for global health and wellness.

Part Four, *Writings and Resources*, contains the entire, unedited collection of letters (1872–1900). It also contains the entire, unedited 1893 essay, "Sick-Nursing and Health-Nursing."

To bring Florence Nightingale into a contemporary context, the book finishes with an epilogue that is a contemporary travelog, "Pilgrimage to Scutari." Nightingale's world-famous work during the Crimean War (1854–1856) began at the Selimiye Barracks, also known as the Barrack Hospital, in Scutari, Turkey. Today, the Barrack Hospital is the Turkish First Army headquarters located in the large suburb of Üsküdar, part of greater Istanbul, on the Asian shore. Through the travelog and the archival and contemporary photographs, the reader is actually able to tour the great halls of the Barrack Hospital and the rooms where Nightingale lived and worked, to explore the Topkapi Palace and the Grand Bazaar where Nightingale sent her assistants for needed supplies for the soldiers, and to tour the nearby Haydarpasa Cemetery where Nightingale requested Queen Victoria's permission to erect a grand obelisk to honor the buried soldiers of the Crimean War.

Today, nurses are challenged to rediscover the essence of our profession. Nightingale's 13 formal letters to her nurses (1872–1900) and her great 1893 essay, "Sick-Nursing and Health-Nursing," are very relevant to the new interest in her profound philosophy, message, and legacy. Thus, we have included them in this book. These works provide the basis of the tenets of healing, leadership, and global action; they show us the steps that we can take as 21st-century citizens to create health for society.

Her Future, Our Present

As we reinterpret Nightingale's legacy, we find that her future is our present. Her integral thought and philosophy are seen today in the art and science of holistic nursing practice, education, and research, and in integrative practice and transdisciplinary dialogues. Her sense of the integration of the art and science in nursing is seen today as nurses engage in evidence-based practice, and as we honor the feminine and spirituality in healing.

Nightingale anticipated the complexity of today's world and recognized that it would take years to evolve an integral way of knowing, doing, and being in the world, a way that calls for a fundamental shift in our consciousness. We are the nurse leaders that she envisioned. We are deepening our understanding of the nurse as an instrument of healing. We are creating total healing environments and sacred spaces in our hospitals, clinics, and schools and in our public buildings, community parks, and town squares. Her legacy resonates today as forcefully as during her lifetime, and it can guide us as we work toward the integration of a healthy world by 2020, where cultural diversity, tolerance, and respect for self and others exist. (See Appendix C for some details on one formal initiative—the Nightingale Initiative for Global Health—under way toward this end.)

Nightingale's story and wisdom reside within each of us and can guide us. Her example is a source of power from the past, through which we can find the vision and strength to assert ourselves at this very challenging moment in history.

Florence Nightingale's Tenets: Healing, Leadership, Global Action

Barbara M. Dossey

Simply put, a tenet is any basic principle, doctrine, or belief that is held as true, generally by a group or profession. Throughout her life and work, Florence Nightingale documented and demonstrated that her major tenet was healing: it is this tenet that ultimately unites nurses and other caregivers and workers in what we now call "health care." To achieve healing at the deepest level, two concomitant tenets—leadership and global action—were in her view essential in order to achieve healthy people and a healthy world. Individuals and their total surroundings were an inherent unity to her.

From this perspective, then, many themes in her books, letters, and monographs can be seen to reveal Nightingale as the architect of what we refer to today as holistic nursing and "total healing environments." (This latter term describes those surroundings and settings that facilitate within an individual the healing process, which is considered as inherent. See Dossey, Keegan, and Guzzetta, 2005a, p. 234).

Clearly, Nightingale's work—influential in her own time—continues to have an impact on us and our world. In fact, her influence on health care is so extensive and pervasive that any of us would benefit from a quick overview, as presented in Table 1-1. Table 1-1A lists these themes as they appeared from her *Notes on Hospitals* (1859, 1863), *Notes on Nursing* (1860), her formal letters to her nurses (1872–1900), and her last great essay, "Sick-Nursing and Health-Nursing" (1893). Table 1-1B lists the specific components of total healing environments that we recognize today (See Dossey, Keegan, & Guzzetta, 2005a; Jonas & Chez, 2003; Knutson, 2005; Moore, 2005; Quinn, Smith, Rittenbaugh, Swanson, & Watson, 2003; Watson, 1999).

Table 1-1.
Total Healing Environments: Florence Nightingale and Today

1-1 A. Florence Nightingale on Total Healing Environments: Themes in Her Writings

Themes Developed in *Notes on Hospitals* (1859, 1863)

The hospital will do the patient no harm. Four elements essential for the health of hospitals

- Fresh air
- Light
- Ample space
- Subdivision of sick into separate buildings or pavilions

Hospital construction defects that prevented health

- Defective means of natural ventilation and warming.
- Defective height of wards.
- Excessive width of wards between the opposite windows.
- Arrangement of the bed along the dead wall.
- More than two rows of beds between the opposite windows.
- Windows only on one side, or a closed corridor connecting the wards.
- Use of absorbent materials for walls and ceilings, and poor washing of floors hospitals.
- Defective condition of water closets.
- Defective ward furniture.
- Defective accommodation for nursing.
- Defective hospital kitchens.
- Defective laundries.
- Selection of bad sites and bad local climates for hospitals.
- Erecting of hospitals in towns.
- Defects of sewerage.
- Construction of hospitals without free circulation of external air.

Themes Developed in *Notes on Nursing* (1860)

Understanding God's laws in nature

- Understanding that, in disease and in illness, nursing and the nurse can assist in the reparative process of a disease and in maintaining health.

Nursing and nurses

- Describing the many roles and responsibilities of the nurse.

Patient

- Observing and managing the patient's problems, needs, and challenges and evaluating responses to care.

Health

- Recognizing factors that increase or decrease positive or negative state of health, well-being, disease, and illness.

Environment

- Both the *internal* (within one's self) and the *external* (physical space). (See the specifics listed in the next 10 » categories.)

» Bed and bedding
- Promote proper cleanliness.
- Use correct type of bed, height, mattress, springs, types of blankets, sheets, and other bedding.

» Cleanliness (rooms and walls)
- Maintain clean room, walls, carpets, furniture, dust-free rooms using correct dusting techniques.
- Release odors from painted and papered rooms; discusses other remedies for cleanliness.

» Cleanliness (personal)
- Provide proper bathing, rubbing, scrubbing of skin of the patient as well as the nurse.
- Use proper hand-washing techniques that include cleaning the nails.

» Food
- Provide proper portions and types of food at the right time, and a proper presentation of food types: eggs, meat, vegetables, beef, teas, coffee, jellies, sweets, homemade bread.

» Health of houses
- Provide pure air, pure water, efficient drainage, cleanliness, and light.

» Light
- Provide a room with light, windows, and a view which are essential to health and recovery.

Table 1-1A. Florence Nightingale on Total Healing Environments: Themes in Her Writings

» **Noise**
- Avoid noise and useless activity such as clanking, loud conversations with or among caregivers.
- Speak clearly for patient to hear without having to strain.
- Avoid surprising the patient.
- Only read to a patient if it is requested.

» **Petty management**
- Ensure patient privacy, rest, a quiet room, and instructions for the person managing care of patient.

» **Variety**
- Provide flowers and plants and avoid those with fragrances.
- Be aware of effects of mind (thoughts) on body.
- Help patient vary their painful thoughts.
- Use soothing colors.
- Be aware of the positive effect of certain music on the sick.

» **Ventilation and warming**
- Provide pure air within and without; open windows, regulate room temperature.
- Avoid odiferous disinfectants and sprays.

Chattering hopes and advice
- Avoid unnecessary advice, false hope, promises, and chatter of recovery.
- Avoid absurd statistical comparisons of patient to the recovery of other patients, and avoid mockery of advice given by family and friends.
- Share positive events; encourage visits from a well-behaved child or baby.
- Be aware of how small pet animals can provide comfort and companionship for the patient.

Observation of the sick
- Observe each patient; determine the problems, challenges, and needs.
- Assess how the patient responds to food, treatment, and rest.
- Help patient with comfort, safety, and health strategies.
- Intervene if danger to patient suspected.

Themes Developed in Formal Letters to Her Nurses (1872–1900)

All themes above in *Notes on Hospitals* and *Notes on Nursing* plus:

Art of nursing
- Explore presence, caring, meaning, and purpose.
- Increase communication with colleagues, patients, and families.
- Build respect, support, and trusting relationships.

Environment
- Include the internal self as well as the external physical space.

Ethics of nursing
- Engage in moral behaviors and values and model them in personal and professional life.

Health
- Integrate self-care and health-promoting and health-sustaining behaviors.
- Be a role model and model healthy behaviors.

Personal aspects of nursing
- Explore body-mind-spirit wholeness, healing philosophy, self-care, relaxation, music, prayers, work of service to self and others.
- Develop therapeutic and healing relationships.

Science of nursing
- Learn nursing knowledge and skills, observing, implementing and evaluating physicians' orders combined with nursing knowledge and skills.

Spirituality
- Develop intention, self-awareness, mindfulness, presence, compassion, love, and service to God and humankind.

Themes Developed in "Sick-Nursing and Health-Nursing" (1893 Essay)

All themes above in *Notes on Hospitals*, *Notes on Nursing,* and her letters to her nurses (1872–1900) plus:

Collaboration with others
- Meet with nurses and women at the local, national, and international level to explore health education and how to support each other in creating health and healthy environments.

Health education curriculum and health missioners education
- Include all components discussed in *Notes on Nursing*.
- Teach health as proactive leadership for health.

Table 1-1. Total Healing Environments: Florence Nightingale and Today

1-1B. Total Healing Environments Today: Holistic and Integral

The Internal Healing Environment

- Includes presence, caring, compassion, creativity, deep listening, grace, honesty, imagination, intention, love, mindfulness, self-awareness, trust, and work of service to self and others.
- Grounded in ethics, philosophies, and values that encourage and nurture such qualities as are listed above and in a way that:
  - Engages body-mind-spirit wholeness.
  - Fosters healing relationships and partnerships.
  - Promotes self-care and health-promoting and health-sustaining behaviors.
  - Engages with and is affected by the elements of the external healing environment (below).

The External Healing Environment

Color and texture

- Use color that creates healing atmosphere, sacred space, and moods that lift spirits.
- Coordinate room color with bed coverings, bedspreads, blankets, drapes, chairs, food trays, personal hygiene kits.
- Use textural variety on furniture, fabrics, artwork, wall surfaces, floors, ceilings, and ceiling light covers.

Communication

- Provide availability of caring staff for patient and family.
- Provide a public space for families to use television, radio, and telephones.

Family areas

- Create facilities for family members to stay with patients.
- Provide a comfortable family lounge area where families can keep or prepare special foods.

Light

- Provide natural light from low windows where patient can see outside.
- Use full-spectrum light throughout hospital, clinics, schools, public buildings, and homes.
- Provide control of light intensity with good reading light to avoid eye strain.

Noise control

- Eliminate loudspeaker paging systems in halls and elevators.
- Decrease noise of clanking latches, food carts and trays, pharmacy carts, slamming of doors, noisy hallways.
- Provide 24-hour continuous music and imagery channels such as Healing Healthcare Systems and Continuous Ambient Relaxation Environment (C.A.R.E.™; website at www.healinghealth.com), with other educational channels related to health and well-being.
- Decrease continuous use of loud commercial television.
- Eliminate loud staff conversations in unit stations and lounges, and calling of staff members in hallways.

Privacy

- Provide sign "Do Not Disturb " for patient and family to place on door to control privacy and social interaction.
- Position bed for view of outdoors, with shades to screen light and glare.
- Use full divider panel or heavy curtain for privacy if in a double patient room.
- Provide a secure place for personal belongings.
- Provide shelves to place personal mementos such as family pictures, flowers, and totems.

Table 1-1B.
Total Healing Environments Today: Holistic and Integral

Thermal comfort

- Provide patient control of air circulation, room temperature, fresh air, and humidity.

Ventilation and air quality

- Provide fresh air, adequate air exchanges, rooftop gardens, and solariums.
- Avoid use of toxic materials such as paints, synthetic materials, waxes, and foul-smelling air purifiers.

Views of nature

- Use indoor landscaping, which may include plants and miniature trees.
- Provide pictures of landscapes that include trees, flowers, mountains, ocean, and the like for patient and staff areas.

Integrative Practice

Throughout hospitals, clinics, schools, and all parts of a community:

- Combine conventional medical treatments, procedures, and surgery with complementary and alternative therapies, and folk medicine.
- Engage in transdisciplinary dialogues and collaboration that fosters deep personal support, trust, therapeutic alliances.
- Offer educational programs for professionals that teach specifics about the interactions of the healer and patient, holistic philosophy, patient-centered care, relationship-centered care, and complementary and alternative therapies.
- Develop and build community and partnerships based on mutual support, trust, values, and exchange of ideas.
- Use strategies that enhance interconnectedness of person, nature, inner and outer, spiritual and physical, private and public.
- Use self-care and health-promoting education that includes prevention and public health.
- Provide support groups, counseling, and psychotherapy, specifically for cancer and cardiac support groups, lifestyle change groups, 12-step programs and support groups, leisure, exercise, nutrition and weight management, smoking cessation, and end-of-life care and bereavement.
- Provide health coaches for staff, patients, families, and community.
- Provide information technology and virtual classroom capabilities.

As we in contemporary health care explore Nightingale's tenets, we will gain new insight into how to heal ourselves, how to facilitate healing, and how to be leaders so that we can better conceive and realize total healing environments that lead to a healthy world. These three tenets call for us to increase awareness of individual and collective states of healing consciousness and to engage in transdisciplinary dialogues that explore holistic nursing and integrative practice. The American Holistic Nurses Association (AHNA) defines holistic nursing in *AHNA Standards of Practice* as follows:

> Holistic nursing embraces all nursing which has enhancement of healing the whole person from birth to death as its goal. Holistic nursing recognizes that there are two views regarding holism: that holism involves identifying the interrelationships of the bio-psycho-social-spiritual dimensions of the person, recognizing that the whole is greater than the sum of its parts; and that holism involves understanding the individual as a unitary whole in mutual process with the environment. Holistic nursing [holds] that the goals of nursing can be achieved within either framework.
>
> The holistic nurse is an instrument of healing and a facilitator in the healing process. … Practicing holistic nursing requires nurses to integrate self-care, self-responsibility, spirituality, and reflection in their lives. This may lead the nurse to greater awareness of the interconnectedness with self, others, nature, and God/Life Force/Absolute/Transcendent. This awareness further enhances the nurses' understanding of all individuals and their relationships to the human and global community, and permits nurses to use this awareness to facilitate the healing process. (AHNA, 2003a; Frisch et al., 2000)

The AHNA defines *integrative practice* as a patient-centered and relationship-centered holistic caring process that includes the client, the nurse, the family, and other healthcare practitioners who incorporate complementary and conventional healthcare services and interventions (AHNA, 2002) .

The American Nurses Association (ANA) also addresses these holistic, integrative concepts in two of its foundational documents, *Nursing's Social Policy Statement* and *Nursing: Scope and Standards of Practice* (ANA, 2003, 2004). Nurses are challenged to integrate these concepts—all concepts with roots in Nightingale's pioneering work—into nursing practice, education, and research through various strategies within traditional education (Dossey, Keegan, & Guzzetta, 2005a), and interactive web-based education (Dossey, Keegan, & Guzzetta, 2005c).

What Will the World Be in 2010 and 2020?

What will our world be in the near future? To actualize Nightingale's vision of a healthy world, nurses will stand at the forefront as they join with others in a vision that is future-thinking and that leads to the steps toward deep healing. (See Appendix C for details on the Nightingale Initiative for Global Health 2010/2020, one such effort.) As elaborated throughout this book, Nightingale often thought about the future and believed that nurses, health missioners, and others who learned how to integrate health into their lives and also learned how to teach health to others were able to move toward creating the necessary steps for a healthy world. Frustrated with many slow reform efforts, in May 1873 she engaged in a flurry of writing and submitted three articles to *Fraser's Magazine*, a progressive literary journal. One of these articles was titled "What Will Our Religion Be on August 11, 1999?" It centered on her belief that, although history unfolded according to certain laws, man could make a difference in the future of humankind:

May 26, 1873.

The eclipse of the sun has begun. 7.36 A.M.
The eclipse of the sun is at its full. 8.28 A.M.
The eclipse of the sun has ended. 9.24 A.M.

After this a dearth of great eclipses of the sun visible in this country succeeds for years. On August 1, 1999, at 12 minutes 20 seconds to 10 A.M., "local time," the next total solar eclipse in England is to occur, we are told.

Supposing us to study the laws under which the Political and Moral World is governed, as we study those under which the solar system, the Material World, is governed, could we arrive at something of the same certainty in predicting the future condition of human society? How it will be with Europe? How it will be with England? How it will be with any one of our homes or institutions on August 11, 1999, at ten o'clock in the morning? (for I would not be particular to a minute).

One thing is certain, that none who now live will then be living here. (Perhaps by that time we many have sufficiently mastered the laws of moral evidence to say with equal certainty that every one who now lives will then be living—'Where'). Another thing is certain, that everything... is so governed, by law as which can be seen in their effects, that not the most trifling action or feeling is left to chance, and that any who could see into the mind of the "All-Ordering Power," as manifested by His laws or thoughts, could of course predict history.

All will be Order, not chance. ... But whether it be the Order of Disorder, so to speak, or the Order of Good Order, depends upon us. And this is practically what we have to consider.

"What will the world be on August 11, 1999?" What we have made it. (Nightingale, 1873, p. 28)

Healing: Bringing Together Body, Mind, and Spirit

As noted at the beginning of this chapter, Florence Nightingale's major tenet was healing. To her, *healing* was a holistic perspective and process of bringing together all aspects of oneself—body, mind, and spirit—to achieve and maintain integration and balance (see glossary, Appendix A). Healing was the essence of nursing and of her work for humankind. She explored the complex nature of healing from many viewpoints. Her source of strength and guidance for doing her work in the world was service to God and others. Nightingale raised questions about what it means to be human, to be cured, to be cared for, and to be healed. She expanded her worldview by studying philosophy and exploring the nature of knowledge and ways of knowing reality.

Nightingale included spirituality as a driving force in healing; it was for her the life principle in humans. It was the thinking, motivating, and feeling part of the human experience; it involved a sense of connectedness with a power that is greater, wiser, and more majestic than the individual self. Her 1872–1900 formal letters to her nurses, also called formal addresses (see Chapter 2 and the formal letters, starting on page 203), show her insight as a classical scholar into the word "spirit" as derived from *spiritus*, which means breath, courage, the soul, life. *Spiritus* is the Latin counterpart of the Greek *pneuma*, meaning breath or air. Spirituality gave meaning to life. These letters also share her worldview, feelings, thoughts, experiences, and *social action* (see glossary) that arose and evolved in her search for the sacred. Spirituality facilitated the interconnectedness with self, others, nature, and God/Life Force/Absolute/Transcendent. It was a unifying force with all that was, and the essence of being and relatedness that permeated all of life.

Nightingale described nursing as healing; nursing was a "calling" and a work of service to others. She believed nursing's concern was the restoration and promotion of health (body, mind, and spirit), the prevention of disease, and assisting patients and families with their needs. Beginning with her classic *Notes on Nursing: What It Is and What It Is Not* (1860a), and continuing with other written works discussed in this book, Nightingale identified and developed concepts related to the nurse, the patient (person), health, and the environment (society). She emphasized that nurses' concerns included the patient's experience, and that spiritual and social support, along with a comfortable and healthy environment, influenced all factors in healing. The active participation of the nurse was part of the healing process.

Nightingale was a *practical mystic* (see glossary) and a spiritual caregiver. (For more detail on this focal issue, see the Pentimento in this chapter and in Chapter 2.) From her preteens into her twenties, she cared for people in the nearby villages who worked or lived on her family estates. Beginning in the 1850s she wrote her philosophical treatise *Suggestions for Thought to the Searchers of Truth Among the Artisans of England*, which she privately printed in three volumes, 829 pages, in 1860 (Nightingale, 1860b, 1860c). The basic premise of her spiritual philosophy was a benevolent God, and she thought that the whole doctrine of a future state depended on it and on our capability of perfection. She characterized her social action thus: "Mankind must discover the organization by which mankind can live in harmony with God's purpose" (Calabria & Macrae, 1994).

In 1872 Nightingale began her book on practical mysticism, *Notes from Devotional Authors of the Middle Ages*. The book was intended to explore the lives of saints and mystics of the Middle Ages, and their social action of healing and spirituality; she wrote the first 87 pages, but never completed it because of more pressing work. She wrote about the mystery and the indwelling presence of God within people:

> *Mysticism: to dwell on the unseen, to withdraw ourselves from the things of sense into communion with God—to endeavor to partake of the divine nature; that is, of Holiness. When we ask ourselves only what is right, or what is the will of God (the same question), then we may truly be said to live in His Light. ...*
>
> *For what is mysticism? Is it not the attempts to draw near to God, not by rites or ceremonies, but by inward disposition? Is it not merely a hard word for "The Kingdom of Heaven is within"? Heaven is neither a place nor a time. There might be a Heaven not only here but now. ...*
>
> *Where shall I find God? In myself. That is the true Mystical Doctrine. But then I myself must be in a state for Him to come and dwell in me. This is the whole aim of the Mystical Life; and all Mystical Rules in all times and countries have been laid down for putting the soul into such a state. ...* (Nightingale, 1872a; Vallée, 2003)

Nightingale's dedication to healing of others was recognized by many. In *Science and Health,* Mary Baker G. Eddy, the founder of Christian Science, described Nightingale's sheer force and the power of her mind and intellect over the physical body in her social action: "It is proverbial that Florence Nightingale, and other philanthropists engaged in humane labors, have been able to undergo, without sinking, fatigues and exposures which ordinary people could not endure. The explanation lies in the support they derive from divine law, that rising above the human" (Eddy, 1895, p. 383).

Nightingale believed that healing could be synchronous, but not synonymous, with curing. Curing to her was the elimination of the symptoms of disease, which might or might not end a person's disease or distress. Her healing framework suggested that it was only nature (understanding God's laws) that ultimately cured (healed) and that the role of the nurse was "to put the patient in the best condition for nature to act upon him" (Nightingale, 1860a). Nightingale saw that breaking the natural laws and her six Ds (dirt, drink, diet, damp, draughts, and drains; see Chapter 5, Table 5-2) were the most common reasons for disease.

In Nightingale's many document and letters, she describes healing as both the internal and external environment; both were key factors that could not be separated (Selanders, 1993, 1998). She believed that the nurse had to develop her (and now his) inner self, the "internal environment." This also applied to patients who would benefit from more understanding about what it meant to learn about and use self-care principles. It was important that nurses change their consciousness through self-care so that they would be more in harmony with self, others, and the universe. The external environment was the physical space where a person lived and where the patient received care. Nurses were responsible for creating a healing environment when possible.

Nightingale encouraged individuals to deepen their spiritual lives. Her 13 formal letters to her nurses from 1872 to 1900 (see Chapter 2 and the full text of these letters starting on page 287), and her 1893 essay "Sick-Nursing and Health-Nursing" (see Chapter 8 and the full text of this 1893 essay starting on page 203), show her ability to synthesize profound insights from her many years of exploring the mysteries of healing and show how to enhance the internal and external environments for healing to take place. Her work explored the role that attitudes and emotions play within healing. Nightingale understood the profound wisdom that was essential for the healing of humankind.

Leadership: The Attributes of Transformation

Nightingale was an inspired leader, and we can follow her example of what happens when our spiritual vision is combined with our vision for now and the future. In today's specialized world, we are often tempted to compartmentalize our lives, putting our professional interests in one corner and our spiritual concerns in another. To Nightingale, fragmenting one's life in this way would have been unthinkable. Her spiritual vision and her professional identity were seamlessly combined. As she put it, "My work is my must." She is, therefore, an icon of wholeness, an emblem of a united, integrated life. By her shining example, she invites each of us to find our meaning and purpose—our own "must"—in our individual journey through life.

With the rapid changes in health care today, Nightingale's leadership can be a source of strength. Nurses must emerge as dynamic leaders that can ensure that healthcare organizations are guided accurately and effectively to create healing environments for patients and their families and for the healthcare team (Porter-O'Grady and Malloch, 2003).

The following eight attributes are recognized today in transformational nursing leaders and can assist us in implementing Nightingale's vision for a healthy world. These eight attributes are listed next and then developed in the rest of this section: self-knowledge, authenticity, expertise, vision, flexibility, shared leadership, charisma, and the ability to inspire others (Ward, 2002). Leadership models and transvisionary leadership are further explored in Chapter 4. (The model of transvisionary leadership blends the transactional and transformational leadership types: the desire to create mutual, permanent change unburdened by cultural constraints or knowledge deficit.)

Self-knowledge

Self-knowledge includes an awareness of one's beliefs, attitudes, values, and weaknesses. It also includes an individual's motivation and the continued search for self-understanding.

Nightingale's self-knowledge is reflected in her profound awareness of her beliefs, attitudes, values, and strengths, and in identifying her weaknesses. (See the Pentimentos in Chapters 4 and 5.) She challenged others to identify their "must," and to fight for care for all people, whether rich or poor. Her constant search for a new level of understanding about what her work should be was often referred to by others as the "Nightingale Power." However, this power was derived from her selfless intent to act as God's instrument. She was a practical mystic in an extroverted world of business and politics, and her introversion was her cloister (B. Dossey, 2000a).

Authenticity

Authenticity is being consistent with one's beliefs and values, and acting on what one believes to be one's truth. This helps to build trusting relationships and leads to successful completion of endeavors.

Nightingale's actions were consistent with her most cherished beliefs and values about humankind. She acted on what she believed to be true and helped her in her many successful endeavors that led to long-lasting friendships.

Her success in making decisions based solely on consideration of the facts is seen in her enduring work—today she is recognized as the first nurse theorist—and in the development of the Nightingale Training School as a model for education and training of nurses. Her authenticity is also seen in her roles as scientist, statistician, contributor to modern hospital design, catalyst for British Army medical reform, and the founder of the first Army Medical School, and as a tireless advocate for sanitation (public health) at home and abroad. She made original contributions to advanced statistics (see the Pentimento in Chapter 6) and published volumes of work that included numerous official parliamentary documents, books, monographs, and pamphlets.

Expertise

Expertise—obtaining the knowledge, skills, and technical ability to achieve a desired goal and become competent—inspires and supports individuals in their professional development and personal growth.

Nightingale's expertise began with her gathering knowledge on basic sanitation, hospital construction, nursing care skills, and conditions in workhouses. Her knowledge base inspired others to develop new ideas and to collaborate on projects to improve health conditions.

Within months of the beginning of the Crimean War (1854–1856), the world's mightiest empire was faced with the rapid destruction of a 27,000-man army mainly by malnutrition, exposure, and disease. At the urgent request of Sidney Herbert, Secretary at War and her personal friend, Nightingale went to Turkey to head the first contingent of British women, nuns, and nurses to ever work in British military hospitals. She transformed these "colossal calamities" into the first successful large-scale example of modern hospital and nursing management. She led in identifying complex organizational and administrative problems that resulted in the British government sending out two Royal Commissions of inquiry—one to Scutari and the other to the Crimea—both staffed by conscientious men with first-rate experience, intelligence, and initiative. When the commissioners arrived in March 1855, they had the power to begin making the necessary changes that Nightingale had identified. Under her leadership, backed by the commissioners' authority, the mortality rate plummeted from 42.7 percent to 2.2 percent in six months as over 18,000 soldiers streamed through Scutari.

Vision

Vision is having the ability to articulate future expectations. It includes having a plan or idea, being able to explain it to others, and aiming at desired outcomes.

Nightingale always had a vision, one that began in her teens. Once she received an allowance from her father, she finally was able to break free of the strictures of her family's expectations. At the age of 33, in her first nurse superintendent role at the Hospital for Gentlewomen in Distressed Circumstances at Harley Street in London, she saw the deplorable state of Victorian healthcare conditions. She envisioned the ideal, and fought to reduce the gap between the two. In her role as an administrator and leader, she challenged the status quo.

As an intuitive, administrative, organizational, and systems genius, she had thoroughly envisioned the models; all she needed was the opportunity and responsibility to create new realities (B. Dossey, 1998c). She completely reorganized and streamlined the physical facility and dramatically improved the quality of patient care, hygiene, and administration of this small, 27-bed hospital.

Her vision was inspired by her intuitions. Probably her greatest and most original intuitions were in perceiving the exact nature of the organizational changes that would be required to humanize and modernize the fields of nursing and hospital administration.

The underlying principle for her revolutionary nursing leadership was expressed in her observation that "The whole reform in nursing both at home and abroad has consisted in this: to take all power over the nursing out of the hands of the men, and put it into the hands of *one female trained* head and make her responsible for everything (regarding internal management and discipline) being carried out" (Abel-Smith, 1960; Nightingale, 1867). Implicit in this principle, without fanfare, was the fact that feminine values and power would be incorporated into the appropriate administrative hierarchies, that women would have a new place in the world. (See Table 1-2 for a summary of the nursing component of her lifetime of social reform accomplishments.)

Flexibility

Flexibility is being able to exist in conditions of uncertainty, ambiguity, and complexity, and to adapt to new situations while assisting others in the midst of constant chaos and changes. It is learning how to divide the labor, explain responsibilities, and be clear in expectations so that others can make a contribution toward the desired task or goal.

Nightingale was an inveterate note-taker, planner, and organizer, and a tireless worker to accomplish her tasks. She always had a system in doing things, order in possessions, the planned life, sustained effort, decisiveness, exercise of authority, settled opinions, and acceptance of routine. She was a master at what today is referred to as time management. Her drive to create real-world structures from her inner vision was motivated by her intuition and mystical vision. She was precise and purposeful, and liked to settle matters so that she could prepare for her next work.

The staggering amount of work that she accomplished from 1857 to 1863, in the face of severe illness and exhaustion, testifies to her persistence. When the window of political opportunity for her reform work was widest open, she seized the moment. She authored, directly and indirectly, and edited over 5,000 pages of published materials that composed the irrefutable case, the indispensable proof related to army problems during the Crimean War. She hand wrote all drafts of her innumerable statistical analyses, publications, reports, letters, papers, articles, abstracts, pamphlets, and other materials, and then she had to proofread all typeset pages before publication.

In 1860, Nightingale started the Nightingale Training School as a secular school using the Nightingale Fund. She insisted that her nurses not impose their religious beliefs on patients; however, she did encourage them to be exemplars of the Christian life and role models for others. She believed that all people had a right to health care regardless of religious affiliation or ability to pay.

Shared Leadership

Shared Leadership implies that power among the members of a group is shared, and that an individual intellectually stimulates others. When leadership is shared, it empowers others to develop creative outlets and new ideas.

Table 1-2.
Florence Nightingale: Nursing Leadership and Social Reform

Specific Areas of Reform	Reform Accomplishments
Nightingale Fund	• November 5, 1853: The Nightingale Fund was created in appreciation of service by Nightingale and nurses during the Crimean War. • June 20, 1856: Fund closed with £44,039 (approximately £2 million, or US$3.4 million, in today's currency). • 1860–1861: Under Secretary Arthur Clough of the Nightingale Fund financially supported the Nightingale Training School along with other aspects of nursing reform. • 1861–1899: Secretary Henry Bonham Carter oversaw the management of the Nightingale Training School with Sarah Wardroper.
Nightingale Training Program	• June 24, 1850: Nightingale began the first secular nurses' training program at St. Thomas' Hospital. • 1860–1887: Sarah Wardroper, as first matron, managed the day-to-day aspects of the training program. • 1875–1895: Mary Crossland, Home Sister, was responsible for moral training and nursing education. • 1860–1872: Richard Whitfield served as first lecturer for nurse probationers. • 1872–1892: Dr. John Croft served as first lecturer under a revised curriculum.
Workhouse nursing	• May 16, 1865: William Rathbone, Liverpool philanthropist, donated £1,200 to start a training program for nurses at Liverpool Workhouse Infirmary. • February 1868: Agnes Jones, a former St. Thomas' nurse probationer and workhouse nursing pioneer, who was the first woman superintendent in Liverpool, died of typhus. • 1865–1868: Nightingale's introduction of trained nurses into workhouse infirmaries laid the foundation for both systematic public health care and governmental provision of healthcare services.
Military nursing	• 1862–1869: Lady Jane Shaw Stewart established and served as first superintendent at Royal Victoria Hospital of the first military nursing service. • 1879: Jane Deeble, second superintendent of Royal Victoria Hospital, took a group of trained nurses to the Zulu War in South Africa, the first such overseas service of trained nurses and the basis for the army's nursing service. • 1914: Nightingale's plan for military nursing service was implemented during World War I.
Midwifery nursing	• 1862–1868: Mary Jones, superintendent of the Lying-In Institute at King's College Hospital, began with 10 lying-in beds. Physician-accoucheures taught probationers. The program was beset by a lack of applicants and numerous political and religious conflicts. • 1876: Nightingale pushed for the establishment of a government midwifery training program. • 1902: The first Midwives Act was passed.
District nursing	• 1874–1878: Nightingale printed a questionnaire (1874) to ascertain the types of nursing being used in hospitals, workhouses, and district nursing in London. The results, published in 1876, emphasized the need for district nursing. • Florence Lees served as the first superintendent for the Metropolitan and National Nursing Association, and was considered the founder of district nursing. • 1910: First preliminary School of District Nursing began at St. Thomas'.

When Nightingale began her drive to create the modern nursing model, her greatest challenge was to develop nurse leaders with whom to share the leadership. She actually had to start from the beginning of developing her well-known record sheet, called "Monthly State of Personal Character and Acquirements of Nurse During Her Period of Service," which was used to assess students at the Nightingale Training School, as seen in Figure 1-1. Most nurses are familiar with these concepts, which remain important today and are valued in contemporary nursing. (Even the Victorian use of leeches, as well as maggots, is making a comeback in modern medicine.) Following the 1860 publication of her 79-page *Notes on Nursing* (Nightingale, 1860a)—which was to teach women in general about health—she published her revised and expanded 229-page *Notes on Nursing* (1860c), which became recognized as the textbook that laid the foundation of the "art and science" of nursing.

Nightingale's leadership and transdisciplinary competence is also seen in her scholarly research in the fields of nursing, medicine, the military, education, social reform, and theology. Nightingale was a researcher par excellence. She possessed an innate, almost intuitive aptitude for mathematics and developed a sophisticated understanding of statistics; one of the great facets of her mind was her ability to understand the meaning and relationships of large volumes of numbers.

Figure 1-1.
Section of Nightingale's "Monthly State of Personal Character and Acquirements of Nurse During Her Period of Service"

Source: London Metropolitan Archives.

Monthly State of Personal Character and Acquirements of Nurse During Her Period of Service

Underneath the following the Five Heads, state the Amount of Excellence or Deficiency , under the Three Degrees, "Excellent," "Moderate," "O".

	1. Punctuality Especially as to administration of food, wine, and medicine.	**2. Quietness**	**3. Trustworthiness**	**4. Personal Neatness & Cleanliness**	**5. Ward Management**
January					
February					
March					
April					
May					
June					
July					
August					
September					
October					
November					
December					
*					

continued

	6. Helpless Patients Moving, Changing, Personal cleanliness of, Feeding, Keeping warm or cool, Preventing and dressing bed sores, Managing position of	**7. Bandaging** Making bandages, Making rollers, Lining of splints	**8. Making Beds** Removal of sheets	**9. Waiting on Operations**	**10. Sick Cooking** Gruel, Arrowroot, Egg flip, Puddings, Drinks
January					
February					
March					
April					
May					
June					
July					
August					
September					
October					
November					
December					

* If defective, state nature of defect in this line.

Her constant, penetrating insights into the underlying truth of innumerable fields and topics, no matter what the popular convention of the day, were remarkable. Nightingale was among a very few at the time to understand that an accurate and thorough use of statistics would be necessary for medical and hospital organization, and nursing management, training, and reform. While refining her statistics from the Crimean War, she pioneered the use of wedge-area charts (see the photograph of one such chart in the Pentimento of Chapter 6). And it was Nightingale's plans for change, backed by her statistical data from the Crimea, that in fact became the great lever for army, nursing, and hospital reform when she returned to England. She championed these and other causes for the rest of her life. Her work in applied statistics lasted for over 40 years and is the reason she is considered one of the women founders of the social sciences (McDonald, 1994).

By the end of her life, she had other nurse leaders with whom to communicate and to share the leadership. However, this had its challenges with these new nurse leaders because of the seven-year debate from 1887 to 1893 over the pros and cons of nurse registration. In mid-1893, Nightingale believed that she had won against the British Nurses Association. She deplored the feud and tried to begin goodwill between both groups. The antiregistration group had the greater number, but the proregistration group had a princess at their head (B. Dossey, 2000a).

Charisma

Charisma is personal charm that enables a person to influence others. Charisma infuses all endeavors that depend on enthusiasm about a group's mission and goals, and leads to respect and loyalty from others.

Nightingale's charisma and her ability to influence others began early in life. One of the people that experienced her charisma and genius in 1847 was Sidney Herbert, who later as Secretary at War in 1854 invited Nightingale to the Crimea as superintendent of nurses. Her charisma is seen in her intellect and her intuition, her flashes of inspiration, her insight into relationships of ideas and meaning of symbols, her originality, her ingenuity, and her fine-tuned insights into the deeper meaning of things, the access to resources of the unconscious, and the visions of what could be. Her charismatic nature as an initiator and promoter of ideas was also seen in her great determination and her utter confidence in her intuition. However, like many great intuitive thinkers, she was impervious to the influence of outside judgment.

Ability to Inspire Others

The ability to inspire others requires the use of one's physical energy to motivate others. It is also the ability to instill confidence and to create cohesive learning environments.

Nightingale had the ability to inspire others. While overseeing her great advances, she was already looking ahead to the next level of reform. Nightingale made her decisions based on a rational, logical analysis of the facts before her. She valued logic above any personal feelings or the feelings of others. She was so logical and frank in her opinions that her truthfulness sometimes overrode her tactfulness, for example, in dealing with nurses at Scutari and in other hospitals in Turkey and the Crimea, and with her loyal friends and colleagues after her return to England in 1856 and for many years to follow.

A master networker, Nightingale's ability to inspire others throughout 1857–1893 is seen in her use of research findings to educate members of parliament and other political and social leaders, so that their healthcare reform could be achieved through proper legislation. Her data analysis was produced in over 100 documents, books, and guidelines that influenced the personal, political, social, and scientific domains.

Other Leadership Attributes

In addition to possessing these eight transformational leadership attributes, transformational leaders are also assertive, active listeners, self-confident, and humble. They are masters of time management and emotional control; they communicate decisively, delegate effectively, and exhibit a genuine love of others; and they thrive in environments that foster networking, change, political awareness, and collaboration (Ward, 2002).

Daniel J. Pesut, president of Sigma Theta Tau International Honor Society of Nursing, has a focus for his presidency (2003–2005): a call to action to "create the future through renewal." Pesut believes that nurse leaders can best create the future through renewal and through conversations of hope and inspiration rather than discontent and regret (Pesut, 2004). He offers six specific initiatives for *renewal through attention* to (1) self, (2) service, (3) scholarship of reflective practice, (4) science, (5) society, and (6) spirit.

Self-care is crucial for thinking creatively and integrating clinical reasoning and the ability to engage in future-thinking to anticipate the future. Self-care requires that we do the necessary inner psychological work that assists us in clarifying our values and commitments. This also helps us move through the "dark nights of the soul and to identify strategies that can guide us through life's ordeals" (Moore, 2004). As the self is renewed through self-care, it is easier to give attention to renewal to service. Service is supported by renewal through attention to scholarship of reflective practice. Reflective practice is supported through renewed attention to the knowledge of science that supports evidence-based practice. Evidence-based care influences and affects the renewal of society at large though attention to the value of the art and science of nursing worldwide. Finally, as nurses rediscover and renew their commitments to self, service, the scholarship of reflective practice, the knowledge derived from science, and conversations about the value of nursing knowledge, nurses will experience the renewal of spirit.

Global Action: Bringing Us All Together

Nightingale's global action was her inspired life's mission, dedicated to serve through healing; to write documents and books; to network with people at the local, national, and international levels; and to shape public opinion about social and political issues to create a healthy world. Through her nursing training school, and in her *Notes on Nursing*, her letters to her nurses (1872–1900), and her 1893 essay "Sick-Nursing and Health-Nursing," she imparted her philosophical foundation that included nurse self-care, nursing art, science, related theories, research, and ethics. Today, this is recognized as holistic nursing that incorporates nursing theory and patterns of knowing, as discussed in the next section. Nightingale's *Notes on Nursing* received wide circulation throughout the world. It was quickly translated into Italian, German, and French. Since there were no international copyright laws in 1860, Appleton & Company in New York published an American edition. This was followed by eight more printings in the next 50 years. The book remains in print today.

At the June 1893 World's Fair, also called the World's Columbian Exposition, held in Chicago, Nightingale's global vision of health for all received further recognition. At this international event, women played a conspicuous and responsible role. Since Nightingale's work was well known by the planners, they sought her counsel, wisdom, and inspiration. Nightingale contributed her remarkable 1893 paper "Sick-Nursing and Health-Nursing," which was read for her at the Congress. (See Chapter 8 and the full text of the essay on page 287). The document proclaimed that the "art of health-nursing" was as important as the "art of sick-nursing." She focused on the need for a new role called "health-missioners," individuals who would go into communities and teach about "positive-health," the "art of health," and the "cultivation of health." The 1893 essay contained her core curriculum, which these health missioners would teach. Today, her curriculum is recognized as holistic nursing, and holistic health and public education.

At the Congress, Nightingale's influence was also seen in the contribution of a Nightingale disciple, Mrs. Dacre Craven (formerly Florence Lees), who had served as the superintendent of the model training school for district nurses in London and whose paper laid the foundation for community health nursing. This historic meeting established a landmark for all future nursing conventions; it was the foundation for the national organization of nurses in the United States and the beginning of formal international collaboration among nurses that became the International Council of Nurses (ICN) in 1899. Today the ICN (based in Geneva, Switzerland) is a federation of 120 national nurses' associations representing millions of nurses worldwide. Its mission is to provide leadership and assistance in resolving present and future healthcare needs.

Nightingale's Tenets: Implications for Contemporary Nursing

To help contemporary nurses better understand and integrate Nightingale's tenets of healing, leadership, and global action, this section explores Nightingale as nurse theorist, Nightingale as integralist, Nightingale as transdisciplinarian, and Nightingale as environmentalist.

Nightingale as Nurse Theorist

Nightingale is recognized as the first nurse theorist (Selanders, 1993a, 1998; Frisch, 2005). Although Nightingale did not write in terms of nursing theory, her life and work have deeply influenced contemporary nursing and all of health care whether we realize it or not. (See also Chapter 5). The goal of nursing theory is to organize knowledge to explain human phenomena and experiences that are relevant to the discipline. Nightingale's documents discussed in this book include her three tenets of healing, leadership, and global action, and descriptions of person (patient), health, the environment (society), and the nurse and nursing.

Meta-Paradigm Concepts: Nursing's Four Domains

Nightingale's work describes the four domains that define the discipline of nursing, which are known as the meta-paradigm concepts. Today, contemporary nursing theorists and nurses in practice, education, and research are developing theories that will advance Nightingale's philosophy and tenets of healing, leadership, and global action from the local to the global level. This can help to bring order out of chaos in health care and to favorably affect society; it can assist in the further development of standards and the scope of practice in professional organizations such as the American Nurses Association, the American Holistic Nurses Association, and other nursing organization subspecialties.

Theory-guided and evidence-based nursing practice can incorporate Nightingale's three tenets to help us achieve the mission of creating total healing environments and relationship-centered care, critical thinking, decision making, and intervention development and evaluation (Chinn and Kramer, 1999; B. Dossey, 1997, 2005; Dossey, Keegan, & Guzzetta, 2005a; Fawcett, Watson, Neuman, and Walker, 2001; Fenton & Morris, 2003; Frisch, Dossey, Guzzetta, & Quinn, 2000; Frisch, 2005; and Watson, 1999). Future expansion of the meta-paradigm concepts in the discipline of nursing will need to be forward-thinking and useful for practice, education, and research.

Patterns of Knowing: Nightingale and Nursing's Knowledge

As a way to organize nursing's knowledge, Barbara Carper (1978) identified the four fundamental patterns of knowing in nursing that are recognized today:

1. *Personal knowing* – The nurse's dynamic process of being whole, which focuses on the synthesis of perceptions and being with self.

2. *Empirical knowing* – The science of nursing, which focuses on formal expression, replication, and validation of scientific competence in nursing education and practice.
3. *Ethical knowing* – The moral knowledge in nursing, which focuses on behaviors, expressions, and dimensions of both morality and ethics intersecting with roles.
4. *Aesthetic knowing* – The art of nursing, which focuses on how to explore experiences and meaning in life with self or another, and which includes authentic presence, the nurse as a facilitator of healing, and the artfulness of a healing environment.

Although Nightingale did not write in terms of patterns of knowing, we can see her influence on contemporary nursing (see Chapter 2). These patterns of knowing help nurses:

- To bring themselves into the full expression of being present in the moment (McKivergin, 2005, Watson, 1988, 1999);
- To integrate aesthetics with science (Chinn and Kramer, 1999; Gaydos, 1999, 2005); and
- To develop the flow of expert experience with thinking and acting (Benner, 1984; Benner and Wrubel, 1989; Benner, Hooper-Kyriakidis, and Stannard, 1999).

These four patterns of knowing have been adapted or supplemented by theorists who suggest that when nurses can move into "unknowing" or "not-knowing," this allows for an authentic encounter (Munhall, 1993). This state occurs because the nurse can be with not-knowing when a patient asks, for example, "When do you think I am going to die?" Other theorists offer different ways of deeper personal knowing and sociopolitical knowing through reflective questioning (Silva, Sorrell, & Sorrell, 1995; White, 1995; Wolfer, 1993).

Nightingale's Call: Nursing as a Spiritual Practice

Nightingale's legacy calls nurses to recognize nursing as a spiritual practice (see Chapter 2). The recognition of nursing as a spiritual practice has also been described by many nurse authors (Barnum, 2003; Dossey, Keegan, & Guzzetta, 2005a; Gaydos, 2005; Henry & Henry, 2004; Koerner, 2003; Macrae, 2001; McKivergin, 2005; Watson, 1999). Nightingale understood the dynamics of spirituality and religion, and how nurses could impart spirituality and honor different religious affiliations simultaneously. She understood the necessity of *not* preaching any type of religious dogma to patients. During the Crimean War, Nightingale honored the many world religions where she served. To understand religious and spiritual beliefs, it is useful to review the chronology of the world's great traditions, founders, historic texts, and philosophers as seen in Table 1-3 on the next page (H. Smith, 1986, 1994). It is important to remember that two of Nightingale's favorite books were the Bible and the *Bhagavad Gita* (The Song Celestial).

Starting in her first position in 1853 as nurse superintendent at the Institute of Sick and Gentlewomen at Upper Harley Street, she held that every sick woman should be cared for regardless of religious affiliation. She also insisted that all soldiers in the Crimean War (1854–1856), regardless of religious affiliation, receive the same level of care. Nightingale stressed the importance of nurses leading an exemplary Christian life and developing a rich inner life.

To explore nursing as a spiritual practice, and the transdisciplinary nature of healing relationships discussed later, it is important to define the terms spirituality and religion. The following definitions were developed by the Samueli Institute for Information Biology (SIIB) (L. Dossey, 2003) and are very useful. *Spirituality* includes the feelings, thoughts, experiences, and behaviors that arise from a search for that which is generally considered sacred.

Table 1-3. Chronology: The Founders, Sacred Texts, and Philosophers of the Great Traditions	
The Vedic Texts of India (Hinduism)	c. 4500–3000 BCE
Krishna (Hindu deity)	c. 1500 BCE
Shinto texts*	c. 1500–1000 BCE
Judaism	c. 1300 BCE
Moses	c. 1300 BCE
King Solomon	c. 970 BCE
The Upanishads (Hinduism)	c. 700–500 BCE
Lao Tse (principal founder of Taoism)	c. 604–515 BCE
Mahavira (principal founder of Jainism)	c. 600 BCE
Buddha	c. 573–483 BCE
Confucius	c. 551–479 BCE
Socrates	c. 470–399 BCE
Plato	c. 427–347 BCE
Mencius (Chinese contributor to Confucianism)	c. 370–290 BCE
Jesus	c. 4 BCE–30 CE
Codex Sinaiticus (earliest copy of the Bible in Greek)	c. 350 CE
Muhammad (founder of Islam)	c. 571–632 CE
Sufism	c. 800 CE
Guru Nanak (founder of Sikhism)	c. 1469–1538 CE

(*Oral tradition dates back to prehistoric Japan. (H. Smith, 1986, 1994)

Spirituality is usually, though not universally, considered to involve a sense of connection with an absolute, immanent, or transcendent spiritual force, however named, as well as the conviction that meaning, value, direction, and purpose are valid aspects of the universe. *Religion* is the codified and ritualized beliefs and behaviors of those involved in spirituality, usually taking place within a community of like-minded people (L. Dossey, 2003, p. 11). These ideas are explored further in Chapter 2.

Healing and Authentic Presence: The Art of Nursing

Today, there continues to be a focus on curing solely with empirical knowledge that is characterized primarily by technology, rationality, objectivity, and a linear cause-and-effect, material worldview. Healing includes the art and science of nursing, and the nurse is an essential therapeutic instrument in the healing process. The art of nursing integrates the healing presence of nurses and modalities such as music, relaxation, pet therapy, and natural light and healing environments as described in Nightingale's *Notes on Nursing*. Healing can occur with curing approaches that use the best of Western medical protocols, treatments, and procedures when necessary or appropriate. This should never be "either/or," but must be "both/and" (Dossey, Keegan, and Guzzetta, 2005a). When the art and science of the profession come together, nurses' intellect, intuition, and healing presence become more dynamic; the interaction of self with another takes on a different quality.

Healing is not predictable. A useful metaphor for a healing moment is that, at such times, the boundaries between two people become fluid. A thread of a story can take a person in a direction that person was not conscious of before the telling of the story. With authentic presence, a nurse can maintain healthy boundaries within this situation, particularly when the nurse integrates self-care and reflective practice on a regular basis. Nursing is indeed an art when the nurse and the patient (and often others, such as relatives, family members, close friends, and practitioners) co-create the circumstances for healing; it is in this "making special" between two people where the healing happens, and where the art of nursing is actualized (Gaydos, 1999, 2005).

Authentic presence is approaching a patient or another in a way that respects and honors that person's essence. A healing encounter is more frequent because there is a coming together of two people in a present moment where a different level of exchange and sharing occurs (Watson, 1999). Authentic presence facilitates a deeper healing experience between the nurse and a patient or among others (McKivergin, 2005). This means that the nurse will ask questions that engage the patient to respond more fully about the present moment.

Nightingale as Integralist

As is evident throughout this book, Nightingale's life and work demonstrate that she was an integralist: she had an integral approach that focused on the individual and the collective, the inner and outer, and human and nonhuman concerns. Nightingale's consciousness spans from the most basic needs of human beings to the vastness of the connection with the Divine. She had the ability to articulate, document, analyze statistical data, design protocols, and envision what a healthy world might be with an integral philosophy and consciousness.

Integral nursing can be defined as an approach that has wholeness as it goal, and is interdependent, dynamic, open, fluid, and continuously interacting with changing variables that can lead to greater complexity and order (B. Dossey, 2005). This comprehensive theory of integral nursing will be the first nursing theory to synthesize nursing's history, which includes Nightingale's legacy and tenets of healing, leadership, and global action, with contemporary nursing and nursing's future. It will assist nurses and nursing practitioners who use various nursing theories engage in deep dialogue for the evolution of the profession. This theory of integral nursing also will serve to effectively interface and position nurses in transdisciplinary dialogues that will assist them in articulating nursing's and nurses' mission and their work. This theory shifts the current focus from the medical model to a comprehensive understanding of the complexity of human nature that nurses and nursing bring to health care and society.

Nightingale as Transdisciplinarian

Nightingale is an example of a powerful transdisciplinarian. She was always analyzing, communicating, exchanging, surveying, involving, synthesizing, investigating, interviewing, mentoring, developing, creating, researching, and teaching. She listened to others, and she created new schemes for what was possible. *Transdisciplinary* dialogues are dialogues in which individuals from various disciplines share knowledge that informs their learning, practice, education, and research. These dialogues also include patients, their families, and all community members and practitioners. Transdisciplinary dialogues are transformative and visionary, facilitating and leading to the creation of total healing environments.

Nurses can be leaders in creating opportunities for transdisciplinary dialogues and approaches to care. A transdisciplinary approach means that professionals and others come together to share knowledge; they emphasize connections with each other rather than specialization: there is "visioning possibilities with," "evolving ideas with," "collaboration with," rather than "competition between and among." There is a commitment to new approaches and the courage and spirit to "walk your talk" with creativity and inspiration. When this is done, all participants acknowledge and respect different approaches to treating symptoms and illness; they see new ways to solve problems, and welcome other possibilities in caregiving with new elements in one's knowing, doing, and being from having engaged with others. It promotes critical reflection that is not sloppy thinking. Healing will never be achieved with an outmoded management culture of fix and cure using the latest technologies at all costs while asking caregivers to work harder and not smarter.

Reflection on self-care and healing are key to shifting to a holistic paradigm of total healing environments. *Reflection* is "thinking about practice," with critical reflection requiring that practitioners "think about how they are thinking about their practice" (Freshwater, 2004). Reflection is viewed as having two dimensions: reflecting on experience after an event occurs and reflecting in action—in real time—during an event. In this latter situation, when a nurse's usual pattern of action is frustrated, the situation must be reframed to decide how best to respond (Johns, 2004). As nurses engage in transdisciplinary dialogue with other disciplines and members of the diverse healthcare team, they are more able to translate Nightingale's philosophy and tenets into relationship-centered care, healing relationships, healing partnerships, and healing communities at the local, national, and international levels.

Relationship-Centered Care

Nightingale's tenets are a guide for nurses as they are challenged to address the complexities within the healthcare system that call for restructure and redesign. The complexity and challenges are enormous. Complexity is often referred to as a phenomenon that occurs at the boundary between order and chaos, or at the edge of chaos (Woodman, 2000). One of the reasons that our healthcare system has failed is that it did not deal with complexity; it remained locked into an autocratic hierarchy where traditional practitioners and other individuals in administrative positions believed that they knew the most appropriate information about protocols and treatments. They did not consider the emerging new story of consumers who wanted to be participants in their own health care and who were informed by the Internet and friends about treatment protocols, or the many nontraditional practitioners and healers who wanted to collaborate and participate with traditional practitioners that were often excluded.

Nightingale stressed the necessity of healing relationships with patients and families and with colleagues. Nurses are well positioned to create a new vision of healing that integrates relationship-centered care into all aspects of the healthcare system. They can come together to explore ways to discuss strategies, education, policies, and research that can lead to integrated health, healing, and integrative practice, as was done at the Gillette Nursing Summit in May 2002 (Krietzer and Disch, 2002).

Relationship-centered care is a process model of caregiving that was developed by the Pew Health Professions Commission (Tresoli and Pew and Fetzer, 1994), and is based on a vision of community. It identifies three types of relationships:

- Patient–practitioner relationship
- Community–practitioner relationship
- Practitioner–practitioner relationship

The word *client* is interchangeable with the word *person* or *patient* in this model; the word *practitioner* is interchangeable with *caregiver*. These integrated relationships are essential in relationship-centered care. Each relationship involves a unique set of responsibilities and tasks that addresses three areas—knowledge, values, and skills.

Relationship-centered care creates the condition of trust in which holistic care can be given and received. It is the human caring process in which the holistic nurse gives full attention and intention to the whole self of a person—body, mind, and spirit—not merely to the presenting symptoms, illness, crisis, or tasks to be accomplished. It is a process of gaining more understanding and insight about a person's experiences and the meaning of those experiences. It also includes experiences and the various meanings of community that include all members of the healthcare team, the patient, and the family. If a relationship-centered care model is to evolve, it requires that the system care for its employees and that self-care be valued. Nightingale reminds us that self-care is essential in quality care and in relationships with self and others. When self-care is part of the healthcare system's mission and values, the burnout phenomenon is reduced.

Nightingale as Environmentalist

Nightingale understood what we recognize today as ecological medicine, which involves not only the health of humans, but also the vitality of all the species and ecosystems with which we are related. It is concerned with not just physical health, but also psychological and spiritual health as well (Asubel, 2004). Asubel, who helped found Bioneers, an environmental organization (see www.bioneers.org), works with the "biological pioneers" who are working to help nature heal and to help us heal ourselves with nature. Bioneers says: "It's all relatives," and that we are "one notion, indivisible," a recognition we need to honor with a "Declaration of Interdependence" (p. 11). In this sense, Nightingale was one of the first Bioneers.

Anthropologist-attorney Carolyn Raffensperger (Raffensperger and Tickner, 1999) has elaborated on the term *precautionary principle*. This is derived from a German word that means "forecaring"—caring into the future—and is akin to the adage "Look before you leap." The precautionary principle says, "When an activity raises threats of harm to human health or the environment, precautionary measures shall be taken, even if some cause-and-effect relationships are not fully established scientifically" (Raffensperger, 2004, p. 44). The precautionary principle boils down to "Better safe than sorry." This is common sense to most people, which is why some experts call the precautionary principle the "duh" principle.

The precautionary principle is found throughout Nightingale's work. In *Notes on Nursing* she provides vivid cautions about what happens to people who are placed in unhealthy environments. She even writes about Dr. Angus Smith's air test, which is a precursor to what we call atmospheric pollution today:

> *...The senses of nurses and mothers become so dulled to foul air that they are perfectly unconscious of what an atmosphere they have let their children, patients, or charges, sleep in. But if the tell-tale air-test were to exhibit in the morning, both to nurses and patients and to the superior officer going round, what the atmosphere has been during the night, I question if any greater security could be afforded against a recurrence of the misdemeanour.*
>
> *And oh; the crowded national school! where so many children's epidemics have their origin, what a tale its air-test would tell! We should have parents saying, and saying rightly, "I will not send my child to that school, the air-test stands at 'Horrid.'" And the dormitories of our great boarding schools! Scarlet fever would be no more ascribed to contagion, but to its right cause, the air-test standing at "Foul"* (Nightingale, 1860a, p. 10).

Nightingale would be thrilled at the work of nurses today who are engaged in environmental issues. For example, nurse Terri Swearingen (2000) and her colleagues who took on the infamous construction of the hazardous Waste Technologies Industries (WTI) incinerator in the Ohio Valley. It was built just 1,100 feet from a 400-child elementary school that sits on a bluff. The WTI incinerator burns over 60,000 tons of toxic waste a year, and spews out mercury, lead, and dioxins through the incinerator stack that blows directly onto the children each day. Although Swearingen and her colleagues were unable to stop the construction of the WTI facility, their work led to a national appraisal of licensing requirements for toxic-waste incinerators.

Nightingale wrote specifically on observations of hazards in the environment and the nurse's responsibility:

> *If you think a patient is being poisoned by a copper kettle, cut off all possible connection to avoid further injury; it has actually been made a question of medical ethics, what should a medical man do who suspects poison?* (Nightingale, 1860a, p. 70)

The emphasis is on "suspects." This is the essence of the precautionary principle: If there is a suspicion about a harmful environment or substance, even though all of the evidence is not in, remove the person from the situation or stop the use of suspected harmful substances.

Nightingale foresaw that nurses and others have a duty and responsibility to take *anticipatory* actions to prevent harm; the burden of proof for a new technology, process, activity, or chemical lies with the proponents, not with the public. The precautionary principle always inquires about alternatives. Precautionary decision making is open, informed, and democratic, and must include all affected parties. The first sentence of the Preface in Nightingale's third edition of *Notes on Hospitals* reads as follows:

> *It may be a strange principle to enunciate as the very first requirement in a Hospital that it should do the sick no harm. It is quite necessary nevertheless to lay down such a principle, because the actual mortality in hospitals, especially in those of large crowded cities, is very much higher than any calculations founded on the mortality of the same class of patient treated out of hospitals would lead us to expect.* (Nightingale, 1863, p. 1)

Nightingale doesn't say a little harm or negligible harm; she says no harm. This anticipates the precautionary principle that emphasizes zero contamination of our environments is acceptable, not minimal or moderate contamination.

Nightingale saw the harm that hospitals could cause. Today, harm in hospitals continues to be a reality. Starfield (2000) states that hospital hazards continue, with 225,000 deaths per year occurring in hospitals, the third leading cause of death each year in the United States, after deaths from heart disease and cancer. The breakdown of these deaths are:

- 12,000 deaths/year from unnecessary surgery
- 7,000 deaths/year from medication errors in hospitals
- 20,000 deaths/year from other errors in hospitals
- 80,000 deaths/year from nosocomial infections in hospitals
- 106,000 deaths/year from nonerror, adverse effects of medications [in hospitals]

These estimates are for deaths only and do not include the adverse effects that are associated with disability or discomfort. Weigart et al. (2000) states that outpatient hazards also exist, with one analysis that estimates between 4% and 18% of consecutive patients experience adverse effects in outpatient settings, with 116 million extra physician visits, 77 million extra prescriptions, 17 million emergency department visits, 8 million hospitalizations, 3 million long-term admissions, 199,000 additional deaths, and $77 billion in extra costs.

Nightingale wrote about nurses' responsibility to educate themselves and others. Today, nurses are educating themselves about the use of toxic chemical products in hospitals, and are leaders and change agents to create a healthy physical hospital space. Examples of what can be done can be found by exploring Michael Lerner's grassroots organizations, The Collaborative on Health and the Environment (www.cheforhealth.org) and Health Care without Harm (www.hcwh.org). The collaborative, which consists of 423 organizations in 51 countries, has helped phase out the hospital incineration of dioxin-containing waste and the use of mercury-containing thermometers, each of which can contaminate a 20-acre lake (Lerner, 2004).

Nightingale focused not just on problems, but also on solutions. Problems besieged England and Europe, and the British Army throughout the British Empire, as well as other parts of the world. Because Nightingale had traveled in Europe, Greece, Egypt, Turkey, and the Crimea, she knew that for Queen Victoria to have a healthy army, the villages near the army stations needed to also be healthy since they shared the same ecological environment. Although she never traveled to India, she worked with British Army officers, civilian servants, and native citizens for over 40 years to educate the women of the villages and towns about health. She obtained data on data sheets that she designed. She then sent these sheets directly to army stations and villages and posted a return date for them to be returned directly to her. Because she analyzed the data, she was recognized as having the most complete perspective of the health of the British army in India. She even educated five British viceroys about public health issues before they took their post in India. She also wrote lengthy letters and articles on the environmental impact of deforestation in India.

Nightingale engaged in what we call today "risk assessment" and on deciding what facts we base environmental decisions. Risk assessment accepts the notion that a certain level of contamination or destruction of the environment is unavoidable. Nurses are working with others to determine the degree of risk that is acceptable and asking questions such as "What is considered safe drinking water in hospitals and in homes?" "How much atmospheric pollution can we get away with in public spaces and in the environment?" However, we must remember that the precautionary principle advocates *zero* degradation of the environment because of the uncertainty of risk assessment.

As Larry Dossey (2004) states, "The hour is late and the task is great. 'Think Globally, Act Non-Locally,' What we do to the world, we do to ourselves. Full realization of this fact can lead to a reformulation of the Golden Rule—from 'Do unto others as you would have them do unto you' to 'Do good unto others because in some sense they *are* you'" (p. 209). The extraordinary healing power of ordinary things is immense (L. Dossey, 2005).

Nightingale's Voice: Why Now?

A central question that nurse clinicians, educators, researchers, and students might ask is, "Where are we headed in healing, and how can Nightingale help us get there?" Today, nurses and others are challenged to focus as Nightingale did, and to envision the new models of healing that are possible in society. Nightingale's example is a source of strength from the past, and a model for how we can assert ourselves in this very difficult moment in human history. The ultimate aim of contemporary nursing is to integrate Nightingale's tenets of healing, leadership, and global action. When we do this we can reconstruct and reweave new patterns and themes into our healing tapestry in nursing practice, education, and research.

Nightingale's work provides ways to explore what it means to be called to a life of service for the greater good of society. We are drawn to her because she is closer to our time, and we can identify with the problems she faced and the challenges she overcame. We, like her, are involved in our own search for meaning. Nightingale's message resonates as forcefully today as in her lifetime. Nightingale is not of the past; her tenets of healing, leadership, and global action, and her way of conceptualizing the world and the Absolute, are still future-thinking. Nurses, healthcare professionals, and others are positioned to reflect critically on how Nightingale's tenets can be brought forward today.

Nightingale's message invigorates the profession with a sense of calling and being of service in healing. Nightingale would not want us to dwell on the past; she would ask us to be concerned with future developments. It helps to remember what Nightingale accomplished without the aid of numerous supportive colleagues, professional nursing organizations, or the information superhighway. If she achieved what she did with her handwritten letters, her publications, and networking with men in power, can you imagine what else Nightingale might have accomplished with a laptop computer, cell phone, fax machine, voice message service, e-mail, Internet access, and a satellite uplink? And we as nurses not only have all of these available technologies in our homes, offices, cars, hospitals, and clinics; we also have numerous professional organizations and networks to assist us.

Nightingale's tenets take her beyond contemporary nursing; she is timeless. As our understanding of Nightingale's tenets expands, we deepen our personal commitment to our work in the world. Our role in today's events will be part of tomorrow.

Pentimento

Florence Nightingale's Life:

Overview

Barbara M. Dossey

Florence Nightingale was born in Florence, Italy, on May 12, 1820, while her parents were on an extended European tour. The Nightingales were a wealthy English family active in politics. While she was growing up there was much conflict between Florence (also called Flo) and her society-conscious mother and sister; her father was more gentle and understanding. As a girl, Florence helped to nurse the poor in the nearby villages. She received a classical education at home from her father, who had been educated at Cambridge, and she became fluent in French, German, Italian, Latin, and Greek. Adept at mathematics, she developed a sophisticated understanding of statistics.

During her teens and twenties Nightingale struggled to find a path to a career. She was also in a serious 7-year courtship with a popular politician and poet. In 1849, she finally broke off the courtship and refused his marriage proposal; she chose to remain single to better serve God and mankind.

In her early twenties Nightingale realized that a new kind of nurse was needed, one who would receive formal training and would function in a new structure of hygiene, efficiency, and organization. She sought out the Kaiserswerth Institute in Dusseldorf, Germany, then the only establishment suitable for her purposes, which she visited for two weeks of observation in 1850, and again for a month of rudimentary training in 1851. Before the age of 30, with no formal training and only the information she had collected personally through her well-placed family friends, many of whom were politicians and physicians, she became one of the most knowledgeable people on hospitals, hospital construction, and health care in Europe.

Nightingale was an intensely introverted perfectionist. She was a brilliant originator and synthesizer of vast amounts of information on nursing, hospital design, sanitation (public health), army medical reform, philosophy, and religion. She understood the importance of statistics and the need to personally collect, analyze, and quantify data on many sanitary, medical, hospital, and nursing issues.

Her epic leadership at the Barrack Hospital in Scutari, Turkey, during the Crimean War (1854–1856) exemplifies how she built the powerful personal and political ties that led to the dispatch of two Royal commissions of inquiry during the Crimean War to solve grievous problems in army structure and organization. Her personal leadership and extensive data gathering, analysis, and administrative solutions were the key to successful army medical reform efforts after the war, and the military sanitation reform in India and throughout the British Empire. She was influential in both civilian and military reforms in England and India for decades, although she worked from her home and never visited these places.

She pioneered the modern administrative role of nurse superintendent during her 22 months (October 1854–July 1856) at the Barrack Hospital. During this period she made three trips to Balaclava in the Crimea where, as in Scutari, she also nursed the most critical patients. Her publications of *Notes on Hospitals* (1859 and 1863) included her work on sanitation and her hospital pavilion plan; her *Notes on Nursing* (1860) was the seminal text for the theory and practice of modern nursing. In 1860 she started the Nightingale Training School in London, which was the first modern secular school of nursing. She was a leader and adviser for the establishment of workhouse nursing and district nursing reform in England. She was a consultant and mentor to many nurses and institutions throughout the world. (See Table 1-2 in this chapter.)

Lea Hurst in Derbyshire, the Nightingale's summer residence.
© Barbara M. Dossey

Embley Park, Romsey, Hampshire, the Nightingales main residence.
© Barbara M. Dossey

By the end of her life, the influence of the Nightingale Training School was felt in 20 countries; the U.S. alone had 1,000 schools. On August 13, 1910, Nightingale fell asleep at noon and did not wake again. Her death certificate recorded the cause of her death as old age and heart failure.

She had lived 90 years and 3 months. The British government offered an elaborate state funeral and burial in Westminster Abbey, but her family declined and honored her request for a simple burial. Nightingale had written in her will that she should be buried in the beautiful 13th-century churchyard at St. Margaret's Church, East Wellow, Hampshire, England, next to her mother and father. On August 20, 1910 a memorial service filled London's St. Paul's Cathedral beyond its capacity.

(Left)
Florence Nightingale in a familiar pose, c. 1839, sketched by her cousin Hilary Bonham Carter.

(Below)
Florence Nightingale (seated with scarf) with Sir Harry Verney (brother-in-law) at Claydon in 1886, with Mary Crossland, home sister (standing behind Nightingale), and the Nightingale probationers.

Lithograph by William Simpson of Florence Nightingale speaking with a medical officer in the Barrack Hospital, 1856. © Florence Nightingale Museum

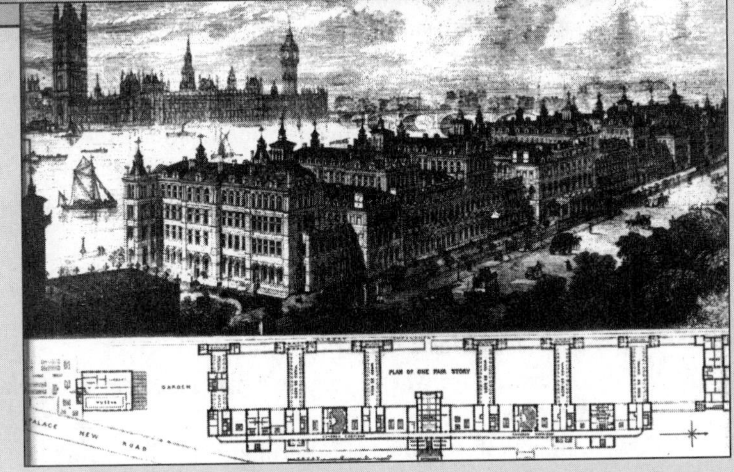

The new St. Thomas' Hospital, which opened in 1871, was built using Nightingale's pavilion floor plan. The Houses of Parliament and Big Ben can be seen across the Thames. © Florence Nightingale Museum

During her lifetime she wrote over 100 books and documents. Ten thousand of her letters form the largest private collection in the British Library in London; another 3,000 to 4,000 are held in private collections (see Appendix C). She is on various Anglican Church calendars throughout the world. In 2001, Florence Nightingale received official recognition in the Episcopal Church of the United States Liturgical Calendar of Lesser Feasts and Fasts in the *Book of Common Prayer* (2004). The inaugural Florence Nightingale Service was held on August 12, 2001, at the National Cathedral in Washington, D.C.

Directions and Reflections

Directions for Future Research

1. Analyze the application and integration of Florence Nightingale's three tenets—healing, leadership, and global action—in practice, education, and research.
2. Investigate how attention to spirituality in clinical practice may influence health outcomes and career satisfaction, retention, absences, and illness.
3. Compare relationship-centered care to traditional care on length of stay, cost, and health services utilization.
4. Collect stories and narratives that provide examples of best practices related to healing, leadership, global action, nursing theory, patterns of knowing, relationship-centered care, and transdisciplinary dialogues.

Reflections on Florence Nightingale's Tenets: Healing

1. How do I define healing?
2. What role does spirituality play in my life?
3. What do I experience when I consciously practice presence with myself and with others?
4. How do I know that healing is happening in my life or in the patients for whom I care?
5. How do I feel when I consider myself as an instrument in the healing process when by myself and with others?
6. How do I care for myself on a daily basis?

Florence Nightingale's 13 Formal Letters to Her Nurses (1872–1900)

Barbara M. Dossey

Alarmed at the lack of moral training and the educational components specific to the "art and science" of nursing, Florence Nightingale wrote 13 formal letters (also called addresses) to her nurses or those who had been in training at the Nightingale Training School at St. Thomas' Hospital, London, from 1872, when she was 52 years old, until 1900, when she was 80. Nightingale's chronic, debilitating illness, her work on other projects, or deaths of relatives or friends meant that in some years she wrote no letter. These annual letters were read aloud to the probationers (student nurses) and graduate nurses by Sir Harry Verney, the Chairman of the Nightingale Fund, who was also her brother-in-law. (See the Chapter 1 Pentimento, Florence Nightingale's Life.) After his death in 1894, they were read by others. Each nurse received a printed copy of the letter marked "For Private Use Only."

The Methodology: Interpretive Biography and Inspiration

The research process applied here is interpretive biography (see Appendix B for the steps in the synthesis process): the studied use of letters, journals, narratives, manuscripts, and other documents that describe turning points in an individual's life (Denzin, 1989). (The 13 unedited letters are found in Part Four.) Unraveling the structure and underlying complexities within these letters, we can discover Nightingale's tenets of healing, leadership, and global action, and place them within the context of her experience during these years. These letters have been quoted many times; however, they have never been examined within the context of Nightingale's mystic spiritual development, her social action as a practical mystic, or their relevance to contemporary nursing.

2

I have been intrigued by Florence Nightingale since 1992, when I was engaged in research for my illustrated biography of her (B. Dossey, 2000a). I found her work for humankind and her discourses on the art and science of nursing stunning. After completing the book, I thought that I was through with Nightingale research. However, my fascination with Nightingale only deepened in August 1999 while I was on a trip with my husband. In the small town of Sheridan, Montana, I received a facsimile copy of my Nightingale book jacket prior to print production. After proofing the cover, I felt relieved to have finally completed all aspects of the project.

From there, I made a stop at an antique shop to look at their old books. The first small, leather-bound book that I pulled from the shelf had a gold-leaf stamp on the spine that read *Science and Health: The Key to the Scriptures* by M.B.G. Eddy (Mary Baker G. Eddy, (1821–1910,) founder of Christian Science). Inside, the copyright was 1895, and this 93rd printing mentioned Nightingale (see Chapter 1). As I pulled this book from the shelf, I knocked to the floor another small, leather-bound book. When I picked it up, the gold-stamped words on the cover read *Imitation of Christ*. I knew immediately that this was a reprint of a work written in 1427 by Thomas À Kempis (1380–1471), the medieval mystic. This little copy was dated 1890.

During a 1998 research trip to the Florence Nightingale Museum in London, I had read Florence Nightingale's 13 formal letters to her nurses, but I did not complete a formal synthesis of them. I also had studied Nightingale's underlined passages in her own large copy of the *Imitation of Christ*. The only connection that I made at this time was that Nightingale valued Christian principles and tried to imitate the life of Christ in her own life and work as seen in these formal letters. But in a flash on this August day, reading this table of contents, three short pages, I saw for the first time the overview of the four sections in the *Imitation of Christ*. I had completely missed this in reading Nightingale's copy. (See the second Pentimento in this chapter: Florence Nightingale: Writing on the Medieval Mystics.) I realized that this book contained the principles that Nightingale had integrated in her formal letters to her nurses from 1872 to 1900. These letters were of a mystic writing to her followers. I had never made this connection. Tears flowed from my eyes, and a chill ran through me. Over the next week, I carefully read this little book. It was clear to me that I would engage in more Nightingale research in the future.

Previous biographers and authors have quoted sentences or short sections from these letters. However, my study adds a new perspective to these letters because they have never been analyzed in the context of Nightingale's mystic spiritual development. Basic to this interpretive biographical study was the assumption that Florence Nightingale was a 19th-century mystic (see the first Pentimento in this chapter: Florence Nightingale: The Practical Mystic). She experienced the five phases of mystical spiritual development in the Western tradition as identified by Evelyn Underhill (1875–1941). Nightingale's social action and contributions are found in her letters, diaries, monographs, books, records, government and military documents, as well as in many secondary sources. In this study I revisit mysticism and mystic spiritual development in order to analyze Nightingale's 13 letters to her nurses in a context that can inform contemporary nursing.

The Letters (1872–1900): Synopses and Excerpts

The following synopses and excerpts reveal Nightingale's "stream of consciousness." The punctuation and the page numbers are those in the original letters.

(*Note: There were no men in the Nightingale School of Nursing at the time these letters were written. Thus, all references to nurses were feminine pronouns. However, her ideas apply to both women and men in nursing today.)*

1872

Nightingale (1872b) describes the nurse, nursing, and the importance of personal progress in the work that is for God:

> For us who Nurse, our Nursing is a thing, which, unless in it we are making progress every year, every month, every week—take my word for it we are going back. … To be a good woman at all, one must be an improving woman; for stagnant waters sooner or later, and stagnant air, as we ourselves, always grows corrupt and unfit for use. … We Nurses may well call ourselves "blessed among women," in this that we can be always exercising all these charities, and so fulfill the work our God has given us to do. A woman who thinks in herself: Now I am a 'full Nurse,' a 'skilled Nurse'—I have learnt "all that there is to be learnt";—take my word for it: she does not know *what a Nurse is* & she never *will* know—she is gone back already. (p. 1)

She observes that nursing is a lifelong professional and personal pursuit: "And at the end of that time a good Nurse will say: 'I learn something every day.'" (p. 1)

For Nightingale, conceit has no place in nursing: "Conceit and Nursing cannot exist in the same person—any more than new patches on an old garment." She reflects on scientific progress and gives an example from her childhood:

> When I was a child, I remember reading that Sir Isaac Newton—who was as you know, perhaps the greatest discoverer among the Stars & the Earth's wonders who ever lived—said in his last hours: "I seem to myself like a child who has been playing with a few pebbles on the sea shore—leaving unsearched all the wonders of the great ocean beyond."

She asks the nurses to reflect on their attitudes about what they have learned:

> By the side of this, put a Nurse leaving her Training-School & reckoning up what she has learnt, ending with: The only wonder is that one head can contain it all. [What a small head it must be, then!]. I seem to have remembered all through life Sir Isaac Newton's words. (p. 2)

She encourages her nurses to be aware of God's purpose in their work, and to value fellow human beings:

> When the head & the hands are very full, as in Nursing, it is so easy, so very easy, if the heart has not an earnest purpose of God & our neighbour, to end in doing one's work only for oneself—& not at all, even when we seem to be serving our neighbours, not at all for them or for God. … What a privilege it is the work that God has given us Nurses to do, if we will only let Him have His own way with us—a greater privilege to my mind than He has given to any woman, except to those who are teachers. (p. 2)

Her focus is on the organization rather than the individual nurse, as she reminds her nurses that nursing is a call from God:

> The very essence of all good organizations is, that everybody should do her own work in such a way as to help & not hinder every one else's work, … the call of God—(for in all work He calls us) of none effect—it is grieving the spirit of God—it is doing our best to make all free will associations intolerable. (p. 4)

Nightingale reflects on the benefits of secular nursing. She asks the nurses to increase their personal responsibility, to deepen their understanding of the meaning in the work, to know one's self, and to remember that the work of nursing is for God:

> Does it not seem to you that the greater freedom of secular Nursing Institutions as it requires (or ought to require) greater individual responsibility, greater self command in each, greater nobleness in each, greater *self possession* in patience;—so, that very need of self possession, of greater nobleness in each requires (or ought to require) greater thought in each, more discretion, & higher not less obedience. (p. 4)

Nightingale shares thoughts on nursing, the nurse, and the patient and society; she also focuses on the art of nursing and personal reflection:

> Lastly, it is charity to nurse sick bodies well—it is greater charity to nurse well & patiently sick minds—tiresome sufferers. But there is a greater charity even than these: to do good to those who are not good to us—to behave well to those who behave ill to us—to serve with love those who do not even receive our service with good temper—to forgive on the instant any slight, real or fancied we may have received, or any worse injury. (p. 8)

The example she set of the love, forgiveness, and patience in the work can be seen in the following passage:

> We cannot 'do good' to those who 'persecute' us for we are not 'persecuted'—if we cannot pray 'Father, forgive them, for they know not what they do'—for none are nailing us to the cross—how much more must we try to serve with patience & love any who use us spitefully to nurse with all our hearts any thankless, peevish Patients! (p. 8)

The Nightingale Training School was very popular in America, and she shares part of a letter from American author Harriet Beecher Stowe (1811–1896), who wrote about Agnes Jones, a Nightingale graduate and a workhouse nurse pioneer who died of typhus in 1868. Jones was dedicated to improving the environment to assist in the healing of the poor:

> We Nurses may well call ourselves "blessed among women" that we can be always exercising these 3 Charities—& so fulfil the work our God has given us to do. … Just as I was writing this came a letter from Mrs. Beecher Stowe who wrote "Uncle Tom's Cabin." She has so fallen in love with the character of our Agnes Jones ("Una") that she asks about the progress of our works—supposing that we have many more Unas—saying that that is "making virtue attractive"—& asking me to tell for them in America about our Unas. (p. 8)

1873

Nightingale (1873a) asks her nurses to integrate their ethical, aesthetic, and personal values and qualities in nursing the patient. She reminds the nurses that they are not to preach religion:

> Let us be on our guard against the danger, not exactly of thinking too well of ourselves (for no one consciously does this), but of isolating ourselves, of falling into party spirit—always remembering that, if we can do any good to others, we must draw others to us by the (not loud but) not unfelt influence

> of our characters, and not by any profession of what we are—least of all, by a profession of Religion. And this, by the way, applies peculiarly to what we are with our patients. … Least of all should a *woman* try to exercise religious influences with her patients, as it were, by a *ministry,* a chaplaincy. We are not chaplains. It is what she is in *herself,* and what comes out of herself, or of what she *is* (almost without her knowing it herself)—that exercises a moral or religious influence over her patients. (p. 2)

She reminds her nurses that they are role models to patients and others:

> No set form of words is of any use. And patients are so quick to see whether a Nurse is consistent always in herself—whether she *is* what she *says* to them. And if she is not, it is no use. *If she is*, of how much use may the simplest word of soothing, of comfort, or even of reproof—especially in the quiet night—(unawares to herself) to the roughest patient, who is there from drink, or to the still innocent child, or to the anxious toil-worn mother or husband! But if she wishes to do this, she must keep up a sort of divine calm, and high sense of duty in her own mind. Christ was alone, from time to time, in the wilderness or on mountains. If *He* needed this, how much more must we? (p. 2)

She conveys ideas on self-care, and how to be reflective and develop the aesthetic qualities of the art of nursing that shape one's personal character. It is important to note that Nightingale provided a private room for each of the nurses:

> Quiet in our own rooms (and a room of your own is specially provided for each one here)—we have bustle every day—a few minutes of calm thought to offer up the day to God—how indispensable it is, in this ever increasing hurry of life! When we live 'so fast' do we not require a breathing time, a moment or two daily, to think where we are going,—at this time, especially, when we are laying the foundation of our afterlife—in reality, the most important time of all? (p. 2)

Nightingale gives many examples of the high purpose of the profession that convey her message about the empirical and personal domains:

> And may I say a thing from my experience? No training is of any use, unless one can learn (1) to feel, and (2) to think out things for oneself. And if we have not true religious feeling and purpose, Hospital life, the highest of all things with these—without them, becomes a mere routine and bustle, and a very hardening routine and bustle. But it would take a whole book for me to count up these; and I am going back to the first thing that we were saying: how shallow a thing is Hospital life—which is, or ought to be, the most inspiring—without deep religious purpose! For, as years go on, we shall have others to train; and find that the spring of religion is dried up within ourselves. (p. 3)

Nightingale often reflects on the importance of prayer to assist with the nurse's ethical, aesthetic, and personal development:

> For, to all good women, life is a prayer; and though we pray in our own rooms, in the Wards and at Church, the end must not be confounded with the means. … For prayer is communion or co-operation with God. … This is the spirit of prayer, the spirit of conversation or communion with God, which leads us in our Nursing silently to think of Him, and refer it to Him. (p. 4)

She speaks of the support of colleagues and Christian friendships:

> The friendships which have begun at this School may last through life, and be a help and strength to us. For may we not regard the opportunity given for acquiring as one of the uses of this place? And Christian friendship, in uniting us to a friend, as uniting us at the same time to Christ and God? (p. 4)

She reminds her nurses that they can center themselves in their busy hospital work and still remember ways to be with God:

> We desire for a few minutes in each day to live in the more immediate presence of God, in presence of truth and justice, and holiness and love. Then is the time to get rid of our vain self-excuses, and see ourselves as we truly are in the sight of God; and to think of others as they are in the presence of God. … These words may seem in a Hospital life 'like dreams.' But they are not dreams if we take them for the spirit of our School and the rule of our nursing. 'To practice them, to feel them, to make them our own.' This is not far from the 'kingdom of Heaven' in a Hospital. (p. 7)

1874

Nightingale (1874a) reinforces the importance of personal qualities in nursing: "Trustworthy, punctual, quiet and orderly, cleanly and neat, patient, cheerful, and kindly." She remarks:

> We scarcely need any other lesson but what explains these to us. *Trustworthy* that is, faithful: Trustworthy when we have no one by to urge or to order us. 'Her lips were never opened but to speak the truth.' Can that be said of us? Trustworthy, in keeping our soul in our hands, never excited, but always ready to lift it up to God; unstained by the smallest flirtation, innocent of the smallest offence, even in thought. … How can we be 'stewards of grace' to one another? By giving the 'grace' of our good example to all around us. … Let us try this—every woman to work as though success depended on herself. (p. 2)

Nightingale explores the importance of an empirical basis for nursing through study and scientific inquiry taught by the ward sisters (nursing instructors), and the hospital physicians and surgeons. She asks her nurses to assess patient problems and needs, and to identify outcomes by incorporating thinking, feeling, and sensory experiences in their work. She stresses the importance of problem-solving and disciplined inquiry:

> Do we look enough into the importance of giving ourselves thoroughly to study *in the hours of study*, of keeping careful *Notes of Lectures*, of keeping notes of all type *cases*, and of cases interesting from not being type cases: so as to improve our powers of observation: all essential, *if we are in future to have charge*? Do we keep in view the importance of helping ourselves to understand these cases by reading at the time *books* where we can find them described, and by listening to the *remarks* made by *Physicians* and Surgeons in going round with their Students? So shall we do everything in our power to become proficient, not only in knowing the symptoms and what is to be done, *but in knowing the* 'REASON WHY' *of* such symptoms, and *why* such and such a thing is done: and so on, till we can some day TRAIN OTHERS to *know the 'reason why.'* (pp. 5–6)

She further comments on the importance of the nurses' notes on lectures and their observations:

> Such observations are a religious meditation: for is it not the best part of religion to imitate the benevolence of God to man? And how can you do this—in this your calling especially—if you do not thoroughly understand your calling, and is not every study to do this a religious contemplation? (p. 6)

She provides an example from the Christian missionary David Livingstone. She reflects on the nurse as a traveler and her influence on society as a model of high morals:

> A Nurse is like a traveller, from the quantity of people who pass before her in the ever-changing wards. And she is like a traveller also in this, that, as Livingstone used to say, either the vices or the virtues of civilisation follow the footsteps of the traveller, and he cannot help it; so they do those of the Nurse. And missioning will be, whether she will or not, the background of her nursing, as it is the background of travelling. The traveller may call himself a missionary or not, as he likes. He is one, for good or for evil. So is the Nurse. … What his influence was, even after his death, you know. … Livingstone always remembered that a poor old Scotchman on his death-bed had said to him: 'Now, lad, make religion the every-day business of your life, not a thing of fits and starts; for if you do not, temptation and other things will get the better of you.' Such a Nurse, one who makes religion the '*every-day business* of her life,' is a 'Missionary,' even if she never speak a word. (p. 11)

Of her life experiences she says:

> Believe me, who has seen a good deal of the world, we may give you an institution to learn in, but it is YOU who must furnish the 'heroic' feeling of doing your duty, doing your best, without which no institution is safe, without which Training-Schools are meat without salt. *You* must be our salt, without which civilisation is but corruption, and all churches only dead establishments. (p. 12)

1875

Nightingale (1875) explores concepts about the nurse, patients, society, and one's ethical, aesthetic, and personal qualities:

> We have three judges—our God, our neighbour, and ourselves. Our own judgment of ourselves is, perhaps, generally too favourable; our neighbour's judgment of us too unfavourable, except in the case of close friends, who may sometimes spoil each other. Shall we always remember to seek *God's* judgment of us, knowing this, that it will some day find us, whether we seek it or not? *He* knows who is *His* nurse, and who is not. (p. 2)

She asks her nurses to pray that God will find more qualified workers for nursing. She gives an example from district nursing, and notes that the hard work requires that nurses practice conscious awareness of wholeness of the individual—body, mind, and spirit.

> Above all, let us pray that God will send real workers into this immense 'field' of Nursing, made more immense this year by the opening out of London *District* Nursing at the bedside of the sick poor at home. A woman who takes the sentimental view of Nursing (which she calls 'ministering,' as if she were

> an angel), is, of course, worse than useless; a woman possessed with the idea that she is making a sacrifice will never do; and a woman who thinks any kind of Nursing work 'beneath a Nurse' will simply be in the way. But if the right woman is moved by God to come to us, what a welcome we will give her, and how happy she will soon be in a work, the many blessings of which none can know as we know them, though we know the worries too! (pp. 10–11)

She expresses the need to build a community of peers while integrating Christian values; she speaks of the unfolding mystery, holiness, and sacredness in the work:

> May we each and all of us Nurses be faithful to the end; remembering this that no one Nurse stands alone! May we not say, in the words of the Prophet, that it is 'The Lord' who 'hath gathered' us Nurses 'together out of the lands'? Should not, therefore, all this Training School be so melted into one heart and mind, that we may with *one* heart and mind act and nurse and sing together our praise and thanksgiving, blessing and gratitude, for mercies, every one of which seems to belong to the whole School. (p. 12)

1876

Nightingale (1876) begins this letter by asking the nurses to rejoice in their success and to grieve over the disappointments in their training; she asks them to work together to find solutions and make the necessary changes. She praises their hard work as told to her by Matron Sarah Wardropper, the medical instructor, the home sisters, and the ward sisters who have had contact with the students on a daily basis. She remarks on the classes that they have attended, and asks them to remember that education must be linked to high purpose:

> What we did last year we may look upon not as a matter of conceit, cut of encouragement. We must not fail this year, and we'll not fail. We'll keep up to the mark: nay more, we will press on to a higher mark. For our 'calling' is a high one (the 'little' things, remember: a high excellence in little things). (p. 2)

She stressed the value of living as a community of healing, and caring for each other:

> Now I say, we live together: let us live for each other's comfort: we are all working together: grasp the idea of this as a larger work than our own little pet hobbies, which are very narrow: our little personal wishes, feelings, piques, or tempers. This is not individual work: a real Nurse sinks self. Remember we are not so many small selves, but members of a community. 'Little children, love one another.' To love, that is, to help one another, to strive together, to act together, to work for the same end, to bring to perfection the sisterly feeling of fellow-workers, without which nothing great is done, nothing good lasts. Might not St. John have been thinking of us Nurses in our Training Schools when he said that? May God be with us all and we be *one* in Him and in His *work*. (p. 3)

She expands on her previous thoughts of what it means to be a nurse:

> If we do the work we don't like from the higher motive till we like it: that is one test of being a real Nurse. … If you wish to be trained or exercise only in that which you like and know you do well, it is needless to say that what you want is not to be Trained Nurses but to do what you like. … If you wish

to do what you like and what you do well for the sake of being praised by others, then you nurse for your own vanity, not for the sake of Nursing. But if you wish to be trained to do all Nursing well, even what you do not like—trained to perfection in little things—that is Nursing for the sake of nursing; for the sake of God and of your neighbor. And remember, in little things as in great, No Cross, no Crown. (p. 3)

She elaborates on the personal qualities that each individual nurse should model in the nursing residence. She speaks of quietness, neatness, not slamming doors, no gossip or unnecessary chatter or loud talking on the stairs. She describes the nurses' dress whether on duty or off:

> Do you remember that Christ holds up the wild flowers as our example in dress? Why? He says: God 'clothes' the wild flowers. How does he clothe them? First, their 'clothes' are exactly suitable for the kind of place they are in and the kind of work they have to do. So should ours be. Second: field flowers are never double: double flowers change their useful stamens for showy petals. And so have no seeds. These double flowers are like the useless appendages now worn on the dress, and very much in your way. Wild flowers have purpose in all their beauty. So ought dress to have:—nothing purposeless about it. Third: the colours of the wild flowers are perfect in harmony, and not many of them. Fourth: there is not a speck on the freshness with which flowers come out of the dirty earth. Even when our clothes are getting rather old we may imitate the flower: for we may make them look as fresh as a daisy. (p. 4)

She continues on cleanliness, health, the environment, and disease:

> When we obey all God's laws as to cleanliness, fresh air, pure water, good habits, good dwellings, good drains, food and drink, work and exercise, health is the result: when we disobey, sickness. 110,000 lives are needlessly sacrificed every year in this kingdom by our disobedience, and 22,000 people are needlessly sick all year round. And why? Because we will not know, will not obey God's simple Health-laws. No epidemic can resist thorough cleanliness and fresh air. (p. 5)

She reinforces her beliefs in the role of the nurse for serving God and society:

> The first thing is to be sure to serve God by helping every fellow-servant of God, and also many who are not servants of God at all—helping them, not by words, but by your acts, to become fellow servants; then to build up, by learning to do every thing to perfection, the real Nurses in ourselves. (p. 5)

She uses the parable of the Pharisees and wonders if there are any among her nurses. She moves on to encourage her nurses to have zeal for God's sake and His work's sake, and to use intention in their work:

> Zeal by itself does not make a good Nurse: it makes a Pharisee. Christ is so strong upon this point of not being conceited, of not nursing to show what 'fine fellows' we are as Nurses, that He actually says 'it is conceited of us to let our hands know what the other does.' What will He say if He sees one of us doing all her work to let not only her other hand but other people know she does it? Yet all our best work which looks so well may be done from this motive. (pp. 5–6)

She had read a medical journal article written by a friend about the Nightingale nurses and how "Mrs. Gamp"—the drunken, brutal, fat, ignorant caricature of a nurse—was gone. She encouraged her nurses to remember that their work was service for God, and to be proud of the school and this new image of nursing, but not to be conceited about being recognized:

> Ah, there's the rub. You see that our name is 'up' for the world. That's what I should like to be left out. This is what friendly critics say of us, and we may be very sure that unfriendly critics say much worse. … Christ made no light matter of conceit. Keep the usefulness, and let the conceit go. (p. 6)

Nightingale asks her nurses to reflect on the art and science of nursing and whether patients are better due to their care:

> Let our Master be able to say some day that every one of the patients has been the better, not only in body but in spirit—whether going to life or to death—for having been nursed by each one of you. (p. 7)

She mentions night nurses, and nurses who have gone abroad, and one who died of typhoid fever, as examples of the sacrifices called for. She challenges each nurse to be brave and have courage in the work:

> In a Nurse's career there is no time to fold hands: it is only the cowardly and the conceited who do that. On, On: there is a hill to climb: there is also a 'Valley of Humiliation' to pass through before we cross the river—before we are welcome home. If Bunyan wrote a 'Pilgrim's Progress,' let us write—not in a book, but in our lives—a Nurse's Progress: for a Nurse is, beyond all others, a pilgrim. On, on: till we can say the course is run: the goal is won: we have got home! (p. 10)

1878

Nightingale (1878) challenges her nurses to see other nursing training schools as friendly rivals because they too are working for the good of society:

> A good Nurse will *test* her Nursing & learn something to the last day of her Nursing life. Wish well to every other Trained & Training Nurse in the world. Oh what a good thing is friendly rivalry! If you stand still, I should wish that every other school should pass you: not that every other school should stand still to let you go ahead. (p. 6)

She speaks of the ethical and the personal domains in nursing and how nurses are role models for patients and others:

> O dear Nurses all, by all means let us mind what we say—but still more let us mind what we do. Let other Nurses only 'see' in us what they had better do themselves, & never what they had better avoid. What we wish *them* to do let them see *us* do. (p. 11)

Beginning in 1861 other hospitals began their own nursing training schools that competed with the Nightingale Training School for qualified women to enter the profession. She challenges her nurses to reflect on their school and work:

> I can tell you that: we are on our trial again after 17 years—whether we win or not depends upon you. Trial is the only thing to prove if we are worth any thing. I hail it. Let us take care not to be left behind. But, if we deserve it, I for one shall say I am glad we are left behind. (p. 12)

She uses an analogy to the brave British soldiers during the Crimean War to call on her nurses to have the same courage in nursing:

> Forward the Light Brigade of St. Thomas' all over the country. (Not heavy in hand with complaints & conceit & self-seeking: *that* we *won't* be). And don't let us be like the chorus at the play which cries 'Forward, forward,' every two minutes: & never stirs a step. May we all be able to say at the next New Year, May God be able to say at our First New Year in His eternity: O the brave charge was made! (p. 13)

1879

Nightingale (1879a) focuses on discipline and humility:

> What makes us endure until the end?—Discipline … Humility—to think our life worth nothing except as serving in a corps, God's nursing corps, unflinching, obedience, steadiness, and endurance in carrying out His work—that is true discipline, that is true greatness, and may God give it to us Nurses, and make us His own Nurses. (p. 2)

She stressed the importance of moral character and continuous training:

> And let us not think that these things can be done in a day or a night, No, they are the result of no rough-and-ready method. The most important part of those efforts was to be found in the patient labour of years. … It is when discipline and training have become a kind of second nature to us that they can be accomplished every day and every night. … Every feeling, every thought we have stamps a character upon us, especially in our year of training, and in the next year or two. … True discipline is to uphold authority, and not to mind the trouble. We come into the work to do the work. … We Nurses are taught the 'reason why.' (p. 3)

1881

Nightingale (1881) focuses on what it means to be a good woman and a nurse, and ways to become involved in the art of nursing with heartfelt caring, compassion, empathy, and mindfulness. Her comments touch on the nurse, the patient, and the empirical, ethical, aesthetic, and personal domains:

> What makes a good woman is the better or higher or holier nature: quietness, gentleness, patience, endurance, forbearance—forbearance with patients, her fellow workers, her superiors, her equals. … You are here to be trained for Nurses—attendants on the wants of the sick—helpers, in carrying out Doctors' orders (not Medical Students) though Theory is very useful when carried out by practice. Theory without practice is ruinous to Nurses. (pp. 1–2)

She explores what it means to be of service to patients and to use intention in the work; she asks the nurses to recognize their influence on others, and to work with and support each other:

> Let us value our training not as much as it makes us cleverer or superior to others, but inasmuch as it enables us to be more useful & helpful to our fellow creatures, the sick who most want our help. Let it be our ambition to be thorough good women—and never let us be ashamed of the name of "nurse." Let us each & all, realizing the importance of our influences on others—stand shoulder to shoulder & not alone, in the good cause. (pp. 2–3)

1883

Nightingale (1883) once again asks her nurses if they are finding meaning and joy in nursing:

> And it is the old, old question too: Are we all of us on our own mettle in our life's work? Joy to us if we are. If not, there *can* only be disappointments. To those of us in earnest in our desire to be thorough workers—thorough women—thorough Nurses [and no woman can be a Good Nurse unless she is a good woman]. (pp. 1–2)

She reflects again on the empirical and the personal domains in nursing training:

> Training is drawing out what you know yourselves. Learn your work thoroughly in your year of training. Store it up & practice it in your brain, eyes & hands, so that you may always know where to find it,—& these—brain, eyes & hands may always be your ready servants. ... If you don't go on you will fall back. Aim higher. (p. 3)

Nightingale asks her nurses to consider the suffering of the patients and what it means to be called to a work of service:

> We Nurses should remember to help our suffering fellow creatures in our Calling—not to amuse ourselves. Let us make our 'Calling' 'Sure.' (p. 5)

She explores thoroughness in nursing, because the work can't be done half-heartedly. She reminds the nurses that the eyes of the world are on the school, and to rejoice in personal success, but also to rejoice in the success of other schools:

> Let us run the race where all may win: rejoicing in their successes, as our own, & mourning their failures, wherever they are, as our own. We are all one Nurse. But see that we fall not off. We must fight the good fight steadily, with all our heart & all our mind & all our strength. ... So may we raise the standard, higher & higher, of thoroughness—(& with thoroughness always goes humility)—of steady, patient, silent, cheerful work. So may we all be on the alert—always on our mettle. Let us be always in the van of wise & noiseless high training & progress. (pp. 5–7)

1886

Nightingale (1886) reviews the progress that the Nightingale Training School has made, and encourages the nurses to move forward in their philosophy of caring and healing. She encourages the nurses to care for themselves, so that they might be more aware of caring for themselves when they are not under the watchful eye of the home sister in their nursing home after they have finished their training:

> What is giving ourselves to our work? It is when duty, intelligence, humanity, religion (or the tie to God,) are all embarked with us in our Work (p. 3). And here I must implore you to remember that God commands us Nurses to keep a sensible but not selfish care of our own bodies. For how can we serve our Patients well, or glorify God in our work, when half-hearted, weary, and dull, as is so often brought on by lack of proper care of the wants of our bodies, fresh air, regularity in going to bed and getting up, taking proper and sufficient food to nourish us, for in a few months you will all be out of this Home. And this caution is needed most by those out of the Home. (pp. 7–8)

She reminds her nurses that they are role models for others and that they must exhibit health, well-being, and high values:

> And how are we to 'teach,' every one of us? How are we to teach the poor Patients, and ourselves, and each other? Not by preaching; by example, by *being* it *ourselves*. ... How much less can we teach goodness, unselfishness, which is the essence of goodness, except by *being* it ourselves! ... To sum up: we teach unconsciously that which we are, whether this be good, indifferent, bad. We do not teach what we preach, but what we are.' (pp. 10, 12)

In her *Notes on Hospitals* (Nightingale, 1863), she integrates thoughts on the nurse, patient, the environment, and health. She elaborates her philosophy and ethics, aesthetics, and personal qualities in care and caring:

> I began my "Notes on Hospitals" with "the first thing in a Hospital is that it should do the Patients no harm." The first thing for a Probationer is that she should do the Patients no harm. She will always be in danger of doing them harm, noticed or unnoticed, if she is not thorough and perfect in every detail of Ward work, of order and cleanliness, and down to the temperature of a hot water bottle (or "up," which you please) or of a poultice. The smallest thing is important to a Patient, to that most delicate instrument, the human body. We are justly horrified at a mistake in giving medicine or stimulant. We are not perhaps so horrified as we should be at mistakes in fresh air, feeding helpless Patients, cleanliness, warmth, order, and all the rest of what we are taught that Nursing helps Nature and the Physician and Surgeon. It is straightness that is so much wanted: straightness of purpose, work, conduct. (pp. 13–14)

Aware of repeating many of her words before, she writes on humility in the work for God:

> I have said nearly these same words before. But let us *do*. Let each of us at the close of every day of this New Year be able humbly to ask of OUR "Great Commander,"—and to lead straight, we must go straight ourselves—did I lead them straight? Did I go straight, and lead straight, in my day's work? (p. 14)

1888

By 1888 Nightingale faced opposition from key nursing leaders and other organizations over nurses' registration. Nightingale did not believe that registration would ensure moral training. The proregistration group had increased nurse training to three years. The antiregistration group, including the Nightingale Training School, required only one year. Nightingale tried to foster goodwill between the associations. The registration battle would continue until 1893, when the proregistration group, now known as the British Nurses Association, was given permission to call themselves "chartered" and not "registered." In 1914, four years after Nightingale's death, the Nightingale Fund Council agreed to establish a three-year training school at St. Thomas' Hospital. Parliament approved a bill that mandated nurses' registration in 1919.

Nightingale's vision of healing included the interdependence of all associations in order to achieve a united nursing mission. She wrote of each nurse's accountability:

> To each and to all I wish the very highest success in the widest meaning of the word in the life's work you have chosen. … We hear much of "Associations" now. It is impossible indeed to live in isolation: we are dependent upon others for the supply of all our wants, and others upon us. Every Hospital is an "Association" in itself. We of this School are an Association in the deepest sense, regulated—at least we strive towards it—on high & generous principles: through organizations working at once for our own & our fellow Nurses' success. For, to make progress possible, we must make this inter-dependence a source of good; not a means of standing still. All "Association" is organised "inter-dependence." We must never forget that the *"Individual"* makes the Association. What the Association is depends upon each of its members. (p. 1)

She challenges her nurses to strive to achieve their full potential through their inner sense of values, goals, authenticity, and sincerity:

> Rules may become a dead letter. It is the spirit of them that 'giveth life.' So is the individual, inside, that counts—the level she is upon which tells. The next is only the outward shell or envelope. She must become a 'rule of thought'—to herself thru' the Rules. Every Nurse must grow. No Nurse can stand still, she must go forward, or she will go backward, every year. (pp. 2–3)

Nightingale urges her nurses to continue to recognize that nursing is a calling and a work of the soul that engages empirical, ethical, aesthetic, and personal values and qualities:

> And how can a Certificate or public register show this? Rather, she ought to have a moral 'Clinical' Thermometer in herself. … Nursing work must be quiet work—An individual work—Anything else is contrary to the whole realness of the work. *Where* am *I*, the individual, in my utmost soul? *What* am I, the inner woman, called 'I'?—That is the question. … Let each one of us take the abundant & excellent food for the mind which is offered us, in our training, our classes, our lectures, our Examinations & reading—not as 'Parasites,' no—none of you will ever do that—but as bright & vigorous fellow workers: working out the better way every day to the end of life. (pp. 3–4)

1897

Nightingale (1897a) focuses on God's blessing and presence, and on patience, self-respect, self-acceptance, and self-love. She addresses the issues of empirics, ethics, and aesthetics. She expresses ideas on life-and-death issues in nursing, and how to honor inner truth, integrity, wisdom, and to always remember that nursing is a calling:

> And what does His blessing mean to us nurses? Does it not mean that, as nursing has to do with life and death (the greatest gifts of God), with the

> body which is the "temple" of the Holy Spirit, all our "works" in it must "begin, continue and end" in Him to His "honour above all things"? If God has given us this calling (nursing to His honour), He has put His honour into our hands. If we let it go down, we are dishonouring Him; we are making it a mere matter of silver and pence. ... A good woman is one who gives the best of a woman—intellectual, moral, practical—to her patients, under the orders of a doctor. (p. 1)

She writes of nursing as work for God, and the importance of developing aesthetic and personal values such as discipline, loyalty, peace, goodwill, humility, kindness, good habits, and joyfulness in the work:

> Would you offer less than your best to God?... What should be the characteristics of the good woman? Discipline. The highest discipline is when every woman on the hospital staff works as one, "as members of one body."... Loyalty to one's corps and one's chiefs. Peace and goodwill to all. Love and humility, for without humility there can be no real love or good will, but much ill will. Kindness. I must add good habits, and I may almost add joyfulness in one's work. Are not these some of the characteristics of the good woman? (pp. 1–2)

She continues: "Nursing should not be a sacrifice, but one of the highest delights of life" (p. 2). She addresses specifics about hospital nursing, workhouse nursing, and district nursing, and discusses the critical time in nursing and the need for progress:

> Nursing takes a whole life to learn. We must make progress in it every year. ... It has been recorded that the three principles which represent the deepest wants of human nature, both in the East and West, are the principles of discipline, of religion (or the tie to God), of contentment. (p. 16)

She warns her nurses:

> Nursing is not an adventure, as some have now supposed: "When fools rush in where angels fear to tread." It is a very serious, delightful thing, *like life*, requiring training, experience, devotion not by fits and starts, patience, a power of accumulating, instead of losing—all these things. We are still only on the threshold of training. (p. 17)

1900

Writing at the age of 80, Nightingale (1900) reveals her continued devotion to God, her thoughts on the ancients, and her vision of healing. We glimpse her serenity in old age and her union with the Absolute. Her deep tenderness for her nurses is revealed as she starts the letter: "My dear Children, You have called me your Mother-chief, it is an honour, to call you my children." She speaks of the greatness of the nursing profession and thanks her nurses for their dedication to their work and for being role models, and reminds them of the Father:

> Always keep up the honour of this honourable profession. I thank you—may I say our Heavenly Father thanks you *for what you do*! "Lift high the royal Banner. It shall not suffer loss" the royal banner of nursing. It should gain through every one of you. It *has* gained through you immensely. (p. 1)

She contrasts the Roman and Christian approaches to nursing and the ethics of caring:

> The old Romans were in some respect I think superior to us. But they had no idea of being good to the sick and weak. That came in with Christianity. Christ was the author of our profession. We honour Christ when we are good Nurses. We dishonour Him when we are bad or careless Nurses. We dishonour Him when we do not do our best to relieve suffering—even in the meanest creature. (p. 1)

She reflects on recent discoveries in nursing, new ideas in medicine, and examples of how to maintain as well as regain health:

> There have been great, I must say, discoveries in *Nursing*: A very remarkable Doctor, a great friend of mine, now dead, introduced new ideas about Consumption, which might then be called the curse of England. His own wife was what was called "consumptive." She had tubercular disease in her lungs. He said to her: "Now you have to choose: either you must spend the next 6 months in your room. Or you must garden every day." (p. 2)

Nightingale lived long enough to witness the evolution of nursing as a respected profession: "*Nursing* is becoming a profession. Trained Nursing no longer an object but a fact" (p. 3). She focuses on the need to educate the public in principles of health:

> But, oh, if *home* Nursing could become an every day fact here in this big city of London, the biggest in the world, in an island the smallest inhabited island in the world. But here in London in *feeding*—a most important branch of it—if you ask a mother who has perhaps brought you a sick child to "look at": "What have you given it to eat?" she answers triumphantly, "O, it has the same as we have!" Yes, often including the gin. And a city where milk, & good milk, is now easier to get than in the country. For all farmers send their milk to London or the great cities. A sick child has been sent to Hospital (and recovered). You ask what it had: 'O, they gave it nothing—nothing'—It is true they gave it nothing, but milk—Milk is 'nothing.' Milk the most nourishing of all things. Sick *men* have recovered & lived upon milk. (p. 3)

She shares the importance of spirituality and the personal presence of God in her life; she celebrates the educated woman as teacher:

> My soul doth magnify the Lord, and my spirit hath rejoiced in God my Savior. The 19th Century (there was a tradition) was to be the century of Woman. How true that legendary prophecy has been. Woman was the home drudge. Now she is the teacher. (p. 4)

A Synthesis of the Letters (1872–1900)

These excerpts show that the letters are written by the mature mind of a practicing mystic to her followers. Nightingale had been reading on the medieval mystics such as St. Catherine of Siena, St. Catherine of Genoa, St. Teresa of Avila, and Thomas À Kempis between 1862 and 1872. As an example of a mystic's writing to his followers, the table of contents from the *Imitation of Christ* by Thomas À Kempis is shown in the second Pentimento in this chapter, Florence Nightingale: Writing on the Medieval Mystics.

Nightingale's 13 letters contain these same concepts. She clearly had in mind a model of the great mystics as she began to write to her nurses on Christian values; how to imitate Christ in their daily activities; how to be an exemplar of a Christian life; and how to be of service to God and society. She often refers to her nurses using military terms such as God's soldiers or God's corps.

Nightingale was a scholar and a seeker of Truth; she spoke and wrote about God (B. Dossey, 2000a; Macrae, 2001; McDonald, 2002a, 2002b, 2002c; Vallée, 2003; Webb, 2002). In 1860 she completed and self-published her philosophical and religious treatise, *Suggestions for Thought to the Searchers after Truth among the Artizans of England* (Nightingale, 1860b, 1860c, 1860d), which she had begun before the Crimean War. The letters contain many concepts from her *Suggestions for Thought*. She believed that she was called to be a deliverer or to be a savior. In this publication, she worked out her definition of savior as one who saves from error (Calabria & Macrae, 1994): "The world never makes much progress except by saviors." Her *social action* (see glossary) was grounded in the belief that "Mankind must discover the organization by which mankind can live in harmony with God's purpose" (p. xvi).

Although the letters are written from a Christian perspective, Nightingale always thought that people should appreciate other cultures and explore different beliefs, rituals, and indigenous practices, lest Western cultural beliefs and values be imposed. She had read and continued to read the literature of world religions and makes reference to these works, such as in her 1897 letter when she writes of the deepest wants of human nature both in the East and West (p. 16). She was familiar with translations of Kabalistic writings in early Judaism (c. 1300 BCE), the Upanishads of Hinduism (c. 700–500 BCE), Buddhist teachings (c. 573–483 BCE), Socrates (c. 470–399 BCE), and Plato (c. 427–347 BCE).

Throughout the letters, the central message of mysticism is revealed. This message is that God can manifest Himself through each person. This goes beyond a single explanation of Christianity as the only way to God. Her view of the Absolute encompassed and transcended expressions of the Divine in terms of specific religions; this is the overarching definition of the mystical tradition. Nightingale had an ecumenical view of religion although her personal view was expressed in Christianity. Her spiritual vision included concepts from other religions; therefore, she cannot be confined to a specific religious tradition.

Three patterns emerge in the synthesis of these letters:

1. spirituality;
2. the meta-paradigm concepts in the discipline of nursing—person, health, environment (society), and nursing; and
3. the fundamental patterns of knowing in nursing—empirical, ethical, aesthetic, and personal—as identified by Carper (1978).

Table 2-1 shows each pattern with identified descriptors found in the letters; many of the same descriptors appear in all three patterns. It is important to remember that Nightingale seamlessly combined her thoughts. In the following discussion of each pattern, the repetition of her thoughts and concepts shows how each pattern is related to and informs the other.

Pattern 1: Spirituality

The letters contain Nightingale's profound concepts that describe a universal spirituality and the holy life lived in communion with God and dedicated to God's service and to society. She articulates her spiritual vision, which she weaves into her philosophy through examples, parables, stories, and examples of care from her experiences as a nurse at Harley Street, at Scutari, and in the Crimea. She also shares her insights as a person with a severe, chronic illness.

The letters contain many references to Christ, God, Father, Savior, Commander, and Master. Her message on spirituality addresses many: God is love, imitate Christ in daily life, humans are created in God's image, follow the scriptures, heaven is within, conquer with love,

Table 2-1.
Florence Nightingale's 13 Formal Letters to Her Nurses (1872–1900): Patterns and Descriptors*

*Note: The following descriptors include both words and clusters of word phrases that can be found in Nightingale's letters (1872–1900). The list also includes the use of interpretive biographical methodology that reflects the author's previous and current Nightingale research and holistic nursing practice, education, and research. (See Appendix B.) Within these letters, Nightingale has provided stories within stories, and the meaning within one letter will change within other letters when she uses the same words to give different explanations of what she means. Thus, there are many descriptors that appear in the same clusters under more than one pattern. The order of the descriptors in Pattern 2 are related to the major emphasis in the letters.

Pattern 1. Spirituality: Descriptors

Imitate Christ.
See the face of God in everyone.
Remember that heaven is within.
Honor the ever-presence of God.
Speak the truth.
God is love.
Recognize nursing as a "calling."
Understand and follow God's laws in Nature.
Be aware that it is more blessed to give than to receive.
Love thy neighbor.
Conquer with love.
Be peacemakers.
Practice loving-kindness.
Commit to a spiritual practice using prayer and reflection.
Practice quietness, inner silence, and solitude.
Recognize goals that benefit humankind.
Examine thyself.
Do no harm.
Practice the Golden Rule.
Learn forgiveness.
Seek wisdom.
Be whole-hearted.
Live and work in unity.
Do not judge others.
Be slow to anger.
Follow the scriptures.
Honor each other.
One is known by one's deeds and not one's religion.
Be truthful.
Show strength, courage, and humility.
Become aware of faith, hope, and charity.
Recognize the divine core of Reality.

(Note: There are many references to Christ, Father, Savior, Master, and Commander.)

Pattern 2. The Meta-Paradigm Concepts in the Discipline of Nursing (Nurse, Person, Environment/Society, Health): Descriptors

Nurse/Nursing

Assess patient problems and needs.
Identify patient outcomes.
Plan, implement, and evaluate patient care.
Incorporate thinking and feeling in nursing actions.
Use problem-solving and questioning.
Identify the purpose of each nursing action.
Implement God's laws in Nature.
Teach health to maintain well-being.
Implement caring from birth to death.
Recognize that nursing is a "calling."
Nursing is distinct from Medicine.
Be accountable, consistent, and truthful.
Protect the privacy and rights of patients.
Display one's stamp of character in every word, thought, and deed.
Integrate core values in personal and professional life.
Display patience, thoroughness, and alertness in one's work.
Be watchful and vigilant.
Honor the patient's independence.
Practice humility, compassion, and love.
Be mindful.
Be caring and compassionate.
Be authentic and sincere.
Honor the pioneers who have come before for their inspiration and wisdom.

Person

Respect each person as a spiritual being.
Honor the wholeness of each person.
Value caring as essential to a person's well-being.
Recognize that a person is constantly interacting with the environment that affects health.

(Pattern 2 continued)

Respect each person's capacity to adapt to greater states of well-being.

Teach individuals about health and well-being.

Honor the dignity of individuals and the diversity of the communities.

Acknowledge the person's choices.

Respect each person's cultural beliefs.

Assist individuals to access their human potential.

Encourage the patient's independence.

(See also the descriptors related to environment/society, below.)

Environment/Society

Promote a healing environment that includes fresh air, ventilation, light, cleanliness, good food, flowers, and music.

Provide a hospital that exists for the patient's health and healing.

Create sacred space.

Build community through cooperation with peers.

Respect the dignity of individuals and the diversity of the communities.

Share one's humanness with others.

Interact with other nursing associations (schools and organizations) to actualize unity and healing.

Be willing to change and evolve.

Honor the meaning, purpose, and vision of intelligent leadership.

Be a mentor and role model to one's peers and others.

Health

Recognize that curing and healing are different.

Be a mentor and coach to patients, families, and colleagues.

Recognize spirituality, health, and well-being.

Interact with other nursing associations (schools and organizations) to actualize healing.

Strive to achieve one's full potential.

Recognize one's connection and devotion to God.

Identify one's inner strengths.

Be aware of love and trust.

Remember that the kingdom of heaven is within.

Honor the ever-presence of God.

Recognize nursing as a "calling."

Honor self-care.

Be self-accepting and have self-respect.

Recognize habits that compromise one's integrity.

Manage stress.

Practice loving-kindness.

Develop personal goals and life plans.

Honor truth, wisdom, and intuition.

Integrate joy, humor, laughter, and play.

Develop an understanding and awareness of wholeness, unity, and oneness.

Practice spiritual renewal through prayers, meditations, and solitude.

Pattern 3. The Fundamental Patterns of Knowing in Nursing (Empirical, Ethical, Aesthetic, and Personal): Descriptors

Empirical Knowing

Assess patient problems, needs, and identify patient outcomes.

Incorporate thinking and feeling in all nursing actions.

Plan, implement, and evaluate patient care.

Use problem-solving and questioning.

Identify the purpose of each nursing action.

Be aware of body, mind, and spirit.

Implement God's laws in Nature.

Participate in health to maintain health and well-being.

Recognize nursing as a "calling" that is distinct from Medicine.

Analyze, document, and interpret observations.

Honor the pioneers who have come before for their inspiration and wisdom.

Ethical Knowing

Be accountable, consistent, and truthful.

Build community through cooperation with peers.

Recognize that curing and healing are different.

Provide a safe hospital environment for the patient's health and healing.

Respect the dignity of individuals and the diversity of the communities.

Respect patients' choices.

Respect the cultural beliefs of a patient.

Protect the privacy and rights of patients.

Honor the patient's independence.

(Continued on next page)

(Pattern 3 continued)

Recognize that nursing is a "calling."

Nursing is distinct from Medicine.

Be a mentor, partner, and coach to patients, their families, and colleagues.

Display one's stamp of character in every word, thought, and deed.

Share one's humanness with others.

Integrate core values in personal and professional life.

Display patience, thoroughness, and alertness.

Be watchful and vigilant.

Honor one's highest moral insights.

Collaborate with colleagues and other nursing associations (schools and organizations).

Aesthetic Knowing

Be mindful and authentic.

Be willing to change and evolve.

Communicate as effectively as possible.

Impart thoughts and images that convey healing and compassion.

Bear witness to the pain and suffering of self and others.

Engage in deep listening.

Recognize nursing as a "calling."

Engage in meaningful conversations about the healing process.

Honor holiness, sacredness, and mystery.

Promote a healing environment (which includes fresh air, ventilation, light, cleanliness, good food, flowers, music, and sacred space).

Personal Knowing

Strive to achieve one's full potential.

Give attention to one's inner sense of well-being.

Honor sacredness, holiness, and connection with God.

Identify inner strengths, caring, love, and trust.

Be nonjudgmental.

See the face of God in everyone.

Remember that the kingdom of heaven is within.

Honor the ever-presence of God.

Recognize nursing as a "calling."

Manage stress.

Implement self-care and simplicity in life.

Value self-care (physical, mental, emotional, social, and spiritual).

Practice self-acceptance, self-respect, and self-responsibility.

Recognize habits that compromise one's integrity.

Set personal goals.

Honor inner truth, wisdom, and intuition.

Be aware of intention, clear thinking, and focus.

Integrate joy, humor, laughter, and play in daily life.

Honor the meaning, purpose, and vision of intelligent leadership.

Be a mentor and role model to one's peers.

Develop an understanding and awareness of wholeness and unity.

Attend to spiritual renewal through prayers, meditations, and solitude.

be peacemakers, speak the truth, it is more blessed to give than to receive, love thy neighbor, loving-kindness, goodness, spiritual practice, quietness, inner silence, solitude, prayer, presence in the moment, goals that benefit humankind, the importance of action rather than words, examine thyself, do no harm, the Golden Rule, forgiveness, seek wisdom, be whole-hearted, live and work in unity, do not judge others, be slow to anger, honor each other, one is known by one's deeds and not one's religion, truth, strength, courage, humility, faith, hope, and charity.

Nightingale believed in the messages contained within Christianity, and envisioned Jesus Christ as the Way of the Spirit, as a great man who could reveal the fundamental truths of God. Her ideas on spirituality are also universal concepts found in all the major world religions (H. Smith, 1986). Her introverted and contemplative nature, and her spiritual strength and force, can be read in every sentence of these letters.

Nightingale's recurring message is one of spirituality and the lifelong process of healing in order to understand the wholeness of human existence. Her emphasis is on moral values. To her, healing was the blending of the nurse's inner and outer life; this blending conveyed the creative expression of unconditional love. This inner peace then allowed the person receiving care to feel safe and more in harmony with self and others. These qualities show an authentic presence that is essential in the healing process. She reminded her nurses that healing occurs when they embrace and transform what was feared or most painful in their lives. She also believed that individuals should become more aware of their interdependence with God and others; this created the conditions for healing; this included learning to trust all of life, both the light and the shadow.

Nightingale asked each nurse to explore the meaning of healing, and to ask each day the steps that they could take to facilitate healing. She reminded them that to be an instrument of healing required daily practice. This would assist the nurse in developing and integrating spiritual qualities on a regular basis. The nurse's interactions with others and an awareness of being of service were what Nightingale saw as creating wholeness and health. She challenged her nurses not to feel helpless, because this could lead to physical illness and mental distress. Rather, she encouraged them to seek mentorship and the support of peers. She addressed spirituality as the basis for self-care, which also included exercising, taking proper nutrition, and managing stress.

Nightingale clearly understood the transpersonal dimension, that which transcends the limits and boundaries of individual identity and possibilities. This included acknowledgment and appreciation of something greater than the individual self. This transpersonal dimension engages one's consciousness, and is embedded in all interpersonal dynamics and relationships. The nurse's lived experience of connection, unity, and oneness with society, the cosmos, or Spirit, is what Nightingale believed led to true healing. Her message on spirituality is combined with her thoughts that emerged related to the nurse, the person, the environment (society), and health found in Pattern 2; spirituality also emerged in the fundamental patterns of knowing in Pattern 3.

Pattern 2: The Meta-Paradigm Concepts in the Discipline of Nursing

In these 13 formal letters Nightingale develops many ideas that will be discussed in this order: the nurse, nursing, and nursing actions; the patient and the family; the environment and society; and health and how to maintain health and prevent disease or illness. Today, these areas are recognized as the meta-paradigm concepts in the discipline of nursing (see Table 2-1).

Nurse/Nursing

Nightingale believed that the profession of nursing was a "calling," and that the nurse was an instrument in the healing process. It is the nurse who places the patient in the best condition for nature to act its healing wonders. Nursing is both an art and a science. Her philosophy of caring and healing embraced the entire life, from birth to death.

She stressed assessing and observing; determining outcomes; identifying the patient's problems, challenges, and needs; planning patient care; and correctly implementing and evaluating patient care. Today all of these areas are recognized as the nursing process. Formal education and skill-based competency allowed the nurse to be in charge of all aspects of nursing. Nightingale believed that nursing at home and in hospitals should be in the hands of nurses and not in the hands of doctors. Nursing was distinct and separate from medicine, as the focus of medicine was on curing with medical and surgical treatments and procedures. Nightingale saw nursing as a caring and healing process where personal interactions could take place if nurses were clear about their intentions. It was this interpersonal caring and healing process that distinguished nurses and nursing from medicine, physicians, and surgeons during the Victorian era.

To Nightingale, nursing was service to God and service to humanity. She believed that the aim of human life was to create heaven—here and now—on earth; her letters reflect that "the kingdom of heaven is within," "we must also create heaven without," and "we are intended to act upon circumstances." To her, surrender and union with God was not an end, but the source of strength and guidance for doing her work in the world. Nightingale conveyed to her nurses that their service to God could also be their strength and guidance. The basic premise of her spiritual philosophy was the concept of a benevolent God.

Person

Nightingale viewed the "person" as the individual who receives care from a nurse. The nurse cared for a person with an illness; she did not care for a disease. Her holistic framework viewed each person as a multidimensional whole—biological, psychological, sociological, and spiritual; she saw each person as unique.

Nightingale saw each person as a holistic being interacting with a family, group, or community. The person engaged in interactions with a nurse; each person's subjective experience about health, health beliefs, and values should be respected.

The nurse was a facilitator and midwife to the person and the community in all phases of living and dying. The relationships between the nurse and a patient could change the individual's awareness, perception, behaviors, and relationship to self, others, and God/Life Force Absolute/Transcendent. It might allow the patient to cope more effectively with stress, with a greater chance of entering into a relaxed and trusting state of mind. The nurse who entered into a caring-healing relationship with a sick person and the family could bring to the encounter an acknowledgment and appreciation of body–mind–spirit dimensions of human existence.

Nightingale gave special attention to the psychological elements that improve health, healing, and the person's peace of mind. *Therapeutic communication* meant appropriate conversation that provided hope, but not false hope. Spiritual elements were characterized by the ability to seek purpose and meaning in suffering, struggle, and the challenges of living and dying. It included the ability to love, forgive, pray, worship, and transcend ordinary circumstances and alienated behaviors. Nightingale believed that the nurse could facilitate the healing process with a dying person until the moment of death.

Nightingale's holistic philosophy valued the worth of each person. A person's spirituality was pervasive, and doing one's best in each moment was essential to caring and healing. She cautioned nurses against idle chatter and false hope with the patient, as well as isolating the sick person from appropriate company.

She saw a person's body, mind, and spirit as inseparable; each person had the capacity to implement self-care practices, and could choose, think, feel, set goals, and make decisions for greater health and well-being. The person was the interpreter of his or her own experience, and the nurse could assist the person in the healing journey, particularly when recognizing the call to be of service to humanity.

Environment (Society)

Nightingale placed no distinct boundaries between one's personal internal environment (the inner self), and the influences of the physical, external environment. She saw each person as constantly interacting with the self, the environment, and society. Society was the system or condition of people living together; it was the critical interacting forces that shaped an individual. Society and its people could benefit from education to create clean, healthy environments, and learn about God's natural health laws for greater health and well-being. Nightingale's health laws also viewed Earth as a living, breathing system that interacted with people; removing waste and not polluting the air, water, or food source should also receive attention if people were to be healthy.

To understand these health laws, education about the physical environment was essential. This included proper ventilation with fresh air and the appropriate temperature, sunlight, clean water, cleanliness of rooms and walls in hospitals and in homes, and management of wastes and odors. Comfort and safety in the environment included personal cleanliness, noise control, clean bedding, mattresses, and beds. The nurse could alter the external physical environment to help the person heal from disease or illness. Nature could then help in the reparative process. The nurse could enhance the external environment to increase healing with such things as flowers and music. Proper nutrition appropriate for each patient was to be considered. Continuity of care was also stressed, such as management and observation of the environment of the sick.

Nightingale emphasized the importance of creating conditions to heal the inner self, the internal healing environment. When each nurse or person created a quiet, clean, external environment, this state of the environment could lead to an inner state of peace, comfort, and reflection that would enhance the person's healing process and well-being.

Health

Nightingale saw health as a dynamic process that was interdependent with the environment, or any disease or illness. She stressed that when one understood God's laws in nature, health generally followed. To her, "a law is nothing more than a thought of God" (Calabria & Macrae, 1994, p. 35). Health was the positive, and pathology was the negative. She believed that disease or illness might be reversed, and that each person should strive toward this goal. It was the nurse's responsibility to place the person in the best position for nature to help in the reparative, healing process. Nightingale thought that in some situations "nature alone cures."

Health was a goal of nursing. Health was seen not only as a state of wellness, but also as using every power one has to the best of one's ability. Nightingale felt that when individuals were ill, they could still have degrees of health through pain management, proper ventilation, light, air, clean water, and proper nursing care.

Nightingale clearly developed concepts related to health promotion, health maintenance and restoration, and high-level wellness in her letters; these ideas were also developed in her *Notes on Nursing* (1860a), and in her last great essay "Sick-Nursing and Health-Nursing" (1893):

> Health is not only to be well, but also to be able to use well every power we have. … Both kinds of nursing [nursing proper and health nursing] are to put us in the best possible conditions for nature to restore or to preserve health—to prevent or to cure disease. … Nursing proper is therefore to help the patient suffering from disease to live—just as health nursing is to keep or put the constitution of the healthy child or human being in such a state as to have no disease. (p. 185)

Nightingale saw health and healing as movement toward wholeness on all levels: physical, mental, emotional, social, and spiritual. She made a distinction between healing and curing. Nightingale felt that healing was always possible, while curing a disease might not always occur. "Curing" was the elimination of the signs and symptoms of disease. This might or might not end a person's disease or distress, since it involved only one dimension of the whole body–mind–spirit system. "Healing" included ways to seek harmony and balance in one's own life, one's family, and one's community. Healing emerged from within the unique body–mind–spirit of the person while living, but also in the dying process. Healing could not be controlled, manipulated, or coerced.

Pattern 3: Fundamental Patterns of Knowing in Nursing

Although Nightingale did not write in terms of the fundamental patterns of knowing in nursing, Nightingale describes the empirical, ethical, aesthetic, and personal domains. For the purpose of this discussion these four concepts will be discussed as the four patterns of knowing in nursing as described by Carper (1978). (See Table 2-1.)

Empirical Knowing

Nightingale saw empirical knowing as a core principle in nursing. This included the explaining and structuring of empirical phenomena to create a formal expression, replication, and validation of scientific knowledge and scientific competence in nursing practice and education; today this would include research. Although her nurses did not engage in research as we know it today, she encouraged her nurses to make observations, implement care, and evaluate what treatments and nursing care improved a patient's health status, and to document anything that was harmful to the patient. She emphasized that nurses could discover information through use of the senses—to hear, see, touch, taste, and smell. She gave specific instructions to her nurses to gather and record data on the patient and the patient's environment in the hospital or in the home. Nightingale herself did engage in research. Her statistics in midwifery and hospital reform are just two examples as discussed in the Pentimento in Chapter 6, Florence Nightingale: The Passionate Statistician.

Nightingale saw the science of healing as a process governed by law; like all physical phenomena, it is regulated by nature and is the manifestation of God. When nurses discovered God's health laws such as proper nourishment, ventilation, cleanliness, and quiet, they were more able to cooperate consciously with intention which helped in the restorative process. She believed that nature alone cures, and what the nurse has to do is to put the patient in the best condition for nature to act upon the individual.

Empirical knowing is expressed in a nurse's practice that integrates scientific theory and competence. She continually asked her nurses to acquire and maintain current scientific knowledge and competency in their practice, and to ask for mentorship from others or to take the responsibility to mentor others. Nightingale stressed the integration of knowledge (theory) in all phases of patient care. She encouraged her nurses to question why symptoms were present, and what procedures and treatments helped or hindered the patient. The first step in assessing each patient was to honor the uniqueness of the person. The patient's problems were identified, and the nurse was to provide patient care based on needs and priorities so that positive outcomes could be achieved. She stressed reassessing and implementing patient care as needed, and evaluating care in a systematic and regular manner. Nightingale also emphasized the difference in "sick-nursing" and "health-nursing," and encouraged health promotion as essential. If a patient was ill, each nurse was to treat the patient and the family as if they were honored guests.

Nightingale encouraged her student nurses and graduate nurses to continually learn new theories that could support all aspects of nursing practice. She called on new leaders to emerge who could transform the hospital system and district nursing, today called public health nursing. This knowledge could advance the science of nursing as well as inform politicians, physicians, and hospital administrators.

Ethical Knowing

Nightingale saw ethical knowing as valuing and clarifying situations to create formal behaviors, expressions, and dimensions of both morality and ethics intersecting with duties; today this would be considered legally prescribed duties. This included daily decisions of right and wrong, what should be done in practice, in personal conduct and behaviors, priorities, responsibilities, and advocacy for the patient, nurse, hospital, environment, and society.

Nightingale identified ethical conflicts where the hospital systems did not allow nurses to do what they believed was right, particularly in identifying unsafe practices or acting as a patient advocate. Nightingale taught that the moral ideal of the nurse was realized when the whole self of the nurse was brought into relationship with the whole of the person receiving care. It was the nurse who must protect the vulnerable patient and who must preserve the humanity and dignity of the individual. In her lifetime, Nightingale was often frustrated over the abuse of nurses and nurse superintendents by physicians and hospital administrators; she tried to resolve these unethical situations. For example, the hospitals used the nurses as essentially free labor, demanding unreasonable hours and responsibilities beyond patient care. Her work brought with it a national and international perspective concerning the ethical issues that nurses faced; these issues still continue in the nursing profession.

Nightingale's letters provide guidelines for the nurse in how to shape personal ethics. She challenged nurses to explore personal principles of conduct in the classroom, in the hospital, and in their free time. She stressed ethical decision-making in both professional and personal realms; what was right and wrong must be recognized as inward values; each nurse was responsible for her own moral conduct, because there was no prescription for it. Each nurse should show ethical knowing as an expression of actions that could be demonstrated, examined, and evaluated. Through reflection and knowing the meaning and purpose in the work, the nurses could gain insight about the highest level of ethical choices and possibilities.

Nightingale encouraged her nurses to hold to an ethic of caring and healing that sought to preserve wholeness. She encouraged them to be role models, maintaining a dignity of self when with colleagues and with patients receiving care, as well as with the family. She saw self-care as part of the ethics of care. She asked her nurses to be aware of those strategies that could maintain their health. She was aware of cultural diversity and recognized each person as a whole body–mind–spirit being. She emphasized that any person should be able to receive care regardless of class, religion, or the ability to pay for services. She insisted on creating a plan of care consistent with cultural background, health beliefs, and values.

Aesthetic Knowing

Nightingale believed that the aesthetic of nursing was crucial to the healing process. She recognized the aesthetic in nursing as the combination of knowledge, experience, instinct, and intuition that connects the nurse with a patient and the family to explore together the meaning of a situation and the human experiences of life, health, illness, or death. She recognized that the aesthetic in nursing could call forth resources and inner strengths from the nurse to be a facilitator in the healing process.

Nightingale stressed that the aesthetic in nursing is made visible through conduct, attitudes, narratives, actions, and caring with patients, families, colleagues, and self. For Nightingale, intention was a volitional act of love and the conscious awareness of creating an image of a spiritual essence and wholeness. Nightingale asked nurses to carry their therapeutic presence with them in every moment. She gave examples of special actions or words that allowed one's spirit to become enfolded in another person's experience.

The aesthetic of nursing also focused on a person's environment. The environment was everything that surrounded the individual of the nurse and the patient, both external and internal. The external physical environment was the actual physical setting of a patient's room and surroundings. The internal healing environment or state was the perceived inner calm and quietness of the nurse or the patient that could be created by reflection, prayer, and time alone.

The aesthetic of nursing included the healing arts such as relaxation; imagery; stories and poetry; prayer; pleasant conversations that could stimulate a variety of new thoughts; music; flowers; small pets as companions for the sick; and good food, sunlight, and fresh air. These were just a few expressions of the experience and symbolic meaning in healing.

Personal Knowing

Nightingale believed that each nurse must understand and develop one's inner self, which led to the dynamic process of becoming whole. This could be achieved through reflection, synthesis of perceptions, and being with self or another with authentic presence. This also included the experience of being with "unknowing," the not-knowing, and events that had not yet emerged such as the understanding of events, situations, dreams, or the experience and perceptions of the self alone or with another person.

Through her own spiritual journey, Nightingale was able to put in very practical terms how her nurses could seamlessly combine their spiritual journey with their professional duties. She helped them to discover courage and fearlessness in charting unknown territories that were touchstones of how to honor a spiritual vision and to reach the highest potential in both nursing practice and daily life. Nightingale asked her nurses to model for others how to "be of service" in nursing, and how to persevere when challenges arose.

Nightingale encouraged each nurse to find strength from within and to delve into a deeper human capacity to find the creative response to life's work, and to explore self-knowledge and steps toward spiritual well-being. Her messages challenged nurses to seek the deepest union between self and God. These core values, at the core of nursing, are eternal and time-honored—compassion, love, empathy.

A recurring message was the lifelong journey of healing and what is required to understand the wholeness of human existence. To her, healing was the blending of the nurse's inner life with her outer life to facilitate her creative expression of love. This inner peace then allows the person receiving care to feel safe and in harmony. These are the steps that show the authenticity of unconditional presence.

Nightingale saw personal knowing in nursing as those strategies that explore the individual self at the physical, mental, emotional, social, and spiritual levels. By knowing self, one is able to practice from an authentic space. She offered descriptions of the authentic self as well as descriptions of the superficial self, such as being shallow in one's thoughts, reactions, or behaviors. She would say that words rarely express the depth of authentic knowing of the self, but rather, that this was between each person and God.

Nightingale wrote about self-reflection, and connections with the Divine. Historically, Nightingale's views have always integrated the spiritual with the technological domains. She reminded nurses that God is a power greater than oneself and influences all aspects of life. She challenged her nurses to find ways to draw near to God by inward reflection, to ask deep questions about healing of the self and others. She repeatedly used the phrase "heaven is neither a place nor a time, but a place within one's self." She asked them to create states where the indwelling presence of God would be manifest to them. To Nightingale, spirituality engaged the nurse's loving-kindness, caring, and compassion as unifying forces in the healing process. Spirituality permeated all of life and was manifested in one's knowing, doing, and being—the interconnectedness with self, others, nature, and God/Life Force/Absolute/Transcendent. She reminded the nurses that they were not chaplains; they should not preach personal religious beliefs and practices to the patients, but should model their values and imitate Christ in their life and work.

Spirituality was at the core of self-care. When the nurse felt loving-kindness, compassion, and tenderness toward self, then self-care activities that led to health and well-being would often follow. These activities included physical exercise, proper nutrition, mental stretching through new learning, tending to emotional needs including frustrations, developing healthy relationships, making healthy choices each day, and taking regular holidays.

She wrote about healthy, supportive conversations as opposed to unhealthy communication such as gossip and unkind remarks. She believed that shared humanity included a sense of connectedness and attention that always reflected each nurse's uniqueness.

The Timely Immediacy of a Timeless Tradition

This chapter introduced Nightingale's formal letters to her nurses (1872–1900), synopses and excerpts from the letters, and a synthesis of these documents. This synthesis yielded two conclusions. The first was the connection between Nightingale's documents and the lives and writings of recognized mystics to their followers, such as Thomas À Kempis (see the Pentimento on page 60, Writings on the Medieval Mystics). The second was the identification of three major patterns:

1. spirituality;
2. the meta-paradigm concepts in the discipline of nursing—person, health, environment (society), and nursing; and
3. the fundamental patterns of knowing in nursing as identified by Carper (1978)—empirical, ethical, aesthetic, and personal.

This synthesis reveals new links between Nightingale and contemporary nursing. Nightingale did describe in detail the importance of the spiritual in nursing and for the nurse; the meta-paradigm concepts in the discipline of nursing; and the fundamental patterns of knowing in nursing.

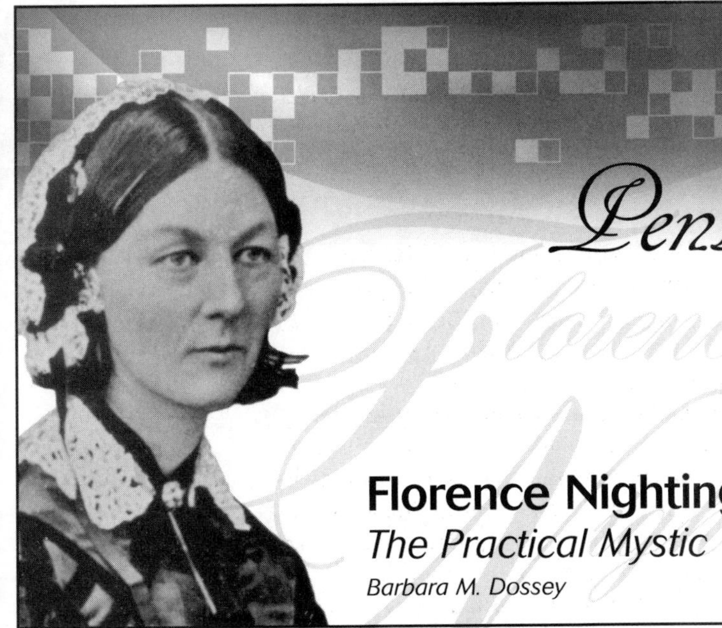

Florence Nightingale: *The Practical Mystic*

Barbara M. Dossey

Florence Nightingale received a clear and profoundly moving Call to serve God at the age of 16. Through a lifetime of hard work and discipline, she became a *practical mystic* (see glossary) in the Western tradition, thereby becoming an instrument of God's love, which was the primary source of her great energy and the fabled "Nightingale power."

Mysticism can be defined as a way of life, as an individual's direct experience of God; a *mystic* is a person who has, to a greater or lesser degree, such an experience (Underhill, 1925, pp. 9–10). The life of such a person is focused not merely on religious practice or belief, but on what he or she regards as firsthand personal knowledge, the love of God, or the Divine Reality of God.

There are degrees of difference between the experience and language of the mystic traditions of West and East. The goal of the Eastern mystic is usually expressed in the terms of "self-realization," in which the self within, and the self that underlies all of life, are found to be one.

But in the Western tradition, God remains in a certain very important sense "the other." The goal of the mystic then becomes that of the "unitive" state, in which the seeker feels wholly united with God (B. Dossey, 2000a, p. 425; Flinders, 1993, p. xxii). For the mystic, God ceases to be an object, and becomes an experience. Moreover, it has come to be recognized that in the Western tradition, mysticism is the supreme human activity. The highest forms of Divine Union impel the self to some sort of active rather than passive life.

Social action is the necessary outcome of the mystic's call; love is the motivating force for the mystic's work in the world. At the same time the mystic's calling, their spiritual development, and subsequent activity constitute phases of a social process involving a withdrawal from the world. A systematic reevaluation of the beliefs, goals, and values of the originating society occurs, and the mystic returns to the world intent on—and equipped to contribute significantly to—reform. Individual mystics articulate the most deeply ingrained ideals and aspirations of their society; it is the mystics' task in life to report the discoveries made to their contemporaries.

The Lives of the Mystics: Historical Agents of Change

Because the experiences of the Christian mystics, and their body of work and historical circumstances, are not familiar to most readers, many authors have misinterpreted Nightingale's private notes, diaries, and letters about God, perfection, and her mysticism. As a prolific diarist, many of her letters and private notes are emotional and passionate, as have been the writings of the great mystics and saints. Authors continue to erroneously assert that Nightingale's emotionalism was due to hysteria, exaggeration, Victorian melodrama, psychopathology, low self-esteem, the need to manipulate and control others, frustration, rage, and/or anger. It is easy to peruse the work of a person who wrote 14,000 letters in her lifetime, select passages out of context, and render uninformed judgment.

However, Calabria (1997, p. 11) has pointed out that if we reduce Nightingale's auditions to nothing more than a symptom of hysteria, etc., we are forced to do likewise to the passionate and stirring accounts of voices and visions as related by St. Teresa of Avila, Blessed Angela of Foligno, St. Catherine of Siena, St. Gertrud of Helfta, and the scores of other women and men throughout history who claim to have experienced transcendence, and whose historical legacy attests to the validity of their experience.

The lives of mystics and saints in the Western tradition are generally not sweet, gentle stories, but tumultuous, complex sagas, because by definition these individuals rose up in history in the spirit of reform. In many instances their mission was to revitalize or reform a church that had grown worldly and lax in religious practice, and which often was corrupt and oppressive. For this reason alone, mystics not only find themselves going against the grain of political convention and authority, but also in following their spiritual Call, frequently pioneer new social and cultural roles.

To be a mystic does not mean a person is a perfect human being. A mystic is one who has been awakened by the Love of God, and is overcome by the depth and purity of this Divine experience. Since they are committed to rid themselves of personal and societal attachments in order to carry out this Divine Will, they often experience tortured relationships with their family, friends, and colleagues.

Five Phases of Spiritual Development in the Life of a Mystic

In her 1911 classic text, *Mysticism,* Evelyn Underhill developed in detail the recognized phases of the spiritual development of a mystic: (1) awakening, (2) purgation, (3) illumination, (4) surrender, and (5) union. There is no timetable to these stages, nor are they always discrete: in fact, there may be a slow unfolding as well as an overlapping of these phases, or they may occur simultaneously. The individual may return to a phase that they have already experienced, the old story of "two steps forward, one step back." The process is similar to an upward spiral, in which the aspirant progresses, only to sometimes drop back, then climbs forward again.

Mysticism is experienced in, or arrived at, approximately the same ways across gender. Nightingale was knowledgeable about the lives and work of both female and male mystics, and often quoted their work. The descriptions of the five stages that follow are only a composite picture, an aid to understanding the process of a mystic's spiritual development. Like nearly all other mystics, Nightingale did not necessarily fit neatly and cleanly into each stage.

Underhill's 1911 text contained no information on Nightingale, as it was 1913 before the official Nightingale biography was released. However, in *Practical Mysticism,* published in 1915, Underhill obviously had read or been provided information from the biography, as she makes three references (pp. x, 102, 162) to

Nightingale's spiritual development, calling her "one of the most balanced contemplatives of the nineteenth-century" (p. 102).

Awakening. In the first phase of mystic spiritual development, there is a conversion of the experience of the ego-oriented self to that of a higher Self, which leads to an awareness or consciousness of a Divine Reality within. This may be an abrupt shift in awareness, accompanied by feelings of joy and exaltation. Nightingale marked the date of her awakening to this higher reality on February 7, 1837, at age 16, when she received a Call from God to be of service. Underhill (1915, p. x) reminds us that the two women who have left the deepest mark upon the military history of France and England—Joan of Arc and Florence Nightingale—both acted under mystical compulsion.

Purgation. The second phase of mystic spiritual development involves great pain and effort. The Self becomes increasingly aware of the Divine Beauty, and realizes by contrast its own imperfection and finiteness. For Nightingale, this stage of her quest would continue for more than a decade. During her travels to Italy, Egypt, Greece, and two trips to Kaiserswerth Institute in Dusseldorf, Germany, she recognized her work in the world and took the steps to break free of her family.

The bench under the cedars of Lebanon at Embley, where Florence Nightingale heard her first Call from God on February 7, 1837.
(© Barbara M. Dossey)

Illumination. The third phase is characterized by the spiritual "betrothal," wherein the soul contemplates union with the Absolute. During the Crimean War, Nightingale struggled in her mission of service to God because of the disharmony and problems between her and the doctors, ladies, nurses, and nuns in the hospital. Underhill says that mystics want to heal the disharmony between the actual and the real, and they feel this disharmony in the white-hot radiance of the faith, hope, and charity that burns in them. Because of this, they are able to work for it with a singleness of purpose and an invincible optimism denied to the ordinary person. It was this fire that drove Florence Nightingale to battle with filth, vermin, and disease in the Barrack hospitals, as St. Catherine of Siena was driven from contemplation to politics, Joan of Arc to the salvation of France, and St. Teresa to the formation of an ideal religious family (Underhill, 1915, pp. 161–162).

Surrender. In the fourth phase of mystic spiritual development, the mystic undergoes a deepening commitment to dissociate from personal satisfaction. This phase is also called the "dark night of the soul" or the "great desolation." The universal human instinct of personal happiness must now be abandoned, and the service to God moves to a deeper level. All great mystics seek to link each finite expression with its origin, the Divine Reality; they search for the inner significance of every fragment of life (1915, p. 102).

Union. The fifth phase is the ultimate goal of the mystic's quest. It is a state of equilibrium characterized by peace, joy, enhanced powers, and intense certitude. Some authorities call this state ecstasy. It is often characterized by various psychic experiences and physical sensations, which are also typical in the stage of illumination. Not all mystics experience increasingly ecstatic states; in fact, for some of the greatest mystics, such as St. Teresa, ecstatic experiences seemed to diminish rather than increase in frequency after the state of union had been attained. An examination of Nightingale's writings indicates that in the last decades of her life, Nightingale manifested the characteristics of the unitive state.

Unitive + Driven = Practical Mystic

Nightingale's life embodied social action and a profound spiritual call and purpose which our world sorely needs. Although gifted with deep mystical insight, she cannot be criticized as resorting to "dreamy mysticism." Her ferocious drive toward reform helped to improve the health of the British soldiers and created a new profession—modern, secular nursing—which has improved the lives of individuals throughout the world. She struggled mightily to break free of the social constraints that inhibited her, just as we must do today.

Florence Nightingale's life has been analyzed by hundreds of scholars. Why have so many individuals been captivated by her for more than a century and a half? Perhaps we sense in her the wisdom that is demonstrated by the great mystics throughout history. We are drawn to her because she is closer to our time, and we can identify with the problems she faced and the challenges she overcame. We, like her, are involved in our own search for meaning and purpose. By her shining example, she invites us to explore our own spiritual development.

Drawing by Parthenope Nightingale, of her sister Florence with her pet owl, Athena. Done c. 1850, the first drawing in which she is portrayed looking squarely at the viewer, and the world, her steel-grey eyes focused out on the work ahead.
(© Florence Nightingale Museum)

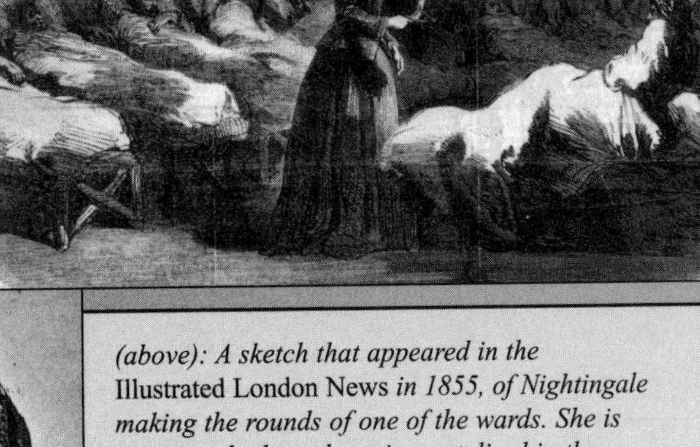

(above): A sketch that appeared in the Illustrated London News *in 1855, of Nightingale making the rounds of one of the wards. She is carrying the lamp later immortalized in the poem "Santa Filomena" by Henry Wadsworth Longfellow.*
(© Florence Nightingale Museum)

(left): Florence Nightingale, age 37, in the photograph her family held to be the best likeness of her.
(© Florence Nightingale Museum)

Note: For more details on Nightingale's mystic spiritual development, see B. Dossey (1998b, 2000a).

Pentimento

Florence Nightingale:
Writing on the Medieval Mystics

Barbara M. Dossey

Nightingale began to read the medieval mystics in her late twenties, and was reading them again between 1862 and 1872. Her spiritual friend and colleague Professor Benjamin Jowett, headmaster and Greek scholar, Balliol College, Oxford, encouraged her to write about their lives. He suggested that she would do a great work and teach the ordinary man a great deal if she pointed out the kind of mysticism that was needed for daily life. He urged her to express the intense feelings that the mystics had about the fusion of faith, truth, the will of God, and the reason in religion and the religion in reason.

CONTENTS.

The First Book.

ADMONITIONS, USEFUL FOR A SPIRITUAL LIFE.

The table of contents from an 1890 printing of the *Imitation of Christ* by Thomas À Kempis. (This edition was published by London's Thomas Nelson and Sons in the year noted. The book was first published in 1427.)

Nightingale was inspired and influenced by this book. The headers of its four main parts clearly point to why this was so: Thoughts Helpful in the Life of the Soul; The Interior Life; Internal Consolation; An Invitation to the Holy Communion.

The Second Book.

ADMONITIONS CONCERNING INWARD THINGS.

The Third Book.

OF INTERNAL CONSOLATION.

The Fourth Book.

CONCERNING THE COMMUNION.

Sometime between 1872 and 1875 Nightingale began her book *Notes from Devotional Authors of the Middle Ages: Collected, Chosen, and Freely Translated by Florence Nightingale* (Nightingale, 1872a; Vallée, 2003). Her book outline and notes indicated that she planned to write specifically on Blessed Angela of Foligno, Madame Jane de Chantal, St. Francis of Assisi, St. Francis Xavier, St. John of the Cross, St. Peter of Alcantara, Father Rigoleuc, St. Teresa of Avila, and Father Surin.

She particularly liked the point that some of the saints made, that they were "not for Church but for God," and that they threw overboard "all that mechanism & lived for God alone." Although she valued the contributions of the Christian mystics, she realized the validity of various modes of religious experience and argued that "you must go to Mohametanism, to Buddhism, to the East, to the Sufis & Fakirs, to Pantheism, for the right growth of mysticism" (Calabria & Macrae, 1994). She wrote that one of her favorite works was an ancient Persian prayer (1872):

> Four things, O God, I have to offer Thee
> Which Thou hast not in all Thy treasury;
> My nothingness, my sad necessity,
> My fatal sin & earnest penitence.
> Receive these gifts & take the Giver hence.

In 1873, she asked Jowett to critique her early work on the mystics. He found the drafts of her translations to be of great interest and gave her some helpful suggestions. He wanted her to shorten her discussion to the "pure gold," leaving out the allusions to herself and her own feelings, but showing the impersonal soul rising to God. He suggested that she call the soul just that, and not use "it," or "itself," which would only cause difficulty about the gender. He encouraged her to add a preface to her book that would show the use of such a book and the spiritual idea. She left an 87-page draft of the preface (quoted in Chapter 1), but the book was never finished.

In May 1872 she wrote the first of 13 formal letters to her nurses (also called formal addresses) that would continue until 1900. She was inspired and influenced by the life of the great mystic Thomas À Kempis (1380–1471); in 1872 she reread his book, the *Imitation of Christ,* first printed in 1427. The table of contents pages from an 1890 printing of the book are reproduced above to give an overview of the book. (An online edition is available at http://www.ccel.org/k/kempis/imitation/ as well as in a form that can be downloaded at http://www.gutenberg.net/etext/1653.) Many of the same themes and patterns contained in this book are found in her formal letters.

As she wrote her formal letters to her nurses, Nightingale clearly had in mind a model of a practical mystic writing to her followers. (See the preceding Pentimento for some details on this topic.) The entire unedited collection of these letters is included in Part Four.

Directions and Reflections

Directions for Future Research

1. Determine whether nurses who understand Nightingale's tenets of healing, leadership, and global action are more likely to recognize and integrate spirituality, nursing theories, and patterns of knowing in clinical practice, education, and research.
2. Explore the influences of Nightingale's tenets on how nurses stay healthy and create health changes.
3. Compare Nightingale's tenets to the nursing theories of nurse theorists.
4. Evaluate Nightingale's tenets in relation to the identification of specific outcomes of care.

Reflections on Florence Nightingale's Tenets: Healing

1. How do my values related to healing influence my nursing practice and personal life?
2. How do I nurture my spirit?
3. How do I assess my wholeness, and how do I describe my physical, mental, emotional, social, and spiritual being?
4. When I use the words God/Life Force/Absolute/Transcendent, what links do I make with Nightingale's message on healing and spirituality?
5. What definitions of nurse, person, environment, and health are a good fit with my own views?
6. What can I do each day to become more aware and to recognize the patterns of knowing in my life and practice?

chapter 3

Nightingale's Foundational Philosophy of Nursing

Louise C. Selanders

Florence Nightingale... For many, this name conjures up an image of a romantic heroine, bravely saving British soldiers from the terrors of substandard health care during the Crimean War. Her contributions to health care continued after the conflict. She established the Nightingale School at St. Thomas' Hospital, London. She reformed the British army's medical establishment and influenced the development of hygienic standards in India, thereby significantly reducing both mortality and morbidity in the subcontinent.

However, a comprehensive view of Nightingale identifies her as an environmentalist, nurse theorist, social reformer, groundbreaking statistician, researcher, and feminist. These terms paint a much broader canvas of the contributions she made during her lifetime, an era in which women were expected neither to substantially contribute to nor to create change. Yet these words do not fully capture the impact of an individual who was integral in the fight to expand the role of women in society as well as to create a positive image for the profession of nursing.

Because modern nursing traces its roots directly to Florence Nightingale, it is important that she be credited with all of her contributions. This is particularly essential in light of persistent claims that Nightingale has little or no significance to ongoing nursing practice and education (e.g., Brooks, 2001; F. Smith, 1982). The solution to this issue is to delineate Nightingale's lasting philosophical foundation of the profession, and to explore how this legacy can serve as a guide for resolving questions of social integration and change, issues which continue to plague the profession. Therefore, this chapter analyzes her professional objectives, develops accurate terminology defining her lasting contributions, and identifies the enduring outcomes of her contributions relative to nursing.

Personal and Professional Beginnings

Florence Nightingale's formative years were those of a wealthy English gentlewoman who was expected to learn to manage a household and to be a loving, supportive, and devoted wife. From an early age, Nightingale sensed she had a greater purpose in life, one that was driven by strong Christian beliefs. Her education was atypical for a woman of the time, with an emphasis on language, philosophy, history, and mathematics. Her knowledge and intellect helped her to avoid what she saw as endless boredom in a rigid social structure.

Nightingale was troubled by the constraints placed upon her by her family and society. She poignantly describes her plight as a woman in a diary of 1847–1849 in which she identifies women as private martyrs who are only able to show a public and carefully constructed face:

> There are Private Martyrs as well as burnt or drowned ones. Society of course does not know them; and Family cannot, because our position to one another in our families is, and must be, like that of the Moon to the Earth. The Moon revolves around her, moves with her, never leaves her. Yet the Earth never sees but one side of her; the other side remains for ever unknown. (Cook, 1913, Vol. 1, p. 59)

In 1850 and 1851, Nightingale spent several months at Kaiserswerth, a German Protestant institution that trained nurses and governesses as well as functioned as an orphanage. This gave her practical experience and the opportunity to observe the healthcare environment and outcomes. This knowledge helped her to formulate nursing as an occupation. In 1853, she took the position of Lady Superintendent of the Hospital for Sick Gentlewomen in Distressed Circumstances at 1 Upper Harley Street, London (B. Dossey, 2000a). This institution was for governesses, who were usually of modest means and unable to avail themselves of private, in-home care. Nightingale established this as a model hospital with emphasis on caring, cleanliness, efficiency, and autonomy of nursing. As the lady superintendent, she saw her chief role as that of patient advocate, a new and radical idea.

These values were more clearly defined during the Crimean War (1854–1856). The 22 months spent in Scutari and the Crimea clearly outlined for her the need to develop nursing as an educated profession. Further, she understood that this would have a more lasting effect on women by developing an outlet that would offer suitable employment in a relatively safe environment. Kaiserswerth, Harley Street, and the Crimea had been a time of education, her post-Crimean period a time she chose for action.

Defining Her Contributions: A Concept Analysis

In the 1913 biography by Sir Edward Cook, Florence Nightingale is described as the "founder of modern nursing," a term that is still commonly used (Vol. 1, p. 439). "Founder" implies that Nightingale was the originator of the profession. Of course, nursing existed in many forms—secular and nonsecular, trained and untrained, formalized and informal—before and during Nightingale's lifetime. It is probable that Cook used the term *founder* both in a complimentary sense and with a degree of ambiguity. Yet this word does not fully convey the far-ranging intellectual nature or continuing significance to nursing that Nightingale's ideas entailed. New terminology that assigns specific parameters to Nightingale's contributions would then be useful in making the argument for Nightingale as a continuing force in nursing.

It can be assumed that Nightingale is a product of both her environment and genetics. It can also be assumed that nursing developed through her leadership because of a confluence of necessity and opportunity. In the Pentimento to this chapter, a new and practical perspective to Nightingale's personality is found that assists in understanding Nightingale's need to quietly and persistently work for social change and the improved welfare of women.

When introducing new terminology to define a concept, a *concept analysis* allows us to systematically examine the characteristics of the idea and the identification of what it does and does not mean. Walker and Avant (1995) describe an eight-step method that is applied in the development of this new terminology. I have applied this method in the following pages to "foundational philosopher," a term applicable to the most essential contributors to any profession, but offered here specifically as a term that can encompass all of Nightingale's contributions to contemporary nursing.

- Step 1: Concept Selection
- Step 2: Purpose of the Analysis
- Step 3: Uses of the Concept
- Step 4: Defining Attributes
- Step 5: Model Cases
- Step 6: Alternative Cases
- Step 7: Antecedents and Consequences
- Step 8: Empirical Referents

Steps 1 & 2: Concept Selection and Purpose of the Analysis. The purpose of the analysis is to identify a word or words that appropriately describe the past, current, and future Nightingalean contribution to the profession of nursing. In this instance, the first two stages of the concept analysis were accomplished in tandem. Through a process of simple vocabulary review, the compound term "foundational philosopher" was developed as the appropriate alternative to "founder." The operational definition was established as "one who first identifies the concepts, assumptions, and outcomes of a profession that are so basic to that profession that they are assumed always to have been part of it." This definition was designed to endure the rigors of both concept analysis and general usage. A "profession" is any vocation that requires a specific knowledge base and advanced education of its participants, and has a high degree of autonomy in an area of expertise. Most often, professions occur in the service sector, consistent with nursing.

Step 3: Uses of the Concept. Because "foundational philosopher" has not been previously identified in English as a compound word, there exists virtually no preconception or commonly accepted use of the term. However, individual definitions of the words are implicit in the understanding of the compound expression. "Foundational" implies the basis or groundwork upon which something or some idea rests. A "philosopher" is an individual who investigates the central ideas of a movement.

Step 4: Defining Attributes. A foundational philosopher has distinguishing characteristics that separate this individual or individuals from others who, although they may accomplish significant acts or achievements within a profession, cannot be considered to be foundational philosophers:

- *Identification of the basic tenets of a profession.* The foundational philosopher, usually through contemplation, insight, or expertise, proposes the basic defining characteristics of a profession or movement. These tenets include core values, outcomes, and societal interaction.
- *Societal need and benefit.* A foundational philosopher is usually motivated by the perceived needs of the profession or movement at the societal level. The intellectual and developmental products of the foundational philosopher address this perceived societal need.
- *Lasting capacity and flexibility.* The tenets proposed as the basis of a profession hold true for extended periods. As the profession develops and changes, the basic tenets still hold true.

Steps 5 & 6: Model and Alternative Cases. Model cases are those that fulfill the defining attributes of the concept. The strength of the model case is dependent on the degree to which the defining attributes can be applied. Additionally, it is advisable to have more than one model case in order to illustrate the strength of the proposed concept.

Walker and Avant (1995) identify a number of alternate subcategories of model cases. The two most relevant in this instance are *borderline* and *contrary* cases. Borderline cases present instances in which it is difficult to determine whether or not, or the degree to which, the defining attributes can be applied, and, indeed, consensus may not be reached as to whether a given instance of a case is determined to be borderline or a true representation of a concept.

More important is the issue of the contrary case—that is, an instance when someone or something definitely does not meet the criteria. It is here that a foundational philosopher is likely to be confused with those persons who are historically significant, but have made contributions that are not conceptually new or are limited to an event or events. The comparison of those who fully fit the criteria to those who do not is helpful in laying and clarifying the parameters of the concept. These are identified in Table 3-1.

Step 7: Antecedents and Consequences. Antecedents are those events or circumstances that must occur prior to an event; consequences are a result of the event. In this case, they are very similar to the defining attributes. Specifically, the antecedents include having the opportunity to contemplate the situation and to determine that there was an unmet social need. The consequences include the development of a new professional opportunity, and the lasting capacity of the basic tenets of the profession to adapt to a changing social situation.

Step 8: Empirical Referents. The last component of the concept analysis is the empirical referents that are defined as "measurable, observable or verifiable components of the concept" (Wade, 1999, p. 314). These are the phenomena that demonstrate the existence of the concept. The critical question becomes how classes or categories of actual phenomena are identified and how, by their existence or presence, they demonstrate the actual occurrence of the phenomena (Walker & Avant, 1995). This may be seen as the most difficult step of the concept analysis, especially if the concept is abstract. In quantitative research, this frequently refers to tools designed to specifically measure presence and intensity of a concept.

In historical research, which is qualitative in nature, the presence or absence of a phenomenon is frequently established through document review. In the case of Nightingale, we are fortunate to have a particularly rich field of resources that includes in excess of 14,000 letters, books, manuscripts, portraits, and extensive personal memorabilia. All of this information falls into the category of primary resources, and has been used by researchers during the last century to document Nightingale's interactions and relationships, trace her travels, and, as is the prerogative of the historical researcher, draw conclusions as to her motivations, values, and intentions. For the purposes of this research, primary documents from 1845–1900 were examined, with the bulk of these papers being dated 1856–1890. In the case of Nightingale, the empirical referents are consistent with the outcomes of practices that she saw as essential and that have endured over time.

Defining the Outcomes of the Concept Analysis

This investigation revealed empirical referents in three areas that specifically relate to the development of nursing:

- the general nature of nursing and nursing practice,
- the nature and value of nursing education, and
- the nature and value of nursing research.

The General Nature of Nursing and Nursing Practice. Nightingale's philosophy of nursing was conceptualized over a period of nearly 20 years extending from her religious calling at 16 through her return from the Crimea when she was 36. Documents published in 1892 and 1893 indicate that, although her thoughts on the basic tenets of the profession had not changed, her philosophy had been broadened and enhanced.

Nightingale's mode of action was not to challenge the basic rules and assumptions of society. Rather, she worked within the system to change those things that seemed to her

Table 3-1. Summary of a Concept Analysis of Florence Nightingale as Nursing's Foundational Philosopher

Analytical Step	Concept Substantiation of "Foundational Philosopher" and Nightingale
Step 1: Concept Selection	Vocabulary review to replace "founder," which was found to not adequately describe Nightingale's contributions.
Step 2: Purpose of the Analysis	Identification of appropriate word(s) that specifically describe Nightingale's contribution to the profession of nursing. No appropriate term existing in the literature. Development of new compound term and operational definition for "foundational philosopher."
Step 3: Uses of the Concept	Proposed utilization in research-based and general usage and to replace "founder of modern nursing" relative to Nightingale.
Step 4: Defining Attributes i) Identification of the basic tenets of a profession ii) Societal need and benefit iii) Lasting capacity and flexibility	i) Identification by Nightingale of importance of all components of a nursing theory—person, health, environment, and nursing—and how these are to interrelate. ii) Initially Nightingale documents the results of nursing care through use of statistics in Crimea. Perceived need for professional nursing is translated into school at St. Thomas' Hospital and development of midwifery, military nursing, and public health nursing as specialties. Continues to use statistics to make arguments for funding and continued educational excellence. iii) Initially, "Nightingale model" carried around the world by graduates of St. Thomas' School. Nursing has a history of continued and uninterrupted development to present time.
Step 5: Model Cases	Nightingale (nursing) Freud (psychoanalysis) Andrew Taylor Still (osteopathic medicine)
Step 6: Alternative Cases i) Borderline ii) Contrary	i) Alternative borderline: • Mary Baker Eddy (Christian Science movement) ii) Alternative contrary: • Dorothea Lynde Dix (Nursing and mental health) • Clara Barton (Nursing and American Red Cross)
Step 7: Antecedents and Consequences	**Antecedents** of Nightingale's development of nursing: Environmental influences: Social status and contacts, family wealth, education, political identity, family value of Unitarian egalitarianism. Experiential development of Nightingale: Kaiserswerth, Harley Street, Scutari, and Crimea **Consequences** of Nightingale's development of nursing: Continued development of nursing as a profession, with increasing emphasis on autonomy of practice.
Step 8: Empirical Referents	Definition of: • General nature of nursing and nursing practice • Nature and value of nursing education • Nature and value of nursing research

without righteous merit. She particularly fought for her perception of the rights of women—the right to an education, the right to meaningful employment, the right to equal status in the family as well as in society (Selanders, 1998b). She also observed that health care was a social atrocity. Nurses were people who could change this situation. The Crimean War provided Nightingale with the opportunity to observe both the reality and the potential for change. Her 22 months abroad was not her one shining moment, as many of her biographers—and her detractors—would have one believe. In fact, it was the staging area for her to create permanent social change (Selanders, 1998a). The philosophical referents relative to the general nature of nursing and nursing practice are listed in Table 3-2.

Table 3-2.
General Nature of Nursing and Nursing Practice

Area of Thought	Philosophical Referent
The General Nature of Nursing	1. Nursing is defined as a unique profession that is both art and science. 2. The basic nursing activity is the alternation of the internal and external patient environment. 3. Nursing is autonomous within the defined scope of practice. 4. Nursing is collaborative with all other healthcare professions. 5. The goal of nursing is to foster health within the patient, which promotes optimal function. 6. Individuals are complex, holisitic beings. 7. Nursing has subspecialties, such as hospital nursing, nursing of children, midwifery, and female nurses in the military. 8. The power of nursing comes from decision-making activities based on empirical observation of the patient. 9. The practice of nursing should not be limited by gender, spiritual beliefs, or values. 10. The nurse should be allowed to develop to the maximum of his or her potential.

Nightingale heavily documented her views regarding nursing. Her papers provide a well-rounded picture of nursing as well as a view of Nightingale's expanding philosophy. Little attention is paid to actual nursing techniques except in *Notes on Nursing,* a volume written not for practicing nurses but for women caring for the health of households. The vast body of her work is theoretical and philosophical. Table 3-3 lists the most important works defining Nightingale's philosophical values relative to nursing. These works represent both the "how" and the "why" of nursing.

Table 3-3.
Nightingale's Most Significant Works Relative to Nursing

1858	*Subsidiary Notes as to the Introduction of Female Nursing into Military Hospitals*
1859	*Notes on Hospitals,* revised 1863
1860	*Notes on Nursing: What It Is and What It Is Not* (with subsequent editions 1860 revised, 1861)
1871	*Introductory Notes on Lying-in Institutions*
1876	*On Trained Nursing for the Sick Poor*
1893	*Sick-Nursing and Health-Nursing:* A paper read at the Chicago Exposition
1895	"Nurses, Training of" and "Nursing the Sick." Two articles from *A Dictionary of Medicine* by Quain
1872–1900	*Addresses to the Probationers*

Nursing Education. Just as the development of administration of nursing services during the Crimean War was not Nightingale's crowning achievement in nursing practice, the establishment of the Nightingale School at St. Thomas' Hospital in 1860 was not her ultimate accomplishment in nursing education. Development of the school was a difficult process, with arguments over location, establishment of the administration of the school, and the financial arrangements that were to be backed by the Nightingale Fund (Baly, 1986). In all of these discussions, Nightingale never suggested that she would assume a role as administrator. While illness may have been a deciding factor in her physical abilities, she clearly wanted to be in a position of developing rather than administering policy.

Although untrained nurses did exist in the early and mid-Victorian times as portrayed by the Dickens stereotype in *Martin Chuzzlewit,* religious sisterhoods provided basic nursing education in the 1830s and 1840s in England. These religious institutions emphasized moral and capable care. A number of Anglican and Catholic sisters were present in the Crimea (Attewell, 1998b). Nightingale, despite her strong religious and spiritual beliefs, strongly advocated for secular nursing education. This philosophy probably arose from difficulties in the Crimea, where nurses were accused of attempting to convert soldiers to a specific religion. Furthermore, Nightingale did not want to require a religious test for students entering nursing education. Rather, she saw this as an opportunity that might be afforded all women despite religious preference.

Nightingale's ideas of nursing education arose from her observations in hospitals across England and the European continent, her training at the Kaiserswerth Institution in 1850 and 1851, her experiences as the nursing administrator at Harley Street in 1853, and the Crimea. It was Nightingale who first formalized a specific curriculum for nurses, thus cementing the link between education and practice. She expected that the educational experience would be a moral and developmental experience as well as educational. The selection process was aimed at students who were considered both academically promising and of proper moral upbringing. Students were to have educational skills such as reading and basic mathematics. In return for signing a letter of agreement to the rules and responsibilities of a student, the school would provide a safe and regulated environment for the young woman. Table 3-4 outlines the specific values held by Nightingale regarding nursing education.

Table 3-4.
The Nature and Value of Nursing Education

Area of Thought	Philosophical Referent
Nursing Education	1. Nursing has specialized educational requirements with theoretical and clinical components. 2. Nurses should be educated by nurses who specialize in education. 3. Nurses should have a grounding in the basic sciences. 4. Nursing education should be controlled by the school, not the hospital. 5. Students are to be regularly evaluated and apprised of this evaluation during the course of the education.

Nursing Research. The arena in which Nightingale would most certainly flourish today is nursing research. She was a consummate researcher, always asking questions and seeking the answers. The most obvious example of this was the data collected during the Crimean conflict, which were used to document numbers of wounded and causes of death. It was her numbers that recorded a death toll of 4,000 from wounds and 16,000 from disease that finally resulted in a government inquiry and eventual reform in the army medical system (Attewell, 1998a).

Research provided the foundation to move the profession forward. She both valued and refined the art of being able to make logical and factual arguments based on data collection. Much of Nightingale's research was based on direct observation—of the patient, of the nurse, of the environment, of the outcomes of care. Table 3-5 identifies the basic referents.

Table 3-5.
The Nature and Function of Nursing Research

Area of Thought	Philosophical Referent
Nursing Research	1. The most basic element of research is empiricism. 2. The nurse should be the primary investigator of nursing phenomena. 3. Statistics provide the basis for logical and factual arguments.

Continuing the Outcomes

Despite belief in the perpetuity of the Nightingalean nursing legacy, it is obvious that the fit in today's world has not always been perfect. Is this because of changes in the profession, or is it the *perception* of the profession as it exists within society?

The Victorians paid particular attention to order, regularity, and predictability in their lives. Nightingale speaks frequently of "universal laws" that govern the cosmos and allow predictability of outcome to actions. In more recent times and with continuing scientific development, diversity has been celebrated as a necessary component of societal improvement. Legitimacy is given to the unpredictable, which encourages us to further describe and assess the anomalous and unpredictable.

What then of Nightingale's concepts as they relate to nursing? Do they meet the needs of an evolving society? First, we must allow that the basic values that she assigned to nursing must be evaluated on individual merit, not age. Health remains the goal of nursing. The patient, however one might define *patient* and whatever the setting, remains the target. The process of nursing continues to be alteration of the internal and external environments. Societal change has altered none of this.

Evolutionary change should not represent a revolt or a search for superiority in thought, any more than Nightingale's lifelong struggle for radical change and reform should brand her a revolutionary or an elitist. Because there is perceived and current value in diversity, this philosophy should provide a platform for the development of ideas, values, and, ultimately, truth.

Florence Nightingale: Then or Now?

Given that society has undergone a transformation in its cultural paradigm, is it possible that the philosophical foundation laid down by Nightingale can survive such a shift? Nightingale did understand and subscribe to the philosophical notions prominent in the 19th century. It is curious to note that she frequently is not given credit for changing with the times. For instance, in her formative years and during the time that she was in the Crimea (1854–1856), she subscribed to the disease transmission theory of miasmatism—that is, that diseases were the result of harmful influences in the environment called miasmas (van der Peet, 1995). This was not in direct opposition to the theory of contagion—the germ theory—but it was very vague and did not explain how disease was transmitted from person to person.

The germ theory did not begin to actively develop until the 1860s, and Pasteur did not generally publish his results until 1878. Nightingale can hardly be faulted for not believing in the germ theory early in her career—but should be given credit for moving with the times. In her article in *Quain's Dictionary,* published in 1895, she talks about germ theory and its impact on nursing practice, the necessity of using antiseptics in the sick room, and how this will improve disease prevention—a part of nursing she saw as essential in maintaining a positive patient environment. Rather than trying to disprove Nightingale's values and ideas, critics should recoginze that the model of evolution of thought that she displayed continues to be of value to the profession in the 21st century.

It is entirely possible that the Nightingalean concepts are as relevant for the 21st as for the 19th century. In fact, the larger issue should be, "Can nursing exist without its historical roots?" The answer probably is no. If nursing were to be perceived as a mature tree with an extensive root system, one understands immediately that if half of the root system were removed—either the historical or the current side—the tree would probably be dislodged and wither. It would appear not to be possible to have nursing lose the ontology of experience, or even the benefits of habit and intuition. Neither can we lose the issues of the moment: entry into practice, staffing requirements, indistinct image, and financial exigencies. Reed (2000) wisely states, when attempting to answer a similar question, "The quest for nursing knowledge, then, occurs not only through the discursive modes of philosophic inquiry and the research process, but also by attending to the embodiment of health processes and practices" (p. 131). This is the description of modernism and postmodernism standing shoulder-to-shoulder and surviving, perhaps even thriving.

Nightingale's legacy is that she was able to foresee and emphasize those values for the profession that transcended the current philosophical paradigm and would be important at any point that nursing was practiced. It is these lessons that we must more acutely listen to, and not discard because they have not been "discovered" in the very recent past. Her intent was not to create a profession for women for the moment. Rather, it was to improve the general state of public health through the identification of practice based on education, empiricism, and the knowledge of the time—whatever time that may be.

The current realities in nursing practice, education, and research present a far different picture. Not only is nursing deeply affected by the issues of the time, it also has been deeply wounded by our culture's attitudes toward women. Characteristics such as empowerment and autonomy, all a part of the original vision for the profession, are not encouraged and frequently are actively repressed, especially in the acute care setting. Those of us who are educators are obligated to start the process of appropriate socialization. Those of us in practice must be gatekeepers, initiators, and innovators. This is the vision. This is the possibility.

Pentimento

Florence Nightingale's Personality Type:

An Exercise in Understanding

Barbara M. Dossey

New and refreshing light can be cast on Florence Nightingale's life and work by examining her personality type. The Myers–Briggs Type Indicator® (MBTI®) reveals that she was an INTJ (*I*ntroverted, I*n*tuitive, *T*hinking, *J*udging) type. MBTI allows us to more clearly understand major areas of Nightingale's life that have been partially unacknowledged or misunderstood: her spiritual development as a practicing mystic; how she managed her chronic illness in order to maintain her prodigious work output; and the strategies she chose to transform her visionary ideas into new healthcare reforms and social realities.

Introduction to Personality Types

The Myers–Briggs Type Indicator, based on Carl Jung's descriptions of psychological types (Jung, 1971), is probably the most widely used personality measurement for non–psychiatric populations in the world today. MBTI is a psychometric questionnaire developed in 1942 by Isabel Briggs Myers and her mother, Katharine Cook Briggs. Myers continued to improve and disseminate the instrument over the next four decades.

Jung suggested that human behavior is powerfully shaped by three sets of preferences: (1) for orienting ourselves in the world (extrovert or introvert); (2) for collecting information (sensing or intuition); and (3) for making decisions (thinking or feeling). Myers and Briggs added a fourth preference—the manner or style in which we like to live our lives (judging or perceiving) (Myers & Myers, 1980, pp. 22–24).

Myers' contribution was developing an item pool and questionnaire that would clearly identify a person's attitudes, feelings, perceptions, and behaviors, thereby revealing the person's preference, and strength of preference, in each of the four dimensions, or pairs of opposites. These four preferences interact to produce the 16 personality types. The four dimensions, or pairs, of the MBTI opposites can be summarized as follows:

- *Extroversion or Introversion (EI) Scale* – The EI scale tells where a person derives his or her energy, in the outer or inner worlds. People who prefer extroversion (*E*) focus on the outer world of people, activities, or things. People who prefer introversion (*I*) like to focus on their inner world of ideas, emotions, or impressions.
- *Sensing or Intuition (SN) Scale* – The SN scale tells how a person acquires information. People who choose to use their five senses to gather information about objects, events, and facts of daily life are sensing (*S*). Those who prefer to focus internally on meanings, possibilities, and patterns and relationships among things, who have a "sixth sense" or just "get it," are i*n*tuitive (*N*).

- *Thinking or Feeling (TF) Scale* – The TF scale tells how a person prefers to make decisions. People who prefer to make decisions that are objective and impersonal, based on logical analysis, are said to be thinking (*T*) types. People who make decisions using a process of personal valuing—considering themselves and others—are feeling (*F*) types.
- *Judging or Perceiving (JP) Scale* – The JP scale describes the manner or style in which we prefer to live our lives. People who seek closure, who like things planned, organized, and settled, have a judging (*J*) attitude. Those people who value a spontaneous and flexible life style, who like to keep their options open, have a perceiving (*P*) attitude.

The existence of these opposites was nothing new, as Jung himself pointed out. But Jung's insight was that an initial choice between the basic opposite pairs *determines the line of development* for how a person gathers information and how they make decisions. This has profound consequences in the field of personality, for it makes possible a coherent explanation for a variety of simple human differences, for complexities of personality, and for widely different satisfactions and motivations. The concept of type sheds light on the way individuals gather information and make decisions, on the things that they value most, on their communication and work styles, and on their behavior patterns (Myers & Myers, 1980, p. 25).

By the 1980s, the Myers–Briggs approach was entering the American workforce as a key human resources tool, demonstrating an effectiveness and efficiency that continues to this day. Its primary utility is to clearly summarize and assess those unique aspects of an employee's personality (and subsequent preferences) in a way that can promote personal and professional development, as well as forecast how each person is most likely to interact with co-workers in a given position. These findings are best applied in fine-tuning job descriptions, team development, career management, and other workplace issues. For individuals, the insights provided by this tool can be applied in way that can clarify and deepen self-understanding.

Likewise, having a grasp of these types helps us more clearly understand major areas of Nightingale's life that have been hitherto partially unacknowledged or misunderstood: her spiritual development as a practicing mystic (B. Dossey, 1998c, 2000a) whose drive to do God's will was the primary source of her motivation, how she managed her chronic illness (1998c) in order to maintain her high work output, and the strategies she chose to transform her visionary ideas into new healthcare reforms and social realities (1998d).

Three-Step Analysis Process to Determine Nightingale's Personality Type

After a six-year study of hundreds of Nightingale's letters and volumes of her work, I developed a three-step analysis process to identify Nightingale's personality type based on MBTI. The first step was to compile a list of Nightingale's behaviors and traits drawn from other scholars' analyses, as well as my own. In the second step, this list was matched to the most appropriate of the 16 personality descriptions of MBTI, which was the INTJ personality type. The third step was to draw conclusions about Nightingale's life and work style based on her INTJ personality type.

Analysis of Nightingale's Personality Type

Florence Nightingale was a visionary far ahead of her time; stubbornly persistent in transforming her visions into reality through tough-minded, logical analysis; and a perfectionist in bringing closure to her goals and objectives, as is evident in most of her photographs, including the one below when she was in her latter years.

In a study of the way Nightingale lived her life and pursued her social action to serve God and humankind, the individual characteristics of her personality reveal that her dominant preferences were introversion, intuition, thinking, and judging. In the language of MBTI, this categorizes her as an INTJ personality type. Her personal history indicates that she had a strong preference for each choice, which further helps us to understand her determined and persevering qualities.

Her successes across many fields are an epitome of her personality type. Inhabitants of the IN quadrant are the most intellectual of all types, with a capacity for seeing farther into the unknown than most people. For the INTJ, the world is a place to create things; their abstract models are as real and objective to them as oak trees and mountains are to other people. The INTJ's motivation from the inspiration of their intuition alone is formidable. In Nightingale, the practical mystic's drive for perfection and her gift of divine energy was articulated through the strength of her personality type.

In contemporary MBTI samples, some of the highest concentrations of collegiate INTJs are found among science and engineering students; in professional life, INTJs are most often research scientists and design engineers (Myers & Myers, 1980, pp. 41–43, 113). Nightingale's great accomplishments in the fields of nursing, sanitation, and statistics reflect the strong design element she brought to all her endeavors, supported by exhaustive and accurate research.

Nightingale at work on her chaise-longue, wearing her customary lace headscarf and shawl.

Because her work was that of an analyst and originator of ideas, it was possible for her to succeed as an introvert working from her bedroom where she lived with a debilitating, chronic illness (*I*ntrovert). Her mission was to improve civilian and military sanitation and healthcare at home, in India, and throughout the British Empire; and to create a whole new idea of what the profession of modern, secular nursing should and could be. She was a visionary before her time (dominant I*n*tuitive). She used her observations of what was, and from these she created logical analyses with compelling data that she had collected to show the flaws, and to justify change (*T*hinking). She had an intense determination to accomplish her projects and visions with detailed plans and organization. She would seek closure on almost everything that she began, and then step to the next level toward perfection (*J*udging).

It is this combination of four preferences that characterizes, and to some extent determines, individual personality type. For Nightingale they form the INTJ type. In each of the 16 types, one preference is dominant—the "captain of the ship"—and a second is auxiliary. For Nightingale's INTJ type, her dominant function was intuition (*N*), supported by thinking (*T*). It is this particular combination that makes the INTJ the most independent of the 16 types. Intuition provides the INTJ with an iconoclastic imagination and an unhampered view of the possibilities; thinking supplies a keenly critical organizing faculty and the craving to translate ideas into reality (Myers & Myers, 1980, pp. 114–115; Nightingale, 1859, 1860b).

According to the MBTI, Nightingale's personality type is best described as an INTJ. MBTI offers a new, practical perspective and fresh insights into Nightingale's complex genius and the way she lived and worked. Understanding her personality type helps us to understand more clearly these areas of her life that have been misinterpreted or misunderstood: her spiritual development as a practical mystic, her management of her chronic illness, and the strategies she chose to create new healthcare and social realities from her visionary models.

3

Directions and Reflections

Directions for Future Research

1. How does the concept of "foundational philosopher" differ from "founder" of a profession?
2. How can nursing education assist in keeping the historical knowledge alive and yet have students be current in today's practice environment?

Reflections on Florence Nightingale's Tenets: Leadership

1. How do I define leadership?
2. How do I lead as a nurse? In practice? In the community?
3. What is the relationship between leadership and philosophy?
4. What is my personal philosophy of nursing?
5. How does my personal philosophy correlate with the philosophy of my employing institution?
6. How can I use my personal philosophy to create change?

Social Change & Leadership: Dynamic Forces for Nursing

Louise C. Selanders

Nursing, as an integral part of society, has developed in response to changing social needs. While most change seems to occur at an imperceptible rate, it is in fact continuous, cumulative, perpetual, and erratic (Baly, 1995). New technology and ideas can combine to create change so significant that social structure and its substrates can be permanently altered within a generation. Occasionally, single events create change in a moment.

Toffler (1980) identified general social change as occurring in three waves. To a large extent, the Western world moved from an agrarian rural model through the industrial urban phase to our current mobile and highly technological society, one that is in the process of being rapidly both united and expanded by computer-networked information and communications systems. Among the social changes of this current phase are changes of labor needs, the loss of certain job categories, and increasing requirements for a more skilled and diversified labor force (Malloch & Porter-O'Grady, 1999; Porter-O'Grady, 1999). These changes have not been isolated, and the world now functions in a global economy. One of the driving forces of international financial markets is the continually rising costs of health care in general and nursing care in particular.

The geography of health care and nursing is also changing in response to societal needs. The system is no longer physician-dependent or hospital-based, and length of stay has declined in many cases from days or weeks to hours (Porter-O'Grady, 2000). The system is described as stressed, with insufficient workers to provide care, especially nurses. Yet nursing is seen as essential to the reduction of patient mortality and onset of complications (L. Aiken et al., 2002). It would seem that nursing has the potential to provide the missing link as the system continues to evolve, and that, in the continually changing environment, nurses are in a unique position to create this change.

Nursing's track record, however, does not demonstrate a readiness to cope with or anticipate change. In this reactive environment, the missing ingredient seems to be leadership at both the micro and macro levels. Florence Nightingale was an effective leader who devised a model of leadership that, although unconventional, does accommodate the needs of current practice. Her experiences in adapting to the unique environment of health care remain relevant in the modern and postmodern milieu of today's practice.

The Many Faces of Social Change

Sociologists do not agree on all of the factors that cause social change. They do agree that it will occur anytime that the supporting super- and substructures of a society shift. Two critical factors are the alteration of population densities and the attitudes that determine cultural values.

Population shifts are due to both preventable and unforeseeable causes. While war, at least loosely defined as a preventable cause, can result in bloodshed for millions, lack of the basic resources of food and water and the presence of communicable disease remain the prevalent causes for catastrophic population change. The plague in medieval times caused the deaths of an estimated 75 percent of the European population—35 million people.

In more recent times, the persistence of contagious disease such as smallpox has changed history. Known to have killed hundreds of millions, it is a scourge that can be traced as far back as a 3,000-year-old Egyptian mummy (Carrell, 2003). Potentially as devastating, AIDS has resulted in the deaths of more than 28 million people worldwide since 1982 and at least 42 million currently are living with the disease (U.S. Department of Health and Human Services, 2002).

Conversely, scientific discovery and worldwide dissemination of knowledge have changed population structures. Infant mortality rates have fallen dramatically, infectious disease has been effectively handled by the development of antibiotics, and research has produced remarkable new techniques to both diagnose and cure disease. The result has been a growing population that lives longer and has larger proportions of dependent people at both ends of the age spectrum, stressing the resources of caregivers and care systems (Baly, 1995).

Cultural patterns are related to religious and racial expectations, occupational and economic stratifications, and family and gender status. Of particular interest to this work is the Victorian era: 1837–1901. It was the time of Nightingale and of the establishment of the modern foundations of nursing. It was also a time of exceptional social change brought on by the industrial age, the importance of "progress" as a conceptual theme, and the development of science and technology. It is said that at the outset of the 19th century, the world was closer to that of the Greeks and Romans than of today. But the steam engine unleashed the power to make and move goods and services, and scientific thought and experimentation allowed technology to move forward at an amazing pace. Within Florence Nightingale's lifetime, communications moved from word-of-mouth to the telephone, and transportation evolved from horseback to manned flight.

The Geography of Women's Work

The Victorian era was above all a time of work. Yet the Victorians were reluctant to recognize women as workers, especially when the work was outside of the home. While work was proclaimed the new religion, this was very narrowly applied to women, who were celebrated as the "Angels of the Hearth" in a firmly structured family organization (Altick, 1973).

If you were to imagine the world of work as a set of concentric circles, the patriarchal household would be at the center and men's work would be at the outside circle, indicating that men would commonly be expected to leave the home to work—perhaps to the field, ultimately to the factory, the mine, or the office. As women began to work for pay, their workplace was another home—usually as a governess or in domestic service. Occasionally, a woman would be called to offer health care in the capacity of midwife or sitter—rarely in the role of healer. This did not disturb Victorian society, as these tasks were considered to be supplemental to standard domestic chores, and thus did not fall outside the sphere of accepted women's work (Hume & Offen, 1981).

A second circle of work would have to be added as women's sphere began to expand with work opportunities, financial exigencies, and the need for a larger workforce. Women were moving from the sphere of the home to the sphere of the marketplace as clerks, secretaries, and occasionally as professionals. This transition, although inevitable, did not happen smoothly. Women were seen as invaders of the male workplace, and the result could only be the destruction of the home, improper care of children, and the decline of the work ethic.

This social change was in a large part initiated by active social reformers, who were primarily female. Some of the most visible were authors such as the Brontës, Jane Austen, Elizabeth Blackwell, and Harriet Beecher Stowe, who evoked possibilities that women had never before considered. These women and other reformers particularly raised social concern because their vocations and their beliefs brought them into direct conflict with the prevailing cultural biases, and therefore they were considered unwomanly.

An additional problem arose when change for women in the workplace was thwarted through the use of legislation specifically directed at factory work conditions, child labor laws, and prostitution. While most would certainly argue that the intent of these laws was to better conditions and eliminate "immoral" practices, in fact they also had the effect of limiting women's work opportunities.

Nursing played an interesting part in this evolution as women moved into a nondomestic setting—the hospital—but frequently assumed "womanly" duties in the care of the sick and injured. While the position was seen as both necessary and appropriate, little or no control over working conditions or autonomy within the position were afforded the bedside nurse. This continued well into the 20th century—and, some would say, today (Aiken et al., 2002; Ashley, 1977).

Change, Nightingale, and Nursing

Enter Florence Nightingale. Philosophically we have to consider Nightingale as a woman of her time who wrote extensively regarding the major themes of the period. From her writing we can determine that she contributed specifically to philosophical beliefs that, if not entirely integrated into society, at least became social themes and subjects of discussion—nursing as a recognized female profession, the relationship of nursing to public health, and the value of egalitarian feminism, especially as it related to the education and employment of women. This is summarized in Table 4-1.

One of the major innovations in Nightingale's system of nursing was providing a place for women to work *with* and *for* women. This was a unique situation, for although women were working, the chain of command was almost always male, including in teaching. Nightingale was particularly insistent about how students would be trained and the surroundings in which they would live, which included the nurses' home, a safe and highly regulated environment. The formalization of the role of matron or head nurse was critical. Although the idea was not new—matrons in hospitals can be traced back to as early as 1526—Nightingale envisioned the role as a blend of supervisor, teacher, administrator, and liaison between the caregiving and educational functions of the nursing staff (Ardern, 2002; Baly, 1986). In fact, it was this role of matron that was responsible for the dissemination of the Nightingale nursing model. While Nightingale is criticized for using only "ladies" in this role, she also seemed to understand that these were women who could create change for the profession through social contacts, fund-raising, and diffusion of knowledge.

Table 4-1.
Philosophical Choice Selection: Nightingale vs. the Prevailing Victorian Perspective

Value	Nightingale's Value	Victorian Value
Value of the Individual	Individuals achieve to the maximum of their potential regardless of gender.	Differential gender expectations are assigned by culture and cannot be individually altered.
Value of Goal Setting	The individual needs to determine goals of substantive achievement based on a philosophical belief system.	Ornamental achievement by women is the expected based on societal norms.
Value of Meaningful Employment	Meaningful employment is the route to individual achievement and is not subject to gender specificity. Value of the employment is not equivalent to remuneration for the employment.	Employment is to be only in the province of the male. Women are too delicate to survive these experiences and must be protected from society's realities.

Social Change and Leadership

James MacGregor Burns (1978) states, "One of the most universal cravings of our time is a hunger for compelling and creative leadership" (p. 1). Leadership is a particular kind of power relationship. It is the reciprocal process of mobilizing resources, human and otherwise, by persons with certain motives and values for the purpose of realizing goals independently or mutually held by leaders and followers (Burns, 1978; Selanders, 1992; Yukl, 1989).

The ultimate outcome of leadership is conflict resolution. Conflict represents a lack of mutuality in process or outcome between the leaders and the followers or among the followers themselves. The conflict may arise within the organization or without. The role of the leader is to resolve the conflict, ideally for the long term and to the satisfaction of both leaders and followers.

Leadership takes many forms. Types such as situational, charismatic, contingency, bureaucratic, and tyrannical leadership all appear in the literature (Burns, 1978; Owens, 1987; Yukl, 1989). Two particular paradigms described by Burns are predominant. The first is *transactional* leadership, which occurs when one or more people take leadership initiative for the purpose of exchanging valued things—such as labor in return for a paycheck. Although bargaining and the resultant practices by the followers may be successful in achieving goals when the perspectives of the leaders and the followers are similar, this type of leadership does not work to build lasting relationships, promote long-term change, or develop mutuality of purpose. Consequently, it is likely that when the immediate need of one of the parties is met, the relationship will either cease or need to be renegotiated.

This differs from the second paradigm, *transformational* leadership, which occurs when one or more persons engage each other in such a way that leaders and followers raise one another to higher levels of motivation and morality (Burns, 1978). This is a change-oriented model that promotes both long-term change and enduring relationships.

Contrasting social structures have moved both the transactional and transformational models forward (Barker, 1991, 1992). The first is the conventional social structure that has existed for centuries, in which the universe is defined as entirely logical and predictable through what is now known as the laws of physics. Further, it is posited that if the laws are both understandable and predictable, then the events of nature can be controlled. As part of the 18th-century Industrial Revolution, and continuing into the Victorian era, these ideals were embraced wholeheartedly in the Western world. Organizational structure evolved utilizing the same principles—that is, that situational control was imperative and that this could best be accomplished through a hierarchical structure embodied in bureaucracy. This provided prime conditions for the emergence of the traditional transactional leadership model that emphasized the power of leadership and the subservience of employees.

A developing and more comprehensive worldview acknowledges that not all elements of society are predictable or understandable (Elkind, 1998; Watson, 1999). This philosophy recognizes the complexity of society, the need for cooperation as opposed to competition within organizations, and the importance of process as opposed to task completion in problem-solving and goal attainment. This viewpoint has resulted in a reduced perceived need to control employees and an increased emphasis on empowerment, lateral management, internal networking, decentralized decision-making, and employee ownership of corporate structures. This worldview is consistent with transformational leadership, which underscores the importance of morality, cooperation, and long-term benefits.

Nightingale as a Visionary Leader

Nightingale both described and exemplified a particular kind of leadership, which in reality is a particular kind of power relationship. *Transvisionary* leadership is a model that blends the transactional and transformational leadership types: the leader desires to create mutual, permanent change, but cultural constraint or knowledge deficit prohibits mutuality as a process. It also requires that the leader have the vision to see the potential in the developing area or profession.

Nightingale was not familiar with the words *transactional* or *transformational*. However, she worked instinctually to change the health of populations and the social condition of women. The tools with which she could create this change were her intellect, her experience, and her access to those who could create this change, through either social perception or parliamentary action. Illness made her acutely aware that leadership without physical presence was possible. Frequently she used her communication and negotiation skills to achieve a goal while working from her sickbed. (See the Pentimento in this chapter for details of Nightingale's lingering illness.)

What differentiated Nightingale's mode of operation from transactional leadership was her need to provide for enduring social change. The most notable examples of Nightingale's application of the transvisionary model were her development of the Royal Commission leading to the reform of the army medical system, and the securing of St. Thomas' Hospital as the site for the Nightingale Training School for Nurses. These were the means to the end—not the end product of her vision. They simply provided the vehicle for her vision of society.

In this model, the leader has expert knowledge that is used as a power base. The constituents are neither educated in the situational specifics nor do they perceive themselves to be empowered, usually because of cultural, social, or organizational constraints. However, they see the leader as one who will assist them in reaching a mutually defined goal through the use of knowledge, position, or opportunity. There tends to be trust and respect between the leader and the followers. Transvisionary leadership implies that the leader does have an active vision of the outcome—one which has not been previously achieved or is commonly considered to be impossible under current circumstances. Part of Nightingale's vision was to perpetuate a line of qualified leaders within the profession. A century and a half later, Maxwell (1998) formalized this concept as his "law of explosive growth," which states that leaders who develop other leaders multiply their growth because every leader they develop will also develop followers. These differ from leaders who only develop followers, from which exponential growth cannot occur.

Nightingale actually sought to utilize all nurses as leaders. In her perception, a flow of leadership would occur as seen in Table 4-2. This demonstrates the typical flow of leadership, from nursing administration to staff nurses to patients. Both staff and patients are considered as constituents—the recipients of leadership—and each can relate directly to the leader. Any constituent can and should provide feedback and restart the cycle, as demonstrated by the arrows in the first column. All participants use a similar conceptual base, but this may be applied differently with different outcomes, representing a variety of depth and permanence.

The Stairstep Leadership Development Model

A leadership technique is not applied in isolation. By definition, there must be leaders and followers. Further, understanding the sequential learning that occurs in order to successfully assume a leadership role enables an individual to move into such a position with greater ease.

There is a series of techniques that individuals use in order to achieve leadership goals. This is identified as the Stairstep Leadership Development Model. This model is partially based on the novice-to-expert concept of Benner (1984). The term *novice* does not imply lack of knowledge in all areas. One can be an expert practitioner of nursing and still have little or no leadership skill or experience. One takes the steps to achieve expert knowledge in a variety of ways—through observation and assessment of leadership situations, through trial and error, through intellectual routes. Knowledge may be gained through purposeful, directed activity or passive observation. Each step demonstrates the necessity to have an increasingly sophisticated set of personal and environmental requisites in order to accomplish the goal of transformational or transvisionary leadership roles.

The ultimate goal of the Stairstep Leadership Development Model is to have the leader and the followers achieve a mutually defined goal with a collective purpose and a long-term effect. This is consistent with transformational leadership, which is enduring and satisfying for both leaders and followers.

Leaders, as in most areas of professional development, generally require development of leadership skills. This model acknowledges that a novice leader, while perhaps having the desire to lead, suffers from a deficit of knowledge and experience. With knowledge, the other essential components—constituents and opportunity—must also be available. Assuming these, there are three potential choices of leadership models available to the leader—transactional, transvisionary, or transformational.

Choosing the appropriate model depends upon the desired outcome, the experience and confidence of the leader, the nature of the problem and constituents, environmental components such as management support, and the opportunity to provide leadership. Any of the three models of leadership can bring attainment of the goal. However, the transactional model may result in short-term gains and diminished satisfaction of the constituents. The transvisionary model provides a middle ground that attempts to maximize constituent satisfaction while utilizing techniques that may be more amenable or available to the leader. All leadership experience adds to the knowledge base of the leader, thus providing a feedback loop.

Table 4-2.
Flow of Leadership to Constituents as Identified by Nightingale

Principal Players	Functions	Outcomes
Nursing Leaders ↓	*Advocates	• Largest degree of impact is with constituents who are being supervised. Analogous to role of profession as a whole. • Advocacy directly for these persons as well as for the profession as a whole.
	Educates	• Education of constituents openly valued, encouraged, facilitated.
	Creates	• Opportunities for change to be created or identified.
	Disseminates	• Broadly based and professional knowledge disseminated to constituents. Facilitates constituents to conduct research and publish.
	Empowers	• Constituents are empowered to create care solutions, identify issues.
Nurses (Constituents) ↓	Advocates	• Constituents advocate for clients relative to care standards, care opportunities, and care outcomes. Functions as a leader with recipients of care as constituency.
	Educates	• Identifies education of clients as a basic nursing function. Actively identifies and pursues personal professional educational needs.
	Creates	• Identifies/creates opportunities for change within the employment setting.
	Disseminates	• Disseminates knowledge both to recipients of care constituency and peers.
← **	Empowers	• Actively empowers constituency in decision-making relative to healthcare issues. Feels empowered to create change within employment setting.
Recipients of Care (Constituents) ↓	Advocates	• Recipients of care learn to advocate for perceived care standard for themselves/significant others.
	Educates	• Recipients of care identify means of educating themselves relative to healthcare status.
	Creates	• Creates opportunities for improving health status of self/significant others
	Disseminates	• Disseminates healthcare information to significant others.
← **	Empowers	• Feels empowered to be in control of own healthcare issues.

* Identical functions are carried out with different constituents, resulting in different outcomes.

** Any constituent can/should provide feedback and restart the cycle.

4

Conclusions: Visionary Leadership

Nightingale understood that the ability to create change depended on a succession of effective leaders. However, nursing, particularly nursing as it occurs in hospitals, seems to have opted out of leadership in many situations and adopted a peculiar form of management that tends to be survival-oriented.

Davies (1992) describes this particular form of management as "coping management," a firefighting approach that is characterized by a strong personal commitment to task, a weak sense of status and position, and a willingness through a "roll-up-the-sleeves" attitude to get done what has to be done. This is a model in which the staff is encouraged to run faster, work harder, do more with less, and not look to the future. The work is led by the head nurse or unit manager who perceives the need to be in the trenches to get the work done. There is the general perception that the administration is unwilling or unable to change. Therefore, for the welfare of the patients, it is essential that "we," the nursing staff, cope. It is a model that guarantees burnout. It fuels the current problems of high turnover, low morale, and feelings of low self-esteem and powerlessness.

This is *not* the model of Nightingale. This was not her vision. But time is quickly going by and we, as nurses, seem unwilling to take up the mantle and provide leadership. We do not have to reinvent the wheel. We simply have to be visionary, not reactive. Consider the processes of change as depicted in Figures 4-1 and 4-2.

Figure 4-1.
The Leadership Development Model

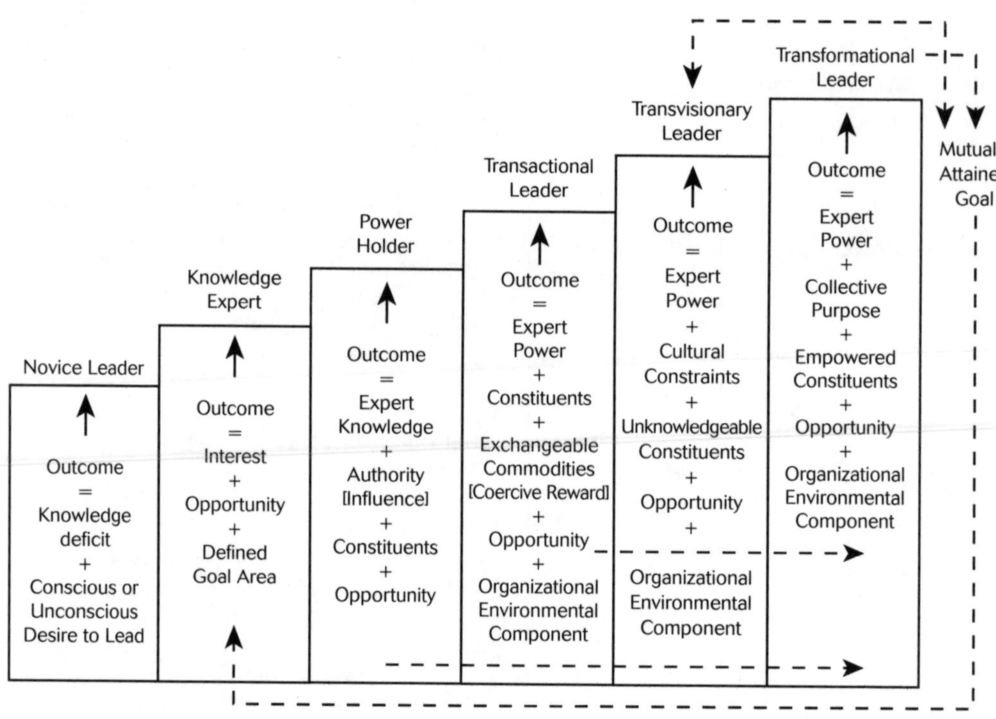

In the evolutionary change paradigm, change is seen as it occurs in nursing today. It is a reactive model that assumes that control over change is either not possible or not practicable. It would appear that the leadership in this situation is either unwilling or unable to envision the future.

Figure 4-2.
Evolutionary Change Paradigm

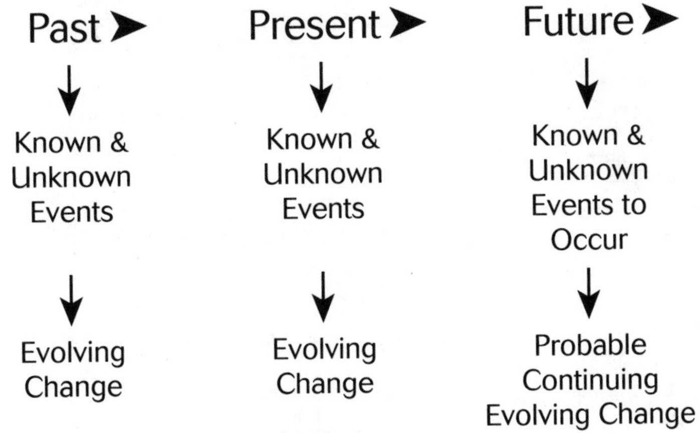

This is markedly different from the situation shown in Figure 4-3. The second paradigm implies that change, at least in some situations, can be controlled. Further, the events of today have an impact on tomorrow, even though there is the understanding that controlled and uncontrolled events will be a part of the future.

The difference between the two paradigms is vision of leadership. Leadership—a dynamic force—has the goal of creating change that betters the situation of both leaders and followers, creating a positive situation for today and tomorrow. This is the model of Nightingale, and it may be the most significant model for nursing's survival in a complex and dynamic social structure.

Figure 4-3.
Controlled Change Paradigm *(adapted from Edward Barlow, Jr. Creating the Future, Inc.)*

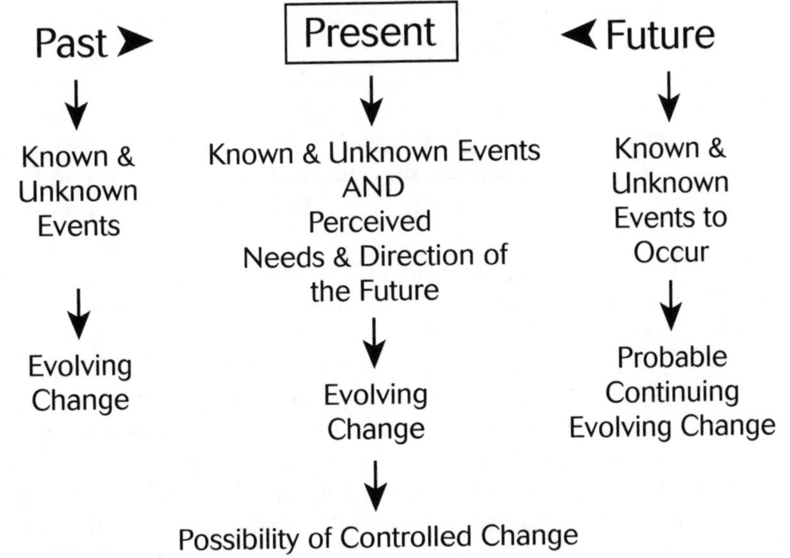

Pentimento

Florence Nightingale:
Her Crimean Fever and Chronic Illness

Barbara M. Dossey

Florence Nightingale fought a decades-long struggle with a debilitating disease contracted during the Crimean War. This chronic condition not only complicated her life, but also led to various posthumous diagnoses, some of which have been used to explain away or detract from her accomplishments. Understanding the symptoms of this disease—recently identified as chronic brucellosis—helps us to more clearly understand Nightingale's symptoms and behaviors during the period from 1855 to 1887 (D. Young, 1995; B. Dossey, 2000a, 1998d).

She was diagnosed with Crimean Fever on May 12, 1855. Her symptoms were fever, extreme fatigue, delirium, and inability to walk or eat. Although she recovered from the initial episode in two weeks, she had to be hospitalized again a few months later with severe sciatica. For the rest of her stay in Turkey, she experienced dysentery, earaches, laryngitis, and insomnia.

Upon her return to England in August 1856, Nightingale had several attacks of symptoms that included palpitations, dyspnea, syncope, weakness, and indigestion. After a second severe fever episode in September 1857, she officially declared herself an "invalid" to lessen the demands on her time and physical strength. From 1857 to 1861 she had several experiences where she felt that death was imminent, after which she even limited time with her family and friends. In December 1861 she had a serious attack with new symptoms where she was unable to walk, and was bedridden for six years with severe spinal pain. Again, during the first six months of 1866, her pain was so severe that she had periods where she could not tolerate having her position changed for 48 hours at a time. In 1867 she began to meet with only one person at a time because she was so weak.

Over the years, Nightingale's critics have viewed Nightingale as a "neurotic" or a "recluse." Others have called her chronic illness neurasthenia (Cook, 1913), stress-induced anxiety neurosis (Cope, 1958; Pickering, 1974), malingering (F. Smith, 1982), chronic lead poisoning (Ference, 1998), chronic fatigue immune deficiency syndrome (Veith, 1990), systemic lupus erythematosus (Veith, 1990), stress and job burnout (Brook, 1990), post-traumatic stress disorder (Brook, 1990), and bipolar disorder (AP, 2003).

However, in 1995, D. A. B. Young, a former principal scientist at the Wellcome Foundation, London, proposed that Nightingale's "Crimean Fever" was what is recognized today as Mediterranean Fever (also Malta Fever), and that this disease is included under the generic name *brucellosis* (D. Young, 1995). Young pointed out that it was important to establish the organic cause of her illness, because there never had been a satisfactory explanation for the behaviors Nightingale manifested after her return from the Crimea. Consequently, some biographers and other commentators have accepted uninformed explanations that could severely damage her reputation.

Common Fevers During the Crimean War

During the Crimean War (1854–1856), the British Army encountered six recognized forms of fever: intermittent fever, remittent fever, simple continued fever, relapsing fever, typhus fever, and typhoid fever. The commonest and most fatal was typhoid fever, with typhus fever being the second. When British troops arrived at Scutari (now Üsküdar, on the Asian shore of the Bosphorus, part of greater Istanbul) and the Crimean peninsula (southern tip of Ukraine), these fevers already existed in both areas; many French, Turkish, and other troops also were ill. Army doctors were skilled at differential diagnosis and were able to distinguish typhoid fever, typhus fever, and remittent fever, which became popularly known as Crimean Fever.

Remittent fever or Crimean Fever had characteristic features of nervous irritability, feverish excitability and delirium, and prolonged gastric irritation. The remission period had two distinct phases from which its name is derived: two periods of exacerbation, the morning and evening, with complete remission in 24 hours (Marston, 1863; D. Young, 1995). Relapse was very common; the resulting chronic, debilitating condition had an extremely protracted and irregular course that required months of convalescence. The overall mortality rate was very low.

Brucellosis did not receive full recognition until 1918 when Dr. Alice Evans established the close association between the causal agents of Malta fever in humans and abortion fever in cattle. These agents were later renamed *Brucella*

Nightingale, en route to the Crimea, tending to a soldier on deck.
© Florence Nightingale Museum.

Florence Nightingale and Charles Bracebridge (her chaperone to Turkey and the Crimea) surveying Sebastopol in May 1855, before her illness. Drawing by Nightingale's sister, Parthe.
© Florence Nightingale Museum

melitensis and *Brucella abortus* (Evans, 1934; D. Young, 1995). Subsequently, additional species of Brucella that can cause disease in humans have been recognized, including *Brucella suis* from swine and *Brucella canis* from dogs. (Dr. Evans became infected while working with cultures of *Brucella melitensis*, and suffered for nearly six years with a diagnosis of neurasthenia before the organism was cultured from her blood. She suffered with recurrent chronic brucellosis for the next 17 years.)

"Crimean Fever" Today: Chronic Brucellosis

Today, remittent fever, also called Malta or Mediterranean fever, is included under the generic name *brucellosis*. Brucellosis exists worldwide and remains endemic in many parts of the underdeveloped world.

The four brucellae that are pathogenic for humans are *Brucella melitensis* found in goats, *Brucella abortus* in cows, *Brucella suis* in pigs, and *Brucella canis* in dogs (Trujillo et al., 1994). Of these, *Brucella melitensis* and *Brucella suis* are the most virulent for humans (E. Young, 1994). Once the pathogens enter the bloodstream, they can localize in the lymph nodes, spleen, liver, and bone marrow. The kidneys and central and peripheral nervous system may also be involved.

Brucellosis has a wide variety of clinical presentation. It can be divided according to its clinical presentation—acute, relapsing, and chronic. Brucellosis is a clinical condition characterized by discrete symptoms and practically no physical signs. The patient may complain of moderate headache, afternoon fever with a slight fatigue, or a slight decrease in appetite.

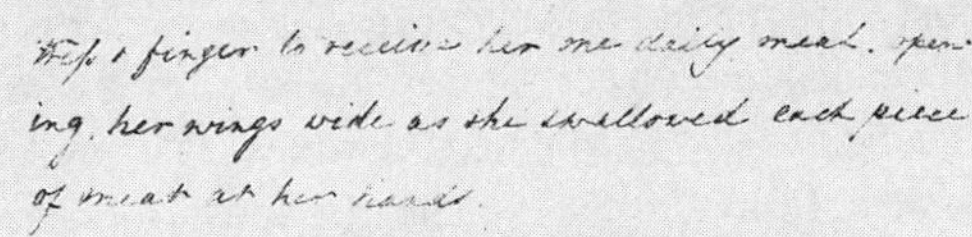

Wrist & finger to receive her one daily meal, open-ing her wings wide as she swallowed each piece of meat at her hands.

The following year she took a second journey into Germany, the waters of Karlsbad having been thought good for her health. She seemed to enjoy her travels & the respect that was paid to her exceedingly, tho objecting to the universal 'Kalbfleisch' as much as others

The strangers in whom she most delighted were Mr L & Mr Bracebridge, both well acquainted with her birthplace, & who always addressed her in Greek, and she spent a great part of every day investigating the shelves in the library, hours indeed she used to remain at the back of the largest quartos. Her toilette (as is supposed to be the case sometimes with literary ladies) suffered much from these excursions, and by the end of the winter she generally had not a feather left in her tail. Her French attendant used to be exceedingly unhappy on such occasions, & remark that company was coming, & that "Monsieur Quiz" (as Athena was occasionally called) was "tout rond et pas beau du tout," & what a pity it was, & could nothing be done?

Two drawings of Nightingale's pet owl, Athena, from the book Parthe created to amuse her sister during her convalescence from Crimean Fever.

The clinical course of the disease will vary depending on the causative species. *Brucella melitensis* is usually the most virulent and invasive (Trujillo et al., 1994). The resulting illness may be followed weeks, months, or even years later by serious complications. The term *chronic brucellosis* is applied when the illness lasts more than a year. It can take two forms: the specific form and the nonspecific form.

Some clinicians prefer to divide patients with chronic brucellosis into three categories:

- Those who suffer recidivant clinical manifestations without specific localization to any organ or tissue; however, laboratory and clinical objective evidence exists that there is active disease. This clinical situation is difficult to differentiate from those patients who received inadequate treatment and are relapsing because of inability to control or eradicate the initial infection.
- Those with chronic symptoms due to localization of the infection in a specific organ or body area.
- Those with general complaints of general malaise, with symptoms of depression and changes in personality, but who show no objective signs of the disease. These patients are frequently classified as having psychoneurotic problems up to 20 percent of the time.

(For further clinical details about this disease, consult the Internet, D. Young, 1995, and B. Dossey, 1998d.)

What Difference Does It Make?

Florence Nightingale's Crimean Fever, contracted in May 1855 while in the Crimea, is recognized today as Malta or Mediterranean fever and is included under the generic name brucellosis. Her letters and diaries from 1855 to late 1887 clearly document that she suffered a variety of significant symptoms that are consistent with the specific form of chronic brucellosis. Since the incubation period of Crimean Fever is two to three weeks, Nightingale appears to have been infected in the Scutari area in April 1855. The most likely source of infection was contaminated food, such as meat, raw milk, cheese, or butter. She and others had reported a high incidence of Crimean fever and contaminated food during April and May.

Although it is obviously impossible to make this diagnosis in retrospect with absolute certainty, her debilitating, chronic symptoms over a 32-year period are compatible with the specific form of chronic brucellosis, both epidemiologically and clinically.

If Nightingale were alive today, she almost certainly would have received a proper diagnosis. Since she became ill in an area where brucellosis was endemic, she would have been tested for this pathogen. Her initial febrile episode would have been managed by antibiotics; and her chronic, severe pain and disability would have been managed more successfully. We must consider the evidence of chronic brucellosis as the cause of Nightingale's debilitating, chronic illness, and not be misled by questionable interpretations that have surfaced from time to time. Dismissing her invalidism as neurosis, without considering organic possibilities, is wildly speculative and risks dishonoring the legacy of a great woman. It is highly unlikely that Nightingale would have become one of the most creative and productive women of the 19th century if her invalidism were due solely to a neurotic cause.

Directions and Reflections

Directions for Future Research

Where in nursing's multiplicity of work settings could the transvisionary model of leadership be successfully used? How could this then evolve into a transformational model for long-term satisfaction of both constituents and leaders?

1. What would be appropriate means by which to measure the success of leadership?
2. In a work setting, compare the measurable outcomes of a positive and dynamic leader to those of a leader who employs the "coping" management style. What is the difference in both patient and staff satisfaction?

Reflections on Florence Nightingale's Tenets: Leadership

1. How important is it to me that I am seen as a leader?
2. How important is it to my profession that I am seen as a leader?
3. How and when am I a leader?
4. Do I feel empowered as a leader? In my work? At home?
5. What is the difference in my environment when I lead as opposed to when I am a constituent?

Leading Through Theory: Nightingale's Environmental Adaptation Theory of Nursing Practice

Louise C. Selanders

During the 1970s, nursing in the United States, and to a lesser extent in Europe, seemed to be consumed by the concept of nursing theory. Late in the decade, conferences were held to introduce large numbers of nurses to the idea. New names seemed to be leading the profession—Rogers (1990), Orem (1995), I. King (1995), Roy (1999), B. Neuman (1995), and Newman (1986). Each introduced a slightly different twist as to what nursing theory was and how it should be introduced into practice and curricula. Myra Levine (1995), herself a nursing theorist, was extremely critical of the process by which theory was brought to the profession:

> In traditional nursing fashion, early efforts were directed at creating a procedure—a recipe book for prospective theorists—that then could be used to decide what was and was not a theory. And there was always the thread of expectation that the great, grand, global theory would appear and end all speculation. Most of the early theorists really believed that they were achieving that. (p. 11)

While the profession dealt with the minutiae of nursing theory and the merits of individual ideas, nursing as a whole seemed to lose sight of the real issues of theory—what is nursing theory, and how and why is it useful to a practice discipline? How has modern nursing survived for more than a century without theory?

The answer, of course, is that nursing theory is not new. The term *nursing theory* may be a child of the mid-20th century, but the ideas that compose nursing theory—and that make it applicable to nursing—were a part of the philosophical thought of Nightingale as early as the 1860s. Defining Nightingale's theory does take a bit of detective work, as modern terminology does not appear in her writings, and the wealth of documentation that she left after nearly 50 years of work and thought on the subject is formidable. However, all of the central elements of theory, regardless of how a theorist defines them, were addressed by Nightingale as they applied to practice.

Why Nursing Theory?

Nurses seem to have difficulty in describing nursing. Often the answers are in our tasks—what we do—and not what we are. Is nursing a profession or an occupation? Does it matter? Indeed it does. The two represent the breadth of employment, social status, social acceptance, and social contribution. There is a rank ordering. An "occupation" is a job—something that may not require any specialized training and may have limited advancement potential. By contrast, a "profession" is seen as providing an essential service to society. The original professions of medicine, law, and the clergy represented the only learned sectors of their time. Professions are now seen to require specialized education, autonomy to practice, a code of ethics through that to act, and formalized regulation (Alligood & Tomey, 2002; McEwen, 2002).

Nursing has also been described as a "practice discipline": an entity that finds its body of knowledge in academia and has a distinctive way of looking at phenomena (McEwen, 2002). It is in this arena that nursing theory becomes essential to the profession. Theory provides the unique perspectives of a discipline and the way it is integrated within society. By providing this perspective, it can organize the data collection necessary to develop the body of knowledge unique to the profession.

Theory, Concepts, and Models

The terminology that surrounds nursing theory can be confusing. Most essential are the terms *theory*, *concepts*, and *models*. A *theory* is a set of interrelated concepts that gives a systematic view of a phenomenon in an attempt to describe it (McEwen, 2002; Torres, 1985). It serves to uncover relationships that may not be apparent to the casual observer. The purpose of a theory for a practice discipline is simply to bring order out of what otherwise might be chaos. Rather than providing care by instincts that cannot be easily documented or predicted, a nursing theory provides the guidelines for decision-making, problem-solving, and intervention development. In the long run, a theory serves as the framework for research, thus leading to refined theory development and improvement in care outcomes.

Theory development progresses through levels. Based on available data and the theory's ability to portray conceptual interrelationships, it is said to be descriptive, explanatory, predictive, or prescriptive, with all theory development beginning at the descriptive level (Kerlinger, 1986; Nieswiadomy, 1993). The ultimate outcome of a theory is to search for truth that leads to the development of a law, something that is truly predictable in nature. This rarely, if ever, occurs in the behavioral sciences.

A theory must be subject to evaluation as to its general utility. Torres (1985) identified a set of characteristics necessary for a theory to be useful in a practice discipline:

- The interrelationships of concepts must provide a unique way of viewing a phenomenon,
- The theory must be logical,
- The theory must be simple but generalizable,
- The theory should be testable,
- The theory should contribute through research to the general knowledge base of the discipline,
- The theory should guide practice, and
- The theory should be consistent with other validated theories.

A *concept* is a complex cognitive abstraction of a phenomenon derived from empirical experience through perception of the environment (Kerlinger, 1986; McEwen, 2002; Nicoll,

1997; Nieswiadomy, 1993). Some concepts may be common to a culture, whereas others vary significantly from individual to individual depending on the lived experience. Concepts familiar to nursing as a genre are *illness*, *wellness*, *caring*, *pain,* and *healer*. Indeed, *nursing* is a concept.

Concepts can be grouped to provide a general worldview that has broad consensus within the discipline (McEwen, 2002; Nicoll, 1997). This grouping of concepts is known as a meta-paradigm. Fawcett (1984) states that each discipline is responsible for identifying those concepts that provide the unique description of the discipline. Despite theoretical pluralism in nursing, it is generally accepted that the meta-paradigm concepts in the discipline of nursing are the following:

- *Person*—the recipient of nursing care that may be referred to as "patient" or "client," and may consist of individuals, groups, and communities.
- *Health*—the person's state of well-being, which can range from high-level wellness to terminal illness or peaceful dying.
- *Environment*—surroundings in which nursing care is rendered that includes both the external and the internal (physical, mental, emotional, social, and spiritual) environment as well as patterns not yet understood.
- *Nursing*—refers to the definitions of nursing and nurse, the actions taken by the nurses on behalf of or in conjunction with patients, and the goals and outcomes of nursing actions.

While the term *model* has been used inconsistently in the nursing literature and occasionally seems to be interchangeable with *theory*, the more accepted usage has been defined as a graphic or symbolic representation of a theory—a picture of the perceived reality. Such representations are useful roadmaps in winding through the maze of verbiage necessary to present a theory.

Nightingale's Development and Philosophical Assumptions

Nightingale was a product of her Victorian environment. As the child of an influential, politically active, and liberal family, she accepted her place in the social order. Family, spiritual reflection, education, travel, and interaction with the influential and famous framed her worldview. She valued the integrity of her family even though interpersonal relationships were frequently difficult and contentious. Her education, while atypical for a woman, was provided at her insistence as well as that of her father. This provided her with a broad range of knowledge in languages, philosophy, mathematics, history, and the classics.

The defining characteristic of Nightingale's upbringing was her profound devotion to God, the sense and practice of spirituality that developed in her childhood and lasted throughout her lifetime. Born into a Unitarian family, she eventually became Anglican: her religious roots seemed to extend beyond organized religious practice to a profound sense of inner spirituality and Christian reflection (B. Dossey, 2000a). She recorded in her diary an encounter with God at age 16 in that He "called her to His service" (Cook, Vol. 1, 1913, p. 15). After this experience, she increasingly sought opportunities to respond to the needs of others, despite her family's objections that these were inappropriate actions for a lady. Her devotion to the Supreme Being continued throughout her lifetime as she continued to seek the divine purpose for which she had been born.

Certain elements of Nightingale's religious beliefs are prominent in her writings. First is the Protestant work ethic. Contrary to the Victorian perception that women were too delicate of mind and body to participate actively in either physical or mental endeavors, Nightingale encouraged work as a means to an end. This was evident as early as her employment as superintendent for the Institution for Sick Gentlewomen in London (1853–1854), and continued throughout her Crimean experience and the development of the Nightingale Training School at St. Thomas (Baly, 1986; Cook, 1913; Nightingale, 1853–1854).

Contrary to the common practice of the period, Nightingale did not use religion as a test for social acceptance. When beginning her superintendency at Harley Street, she vehemently objected to the rule that each patient must be a member of the Church of England. In her view, people from all religions—or no religion—were in need of health care, and no one had the right to limit access on such grounds. It is probable that she would have left this post had she not been able to obtain a rule revision from the governing body. After her Crimean experiences, she concluded that nursing education should also be a secular endeavor, in that church affiliation should not affect the student selection process (Baly, 1986). Nightingale's actions should not be perceived as a denial of the importance of religious beliefs. Rather, it was her perceived need to be inclusive of all people as she assisted individuals to achieve their potential.

Assumptions are ideas that are accepted as true without empirical testing (Walker & Avant, 1988). Philosophical assumptions are those based on the inherent beliefs of an individual or organization. Seven Nightingalean philosophical assumptions—summarized below—serve as the basis for the theory development.

Natural Laws

The presence of universal natural laws that govern the manner in which the world works is reflected in Nightingale's profound belief in God. She defined a law as "the thought of God" (Cook, Vol. 2, 1913, p. 396). Further, she states that one must be careful as to what is called a law. For example, the Ten Commandments are said to be laws of God, yet they are frequently broken without apparent or immediate consequence. By definition, then, they therefore cannot be laws. As discussed in Chapter 3, "universality" was a prominent notion of the period, and for those subscribing to this principle it was useful in bringing order to the universe.

The laws of life are definable through experience and research, including statistical analysis. In her last major canon in *Notes on Nursing,* Nightingale (1860a) speaks of the necessity of empirical observation as a major function of nursing care. After her Crimean experience, she saw the need for keeping statistics on nursing care. She concluded that one should engage in data collection and analysis as a part of nursing so that the most effective means of obtaining and retaining the health of the patient might be identified.

Humankind Can Achieve Perfection

While Nightingale believed deeply in the presence and power of God, she also believed in self-determination, self-realization, and, ultimately, the perfectibility of humankind. The route to perfection was through strict adherence to natural laws.

When related to health care, the seeking of perfection meant that people sought perfect health. It was the role of the nurse to alter the environment in such a way as to obey the natural laws, thereby providing the environment in which perfection might be achieved.

Nursing Is a Calling

Nightingale defines a "calling" as doing work in such a way as to do what is right and best. Indeed, the work of nursing is so important that it should be thought of as a religious vow. Work is to be done with enthusiasm (Nightingale, 1893), not merely for money or because it is a popular avocation.

Nursing Is an Art and a Science

By identifying these two components of nursing, Nightingale instills the expectation that nursing will be practiced by educated individuals utilizing current research and methods (the science) as well as through compassion and common logic (the art).

Nursing Is Achieved Through Environmental Alteration

Nightingale identified the components necessary for the maintenance of health in her canons found in *Notes on Nursing* (1860a). Through environmental alteration, one is able to put the patient in the best possible condition for nature to act, thereby facilitating the laws of nature.

Nursing Requires a Specific Educational Base

The idea that nursing required specific education was revolutionary in 19th-century England. Nightingale's focus on nursing education underscored her belief in the value of educating women in general (Selanders, 1998b).

Nightingale emphasized the need to blend theoretical and clinical experiences as part of the educational package, stating, "Neither can [nursing] be taught in lectures or by books [alone] although these are valuable accessories, if used as such: otherwise what is in the book stays in the book" (Nightingale, 1893, p. 24).

Nursing Is Distinct and Separate from Medicine

Although the physician and the nurse may deal with the same population, nursing is not to be viewed as subservient to medicine, as the purpose of the two is distinctly different. Nursing's focus is caring through environmental alteration, while medicine's focus is cure of the disease. This is not to deny that nursing and medicine are most effective when working in a collaborative manner for the purpose of achieving patient health.

Nightingale's Theory of Nursing

Nightingale did not specifically write in terms of the meta-paradigm concepts in the discipline of nursing. However, each component is addressed in her various documents.

Environment

Environment is the umbrella concept in the Nightingale theory of nursing. It was her contention that the environment could be altered in such a manner as to improve conditions so that the natural laws would allow healing to occur. This grew out of her empirical observation that poor or difficult environments led to poor health and disease.

Her definition of environment was anything that, through manipulation, assisted in putting the individual in the best possible condition for nature to act. Therefore, the environment had internal and external components. Nightingale was as concerned about elements that entered the body—food, water and medications—as those that affected the external being, such as ventilation, light, noise, stimulation, and room temperature. She saw ventilation as the most important of these elements. This reflected conditions in Victorian England, where the air quality was generally poor, especially in the big cities because of coal burning. A common belief was that "night air" would invite disease, so houses were generally tightly shut.

Nightingale wrote her most famous publication, *Notes on Nursing: What It Is and What It Is Not* (1860a), for the express purpose of teaching the general public, and especially women who were responsible for household management, how to maintain appropriate conditions within the home. In the preface she writes:

> The following notes are by no means intended as a rule of thought by which nurses can teach themselves to nurse, still less as a manual to teach nurses to nurse. They are meant simply to give hints for thought to women who have personal charge of the health of others. Every woman, or at least almost every woman, in England has, at one time or another in her life, charge of the personal health of somebody, whether child or invalid—in other words, every woman is a nurse. (p. 1)

Nightingale's basic tenets for maintenance of health are listed as her canons in *Notes on Nursing*. Table 5-1 identifies modern concepts and Nightingale's canons.

Table 5-1. Comparison of Nightingale's Canons & Modern Practice Concepts

Nightingale's Canons	Modern Concepts
Ventilation and Warming Light Cleanliness of Rooms and Walls Health of Houses Noise Bed and Bedding Personal Cleanliness	Physical Environment
Variety Chattering Hopes and Advices	Psychological Environment
Taking Food What Food?	Nutritional Status
Petty Management Observation of the Sick	Nursing Care Planning and Management

Person

The person is the individual receiving nursing care, commonly referred to as the "client" or "patient." Nightingale believed that the patient of nursing was an individual, although this was broadened with the development of nurse visitors (public health nurses), who dealt with the welfare of the family unit.

Even in the 19th century, Nightingale perceived that people were multidimensional beings composed of biological, psychological, social, and spiritual components. Typically it was the physical component that was addressed by both medicine and nursing in the attempt to alleviate disease or repair the effects of trauma. However, Nightingale clearly saw the need to address the psychological and social components, which included thought processes, self-concept, feelings, intellect, and social interaction. She warned against the lack of variety (stimulation) in the sick room, and demonstrated that psychological processes could, in fact, cause illness.

Nightingale did not specifically address the place of spirituality in the health of the individual. Because her own spirituality was so intimately tied to her perception of people and their inherent rights to health care, it is an implicit rather than overt element in her description of people.

Holism is defined as the perception that an integrated whole has a reality independent of and greater than the sum of its parts (Dossey, Keegan, & Guzzetta, 2005a). While not using the term, Nightingale did perceive human beings to be holistic. Figure 5-1 depicts the classic view of a multidimensional, holistic individual. Each sphere is essentially equal, with the holistic person being integrated in the center.

Figure 5-1.
Multidimensional Holistic Person

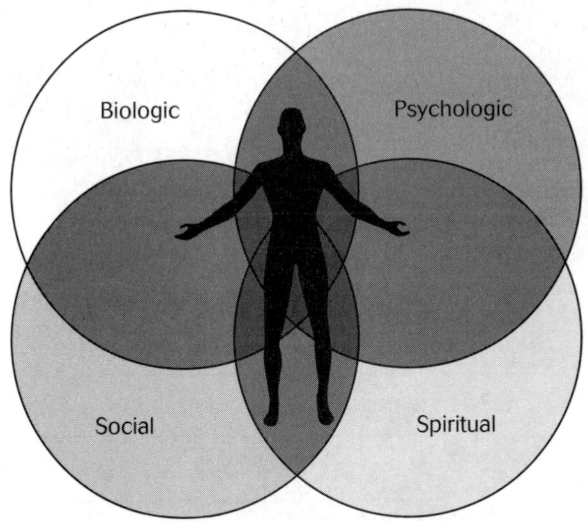

Figure 5-2 illustrates Nightingale's concept of holism with predominant biological and psychological spheres and a less prominent social sphere. In the center is the integrated individual who becomes the focus of nursing care. Surrounding this integrated individual is the spiritual sphere, which is assumed to be pervasive.

Figure 5-2.
Holistic Person as Conceived by Nightingale

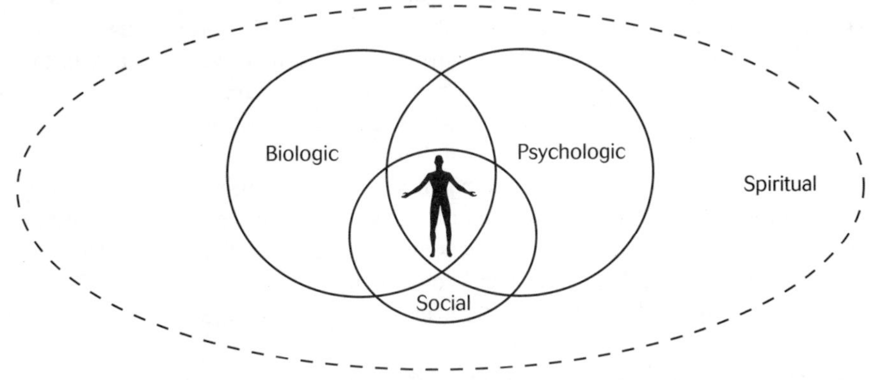

Health

Nightingale (1860a) states that health is "not only to be well, but to be able to use every power we have to use" (p. 26). This is consistent with the modern perception of health as a relative state, with ultimate health being the best a person can be at any given time. The conditions that govern the state of health are the natural laws.

Disease is portrayed with greater etymological accuracy as "dys-ease," or the absence of comfort. Nightingale (1893) also stated that disease was a "reparative process," indicating that symptoms alert one to the presence of illness, thus allowing appropriate interventions. Breaking the natural laws would cause disease. The most common reasons that disease might occur are summarized in Table 5-2.

Some other aspects of Victorian England's perspectives on the transmission of disease and the development of Nightingale's own perspectives are discussed in this chapter's Pentimento.

Table 5-2.
Nightingale's "Six D's of Dys-ease"

Dys-ease Element	Comments
Dirt	General hygiene, cleanliness in the home, interpersonal contact
Drink	Cleanliness of drinking water
Diet	The need for a proper and balanced diet
Damp	The need for a dry, warm environment
Draughts	The belief that drafts can precipitate disease
Drains	The need for proper drainage and sewer systems

Nursing

The goal of nursing is to place the patient in the best possible condition for nature to act. This is accomplished through alteration of the environment to reinforce the natural laws.

Nightingale divided nursing into two arenas. In the first, called "health nursing" or "general nursing," she placed those activities that promoted *health*. These were outlined in the canons (chapter titles) of *Notes on Nursing* and were carried out in all caregiving situations whether the individual was specially educated or not. The use of the term "canons" is probably not coincidental. One definition of canon is a church law. Therefore, it is plausible that the laws of health were considered as sacrosanct as the laws of the church, with serious consequences if broken.

The second type of nursing is "nursing proper," which is reserved for those individuals who are educated in the art and the science of nursing. By being specifically educated, the nurse is able to solve problems in a logical manner known today as the nursing process. This would be reserved today for those who are both specifically educated as nurses and licensed to practice.

Nightingale's Model for Nursing Practice

The theory of nursing care developed by Nightingale has been termed the "environmental adaptation theory," indicating that the role of the nurse is to alter the internal and external environments in order to maximize the patient's health (Selanders, 1993, 1998a). The model for practice gives a pictorial view of how nursing care can be rendered on a systematic plan known as the nursing process. Figure 5-3 illustrates Nightingale's nursing process as a four-step sequence: observation, identification of the needed environmental alteration, implementation of the alteration, and identification of the current health state. In a feedback loop, the evaluation of the effectiveness of the intervention then restarts the process as the identification of the patient's health state. This is repeated as frequently as is necessary to achieve the goal of improved health.

Figure 5-3.
Nightingale's Model for Nursing Practice

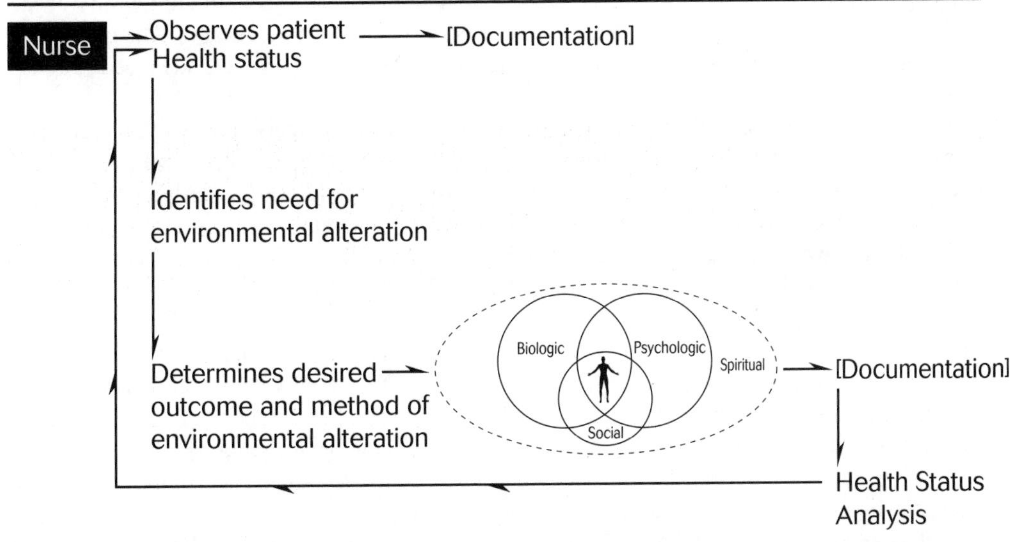

This model functions in health nursing as well as nursing proper, including health promotion, illness prevention, health restoration, and rehabilitation as appropriate activities in which the model can be implemented. It is assumed that health needs are met through the introduction of the 13 canons as well as the needs created by illness. For current usage, the spirit of the canons, not the specifics of care, needs to be observed. Nurses are no longer taught wall-liming or how to brew beef tea—both care standards of the 1860s. However, a clean environment and proper nutrition are as important today as 150 years ago.

Nightingale was resolute that documentation accompany all phases of nursing. Consequently, this is seen as an adjunct phase to each step of the process. This served two very practical purposes. Not only did it provide a roadmap to a patient's progress and provide indicators for care needs; from a retrospective view, it allowed auditing of patient outcomes and determination of appropriate care standards for client conditions. This was the forerunner of care mapping and evidence-based outcome. Nightingale often was able to assemble quantitative data from patient documentation that she could use to lobby for care improvements.

In this model, the nurse is the more active participant in the nurse–patient relationship. This does not exclude mutuality of care or outcome. However, the nurse would be responsible for initiating the process of mutuality.

Evaluating the Model

General evaluation of the model should first be done in relation to Torres' (1985) criteria. In each instance, the model meets the standard. The first is that the interrelation of concepts should provide a unique way of looking at the phenomena of nursing. This is combined with the idea that theory should guide practice. It is hard to argue that Nightingale did not provide a unique way of looking at nursing as she was the first to philosophically consider nursing as a profession. Clearly she is able to guide practice through the practical application of environmental adaptation that gives the nurse a clear message as to how, when, and where nursing should be practiced.

The most important of these benchmarks is that the theory be logical and generalizable. Nightingale's basic tenets of nursing practice have served the profession well for one and a half centuries. Many practice nursing without realizing that most of what they do is actually based in her philosophy.

Environmental alteration has served as a framework for research studies. Many do not identify Nightingale as the organizing framework, failing to recognize the origins of the nursing model. One example of a qualitative study that identified the continuing utility of the nursing model was completed by Dennis and Prescott (1985). Application studies in practice settings such as labor and delivery and in the treatment of insomnia by advanced practice nurses have also occurred (Baker, 1997; Hayes, 1983).

The last of Torres' (1985) criteria indicate that the theory under consideration should be consistent with other validated theories. One of the most commonly recognized conceptual models used to describe human needs and behavior was developed by Abraham Maslow (Kozier, Erb, & Oliverieri, 1991). He cited five levels of needs based on how critical to survival each was. Although an individual continues to develop throughout life, one set of needs tends to predominate over others and occupy the majority of an individual's activities.

The Nightingale model is philosophically consistent with Maslow in that it consistently assists in meeting the needs of patients. Figure 5-4 demonstrates that health nursing as found in the 13 canons provides the basis for meeting the most basic physiological and safety and security needs. Nursing proper, the province of the educated nurse, not only employs these basic strategies but also works to address the higher-level psychological needs of love, belonging, and self-esteem. Furthermore, Nightingale addressed self-actualization through the identification of nursing as an educated avocation for women.

It should be recognized that the Nightingale model is one of a series of theories developed for nursing. These should not be viewed as competing theories, and practitioners should not be placed in the position of needing to choose a single framework from which all practice will emanate. The more logical view is theoretical pluralism. That is, the nurse should be able to identify the most appropriate theoretical basis for an individual practice. This assumes that theoretical pluralism is taught in the educational setting, is identified as essential in the practice setting, and is valued by the practitioner. Leadership through theory occurs when the nurse is able to identify the theoretical basis of practice, plan nursing interventions, evaluate outcomes, and articulate to others both the reasons and expectations of care. This is nursing at the most practical level. This is the nursing of Nightingale.

Figure 5-4.
Needs According to Maslow and Nightingale

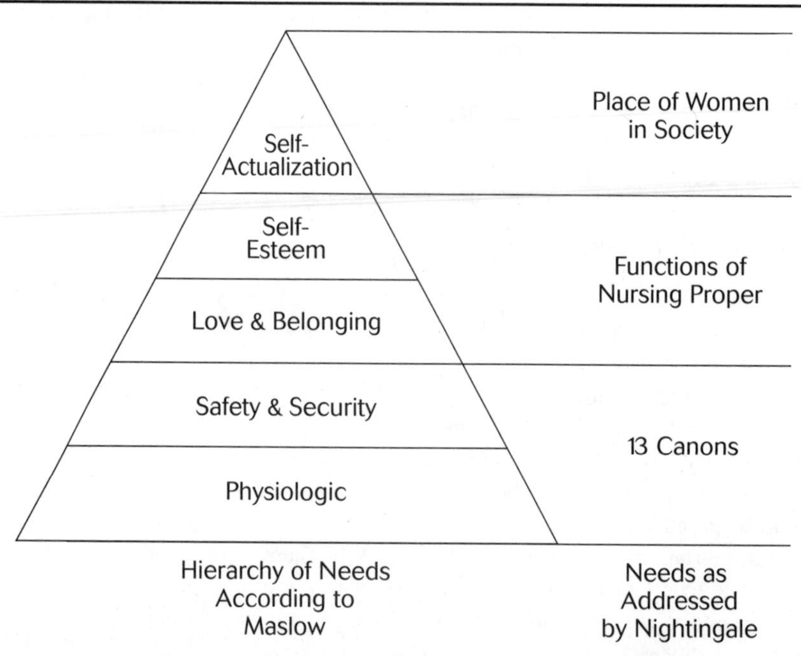

Pentimento

Florence Nightingale, Dirt, and Germs

Louise C. Selanders

The 19th century saw great advances in industrialization, transportation, communication, and science. Yet with all of this progress, the Victorians could not seem to effectively protect or isolate themselves from communicable disease. Population growth and concentration, poor sanitary practices, and faulty understanding of disease transmission aggravated high mortality rates. The repeated epidemics that killed thousands were sufficient reason for a persistent, perhaps obsessive, concern with health and its maintenance.

Public outcry led to the appointment of sanitary commissioners in London, the most famous of which was Sir Edwin Chadwick. He also produced the *Report on the Sanitary Conditions of the Labouring Population of Great Britain*. Chadwick's statistics reveal that in 1839, for every person that died of old age in Great Britain, eight died of specific diseases. Cholera, typhus, typhoid, tuberculosis, and influenza—all communicable diseases—were endemic in the population.

Nightingale's perception of disease transmission, like much of her knowledge, evolved during her lifetime. She is frequently criticized for continuing to believe the miasmatic theory to her deathbed, a claim that is not supported by the primary literature (Halliday, 1999; van der Peet, 1995). Her understanding of germ theory was not unlike that of much of the Western world at the time.

Theories of Disease Transmission

In the 1830s and 1840s, contagious diseases were endemic in the Western world. "Fevers," which described the major symptom of a number of disorders, were always present in the population, including influenza, cholera, tuberculosis, typhus, and typhoid. The scourge of smallpox had declined due to the practice of vaccination (Carrell, 2003; Fenn, 2001). Cholera took 52,000 lives in Great Britain in 1848–1849, 1853–1854, and 1866. Understanding how diseases were transmitted became a social imperative. Two major theories evolved.

Miasmas and Bad Air

The most widely accepted thought on disease transmission in the early- and mid-Victorian period was the miasma theory, which held that certain properties of air, when inhaled into the lungs, caused disease. Spontaneous generation was thought to be responsible for toxins in noxious air. Therefore the Victorians were concerned about control over the air they breathed, causing such customs as tightly closing up houses at night to avoid the hazards of "night air." In explaining the need for good air and circulation, a professor of chemistry stated, "The free currents of air which are necessarily in constant circulation from their proximity to the majestic Thames … have been considered (and not improperly) as a great cause of salubrity of the metropolis." Believing that perhaps all negative health consequences were caused by bad air, he wrote, "From inhaling the odour of beef the butcher's wife obtains her obesity" (Halliday, 1999, p. 17).

Germs and Contagion

The germ theory of disease transmission evolved over a period of several decades. It professed that some diseases are caused by microorganisms that grow by reproduction as opposed to being spontaneously generated in the air. Support for this theory came from Ignaz Semmelweis, a Hungarian physician practicing obstetrics in Vienna. He noticed a stark difference between the high mortality rates from puerperal fever in patients cared for by medical students and the low mortality of those cared for by midwifery students. He concluded that disease was being transported on the unwashed hands of the medical students. By demanding that they wash their hands, he was able to reduce the mortality rates of the medical students' patients (Nuland, 2003).

Germ theory was boosted by the work of Louis Pasteur, a French scientist. His work in fermentation caused him to conclude that germs were not produced through spontaneous generation. His initial work was reported in 1857, and more definitively in 1878. Although not the predominant thought on disease transmission, miasmatism had supporters well into the 20th century.

Nightingale and the Major Figures in Disease Transmission

Sir Edwin Chadwick (1800–1890) was both a social reformer and a sanitarian. Educated as a lawyer, he worked as a young man in journalism. It was here that he became aware of the slums of London and of the plight of the truly poor. From this beginning, his efforts as a public servant focused both on the needs of the poor and on public sanitation. He was instrumental in the establishment of workhouses and fair public compensation for the poor.

In his 1838 *Report on the Sanitary Condition of the Labouring Population of Great Britain*, he outlined public health conditions of the time and the economic consequences of not remedying the deficiencies (Halliday, 1999). The first and probably the most important of his concerns was the relationship between unsanitary living and the onset of disease.

Chadwick was a staunch and lifelong miasmatist who held virtually no regard for medical science, stating that "sanitary science was a subsidiary department of engineering, a science with which medical practitioners could have little or nothing to do" (Small, 1998, p. 38). In his view, it was better to have clean sewers even though the system dumped sewage into the Thames. This practice spread waterborne disease, especially cholera. Frequently antagonistic to those who did not share his opinion, Chadwick was able to enforce his point of view as the sanitary commissioner of London. Nightingale and Chadwick shared many of the same beliefs, including the need to improve the environment for the purpose of improving public health. Her methods of operation, however, were starkly different from Chadwick's. While Nightingale believed in negotiation and working within the existing system to bring about long-term improvement, Chadwick was intolerant of opposing views and contentious in his personal relationships. He was removed from public office in 1854, and never held another public post.

Dr. William Farr (1807–1883) was born into modest circumstances. He was educated as a physician, and his French education emphasized hygiene, a topic unrecognized by the London medical establishment (Small, 1998). Finding his medical practice very difficult, he turned his attention to medical statistics and became the first compiler of abstracts in the General Register Office, which was responsible for the systematic recording of births, marriages, and deaths. It was up to Farr to summarize the data collected.

Originally a supporter of the miasmic theory, Farr helped to collect statistics on the cholera outbreak of 1849, which caused nearly 15,000 deaths. In the outbreak of 1853, he again collected statistical data that helped to show that there was a relationship between cholera victims and their proximity to the Thames. While he was not yet a believer in the contagion theory, his data helped Dr. John Snow demonstrate a pattern of water usage and cholera. By the 1866 outbreak, Farr, now a convert to germ theory, used his data to show that the common factor in contracting the illness was a water reservoir.

Farr was introduced to Nightingale shortly after her return from the Crimea (Small, 1998). Nightingale too was an advocate of statistical data. Farr offered her new methods of classifying information such as "deaths per thousand living" (Small, 1998). He was a supporter both of Nightingale and of the causes that she put forward, particularly the development of nursing (Cope, 1958).

Dr. John Snow (1813–1858) was a physician and anesthetist practicing medicine in London. He originally gained recognition by administering anesthesia to Queen Victoria during the birth of her son, Prince Leopold, in 1853. Announcement of this event in the newspapers helped to standardize anesthesia as a practice in both childbirth and surgery.

During the 1848–1849 cholera epidemic, Snow developed a theory of disease transmission quite different from the prevailing miasmic theory. To him, cholera seemed to be a disease of the intestinal tract: therefore, it must be taken in orally, multiplied in the gut and spread through the fecal–oral route. He further reasoned that the common intake agent was contaminated water drawn from wells throughout the city. During the 1853–1854 epidemic, he was able to test this hypothesis through plotting out instances of cholera, water sources to individual homes, and water sources to the wells. He was able to determine that the vast majority of cases had drunk water from a specific location—the Broad Street pump. After the pump handle was removed and water access restricted, the instance of the disease dropped nearly to zero. Dr. Snow published his results, and work by scientists such as Robert Koch helped to solidify the theory. There is no documentary evidence that Nightingale personally knew John Snow or his work, possibly because of his early death in 1858.

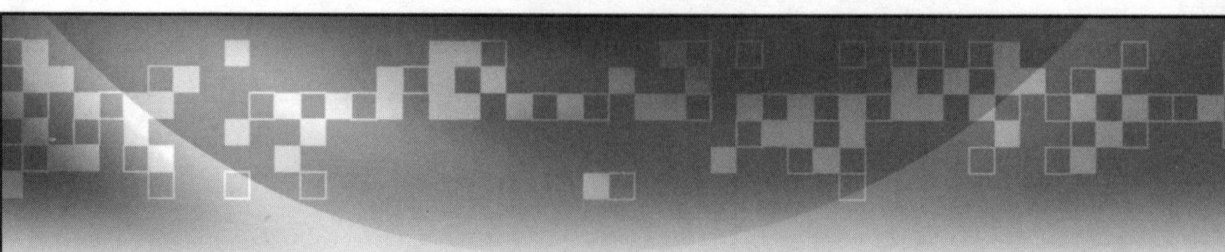

Nightingale, Dirt, and Germs

Nightingale's awareness of the environment's effect on the spread of disease is conspicuous in her statistical analysis of deaths during the Crimean War. She had been greatly influenced by the work of Adolphe Quetelet, the Belgian statistician, astronomer, mathematician, and sociologist who had demonstrated that patterns of behavior in groups of people could be interpreted by the laws of probability, thereby defining the "average person" (Keith, 1998; McDonald, 1994). Her experiences led to *Notes on Nursing,* which set out her observations and conclusions regarding care of the sick and injured for the general population (Skretkowicz, 1996).

Nightingale also stressed the importance of personal cleanliness in *Notes on Nursing* and created a standard of how handwashing should be done by nurses:

> *Every nurse ought to be careful to wash her hands very frequently during the day. ... One word as to cleanliness merely as cleanliness. Compare the dirtiness of the water in which you have washed when it is cold without soap, cold with soap, and hot with soap. You will find that the first hardly removed any dirt at all, the second a little more, the third a great deal more...that by simply washing or sponging with water you do not really clean your skin. Take a rough towel, dip one corner in very hot water,—if a little spirit be added to it will be more effectual,—and then rub as if you were rubbing the towel into your skin with your fingers. The black flakes which will come off will convince you that you were not clean before, however, much soap and water you have used. These flakes are what required removing.* (Nightingale, 1860a, p. 53)

In the 13 canons of *Notes on Nursing,* Nightingale's priorities for care are consistent with miasmatism (Nightingale, 1860a). Her greatest concern was adequate ventilation. This concern was still apparent in her 1893 treatise for the Columbian Exposition.

Nightingale identified the "Six D's" that were most likely to cause disease: dirt, drink (impure water), diet, damp, draughts, and drains (improper drainage and sewage removal). These were the environmental agents that disturbed natural law and thus disturbed health. Most early nursing care was aimed at removing these stressors, thus improving the patients' vital capacity and putting them in the best possible condition for nature to act.

In 1860 during the same period of beginning her Nightingale Training School at St. Thomas' in 1860, Nightingale was simultaneously working to decrease the filthy and overcrowded conditions in the workhouses through major workhouse nursing reform, and drafting documents for workhouse legislation through 1860–1867. With the Nightingale Fund Committee, she began a midwifery training program at King's College Hospital. With trained midwives, physician accoucheurs, and proper sanitary precautions, Nightingale felt mothers and their babies could have a healthy birthing process because childbirth was a normal condition of life. Nightingale realized that lying-in hospitals needed vast improvements.

In October 1871 Nightingale published her *Introductory Notes on Lying-in Institutions*, a remarkable 110-page work that provided information for improvements in the construction and management of these institutions. Two pages from this work show her statistics and a portion of a data collection form. This work also included information on

PROPOSED REGISTRY 75

TABLE XVI.—*Proposed Registry of Midwifery Cases.*

Name	Age	Residence	Married or Single	No. of Pregnancy	Date when last Child was Born	Date of Admission	Period of Gestation	Date of Commencement of Labour	Duration of Labour, in hours	Nature of Delivery	Presentations	Complications of Delivery	Operation, if any	Accidents or Diseases, if any, after Delivery: Nature of Accident or Disease	Date of Attack	Duration	Result and Date	Births: Single, Twins, or Triplets	Infant Born Living or Dead	Sex of Child	If Infant Dead after Birth, Cause of Death, and Date	Date of Removal from Lying-in Department	No. of Days in Lying-in Department	Date of Discharge from Institution	Remarks

…in a woman discharged from the institution within a month from the time of her delivery, a record of this death, …d in the column of Remarks. In the same column should be entered remarks on abnormal configuration, or on which might influence the result of the delivery.

Proposed Registry of Midwifery Cases (upside-down, as it appeared originally), which Nightingale hoped would encourage midwives to record significant observations. Printed in Florence Nightingale (1871). Introductory Notes on Lying-in Institutions. *London: Longmans, Green & Co.*

PREFACE. ix

The following table gives the actual fates and dates :—

Midwifery Statistics, King's College Hospital.

Year	Total Deliveries	Fatal Cases: Date of Birth	Nature of Labour	Cause of Death	Date of Death	Deaths to Labours
1862	97	Nov. 6	Natural	Puerperal peritonitis	Nov. 25	1 in 32·3
		„ 30	Twins	Phthisis and puerperal fever	Dec. 27	
		Dec. 10	Natural	Puerperal peritonitis	Dec. 20	
1863	105	Jan. 10	Natural. Child still-born	Puerperal fever	Jan. 16	1 in 52·5
		April 29	Natural	Puerperal fever	May 20	
1864	141	Feb. 16	Natural	Puerperal fever	Feb. 25	1 in 47
		April 14	Induced	Pyæmia	April 29	
		Dec. 1	Born in cab	Hæmorrhage	Dec. 7	
1865	163	Jan. 30	Natural	Embolism	Feb. 12	1 in 32·6
		Feb. 8	Natural	Puerperal fever	Feb. 18	
		June 24	Forceps	Puerperal metritis and pelvis cellulitis	July 30	
		Oct. 20	Forceps	Laceration of perinæum, puerperal fever	Nov. 8	
		Oct. 29	Natural	Puerperal fever	Nov. 9	
1866	150	Jan. 10	Natural	Gastro-enteritis	Jan. 20	1 in 30
		Mar. 24	Natural	Retained placenta, puerperal fever	April 10	
		Oct. 8	Placenta prævia. Turning	Emphysema and bronchitis	Oct. 10	
		Nov. 10	Forceps	Peritonitis	Nov. 15	
		Dec. 4	Natural	Puerperal fever	Dec. 31	
1867	125	Jan. 10	(Had erysipelas when admitted*)	Puerperal fever	Jan. 30	1 in 13·8
		Feb. 7	Natural	Considerable hæmorrhage, puerperal fever	Feb. 22	
		„ 8	Natural	Puerperal fever	Feb. 22	
		April 12	Turning	Puerperal fever	April 22	
		May 18	Natural	Pyæmia	May 27	
		June 4	Natural	Puerperal fever	June 19	
		July 26	Natural	Puerperal fever	Aug. 11	
		Nov. 5	Twins: 1st dead, 2nd by turning	Puerperal fever	Nov. 10	
		„ 8	Forceps	Laceration of vagina, puerperal fever	Nov. 14	
Total	781	—	—	—	deaths: 27	1 in 28·9

* 'So was confined in No. 4 ward.'

Some of the midwifery statistics from King's College Hospital that Nightingale compiled and used in her Introductory Notes on Lying-in Institutions.

personal and ward hygienic procedures, and her proposed floorplans for lying-in wards with more sinks than usual for use with delivery and cleaning the lying-in room with lime wash. She had detailed management instructions for the mother's and baby's baths as well as cleaning of the bed linen, beds, ward furniture, and lime wash of ward floors and walls. She described specific instructions for lying-in wards as compared to the general hospitals:

> *Hot and cold water to be constantly at hand, night and day...The necessary consumption of hot and cold water is at least double or triple that of any general hospital. Sinks and W.C. sinks must be everywhere conveniently situated.* (Nightingale, 1871, p. 81)

Nightingale came to two major conclusions in *Notes on Lying-In Institutions*: that the death rate for women delivering at lying-in hospitals was greater than for women giving birth at home, and that the high mortality in midwifery practice was largely preventable:

> ... *One feels disposed to ask whether it can be true that, in the hands of educated accoucheurs, the inevitable fate of women undergoing, not a disease but an entirely natural condition, at home, is that one out of every 128 die?* (Nightingale, 1871, pp. 9–10)

Nightingale, like many physician accoucheurs and other authorities, were on the trail to solving the mystery to puerperal fever. Nightingale advocated eliminating medical students from delivery rooms and even had a section in *Notes on Lying-in Hospitals,* "Should Medical Students Be Admitted to Lying-In Hospitals?" She recognized that admitting medical students from general hospitals or from anatomical schools to practice or even to visit in midwifery wards without special precautions caused grave danger to the mother. Although these recommendations were made, medical students continued to be admitted as seen in these following quotes:

> ... *It is one of the contingencies necessarily due to connecting together the teaching of midwifery to students, with other portions of clinical instruction, that no precautions can prevent a student from passing from a bad surgical case, or from an anatomical theatre, to the bedside of a lying-in woman, while sad experience has proved that the most fatal results may ensue from this circumstance. Of course risks of this kind are greatly increased when there are lying-in wards in general hospitals—especially if a medical school be attached to such a hospital.* (Nightingale, 1871, p. 25)

> ... *Applying the same principle to lying-in wards to which medical students are admitted, there can be no doubt that a responsibility of the very gravest kind attaches to all teachers and managers of lying-in hospitals who do not satisfy themselves that students admitted as pupils have nothing to do, either with general hospital practice, or with anatomical schools, during this period. Midwifery instruction should be treated as a matter quite apart.* (Nightingale, 1871, p. 70)

> ... *This risk has not been overlooked in the arrangements for the lying-in wards at King's College Hospital, under which, while*

intended solely for the training of midwifery nurses, provision was made for a limited and regulated attendance of students; but, when enquiries came to be made into the probable cause of the high death-rates, it was found that the restrictions laid down as to the admission of students had been disregarded; also that there was a post-mortem theatre almost under the ward windows. (Nightingale, 1871, p. 26)

She believed that childbirth was a natural process and the best possible place for delivery should be carried out in homes under clean conditions:

In short, the entire result of this enquiry may be summed up, in a very few words, as follows:—A woman in ordinary health, and subject to the ordinary social conditions of her station, will not, if delivered at home, be exposed to any special disadvantages likely to diminish materially her chance of recovery. But this same woman, if received into an ordinary lying-in ward, together with others in the puerperal state, will from that very fact become subject to risks not necessarily incident to this state. These risks in lying-in institutions may no doubt be materially diminished by providing proper hospital accommodations, and by care, common sense, and good management. And hence the real practical question is, whether it is possible to ensure at all times the observance of these conditions. (Nightingale, 1871, p. 67)

In 1895, two articles by Nightingale were published in *A Dictionary of Medicine,* edited by Quain. In "Nursing the Sick," Nightingale refers to the ideas of germ theory, using words such as *antisepsis*, *disinfectant*, and *germs*. She suggests carbolic acid, chlorinated soda, and boiling water as safe means of disinfection. These are also alluded to in "Sick-Nursing and Health-Nursing." (Nightingale, 1893). She states:

Absolute cleanliness is the true disinfectant; but chlorinated soda, if disinfectants are to be used is about the best. Always have chlorinated soda for nurses to wash their hands, especially after dressing or handling a suspicious case. [Quoting a surgeon] 'It may destroy germs at the expense of the cuticle; but if it takes off the cuticle it must be bad for the germs.' Fire is the right way, if the thing is so bad that it wants a disinfectant. Hair (and all hospital beds should be of hair) should be heated to about 350°, teased, and exposed to air. Boil, wash, scour with much soap and water and, say, chlorinated lime; then dry and expose to air all bed ticking, blankets, cover lids, etc. (Nightingale, 1895, p. 240)

While Nightingale would not be considered an ardent contagionist, she clearly did understand the basic concepts of germ theory, and urged that these concepts be taught to nursing students alongside the principles of sanitation. Nightingale never did give up her passionate beliefs about the environment and its relationship to health. There is much about miasmatism that is at least implied in germ theory. Miasmatism does not expressly take into account the scientific basis of germ theory, but cleaning the environment does increase the probability of improving the general public's health. One only has to look at the mortality statistics from the Crimea to understand the positive effects of cleanliness.

Directions and Reflections

Directions for Future Research

1. How does theory differ for a practice profession as opposed to a science that requires bench research?
2. How is theory utilized in your setting?
3. Compare your definition of nursing with others in the profession, the current ANA definition, Nightingale's definition, and the definition found in your State Nurse Practice Act. How are the definitions similar to or different from your definition?
4. In your practice setting, design a quantitative or qualitative study to assess the effectiveness of environmental adaptation. How are internal and external components of the environment measured differently?

Reflections on Florence Nightingale's Tenets: Leadership

1. How do I define theory?
2. How do I define nursing theory?
3. How do I personally use theory in practice?
4. Should the profession of nursing adopt a single theoretical base as opposed to theoretical pluralism?

Florence Nightingale's Artifacts: Myths and Meanings

Alex Attewell

Toward the end of her long and productive life, Florence Nightingale was asked to lend for exhibition her "representations" of the Crimean War. What were these "representations" to be? In reply, Nightingale introduced an ambiguity; the organizers had in mind her portrait and her Crimean possessions, which could be used to authenticate the world-famous myth of the Lady of the Lamp. She declared, however, that her true representations were the Crimean legacy of improved army health, the advent of trained nurses, and the improvement of sanitation and hygiene.

This chapter examines the representations in both senses of the word and shows how Florence Nightingale used the power of her myth to promote her legacy to society. This is an important aspect of her leadership that hitherto has remained relatively unknown. Today Florence Nightingale's image and artifacts are still with us and are capable of challenging and inspiring us to rediscover her legacy, and her leadership style.

The Reclusive Campaigner

At the end of the Crimean War in 1856, Florence Nightingale's intentions were either to oversee nursing in a large hospital or to travel to India to promote the health of the army. Her poor health, however, prevented both. Instead she campaigned from the seclusion of her sickbed. She developed a highly efficient working method, gathering reports and statistical information from the government and personal contacts as a means of exerting influence on government policy. She took reclusiveness to extraordinary ends:

- Once she refused to see Prime Minister Gladstone when he called on her without an appointment.

- She worked on nursing reform with her cousin Henry Bonham-Carter by correspondence for 13 years before granting him a personal audience.
- She founded the first modern nurse training school, the Nightingale Training School, at St. Thomas' Hospital, but only visited once.
- Her remarkable research methods established her as the authority on health in India, although she never visited the country.

Florence Nightingale succeeded in supporting causes from arm's length through journalism and indirect influence on the press, through her contacts with politicians and civil servants, and through personal influence on the many nurses, doctors, engineers, and other experts she had worked with. Her physical presence was not a necessary part of her working method. In a campaigning style that emphasized influence rather than the use of direct power, it probably helped that Florence Nightingale remained unseen. If she gave so little regard to showing herself in public, it is hardly surprising that she was reticent about sitting for portraits. In general she refused to sit for portraits unless she felt obliged to by the circumstances of the request. Her loyalties had the effect of creating associations between her pictorial representations and the causes she espoused, as is evident from a short list of post-Crimean portraits:

- The 1856 photograph was commissioned by Queen Victoria, her committed supporter.
- The 1862 marble bust by Sir John Steell was commissioned by the soldiers who had been Florence Nightingale's patients in the Crimea.
- The 1887 oil portrait by Sir William Richmond and the incomplete Watts portrait of 1864 were commissioned by Florence Nightingale's brother-in-law Sir Harry Verney, who was a loyal supporter in Parliament.

The artist Jerry Barrett went to Turkey to make sketches toward an oil painting of the main protagonists at Scutari. Florence Nightingale had no time to sit while she was there, and her time was no less precious on her return. Barrett had no choice but to base the central figure of his impressive "Florence Nightingale at Scutari, The Mission of Mercy" on a photograph (Nightingale, 1856).

The National Portrait Gallery was established in 1856, at the conclusion of the Crimean War, with the idea of honoring great individuals whose achievements visitors could contemplate and perhaps emulate (Kavanagh, 1990). Florence Nightingale was an obvious subject for inclusion in the gallery, but even after her death in 1910 the gallery found it difficult to acquire an original portrait. The trustees had to settle for a slight portrait cut from the sketchbook of the gallery's first director, Sir George Scharf. Scharf had managed to draw Nightingale while visiting Embley Park, the family's Hampshire home, in 1857 (Saumarez-Smith, 2001).

Two letters Nightingale wrote over 40 years after the Crimean War show that she used her image—her "relics" and "representations"—as a lure to capture public interest in her causes. Imre Kiralfy, an entrepreneurial showman, was the organizer of the Victorian Era Exhibition held at Earl's Court in 1897 to celebrate the 60 years of Queen Victoria's reign. Kiralfy apparently delegated the task of obtaining Florence Nightingale's image for display in the nursing section to Lady Wantage, an acquaintance of Nightingale's and a pioneer of the Red Cross in Britain. The initial request was met with the following invective from Florence Nightingale:

> Oh the absurdity of people and the vulgarity! The 'relics,' the 'representations' of the Crimean War! What are they? They are, first, the tremendous lessons we have learnt from its tremendous blunders and ignorances. And next they are trained Nurses and the progress of Hygiene. These are the 'representations' of the Crimean War. And I will not give my foolish portrait (which I have not got)

> or anything else as 'relics' of the Crimea. It is too ridiculous. You don't even judge the victuals inside a public-house by the sign outside. I won't be made a sign at an exhibition. (1897b)

The second letter, to her sister's stepson, developed the theme. The real "relics" of the Crimean War were the Royal Commission on the health of the British army, which provided for "great improvements in the soldier's daily life"; the training of nurses, "both in character and technical skill and knowledge"; and hygiene and sanitation, the lack of which caused the deaths of thousands of soldiers from disease during the Crimean War (1897c).

The idea of her portrait or Crimean possessions on public show filled Florence Nightingale with horror. The idolatry of the "the lady with the lamp" image offended her religious beliefs and was a source of angst.

Also, she was intolerant of the nostalgia that the Victorian Era Exhibition implied; she was constantly impatient for progress in her work and was unwilling to bask in the glory of past achievements. Even 40 years after the Crimean War, she considered that the true representations of the Crimea were still very much alive as the themes of her life's work: the health of the army, the training of nurses, and the advancement of hygiene.

Her Real Work vs. Her "Relics"

Her friend Benjamin Jowett, the renowned classics scholar, accurately described her work as consisting of "many beginnings and ravelled threads to be woven in and completed" (Jowett, 1867). To a remarkable extent Florence Nightingale succeeded in drawing together the threads of her life in the 1890s. Her post-Crimean work to reform the health of the British army had led to an interest in the army in India, and hence to the wider Indian population. In 1892 she wrote on rural health education for India, concluding her thoughts on health lectures in 1893 and on health missioners in 1896. The subject matter of health promotion was also the end point of her life's work in nursing. In 1860, the year of the founding of the Nightingale Training School, she bridged the subjects of health in the home and in the hospital in the first edition of *Notes on Nursing*. She developed the themes again in her articles for *Quain's Dictionary of Medicine* in 1882, this time bringing in the latest thinking about germs. Her last important writing on nursing, "Sick-Nursing and Health-Nursing" (1893; discussed and reproduced in this book), comes together in a climax with her last thoughts on hygiene in *Health Teaching in Towns and Villages, Rural Hygiene* (1894) and the conclusions of her

Bronze bust of Florence Nightingale was cast from the original 1862 marble bust by Sir John Steell commissioned by veterans of the Crimean War.
© Florence Nightingale Museum

Indian work in health education. The message of her final writings has been summarized by Dr. Thomas Lauder Brunton and Lucy Seymer as establishing that the axiom "prevention is better than cure" is true within the area of health (Brunton, 1911; Seymer, 1954).

The Nightingale "relics" chosen by the organizers of the 1897 exhibition were the marble bust by Sir John Steell and the Crimean carriage, which she used to visit the hospitals (Thornton, N.D.). The white marble bust is in the classical Roman style, approximately life-size, on a pedestal. The style and material of the bust capture Florence Nightingale's greatness, but in her downward glance it also has a reticent and humble aspect. It is surprising that a bust was ever made, but the circumstances of the commission were uniquely persuasive. In 1862 Florence Nightingale consented to sit for the sculptor, Sir John Steell, for two reasons. The first and most important was that the bust was commissioned by the common soldiers who had been Florence Nightingale's patients during the Crimean War. In a rather touching manner, the bust was paid for by many small subscriptions. The second reason was that Florence Nightingale, who already knew and liked Steell, did not have to interrupt her work on army health in India for more than two short sittings (Woodham-Smith, 1950). The soldiers presented Florence Nightingale with the bust, but it would seem that she did not keep it with her, instead entrusting it to the care of her sister Lady Parthenope and her husband Sir Harry Verney, who lived at Claydon House in Buckinghamshire.

Florence Nightingale's Crimean carriage was saved after the war by Alexis Soyer, the publicity-conscious chef who improved the hospital diets at Scutari. The press had already closely identified the carriage with Florence Nightingale's mission:

> It is very light being composed of wood battens framed on the outside and filled with basketwork so much the fashion now in England. The interior is lined with a sort of waterproof canvas. … It is fitted with patent brakes to both the hind wheels, so as to let it go gently down steep hills. From its appearance, it has been well tested and proved itself, not withstanding its rough appearance, a good friend to hundreds of our unfortunate countrymen. (*Illustrated London News*, 1856)

Florence Nightingale's Crimean carriage at Lea Hurst in the early 1900s.
© Florence Nightingale Museum

If Florence Nightingale had had her choice, this vehicle probably would have vanished from history. Instead, in contrast to Florence Nightingale's own quiet arrival in England, when the carriage rolled off a ship at Southampton, the mayor of the town paraded it around the streets. The carriage was briefly a proxy for the retiring national heroine, but as soon as Florence Nightingale realized how it was being treated she had it hidden away in the stables of her Derbyshire family home, Lea Hurst. Like the bust, it remained beyond the public gaze for the next four decades.

While setting obstacles before the exhibition organizers of 1897, Florence Nightingale imbued her Crimean carriage and the bust with her ideology. After initial protestations about the loan, she lectured Lady Wantage extensively on the continuing importance of her work. When Florence Nightingale did eventually accept Lady Wantage's petition, it was because she conceded that the report of the Royal Commission on the health of the army made a dull exhibit. The carriage and the bust were, in contrast, dramatic exhibits that could be used to encourage an interest in Florence Nightingale's "true relics": army health, trained nursing, and hygiene. The obstacles that Florence Nightingale placed before the request may to an extent explain why her Crimean carriage and bust were shown in a contemporary setting, placed center stage among the latest nursing equipment, and not with Sister Dora in the historical section on women's work.

"The Battle of the Nurses": How to View Nursing?

Florence Nightingale's desire to direct the meaning of her "relics" needs to be interpreted within the wider context of nursing at the time. The dominant subtext of the nursing section of the Victorian Era Exhibition was in fact already attuned to her views. Eva Luckes, the matron of the London Hospital, was one of the organizers of the exhibition. She was, with Nightingale, one of the leading campaigners against the registration of nurses during what was known as the "Battle of the Nurses," which raged between 1887 and 1893.

The registration of nurses has been written about extensively within the literature on Florence Nightingale and in nursing history generally (Baly, 1997; McGann, 1994). In the light of subsequent events she appears to be a reactionary on this issue. (This is discussed in Chapter 8.) She and her allies among the hospital and nursing hierarchy were out of touch with the views of the majority of nurses who sought the professional status that a legally restricted register of qualified nurses promised. However, the objections that she raised are still worthy of consideration today: her misgivings that training and education might end upon registration is still a real concern that has been addressed recently with the emphasis in America and Britain on continuing post-registration education. Nightingale also criticized proregistration nursing as profit-oriented and separated from the spiritual values that had brought her to nursing at the start of her career. As we can see from the writings of Dossey and Selanders, the holistic and spiritual dimensions of nursing are once again being valued, in a new context that goes beyond the registration debate of the 1890s (B. Dossey, 2000a; Selanders, 1993).

The "Battle of the Nurses" appears to have colored the nurses' perceptions of the exhibits on show in 1897. An article in *The Nursing Record and Hospital World*, which was edited by Ethel Bedford-Fenwick, the leader of the registrationists, expressed surprise that Florence Nightingale's relics did not appear in the "historical" section (*Nursing Record*, 1897). In a letter to the editor in the following issue, one nurse criticized the exhibition for lacking scientific organization of the "nursing appliances and nursing inventions." This was a nuance that was meaningful to the nurses of the day, but that was probably lost on non-nurses. A review of the exhibition in the leading medical journal, *The Lancet*, did not detect any faults in the organization and found a great deal of scientific interest in the milk sterilizers, feeding bottles, and incubators on display in the neonatal nursing section (*Lancet*, 1897).

Scientific knowledge had also been an aspect of the ideological battle surrounding registration during the World's Columbian Exposition in Chicago in 1893. Mrs. Bedford-Fenwick received two gold medals for her organization of the nursing exhibition held in the Women's building. Her display of medical glassware designed for an aseptic environment was particularly singled out for praise (*Nursing Record*, 1893). The subtext of the scientific nursing direction, in Britain at least, was the identification of first antiseptic and then aseptic practices as the cornerstone of progressive nursing knowledge. Implicitly this knowledge stood in contrast to the "prevention is better than cure" approach that had typified the sanitary nursing approach of Florence Nightingale.

The crude ideologies evident in the exhibitions of both 1893 and 1897 suggest that there was a straightforward polarization of opinion between those who believed in germs and those who did not. Reality was more complicated. Through *Notes on Nursing* and her backing for district nursing, Florence Nightingale endowed nursing with a body of public health knowledge. This was based on the empirical observation that stagnant water and dirty, poorly ventilated environments caused disease. According to Porter, Nightingale and the sanitary engineers, who were responsible for improved sewers and drains, did more to reduce mortality in the 19th century than the medical profession with their as yet limited therapeutics (Porter, 1987). After Pasteur's fundamental work on bacteriology in the 1860s it is sometimes assumed that medical science and nursing changed overnight, but this was not the case. Florence Nightingale, contrary to the opinion of historians, did understand germ theory (see the Pentimento at the end of Chapter 5 for details on this controversy) as early as 1882, and among other practices, she advised nurses to use chlorinated soda as a disinfectant (Vicinus & Nergaard, 1989). On the other hand, her new understanding did not undermine her firmly held belief in the value of prevention, which she articulated with exceptional clarity in "Sick-Nursing and Health-Nursing" (1893):

> The work we are speaking of [health lectures in the community] has nothing to do with nursing disease, but with maintaining health by removing the things which disturb it, which have been summed up in the population in general as 'dirt, drink, diet, damp, draughts and drains.'

The Columbian Exposition was a critical point for both British and American nursing in different ways. Celia Davies has recounted how the professionalizing strategies of the British and American nurses remained distinct during 1893, despite the fact that both groups were represented in Chicago (Davies, 1983). The British made their mark in the Congress of Representative Women, while important decisions on the future organization of American nursing were made at the subsection meeting, Nursing the Sick, at the International Congress of Charities.

In many senses the representations of Florence Nightingale in the 1890s have fixed her in our consciousness, and there are still many ambiguities. Was she a reactionary or a visionary, progressive or anti-scientific? Writing 55 years later, Isabel Stewart voiced the reasonable judgment that the views Florence Nightingale expressed in 1893 were "ultramodern" in terms of her philosophy of nursing, but were conservative with regard to nursing organization (Stewart, 1948).

Postscript

At the 1912 meeting of the International Council of Nurses, Ethel Bedford-Fenwick proposed the creation of an educational memorial to Florence Nightingale. This came into being in 1934 as the Florence Nightingale International Foundation (Florence Nightingale International Foundation, 1934). It is clear from the reported discussions that Florence Nightingale's own perception of her representations held sway: the memorial was not intended to be a static shrine; rather, it was to embody the movement to promote people's health to which she devoted her life.

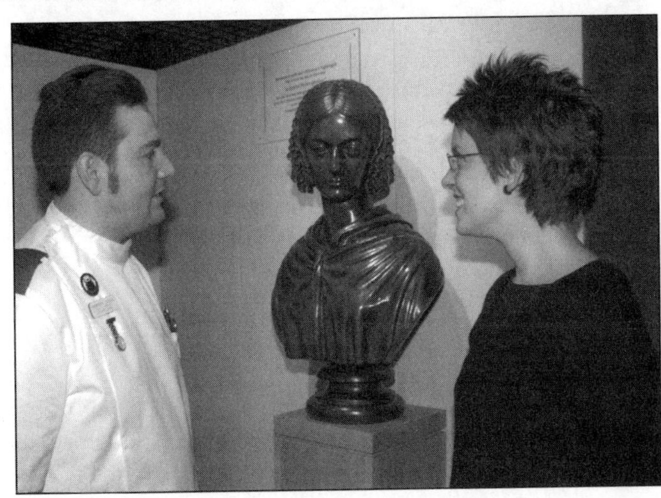

The Florence Nightingale Foundation's Nurse's Day event at the museum: May 12, 2004, with student nurses from Homerton College, Cambridge, and King's College London. *© Florence Nightingale Museum*

Miss Adelaide Nutting, who had been closely involved in the Chicago Congress in 1893, was responsible for interpreting the requirements for Florence Nightingale's memorial. Her words, from two papers she wrote in 1929 and 1946, capture the essence of Florence Nightingale's continuing relevance, and apply to this day:

> Florence Nightingale belongs not alone to England and the English people. She is one of those whose home is the universe. Her work is the heritage of all humanity.
>
> Her ideas have taken shape in great reforms, movements of vast benefit to mankind, and almost worldwide in range. Her achievements, massed one upon the other, were concerned chiefly with conditions affecting health and physical well-being of the people everywhere, but her ideas reached fruitfully into many areas of life, and show a mind of amazing vigour and independence, originality and energising power.
>
> She is a living force today of true magnitude, and it is important that her contributions to the thought and life of the present should be more fully recognised, understood, and securely established. It seems equally important that her ideas and work should be carried to further and higher development. It would be no true loyalty to her or to them, to hold these to the forms and methods in which they took shape and were clothed at the time when she first advanced them. Her dynamic and searching mind would have been the first to question any static view of the vital problems and conditions with which she was concerned throughout the greater part of her life. (Nutting, 1946)
>
> I would like to suggest, as a possibility, the establishment of … an International Centre for study and research in nursing and the kindred problems of hospitals and public health, upon which things Florence Nightingale's mind played with such amazing power and originality.
>
> One of the first acts of such a foundation would be to secure the right place in which to house it and from which to carry on its work, to gather together there all her books, letters, manuscripts, portraits, personal belongings, and other things intimately associated with Miss Nightingale's life and work. (Nutting, 1929)

Pentimento

Florence Nightingale:
The Passionate Statistician

Barbara M. Dossey

Florence Nightingale originated the process of modern nursing research. She believed that statistics was the only way to organize what we now term a holistic healthcare system. For example, if the water supply or soil around a town was contaminated, then the people of the region would be unhealthy. She pioneered the use of evaluative statistics; her research was holistic in that she intertwined nursing with all facets of society. Her passion was directly linked to God, who was a God of order; the laws of God were to be understood by man in order to have the highest degrees of health.

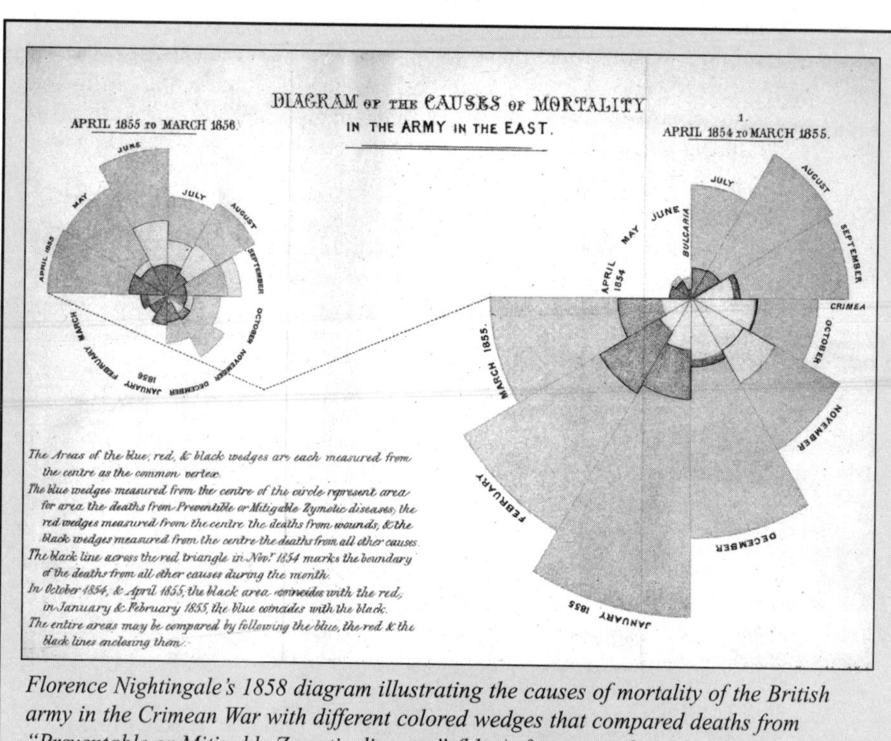

Florence Nightingale's 1858 diagram illustrating the causes of mortality of the British army in the Crimean War with different colored wedges that compared deaths from "Preventable or Mitigable Zymotic diseases" (blue), from wounds (red), and from all other causes (black).

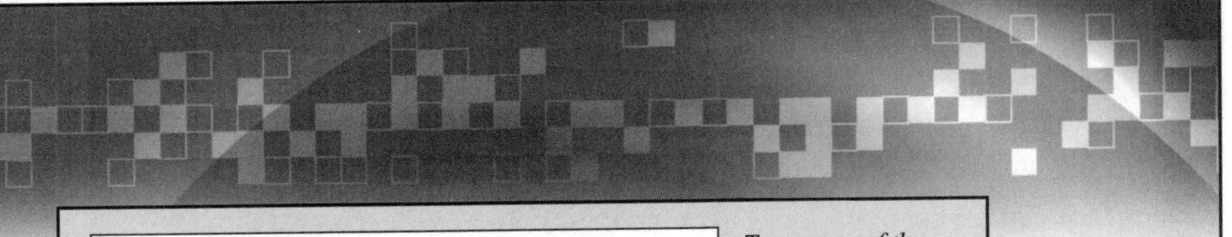

ANSWERS TO WRITTEN QUESTIONS

ADDRESSED TO MISS NIGHTINGALE BY THE COMMISSIONERS APPOINTED TO INQUIRE INTO THE

Regulations affecting the Sanitary Condition of the Army,

Reprinted (with some alterations) from the Report of the Royal Commission.

I.—Sanitary State of the Army and Hospitals.

HAVE you, for several years, devoted attention to the organization of civil and military hospitals?

Yes, for thirteen years.

What British and foreign hospitals have you visited?

I have visited all the hospitals in London, Dublin, and Edinburgh, many county hospitals, some of the naval and military hospitals in England; all the hospitals in Paris, and studied with the 'sœurs de charité;' the Institution of protestant deaconesses at Kaiserswerth, on the Rhine, where I was twice in training as a nurse; the hospitals at Berlin, and many others in Germany, at Lyons, Rome, Alexandria, Constantinople, Brussels; also the war hospitals of the French and Sardinians.

When were you sent out to the British war hospitals at Constantinople?

We arrived at Constantinople on November 4, 1854, the eve of the Battle of Inkermann.

What hospitals did you find occupied there by the British?

Two large buildings on the Asiatic side, near Scutari, viz., a Turkish barrack and a Turkish military general hospital, both of which had been given over by the Turkish government for the use of the British troops.

How many patients did they contain at that date?

The Barrack contained 1500, the General hospital 800 patients, total 2300.

By how many nurses and ladies were you accompanied?

By 20 nurses, 8 Anglican 'sisters,' 10 nuns, and 1 other lady.

Where did you take up your residence?

We were quartered the same evening in the Barrack hospital, and two months afterwards, a reinforcement of 47 nurses and ladies having been received from England, we had additional quarters assigned us in the general hospital, and later at Koulali.

Two pages of the 1858 Royal Commission Report showing Florence Nightingale's answers to written questions submitted to her. Printed in Florence Nightingale's (1859) Notes on Hospitals, *p. 23, 29.*

before the Royal Commission. 29

To what do you mainly ascribe the mortality in the hospitals?

To sanitary defects.

Will you now state what the rate of mortality was? And how you have calculated it?

I have calculated it, (1.) on the cases treated; (2.) on the sick population of the hospitals.

I beg to put in a Table.

Average of Weekly States of Sick and Wounded, from October 1st to January 31st, deduced from those given by R. W. Lawson, Deputy Inspector-General, Principal Medical Officer, Scutari.

Date.	No. of Days.	Sick Population of the Hospitals (mean of weekly numbers remaining)	Cases treated (mean of admissions and discharges including Deaths.)	Deaths.	Mortality.	
					Annual rate per cent. per annum on the sick population	Per cent. on cases treated.
1854.						
Oct. 1st to Oct. 14th . .	14	1,993	590	113	148	19·2
Oct. 15th to Nov. 11th . .	28	2,229	2,043	173	101	8·5
Nov. 12th to Dec. 9th . .	28	3,258	1,944	301	121	15·5
Dec. 10th to Jan. 6th (1855)	28	3,701	3,194	572	202	17·9
1855.						
Jan. 7th to Jan. 31st . .	25	4,520	3,072	986	319	32·1
	123	3,140	10,843	2,145	203	19·8

February, 1855 *

Hospitals.	Sick Population.	Cases treated.	Deaths.	Rate of Mortality per cent.	
				Annually on sick Population.	On cases treated.
Scutari and Koulali	4,178	3,112	1,329	415	42·7
Koulali alone . .	648	581	302	608	52·0

* This mortality is considerably understated. If to the Adjutant's Head Roll of Burials for Scutari, page 26, which is probably the correct return, had been added the Medical Officer's Return of Deaths for Koulali, here given, which is the only one we have, the total deaths would have been, not 1329, but 1453; and the rate of deaths on cases treated, not 42·7, but 46·7 per cent.

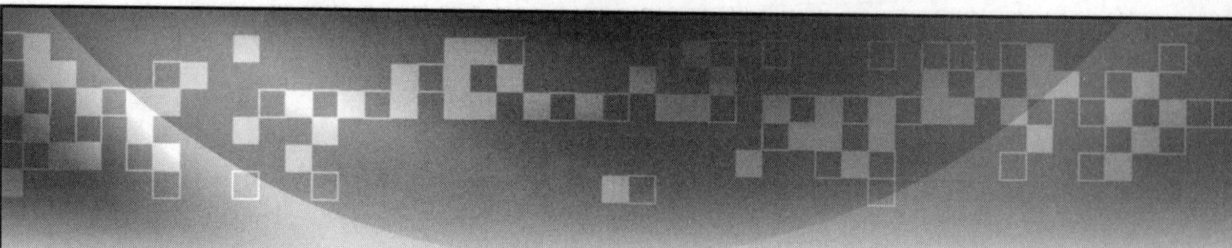

Her research in applied statistics for over 40 years had a direct impact on the 19th-century public healthcare system, as well as medical, nursing, and army reform; the effects on healthcare reform have continued into the 21st century. Eight areas of Nightingale's research demonstrate the depth and breadth of her statistical achievements, and her influence in many fields of research:

1. The collection and presentation of data for the Royal Commission on the Sanitary State of the Army in the East (1858, 1859).
2. Reform of hospital statistics and the establishment of uniform criteria for reporting disease (1860).
3. Fighting the Contagious Disease Acts for the compulsory inspection and treatment of prostitutes (1862).
4. The collection and analysis of data for the Royal Commission on the Sanitary State of the Army in India (1863).
5. Data collection on the mortality and morbidity of native children in colonial schools (1863).
6. Analysis of data on surgical outcomes (1863).
7. *Introductory Notes on Lying-In Institutions* (1871).
8. Surveys on types of nursing in London hospitals, workhouses, and district nursing, the practice of different sisterhoods and religious organizations, and the types of nursing training programs (1874–1878).

Nightingale's research contributions were first recognized by her colleagues in 1858, when she became the first female member of the London Statistical Society, later known as the Royal Statistical Society. In 1874 she was elected an honorary member in the American Statistical Society. At Oxford University in 1891 she attempted, with a colleague, to establish a chair in social physics and its practical application. This position was intended for the education of people entering public service throughout the British Empire. However, she was never convinced that her joint endowment would be used for research in social physics; hence, she withdrew her support. In 1997, her work in statistics was finally honored at Oxford University with the establishment of an annual Florence Nightingale Lecture in Statistics.

B.—Proposed Hospital Statistical Form.

This Sheet will serve for the Classification of Cases in Hospitals under the following headings:—"Remaining, 1st January"—"Admitted"—"Cured (or Relieved)"—"Dead"—"Discharged incurable, for Irregularities, or at their own Request"—"Remaining, 31st December"—"Duration of Cases in Days."

Write the Name of Hospital, the Sex, the required Heading, and Date with the Pen.

Ages	Months. 0	Months. 3	Months. 6	1	2	3	4		10	15	20	25	30	35	40	45	50	55	60	65	70	75	80	85	90	95 and upwards.	Total.
CLASS I.—Order I. (Zymotic Diseases.)																											
1. Small Pox																											
Measles																											
Whooping Cough																											
Croup																											
Scarlatina																											
Quinsy																											
Diphtheria																											
Coryza, Catarrh, Influenza																											
Ophthalmia (purulent) ..																											
Erysipelas																											
Metria (puerperal Fever)																											
Pyæmia																											
Hospital gangrene																											
Carbuncle, Boil																											
Dysentery																											
Diarrhœa																											
Cholera																											
Typhoid Fever (typhia) ..																											
Typhus																											
Relapsing Fever (typhinia)																											
Ague																											
Remittent Fever																											
Rheumatism																											
OTHERS																											
Order II.																											
Gonorrhœa																											
Primary Syphi[illegible]																											
Secondary Sy[illegible]is																											
Tertiary S[illegible]																											
OTHERS																											
[illegible] III.																											
Scurvy																											
Purpura																											
Alcohol { a. Delirium tremens ..																											
Alcohol { b. Intemperance																											
OTHERS																											
Order IV.																											
Thrush																											
Porrigo																											
Scabies																											
Worms																											
OTHERS																											
CLASS II.—Order I. (Constitutional Diseases.)																											
Gout																											
Dropsy																											
Cancer																											
Canker (noma)																											
Mortification																											
OTHERS																											
Order II.																											
Scrofula																											
Tuberculosis Mesenterica																											
Phthisis																											
Hæmoptysis																											
Pneumothorax																											
Hydrocephalus (with tubercular deposit) ..																											
OTHERS																											
CLASS III.—Order I. (Local Diseases.)																											

Most of the diseases in the following marginal list are of less frequent occurrence in hospitals; and all, with some exceptions, are *classed as* "Others" in their respective orders in the left-hand column. They will be distinguished in abstracting the diseases by writing the *ages* of the persons attacked, cured, or dead, &c., against the particular disease in the margin below. Thus, a person aged 16 would, if admitted for "*mumps*," be indicated in the body of this sheet by *a tick* against "Others" of Class I. Order I.; and his age *(16)* would be written against "mumps" in the margin. And so of other diseases. The diseases not found printed in the margin must be written in their proper compartments. A summary of the facts in the margin should be given in an appendix to the general Table.

[illegible]
dysentery with abscess of liver (placed to *dysentery*)
yellow fever

Order II.

leprosy (Greek elephantiasis)
yaws
glanders
hydrophobia
malignant pustule
necusia*

* *Infection by puncture in dissection, or by handling the parts of dead animals.*

Order III.

rickets
bronchocele
cretinism
ergotism

Order IV.

phthiriasis
Hydatids, tape worm, and other entozoa should be distinguished here. In the capital table they will be added to the head "Worms."

CLASS II.

Order I.

anæmia
lupus
dry gangrene

Portion of proposed Hospital Statistical Form, one of Nightingale's Model Hospital Forms developed in 1859 with detailed instructions provided on the right-hand side. Printed in Florence Nightingale (1862), Hospital Statistics and Hospital Plans, *reprinted from the Transactions of the National Association for the Promotion of Social Science (Dublin Meeting, August 1861). London: Emily Faithful & Co.*

Directions and Reflections

Directions for Future Research

1. Survey nurses in various countries to determine how they have been influenced by Florence Nightingale's legacy and leadership.
2. Determine an effective way to integrate Florence Nightingale's historical research in core nursing courses.
3. Analyze various teaching strategies to integrate Florence Nightingale's visionary leadership in core nursing courses.
4. Develop strategies to evaluate the outcomes of integrating Florence Nightingale's legacy and leadership in nursing practice, education and research.
5. Determine if nurses are empowered in their nursing practice, education, and research by becoming informed about Florence Nightingale's legacy and leadership.

Reflections on Florence Nightingale's Tenets: Leadership

1. What are my values and beliefs, or my biases and attitudes, on Florence Nightingale's legacy and leadership for contemporary nursing?
2. How can I determine if I am offering accurate information on Florence Nightingale's legacy and leadership for contemporary nursing?
3. Identify my thought patterns and belief system that affect me as a leader.
4. Can I find a mentor or personal coach to help me enhance my leadership skills?
5. How are the growth and development of my leadership skills reflected in the events of my life?

7 At the Millennium Crossroads: Reigniting the Flame of Nightingale's Legacy

Deva-Marie Beck

While the basic facts of Florence Nightingale's life are presented in the first Pentimento in this book (page 24), readers also will benefit from a broader perspective of her life to best appreciate her global vision for nursing and its ongoing relevance to human health. This chapter, then, reviews that long and productive life in the context of Nightingale's own time and examines from that perspective several key issues in 20th-century health care.

A Hidden Panorama, A Global Vision

Nightingale began her work at a neighborhood hospital in London, and established her career during the Crimean War. She published a little book that is still in print, often quoted by nursing students, and frequently cited in the nursing literature. Later, she oversaw the growth of a school that would become a cornerstone for modern nursing education. These examples are like well-worn cameos cherished as keepsakes—stories of the beginnings of modern nursing as it is practiced even now, more than a century later.

In the Crimea, Nightingale carried a lamp to light her rounds during night shifts at Scutari hospital in Constantinople. Her lamp was a simple cylinder, wrought with an open metal framework to carry one lighted candle. It was covered with a thin parchment to keep the flame from blowing out as she walked along the drafty passages, and to keep the firelight from being too bright in the soldiers' eyes. Later, several men wrote home about how much her nightly rounds meant to them. This story caught the hearts of families who worried about their sons and husbands on a battlefield far away. Her flame became a symbol, first of her exemplary caring during a deeply troubled period and then of the illumination her insights have brought to later times. The candle carrying her legacy is still lit, illuminating the story of her life.

Thus Nightingale became the most recognized nurse in history. But these stories have been drawn from the much larger panorama of her 50-year career. Beyond her own neighborhood and her country's battlefield, Nightingale took nursing further still, to villages and cities around the world, to the halls of leadership and to behind-the-scenes discussions that would shape the history of health care. Although she wrote one famous book, she also wrote 20 others, hundreds of monographs and articles, and at least 14,000 letters (McDonald, 2000). Together, they compose an opus of written contributions not just to the evolving field of nursing, but also to related health disciplines, rarely matched by any of her contemporaries, male or female, in any field (B. Dossey, 2000a). Her tremendous body of work is just now becoming available to 21st-century readers.

This larger Nightingale panorama that she called *nursing* has remained essentially hidden behind that album of familiar stories about her career. Dolan's extensive review of nursing history has touched upon this, calling Nightingale "one of those rare and gifted people who transcend the period of their own existence and whose plans and accomplishments represent the thinking of a much later period in history" (1968, p. 211). She suggests that the Nightingale panorama be brought out again, to be studied for relevance to caring today. The light shining from Nightingale's life can spread across the field of her lesser-known work to further illuminate the health issues we face today.

The 21st century has become, like centuries before, both the best and worst of times. Current healthcare issues are complex—brightened by successes, yet fraught with significant risks. As a global thinker, Nightingale would have loved 21st-century globalization and its challenges. She would have been keen to learn about emerging trends. She noted cultural, social, and economic concerns, particularly in relation to health and to the discipline of nursing. She urged nurses to progress in their practice, to think outside their official domains.

As Nightingale's panorama is unfolded, her tenets become visible. Nightingale's insights support the now-established premise of comprehensive care of the sick and injured. Yet her own nursing career also encompassed the earth, envisioning comprehensive care for humanity.

Modern nursing is at a crossroads. Faced by difficulties, we can struggle along, as nurses have before. Or we can pause to consider, and determine what nursing could become. Nightingale's world needed her. Our world needs nursing. What she learned can expand the choices nurses can make in our nursing practices to serve humanity's needs. Nurses can, like Nightingale, become global visionaries for the health of humanity. As we stand at our crossroads, her light can help us see.

In Her Time and Ahead of Her Time: Nightingale's 19th-Century Context

Florence Nightingale lived and worked in response to her times. Yet she was also ahead of her time. She lived a unique life, insisting on pursuing a career even though her wealthy family could have provided her with a lifetime of leisure. Because she was a woman, this choice to work outside her home was all the more unusual. Most of her aristocratic contemporaries were wives, mothers, and grandmothers, hostesses within their own household spheres, with many servants. Nightingale was also a vanguard woman because she chose nursing, a role that was considered the work of desperate, impoverished women who lived on the street like prostitutes. In addition to these unusual choices, Nightingale's career was unique beyond anyone in her time. As noted above, she was also one of the most prolific authors of the 19th century. In addition to being an early role model for nursing, Nightingale was also a leader in several other fields that would emerge in her time, including social work and statistical analysis. She responded to the culture of the 19th century by envisioning what could be changed and working with her talents and the resources available to her to evolve the healthcare culture of the 20th century and beyond (Attewell, 1998b; Baly, 1986; Cook, 1913; B. Dossey, 2000a; Selanders, 1992, 1993, 2001; Woodham-Smith, 1953).

Anticipating Transdisciplinary and Holistic Perspectives

In the 19th century, wealthy British men were educated in several classical disciplines, including philosophy, history, languages, science, and mathematics. They were taught to read and write well, not only in English, but also in Latin and Greek. In the 20th century, this well-rounded approach to higher learning would become more specialized, typically focused on one specific discipline like medicine, law, or engineering.

Through their study of philosophy and history, 19th-century scholars and leaders also studied culture and religions. They discussed the prevailing attitudes and religious issues of their day, as well as spiritual perspectives from history. They watched social issues and interpreted their times in the context of earlier times. Although the terms *interdisciplinary* and *holistic* aptly describe these 19th-century perspectives, these words would not come into use until the 20th century. According to the Oxford English Dictionary, the word *interdisciplinary* was created in 1937 to refer to a combination of two or more academic, scientific, or artistic fields of study. The word *holistic*—understanding life in terms of interacting wholes that are more than the mere sum of their parts—was coined in 1926 by Gen. J.C. Smuts. The word *holism* has evolved to encompass physical, emotional, mental, social, cultural, and spiritual perspectives. Nightingale's thoughts anticipated these later perspectives of holism and interdisciplinarity. In this book, however, the term *transdisciplinary* is used to imply a deeper dialogue across disciplines to share knowledge that informs their learning, practice, education, and research. These transvisionary dialogues are transformative and visionary to bring about actions to create total healing environments and global health. Beginning with the well-rounded, classical education that she received from her father, a Cambridge scholar, Nightingale studied many subjects at length. She was fluent in German, French, Italian, Latin, and Greek, and often consulted ancient texts in their original language (Woodham-Smith, 1953). She studied philosophy, history, science, and mathematics, a subject she had to fight hard for permission to learn (B. Dossey, 2000a). Today, her own basic education would be considered to be at the level of advanced interdisciplinary graduate work. She continued throughout her life to build upon this foundation, to study and to learn in many fields of interest.

During her youth and into her twenties, she also gained what would now be considered a holistic exposure to many cultures, traditions, and spiritual perspectives during several extended trips to Europe, to the eastern Mediterranean, and to North Africa (Calabria, 1997; B. Dossey, 2000a; Macrae, 1995). She continued to study the sacred texts of many religions throughout her life. She was well versed in the critical social and political concerns of her day. Throughout her lifetime, many of her friends were renowned politicians, leaders, philanthropists, philosophers, and educators in Britain, Europe, the United States, and the British Commonwealth (B. Dossey, 2000a).

Throughout her life, Nightingale was a scholar and a correspondent with scholars. She collaborated with William Farr, the leading medical statistician of her time; with John Stuart Mill, regarded by many as the foremost British philosopher of that era; and with Adolphe Quetelet, the Belgian "statistician, astronomer, mathematician, and sociologist considered the founder of the modern science of social statistics" (B. Dossey, 2000a, p. 228). Through her association with Quetelet and her independent study, she well understood the use of statistical data to improve health outcomes and policies regarding health. Many of her written works build upon this expertise. For more than 30 years, she maintained a close friendship with Benjamin Jowett, the highly regarded headmaster and theologian at Balliol College of Oxford. Jowett and Nightingale sustained their relationship mostly through correspondence that touched on many disciplines, as well as philosophical, spiritual, and cultural perspectives (B. Dossey, 2000a; Quinn & Prest, 1987; Selanders, 1992).

From these and other similar experiences, Nightingale's interests and talents would develop into a wide range of endeavors to support human health. After her return from the Crimea, she spent more than three decades working on comprehensive health policy issues, not only for Great Britain but for India, Canada, Australia, and New Zealand. She often played a consultative role in support of the British army throughout the world, and advised the Union army during the American Civil War. She designed hospitals; spearheaded the use of statistics to improve health outcomes; advised Commonwealth leaders regarding the economies, cultures, and spiritual practices of indigenous peoples; and helped to develop what would later be termed *social medicine* (I. Cohen, 1984; B. Dossey, 2000a; Duhl, 1996; Keith, 1988; Seymer, 1954). From today's vantage point, Nightingale was an exemplary interdisciplinarian with a quintessentially holistic point of view.

19th-Century Culture and Women's Roles

Ahead of her time in so many areas, Nightingale was also a product of her time and limited by her time. Throughout her life (1820–1910), and even at the time of her death, women had not achieved many of the rights they enjoy now. Nightingale acquired a thorough classical education and fought vigorously to include advanced mathematics in her studies. Most girls, even in her aristocratic sphere, did not receive an education beyond basic reading. In 1878, women were finally allowed to obtain a degree at the University of London for the first time and also admitted to lectures at Oxford. It was widely believed that women did not have the intellectual capacity for university-level studies (Selanders, 1992). During the 19th century, most women were not allowed to inherit property, retain wealth of their own, or have any significant legal standing (B. Dossey, 2000a; Selanders, 1998a). Women in North America were still fighting for the right to vote for several years following Nightingale's death.

Secular nursing was a bold concept even at the end of Nightingale's career. By the late 19th century, women could be respectably employed outside their homes. Nightingale pioneered and modeled this trend with her own life, realizing that prior to her time the only viable way to accomplish an "alternative" feminine career was through entrance into a religious order. The possibility of women having a full-time career as well as a married life had not yet been fully envisioned, even by Nightingale. In the 19th century, of course, contraception was not available to allow women to live relatively free of the responsibilities of raising a family. The traditional responsibilities of a household barred them from a secular career as demanding as Nightingale knew nursing to be. When read superficially, Nightingale's discussions about her own cultural limitations may seem irrelevant to current conditions. Her readers could easily forget to look for a deeper, timeless relevance in her work and be tempted to leave her insights on museum shelves. The milieu in which women lived in the 19th century, in comparison to the lifestyles women enjoy at the turn of the 21st century, is a significant factor in understanding why so much of her work is unknown to today's nurses (Selanders, 1998b; Vicinus, 1972, 1977).

It is also significant to note that Nightingale consistently used the feminine pronoun in her writing, using *her*, *hers*, and *she* in her discussions of nursing, without reference to *him*, *his*, and *he*. One recent observation suggests that she even "fought to keep men out of nursing" (Sullivan, 2002). In her recent thorough overview of Nightingale's life and work, Dossey (2000a) does not mention this anti-male perspective. Neither is this anti–male nurse language evident in Nightingale's "Sick-Nursing and Health-Nursing" (Beck, 2002; Nightingale, 1893). In Nightingale's lifetime, the idea that men and women could assume each other's traditional roles was yet to evolve. She simply did not include men in her vision of health promotion and nursing, although she did work with men who shared this vision with her. Nightingale assumed that nursing and health promotion would always remain women's domains. These assumptions were woven into her concepts and integral to her language.

Some researchers have been deterred from studying Nightingale's primary documents by her occasionally archaic language. For others, the notorious Victorian constraints on women would seem to make her opinions irrelevant today. It is important to ignore these impediments and take advantage of her timeless intellect and insights.

The Emergence of Nursing: Nightingale's Premises

Nightingale's *Notes on Nursing: What It Is and What It Is Not* (1860a) has often been referred to as her basic treatise on modern nursing practice; indeed, her title implies this. *Notes on Nursing* remains her most famous publication, and is probably the most widely read book on nursing ever written, continually in print since 1860 (Skretkowicz, 1996). However, she originally wrote this little volume for general readers to improve their own household health. Because her topic was aimed at a general audience and useful to every household, and because she was already known for her Crimean contributions, the book became an "instant best-seller"; more than 15,000 copies sold in the first few months. It was only later revised by Nightingale to be used as a specialized nursing text (B. Dossey, 2000a; Selanders, 1993; Skretkowicz, 1996). The style of this book illustrates how Nightingale focused on the need to bring theory to practice—how to make people more comfortable, to increase their chances of recovery, to promote and maintain their health. Within these practicalities, she stated nursing principles that can now be understood as holistic approaches, with attention to physical, emotional, mental, and spiritual well-being (B. Dossey, 1998a, 2000a, 2002; Roy, 1992; Watson, 1999).

In Nightingale's career the concept of nursing did not coalesce into the profession practiced today. Indeed, in her mind the entire experience of womanhood was often synonymous with the concept of "nursing." She did not specialize the terms *nurse* and *nursing* into the employment roles and boundaries understood now.

However, Nightingale's definition of *sick-nursing* was already forming into the role most common to current understandings of *nursing*, and she warned of related problems with emphasizing sick-care, rather than health-care. She saw "health-nursing" as a far wider, more encompassing approach that addressed the whole of human health at both *micro* (individual) and *macro* (societal) levels. Nightingale herself had embodied both. She became famous for her "sick-nursing" in the Crimea, but her vision, even there, was one of "health-nursing," creating "the best possible conditions for Nature to restore or improve health" (1893, p. 186). In addition to providing exemplary bedside care in the Crimea, she also filled leadership, diplomatic, administrative, and policy roles. Although she was concerned with providing excellent care for "her soldiers," and seeing to their nutrition, their pain, their rest, and their wounds, she would also address their welfare in other matters, including their environment, their isolation, their fear of death, their economic circumstances, and other social issues such as gambling and prostitution (B. Dossey, 2000a).

While almost all nurses today can quote "the best possible conditions" as Nightingale's premise, her own macro experiences and her applications of this idea are no longer firmly embedded in nursing culture. Most current nursing education and clinical practices no longer retain these macro perspectives, which Nightingale saw as her basic premise for "health-nursing."

While she is most famous for her role in nursing, Nightingale made monumental contributions to health promotion, an area where present-day nurses who work within the specialty titled "public health nursing" are only one small group among dominant professional players (Beck, 2002). Nightingale's broader contributions have been detailed in *Scientific American,* with particular attention to her use of statistics. The article made note of Nightingale's innovative use of "exploded wedge diagrams," often called "pie charts" (I. Cohen, 1984; Small, 1998). Her work was well received by statistics experts from around the world at the International Statistical Congress of 1860, where she submitted two papers on hospital statistics (B. Dossey, 2000a). The Pentimento on page 122 (Chapter 6) summarizes this work.

Nightingale Anticipates Contemporary Nursing Practice

Since Nightingale's time, the majority of nursing practices have evolved into the very "sick-nursing" domains that she identified in 1893. Notable exceptions include home health and public health nurses, maternity and well-baby nurses, complementary therapy (CAM) nurses, and advanced practice nurses who have a wellness orientation. Much of modern nursing practice has evolved into specialty areas, each with a narrower focus on specific populations and procedures. This specialization has further influenced nurses to work almost entirely at the micro level of individual health concerns. While most nurses today would assume this focus on individual health as a given, Nightingale would not have done so. Her work always took into account larger cultural, political, and economic factors at community, national, and international levels of health (Benson & Latter, 1998; Kleffel, 1991; Robinson & Hill, 1995; Rush, 1997; Spellbring, 1991). Nightingale's many written works, including "Sick-Nursing and Health-Nursing" and numerous other articles and books, encompass her wider, macro perspectives. As 21st-century nursing becomes more narrowly focused on individual micro health, many of Nightingale's earlier insights no longer seem to apply to current practice (Beck, 2002; Rafael, 1999; Rush, 1997). Much of her significant work has been forgotten in contemporary nursing practice.

Nightingale's "Must": A Timeless Spiritual Imperative

Throughout her life, Nightingale heeded a deep spiritual "calling," maintaining her own ongoing communion with her sense of God, for her a very personal and intimate presence. In her sixteenth year, on February 7, 1837, as Nightingale was to recall many times thereafter, she received a direct "call from God," probably while sitting under two "majestic" cedars of Lebanon, a site that was one of her favorite places for contemplation of nature (Cook, 1913; B. Dossey, 2000). From this moment on, she began to build her own bridge between the spiritual and practical worlds. As she described it, "the 'kingdom of heaven' is within, indeed, but we must also create one without, for we are *intended* to act upon our circumstances" (cited in Calabria & Macrae, 1994, p. xviii). This specific relationship between spiritual experience and practical application was uncommon, even in the overtly religious society of Victorian England. Nightingale summed up her dual focus on mysticism and action in one word: her "must."

Far-Reaching Vision

One of Nightingale's least known yet most visionary articles portrays this "must" as a conscious blend of spiritual commitment and social action. The intriguingly titled "A Subnote of Interrogation: What Will Be Our Religion in 1999?" was published in *Fraser's Magazine* in 1873. She asked,

> What will the world be on August 11, 1999? What we have made it.... What 1999 will be, whether all these things are the same then as now, or worse, or better, depends, of course, in its proportion upon what we are doing now, or upon what we are *not* doing now.... in 1999, shall we not wish to have worked out what life, family life, social life, political life, *should* be? and not to have taken for granted that family life, social life, political life are to be as they are...if we are really to succeed in it, really to succeed in bringing about a little corner of the kingdom of heaven. (pp. 28–31)

Nightingale's writings often reflected upon the timelessness of spiritual perspectives. Her "must" became the foundation of her work in her world. Seeing her "must" as touching her time and far-reaching across time, she urged her readers to identify their "must" in the context of the times they lived in. She urged us to allow our own spiritual lives to also be the foundation of our professional lives. She urged us to remember that our work can have an impact a hundred years from now.

Transcending History

In 1860, Nightingale asked her readers to consider this with her:

> It did strike me as odd, sometimes, that we should pray to be delivered "from plague, pestilence and famine" when all the common sewers ran into the Thames, and fevers haunted undrained land, and the districts which cholera would visit could be pointed out. I thought that when cholera came, we might improve these causes, not that God would remove the cholera. (cited in Macrae, 1995, p. 9)

Watson notes that Nightingale's life and work represent a timeless blend of mysticism, art, science, and social action that "called forth and made explicit the connections between and among all aspects of self, other, humanity, the environment, nature, and the cosmos, as a means of learning, understanding, and connecting health, caring, and healing" (Watson, 1998, p. 292). Nightingale's life became a blueprint for the "interrelationships among the personal, the political, the social, and the scientific" (Watson, 1992, p. 84). Like Dolan, Watson has connected Nightingale's timelessness to our experience: she "transcends history and invites us to enter the future," and to "reach past this era and lure us into her prophetic vision that is already upon us" (1998, p. 294).

Burkhardt has commented that famous people and events are not always understood in the context of their times, but are more likely filtered "according to lenses through which we see them" (1998, p. 165). She postulates that the current "lenses of science or the ideals regarding women's roles and behaviors or [a] lack of comfort with blending the spiritual with the secular" (p. 165) may be keeping today's audience from a thorough understanding of Nightingale's spiritual commitment and its profound impact on her work. However,

> Nightingale was able to see that science and mysticism are inextricably connected and that healing requires attentiveness to body, mind, spirit and environment. She also recognized the primacy of *love* in healing and that service to humanity is service to the source of life, whether the source be called God, Goddess, the Absolute or Higher Good. (1998, p. 165)

Nightingale's "must" gave her the vision and strength needed for her life of service. This sense of direction never appeared to leave her, even as she faced severe challenges: her doubts as a youth, her choice to stand against her family's wishes, her endurance during the Crimean War, and her decades of painful chronic illness (B. Dossey, 2000a; Widerquist, 1992). Her "must" became her compass and her guiding star. Understanding these aspects of Nightingale's life brings additional meaning to her endeavors, and provides a deeper comprehension of the practice of nursing that she envisioned and worked to establish.

An Ordinary Woman Meets Her Extraordinary Times

Nightingale's *practical mysticism* (see the Pentimento on page 55) embodies all her personal and professional experiences. Her own profound spiritual perspective can be understood as a crucial source of her resilience and her accomplishments. Her experiences as an ordinary woman with ordinary human frailties and desires interacted with her times to create a legend. She focused daily on the application of her "must" to the needs of her time. Her legend was built on her daily decisions to apply her "must" to the work at hand.

In the generations since her time, Nightingale's legend appears to reach beyond our ordinary nursing careers. Her work seems vast beyond what is attainable today. Yet ordinary nurses live in extraordinary times as well. As we face the healthcare challenges of the early 21st century, Nightingale's dedication can inform our practice, both professional and spiritual. Her legend can serve each of us in our time. As we daily live our personal and professional lives, Nightingale's spiritual *and* practical life can temper our ordinary frailties and desires. Just as her life still influences the 21st century, our spiritual and practical lives can affect future generations.

Revisiting the 20th Century: Health and Disease Become Separate Paradigms

At the beginning of the 20th century, lifestyles of women were beginning to change, gaining a new strength and conviction (Achterberg, 1991; Baly, 1986). Educational choices were opening, if slightly, not only for women, but also for marginalized people of color and those from impoverished backgrounds (Merriam, 1969). Humanitarian and philanthropic efforts were acknowledged as important contributions to the world (Birnbach, 1986; Burdett-Coutts, 1893). The formation of the International Red Cross had begun with the first Treaty of Geneva, written in 1864 and signed by Britain in 1870. This treaty, later referred to as the first Geneva Convention, required for the first time in history that neutrals attend to the wounded on both sides, in order to limit the sufferings inherent in war. Henri Dunant, the founder of the International Red Cross, attributed his inspiration for all of these efforts directly to his knowledge of the work of Florence Nightingale (B. Dossey, 2000a).

By the early 1900s, awareness of sanitation and related policies and changes in infrastructure had improved the health of humanity and extended life expectancy considerably. Prevailing nursing practice had contributed significantly to these sanitation efforts, and those working in support of nursing had also made impressive gains. Both national and international nursing organizations had been founded, and new forms of health care were emerging (Kalnins, 1999). By the time of Nightingale's death in 1910, schools of nursing that used her curricula were flourishing across the British Commonwealth and in 20 other countries. "Health visiting" was established throughout the rural districts of Britain (B. Dossey, 2000a). The Victorian Order of Nurses (VON) established district nursing across Canada, and was involved in both disease prevention and health promotion, besides caring for sick populations (Pringle & Roe, 1992; Victorian Order of Nurses, 1996).

By 1914 the American nurse Lillian Wald had coined the term *public health nursing* and had, with her colleagues, developed prototype best practices in support of health in urban areas. By 1919, Wald had established the Henry Street Settlement as a neighborhood nursing center with a staff of 54 nurses who were responsible for approximately 15,000 patients (Naylor & Buhler-Wilkerson, 1999). Wald also addressed many health issues with a wide range of activities, including lobbying for healthcare funding for the poor, establishing school nursing and rural nursing, and influencing concerns about child labor and welfare (Novak, 1991; Rafael, 1999). Other public health organizations had been so successful in developing preventive health programs that Wald was able to convince the Metropolitan Life Insurance Company to "provide the service of trained nurses as an additional benefit to its industrial policyholders" (Buhler-Wilkerson, 1983, p. 91). Her arguments were founded on effective nursing outcomes that she and her colleagues had documented. In 1914, nearly 2,000 agencies had hired public health nurses to support the health of people in "department stores, industries, insurance companies, boards of health and education, hospitals, settlement houses, milk and baby committees, hotels, and playgrounds, as well as visiting nurse associations" (Buhler-Wilkerson, 1983, p. 91). Wald "drew upon contemporary ideas that linked nursing with social welfare and the public" (Reverby, 1993, p. 1662). Although Wald created a prototype universal public healthcare service in the United States based upon the paradigm of promoting health, with nurses as both leaders and autonomous caregivers, her vision was soon to be replaced by another "changing political and cultural infrastructure" (Buhler-Wilkerson, 1993, p. 1786).

Shifting to a Biomedical and Industrial Perspective

As Nightingale had anticipated in 1893, a focus on the medical treatment of sickness began to displace the previous emphasis on promoting health. This perspective emphasized the use of pharmaceuticals, the work of physicians, and their mandate to diagnose and treat disease. Rafael (1999) has detailed some of the factors involved in this change. As the biomedical approach to health gained in prominence, the wider, more inclusive approach of public health nursing to promote healthy factors outside medical jurisdictions was replaced by an increasingly reductionist reliance on disease treatment procedures. The *Flexner Report* of 1910 widely publicized, with the assistance of corporate and philanthropic funds made available to physicians, the value of medicine over health promotion strategies established by nurses (Buhler-Wilkerson, 1983, 1985; Rafael, 1999).

Over the following decades, the biomedical approach became the predominant premise for general expectations of healthcare delivery, eclipsing the contributions of public health nurses who based their work on different premises. Successes in public health promotion by nurses and other public health professionals have, for the most part, been obscured by the larger awareness about health care and what it delivers to the world. Likewise, over the same decades, nursing's promotion of health and healing—specified by Nightingale as a unique pattern distinct from medicine's focus on disease—began to lose focus. Beginning with the *Flexner Report*, the tapestry of heath care—two interweaving yet distinct patterns, the medical and the nursing disciplines—was reduced to only one pattern. The significance of nursing's uniqueness was disappearing, even to nurses themselves (Beck, 2002; Buresh & Gordon, 2000; Neuman, 2002).

Sickness and the Profit to Be Made

The delivery and financing of health care has been massively influenced by the expanding role of complex technology in medicine. As technology has advanced, the concept of health care has become almost synonymous with the ongoing sales of improving medical technologies, such as heart monitoring machines, computers to deliver pharmaceuticals, and the advance of medical diagnostic imaging technologies including CAT scanners and MRIs. While, in the minds of many people, their health is dependent upon the latest and best technology, in the minds of investors, health care is merely a potential source of profit. By the 1990s the "healthcare sector" had been openly acknowledged as an important portfolio component. Profits to health sector shareholders and salaries to healthcare CEOs and CFOs have even been deemed the real reason for the healthcare industry to exist (Benetar, 1998; Stern, 2001).

As disease-oriented practice prevailed, the 20th-century health culture also became, for the most part, a narrowly focused set of concepts that described how the body got sick, and resulting protocols and expenditures dealt with sickness as it arose. This has been particularly true as more technologies have been invented, refined, and sold to support the treatment of sickness. There have been few financial incentives to change this system. A great deal of profit has been created within this domain, often referred to as the *biomedical–industrial complex*. Treating sickness, managing chronic disease, and keeping dying people alive longer has become a "growth industry" for biomedical companies, hospitals, HMOs, and healthcare professionals alike. The "care" in health care has been eclipsed by profitability (Barlow, 2002; Fagin, 2001). This phenomenon, which has become one of the most significant issues for worldwide health care, was anticipated by a nurse, Florence Nightingale, who wrote in 1893 that "competition, or each man for himself ... is the enemy of health" (Nightingale, 1893).

Nurses Become Reactive Instead of Proactive

With this biomedical–industrial turf firmly established, most nurses have been caught up in their own roles in support of technology and their financial stakes in their own careers. Nurses have seen less and less relevance in their original *autonomous,* broader-based, health-focused mandate as developed by Nightingale, Wald, and others at the beginning of the 20th century. Nightingale and Wald embodied a nursing approach that *pro*actively worked to promote the conditions that improved health. As the biomedical model took hold, nursing's predominant approach was molded into a *re*active one—a role that, with physicians at the helm, reacts to treating disease after it has occurred. While some nurses have worked outside the purview of this biomedical culture, most have not.

At the end of the 20th century, therefore, the majority of nurses could only relate to their reactive disease management roles within the limitations of the clinical arena. Despite repeated attempts to correct this discrepancy through nursing education and research (Rush, 1997), nursing's clinical practice has lost its original premise to proactively nurture health before sickness arises. Despite the proactive health promotion mandate introduced to secular nursing by Florence Nightingale and strengthened by Lillian Wald and others in their time, nurses are, even at the start of the 21st century, practicing mostly within the paradigm of technical medical treatment rather than from a paradigm that emphasizes proactive health care. Nightingale's 1893 concerns about the predominance of "sick-nursing" over "health-nursing" have been fully realized.

The Health of the Global Commons

Despite the 20th-century trend toward biomedical approaches and financial rather than human considerations in health care, another significant phenomenon, called *new public health*, has emerged. Developed by an international community of health promotion educators and policy-makers, this approach encompasses the health of all of humanity (Baum, 2003). It emphasizes that all people have common health concerns. This paradigm identifies health as a global resource as significant as other resources such as land and minerals. As such, health is a collective public good like air and water that can benefit all humanity. Global health becomes the concern of everyone living within the global commons and a common ground on which to share common concerns (Kickbusch, 1997, 2000).

In addition, the new public health paradigm explicitly acknowledges that human health reflects an infinite variety of human expressions—a continuum of human potential that can span, like life itself, the full range of human experience (WHO, 1986). From this perspective, health stems not just from the treatment of disease but from a variety of interrelated factors, including social, economic, environmental, emotional, mental, and spiritual (Beck & Wright, 1996). The new public health paradigm correlates with Nightingale's global vision. Building on her global perspective, the worldwide nursing community can benefit from and contribute to these developments. (See the Pentimento on health determinants, page 142.)

Globalization Is Everyone's Trend

The concept of health of the global commons is yet another aspect of the globalization trend that affects many areas of human endeavor. Where once people thought about and worked within the narrow confines of their communities and regions, now people are interacting within wide geographic and cultural contexts. Information is instantly available to more and more people on the Internet. Issues involving the global nursing shortage—such as recruitment of nurses to wealthy countries and the corresponding loss of nurses to poorer countries—illustrate the impact of globalization on the healthcare sector. Because nurses are the largest group of healthcare professionals in the world (WHO, 1998), the health of the global commons may, and perhaps should, become one of nursing's key practice arenas.

The *Declaration at Alma Ata*, or "Alma-Ata" as it was later nicknamed in the health promotion literature, is the first international health treaty to recognize an interdisciplinary definition of health, including mental and social as well as physical dimensions (WHO, 1978). It also acknowledges the contributions of a wide range of diverse regional systems of health care and healthcare professionals. Despite its limitations—it states the significance of human health without specifying how health would be accomplished—the Alma-Ata marks the beginning of a significant global shift in awareness of the value of human health. It establishes a correlation of detrimental social and economic factors with disease. For the first time, it declares that health is significant to everyone, the human *right* of everyone, and that health is of itself a significant social goal for all of humanity.

Nightingale's scope encompassed these issues. She saw health in social and economic terms as well as in physical, emotional, mental, and spiritual terms. She also recognized that the health of nations was directly connected to the health of individuals and that "health-nursing" should be practiced on this scale (Nightingale, 1893).

New Public Health, Nightingale, and Nursing

Rafael (1999) has pointed out that many of the interrelated concepts described in the three global health documents (see the Pentimento on health charters, page 146) were understood, developed, and advocated by Nightingale throughout her career. In additional examples, Nightingale addressed environmental reforms in the poor workhouses of her time and made it possible for students from her school to observe and work in these places (Monteiro, 1991). Her first district nurses' training school included one year devoted to district and community health promotion. This curriculum emphasized nurturing the patient's self-care, and addressed individual, social, and health reforms (Laffrey & Page, 1989; Monteiro, 1991). Nightingale was quite interested in the economic relationship between health and poverty (Nightingale, 1869, 1879d, 1893). She noted connections between economic states and "states of mind," and encouraged nurses to work for related social reforms (Erickson, 1996). Although she is sometimes accused of being against advanced education, particularly for nurses (Sullivan, 2002), Nightingale was keen on using a wide variety of educational formats and levels to promote health, both for health professionals and for the general public. She advocated for health education at both micro and macro levels in many of the interdisciplinary arenas she addressed (B. Dossey, 2000a; Nightingale, 1860a, 1893, 1894a). Her approach to health was akin to today's holistic approaches, and she applied this premise to her entire body of work (B. Dossey, 1998a, 2000a).

Selanders (1993, 1998b) has observed that while many other nursing theorists look primarily upon the nurse–patient interaction, Nightingale also addressed the environment surrounding this interaction. Selanders has further noted that one of Nightingale's most significant contributions to nursing was her emphasis on the environment's influence on health. With a philosophy remarkably similar to emerging global health understandings of health determinants as detailed in the Jakarta Declaration (WHO, 1997), Nightingale urged her readers to notice whether environments were detrimental to or supportive of health. Like the Jakarta Declaration, Nightingale expected that her readers would take their own initiative to change their environments if this change could be beneficial to their families and communities. Indeed, Nightingale believed this study of health-determining environments to be as important as, if not more important than, the study of physiology. As noted earlier, Nightingale downplayed disease and emphasized health, remarking that "pathology [only] teaches the harm that disease has done, but it teaches nothing more," and noting that "health is the positive of which pathology is the negative" (1860a, p. 74).

Nightingale anticipated this premise of health determinants in the initial pages of "Sick-Nursing and Health-Nursing." She elaborated on two ways to create healthy environments. The first was to improve the surroundings of the sick as much as possible, to facilitate "nature's attempt to cure" and "nature's way of getting rid of the effects of conditions which interfere with health." This definition underscores her assumption that the environment is a significant factor. Her second approach, "health-nursing," encompassed both the micro level of nurturing individual health and the macro level of nurturing societal conditions—all the positive health determinants—so "as to have no disease" in the first place (1893, p. 186).

Rafael (1999) has noted the many difficulties nurses have had since Nightingale's time in remaining proactive *and* visible in the many areas of health that Nightingale influenced. However, he also notes that nurses and their premises of practice remain uniquely suited to contribute to these areas, and that nurses can therefore continue in clinical, educational, and research areas to apply this Nightingalean legacy to the health of the global commons. With the profession of nursing and health care at a significant crossroads, nurses can—if we wish to do so—make key contributions to humanity's health in this new millennium.

At the Millennium Crossroads: Advocacy for the Health of People

Throughout her career, Nightingale worked as an individual nurse and an individual global citizen–activist to advocate for human health. She embodied the kind of caring and citizenship that was needed in her time and is needed now. She collaborated with leaders and innovators in many sectors: military; higher education; clergy; hospital and community planning and administration; philanthropy; local, national, and international public policy; technical invention; and communications (B. Dossey, 2000a). She worked in both large and small ways, at individual levels, at societal levels. She established holistic and interdisciplinary nursing competencies that can be replicated in contemporary practice. She demonstrated what is possible for one single health advocate to do, both locally and globally.

Nurses as Health Advocates

Kleffel (1991) has urged nurses to return to their Nightingalean roots and the concept of influencing the environment—read *health determinants*—as a substantial component of nursing knowledge and practice. Again, reflecting on Nightingale's life and work, Kleffel emphasized that nurses already:

> care for individuals with conditions that originate in the environment, such as injuries from hazards in the home, work place, or school; injuries in war; illnesses due to exposure to toxic wastes, water and air pollution; substance abuse, suicide attempts, malnutrition, and everyday human interactions such as ageism, sexism, and a lack of human rights. (p. 40)

However, nurses can also broaden our base of understanding to incorporate the greater environments (again, read *health determinants*) affecting human health. In 1986, Chopoorian (as cited in Kleffel) remarked that currently

> nursing theories do not have explanations for phenomena such as riots motivated by racism or for violence against women, children, and the elderly in society. …[N]urses do not show public outrage about the origins of their clients' most serious problems, especially as they are witnesses to the most painful aspects of these problems. (pp. 40–41)

In 1893 Nightingale called for the kind of "health-nursing" that could solve many of the health challenges we understand now, a century later. As though she could see clearly the larger health concerns humanity would face, and the limitations of biomedical–industrial approaches to these difficulties, Nightingale reminded her readers how to frame health issues. In *Notes on Nursing,* she wrote these lines, familiar to most nurses:

> Pathology teaches the harm that disease has done. But it teaches nothing more. We know nothing of the principle of health, the positive of which disease is the negative, except by observation and experience and nothing but observation will teach us the ways to maintain health or bring back the state of health. (p. 74)

Given the health concerns facing humanity at the crossroads of this new millennium, Nightingale's familiar words could well take on deeper meaning.

Throughout her career, Nightingale remained convinced that it is "nursing [that] is putting us in the best possible conditions for nature to restore or preserve health" and that the comprehensive and valuable discipline of "health-nursing" would be the best approach to addressing the kinds of health concerns people will continue to have.

> Call it health-nursing or general nursing—what you please. [But] upon womankind the national health depends. She must recognize the laws of life [and] the laws of health. (1893, p. 185)

McBeath has noted that "most influences on health lie beyond the reach of medical care and health education…[thus we healthcare professionals should redirect] our energies to the importance of policies that promote public action toward improving the several aspects [determinants] of ordinary life that are the real precursors of health" (1991, p. 1564). Maben and Macleod-Clark (1995) have established that nurses now require new information, new orientations, new skill sets, and new tools with which to employ these skills. Robinson and Hill (1995) and Lindsey and Hartwick (1996) have concluded that effective contemporary nursing practice can evolve from an emphasis on *re*actively attempting to fix the problems of disease (in support of the physician's mandate), to *pro*actively advocating for establishing healthful conditions. Nightingale called for both approaches to nursing. She saw the value of maintaining excellent "sick-nursing" care in all of its forms. She called for new forms of "health-nursing" that could foster health *before* a person fell sick (Nightingale, 1893).

Recognizing the magnitude of the health problems of our time, nurses—and everyone concerned with human health—now stand at a crossroads. Does health care exist to make a profit or does it exist to serve people? To consider our best course, nurses of all specialties would do well to revisit Nightingale's life and philosophy as a model for what we, as "empowered" caregivers, might do. As advocates for health care, nurses in many different arenas can be empowered *to assist humanity to make the choice for people* and thus, to make a significant contribution to 21st-century health care, including the sustainability of the nursing species.

Reigniting the Flame of Nightingale's Legacy

The light of Nightingale's compassion and caring still shines for those who would study her life and insights. In the Crimea, she carried one small candle throughout long nights to bring her caring to one wounded man at a time. Yet later her same caring would shed light on larger issues, encompassing the health of entire nations. Her approach was, as much as possible, *proactive* promotion of health and prevention of disease, across the micro to macro continuum. And with these principles, she worked in many health arenas: bedside nursing, nursing education, hospital design, military provision, economic strategies for the poor, public education, community development, agriculture, land use and transport planning, concern for cultural diversity, and the use of statistical data to improve health outcomes (Nightingale, 1863, 1869). She shed light on the problems of her time by corresponding with experts in many fields and leading policy initiatives (Simpson, 1977). Acting at the level of what would be identified today as health minister, she consulted many powerful leaders, including Queen Victoria, several prime ministers, governors, secretaries of war and state, commanders-in-chief, and five Indian viceroys, and briefed them with her considered recommendations (B. Dossey, 2000a).

If We Are Daunted

But many have remarked that the panoramic scope of Florence Nightingale's story makes her life and work all the more daunting to contemporary nurses. Even when one looks just at her Crimean War experience, she appears to be a superhuman figure. This chapter is intended to highlight the Nightingale panorama, not to suggest that all nurses become the Florence Nightingale described here, or that the full range of her experiences is what all nurses must now do. This chapter has attempted to introduce Nightingale's wider nursing career, and the premises she held throughout her career, into the 21st century.

With increasing globalization, many more people can now think like Nightingale did. With high-speed, long-distance communications and travel commonplace, our increasingly global perspective is closer to Nightingale's perspective. While most of her neighbors thought about people on their own street, or perhaps in their town, Nightingale was continually in touch with people in lands around the earth.

Today there is increasing awareness that local action can affect global concerns. "Think globally, act locally" is a widely used axiom. Although many people now work on global issues, local action is regarded as the best way to address these concerns in a sustainable way. Nightingale worked, for instance, on the global issue of improving sanitation, provisions, and services in support of the British army, but she started on this issue by working in the field, at the local level, in one hospital in Scutari. She accomplished a great many things during her career. However, a closer look shows that she was applying that "think globally, act locally" axiom. Even when she was working on health issues for the whole of India, she was also looking at the success or failure of strategies at the village level and considering individual people living in that village.

Keeping Her Distinctions in Mind

This chapter's intention is also to recall the value of Nightingale's principles for nurses and for nursing, again in the context of our time. While she understood the full range of human suffering from long personal experience, she maintained her focus on returning people to health and on proactive ways to stay healthy, rather than on treating diseases. In Nightingale's mind, this distinction was the difference between thinking like a nurse and thinking like a physician. To Nightingale, nursing focuses on people and their health; medicine focuses on disease and its treatment.

Since Nightingale's time, there have been such massive developments in the ways diseases are treated that these distinctions have blurred. With so many nurses now working in clinical settings that focus on the treatment of disease—even though this treatment is called *health care*—even nurses have lost sight of Nightingale's principles. Even in the most technical disease treatment settings—where a patient is ventilator dependent and relying on complex, computer-delivered medicine regimens—the attending nurse is doing far more than assisting the doctor to treat acute disease. The attending nurse is helping that person to recover, to heal, and, if possible, to return to optimum health. A return to Nightingale's vision is a return to remembering how significant this distinction is for nurses themselves, as well as for their physician colleagues, for hospital administrators, and for the public at large.

In addition, because new public health initiatives based on global perspectives are just beginning to be applied at local levels, nurses can, with our mandate to promote health, discover ways to participate. A careful look at Nightingale's work in support of health, abroad and at home, shows that she anticipated our 21st-century opportunities to address global health with our nursing discipline. She recommended transdisciplinary, collaborative strategies that are quite similar to current "Healthy Cities" approaches. Since her time and before, nurses have been celebrated for our ability to apply theory to local, real-life situations. Even when considering the health of the global commons, local applications will always be needed and welcomed. As nurses incorporate Nightingale's global vision with our expertise at local levels, we can *think global health and act local health*—to make significant contributions to the health of people in the 21st century.

Tenets for the Health of People

Although Nightingale's work was vast in scope, a closer look at her panorama shows that she took each day at a time, addressing the project in front of her with passion. Sometimes her caring would be at the bedside of a soldier, sometimes before the throne of a queen. Rather than practicing at a specific place—like a hospital or clinic—Nightingale's nursing domain was the health of people, wherever she found them in need of caring. Nightingale's tenets remain nursing's legacy. Today's nursing can emerge from these tenets to encompass a wide range of nursing roles: from bedside care to collaborating on "Healthy Cities" projects, briefing leaders and being leaders in our time, both locally and globally. In the 21st century, our opportunities are almost unlimited.

Every nurse alive today, and indeed everyone, can benefit from a review of Nightingale's panorama. Each can choose the image of Nightingale most relevant to him or her, and become a unique inheritor of Nightingale's legacy. In a keynote address to the delegates who attended the 1996 United Nations Human Settlements Summit "International Tribute to Florence Nightingale at Scutari," convened in Istanbul at the barracks where Nightingale began her work, Beck noted the connections between what Nightingale accomplished and what is possible to accomplish in the 21st century:

> Florence Nightingale saw 19th century problems and created 20th century solutions. We see 20th century problems and we can, like she did, create 21st century solutions. This is the challenge and opportunity of our future—to bring our individual caring and commitment to health and well-being for ourselves, for our patients and clients, for our communities and for our Planet Earth. (1996b)

Early in her life, Nightingale asked, "What can one person do to help?" (B. Dossey, 2000a, pp. 48–49). She answered by igniting the flame of her dreams—to live a life of experience, research, and writing; to formulate a vision of the health of humanity; and to act on that vision. In our time, her questions remain our questions: "What will be our health in 2099?" "What can we do to help?" Our answers could well be the same.

Pentimento

Florence Nightingale

The Lens of Health Determinants:

Nightingale's Dual Focus on Negative and Positive

Deva-Marie Beck

Although the term *health determinants* has come into use nearly a century after the life and work of Florence Nightingale, she focused on the underlying concept throughout her nursing career. She identified the significant value in determining and changing those conditions that could make people sick. At the same time, she called for determining and sustaining those conditions that could keep people healthy or help them recover.

Nightingale focused through the lens of creating health-determining factors rather than through the lens of treating disease, after the fact, because "pathology [merely] teaches the harm disease has done. But it teaches nothing more." She noted that "if Life Insurance and such societies, were they instead of having the person examined by the medical man, to have [the] houses, conditions, ways of life, of these persons examined, at how much truer results would they arrive!"

As early as 1860 when she published *Notes on Nursing: What It Is and What It Is Not,* she established the connections between human health and the quality of human environments. Writing for the general public, and particularly for women, Nightingale used *Notes on Nursing* to discuss the household environment and the physical conditions that sustain the "health of houses… pure air, pure water, efficient drainage, cleanliness, and light." Because she was writing for readers who lived in the cool, damp climate of Britain, she also identified warmth as a key factor for maintaining health. She noted that negative health conditions could be found in wealthy neighborhoods as well as in destitute places. "I have met a strong stream of sewer air coming up the back staircase of a grand London house from the sink, as I have ever met at Scutari."

Nightingale also noted positive and negative emotional environments. In *Notes on Nursing*, she discussed the negative influence that "apprehension, uncertainty, waiting, expectation, [and] fear of surprise" can have on patients. She strongly suggested the use of calm as a positive emotional environment. In "Sick-Nursing and Health-Nursing," she discussed the health-sustaining value of family, friends, and social support—the positive "bonds of sympathy" and the "esprit de corps" people can have with each other. Also focusing on education and applied learning, Nightingale identified the value of positive mental environments where the factors supporting health could be easily taught and well-understood by individuals in their homes.

By 1893, Nightingale was also addressing larger economic and cultural issues, establishing these as appropriate topics for nurses to study and apply. She acknowledged the value of positive emotional influences on health, again widening her focus to speak of the health of humans in social terms. She spoke to her sense of larger family and her sense of community. She continued to appreciate the positive health factors in learning, specifying these details to be taught to individuals. Yet, she extended her concern to ignorance and apathy in general and asked her readers to address these as well. She assumed that the significance of health education should inform the development of health policies that would apply to larger populations, not just in the teaching of the details to one individual at a time. She identified "competition, or each man for himself" as "the enemy of health" and specifically encouraged cooperation as the positive health-determining antidote. She saw that true health outcomes rely on our ability to collaborate in positive ways. "As far as we are successful, our success lies in combination."

Based upon her focus on healthy environments, Nightingale saw nursing—rather than a practice of treating disease—as a practice to improve the conditions supporting recovery and health. In "Sick-Nursing and Health-Nursing," she repeated this lifelong theme: "sickness or disease is Nature's way of getting rid of the effects of conditions which interfered with health. It is Nature's attempt to cure. We have to help her." She identified the practice of sick-nursing as changing negative conditions to "prevent or to cure disease or injury." She noted that nature—and the environments that support nature's mechanisms—are the true curative, not doctors' procedures, nor medicines. Nightingale saw health-nursing as a practice "to keep or put the constitution of the health of the child or human being in such a state as to have no disease." She identified the common denominator between the practices of sick-nursing and health-nursing—"both kinds of nursing are to put us in the best possible conditions [health determinants] for Nature to restore or to preserve health."

In *Notes on Nursing*, Nightingale wrote for readers who would take her words and apply her experience to improve conditions for individuals, in families, and within their households. Later, this text was developed for applications to professional nursing education and is still read—as Nightingale's major influence on nursing—by nursing students, more than a century later. This book of hers was intended as a lens for understanding how to improve small, one-on-one environments. Contemporary nurses—who retain this narrower lens—see the practice of nursing as working with individuals only.

To write "Sick-Nursing and Health-Nursing," Nightingale was practicing nursing in the broader arena of a global meeting: the Columbian Exposition. During her last years of writing about nursing, she retained the same clear focus on negative

Nightingale's Negative Health Determinants

Stagnant Water

© *World Health Organization, Pierre Virot, photographer*

Impoverished Conditions
© *World Health Organization, Pierre Virot, photographer*

Secondhand Smoke
© *World Health Organization, Pierre Virot, photographer*

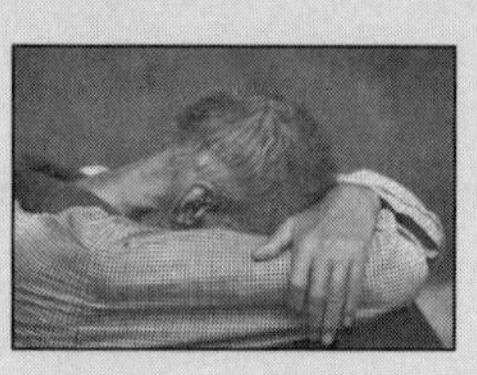

Isolation
© *World Health Organization, Pierre Virot, photographer*

Air Pollution

and positive conditions influencing health, discussing the "want of cleanliness, want of fresh air, careless dieting and clothing, want of white-washing, dirty feather beds and bedding—in one word, want of household care of health." Yet, for Nightingale, the nursing practice of maintaining the cleanliness and fresh air in one bedroom also extended to sustaining the scope of cleanliness and clean air to a community and a nation. "The work we are speaking of has nothing to do with nursing disease, but with maintaining health by removing the things which disturb it, which have been summed up in the population in general as 'dirt, drink, diet, damp, draughts, drains.' "

Beyond the study of *Notes on Nursing,* those who wish to broaden their scope to include wider human health lenses can look to Nightingale's later work with fresh insight. Across her long and varied career, Nightingale further

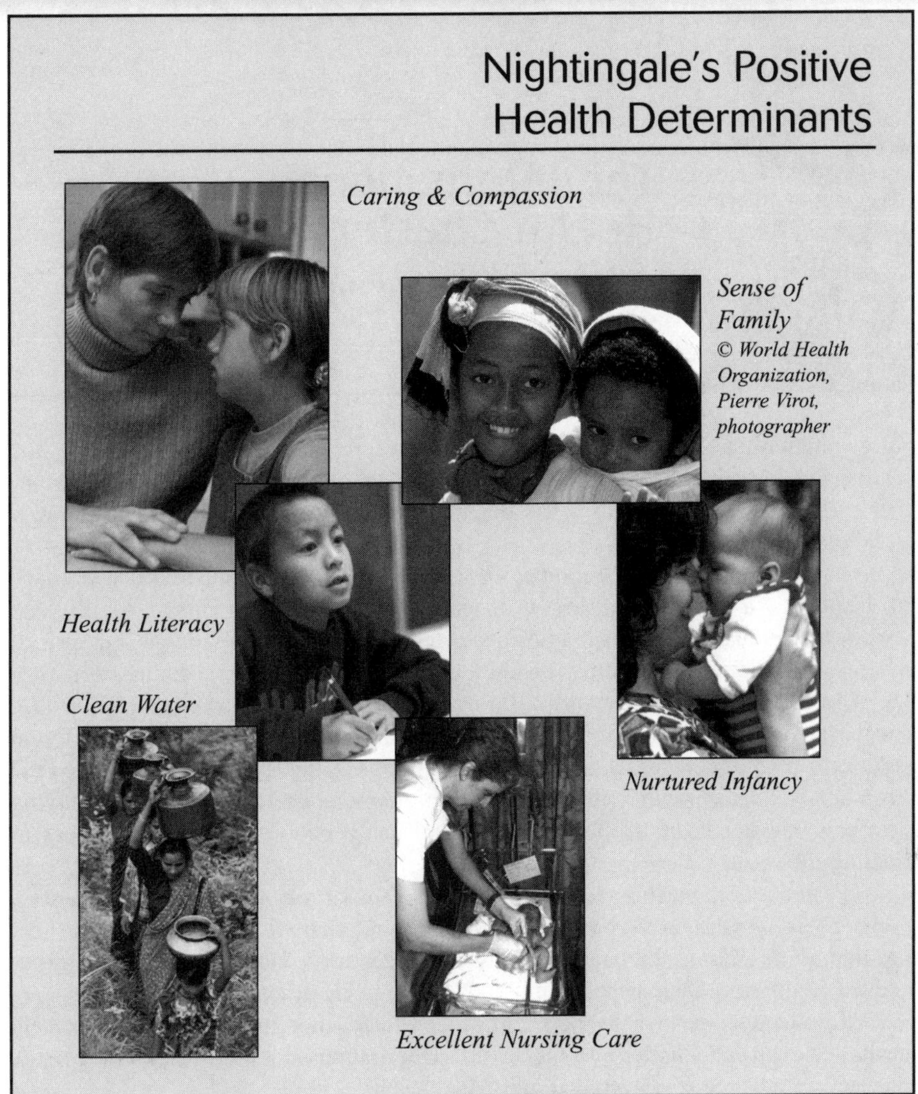

developed the continuum between one human being and the whole of humanity. Indeed, she saw this wider continuum as nursing's fullest arena. Along this full span, she retained her basic premise that all nursing practice is to put and maintain "the best possible conditions"—that is, health determinants—in place for people to recover *and* to thrive.

Nurses—who are seeking to take global action—can see the practice of nursing from these perspectives. Because nursing's focus has always been on creating environments for recovery, and healing, as we discover Nightingale's wider lens, we can also evolve caring practices to create better, health-sustaining conditions for each human being, as well as all of humanity.

Pentimento

The International Health Charters:
A New Global Health Language for Nurses

Deva-Marie Beck

Three international health charters—created in a series between 1978 and 1997, and named for the places where they were ratified—represent the first time in history that the topic of human health has been addressed in the form of global treaties between countries.

The first, titled the *Declaration at Alma Ata* (WHO, 1978), focused on the primacy of health as a fundamental right of each member of the human family and acknowledged that health was not just dependent upon physical conditions, but also on mental (and emotional) as well as on cultural, social, and economic conditions.

The second, titled the *Ottawa Charter for Health Promotion* (WHO, 1986), specifically noted that endeavors focusing on health promotion are entirely different from efforts to treat disease. Given this premise, the Ottawa Charter established the need for transdisciplinary collaborations to promote health, rather than leaving health in the hands of people focused specifically on biomedical approaches to treating illness.

The third, titled the *Jakarta Declaration on Health Promotion for the 21st Century* (WHO, 1997), builds on the premises of the other two charters. It further describes that health must be addressed proactively, before diseases arise, and that innovative ways to address health must include collaboration between many disciplines and sectors.

All three documents note the significance of education to influence and promote health. The Ottawa Charter and the Jakarta Declaration both emphasize that people, themselves, must be empowered at individual levels.

Relevance to Nursing

While the nursing profession has not recently been focused on the global arena of health, nor upon these international charters, the language of these documents calls for implementing areas of expertise that are inherent to nurses and to nursing. Also, the concepts developed in these charters reflect the ideas that Florence Nightingale established for nurses. In addition, these documents establish a leadership mandate to address health concerns—not just for governments nor for any single profession—for everyone who wishes to bring their talents and abilities for collaborations to secure human health. The Jakarta Declaration, in particular, calls for innovative approaches to create new health-supporting partnerships.

On the basis of the language of these charters, nurses have—if we wish this—a broader and stronger mandate to bring our significant talents to all health promotion endeavors. Using these charters as a language base, nurses can work—autonomously, as well as within new transdisciplinary collaborations—to create and implement a global vision for human health.

The following excerpts highlight language of specific interest to nurses from all three charters.

From the 1978 Declaration at Alma Ata

[Health] involves, in addition to the health sector, all related sectors and aspects of national and community development … [and] requires and promotes maximum community and individual self-reliance and participation in the planning, organization, operation and control of primary healthcare.

[Health] relies, at local and referral levels, on health workers, including physicians, nurses, midwives, auxiliaries and community workers … as well as traditional practitioners as needed … to work as a health team and to respond to the expressed health needs of the community.

An acceptable level of health for all the people of the world … can be attained through a fuller and better use of the world's resources, a considerable part of which is now spent on armaments and military conflicts. A genuine policy of independence, peace, détente and disarmament could and should release additional resources that could well be devoted to peaceful aims and in particular to the acceleration of social and economic development of which primary healthcare, as an essential part, should be allotted its proper share.

Health, which is a state of complete physical, mental and social wellbeing, and not merely the absence of disease or infirmity, is a fundamental human right and which the attainment of the highest possible level of health is a most important world-wide social goal whose realization requires the action of many other social and economic sectors in addition to the health sector.

The promotion and protection of the health of the people is essential to sustained economic and social development and contributes to a better quality of life and to world peace. [It includes, at least,] education concerning prevailing health problems and the methods of preventing and controlling them; promotion of food supply and proper nutrition; an adequate supply of safe water and basic sanitation; maternal and child healthcare, including family planning; immunization against the major infectious diseases; prevention and control of locally endemic diseases; appropriate treatment of common diseases and injuries; and provision of essential drugs.

From the 1986 Ottawa Charter for Health Promotion

Health is seen as a resource for everyday life, not the objective of living … a positive concept emphasizing social and personal resources, as well as physical capacities. Therefore, health promotion is not just the responsibility of the health sector, but goes beyond healthy lifestyles to wellbeing.

Good health is a major resource for social, economic and personal development and an important dimension of quality of life. Political, economic, social, cultural, environmental, behavioural and biological factors can all favour health or be harmful to it. Health promotion action aims at making these conditions favourable through advocacy for health.

This includes a secure foundation in a supportive environment, access to information, life skills and opportunities for making healthy choices. People cannot achieve their fullest health potential unless they are able to take control of those things which determine their health. This must apply equally to women and men.

Our societies are complex and interrelated. Health cannot be separated from other goals. The inextricable links between people and their environment constitute the basis for a socioecological approach to health. The overall guiding principle for the world, nations, regions, and communities alike is the need … to take care of each other, our communities and our natural environment.

Health promotion works through concrete and effective community action.… At the heart of this process is the empowerment of communities, their ownership and control of their own endeavours and destinies. Community development draws on existing human and material resources in the community to enhance self-help and social support; … this requires full and continuous access to information, learning opportunities for health, as well as funding support.

Health promotion supports personal and social development through providing information, education for health and enhancing life skills. By so doing, it increases the options available to people to exercise more control over their own health and over their environments, and to make choices conducive to health.

Enabling people to learn throughout life, to prepare themselves for all of its stages, and to cope with chronic illness and injuries is essential. This has to be facilitated in school, home, work, and community settings.

The role of the health sector must move increasingly in a health promotion direction, beyond its responsibility for providing clinical and curative services. Health services need to embrace an expanded mandate which is sensitive and respects cultural needs. This mandate should support the needs of individuals and communities for a healthier life, and open channels between the health sector and broader social, political, economic, and physical environmental components.

Reorienting health services also requires stronger attention to health research as well as changes in professional education and training. This must lead to a change of attitude and organization of health services, which refocuses on the total needs of the individual as a whole person.

Health is created by caring for oneself and others, by being able to take decisions and have control over one's life circumstances, and by ensuring that the society one lives in creates conditions that allow the attainment of health by all its members.

Caring, holism, and ecology are essential issues in developing strategies for health promotion. Therefore, those involved should take as a guiding principle that, in each phase of planning, implementation, and evaluation of health promotion activities, women and men should become equal partners.

From the 1997 Jakarta Declaration on Health Promotion for the 21st Century

Health is a basic human right and essential for social and economic development. Increasingly, health promotion is being recognized as an essential element of health development. It is a process of enabling people to increase control over and to improve their health.

Pre-requisites for health are peace, shelter, education, social security, social relations, food, income, empowerment of women, a stable eco-system, sustainable resource use, social justice, respect for human rights, and equity. Above all, poverty is the greatest threat to health.

Health learning fosters participation. Access to education and information is essential to achieving effective participation and the empowerment of people and communities.

New responses are needed. To address emerging threats to health, new forms of action are needed. The challenge for the coming years will be to unlock the potential for health promotion inherent in many sectors of society, among local communities, and within families.

Co-operation is essential. Specifically, this requires the creation of new partnerships for health on equal ground between the different sectors at all levels of governance in societies.

Greater investment for health, and re-orientation of existing investments—both within and between countries—has the potential to significantly advance human development, health, and quality of life. Investments in health should reflect the needs of certain groups such as women, children, older people, indigenous, poor, and marginalised populations.

Existing partnerships need to be strengthened and the potential for new partnerships must be explored. Partnerships offer mutual benefit for health through the sharing of expertise, skills, and resources.

Health promotion is carried out by and with people, not on or to people. It improves both the ability of individuals to take action, and the capacity of groups, organizations or communities to influence the determinants of health. Improving the capacity of communities for health promotion requires practical education, leadership training, and access to resources. Empowering individuals demands more consistent, reliable access to the decision making process and the skills and knowledge essential to effect change. Both traditional communication and the new information media support this process. Social, cultural, and spiritual resources need to be harnessed in innovative ways.

7

Directions and Reflections

Directions for Future Research

1. Identify relevancies between the work and insights of early nursing activist role models, such as Clara Barton, Margaret Sanger, and Lillian Wald, and the healthcare issues of the 21st century.
2. Identify common themes relevant to contemporary nursing practice from collected stories of nurses working in international healthcare arenas, such as the Peace Corps, the United States or Canadian Armed Services, or the International Red Cross.
3. Explore the ideal sustainable environment for the nursing species. Collect stories from nurses who have been "endangered" by unsustainable working environments to identify issues and themes from the clinician's perspective.
4. Review the emerging health determinants literature for relevance to contemporary and earlier nursing theories.

Reflections on Florence Nightingale's Tenets: Global Action

1. Which, if any, Nightingale story do I resonate with? Why?
2. How do I define my own "must" or personal mission statement?
3. How do I apply my sense of mission to my life, personally and professionally?
4. If I could do anything with my nursing career, what would it be?
5. What, if any, global health challenges directly impact upon my career or life?
6. If I could envision a nursing arena for global health, what would that look like?
7. What words or phrases from the *Declaration at Alma Ata,* the *Ottawa Charter of Health Promotion*, or the *Jakarta Declaration on Health Promotion for the 21st Century* inform my nursing practice?

Sick-Nursing & Health-Nursing: Nightingale Establishes Our Broad Scope of Practice in 1893

Deva-Marie Beck

This chapter is the first historical study of Florence Nightingale's last major publication, the 1893 essay, "Sick-Nursing and Health-Nursing" (reproduced starting on page 287). Although this work has never been studied in depth, it represents the culmination of Nightingale's career. As such, it reflects the broad scope of her nursing practice. She addressed the topics of sick-nursing and health-nursing from the perspective of over 40 years' experience. Her premise is that these topics were significant because they encompassed a whole world of human need and suffering, with "such stupendous issues as life and death, health and disease" (Burdett-Coutts, 1893, p. 187).

Writing at the Culmination of Her Career

At the age of 73, Nightingale wrote this essay upon invitation as part of a formal Royal British Commission contribution to the 1893 Chicago World's Fair, also called the Columbian Exposition. For the first time, such an event featured women's contributions to humankind with specific exhibits and meetings. (See the first Pentimento in this chapter for details on this essay and how it came to be lost in the ongoing controversy over registration of nurses.)

Earlier in her career, as she was writing *Notes on Nursing: What It Is and What It Is Not* (1860a), Nightingale developed her ideas for a general audience. That "little book" immediately became a best-seller and remained so through the remaining 50 years of her life. The wide and lasting popularity of this publication confirmed that her insights were valuable to a general readership (Selanders, 1993). Thirty years later, when she wrote "Sick-Nursing and Health-Nursing," she knew that her reading audience could be larger still. The Chicago Exposition was the first worldwide event that formally honored the contributions of women. In contributing this essay,

(The page citations that are italicized in this chapter are from the essay's original source, Burdett-Coutts 1893, not this book.)

Nightingale concurred with her friends Lady Burdett-Coutts and Queen Victoria, who believed this fair to be significant for women of the world. In the essay, Nightingale recognized the fair, and the American hosting of the fair, as significant new developments that could promote wider collaborations among women that were poised "to be taught to the whole world." She wrote her manuscript from this vantage point, and put her passion into the words, "in the future, which I shall not see, for I am old, may a better way be opened!" (1893, *p. 198*).

In *Notes on Nursing,* Nightingale's remarks were directed to individual, *micro-level* care. In "Sick-Nursing and Health-Nursing" she continued to address individual care, yet here she ranged beyond the micro-level scope of practice to encompass the macro-level arena. Nightingale asked readers across this continuum to join her. She urged individual caregivers "to recognize the laws of sickness, the symptoms of disease, or the symptoms … not of the disease, but of the nursing, bad or good." In the same paragraph, she also addressed health leaders and health policymakers, because "upon womankind, the national health, as far as the household goes, depends" (*p. 185*). Nightingale embodied both perspectives. She understood that her reading audience could range from one individual to the whole of humanity, and to leaders at all levels. She had experienced and developed, and so was able to envision, broad scopes of practice that could range across the breadth of health issues.

Nightingale began by citing a human "want" that is "nearly as old as the world, nearly as large as the world, as pressing as life or death" (*p. 184*), referring to relief from disease and suffering. She continued in the same paragraph by citing wants that are "older still and larger still," the feminine desire to nurture children in their "delicate" infancy, and the human desire to be well, to flourish, to thrive.

Nightingale quickly moved on to another key observation, one that reflected her views of comprehensive health promotion. "But since God did not mean mothers to be always accompanied by doctors, there is a want older still and larger still." She also realized that although "science" had begun to address health, the accompanying "art" was not yet fully understood. She called this the "art of health": one that concerned "every family in the world." This art should be well understood and practiced by everyone responsible for tending children and families. She named "every mother, girl, mistress, teacher, child's nurse, every woman" (*p. 184*). With these remarks, she called for establishing a world of "health-nursing."

"To Be Able to Use Well"

Focusing on her commitment to well-being, Nightingale then asked her readers to consider her most pertinent question, "What is health?" Her answer: "Health is not only to be well, but to use well every power we have" (*p. 186*). We should pause to consider the context of Nightingale's own experience, to clarify what she meant by being able "to use well, every power we have."

Nightingale had applied these words to her own work throughout her life. By the time she wrote this essay, she had written thousands of letters. She was a consummate networker, writing to leaders at all levels of government, to policymakers, philanthropists, journalists, inventors, clergy, and educators, as well as to a wide circle of friends and family. She used the power of her networks to accomplish her objectives (B. Dossey, 2000a; McDonald, 2000). Additionally, she may well have been referring to her belief in spiritual resources when she referred to "every power we have."

With this definition of health established, Nightingale detailed the health priorities she believed should be in place around the world. She had a cosmopolitan worldview, acquired through her fluency in five foreign languages, extensive travel for pleasure and work, and a lifelong study of cultural and spiritual traditions different from her own. Nightingale emphasized the significant connection between worldwide health and women who cared for infants and children. She focused on the need to support this caregiving, including education about early childhood needs. "The human baby is not an invalid, but is the most tender form of animal life" (*p. 186*). With a sarcasm indicative of her moments of frustration, she also remarked that, despite the obvious value of this kind of education, women were "supposed to know it all by instinct, like a bird" (*p. 185*). She acknowledged that, in her time, public opinion had been harnessed effectively for better health conditions, particularly through improved drainage and sanitation. However, she reminded her readers that the general public was "not at all awake" to the importance of teaching the mothers and girls who were responsible for healthy household conditions. She asked, "where, then, is the remedy for this ignorance?" (*p. 191*). Wishing for more people qualified to advocate for the concerns which "touch the very health of everybody from the beginning" (*p. 185*), Nightingale looked for widespread, systematic teaching about health in infancy. She called for education programs developed and implemented by knowledgeable "health-nurses" and aimed at everyone involved in early child care, on a global basis.

Leadership for Health

Nightingale demonstrated her understanding of larger, macro-level health issues: "How to keep the baby in health [is] certainly the most important function to make a healthy nation." She added that this key theme was only one aspect of the broader field of "health-nursing." Returning to her introductory remarks about the "art of health," Nightingale elaborated on the many advances that had taken place in her lifetime, including large organizations, bodies of literature, medical officers of health, and "immense" sanitary works. She added, however, that these same developments had not included a network of support systems for "health at home." She reminded her readers that the contributions of women, "by whom everybody is born," had not yet been adequately acknowledged (*pp. 185–186*).

Nightingale asked her readers to consider a key health leadership question: "How to bring these great medical officers to bear on the families, the homes and household, the habits of the people, rich as well as poor?" She observed that this question had not been properly studied. She also added a philosophical aside that human beings are inclined to be "convinced of *error*" before they can be "*convinced of right*." Reflecting on her spiritual scholarship, she recalled, "the discovery of sin comes before the discovery of righteousness" (*p. 185*). Nightingale noted that although concern for health should look first at the lack of healthy conditions rather than the disease process, this approach was not valued. She remarked pointedly that "everything comes before health" and "we do not look after health, but after sickness" (*p. 185*).

Nursing, Caring, and Advocacy in Health Promotion

Asking rhetorically "what is nursing," Nightingale answered first by stating her key premise that there are two kinds of nursing—one that addresses sickness, and one that addresses health and health promotion. However, after making this distinction, she added that both kinds of nursing work toward the same end, that of putting people "in the best possible conditions for Nature to restore or to preserve health—to prevent or to cure disease or injury." She reiterated one of her major lifetime distinctions between nursing for illness and nursing for health. Her goal for "sick-nursing" was always to assist the suffering so that they lived through this "natural" illness process. Her goals for "health-nursing" were to strengthen the conditions supporting health and wellness, and to nurture those conditions—those positive health determinants—so "as to have no disease" (*p. 186*) in the first place.

For the wider audience of a World's Fair and in the context of specifying the scope of "sick-nursing' and "health-nursing," Nightingale returned, almost verbatim, to her own *Notes on Nursing,* first written for mothers and homemakers in Britain. In both works she listed her health-promoting factors or nursing "canons." But before citing this list once more, she took extra care to remind her readers about nursing's unique mandate to address these factors. She believed that beyond the giving of medicine or surgical applications, according to physicians' "orders," the profession of nursing, as focused on health promotion, should be an autonomous one. She herself demonstrated nursing's autonomous role when she advocated for health issues. Her health promotion list included: "the proper use of fresh air (ventilation), light, warmth, cleanliness, quiet, and the proper choosing and giving of diet, all at the least expense of vital power to the sick." She explained that while these factors certainly related to "sick-nursing," their application would always be more significant to the practice of "health-nursing" because in these settings practitioners supplied the "same proper use of the same natural elements, with as much life-giving power as possible" (1893, *p. 189*). Again, she stressed that these endeavors were to be aimed at helping people to become healthy and to remain so.

Nightingale used the metaphor of indoor gardening. She noted that people care for their "[house]plants, which we know very well, perish in rooms [which are] damp and close," but that these same nurturing, caring environments, which can also improve and support the health of human beings, are not given enough priority. She cited statistics of infant mortality, as an early benchmark in health promotion research. She chose this example because the "life-duration of babies is the most 'delicate test' of health conditions" (*p. 190*).

Continuing from her health advocacy premise, Nightingale asked her readers to consider the numbers of children, both in cities and in rural areas, who died in the first years of life. She commented that "tons of printed knowledge" was already available, and that the "causes of enormous child mortality" were already well documented. She listed several related factors, including unclean clothing and bedding, want of fresh, clean air, and careless food intake: "in one word, want of *household* care of health." She reminded her readers that the remedies to these oversights were also well documented. She questioned why this same knowledge had not been adequately "brought into the homes and households and habits of the people, poor or even rich" (*p. 190*).

Larger Nursing and Health Promotion Issues

Nightingale warned that people still did not believe in "sanitation as affecting health." She observed that some still believed sanitation efforts were a "mere fad." People would rather "believe in catching cold, and in infection, [by] catching complaints from each other." She returned to her essay's principal theme, reminding her readers that all of these issues have everything to do with health-nursing and "nothing to do with nursing disease." She recommended that the ideal remedy would be the training and employment of "health-nurses" to teach the public about health issues. She believed that investments in "sick-nurses" to care for people after they catch disease were less useful. She also reiterated the transdisciplinary nature of health promotion and the value of transdisciplinary approaches to health-nursing (*p. 192*).

She reminded her readers that health promotion efforts could be characterized as the six "Ds"—"dirt, drink, diet, damp, draught, [and] drains" (*p. 192*). This list of Ds might strike today's readers, who live in places where sanitary measures like sewage treatment and clean-running tap water are the norm, as only a quaint tribute to long past public health accomplishments. However, for the poor of the world, who still often rely on latrines or open areas of toileting and have to carry water, sometimes long distances, for drinking and bathing, this list remains significant to their health. The massive electrical blackout that occurred in North America in 2003, and other seasonal hurricanes that disable powerlines and threaten clean water supplies for millions, highlight these concerns. People from Ontario to North Carolina were vulnerable to basic sanitation problems. In all areas of the world, Nightingale's "dirt, drink, diet, damp, draught, [and] drains" remain perennial health issues.

Nightingale acknowledged that in the last decade of the 19th century human beings were "finally awakened" to the need to address external health issues. However, she also acknowledged that her own vision of health promotion was "still far from the mark." She discussed the correlation between the lack of value for women's contributions to society and the lack of value for health promotion in general. She also observed that even women themselves forgot to value their own contributions to health and health, itself. Expressing her continued frustration, she warned her readers that "so-called civilization" had already made significant progress, in "direct opposition to the laws of health." She stated that women themselves had contributed to this trend by persisting in the belief that "health [is] something that grows by itself" without requiring careful attention. She reminded her readers that we should, instead, value women and their ability to nurture, "in whose hands rest the health of [all] babies" (*p. 189*).

Painting this health promotion picture with her broadest strokes, Nightingale emphasized the significant role of every mother and her potential to be a "health-nurse" in support of healthy populations. She made this issue her foundation for sustaining a truly healthy world. She observed that the role of "sick-nursing" to assist with disease treatment touched only the merest trace of her fuller vision of "health-nursing." The breadth of her picture for all of her readers included caring about and being fully involved in health leadership for all nations, all races, and all classes. She believed that this leadership could create those positive health determinants that not only supported recovery from illness, but also fully supported our ability to bring healthy generations into the world.

Nightingale's Tensions

Are Nightingale's observations in "Sick-Nursing and Health-Nursing" still applicable? Do her recommendations still apply to nurses and their problems? To answer these questions, we can identify several "tension" themes in Nightingale's discourse. The seeming contradictions of these tensions may have contributed, in part, to the fact that some nurses consider Nightingale's ideas less than relevant for our times.

Sickness versus Health

Nightingale reiterated that the discipline of nursing focuses on people and their health needs, differentiating this from the discipline of medicine that focuses on the study of disease conditions and how to treat them. In defining sickness, she was consistent with her earlier works. "Sickness or disease is Nature's way of getting rid of the effects of conditions which interfered with health" (*p. 186*). She emphasized the distinction between "nursing sickness," an endeavor that addresses illness conditions, and "nursing the sick," an endeavor that focuses on the people who have health concerns due to their condition.

She acknowledged that "sick-nurses" must also be able to recognize the laws, causes, and symptoms of disease. She reminded her readers to always consider whether the nursing care itself—good or bad—had contributed to either the worsening of the condition, or the recovery toward health.

Nightingale elaborated on her distinction between sickness and health by describing the realm of "health-nursing." She explained that, although similar to "sick-nursing," "health-nursing" is far more comprehensive. "Health-nursing," which encompasses the health of humanity, nurtures each person to "be well" and encourages each nurse to "use well" all resources available to her. She elaborated on this wider scope of practice and what it could mean to nurses and to health. She identified these premises as the laws of health, even "laws of life."

Profit versus Caring

By the time she wrote "Sick-Nursing and Health-Nursing," Nightingale could look back at a generation of nurses who had been trained since her own early efforts to advance nursing care and education. From this vantage point, she addressed what she called the "dangers" of a second significant tension—profit versus caring. She voiced concern that the money to be made in hospital care might be at the expense of patients and nursing students. Nightingale noted that "forty or fifty years ago, a hospital was looked upon as a box to hold patients in. …the first question never was: 'Will the hospital do them no harm?'" While acknowledging that "enormous strides" had been made, at least to improve sanitary conditions for patients, she noted that "now there is danger of a hospital being looked upon as a box to train nurses in," and warned that "enormous strides must be made not to do them harm." She cautioned that students should not be used as cheap labor thrown into hospital wards to "pick up" as they can, "without receiving adequate supervised training first." She strongly advocated investment in an educational system that would provide student nurses "something that can really be called an 'all-around' training" (1893, *p. 196*).

It is important to recall that Nightingale had witnessed the usury of both patients and students by hospitals for decades. She had seen the increasing trend toward this usury, with a corresponding shift of priority to making money, rather than one of providing caring service. Within the evolving field of nursing education, the usury of students had become one of her greatest concerns. She also addressed the nurses themselves, reflecting that by the early 1890s there were already major concerns about the quality of nurses and the nursing field. She noted new reasons why people were choosing to become nurses. She warned of the danger of making this choice for what she called "fashion," rather than from the earnest desire to care for humanity. While she agreed that women need money as much as anyone, Nightingale warned about "mere money-getting." She added, "yet man does not live by bread alone, still less woman" (*p. 196*), and "woman does not live by wages alone." Sullivan (2002) has recently claimed that Nightingale "encouraged low wages" for nurses. She did warn against putting "mere money-getting" above serving the needs of people, and a possible "want of earnestness" in caring about people (*p. 193*). However, the *level* of wages to be paid to nurses was not mentioned in this essay.

Obedience versus Autonomy

An issue discussed by Nightingale scholars since her time is the tension between "obedience" and "autonomy." Many have criticized Nightingale's seeming strict stance about obedience (Baly, 1986; Katz, 1969; Muff, 1982). Selanders (1992) has noted that Nightingale's emphasis on developing a home for nurses to live together while off-duty "contributed to the atmosphere of absolute obedience" (p. 96). Many of the young women who first attended the Nightingale Training School had recently moved from their own sheltered home environments. These women characteristically "had little or no experience in decision-making and … had limited educational experience" (1893, *p. 106*).

Selanders reasoned that "Nightingale saw the need 'to take care of [her] nurses,' [perhaps] assuming that they were not capable of taking care of themselves." Her desire to provide what she perceived to be necessary guidance may have been the reason why she has been so consistently accused of demanding strict obedience from her nurses. "Had nursing not evolved in such a controlled setting where subservience was the expected norm, the potential of [autonomous] nursing practice might be more evident today" (1992, p. 105).

However, Nightingale herself exhibited altogether different behaviors. In many areas of her own career, she worked autonomously, accepting her own authority on matters which she had studied carefully. With regard to Nightingale's life and work, and her expectations of others, a tension still exists between her supposed standard of obedience and her own remarkable ability to work and influence others from a position of autonomy. Only one reference to the word "obedience" appears in the essay:

> Training is to teach the nurse how to handle the agencies within our control which restore health and life, in strict, intelligent obedience to the physician's or surgeon's power or knowledge; how to keep the health mechanism prescribed to her in gear. (*p. 187*)

She qualified *obedience* with the adjective *intelligent,* explaining that this intelligence included a detailed nursing knowledge of "the health mechanism." Nightingale expected her students (and the readers of her essay) to independently understand human "health mechanism[s]." She saw this independence as arising from the difference between nursing's discipline and medicine's discipline. She remarked that an effective "treatment of patients will not be attained" (*p. 187*) without a clear understanding of the nurse's role within the "sick-nursing" domain. She urged her readers to address physicians' orders with a loyal, but also independent, sense of nursing judgment and an equally independent concern for patients' internal and external environments.

Profession versus "Calling"

Nightingale characterized nursing as a "calling," a concept which she believed to be very different from what other people were, for the first time, terming a "profession." She questioned her readers,

> What is it to feel a calling for anything? Is it not to do our work in it to satisfy the high idea of what is right and best, and not because we shall be found out if we don't do it?" (*p. 193*)

She described a "calling" as a life of caring, that deep desire to serve with an involvement of one's whole being—physically, emotionally, mentally, and spiritually.

Nightingale connected the term *profession* with the "danger" of mediocrity. She cautioned against settling for job-description work patterns, rather than allowing nursing to grow, deepen, and evolve as a "calling." She warned that "no system can endure that does not march," asking, "are we walking to the future or to the past? Are we progressing or are we stereotyping? ... How then, to keep up the high tone of this, to 'make your calling and election sure?'" Her answers spoke of "fostering that bond of sympathy" between colleagues, and a "community of aims and of action in good work" built on this bond. Nightingale also urged her readers to clarify their own "calling" for themselves through reflection. This was the approach that she herself had taken throughout her life. She reminded her readers to continue to "press toward that mark of your high 'calling'" (*p. 196*).

Returning to her concern about what the nursing profession might degenerate into, Nightingale wrote, "we have scarcely crossed the threshold of uncivilized civilization in nursing," and that "there is still so much to do" (*p. 196*). During a 2001 scholarly debate about this essay, nursing educator Margaret A. Burkhardt and Nightingale biographer Barbara M. Dossey discussed nursing's present understanding of the term *profession*, as compared with Nightingale's earlier concerns regarding this term. Dr. Burkhardt posited that nursing's current standard of profession might well be closer to Nightingale's own standard than it was in her time. Dossey readily agreed that Nightingale would have approved of our evolving sense of 21st-century nursing praxis (Burkhardt & Dossey, personal communication, July 2001).

Duty versus "Must"

Dossey (1998a, 1998b, 2000a, 2000b) has emphasized that Nightingale called her work her "must." Nightingale often used this phrase to capture her sense of commitment to the "call from God" that she experienced at age 16. Although she did not mention her "must" in the essay, this concept and that of "duty" form another significant Nightingale tension. Several scholars have expressed a belief that Nightingale was such a strong proponent of "duty" that she demanded it unyieldingly of her students and her followers (Small, 1998; F. Smith, 1982), and that this has restricted Nightingale's influence over nursing's evolution. Reverby (1987) has discussed this restriction in detail, describing this "duty" as so malignant in its implications that women are expected "do their duty" in obligation to their fathers, husbands, sons, family and, in the context of the nursing profession, to physicians and hospital administrators.

Nightingale mentioned "duty" only once in this essay, and took the trouble to clarify her meaning. She was writing of the wide range of transdisciplinary and holistic competencies required of nurses to do their jobs effectively. These competencies included

> method, self-sacrifice, watchful activity, love of the work, devotion to duty (that is, the service of the good), the courage, the coolness of the soldier, the tenderness of the mother, the absence of the prig (that is, never thinking that she has attained perfection or that there is nothing better). (1893, *p. 195*)

Nightingale clearly distinguished the word *duty* as something positive: "that is, the service of the good." This definition is consistent with other examples from her life. Nightingale's own choices were made from an autonomous duty to her God (B. Dossey, 1998a, 2000a). In this instance, Nightingale was referring to that duty that one feels from within—that internal calling to make a difference in a world of need. She also referred to physicians on this same page, but did not mention a duty to them. Nor did she require a duty to herself or her standards. Nightingale's word *must* and her sense of duty might seem to have directly opposite meanings. However, her own clarification of duty as a "service of the good" indicates that she understood her duty and her must as similar, spiritually meaningful things. Nightingale's "must" was to serve her God; duty was not subservience to others, but a "must" found within one's own soul.

Nightingale's Health Determinants

In both *Notes on Nursing* and "Sick-Nursing and Health-Nursing," Nightingale focused on what she called *canons*—the factors that support recovery, health, and healing. Nightingale's health canon concept is strikingly similar to the modern use of the concept of health determinants. Selanders (1993) has pointed out that Nightingale paid careful attention to the environments of health. She envisioned that, like her, nurses would proactively improve these key determinants to patients' recoveries from illness, and to people's maintenance of health and well-being. In 1860, Nightingale emphasized that personal and collective excellence in nursing care were a major micro-level determining factor in recovery, healing, and health. In 1893, she took this stance again, and she also took a wider macro-level stance, focusing on the "health determinant" of larger policies that support nursing and caring excellence. (See the second Pentimento in this chapter for a brief discussion on the topic of health determinants.)

Commitment to Caring Excellence and "Vital Force"

Nightingale made a significant statement about the value of nursing care and the necessity of vigilance to sustain excellence of care. She urged nurses to remember that, while the physician prescribes the "vital force" for support, it is the "nurse [who] supplies it" (*p. 186*). To build upon her own meaning of the term *vital force*, Nightingale returned to one of her major spiritual themes, that the Creator "makes health" and "makes disease." Here, she reminded her readers about the connection between vital force for health and Spirit, and the importance of practicing nursing from this perspective. Nightingale's reference to "vital force" was specific to her sense of the human spirit residing in, and expressing itself through, the physical body. She identified two of nursing's roles as watching and encouraging this human spirit in significant ways. (It should be noted that she was not referring to healing waters or any products that used the terms *vital force* or *vitalism* as promotional jargon.)

Nightingale believed that nursing's assumptions, approaches, and skills are the very things on which "physicians or surgeons must depend" for their own success or failure. She again stressed one of her key themes: sickness was merely "nature's way of getting rid of the effects of conditions which [have] interfered with health." Her principle was to see Nature as delivering health, and disease as merely an "interference" with this supply. She reminded her readers that "nature attempts to cure," but that "we have to help her." Nightingale saw that nursing care was the best way to provide this essential "help" (*p. 186*).

She also emphasized the time, energy, and commitment required to provide quality nursing care. She reminded her readers that a physician or surgeon comes to visit a patient briefly, only once or twice a day, if that often. The doctor's role is simply to "give his orders." The nurse's role, however, is to remain with the patient, to deliver care "with intelligence of conditions, every minute of the twenty-four hours" (*p. 195*). One can almost hear her say "twenty-four/seven."

Nightingale recognized the demanding but rewarding nature of the caring excellence required of nurses. From her own experience, she understood the stress involved in this calling, and what it took do the job well. She emphasized the comprehensive capabilities required to bring excellence to caring, and she underscored that the value of nursing's service to the world is underestimated. Nightingale focused on her commitment to nurses, reminding us that we should be honored for what we deliver—the "supply" of "vital force" to the health and well-being of humanity (*p. 195*).

Caring Excellence in Training

Nightingale defined training as teaching "the nurse to help the patient live." She acknowledged that the practice of "sick-nursing" had become, even in her lifetime, a tough assignment, particularly because she had witnessed a significant increase in the number of procedures required in the practice of "sick-nursing." Her observation in 1893 echoes a familiar one nurses could make today: "a good nurse of twenty years ago had not to do the twentieth part of what she is required by her physician or surgeon to do now" (*p. 186*). Nightingale further acknowledged that an increase in the list of procedures required of the "sick-nurse" must be matched by an increase in the length and quality of training to ensure the "sick-nurse's" ability to provide excellent care.

Nightingale recalled another of her lifelong themes, the value of experiential learning. She reminded her readers that the ability to create and maintain healthy conditions, both in family and in community, can be learned only through an extensive immersion in these same environments. To illustrate her point, Nightingale first cited the prevailing opinion of some "eminent medical officers." She quoted these "officers" who had claimed that "ambulance, nursing and fashionable hygienic lectures of the day" would be sufficient community health education. She discounted this "eminent" opinion that a "sprinkle" of community experience would be enough on-site training. On the contrary, her own hard-earned experience made clear that lectures alone are "not instruction and can never be education" (*p. 191*). Building on this point, she reminded her readers that nursing's focus on people is precisely the reason why nursing can be taught only in the people environment (e.g., the bedside, the clinic, the home, and the community). She also cautioned that while books and lectures can be valuable accessories, they are never a substitute for the experience of being with the people for whose care nurses are training. "Otherwise, what is in the book, stays in the book" (*p. 184*).

These themes are familiar to everyone who has read Nightingale's early work. They are reminiscent of her oft-quoted preface to *Notes on Nursing*: "I do not pretend to teach her (the reader) how, I ask her to teach herself, and for this purpose I venture to give her some hints." This value placed upon experiential learning is a well-known legacy of Nightingale and is embodied in almost every aspect of modern nursing practice. Nightingale reminded her readers yet again that if persistent difficulties are to be found, nurses must look first to discovering any faults in their nursing care before they blame a disease for the problem.

With these points in mind, Nightingale saw nursing training as learning how to bring caring excellence to recovery, healing, and health—to "observe exactly, understand, do, to know exactly, and to tell, exactly." She reemphasized the importance of nursing endeavors, reiterating that nursing practice encompasses "such stupendous issues as life and death, health and disease" (1893, *p. 187*).

Excellence in Training Environments

Using the hospital setting as another case in point, Nightingale also took the time to cover the factors that create excellent nursing training environments. First, she called for an administrator who had already mastered nursing as a discipline. She pointed out that this nursing administrator must be granted the authority to act independently on behalf of an administrative committee or hospital board. She cautioned that a good administrator must be able, together with this group, to consult with physicians for their opinions. However, she stressed that this same administrator must also be encouraged to act independent of the physicians' disease-treatment mandate. Nightingale held that nursing's mandate for health and healing must be empowered at these levels. Second, nursing training should include a familiarity with medical environments, and nursing students should also learn from teachers versed in medical disciplines. Third, supervision of training in all aspects of the care of patients should come from nursing leaders who have themselves received excellent nursing training and experience. She saw the importance of the principle that nursing administrators and staff should follow a well-defined chain of command, first within their own ranks, then to the hospital's officers. Nightingale's many years of experience working with and consulting for the British army can be detected in these comments (B. Dossey, 2000a).

Nightingale returned to the garden analogy that she used several times in the essay. Referring to the skill of creating a garden, she asserted that a garden's beauty is not ensured simply because of its size, nor is a garden's quality guaranteed just because of the length of time it has been growing. Likewise, neither the length of nurses' training time nor the size of a training institution guaranteed teaching excellence in and of itself. She advocated nursing's distinct premise, to nurture "the best possible conditions for Nature to restore or to preserve health—to prevent or to cure disease or injury," as the best foundation on which to build excellence in nursing training.

Concerns for "Registration" and Nursing Excellence

Nightingale stated her often misunderstood concerns for the "registration" of nurses. She opposed registration as an artificial and coldly administrative way to place people in nameless registers. She questioned registration's ability to certify nursing excellence from a distant bureaucracy. Her concern was that the human face and human heart would be lost in the triviality and anonymity of office registers. She was also concerned with the regulation of nursing registration standards, asking "who is to guarantee our guarantors?" (*p. 197*).

She also laid out her concerns about adequate registration examinations. To make her point, Nightingale paraphrased others who had remarked that since plumbers, carpenters, and engineers can be given examinations to certify their proficiency, nursing competencies could also be measured by certification exams alone. Returning to one of her favorite themes, Nightingale reminded her readers that while other professions have to do with electrical and gravitational forces, nursing has to do with "living bodies" and "living minds," for "life is not vegetable life, nor mere animal life, but it is human life—with living, that is conscious forces" (*p. 195*). She frequently returned to the topic of registration. Her comments provide additional insight into Nightingale's famous, and perhaps to today's readers baffling, refusal to support the official registration of nurses in her time. She worried that if nurses were simply "registered" with bureaucracies to ensure the quality of our work, they could lose the humanity essential to excellent service for sickness and health.

Caring Excellence Nurses Give to Themselves and Each Other

Nightingale also used her essay as a forum to make sure that nurses remembered to care for themselves and for each other. She asked her readers a question from the core of her vision: how will nurses hold that "sense of keeping up to the highest attainable in tone and character?" (*p. 194*). She further asked them to consider what would be the best way to make sure that this level of "calling" becomes a standard of nursing practice? How are nurses to be sure that they choose and sustain their careers from the depth of their hearts and their souls?

Nightingale's answer derives from her awareness that caring excellence begins within the caregivers themselves. She returned to her own sense of that esprit de corps or "bond of sympathy" that can occur within the ranks of nurses in their place of work and in their homes and gathering places. In Nightingale's time, nurses were most often single women. She herself had lived with this choice for decades and knew firsthand of its emotional hardship (B. Dossey, 2000a). With her remarks about "bonds of sympathy," she emphasized the importance of single women living together in places where they could share the camaraderie of being each other's family. She saw the value of strong bonds between nurses, supporting each other, and sharing a sense of collective space in their communities. She described places where fully trained nurses and students might reside together, and where private duty nurses could return to a "common home between their assignments" (*pp. 193–194*).

In this context, Nightingale also developed her theme of "high home helps" (*p. 193*), defining these as necessary emotional and spiritual environments that should be provided in "constant sympathy" for and between nurses, to help them to meet the challenges of their work. For emphasis, she returned to what she had said earlier, "man cannot live by bread alone, still less woman" (*p. 196*).

Nightingale continued by adding her concerns that nurses would only be able to achieve excellent education and caring practice standards by making sure that "every sick person [would] have the best chance at recovery." She repeated that the hospital approach to illness—however effective it might seem—would only be an "intermediate stage of civilization" (*p. 198*). She believed that the creation of newer methods for support in home environments was the best way to provide for the "sick population" as a whole. She envisioned home-based "sick-nursing" roles as a major component of this eventual outcome.

Nightingale believed that nursing in all forms—in hospitals, on private duty, and in support of health promotion at community levels—would deteriorate if its esprit de corps and sense of "calling" were lost. She wrote that in addition to wages, nurses need "wise and loving" nurturing between assignments. She expressed concern that otherwise nurses would look to "*what* they can get" rather than what they can give to the people while at work. She cautioned, too, about nurses being "put upon" (*p. 194*). She warned of a time when nurses would give of their caring, but not receive in return the care and concern they also deserve from others—from their families, from their wider employment and professional support systems, and, perhaps most importantly, from a grateful society.

Caring Excellence = Health Education in the Community

Nightingale described prototype educational projects that were already operational in several rural districts in Britain, in which women called "health-missioners" provided detailed instruction to village mothers. She included information about sanitation for persons and homes, including clothes and bedding. She paid particular attention to the health of prenatal and postnatal mothers and their infants. This community-based training provided village-based lectures, supplemented with personal, interactive instruction in the homes of the people involved. These kinds of instruction were "conversation[s]" emphasizing sanitary household conditions and essential personal health principles with specific "reference to skin, to circulation, [and] to digestion." She also recommended lessons in "what to do in emergencies, or for accidents—particularly in the case of small children and infants—before medical help arrives," (1893, *pp. 192–194*).

To make this "health-visiting" education available to her readers, Nightingale included a comprehensive addendum at the end of the essay. This addendum described the responsibilities of "District Nurses" and training for "Health Missioners." She also included a "Syllabus of Lectures to Health Missioners" that these practitioners could in turn share with all women in their communities. This syllabus contained a thorough overview of items to be considered as the women themselves maintained health within their homes, with "extra lectures" added to address emergencies (*pp. 199–205*).

Nightingale's main concern was the effective application of these topics to the places and situations where these efforts were needed, particularly in home environments. To this end, she kept specific outcomes in mind. She urged her readers to ask, "did they [women in the community] practice the lecture in their own homes thereafter, did they really apply themselves to household health and the means of improving it?" She reminded nurses about the value of their involvement in community settings: "is anything better worth practicing for mothers than the health of their families?" (*pp. 191–192*).

Nightingale Anticipates Holism and Transdisciplinarity

Her first few paragraphs demonstrate that Nightingale anticipated contemporary transdisciplinary and holistic approaches. Though she began, even in her title, by making a distinction between "sick-nursing" and "health-nursing," she reflected her sense of inclusiveness by quickly clarifying that "both kinds of nursing are to put us in the best possible conditions for Nature to restore or to preserve health." By defining health as "not only to be well, but to be able to use well every power we have" (*p. 186*), she demonstrated her commitment to both artistic and scientific approaches, and her commitment to the holism of nursing and caring.

In contrast to what some other scholars have said of Nightingale (e.g., Reverby, 1987), that she understood only the "art" of nursing, she opens her essay with her own transdisciplinary perspective: "A new art and a new science has been created since and within the last forty years" (*p. 184*). Although earlier in her life she had described nursing as "one of the fine arts, I almost said, the finest of the Fine arts" (1868, p. 326), by 1893 she had also learned and practiced the science of statistics to a remarkable degree. By this time, she had authored more than 10 significant, voluminous reports that included detailed analyses of health outcomes and solid, evidence-based recommendations for improvements to health in a number of areas (B. Dossey, 2000a).

Holistic Issues

Nightingale described the transdisciplinary nature of the calling of nursing as the ability to synthesize a wide range of talents. Among these were vigilance, skilled knowledge of technique, intellect, the courage to meet life's difficulties head-on, and a wide range of passions that encompass a devotion to serving life. She also cited nurses' need for a balanced mix of detachment and tenderness, and called for their commitment to the best in life without being self-righteous or self-satisfied with a fixed or immovable standard. She saw their practices as holistic in nature and urged them to maintain a "threefold interest" in physical issues: "a technical (practical interest) in the patient's care"; mental issues: "an intellectual interest in the case"; and spiritual issues: that "high calling" necessary for a heartfelt interest in the person being served (*p. 195*).

Nightingale valued the breadth of nursing, noting the danger of nursing becoming only a mental endeavor of theory, "taught by book and lecture" alone (*p. 194*). Nightingale herself had mastered a thorough classical education, equivalent to today's advanced graduate study. She applied herself to the knowledge and application of many academic disciplines. However, she has been criticized for being "against advanced preparation for nurses" (Sullivan, 2002). Nightingale stated that "book-learning" was never adequate in and of itself. "No theories, no book-learning can ever dispense with this [experience] or be useful for anything, except as a stepping stone" (*p. 197*). She particularly felt that experience was even more important for the issues of health. She reminded her readers that academic approaches are useful only to bring intelligence to the practical work. She believed that mental disciplines should always be used to serve practical situations. "Neither can it [nursing] be taught by lectures or books, though these are valuable accessories if used as such; otherwise, what is in the book stays in the book" (*p. 184*).

Returning to her gardening metaphor, Nightingale asked her readers if books describing the purpose of "artificial and natural manures" were enough to make someone into a horticultural expert. She also saw a danger of being satisfied with naming nursing problems and considering that this "diagnosis" would become an end in itself. She warned about spending too much time in understanding a disease as it presents itself, rather than focusing on cultivating the holistic "resource[s] or intelligence" to mitigate disease effects. She added that there are "a thousand and one" holistic ways to apply the resources that nurses wield, "even when there is no cure" (*pp. 194–195*).

Nightingale lamented that what we now term holistic health perspectives—and how to work with them, rather than against them—are not "*practically* taught" (*p. 190*). She explained that in her time, there had not been adequate study of how the body is designed holistically to work with the mind, and how these relationships can be healthy or unhealthy. She also shared her desire to apply the knowledge of holistic determinants to keeping children healthy.

Socioeconomic Issues

Nightingale cited the importance of socioeconomic issues as well. She cautioned that many negative health determinants are related to poor community infrastructure and design, and to poorly prioritized administrative and bureaucratic choices. She further demonstrated her familiarity with broader transdisciplinary determinants of health by offering an example from the workplace. Anticipating the language of the late 20th century, she cautioned employers that "health is their only capital," and that any and all means should be employed to secure the "prime agents of health" for their employees. The broader meaning of "capital" beyond a monetary definition, and proposals to include environmental, social, and human capital in the assessment of worth, have only recently been considered by economists and other related policymakers (Wright, 1995). Nightingale stated her opinion that workplace health was worth employees' efforts to unionize and "almost worth" (*p. 191*) striking for.

Nightingale mentioned another socioeconomic health determinant, this time from her familiarity with the education sector, citing crowded school conditions where "children's epidemics have their origins." She rebuked those who would attribute "current contagion" to a mere "something being much about this year" and "in God's hands." She emphasized that humans have been created to do God's work in the world: "so far as we know, He has put them [the children at risk] into our own [hands]" (*p. 191*). She regretted that "the chief 'epidemic' that reigns this year is 'folly.'" Moving beyond this pointed aside, Nightingale immediately brought her readers to the core of her wish that an informed and caring citizenry become actively involved in concerns about health: "You must form public opinion … officials will only do what you make them. *You*, the public, must make them do what you want" (1893, *p. 191*).

Continuing with her socioeconomic theme, Nightingale warned that allowing competition, the selfish approach of "each man for himself," to dominate our choices about health care would ultimately create a situation where the "devil [is] against us all." We are told that competition is a necessary evil, but selfish priorities are "the enemy of health." In fact, she continued, the "antidote" for this selfishness would be collaborative efforts to accomplish "all that makes life useful, healthy and happy" (*p. 197*).

Discussing the full continuum of individual and collective issues, Nightingale again admonished nurses to keep their own socioeconomic priorities straight—to not "look upon patients as made for nurses, but upon nurses as made for patients." Otherwise, she warned, nursing could become merely a retail service similar to that of being a milliner or a women's hat dispenser. She conceded that this retail approach to the job would provide "a life of freedom, with an interesting employment, for a few years." But she returned to her conviction that nursing must be seen and practiced as an in-depth, holistic way of life. She worried that the practice of nursing would become a superficial mode for doing "as little as you can and amus[ing] yourself as much as you can." Making sure nurses understood their responsibilities in this respect, she also warned of a time when they would feel emotionally and financially unsupported, undervalued, not receiving back what they give to society (*p. 194*).

Nightingale's Vision Detailed "Unity in Community"

Nightingale laid the foundation for a far-reaching understanding that the "health of the unity is the health of the community. Unless you have the health of the unity there is no community health." She stated that the notion of "independence" was an illusion that did not promote health. She urged her readers to promote health by forming partnerships because, "As far as we are successful, our success lies in combination." To illustrate this point, Nightingale mentioned the Chicago World's Fair as an excellent example of interdependence between representatives from "all parts of the world, to prove the dependence of man on man." She credited the people of the United States and praised the Columbian Exposition as a model that has "taught [these collaborative lessons] to the whole world" (*p. 197*).

Art and Discipline

In true transdisciplinary fashion, Nightingale used her knowledge of the artist's creativity to picture her vision for nurses, as she returned to her theme of nursing as art. She described painting as the mixing of colors through knowledge, practice, and experience, furthering her premise that the practice of nursing should be valued by nurses as well as by everyone else as a superb art because "you have to do with living bodies and living minds, and feelings of both body and mind" (*p. 195*).

Nightingale also cast her definition of discipline in broad moral terms. She mentioned a nursing educator whom she regarded highly, saying that true discipline embraces a holism of human experience: the full, evolving development of physical, moral, and spiritual faculties. She also saw discipline as enabling humans to gain a greater understanding of the workings of "Nature's laws," which she believed were synonymous with "God's laws." In her view, discipline was not only the ability to bring precision, method, order, and stewardship to physical surroundings, but also the ability to bring emotional grace and calm, even to harried situations. For Nightingale, discipline encompassed the ability to "have patience with our circumstances and ourselves" (*p. 187*).

Nightingale also conceived of discipline as an ability to continue to learn, becoming yet more finely tuned to the service of humanity. She defined discipline in holistic terms as the ability to be emotionally centered and focused on the quality of what can be accomplished rather than becoming overly anxious to see results. She shared her belief that all of these facets of discipline are God's gifts to provide people with the "patience and steadfastness" (*p. 187*) that life requires.

Nightingale also developed the theme of nursing's integrity. She acknowledged that rising technical demands were already being placed on nurses by physicians and by their employers and that these demands would, in turn, require us to uphold more rigorous nursing practice standards. She underscored her premise that these same standards, however they might be instituted and maintained, will never replace the individual integrity of each nurse, and their practice and life experience. She illustrated this point by describing the wide disparity often seen, even in her time, between theoretical education and the ability to test well on exams—and a nurse's capability to deliver applied theory to excellent caring for those in need.

Creating Heaven on Earth

Near the conclusion of the essay, Nightingale returned to one of her most cherished themes, that of working to bring vision into reality, heaven to earth, by paying close attention to the details of health. She reminded her readers of the issues that would always be at stake: the "superstitions of centuries" and the "bad habits of generations" that will never be "cured" with academic pursuits isolated from the real world of suffering. With "every stroke of the work done, there should be felt to be an illustration of what has been learnt elsewhere—a driving home, by experience not to be forgotten, what has been gained by knowledge too easily forgotten" (*p. 197*).

Nightingale's clear recognition of and commitment to the spiritual component of human experience is evident in her repeated references to a "calling." She saw a calling as "our work to satisfy the high idea of what is *right and best.*" She contrasted this "high idea" with a prevalent shallow notion of doing something just "because we shall be found out if we don't do it." She compared her sense of calling to that "enthusiasm" found in proud craftsmanship, and to the creation of beautiful art forms and the work of artisans—"from a shoemaker to a sculptor" (*p. 193*).

Nightingale alluded to her often-quoted statement that nursing itself was one of the finest forms of art ever created (1868). She emphasized the importance of practicing nursing as a holistic "art," so finely honed that it is valued both by those who practice it and by everyone who benefits from it. She again evoked the artisan metaphor: "now, the nurse has to do not with shoes or with marble, but with living human beings" (*p. 193*).

Nightingale saw calling as that assurance needed against the "dangers" that had arisen during her watch over the beginning years of modern nursing. Already, in these first decades of her field, she was concerned that nursing had become "stereotyped" into a structure that could not, because of its already set patterns, grow and evolve from a spiritual core. In her time, nurses had "scarcely crossed the threshold of uncivilized civilization in nursing" (*p. 198*).

Nightingale fervently hoped that nurses would fully understand that they are, in all of their endeavors, working with the support of higher, Divine powers. She allowed her own deep spiritual convictions, and her own profound sense of being so sustained, to shine through her discourse. She referred to the Divine Spirit as the "Supreme Moral Governor" who supports their endeavors—"envelop[ing]" nurses "round" with the power they need to succeed (*p. 198*).

Referring again to the dangers of focusing on fashion and of making money for its own sake, Nightingale urged nurses to maintain their spiritual motivation to work in the service of the Divine. She saw this higher motivation as the only way to avoid these dangers. She also warned of the danger of becoming too involved in "personal mortifications" about the difficulties nurses faced. However, she also warned against taking too much pride in their proficiency, in their training schools, in the achievements of their colleagues (especially physicians), or in the reputation of their hospitals. Nightingale painted a picture of the "highest grade" which a nurse can achieve, that of "graduating" to become a "fellow-worker with the Supreme Good, with God" (1893, *p. 198*).

Modern readers may take issue with Nightingale's frequent references to her own spiritual perspectives. Her language, taken out of the context of a wider understanding of her life and her universal approaches to spirituality, can sound as though she is proselytizing only one spiritual way for all nurses to follow. Instead, Nightingale's intent was to refer to the timelessness and profundity of nursing's relevance to humanity, from whatever spiritual perspective individual nurses might bring to their practice.

Remembering the importance of the "calling" of nursing and the caliber of nurses themselves, Nightingale returned to her visions for the health of humanity. She referred to her time as a "threshold" for better approaches to come. "In the future which I shall not see, for I am old, may a better way be opened! May the methods by which every infant, every human being will have the best chance at health ... be learned and practiced." Touching a time and space beyond her own, Nightingale directed her vision across the boundaries of any one lifetime, or any one way of approaching the challenges of keeping humanity healthy. "May we hope that, when we are all dead and gone, leaders will arise who have been personally experienced in the hard, practical work, the difficulties and the joys of organizing nursing reforms, and who will lead far beyond anything we have done!" (*pp. 198–199*).

Nightingale closed with an analogy that is often used today, that of the atom as a single unit of the whole. In words quintessentially characteristic of her own mystical social activism, Nightingale returned to her sense of the value of nurses and women—and for our time, caregivers of both genders, and of all disciplines—as conscious, effective "atoms" in a vast ministry of service to the "Highest." She concluded her last major essay with a vision of heaven on earth: seeing each person as a beautifully unique "atom," but never alone in our individual and collective efforts to make a difference in our time (*p. 199*).

From Nightingale's Time to Our Own

Based upon her long career, which spanned a broad scope of nursing practice, Florence Nightingale wrote "Sick-Nursing and Health-Nursing" to share her insights with the world at the 1893 International Columbian Exposition. At that time, women were filled with hope. They saw the World's Fair as a signpost of acknowledgment for their past contributions as well as a beacon for their budding participation in society outside their homes. Nightingale's themes reflected this hope. As she wrote, she thought about nursing's past and envisioned nursing's future. Using this sense of history, she spoke of the timeless, common needs of humanity for the relief of suffering as well as for a healthy life. She saw nursing as pivotal to these needs, and nurses as major contributors to the world's well-being. She spoke of the challenges she had faced, knowing that many of her concerns about the field of nursing, and for nurses themselves, would remain relevant to the challenges of the future.

A century later, we have looked back at Nightingale's perspectives in the context of nursing since her time. We have noted the contemporary relevance of many of her insights as well as the tensions inherent within them. Many of these tensions remain with nurses today.

For instance, Nightingale knew that women in her time were just beginning to fill roles outside their homes, and she discussed the tension between obedience and autonomy. She knew her culture emphasized obedience to the authority of men, but she had experienced the autonomy women can gain when they preserve their own perspectives and contribute to the world from the value of their own experience. This tension between obedience to the authority of physicians and hospital administrators and the autonomy nurses gain from the knowledge and wisdom of their own discipline continues in nursing today. Nightingale noted the importance of following physicians' orders when their expertise provided needed knowledge. However, she emphasized that nursing knowledge and nursing perspectives should be the primary, autonomous guide for nursing practice.

Nursing historians have sometimes criticized Nightingale's concept of duty. In their view, she was limited by a culture in which women felt duty-bound to their fathers, husbands, families, and homes. But Nightingale did not see nursing as a duty to be transferred from home, father, husband, and family to hospital, doctor, and patient. She saw nursing as her "must"—her Spirit's commitment to humanity. Likewise, in Nightingale's time, the word profession was not elevated to the status it holds today. She noted the tension between profession as just a job and nursing as a calling. From her own profound sense of this calling, she urged her readers to remember the importance of committing one's spirit to the practical needs of humanity.

She also anticipated one of the key healthcare issues of our time: the tension between the money to be made and the caring service to be provided. She worried that money would take priority over caring, and she knew that if this were to happen, both nurses and patients would pay the price. She was concerned that nurses themselves would think only of what money could buy them and of themselves as retailers of health care. Acknowledging that money was important to everyone, she saw caring as more important still. She urged nurses to see their contributions as far more significant than the work of a seller of hats or the maker of shoes. She saw nursing as greater than the work of a master sculptor in service to the beauty of marble. She saw nursing as service to the beauty of "living bodies and living minds."

Nightingale saw two intertwining roles for nurses: the promotion of healing and health, and the alleviation of suffering from sickness and injury. She saw the tension between these two roles, and worried that a focus on sickness would take priority over a focus on health. She carried this theme throughout her career, seeing the focus on sickness as primarily medicine's domain. She acknowledged that nurses should continue to provide excellent care for the sick, but she saw nursing's focus on health and the return to health as the critical difference between nursing and medicine.

Nightingale's "Sick-Nursing and Health-Nursing" conveyed to the people of her time her life's knowledge of this field and her calling. It also displayed her conviction that nursing was and would always be critical to the people of the world. Given our 20th-century experience and our hopes for the 21st century, nurses can still benefit from Nightingale's wide range of insights. She looked to our own time with fervent hope, and saw nurses as leaders achieving gains for human health far beyond what she had accomplished. She knew this would be a challenging task. She knew that the earth would always need the heaven that people who care can bring with their caring.

Pentimento

The 1893 Columbian Exposition World's Fair:

A Nightingale Essay Is Forgotten in Controversy

Deva-Marie Beck

The Columbian Exposition World's Fair was convened in Chicago in 1893. The name "Columbian Exposition" referred to the Fair's theme, which highlighted 400 years of human progress—between Columbus's time in 1492 and the event itself. Here, for the first time, women's contributions to the benefit of humankind were honored with specific exhibits, events, and meetings. Many of these were convened at an official exhibition building, christened "Women's Hall." This building was designed by a woman architect—again a first for women—and landscaped with a surrounding moat and flower gardens.

Aware of this theme and its significance for women, Lady Angela Burdett-Coutts, a prominent British philanthropist, was one of the British representatives to the Fair. In this position, Baroness Burdett-Coutts submitted—at the behest of Queen Victoria—the Royal British Commission's contribution in the form of an anthology titled *Woman's Mission: A Series of Congress Papers on the Philanthropic Work of Women by Eminent Writers*. One of the "eminent writers" collected in this work was Burdett-Coutts' friend and colleague, Florence Nightingale, who submitted her essay titled "Sick-Nursing and Health-Nursing" to the anthology. Written in Nightingale's 73rd year, "Sick-Nursing and Health-Nursing" represented the culmination of her lifetime of experience, study, research, and analysis, and specifically encompassed her vision for the future of both nursing and health promotion. (It is reproduced in this book on page 287.)

Much earlier, in 1860, Nightingale had written *Notes on Nursing: What It Is and What It Is Not,* in which she developed her initial nursing experience for a general audience. Upon its release, this little book immediately became a best-seller and remained in popular print throughout her lifetime. With the broader topics of "Sick-Nursing and Health-Nursing," Nightingale understood that her audience could be larger still. Knowing that the Chicago Exposition would convene the first-ever official international convocation honoring the contributions of women, Nightingale joined Lady Burdett-Coutts in a British contribution they believed would have wide appeal. In her essay itself, Nightingale specifically recognized the Fair, and the American hosting of the Fair, as new developments that promised broader collaborations "to be taught to the whole world."

The most controversial feature of Nightingale's 1893 essay was her firm stance against the registration of nurses. Nightingale did not believe that confirming a registration number—even from a thorough exam of book-learning—would be enough to give nurses what they needed to accomplish their challenging work or to assure the public of the quality of nursing care. From this position, Nightingale solidly opposed the nursing registration issue and used her considerable fame and respect to block it. Other stakeholders—particularly hospital administrators who stood to gain from having their own controls over the nursing workforce—stood with her against the issue of nursing registration for their own business-driven reasons.

At this same Columbian Exposition, an International Nursing Congress was also convened for the first time in history. Here, the very issue of nursing registration became the key focus of discussion. This Congress was attended by several influential nursing leaders who were politically savvy to the most critical issues of their times. They viewed registration as an imperfect, but significant way for nurses to secure their

Woman's Building From *Conkey Complete Guide to the World's Columbian Exposition*, *W.B. Conkey Company: Chicago, 1893.*

"It is fitting that the close of the nineteenth century should focus and illustrate in definite form, the share which women have taken in its development."

Lady Angela Burdett-Coutts
Editor, Woman's Mission
XXX
Royal British Commission
Columbian Exposition, 1893

Baroness Burdett-Coutts quote
From the private collection of Deva-Marie Beck

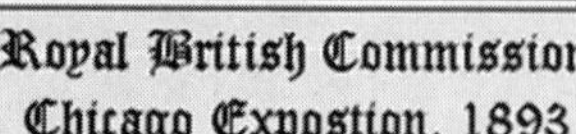
Royal British Commission
Chicago Expostion, 1893

WOMAN'S MISSION

A SERIES OF CONGRESS PAPERS ON THE

PHILANTHROPIC WORK OF WOMEN

BY EMINENT WRITERS

Woman's Mission
From the private collection of Deva-Marie Beck

own collective control over their professional destinies. Notable to these efforts was the leadership of British nursing activist Ethel Gordon Fenwick, former matron of St. Bartholomew's Hospital in London. Since 1887, Fenwick had crusaded to register nurses in Britain because she believed this approach was in the public's and nurses' best interests. Because of these efforts, Fenwick was already well known in Britain as Nightingale's leading opponent on this issue.

While en route to the Exposition, Fenwick stopped first in Baltimore to gain the backing of Isabelle Hampton (later Hampton-Robb), who was a Bellevue graduate and who had become the superintendent of the original nursing training school at Johns Hopkins Hospital. Hampton joined Fenwick in Chicago and gave a keynote address envisioning uniform standards for nursing education. Hampton was the only woman to officially speak at the Fair. Lavinia Dock, also a Bellevue graduate and Hampton's assistant at Johns Hopkins, attended the Exposition as well. Living long into the 20th century, Lavinia Dock would go on to speak, even into the late 1940s, of the pivotal 1890s and of the significance of their original meeting at the Chicago Exposition as the "seedling" of the nursing profession's further growth into contemporary times.

In a 1949 edition of her work, Isabelle Hampton noted her admiration for the depth and breadth of Nightingale's contributions in nursing education. She also expressed respect for Nightingale's work by corresponding with her about developments in improved preparation for nurses, particularly nursing educators, and for better quality patient care. Ethel Gordon Fenwick later proposed and helped to establish the International Council of Nurses (ICN) in 1899. In this wider sphere, Fenwick dramatically honored the contributions of Nightingale by actively supporting the creation of the ICN's Florence Nightingale International Foundation.

But, in 1893, the urgency to accomplish a platform that would provide them with some new measure of control over nursing's future—which Fenwick, Hampton, and Dock established during that time—won the day at the Chicago Exposition. Ironically, these women were in an excellent position to actively address

Nightingale's wider concerns for the significant impact that both "sick-nurses" *and* "health-nurses" could have on human well-being. Instead, they were trapped in the limitations of their times.

As representatives of the emerging nursing leadership of the 20th century, Fenwick, Hampton-Robb, and Dock saw the "trees" of their understandable but necessarily short-term concerns for control and professional turf, and they acted decisively on this perspective. Nightingale saw the wider "forest" scope of human health as a much larger, longer-term, and ultimately more-pressing concern. She expressed her ideas in depth in her almost-forgotten essay, "Sick-Nursing and Health-Nursing," ideas that were substantively lost in the 1893 scuffle. And although nurses now have a registration process by which to continue some measure of control over our profession, larger issues—about the health of humanity, which Nightingale believed to be far more significant—remain.

Columbian Exposition
From *A Week at the Fair: Illustrating Exhibits and Wonders of the World's Columbian Exposition.*
Rand McNally & Co.: Chicago, 1893.

"Upon womankind the national health — as far as the household goes — depends."

Florence Nightingale

"Sick-Nursing and Health-Nursing"
submitted in 1893 to the
Columbian Exposition
Chicago World's Fair

Nightingale quote
From the private collection of Deva-Marie Beck

(*Sources:* Burdett-Coutts, 1893a; Nightingale, 1860a; Seymer, 1954)

Pentimento

Health Determinants Now:
A Perspective for Health Promotion

Deva-Marie Beck

The term *health determinants* represents a comprehensive perspective recently established by the international health promotion community. Health determinants are those factors, conditions, and environments that affect health by supporting or detracting from it. This concept has evolved over the past several decades—within a growing network of health promotion educators, researchers, and health policy advisers—through formal discussions, regional and global conferences, and the establishment of an international body of literature.

Beyond either seeing health only as the absence of disease or attempting to create health merely by treating disease after it has occurred, the health determinants lens identifies those negative conditions leading to disease and positive conditions supporting healing and improving health. Examples of positive health determinants include adequate supply of fresh food and clean water, strong maternal nurturing of infants and children, positive social networks, education and the conditions that encourage learning, thriving economic conditions, and natural environments.

Conversely, examples of negative health determinants that contribute to the onset of disease include secondhand smoke and air pollution, lack of nourishing food, stagnant water, and impoverished conditions, particularly for women and their infants and children. Other negative examples include isolation, loneliness and the emotions of hatred and fear, ignorance and the factors that block learning, distressed conditions found in places ravaged by natural disasters such as storms or earthquakes, and man-made disasters such as toxic spills and war-torn areas.

Recent research has identified that the international shortage of nurses directly affects health. A lack of nurses significantly contributes to increased nosocomial infections, untoward drug reactions, and even patient mortality. While these findings are no surprise to nurses themselves—particularly to those who work in hospitals—this shortage has become a significant marker for an improved understanding about the connections between environment, health, *and* the value of the people who sustain hospital caring environments. One of the key roles of the nursing discipline is to monitor and maintain quality conditions conducive to recovery and healing. Without the ongoing interventions of excellent nursing care, disease processes are more likely to be exacerbated. This example can be seen from a health determinants perspective. A significant global nursing shortage can be identified as a widespread negative health determinant. The global presence of quality nursing care is a positive health determinant for all of humanity.

The origins of the health determinants paradigm are usually ascribed to the work of Thomas McKeown—a British philosopher of social medicine—who identified that declining disease and death rates were more directly related to improvements in factors such as nutrition, family planning, and adequate housing, rather than to medical interventions. This insight informed the work of Marc Lalonde, a Canadian health minister who submitted a related health policy white paper for the Canadian government in 1974. The release of the Lalonde report became a watershed event for Canadian and international health promotion, contributing to an emerging global consensus about the value of health promotion efforts and the significance of convening the first international health conference at Alma Ata in Kazakhstan in 1978.

All of these early discussions called for a broader understanding of health and for the establishment of transdisciplinary collaborations—that would include, but not be limited to, traditional healthcare professionals—between many disciplines addressing human well-being. These disciplines have included educators, community service and city leaders, and people working in architecture and urban planning, transportation, parks and recreation, law enforcement, and waste disposal.

The worldwide Healthy Cities movement—birthed in the 1980s in Berkeley and Toronto in collaboration with the European Regional Office of the World Health Organization—is a thriving outgrowth of the health determinants perspective. One example of a Healthy Cities project is the New Mexico Partnership for Healthier Communities, a collaborative effort between community service groups, educators, and tribal representatives serving eight sovereign indigenous nations. This collaboration has significantly improved the health of New Mexicans by reducing the negative health determinants of domestic violence and substance abuse through increasing positive health determinant options with improved educational opportunities and nurturing a stronger sense of family and community.

Although the health determinants approach resonates with the premises of the nursing discipline, contemporary nurses have rarely been involved in this recent larger-scale health determinants paradigm. Throughout most of the 20th century, the nursing lens has focused primarily on influencing the health of individuals with excellent care in support of the biomedical model in the treatment of disease. Nurses have also been actively involved in promoting individual health by encouraging lifestyle changes such as smoking cessation and the reduction of cardiac risk factors.

This narrower lens on the health of individuals has kept nurses out of the health determinants discourse that predominantly focuses on wider community, regional, and global conditions. However, throughout nursing's history, and widely discussed in nursing literature, nurses have noted and intervened to address these same health determinants on smaller scales. Nurses note, for instance, how the lack of family support, loss of jobs, lack of knowledge, and high-stress environments, such as impoverished neighborhoods, negatively affect the health of individuals. Likewise, nursing practice actively encourages fresh air, increased exercise, and adequate nutrition and hydration.

Nurses also acknowledge the value of nurturing specific caring and compassion environments, maternal-child bonding, and family and social-support networks. The

Nightingale's Positive Health Determinants

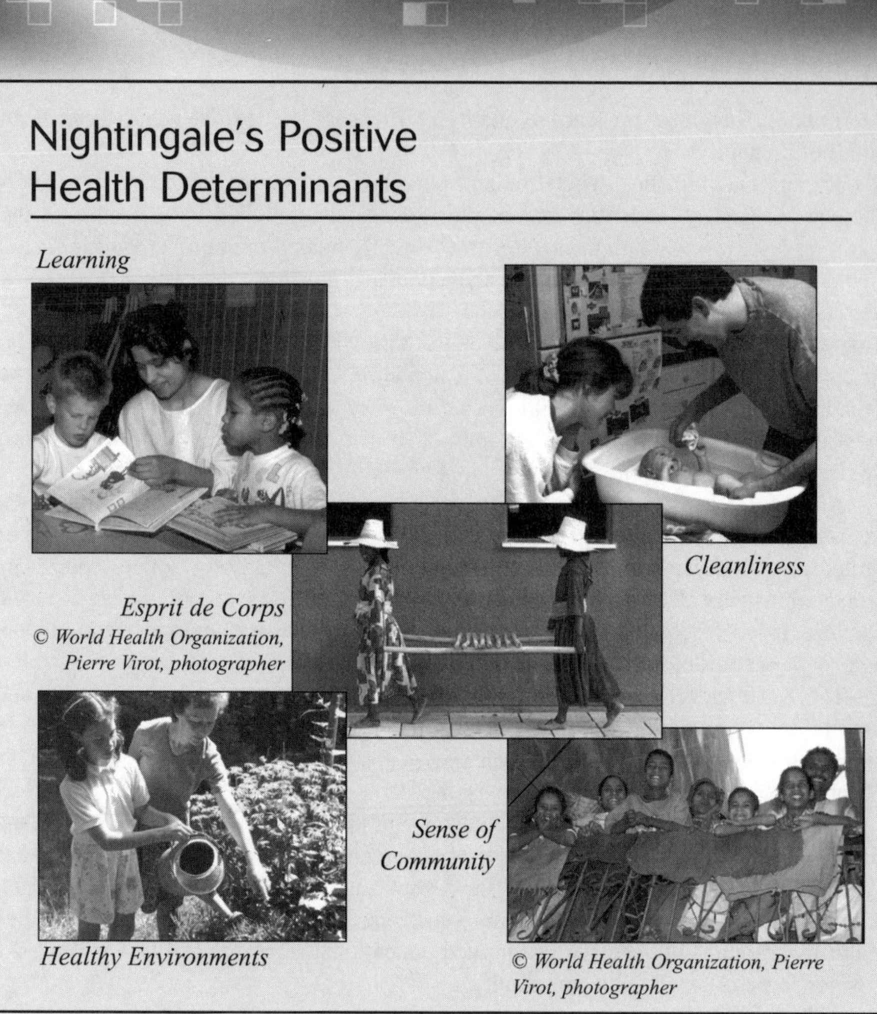

Learning

Cleanliness

Esprit de Corps
© World Health Organization, Pierre Virot, photographer

Sense of Community

Healthy Environments

© World Health Organization, Pierre Virot, photographer

practice of nursing is based on the facilitation of patient learning and improved understanding of health issues, across the lifespan. Nurses see all of these positive health determinants as key elements for the success of recovery from disease and for the improved ability to thrive with chronic conditions. Because of these well-established nursing premises, nurses are ideally suited—if they could and would take the opportunity to widen their lenses and join collaborations like those described above—to actively participate in establishing positive health determinants and mitigating negative health determinants on a larger scale.

Likewise, the existing health determinants literature often notes that—because health promotion discourse is often discussed at wider policy levels and on the scale of entire populations—the detailed application of health determinants theory often goes unrealized in actual practice. With the active participation of nurses—as those health professionals who have practical caring applications well established—applied partnerships to decrease negative health determinants and increase positive health determinants could have a major impact on human health in the 21st century.

(*Sources:* Edwards, 1999; Kickbusch & Quick, 1998; Lalonde, 1998; McKeown, 1979; Norris & Pittman, 2000; Quinn, 2002; Rafael, 1999; Wallerstein, 1992)

Directions and Reflections

Directions for Future Research

1. Investigate one or two of Nightingale's lesser-known writings to determine its relevance and implications for nurses, patients, and the promotion of public health. Nightingale wrote a great deal, much of which has not been explored for relevance to contemporary nursing and healthcare issues.
2. Compare and contrast women's issues in 19th-century, early 20th-century, and modern cultures. Compare attitudes of nurses from each of these eras. Identify common themes and explore the relevance of these themes to the future of the nursing discipline.
3. Investigate the connections between health and socioeconomic issues from the patient's perspective. For example, query levels of the self-reported, subjective sense of health in correlation with levels of economic well-being. Compare these reports on the individual, micro level with findings gleaned from macro-level, socioeconomic studies.
4. Investigate the notions of "nursing as science" and "nursing as art" as understood by nursing clinicians, educators, administrators, and policymakers. Identify common themes and relevance to nurse recruitment and retention.

Reflections on Florence Nightingale's Tenets: Global Action

1. How do I connect my nursing practice to the larger needs of society?
2. How does my working environment contribute to or detract from my ability to provide caring excellence for my patients and clients?
3. If I could change anything about my career environment—other than leaving it for another job—what would it be? What practical steps could I proactively take to make that change? If I encountered obstacles in this change, what would I do to surmount these?
4. How do I create a sense of caring community in my working environment and with my colleagues? What could I try that has not been done before?
5. To me, is nursing a science or an art? Or is it both? Why?
6. Do my spiritual beliefs influence my nursing practice? If so, how?

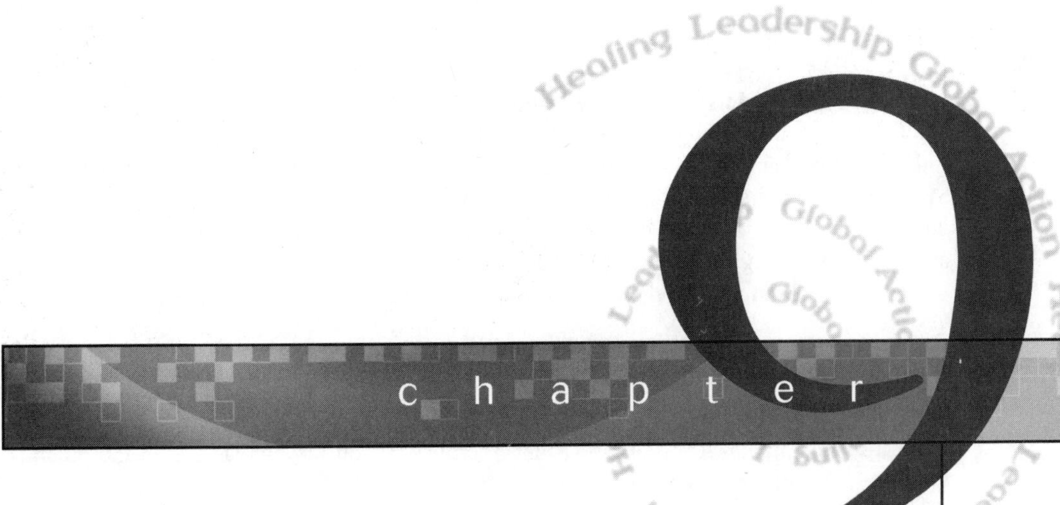

21st-Century Citizenship for Health: "May a Better Way Be Opened!"

Deva-Marie Beck

In the future which I shall not see, for I am old, may a better way be opened! May the methods by which every infant, every human being will have the best chance at health … be learned and practiced. (Nightingale, 1893, p. 198)

With these words, Nightingale looked forward to the coming decades and centuries. She envisioned people who could evolve nursing's scopes and standards of practice by continually upgrading our ways, means, and arenas for promoting the health of human beings.

The Tenets of Nightingale's Legacy

As nurses look to the contributions we can make in our generation, Nightingale's life is a blueprint for the foundations we can build. As a nurse, she made major contributions to nursing theory, education, research, statistics, and public health. She was also a visionary author who wrote about a broad range of health topics. She called for providing health care mostly at home rather than in hospitals, for enlarging our role as health educators, and for improving the health of regional populations, as well as the health of individuals.

Nightingale collaborated with other disciplines to promote health in a variety of ways and in numerous arenas. She was a media expert shaping public opinion about the value of nursing and health issues. She was a health policymaker collaborating with others to improve the environment and to promote cultural understanding. She was an international networker, constantly communicating with her friends and colleagues in the service of health around the world. She was an adviser to national leaders in many countries. She was a global citizen who understood that one person can make a significant difference in the health of humanity. With all these perspectives and accomplishments, she modeled a broader scope of nursing practice, which she labeled "sick-nursing" and "health-nursing."

Nightingale understood that the health of nations and of our world is dependent upon the health of individuals. She advocated for broadly based health literacy and knowledge. She linked environmental and economic concerns to sustainable health. She saw nurses fulfilling their roles, as she had done: as health promoters, as health educators, as leaders, and as major contributors to the issues of human health from personal to global levels. This is the breadth and depth of her legacy for nursing and for health care. This is also her legacy for us and for our time. ("Sick-Nursing and Health-Nursing" is reproduced in this book; see page 287.)

The Magnitude of Our Health Issues

Today the magnitude of health problems, in our communities as well as in our world, may seem insurmountable. Antibiotic-resistant microbes are on the increase, with the potentially virulent return of small pox, dengue fever, tuberculosis, and new strains of malaria, and with the recent onset of new killer diseases such as AIDS and SARS. Beyond these disease-vector issues, health issues also encompass economic and social issues. Our health problems are compounded by the precipitous rise in healthcare costs. Human health is also assailed in the many war-torn regions of the world.

These conditions, added to the looming impact of the significant shortage of nurses, nursing educators, and other healthcare professionals, seem overwhelming, perhaps beyond our reach to even consider, let alone try to plan or implement what must be done to address them. Despite all of our technical advances and perhaps, in part, because of them, our health concerns are as immense as in Nightingale's time. They remain "nearly as old as the world, nearly as large as the world, as pressing as life or death" (1893, p. 184).

Looking at Nightingale's achievements, it is tempting to say that she was an exception, a genius, an extraordinary woman, someone who did far beyond what any of us can do in our time.

Yet the sustainability of the human race requires that at least some people, as concerned citizens and as committed health advocates, see the world as Nightingale saw it. For her, the world was a global arena where local, smaller health-promotion-focused solutions were created as models of success. Across her career, she worked on a series of local projects, from serving in a Crimean battlefield hospital, to providing adequate provisions and conditions for British soldiers, to developing a system of secular nursing education, to collaborating to improve health outcomes in numerous small projects across the English-speaking world. Nightingale's overriding strategy was to address the magnitude of global health problems with local health-promoting solutions and to collect the data necessary to improve her plans.

"Still Far from the Mark"

Nightingale marked the beginnings of sick-nursing. Since her time, especially in the Western world, where sick-nursing and sophisticated sick-treatment compose a significant amount of health care in hospital settings, the practice of sick-nursing has become almost synonymous with most of the varieties of specialty nursing practice. Nightingale saw that the treatment of sickness was a *re*active approach that addressed problems after they occurred: "everything comes before health," and human beings are inclined "not [to] look after health, but after sickness" (p. 185).

Nightingale also saw the promotion of health as a *pro*active approach that sought to improve and change conditions, to help people recover faster and to keep people healthy in the first place. She identified this proactive approach as the more inclusive practice of health-nursing. She acknowledged that nurses and humanity were "still far from the mark" to fully implement this practice.

Similarly, Nightingale feared that the health arena would become yet another means of making money, rather than a way of caring for people. By 1893, she had observed the trend toward making a profit first over providing a caring service. She warned that value could be placed on sickness because of the money to be made from treating sickness conditions. She noted that people had forgotten to ask, "will the hospital do them [the patients] no harm?" To illustrate her point, Nightingale cited an example of hospitals making profits at the expense of using untrained or poorly oriented staff in hospital wards to "pick up" as they can (p. 188).

This concern continues today, as investment analysts view health care as an industry, valued for its ability to make profits for shareholders (Stern, 2001). Reverby, a nursing historian, elaborates on this problem by showing how health care was characterized in the past versus how it is perceived now. "The mantle of service … which for so long covered hospitals and other healthcare facilities has slowly been removed. … Now they are expected to run according to capitalistic logic as much as an automobile plant or department store" (Reverby, 1979, p. 206).

Fagin (2001) has recently addressed the "burden of caring." Like Nightingale, she notes the tendency to prioritize the profit to be made on disease at the expense of patients and their caregivers. In a business-focused climate, the priority for providing good care can become lost in the drive to make sure that shareholders, who have other options to invest their money, see enough profit to keep their investments in the healthcare sector. Barlow (2002) has also commented on the priority of paying the multimillion-dollar salaries that CEOs and top-level managers of healthcare corporations command, both in nonprofit and for-profit healthcare organizations. Competition from other sectors drives compensation in the healthcare sector.

Calling for a Caring Focus

If we focus on competition in our work, caring fades from considerations about how to solve increasingly serious healthcare problems, including the eroding quality of care provided by hospitals and the increasing worldwide shortage of nurses and nursing educators (Kimball & O'Neil, 2002; Kingma, 2001). Nightingale warned her readers that "competition, or each man for himself, and the devil against us all, may be necessary, we are told, but it is the enemy of health" (1893, p. 197). She reminded her readers to focus on the caring in health care.

Even as she noted her concerns for competition, Nightingale also urged her readers to implement care by thinking and working proactively. She asked nurses, and indeed the general public, to properly understand the factors required to sustain quality health care. Even as she recognized the ongoing need for excellent "sick-nursing" care to support people who are ill, she also noted the crucial need for "health-nursing" as an approach to bringing caring to wider arenas.

Identifying competition as the "enemy of health," she called for her readers to become advocates for an "antidote" mindset. She urged her readers to collectively care by becoming a strong voice for the value of health. She saw "health-nurses" as proactive leaders involved in creating a stronger collective consciousness about the importance of focusing on health first, rather than treating disease after it occurs.

Nightingale Focuses on Promoting Health Rather Than Treating Sickness

Throughout her career, Nightingale wrote about how humans tend to value the treatment of disease over the promotion of health. In *Notes on Nursing* (1860a), she reminded her readers that the study of pathology merely teaches us negative results or the "harm disease has done, but, nothing more" (p. 74). Instead, she recognized the positive value of identifying, delivering, and strengthening the factors that support health. Throughout her career she emphasized positive health-determining patterns—the creation of health-promoting environments at the bedside, within the home, in the community, across regions and nations, and for the world.

"Sick-Nursing and Health-Nursing" was written specifically to illustrate this theme. In the 1890s, Nightingale was in her seventies. She had completed numerous health-related projects in Britain and overseas. She had also spent decades analyzing the fieldwork of others who brought their data and experiences to her for recommendations as to how to improve their health services.

Nightingale saw all of these contributions as "nursing." She went on to identify the sub-topics of "sick-nursing" and "health-nursing," and to describe the cohesive relationship between them. She called upon us to connect the entire span of our potential nursing domains. For instance, in the Crimea Nightingale faced the sick-problem of vast numbers of dying soldiers. However, she did not solve this problem by bringing more people to deliver sickness treatments for their wounds. Instead, she and her colleagues solved the problem, over time, by recognizing the unsanitary situation as a sickness determinant or negative health determinant. They then shifted their focus to the creation of cleaner conditions as a positive health determinant. Nightingale's solution was established not through a treatment of the sickness problem, but by shifting from the old sickness environment to a new environment where the determinants of health were promoted (B. Dossey, 2000a). Although this example is Nightingale's most visible legacy even now, more than a century later, the paradigm she saw—to shift nursing from sickness treatment to health promotion, from sickness determinants to health determinants—remains mostly invisible in analyses of and conclusions about today's similar dilemmas. This is particularly true if we look only at sickness treatment, even if it is labeled "health care." For example, when faced with a spreading microbe such as multi-resistant staphylococcus aureas (MRSA), the sickness-determinants approach looks to create a new antibiotic to kill it. The health-determinants approach identifies ways in which the infected environment can be changed and works to discover how the body's immune system can be strengthened against the infection. Both approaches are important. But the health-determinants approach is often overlooked and under funded.

"Health for All"

In 1893, Nightingale noted that a longing for health was a common hope experienced by everyone everywhere. She also saw the longing to know how to live a healthy life, beyond the treatment of disease, and how to pass this knowledge on to future generations. "Since God did not mean mothers to be always accompanied by doctors, there is a want older still and larger still ... it is an art which concerns every family in the world ... the art of health" (1893, p. 186).

Nightingale called for nurses to apply ourselves to helping people stay healthy and regain health. Just as she had done for the soldiers during the Crimean War, she called for us to promote health at the individual level. Just as she did for decades following the Crimean War, she called for us to work on the larger collective, and even global, level. Nightingale clearly demonstrated the significance of caring for individuals. Yet she saw that her caring would be more effective if she also cared for people by working to change policies, influence public opinion, consult with people in key positions, and inform regional and national leaders about the importance of health issues.

Nursing's Focus

However, since Nightingale's time, the discipline of nursing has lost sight of the individual-to-global continuum. Rush (1997) has noted that nurses are now conditioned to focus their efforts, in education and in practice, at the micro level of individuals and families. Noting Nightingale's legacy as a global figure in these larger practice arenas, Rafael (1999) wonders if it is still possible for nurses to affect the macro determinants that promote health. How can we follow Nightingale and address, across the continuum of "sick-nursing and health-nursing," the full range of opportunities to promote health and healing at both micro and macro levels?

Nightingale herself gave us an approach to take. Instead of focusing on *who* provides disease treatment or specifying *where* health care is provided, Nightingale established, for nurses, the *how* to effectively promote health. She called on us to focus, in all practice settings, on the improvement of healthy environments. Selanders (1993) reminds us that Nightingale was the first nursing theorist to understand that a person's physical, emotional, mental, and spiritual environment can be either nurturing or detrimental to healing and to health. Selanders sees that one of our prime contributions to health care is to proactively determine if environments are detrimental to the recovery of health, and to change or adapt these if the environment can be improved.

In her own career, and in support of efforts by others across the British Commonwealth and in the United States, Nightingale showed that nurses could improve health environments for individuals, as well as for communities, regions, and even nations. She presented both "sick-nursing" and "health-nursing" as "kinds of nursing [that] are to put us in the best possible conditions [we could say *the best possible health determinants*] for Nature to restore or to preserve health—to prevent or to cure disease or injury." She concluded that health was "not only to be well, but to be able to use well every power we have" (p. 186). Nightingale's definition of health could be paraphrased, *positive health determinants* are those conditions that not only keep us well, but also are the very conditions *that we can influence by using well, every power we have to use.* Working from Nightingale's tenets, we can focus on promoting healthy environments across the human continuum. Nurses can assume, as Nightingale did, that our knowledge and experience is valuable to the wider general public, as well as for individual patients and their families. Like Nightingale, we can be health promotion experts in the community and contribute our expertise to media coverage, to town hall discussions, and to decisions made at regional and national meetings. With our mandate to improve health environments, we can educate leaders and even take leadership roles ourselves.

Nightingale called for nurses to be aware of the pressures placed on healthy environments. She warned that health and health promotion endeavors can be forgotten, and even abandoned. Particularly, she saw the need for "sick-nurses" and "health-nurses" to watch for and speak up against economic pressures that threaten health. To those who would respond that financial concerns are more important than human concerns, Nightingale cautioned business and policy leaders that healthy people are a significant resource. Thus, ultimately, "health is [our] only [true] capital" (p. 190). She reminded nurses that our health promotion arenas are as important as any other sector of human concern and that our knowledge encompasses "such stupendous issues as life and death, health and disease" (p. 187). As experts in the field of health, nurses can grow beyond their typical "sick-nursing" arenas, to also take a proactive role for "health-nursing" in their communities, regions, nations, and on the planet.

Recommendation #1: Make health—and influencing positive health determinants—a top priority in human affairs.

Nursing = Nurturing That "Vital Force"

Nightingale observed that the "vital force," or living impulse for health, begins at the individual level. She saw nurses as the nurturers of this life-spark, particularly during illness, when people are feeling fragile and vulnerable, and wondering whether life is worth the effort it takes to recover. Nightingale reminded her readers that during these times a special vigilance is needed to support people around the clock as they regain their health.

Reinforcing the Significance of Nursing

Even as nurses perform numerous complicated biomedical tasks required in contemporary hospital, clinic, and home-care settings, we are also constantly attending to our patients' recovery and interacting with them. In addition to watching monitors, lab values, and vital signs, we are attuned to the nuances of people's comfort, age, energy levels, attitudes, beliefs, level of education, and culture. Even as we address physical needs, we are simultaneously concerned with psychosocial, emotional, and spiritual needs. Although we work primarily in disease-treatment settings, we are always also working to maintain an underlying health promotion environment, even if this means a brief hand-hold for a patient rolling to surgery. We watch for opportunities to intervene with well-chosen words, an outreach of touch, and our calm presence and confidence during difficult procedures. Nurses are the ones sustaining a culture of caring in health care.

The often chronic and now acute nursing shortage further demonstrates the significance of our contributions. They are now noticed because they are missed when we are missing. When we are not there, infections rise, tempers rise, and people get sicker more often instead of recovering, even from minor illnesses. A critical connection between high patient/nurse ratios and patient mortality has been established (Aiken et al., 2002).

Various reasons are now being cited for this shortage, including women's increasing ability to choose alternative careers, and aging "baby boomer" clinical nurses, nursing educators, and researchers ready to retire over the next decade. Other national and international factors have also been identified, including budget-balancing amendments, trade agreements, migration patterns, and currency values.

These factors underlie the nursing shortage and worldwide healthcare crises (Disch, 2002; Kingma, 2001). Nurses have not been valued, nor have we ourselves remembered to value our comprehensive, holistic contributions to society. Even in settings where there is an extreme reliance on physician-prescribed biomedical machinery and sophisticated pharmacology to keep an individual patient alive, nursing is the discipline that maintains its vigilance for the well-being of that patient and for the maintenance of an environment that supports that patient's well-being. Nightingale noted that nurses are a vital and irreplaceable link in the healthcare chain. Without nursing, most of the focus on the recovery of health vanishes from health care. Without nursing, much of the care in health care simply disappears (Lang & Jennings, 2002; Needleman et al., 2002; Wakefield, 2001).

Valuing and Nurturing Our Contributions

In Nightingale's opinion, practitioners of the nursing discipline should never be underestimated. As in her time, we remain alert to the "vital force" that attends Nature's success or failure in recovery, and in end-of-life conditions, "even when there is no cure" (p. 195). Particularly in the current climate of nursing shortages, low nursing morale, and high nursing recidivism, and the prospects of these conditions worsening in the coming years (Fagin, 2001), Nightingale's words about the value of nursing's "vital force" for health care need to be on the lips of everyone who practices any form of nursing.

Within our practicing ranks, and particularly as nursing educators and nursing administrators, we must sustain a profound sense of the value of our contributions by *prioritizing support for one another in everything we do.* We must practice "care for the caregivers" (Kibrick, Beck & Burkhardt, 2003). The nursing shortage has given us the opportunity to return to Nightingale's premise that we must honor what nurses bring to the health of each person living on the planet.

Recommendation #2: Value and sustain nurses and their caring in health care.

Community Health: Creating Collaboration

Although Nightingale expressly valued nurses for their contributions to human health, a careful reader will find that her remarks were addressed to everyone interested in the topic of human health. To take full advantage of Nightingale's principles, health promoters from many disciplines need to look beyond her "nurse" and "nursing" language. Her words are relevant for medical social workers, public health professionals, teachers, and human rights and social justice advocates. Her ideas are useful to service clubs, such as Rotary International and St. Johns Ambulance, and to community leaders of all kinds. In fact, Nightingale's entire career, which was characterized by collaboration with representatives of many of the above disciplines, can serve as a model for effective health promotion. As a nurse, Nightingale understood that she could be a more effective health promoter if she reached out to her colleagues from other disciplines. Instead of waiting for others to find her, she found them and took the lead to organize projects on which they could work together. In this way, Nightingale established a transdisciplinary basis for her nursing practice and evolved her transdisciplinary approaches as she went along.

Nightingale as Transdisciplinary Collaborator

Throughout her transdisciplinary career, Nightingale developed programs and oversaw their implementation. She also researched the outcomes of these projects to determine if her ideas and applications would be valuable on a larger scale. After the Crimean War, she collaborated to create new standards for provisions for the British army, developed procedure manuals based on these collaborations, and followed up to ensure that the supplies the troops needed were available and ready for use. Later she collaborated with community leaders on the planning of projects to be developed in villages across India. Over several decades, although she remained in Britain, Nightingale maintained an active role in these projects, insisting on regular briefings from the field. In these projects, she addressed economic and environmental issues as well as more traditional health topics. She read extensively about these disciplines and published her own impressions in an editorial piece for the *Illustrated London News* (Nightingale, 1874b). In the summer of 1879, she published a series of articles that addressed economic and environmental issues from a health perspective, collectively titled "A Missionary Health Officer in India," in *Good Words* magazine (1879b, 1879c, 1879d).

Nightingale saw the importance of working with other experts who could contribute to her projects. These experts included educators and other academics; local, regional, and national leaders; physical and social scientists; mathematicians; sanitation engineers; urban planners and builders; philanthropists; clergy; planners and implementers of health policy; communicators; writers; inventors; and citizen-activists (B. Dossey, 2000a).

Flynn (1997) has noted that people, including nurses, who are involved in health education and in the education of healthcare professionals "need to take transdisciplinary education seriously" (p. 5). She cites programs where both nursing and medical students study community health by collaborating in the field with community leaders, including those from the disciplines of law, business, recreation, transportation, and urban planning, to develop and support "Healthy Cities" projects. Flynn notes that the "preparation of future health professionals will be limited" until these kinds of strategies and programs are developed and put into place for "students and faculty [to] participate in transdisciplinary education and practice with communities" (p. 5).

Community Perspectives from a Global Vantage Point

Nightingale called for nurturing an esprit de corps between differing peoples. She addressed the connections between health and aboriginal cultures for the peoples of New Zealand and Australia (Keith, 1988). She also created connections between community health promoters and people from business and public service sectors (B. Dossey, 2000a). She forged new methods of understanding between peoples and fostered cross-cultural, community-based projects around the world. To convey the breadth of these endeavors, she said that "the health of the unity is the health of the community. Unless you have the health of the unity there is no community health" (1893, p. 197). She saw the value of collaborating with people from many other walks of life to create and maintain positive health determinants in the community, including education, recreation, and transportation: "to secure the best air, the best food, and all that makes life useful, healthy and happy (p. 197). Nurses and other health promoters must create caring communities with others of like mind and heart. We can create new educational projects for our colleagues and for people of all ages in our communities. We can create formal and informal dialogues between peoples of differing perspectives. We can create new clinical practice arenas in places where people need our expertise and caring. We can develop new research frameworks that emphasize the value of what we do. We can demonstrate innovative ways to address the health needs of the 21st century. Together, we can proactively forge new, transdisciplinary alliances to serve health better.

Recommendation #3: Collaborate—across disciplines and across cultures—for promoting health in community settings.

Her Future Is Here: Education for Global Health

Nightingale looked to the future for better ways to support human health. She believed that all levels of education were essential to these endeavors. She spoke of the importance of education for both the theory and the practice of nursing. She also encouraged teaching of people in general. She valued learning as an essential component of all health promotion efforts, including opportunities to learn through experience. She noted a direct link between lack of education and the health problems found in the "families, the homes and household and habits of people" (p. 185). Discussing the critical connections between health and the role of those who provide care to infants and children, Nightingale also emphasized the need for creating educational programs that support quality child care, including meticulous details about early childhood needs. "The human baby is not an invalid, but is the most tender form of animal life" (p. 186).

McDonald (1998, 2000), who has created an Internet site (see Appendix C) that will ultimately compile all of Nightingale's works, including her 14,000 known letters, has cited one of Nightingale's private notes that underscores her belief that education is crucial to health:

> Oh teach health, teach health, teach health, to rich and poor, to the educated, and, if there be any uneducated, oh teach it all the more: to men—to women especially—to mothers, to young mothers especially … for the health of their children comes before Greek and grammar. (Nightingale, 1894b)

Micro and Macro: Teaching Health at Personal, Community, and Global Levels

Through much of her career, Nightingale promoted health education aimed at helping people to be healthy and to stay healthy. For her, the concept of health education applied both to individuals and to the world. In "Sick-Nursing and Health-Nursing," she demonstrated her ability to cover a wide health continuum, discussing a broader, macro-level health agenda, while, at the same time, showing her micro concern for the health of individuals. "How to keep the baby in health [is] certainly the most important function to make a healthy nation" (p. 186). In one sentence she linked personal micro health and the macro health of everyone on the planet. She saw one baby as representative of all babies. She recognized that even the largest health issues are composed of individual health concerns.

Nightingale knew that solutions to global problems must include local issues. To do this, she built educational bridges between the health of individuals in their communities and the health of communities in the world. She emphasized the importance of experiential education, rather than relying on theory alone. She discussed this individual–community–global connection with a local experiential health education project that could be applied to communities across the planet. (See the Syllabus from her 1893 essay starting on page 299.)

Nightingale based these premises in part on her own involvement in community education projects in India (B. Dossey, 2000a). From this experience, she knew that significant health outcomes could be promoted even through informal, conversational teaching initiatives in individual homes, within families, and in small neighborhood groupings. Nightingale detailed the work of women educators, called "health-missioners," who could speak in detail with village mothers about the maintenance of health-promoting environments in their homes and for their families. For example, she suggested instruction in determining the health of the body, as well as how to keep village, home, bedroom, kitchen, and garden environments healthy. She maintained that knowledge must always be confirmed by real-life experience.

In addition to urging her readers to educate people about their own health, Nightingale suggested educational programs to keep officials and leaders informed about health issues "from the voice of the people."

Health Status, Poverty, and Education

Nightingale demonstrated that health education initiatives could be successful health promotion tools in impoverished neighborhoods. She noted that poorer people could enhance their health and their quality of life, if they were given appropriate opportunities to learn. "Teach health, to rich and poor, to the educated, and, if there be any uneducated, oh teach it all the more" (Nightingale, 1894b).

Mustard and Frank (1998) have connected health status and education in low levels of income. They have noted that poverty does not necessarily imply poor health status. A number of studies indicate that when women are educated sufficiently to experience some sense of control over their lives and those of their children, infant and child mortality rates decrease. Countries that have prioritized women and children in their culture and social environment have a better health status.

One of the most significant health promotion strategies available today is the very strategy Nightingale called for—to "teach health, teach health, teach health" (Nightingale, 1894b). She recommended other related health promotion strategies—including community development projects and local education initiatives (B. Dossey, 2000a).

Nursing's Education Legacy

Nightingale bequeathed to nurses a health education legacy. In keeping with her emphasis on the value of health education for "everybody [who] is born," nurses and other citizen-activists concerned with human health should strive to positively influence literacy and particularly "health literacy." These strategies can include developing health and holistic health education modules for all levels of learning: preschool, K–12, college, graduate school, and (not to be underestimated) the emerging trend of adult lifelong learning. The health education programs that nurses develop can take a variety of formats, including teaching about health on the Internet. Health education components could include healthy physiology; diet, exercise, and body mechanics; the value of rest, recreation, family, and social support; spiritual issues; and the significance of positive attitudes and beliefs about health. Teaching strategies could include experiential settings like community field trips, study tours, and spending learning time in natural environments. Traditional classroom possibilities include on-site teaching in schools and recreations centers, at workshops and seminars, at "learning annex" community centers, and through health educational web sites and community–cable television programming. With health promotion as the basis upon which our "health-nursing" is practiced, all of these educational forms of supporting human health are within our nursing domain and mandate.

However, Nightingale warned of the danger of being satisfied with "book-learning and lectures" alone. Applied knowledge was a key component of her learning strategies. She understood that:

> Book-learning is useful only to render the practical health of the health workshop intelligent, so that every stroke of the work has [been] done, [such that] there should be felt to be an illustration of what has been learnt elsewhere—a driving home, by experience, not to be forgotten, what has been gained by knowledge too easily forgotten. (p. 197)

Nurses, nursing educators, citizen-activists, and health promoters from all sectors should look seriously at collaborating with Kickbusch (2001a) and others in the local development of global "health literacy" strategies and related practical applications to teaching people about personal and community health.

Recommendation #4: Think globally, act locally to create health literacy for both genders and for all ages.

From Invisible to Visible

Nightingale identified another key strategy for promoting health—the strategy to make health issues visible to the public and, particularly, to public officials. She urged her readers to take action: "You must form public opinion. The generality of officials will only do what you make them. You, the public, must make them do what you want" (1893, p. 191). These remarks were based on her experience in briefing local, regional, and national leaders with the health expertise she had gained and the knowledge she and her colleagues had collected in the field.

She also based these recommendations on her own efforts to influence public opinion through letters to the editor and editorial pieces for newspapers, and through correspondence with journalists. Because she was willing to explore the use of media in new ways, we can actually hear Nightingale's voice on several websites (including Country Joe McDonald's tribute to Nightingale, www.countryjoe.com). This recording was recorded by Colonel George Gouraud, Thomas Edison's assistant in London (B. Dossey, 2000a; p. 398).

Nightingale Behind the Scenes

Most of Nightingale's work still remains unheralded. Despite her desire to form public opinion about health, she worked, for the most part, behind the scenes. For decades, she quietly chaired and participated in meetings about health promotion with officials from Britain, India, Canada, New Zealand, and Australia. Unbeknownst to almost everyone, she analyzed data about the health of the British army and wrote numerous books on the topic. In addition, it was not widely publicized that Nightingale herself designed the first St. Thomas' Hospital on the Thames waterfront, and worked extensively with William Rathbone, a widely respected philanthropist and reformer, to develop extensive health projects for the working poor (B. Dossey, 2000a).

Although Nightingale was reclusive by nature and purposely shunned publicity, she also was working within the constraints of her times. Women, with the exception of the Queen, were not allowed to speak at Parliament. Women of means were not supposed to work outside the home, or even there. During Nightingale's time, it was expected that women's efforts would be invisible. She did not hold public positions, but worked behind the scenes, allowing those who worked with her to take the credit. To influence her causes, Nightingale had to utilize "referent power"—to make a public impact by collaborating, in private, with men who exerted external influence from their collaborations with her (B. Dossey, 1998b, 2000a; Selanders, 1992, 2001).

The recent controversy as to whether Nightingale actually contributed to the decreased death rate of Crimean soldiers after sanitation was improved there (Small, 1998) is an example of her work behind the scenes. Although other sanitation engineers and statisticians were involved in these improvements and deserve credit for their part, it was Nightingale who first invited them to apply their expertise. It was Nightingale who quietly collaborated with them as they implemented their recommendations. It was Nightingale who worked for decades thereafter to make certain that British army reforms included sanitation and related provisions issues, despite significant opposition from men in power at that time (B. Dossey, 2000a).

Nurses Behind the Scenes

Although the 21st century is different from the 19th in many dramatic ways, women still work behind the scenes, influencing their brothers, husbands, and sons to make visible contributions and take public credit based upon this unrecognized input. Health promotion work like Nightingale's continues unheralded and invisible. Her example of quiet endeavor continues to influence nursing's culture. Much of today's health care is performed by nurses, yet physicians have been the ones who are mostly credited with the work, because they are more inclined to publicize their contributions.

Buresh and Gordon (2000) address this issue. They have noted that for many decades nurses have been conditioned by our culture and by our mentors to remain silent about what we see and about what we have accomplished. We commonly describe our work as "just nursing," instead of acknowledging the immensity of our contributions to health. Our nursing culture has conditioned us to believe in the virtues of this silent approach, to respect the confidentiality of our interactions with patients, to keep what we do and think hidden.

Although the discipline of medicine has had no such constraints, nursing has consistently shied away from making our contributions and the theoretical foundations of our practice visible to the public. Buresh and Gordon also note the irony that the largest and most-respected healthcare profession "has been shown to be vastly under-represented in news coverage … virtually missing from health reportage." According to their findings, "practically everyone has had more of a public voice on health and healthcare than nurses" (p. 2). They call this a "disturbing discovery," with "far-reaching implications," and wonder how anyone will ever understand the value that nurses bring if this situation does not change.

> When medicine is consistently depicted as the center of the healthcare universe, then physicians will get credit for every contribution to healthcare, even in those instances when credit should go to nursing or other profession[s]. (pp. 2–3)

Calling for Nursing's Voice

Reflecting on the reticence of Nightingale, Buresh and Gordon have acknowledged that "over the last decade we have come to believe that there is a profound ambivalence in nursing about whether it is even advisable to be more visible, more vocal, and to have a larger role on the public stage" (p. 5). One remedy for this would be to create nursing's "voice of agency" (p. 35).

They point out that "agency" comes from the Latin verb *agere,* meaning to drive, lead, act, or do. "Agency is the capacity for acting or the condition of acting or asserting power" (p. 35). Despite her own ambivalence about public involvement in health issues, Nightingale called for this approach in "Sick-Nursing and Health-Nursing." She specifically called for her readers' voices to be heard, reminding us that "you must form public opinion" (p. 191). She knew that if those who care do not take this point, no one else will. In order to sustain relevant, "contemporary caring work," Watson (1999) likewise believes that the

> caring knowledge of women and nursing [can] no longer remain hidden... [and that] work today, again, requires strong voices, a being in the world, courageously and convincingly conveying a new proclamation for reform in personal, public, political and social thinking and acting [in support of the health of people] of our time. (p. 264)

Until now, disease has been visible, and treating disease has been visible. Sickness factors and sickness determinants have been visible. Conversely, health has been invisible, and those who support and nurture health have been unsung. A classic example is the contemporary management of diabetes. When telling the public the diabetes story, much is made of the discovery and refinement of insulin by physicians and pharmaceutical researchers. The sickness factor of the failure of the pancreas to secrete insulin and the resulting sickness treatment to replace insulin are given the credit for successful diabetes outcomes. Often omitted are the details of how nurses have for decades carefully supervised the use of insulin in hospitals and taught patients to safely manage their own blood sugar levels, their insulin doses, their diets, and their exercise. Health-promoting factors such as thorough teaching and the value of positive health determinants—in the case of diabetes, improved diet and exercise—have been mostly unrecognized until now.

Nursing's Communications Legacy

As we learn to communicate through public media, these new skills can easily transfer to our already established communication abilities. In the 21st century, information is making a significant impact on the culture of humanity. Nurses can and should participate in this emerging culture. Our new communication channels can include websites, e-mail, radio talk shows, letters to the editor, and newspaper human interest stories. Throughout the United States, for instance, local cable television channels continue to seek neighborhood involvement in their programming. In these settings, nurses, health educators, and citizen-activists should be encouraged and trained to become media-based health promotion advocates—to create, produce, and air their ideas for the value of health in their communities. Although these ideas are new, and perhaps scary to many, they are in keeping with Nightingale's vision that we are the ones to "form public opinion."

Recommendation #5: Make media a catalyst for nursing and for health.

"To Be Well, To Use Well"

Nightingale asked her readers to consider the full impact of what nurses and other health advocates can bring to humanity: "[we] have to do with living bodies and living minds, and feelings [both emotions and sensations] of both body and mind" (1893, p. 195). With this sentence, she also emphasized her conviction that health is fundamentally influenced by holistic—physical, emotional, mental, and spiritual—determinants. In addition to physical factors such as light, diet, exercise, and clean air and water, health depends on family and friendships. Mental health is improved through the use of positive language (B. Levine, 1991; Hawkins, 2002) and through education and increased understanding (Kickbusch, 1999). People of all spiritual traditions can enhance their health with prayer, sacred ceremony, and their own unique faith in Divine power (L. Dossey, 1993).

Dwelling on her own personal commitment to the holistic determinants of health, Nightingale asked the most pertinent question of her essay: "What is health?" Her answer: "Health is not only to be well, but to use well every power we have" (p. 186). She honored personal health and the things that each of us can do for ourselves—and for each other—to be healthy. Yet she also saw individual health as a means to serve others, rather than an end in and of itself. When we are well, we can better contribute our own unique talents to the world.

Nursing's Social Legacy

Nightingale bequeathed to nurses a social legacy. She reminded us that, if we address the health of one baby, we address the health of a nation. She urged us to understand and influence the health of humanity, as well to understand and influence the health of one human being. We are already acting locally; all we need to do is apply our skills and our knowledge to thinking globally. When Nightingale wrote that "health is not only to be well, but to use well, every power we have to use," she was writing her words for all of us—the "sick-nurses" and "health-nurses" of the world.

All of us have our own personal health to address; most of us will be concerned with the health of our families. Many of us will continue to address individual micro health in home-care, in hospitals, and in clinics. But, in the near future, many more of us will work on macro health for our neighborhoods and communities, and many more will address wider global health issues, including the cultural, social, economic, and environmental components of health. To do so, we will use an array of communication, networking, and educational tools that are becoming available to the citizens of the earth. To do so in the Nightingale tradition, we must keep our physical, emotional, mental, social, cultural, environmental, economic, and spiritual endeavors in mind.

Recommendation #6: Keep health holistic and transdisciplinary.

Advocacy and Citizenship for Health

In the final pages of her biography of Nightingale, Dossey (2000a) cited the tribute by Mahatma Gandhi:

> It is said that she did an amount of work which big and strong men were unable to do. She used to work nearly twenty hours, day and night. When the women working under her went to sleep, she, lamp in hand, went out alone at midnight to the patients' bedside, comforted them and herself gave them whatever food and other things were necessary. She was not afraid of going even to the battle-front, and did not know what fear was. She feared only God. Knowing that one has to die someday or other, she readily bore whatever hardships were necessary in order to alleviate the sufferings of others. (1994, pp. 61–62)

Gandhi applied in his own life what he described in his tribute to Nightingale. Many of his words would have later been appropriate for a tribute to Gandhi himself. Health advocates often quote him as saying that "we must be the change we wish to see" (Gazella, 2003). With decades of her own similar experiences in mind, Nightingale wrote "Sick-Nursing and Health-Nursing," wanting her readers to understand what she understood—that if we want the world to be a better place, we must each look for and act upon ways to make it better. She saw nursing in all of its forms as this "calling," this advocacy, this citizenship for the sake of human health.

Nightingale's "Calling"

Nightingale urged her readers to remember their "calling"—that sense of core purpose or direction one feels from within. She asked, "what is it to feel a *calling* for anything?" and "is it not to do our work in it to satisfy [our] high idea of what is *right* and *best*, and not because we shall be found out if we don't do it?" (p. 193). She encouraged her readers to do as she had done, to make their calling their professional mandate, an internal commitment coming from within, rather than as an external, "registered nursing" norm dictated from without (p. 193). She urged us to have a clear sense of our purpose in the world, lest we determine our life direction because of the expectations of others or because of the norms our culture gives us. She also asked each of us to set our own standards for our professional lives rather than to allow our "registration" or other benchmark, like certification or practice status, to guide our level of service. Nightingale herself defined the scope of her nursing career in this way. Her internal commitment to health directed her choice to seek ongoing education and experience that continually prepared her to strengthen and broaden her fields of service. Her calling guided her professional choices, her practice roles as a nurse who promoted health not only at the bedside, as an administrator and as a nursing educator, but also as an author, a policymaker, and a national and international adviser.

She understood that her calling, while it certainly involved her physical, emotional, and mental commitment, was essentially spiritual. She felt spiritually guided to do her work because she heard "God's voice" on three distinct occasions throughout her life, starting when she was just 17 (B. Dossey, 2000a). The flame she was so famous for carrying in her lamp at Scutari was, for her, a Divine spark that had been ignited within her as a girl. Honoring this, she practiced consistent prayer and meditation, and read sacred texts from many religious traditions. Later in life she kept both the Bible and the sacred Hindu text, *Bhagavad Gita*, beside her bed, and made notes in the margins. She was vigilant to that sense of Divine guidance as she faced her own dark times, including years of disapproval from her mother for becoming a nurse and decades of chronic illness and pain. She allowed that spark to shed light on the health issues of her time, as she advocated for individual and public health care, as well as for human rights and social justice.

Global Health, Local Health: Remembering Our "Musts"

Chinn (2002) has stated that nurses—with our wealth of knowledge and expertise regarding health care and the promotion of health—can make key contributions to this arena of global citizen advocacy:

> The world has never been simple, but now no one can act as if it is. Nurses bring important insights to bear on the challenges that are now before us, and on the new challenges that face everyone where knowledge is concerned. (p. v)

Nightingale was the kind of citizen-activist Chinn envisions for nursing in our time. She did not wait for directives from physicians or hospital administrators or even from her own colleagues. From her own sense of calling, she acted on her commitment to humanity, on directives from within. Many have respected Nightingale for this kind of citizen-activism, recognizing how much she accomplished and what a visionary she was. But many have also mused, "I could never be a Florence Nightingale." They believe that she made too great a sacrifice, denied herself too much, and nearly killed herself in the process. Yet a careful study of her personal writings, particularly her diaries, letters, and Bible annotations, indicate that at each moment of choice she simply said "yes" to her own "must." Indeed, she did face tough choices. Yet even then she chose to carry on with her profound sense of doing what she was born to do (B. Dossey, 2000a).

When Nightingale asked her readers, "How then, to keep up the high tone of a calling, to 'make your calling and election sure'?" (1893, p. 196), she was acknowledging the inherent value of trusting and honoring our *spiritual* perspectives within our professional practices. Rather than taking what she would have said was best for her, Nightingale also urged her readers to go within and answer their own sense of calling, to ascertain where they could be of service, where they could fulfill their must, where they could make their difference.

Watson (1999) describes the significance of bringing spiritual and caring perspectives to the human and ecological sufferings that have become global health concerns. She also notes that a modern understanding of Nightingale's broad scopes of nursing practice, and honoring the timelessness of Nightingale's holistic insights, can be a catalyst for innovative approaches to individual, community, and global health. Each of us should go within to discover our own musts, our callings that best combine our talents with committed action to address the health needs of the world, whether we are "sick-nurses," "health-nurses," other health professionals, or global citizens.

Recommendation #7: Answer your own calling.

Healing

Koerner (2001) elaborates on the value of following Nightingale's example to evolve new ways to support healing. She notes that nurses should bring our voices, knowledge, and expertise to the efforts of civil society:

> Wherever there are people, nursing has the opportunity to support health and well-being in partnerships with others.... Through cooperation and cocreation, a synergy will be formed that can transform the total well-being of society. Alone, nursing cannot do it. Without nursing it cannot be done. (p. 26)

As nurses, we know that healing must be addressed with a significant *caring* component. We understand that recovery and health are affected by the environments we create—physically, emotionally, mentally, and spiritually. We deal with human distress, injury, and disease. However, we also know that healing requires the conscious promotion of health-supporting factors such as comfort and rest, relief of pain, adequate fluids and nutrition, clean air, use of sunshine and light, exercise, applied knowledge of health processes, and emotional and spiritual support. We know that when they are provided, these positive *health determinants* become, in and of themselves, significant solutions to the problems of disease. We know that communication and education are essential approaches to promoting healing and recovery and to sustaining health.

Leadership

The *Ottawa Charter for Health Promotion* gives us, as citizens of our nation and our world and as nurses, a mandate for health leadership. It declares that "health promotion is carried out by and with people, not on or to people … social, cultural, and spiritual resources need to be harnessed in innovative ways" (WHO, 1986). Since Nightingale's time, we have used our knowledge and our skill to work on the "people" side of health. We have practiced primarily with individuals, with small groups such as families, and with local communities. In the 21st century, we can follow Nightingale's tenets and bring the priority of people's health to regional, national, and global arenas as well.

Knowledge is power, and we have critical knowledge to take the lead in our efforts for global citizenship. With our caring expertise, we can make a significant contribution to the growth of a worldwide civil society of committed, caring, and compassionate citizens. We can share our able hands and our pertinent voices with established nongovernmental organizations (NGOs) who are working on health issues. We can also form our own innovative NGO communities. We are good at facilitating teams of people to accomplish healthcare objectives. We can transfer these skills from hospitals and clinics to town meetings, regional conferences, and even to global summits. We are excellent collaborators. We can collaborate with other disciplines, such as those working on environmental cleanup, human rights, and social justice, to add our relevant health promotion mandate to these efforts. We can work, as many are already doing, by thinking globally and acting locally. We can establish local best practices to promote health and then, through the use of media and the Internet, share the results so that our successes can be replicated on a global scale. Because we have always been involved in health education, it is natural for us to participate in global "health literacy."

Our voices are trusted (ANAnova, 2002) because we have won and sustained that trust by effectively caring for people's health for a long, long time. Now we can move beyond our bedside arenas to administrative, financial, legislative, and health regulatory arenas, and use our trusted voices to call for health as a public issue, a political issue, a voter priority. With all of these suggestions, and with many more approaches yet to be discovered, we can take the lead to practice exemplary nursing. We can even be the leaders ourselves.

Global Action

Like Nightingale before us, we must focus on the value of excellent caring in all aspects of "sick-nursing." At the same time, we can also broaden our scopes beyond the limited practice of "sick-nursing" to understand and practice "health-nursing." As "health-nurses" we can see the value of identifying and implementing positive health determinants. That same list—"comfort and rest, relief of pain, adequate fluids and nutrition, clean air, use of sunshine and light, exercise, applied knowledge of health processes, and emotional and spiritual support"—can be brought not only to our traditional practice areas and individual patients, but also to regional and global arenas and the whole of humanity. The practice of "health-nursing" requires a broader proactive perspective, a global vision that points to the value of bringing, financing, and maintaining positive health determinants to people at local, regional, and global levels. We have always shared a vision for healing and for health. Global action is simply the widening of our scopes to communicate what we know to the public, to share the value of our perspectives and the effectiveness of our practices with our wider world.

Given the magnitude of the health challenges faced by humanity—the increase of infectious diseases and environmental toxins, the rising cost of health care, poverty and war that contribute to disease—it is tempting to feel overwhelmed by the problems facing us. It is easy to lose our vision. Throughout her life, Nightingale recognized that people do get discouraged, and rightly so. In her last essay, titled "Health Teaching in Towns and Villages,"

Nightingale addressed this discouragement by asking her readers to consider the ongoing value of what they can bring over the short term to longer-term solutions. "If we can transform, by a few years of quiet, persistent effort, the habits of centuries, our progress will not have been slow, but amazingly rapid" (1894a, p. 377). In her time, the quality of human health was precarious, just as it is today. Nevertheless, Nightingale did not let her sense of being overwhelmed stop her. She continued on, despite obstacles of all kinds, by daily following her must, trusting her talents, retaining her global vision, and, in so doing, "pressing toward the mark of [her] high calling" (1893, p. 196).

The health problems of today require renewed vision and the participation of committed citizens who take an active role in the promotion, locally and globally, of human health. In Nightingale's footsteps, we can recall that we have a significant breadth and depth of knowledge and skill to share in these endeavors. For centuries, healing has been our natural arena. We have been excellent healers. Great improvements in human health have come from our service. Now we can tap that knowledge more effectively by also becoming excellent leaders at all levels of need in our advocacy for human health.

Thus, with Nightingale's tenets, we too can be global visionaries and global change agents. We can focus our collective callings for the sake of 21st-century health care and related social, ecological, and human rights issues. We can continue the practices we have established. We can also be innovative and create new practice arenas. We can model the fulfillment and satisfaction of being nurses, of bringing health and healing to our world. Nightingale passed the vision to us—to remember who we are, what we can do, who we care for and why:

> May we hope that, when we are all dead and gone, leaders will arise who have been personally experienced in the hard, practical work, the difficulties and the joys of organizing nursing reforms, and who will lead far beyond anything we have done! (Nightingale, 1893, p. 199)

Recommendations

Recommendation #1: Make health—and influencing positive health determinants—a top priority in human affairs.

Recommendation #2: Value and sustain nurses and their caring in health care.

Recommendation #3: Collaborate—across disciplines and across cultures—for promoting health in community settings.

Recommendation #4: Think globally, act locally to create health literacy for both genders and for all ages.

Recommendation #5: Make media a catalyst for nursing and for health.

Recommendation #6: Keep health holistic and transdisciplinary.

Recommendation #7: Answer your own calling.

Pentimento

Tributes to Nightingale's Legacy: *International Celebrations to Honor Nursing*

Deva-Marie Beck

In Britain

Each year, a Commemoration Service is convened at Westminster Abbey in London on a date close to Florence Nightingale's birthday, the 12th of May. Open, by early reservation, to all who wish to attend, the Abbey is filled with approximately 2,000 people, mainly nurses, midwives, health visitors, and government ministers. During this service, British nurses are honored in a unique ceremony where a lamp is taken from the Nurses' Chapel in the Abbey and carried by a senior member of the profession who is escorted by a procession of nurses, usually student nurses. Together, these nurses process to the front of the Abbey where the lamp is handed from one nurse to another and then to the dean of the Abbey, who places it on the high altar. This ritual signifies the passing of knowledge from one nurse to another.

This service is sponsored by the Florence Nightingale Foundation, whose story is linked with the early history of the International Council of Nurses (ICN) and the Florence Nightingale International Foundation, as well as with the League of Red Cross Societies in Geneva and its national societies in many countries. At the time of Nightingale's death in 1910 at the age of 90, the international nursing community paid tribute to her life and work. During the 1912 ICN Congress convened in Cologne, Ethel Bedford Fenwick proposed an educational foundation as a memorial to Nightingale. She envisioned this memorial as a way to enable nurses "to prepare themselves most fitly to follow in her footsteps."

In Turkey, at a United Nations Summit

In 1996, Florence Nightingale and nurses were honored at a United Nations summit for the first time. The setting was Istanbul (Constantinople) where, in November 1854, Nightingale arrived to serve at Scutari Barracks, a still-active military base, now staffed by the Turkish First Army. During Nightingale's time, Scutari was the only military hospital for the Crimean War. Here, Nightingale worked for 22 months, attending to the wounds and needs of the soldiers. Situated on the Asian side of the city—across the narrow channel of water still known today as the Bosphorus Strait—Scutari remains near the oldest part of the city, close to ancient sacred sites, including the Blue Mosque and the Aya Sophia, the first cathedral in Christendom, built in the 3rd century.

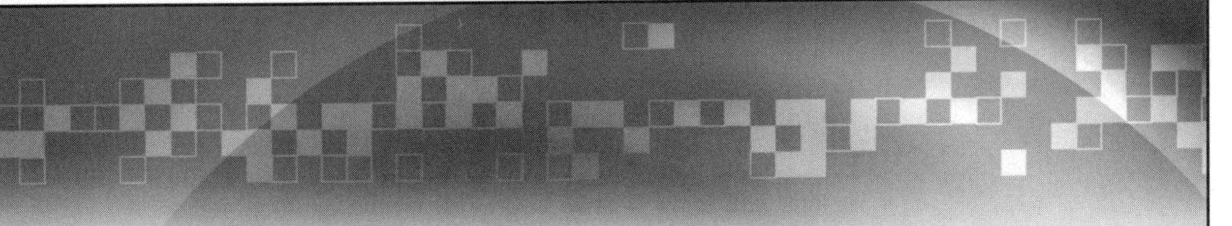

Although in the West Nightingale is most remembered for what she did for her own countrymen, she worked tirelessly for the welfare of all wounded soldiers under her care, regardless of nationality, religion, or ethnic background. Thus, she is highly regarded in the Arab world as well.

In 1996, Istanbul became the host city for "Habitat II"—the United Nations Human Settlements Summit. Here, representatives of governments and of civil society from around the world convened to discuss the challenges inherent to human habitats—from the smallest village to the megalopolis. To highlight the connections between health and nursing's contributions to the conditions found in human dwellings, the United Nations International NGO Health Caucus cosponsored—with the Turkish First Army and the Wellness Foundation from North America—"An International Tribute to Florence Nightingale at Scutari."

Here, student nurses from the Red Crescent School of Nursing in Istanbul created a "Nurses Throughout Time" candlelighting ceremony in which costumed participants represented nursing from ancient to contemporary times, each lighting a candle from the candle held by the student who depicted Florence Nightingale. In addition, representatives from the Turkish Ministry of Health, the Florence Nightingale College of Nursing at the University of Istanbul, St. Johns Ambulance, the worldwide "Healthy Cities'" movement, and the Wellness Foundation spoke about the Nightingale legacy in the context of wider human health issues. Beyond the treatment of disease, speakers

Lifesize diorama of Nightingale at Scutari, Turkey
(Displayed at the Nightingale Museum in London.)
Courtesy of Florence Nightingale Museum

The Blue Mosque in Turkey

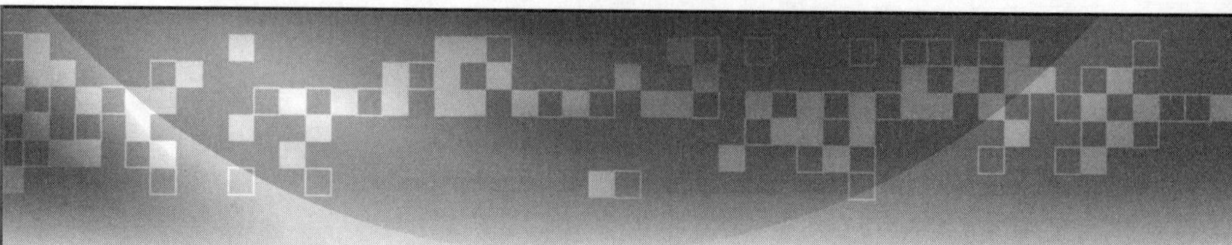

highlighted the activities of contemporary global citizens who work—like Nightingale did in her time—to keep the issues affecting all of humanity in the forefront of human consciousness.

In Washington, D.C.

The National Cathedral in Washington, D.C.—where a Florence Nightingale stained glass window features panels depicting several scenes from her life—has become a sacred site for honoring nurses and nursing in Nightingale's footsteps. On August 12, 2001, the First Inaugural Service Commemorating Florence Nightingale was convened, including presentations from former U.S. Surgeon General Dr. David Satcher, three American Nightingale scholars, and the participation of national nursing and student nursing leaders. Remembering the contributions of Nightingale and all of the nurses who have been inspired to follow her example, this service marked the first time that the Episcopal Church officially recognized her with a "Lesser Feast Day" officially placed on their church calendar—to honor both Nightingale and nursing on August 13, the date of her death in 1910.

An excerpt from the remarks of Nightingale scholar Barbara Dossey summarizes the intent of this service:

> Today we honor an extraordinary human being. Like a fiery comet, Florence Nightingale streaked across the skies of nineteenth-century England and transformed the world with her passage. She was a towering genius of both intellect and spirit, and her legacy resonates today as forcefully as during her lifetime. ... But why does Nightingale deserve to be included in the Calendar of Lesser Feasts and Fasts in the Episcopal Church of the United States of America? The reason is because of the unique way in which her spiritual vision intertwined with her work in the world.

On the Internet and Around the World

In 2000, the American Holistic Nurses Association (AHNA) initiated an "Annual World-Wide Commemorative Moment for Florence Nightingale and Nursing" at noon (local time) on May 12. Each year, on the Internet, the AHNA re-announces this event by inviting all nurses around the world to "pause, take a moment of silence or create a healing ceremony or ritual in celebration of and dedication to the heart and spirit of nursing." During this 24-hour period each year, more and more nurses are being invited to remember Nightingale's legacy for contemporary nursing by remembering the strength and honor of nursing's vision. The Internet invitation urges participants to "reconnect with the fire and the soul, the sense of calling in nursing" and to "acknowledge the interconnections and oneness of nurses in personal, political, social and scientific domains." The invitation posts several suggestions for how to celebrate this collective "Nightingale Moment," including collaborating with hospitals, home care agencies, and other health-related facilities and convening city council hearings and creating town meetings to highlight recent healthcare trends and, particularly, to feature the contributions of nurses to health care.

Stained glass windows depicting scenes of Nightingale at the Crimea in the National Cathedral in Washington, D.C.
Photographer: Jim Hawkins

(*Sources:* AHNA, 2003b; Beck, 1996a, 1996b; Dossey, 2001; Florence Nightingale Foundation, 2003; Wellness Foundation, 2002).

Pentimento

Florence Nightingale

Remembering Nursing's Broad Scopes of Practice:
From Micro to Macro

Deva-Marie Beck

In earlier times, nurses have taken the scope of their practice to promote health and healing on the scale of the community to national to international levels; that is, macro levels. For instance, during the early development of Ottawa in Canada (then called Bytown) in the 1840s, Elizabeth Bruyere and the nursing sisters of her order—the Grey Nuns—used their health mandate not only to establish and run the Bruyere Hospital, which continues to operate today, but also to create educational programs for the community's children, regardless of race or language, and to take an active leadership role in the quality development of their town. Bruyere and other early contributors to Canadian nursing efforts have been honored in a national memorial unique to Canada. Mounted in the Hall of Honor of the Centre Block—the central building of the complex of Parliament buildings in Ottawa—the national Canadian Nursing Memorial is a life-size marble bas-relief created specifically to remember the wide range of nursing practice in Canada. The memorial's inscription reads, "Led by the Spirit of Humanity across the seas, woman, by her tender ministrations to those in need, has given to the world the example of heroic service embracing three centuries of Canadian history."

During the Civil War, nurses practiced beyond a micro-level focus to treat the wounds of individual soldiers. Cordelia Harvey was a nurse who worked to rehabilitate the wounded Union forces along the Mississippi River. After practicing in several hospitals and noting that the Union men were dying due to their difficulty adjusting to the hot, sultry climate, she petitioned President Lincoln directly for support to build a northern military rehabilitation hospital. Lincoln, who was concerned that moving wounded soldiers would encourage their desertion, rejected the plan and several of her requests. Despite a clear "no" from her president, Harvey continued with her petitions, keeping the larger, macro-level welfare of the soldiers as her top priority. Her repeated letters focused on the severe conditions she continued to observe, warning Lincoln with blunt language saying, "I come to you from the cots of men who have died, who might have lived had you permitted. This is hard to say, but it is none the less true." Because of Harvey's perseverance, Lincoln finally issued an order for establishing a military rehabilitation facility in Wisconsin.

Clara Barton is another famous example from that time. In addition to practicing at the micro level to care for individual soldiers on the battlefields around Washington, D.C., Barton worked at the macro level throughout the Civil War to demand that national leaders make adequate provisions available to the wounded. Based on her

Nursing on the Micro Level

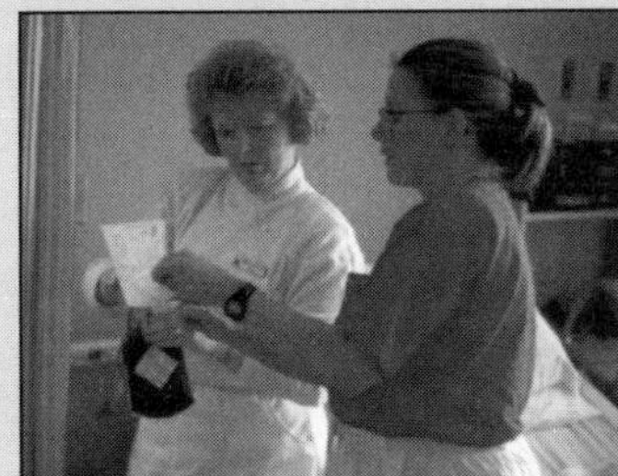

Double-Checking Blood

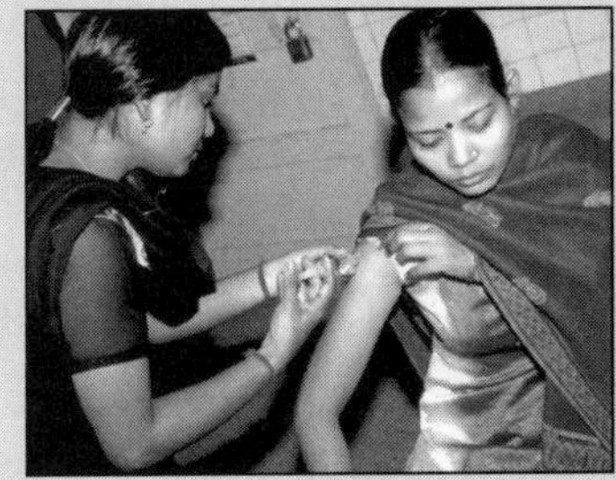

Streptomycin in India
© World Health Organization, Pierre Virot, photographer

experiences during the American Civil War, Barton later traveled to Europe to meet and learn from Henri Dunant—a Swiss banker and philanthropist who had also personally nursed the wounds of victims on the front lines of the Italian War of Independence in 1859. Because of his micro-level exposure to the suffering of the wounded, Dunant was able to create new macro endeavors, founding the International Red Cross and establishing the foundations for the Geneva Convention, the first international treaty to establish a neutral basis for serving war victims, both armed forces and civilians.

Throughout her association with Dunant, Barton was able to benefit from his innovative experience to create an independent, civilian-based humanitarian organization dedicated to caring for the wounded on both sides of regional and national conflicts. With this knowledge, Barton returned to the United States to found the American Red Cross, which has since provided humanitarian aid to victims of war, as well as for victims of natural disasters such as floods and earthquakes.

Like Florence Nightingale, whose macro-level nursing practice had directly inspired Henri Dunant's efforts, Clara Barton saw nursing as a practice continuum, from serving the health of one individual to serving the health of humanity. The leadership legacy of all three of these nursing pioneers is featured in a permanent exhibit at the International Red Cross and Red Crescent Museum in Geneva.

The Florence Nightingale Stained Glass Window, located in the north transept of the National Cathedral in Washington, D.C., also acknowledges the wider macro-level scope of nursing practice. In addition to panels depicting Nightingale's work in the Crimea and her micro-level practice of nursing in a hospital setting, the window also features a panel depicting her macro-level practice to design St. Thomas' Hospital in London. One panel, titled "Notes on Nursing," shows Nightingale writing at her desk. When the window was installed in 1938, the window's designers knew that Nightingale had penned her famous book by that title. However, at that time, they did not realize that they were also depicting Nightingale's wider focus on health, as she hand-wrote more than 14,000 letters—to network with friends and colleagues about health issues—now cataloged in private collections around the world and soon to be made available on the Internet.

Nursing on the Macro Level

Attending a World Health Assembly
© World Health Organization, Pierre Virot, photographer

Walking for Health
© World Health Organization, Pierre Virot, photographer

During a recent commemorative service honoring the contributions of nursing and Nightingale at the National Cathedral in Washington, D.C., Nightingale biographer Barbara Dossey asked, "If she achieved what she did with her handwritten letters, publications, and by networking men in power, can you imagine Nightingale with a laptop computer, cell phone, fax machine, voice mail system, e-mail, Internet, CD-ROM, information superhighway, and a satellite uplink?"

Contemporary nurses most often focus on the micro-level aspect of their scopes of practice in the care of individuals, frequently taking meticulous note of mini-micro details such as double-checking the labels of blood products before they are administered and safely administering complex antibiotic regimens. Yet, a macro global overview of health also remains within nursing's domain. Even though nurses most often think of their tools in terms of syringes and blood pressure cuffs, the information technology tools mentioned above by Dossey can also be health promotion tools available to nurses who practice at global levels.

With globalization as a growing trend in many sectors of human experience, the opportunities for individuals to participate at the global scale continue to increase. Citizen involvement in global issues continues on the rise, and nurses who keep informed about and speak to the wider health challenges—including the severe global nursing shortage—can make a significant contribution at the macro level. Nurses can participate in and bring their voice to briefings at regional, national, and international forums. They can also use their mandate to promote human health by calling for and collaborating with others who are working on the contemporary issues of social justice, human rights, ethics, the environment, peaceful conflict resolution, and literacy and education—all topics directly related to the health of humanity.

(*Sources*: B. Dossey, 2000b, 2001; Gibbon & Matthewson, 1947; Mayou, 2003; McDonald, 2000; Rogge, 1986)

Directions and Reflections

Directions for Future Research

1. Compare nursing theorists and their theories according to their assumptions regarding individual (micro) and societal (macro) health.
2. Bring nursing-framed inquiries to collaborative, transdisciplinary community projects such as the Healthy Cities movement.
3. Develop a health literacy curriculum for a specific population such as nursing mothers, victims of domestic violence, or HIV-positive patients who wish to optimize their quality of life. Demonstrate the effectiveness, based on health outcomes, including emotional, mental, and spiritual health, of nurse-designed and nurse-taught health literacy projects.
4. Determine whether nurses who also have media and communication skills have a more positive view of nursing than those without these skills.
5. In collaboration with urban service clubs such as Rotary International and Lions Club, or international NGOs such as Amnesty International and the Sierra Club, develop practical ways in which nurses can learn about and work on global health issues, or issues related to health, such as the environment or social justice. Investigate health outcomes of these projects as well as levels of stress and career satisfaction of project participants.
6. Collect stories from nurses who can identify their own sense of calling. Identify common themes and relevance to nursing retention and recruitment.

Reflections on Florence Nightingale's Tenets: Global Action

1. If I am fulfilled in my nursing career, what steps do I take to recruit others into nursing? What do I tell them? What do I warn them about? If I am dissatisfied with nursing, what one thing would I change to retain nurses, including myself?
2. Does my nursing practice focus on the promotion of health or the treatment of disease? Am I satisfied with this? Why? If not, how would I change it if I could?
3. How do I or could I serve my community with my talents? Are these talents related to my nursing practice or my nursing perspective?
4. If I could create a health literacy project, what audience or patient population would I write for? What points would I include in the project? What would be my teaching methods?
5. What ways could I contribute to media coverage of nursing and related health issues?
6. What is my global vision of health? Are there connections between my nursing practice and health on a global scale?

The Letters

Florence Nightingale's Formal Letters to Her Nurses (1872–1900)

This section contains the typescripts of the series of 13 formal letters (also called addresses) that Florence Nightingale wrote to her nurses—the probationers (student nurses) who were in training at St. Thomas's Hospital, London, and the graduate nurses who had been trained there. The first letter was written in 1872, when she was 52 years old; the final letter of 1900 was composed when she was 80. All told, she wrote one almost annually in 1872, 1873, 1874, 1875, 1876, 1878, 1879, 1881, 1883, 1886, 1888, 1897, and 1900. Her chronic, debilitating illness, her work on other projects, or the deaths of relatives or friends meant that in some years she wrote no letter.

Chapter 2 comprises a formal study of these letters, primarily in the context of Nightingale's mysticism and mystic spiritual development, which shows how the letters can directly address contemporary nursing. She clearly had in mind a model of the great Western mystics as she began to write to her nurses on Christian values, how to imitate Christ in their daily activities, how to be an exemplar of a Christian life, and how to be of service to God and society. Although clearly written from a Christian perspective, these letters also reveal an ecumenical sense of religion and a universal sense of spirituality. Nightingale always held that people should appreciate other cultures and explore different beliefs, rituals, and indigenous practices. She had read and continued to read the literature of world religions, and these letters clearly reflect this depth and breadth of vision.

The note that precedes each letter as reproduced on the following pages originally appeared in each letter as a footnote on the first page: the handwritten letters were read aloud to the nurses by Sir Harry Verney, the chairman of the Nightingale Fund. (After his death in 1894, the two final letters were read by others.) Each nurse also received a printed copy of the letter.

Note: Every attempt has been made to faithfully reproduce these letters from the originals. This means that variations in punctuation and spelling have been retained. Points of explanation have occasionally been added to increase clarity and readability.

(*Source*: The originals of these letters are archived in the collection of the Florence Nightingale Museum in London, England, and reproduced here courtesy of the museum. See Appendix C for information regarding the museum.)

1872

NOTE.—This Address was read by Sir HARRY VERNEY, the Chairman of the Council of the Nightingale Fund, to the Probationer-Nurses in the School at St. Thomas' Hospital, on the 8th May, 1872.

FROM: MISS NIGHTINGALE
TO THE:
PROBATIONER-NURSES IN THE 'NIGHTINGALE FUND' SCHOOL, AT ST. THOMAS' HOSPITAL AND THE NURSES WHO WERE FORMERLY TRAINED THERE.
Printed for Private Circulation.

I.—For us who Nurse, our Nursing is a thing, which, unless in it we are making *progress* every year, every month, every week,—take my word for it we are going *back*.

The more experience we gain, the more progress we can make. The progress you make in your year's training with us is as nothing to what you must make every year *after* your year's training is over.

A woman who thinks in herself: 'Now I am a 'full' Nurse, a 'skilled' Nurse—I have learnt all that there is to be learnt'; take my word for it she does not know *what a Nurse is*, and she never *will* know: she is *gone* back already.

Conceit and Nursing cannot exist in the same person any more than new patches on an old garment.

Every year of her service a good Nurse will say: 'I learn something every day.'

I have had more experience in all countries and in different ways of Hospitals than almost any one ever had before (there were no opportunities for learning in *my* youth such as you have had); but if I could recover strength so much as to walk about, I would begin all over again. I would come for a year's training to St. Thomas' Hospital under your admirable Matron, (and I venture to add that she would find me the closest in obedience to all our rules), sure that I should learn every day, learn all the more for my past experience, and then I would try learning every day to the last hour of my life:—

'And when his legs were cuttit off,
'He fought upon his stumps,'

says the ballad; so when I could no longer learn by nursing others, I would learn by being nursed, by seeing Nurses practise upon *me*. It is all experience.

AGNES JONES, who died as Matron of the Liverpool Workhouse Infirmary, (whom you may have heard of as 'Una,') wrote from the Workhouse in the last year of her life: 'I mean to stay at this post forty years, God willing: but I must come back to St. Thomas' as soon as I have a holiday; I shall learn so much more, (she had been a year at St. Thomas') 'now that I have more experience.'

When I was a child, I remember reading that Sir Isaac Newton, who was, as you know, perhaps the greatest discoverer among the Stars and the Earth's wonders who ever lived, said in his last hours: 'I seem to myself like a child who has been playing with a few pebbles on the sea-shore, leaving unsearched all the wonders of the great Ocean beyond.'

By the side of this put a Nurse leaving her Training School and reckoning up what she has learnt, ending with—'The only wonder is that one head can contain it all.' [What a small head it must be then!]

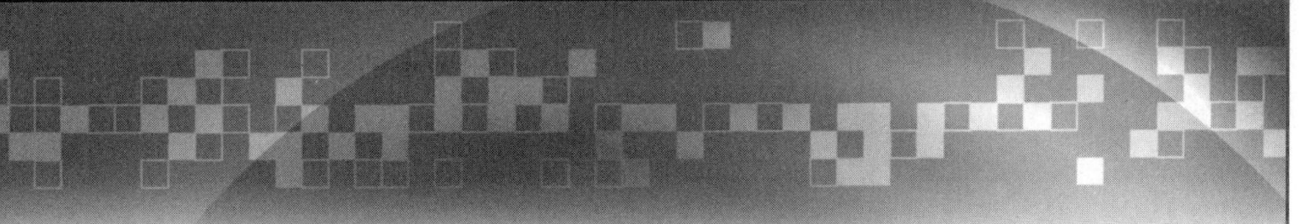

I seem to have remembered all through life Sir Isaac Newton's words.

And to nurse—that is, under Doctors' orders, to cure or to prevent sickness and maiming, Surgical and Medical,—is a field, a road to which one may safely say: There is no end—no end in what we may be learning every day.*

I have sometimes heard:—'But have we not reason to be conceited, when we compare ourselves to ——— and ———?' (naming drinking, immoral, careless, dishonest Nurses.) I will not think it possible that such things can ever be said among *us*. Taking it even upon the worldly ground, what woman among us, instead of looking to that which is higher, will of her own accord compare herself with that which is lower—with immoral women?

Does not the Apostle say: 'I count not myself to have apprehended: but this one thing I do, forgetting those things which are behind, *and reaching forth unto those things which are before, I press toward* the mark for the prize of the *high calling* of God in Christ Jesus; and what higher 'calling' can we have than Nursing? but then we must 'press forward,' we have indeed *not* 'apprehended' if we have not 'apprehended' even so much as this.

There is a little story about 'the Pharisee,' known over all Christendom. Should Christ come again upon the earth, would he have to apply that parable to us?

And now, let me say a thing which I am sure must have been in all your minds before this: if, unless we improve every day in our Nursing, we are going back: how much more must it be, that, unless we improve every day in our conduct as Christian women, followers of Him by whose name we call ourselves, we shall be going back.

This applies of course to every woman in the world; but it applies more especially to us, because we know no one calling in the world, except it be that of teaching, in which *what we can do* depends so much upon *what we are.* To be *a good Nurse* one must be *a good woman*; or one is truly nothing but a tinkling bell. To be a good woman at all, one must be an improving woman; for stagnant waters sooner or later, and stagnant air, as we know ourselves, always grows corrupt and unfit for use.

* There is a well known Society abroad, (for charitable works) of which the Members go through a two years' probation on their first entering, but after ten years they return and go through a second probation of one year. This is one of the most striking recognitions I know of the fact, that progress is always to be made: that grown-up people, even of middle age, ought always to have their education going on. But only those *can* learn *after* middle age who have gone on learning up to middle age.

Is any one of us a *stagnant woman?* Let it not have to be said by any one of us: I left this Home a worse woman than I came into it. I came in with earnest purpose, and now I think of little but my own satisfaction and a good place.

When the head and the hands are very full, as in Nursing, it is so easy, so very easy, if the heart has not an earnest purpose for God and our neighbour, to end in doing one's work only for oneself—and not at all, even when we *seem* to be serving our neighbours—not at all for them or for God.

'In the midst of this multiplicity of works and of women,' said an excellent Matron, 'much may go wrong; if,' she added, 'self is the only object.' Then it is 'all *go* and all *do*,' and 'no food' for the best part of us.

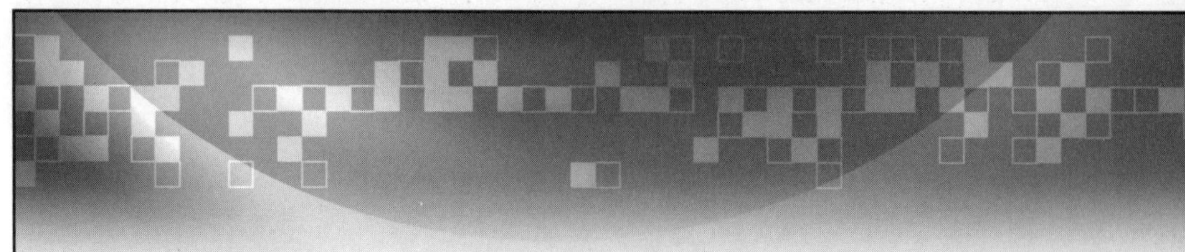

I should hardly like to talk of a subject which, after all, must be very much between each one of us and her God,—which is hardly a matter for *talk* at all, and certainly not for me, who cannot be among you (though there is nothing in the world I should so dearly wish), but that I thought perhaps you might like to hear of things which persons in the same situation, that is, in different Training Schools on the Continent, have said to me.

I will mention two or three.

(1). One said, 'The greatest help I ever had in life was, that we were taught in our Training School always to raise our hearts to God the first thing on waking in the morning.'

Now it need hardly be said that we cannot make a rule for this; a rule will not teach this, any more than making a rule that the chimney shall not smoke will make the smoke go up the chimney.

If we occupy ourselves the last thing at night with rushing about, gossiping in one another's rooms; if our last thoughts at night are of some slight against ourselves, or spite against another, or about each other's tempers, it is needless to say that our first thoughts in the morning will not be of God.

Perhaps there may even have been some quarrel; and if those who pretend to be educated women indulge in these irreligious uneducated disputes, what a scandal before those less educated to whom an example, not a stone of offence, should be set!

'A thousand irreligious cursed hours,' (as some poet says,) have not seldom, in the lives of all but a few whom we may truly call Saints upon earth, been spent on some feeling of ill will. And can we expect to be really able to lift up our hearts the first thing in the morning to the God of 'good will towards men' if we do this?

I speak for myself, even more perhaps than for others.

(2). Another woman once said to me—

I was taught in my Training School, never to have those long inward discussions with myself, those interminable conversations inside myself, which make up so much more of our own thoughts than we are aware. If it was something about my duties, I went straight to my Superiors, and asked for leave or advice; if it was any of those useless or ill-tempered thoughts about one another, or those that were put over us, we were taught to lay them before God and get the better of them, before they got the better of us.

A spark can be put out while it is a spark, if it falls on our dress, but not when it has set the whole dress in flames. So it is with an ill-tempered thought against another. And who will tell how much of our thoughts these occupy?

I suppose, of course, that those who think themselves better than others are bent upon setting them a better example.

II.—And this brings me to something else that I may have said before: [I can always correct others though I cannot always correct myself]—it is about jealousies and punctilios as to ranks, classes and offices, when employed in one good work. What an injury this jealous woman is doing, not to others or not to others so much as to herself—she is doing it to herself! She is not getting out of her work the advantage, the improvement to her own character, the nobleness (for to be useful is the only true nobleness) which God has appointed her that work to attain. She is not getting out of her work what God has given it her for; but just the contrary.

[Nurses are not children, but women; and if they can't do this for themselves, no one can for them.]

I think it is one of Shakespeare's heroes who says, 'I laboured to be wretched.' How true that is! How true it is of some people all their lives; and perhaps there is not one of us who could not say it with truth of herself at one time or other: I laboured to be mean and contemptible and small and ill-tempered, by being revengeful of petty slights.

A woman once said: 'What signifies it to me that this one does me an injury or the other speaks ill of me, if I do not deserve it? The injury strikes God before it strikes me, and if He forgives it, why should not I? I hope I love Him better than I do myself.' This may sound fanciful; but is there not truth in it?

What a privilege it is; the work that God has given us Nurses to do, if we will only let Him have His own way with us—a greater privilege to my mind that He has given to any women, (except to those who are teachers), because *we* can always be useful, always 'ministering' to others, real followers of Him who said that he came 'not to be ministered unto' but to minister. Cannot we fancy Him saying to *us*, If any one thinks herself greater among you, let her minister unto others.

This is not to say that we are to be doing other people's work. Quite the reverse. The very essence of all good organisation is, that every body should do her (or his) own work in such a way as to help and not to hinder every one else's work.

But, this being arranged, that any one should say, I am 'put upon' by having to associate with so-and-so; or, by *not* having so-and-so to associate with; or, by not having such a post; or, by having such a post; or, by my Superiors 'walking upon me,' or, 'dancing' upon me, (you may laugh, but such things have actually been said); or &c., &c.—this is simply making the peace of God impossible—the call of God (for in all work He calls us) of none effect; it is grieving the Spirit of God; it is doing our best to make all free-will associations intolerable.

In 'Religious Orders' this is provided against by enforcing blind, unconditional obedience through the fears and promises of a Church.

Does it not seem to you that the greater freedom of secular Nursing Institutions, as it requires (or ought to require) greater individual responsibility, greater self-command in each one, greater nobleness in each, greater *self possession* in *patience*—so, that very need of self-possession, of greater nobleness in each, requires (or ought to require) greater thought in each, more discretion, and higher, not less, obedience? For the obedience of intelligence, not the obedience of slavery, is what *we* want.

And you who have to be Head Nurses, or Sisters of Wards, well know what I mean, for you have to be Ward *Mistresses* as well as Nurses; and how can she (the Ward Mistress) command if she has not learnt how to obey? If she cannot enforce upon herself to obey rules with discretion, how can she enforce upon her Ward to obey rules with discretion?

The slave obeys with stupid obedience, with deceitful evasion of service, or with careless eye service. Now, we cannot suppose God to be satisfied or pleased with stupidity and carelessness. The free woman in Christ obeys, or rather *seconds* all the rules, all the others given her, with intelligence, with all her heart, and with all her strength, and with all her *mind*.

'Not slothful in business; fervent in spirit, serving the Lord.'

III.—And of those who have to be Ward Mistresses, as well as those who are Ward Mistresses already, or in any charge of trust or authority, I will ask, if Sisters and Head Nurses will allow me to ask of them, as I have so often asked of myself—

What is it that made our Lord speak 'as one having authority'? What was the key to *His* 'authority'? It is not the charge or position itself, for we often see persons in a position of authority, who have no authority at all; and, on the other hand, we sometimes see persons in the very humblest position who exercise a great influence or authority on all around them.

The very first element for having control over others, is, of course, to have control over oneself. If I cannot take charge of myself, I cannot take charge of others. The next, perhaps, is—not to try to 'seem' *any*thing, but to *be* what we would *seem*.

A person in charge must be felt more than she is heard—not heard more than she is felt. She must fulfil her charge without noisy disputes, by the silent power of a consistent life, in which there is no *seeming*, and no hiding, but plenty of discretion. She must exercise authority without appearing to exercise it.

A person, but more especially a woman, in charge must have a quieter and more impartial mind than those under her, in order to influence them by the best part of them and not by the worst.

We (Sisters) think that we must often make allowances for them, and sometimes put ourselves in their place. And I will appeal to Sisters to say whether we must not observe more than we speak, instead of speaking more than we observe. We must not give an order, much less a reproof, without being fully acquainted with both sides of the case. Else, having scolded wrongfully, we look rather foolish.

The person in charge, every one must see to be just and candid, looking at both sides, not moved by entreaties, or by likes and dislikes, but only by justice, and always reasonable, remembering and not forgetting the wants of those of whom she is in charge.

She must have a keen though generous insight into the characters of those she has to control. They must know that she *cares for* them even while she is checking them; or rather that she checks them *because* she cares for them. A woman *thus* reproved is often made your friend for life; a word dropped in this way by a Sister in charge (I am speaking now solely to Sisters and Head Nurses) may sometimes show a probationer the unspeakable importance of this year of her life, when she must sow the seed of her future nursing in this world, (for although future years of importance to train the plant and make it come up, yet if there is no seed nothing will come up) and of her future life through eternity.

Nay, I appeal again to Sisters' own experience, whether they have not known patients feel the same of words dropped before *them*.

We had in one of the Hospitals which we nurse, a little girl patient of seven years old, the child of a bad mother, who used to pray on her knees (when she did not know she was heard) her own little prayer that she might not forget, when she went away to what she already knew to be a bad life, the good words she had been taught. [In this great London, the time that children spend in Hospital is sometimes the only time in all their lives that they hear good words.] And sometimes we have had patients, widows of journeymen for instance, who had striven to the last to do for their children and place them all out in service or at work, die in our Hospitals, thanking God that they had had this time to collect their thoughts before death and to die 'so comfortably,' as they expressed it.

But, if a Ward is not kept in such a spirit, that patients can collect their thoughts, whether it is for life or for death, and that children can hear good words, of course these things will not happen.

Ward management is only made possible by kindness and sympathy. And the mere way in which a thing is said or done to patient, or probationer, makes all the difference. In a Ward too, where there is no *order* there can be no '*authority*,' there must be noise and dispute.

Hospital Sisters are the only women who may be in charge really of men. Is this not enough to show how essential to them are those qualities which alone constitute real authority?

Never to have a quarrel with another; never to say things which rankle in another's mind; never when we are uncomfortable ourselves to make others uncomfortable—for quarrels come out of such very small matters—a hasty word, a sharp joke, a harsh order—without regard to these things, how can we take charge?

We may say, so and so is too weak, if she minds that. But, pray, are we not weak in the same way ourselves?

I have been in positions of authority myself and have always tried to remember, that to use such an advantage—for they cannot 'oust' me, I can 'oust' them—inconsiderately, is—cowardly. To be sharp upon them is worse in me than in them to be sharp upon me. No one can trample upon others, and govern them. To win them is half, I might say the whole secret of 'having charge.' If you find your way to their hearts, you may do what you like with them; and that authority is the most complete which is least perceived or asserted.

The world, whether of a Ward an Empire, is governed not by many words but by few; though some, especially women, seem to expect to govern by many words—by talk, and nothing else.

There is scarcely anything which interferes so much with charge over others as rash and inconsiderate talking, or as wearing one's thoughts on one's cap. There is scarcely anything which interferes so much with their respect for us as any want of simplicity in us. A person who is always thinking of herself—how she looks, what effect she produces upon others, what others will think or say of her—can scarcely ever hope to have charge of them to any purpose.

We ought to be what we want to seem, or those under us will find out very soon that we only *seem* what we ought to be.

If we think only of the duty we have in hand, we may hope to make the others think of it too. But if we are fidgety or uneasy about trifles, can we hope to impress them with the importance of essential things?

There is so much talk about persons now-a-days. Everybody criticises everybody. Everybody seems liable to be drawn into a current. Has there been such a current in our Probationers' Home?—a current against somebody?—or in favor of everyone doing what she likes, pleasing herself, or getting promotion?

If any one gives way to all these distractions, and has no root of calmness in herself, she will not find it in any Hospital or Home.

'All this is as old as the hills,' you will say. Yes, it is as old as Christianity; and is not that the more reason for us to begin to practise it to-day? '*To-day*, if ye will hear my voice,' says the Father; '*To-day* ye shall be with me in Paradise,' says the Son; and He

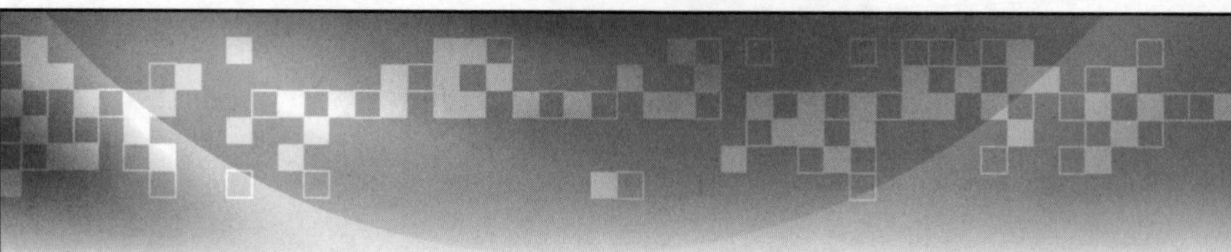

does not say this only to the dying; for Heaven may begin here, and 'The kingdom of heaven is within,' He tells us.

I have returned now to the probationers, as you see.

Most of you here present will be in a few years in charge of others, filling posts of responsibility. *All* are on the threshold of active life. Then our characters will be put to the test, whether in some position of charge or of subordination, or both. Shall we be found wanting? unable to control ourselves, therefore unable to control others? with many good qualities, perhaps, but owing to selfishness, conceit, to some want of purpose, some laxness, carelessness, lightness, vanity, some temper, habits of self indulgence, or want of disinterestedness, unequal to the struggle of life, the business of life and ill adapted to the employment of Nursing which we have chosen for ourselves, and which, almost above all others, requires earnest purpose, and the reverse of all these faults. Thirty years hence, if we could suppose us all standing here again passing judgment on ourselves, and telling sincerely why one has succeeded, and another has failed; why the life of one has been a blessing to those she has had charge of, and another has gone from one thing to another, pleasing herself, and bringing nothing to good—what would we give to be able *now* to see all this before us?

Yet some of these reasons for failure or success we may anticipate now. Because so and so was or was not weak or vain; because she could or could not make herself respected; because she had no steadfastness in her, or on the contrary, because she had a fixed and steady purpose; because she was selfish or unselfish, disliked or beloved; because she could or could not keep her women together or manage her patients, or was or was not to be trusted in Ward business. And there are many other reasons which I might give you if it were right, or which you might give yourselves for the success or failure of those who have passed through this training school for the last eleven years.

Can we not see ourselves as others see us?

For the 'world is a hard school-master,' and punishes us without giving reasons, and much more severely than any Training School can, and when we can no longer perhaps correct the defect.

Good posts may be found for us; but can we keep them so as to fill them worthily?—or are we but unprofitable servants in fulfilling any charge?

Yet many of us are blinded to the truth by our own self-love even to the end. And we attribute to accident or ill-luck what is really the consequence of some weakness or error in ourselves.

But can we not see ourselves as God sees us? is a still more important question. For while we value the judgments of our superiors, and of our fellows, which may correct our own judgments, we must have also a higher standard which may correct theirs. We cannot altogether trust them, and still less can we trust ourselves. And we know, of course, that the worth of a life is not altogether measured by failure or success. We want to see our purposes, and the ways we take to fulfil such charge as may be given us, as they are in the sight of God.—'Thou God seest me.'

And thus do we return to the question we asked before—how near can we come to Him whose name we bear, when we call ourselves Christians*?—to His gentleness and goodness—to His 'authority' over others—in following Him whom we would fain make our pattern?

And the highest 'authority' which a woman especially can attain among her fellow women must come from her doing God's work here in the same spirit, and with the same thoroughness, that Christ did, though we follow him but 'afar off.'

IV.—Lastly, it is charity to nurse sick bodies well; it is greater charity to nurse well and patiently sick minds, tiresome sufferers. But there is a greater charity even than these:—to do good to those who are not good to us, to behave well to those who behave ill to us, to serve with love those who do not even receive our service with good temper, to forgive on the instant any slight, which we may have received, or may have fancied we have received, or any worse injury.

If we cannot 'do good' to those who 'persecute' us—for *we* are not 'persecuted'; if we cannot pray 'Father, forgive them, for they know not what they do'—for none are nailing us to a cross—how much more must we try to serve with patience and love any who use us spitefully, to nurse with all our hearts any thankless peevish patients!

We Nurses may well call ourselves 'blessed among women,' in this that we can be always exercising all these three charities, and so fulfil the work our God has given us to do.

P.S.—Just as I was writing this came a letter from Mrs. BEECHER STOWE, who wrote *Uncle Tom's Cabin*. She has so fallen in love with the character of our AGNES JONES ('Una') which she had just read, that she asks about the progress of our work, supposing that we have many more Unas, saying that that *is* 'making virtue attractive,' and asking me to tell for them in America about our Unas.

Shall we ask her to write for us? She says that her brother, the Rev. HENRY WARD BEECHER, of whom you may have heard as a preacher, has re-issued our 'Una 'with a notice by himself, which she will send us. They wish to 'organise a similar movement' in America—a 'movement' of Unas—what a great thing that would be! Shall we all try to be Unas?

She ends, as I wish to end,
Yours, in the dear name that is above every other,
FLORENCE NIGHTINGALE.
London, May 1872.

* There is a most suggestive story told of one, some 300 years ago, an able and learned man, who presented himself for admission into a Society for Preaching and Charitable Works. He was kept for many months on this query:—*are you a Christian?*—by his 'Master of Probationers.' He took kindly and heartily to it; went with his whole soul and mind into this little momentous question, and solved it victoriously in his own course, and in his after course of usefulness for others. Am I a Christian?—is, most certainly, the first and most important question for each one of us Nurses. Let us ask it, each of herself, every day.

1873

NOTE.—This Address was read by Sir HARRY VERNEY, the Chairman of the Council of the Nightingale Fund, to the Probationer-Nurses in the School at St. Thomas' Hospital, on the 23rd May 1873.

LETTER
FROM: FLORENCE NIGHTINGALE
TO THE:
PROBATIONER-NURSES IN THE 'NIGHTINGALE FUND' SCHOOL,
AT ST. THOMAS' HOSPITAL AND THE
NURSES WHO WERE FORMERLY TRAINED THERE.
Printed for Private Circulation.

May 23, 1873
MY DEAR FRIENDS,

Another year has passed over us. Nearly though not quite all of us who were here at this time last year have gone their several ways—to their several posts; some at St. Thomas', some to Edinburgh, some to Highgate. Nearly all are, I am thankful to say, well, and I hope we may say happy. Some are gone altogether.

May this year have set us all one step farther, one year on our way to becoming 'perfect as our Father in Heaven is perfect,' as it ought to have done.

Some differences have been made in the School by our good Matron, who toils for us early and late—to bring us on the way, we hope, towards becoming 'perfect.'

These differences are, as you see: I leave it to you to say, *improvements*—our new Medical Instructor having vigorously taken us in hand and giving us his invaluable teaching: 1. In Medical and Surgical Nursing; 2. In the elements of Anatomy. I need not say: Let us profit.

Next, in order to give more time and leisure to less tired bodies to avail themselves of it, the Special Probationers have two afternoons in the week off duty for study, for the course of reading which our Medical Instructor has laid down. And the Nurse-Probationers have all one morning and one afternoon in the week to improve themselves, in which our kind Home Sister assists them by classes. And, again, I need not say how important it is to take the utmost advantage of this. Do not let the world move on and leave us in the wrong. Now that, by the law of the land, every child between five and thirteen must be at school, it will be a poor tale, indeed, in their afterlife for Nurses who cannot read, write, spell, and cypher well and correctly, and read aloud easily, and take notes of the cases for the Doctors or for themselves—now especially when the Nurse is often required to take the temperature of cases, and the like. Only this last week, I was told by one of our own Matrons of an excellent Nurse of her own to whom she would have given a good place, only that she could neither read nor write well enough for it.

And may I tell you, not for envy, but for a generous rivalry, that you will have to work hard if you wish St. Thomas' Training School to hold its own with other Schools rising up.

Another difference will be, that those of our Special Probationers who have completed half their time of training, will be released from some of the Ward work, which is not exactly adding to their training or knowledge, while it takes away their bodily strength for the after-work of Sisters or Matrons, and of training others, to which they are destined.

In a former time in our School the Nurse-Probationers took the Special Probationers under their protection, and saved them from doing the hardest work; and the 'Special' Probationers took the Specials; but each gave to the other what she could. You will tell me whether we are wrong in thinking such a spirit a good one, and whether, if it is, it has departed from among us.

No 'Special' (or hardly any) has ever been found to shirk her work. In that I believe we are all agreed. Indeed, a little bird has whispered that the 'Special' was so willing, the Patients actually preferred asking her for little services.

But that is a little secret among ourselves, you know.

And it is not only the 'Special' who may be of much use to the Nurse-Probationer, or—the other way. The older Probationer may be, and sometimes has been, of very great use to her junior in the School. I can remember instances of this: one (she is not now with us here, but she still belongs to our Society) who,—as a Senior Nurse-Probationer, helped, taught, and spared her juniors in the Wards. For much may be done in sparing a young woman, entering a Ward for the first time in her life, the worst parts of her business till she is more at home in her work, instead of, as is sometimes done (I hope *not* with us), throwing upon her, as a kind of fag, the nastiest things to do.

We must try to avoid the mistake of dividing this or any other 'Home' or School into those who are like us and those who are not.

Let us be on our guard against the danger, not exactly of thinking too well of ourselves (for no one consciously does this), but of isolating ourselves, of falling into party spirit—always remembering that, if we can do any good to others, we must draw others to us by the (not loud but) not unfelt influence of our characters, and not by any profession of what we are—least of all, by a profession of Religion.

And this, by the way, applies peculiarly to what we are with our patients.

Least of all should a *woman* try to exercise religious influence with her patients, as it were, by a *ministry*, a chaplaincy. We are not chaplains. It is what she *is* in *herself*, and what comes out of herself, out of what she *is* (almost without her knowing it herself)—that exercises a moral or religious influence over her patients. No set form of words is of any use. And patients are so quick to see whether a Nurse is consistent always in herself—whether she *is* what she *says* to them. And if she is not, it is no use. *If she is*, of how much use may the simplest word of soothing, of comfort, or even of reproof—especially in the quiet night—be (unawares to herself) to the roughest patient, who is there from drink, or to the still innocent child, or to the anxious toil-worn mother or husband! But if she wishes to do this, she must keep up a sort of divine calm, and high sense of duty in her own mind. Christ was alone, from time to time, in the wilderness or on mountains. If *He* needed this, how much more must we?

Quiet in our own rooms (and a room of your own is specially provided for each one here)—we have bustle enough during the day—a few minutes of calm thought to offer up the day to God—how indispensable it is, in this ever increasing hurry of life! When we live 'so fast,' do we not require a breathing time, a moment or two daily, to think where we are going,—at this time, especially, when we are laying the foundation of our afterlife—in reality, the most important time of all?

And I am not at all saying that our patients have everything to learn from *us*. On the contrary, we can, many a time, learn from them, in patience, in true religious feeling and hope. One of our Sisters told me that she had often learnt more from her patients than from any one else. And I am sure I can say the same for myself. The poorest, the meanest, the humblest patient may enter into the kingdom of Heaven before the cleverest of us, or the most conceited. For, in another world, many, many of the conditions of this world must be changed. Do we think of this?

We have been, almost all of us, taught to pray in the days of our childhood. Is there not something sad and strange in our throwing this aside when most required by us, on the threshold of our active lives? Life is a shallow thing, and more especially *Hospital* life, without any depth of religion. For it is a matter of simple experience that the best things, the things which seem as if they most would make us feel, become the most hardening if not rightly used.

And may I say a thing from my own experience? No training is of any use, unless one can learn (1) to feel, and (2) to think out things for oneself. And if we have not true religious feeling and purpose, Hospital life, the highest of all things *with* these—*without* them, becomes a mere routine and bustle, and a very hardening routine and bustle. One of our past Probationers said: 'Our work must be the first thing, but God must be in it.' 'And He is not in it,' she added. But let us hope that this is not so. I am sure it was not so with *her*. Let us try to make it not so with any of us.

There are three things which one must have to prevent this degeneration in oneself. And let each one of us, from time to time, tell, not any one else but herself, whether she has these less or more than when she began her training here:—

One is the real deep religious feeling and strong personal motherly interest for each one of our patients. And you can see this motherly interest in girls of twenty-one—we have Sisters of not more than that age who had it—And *not* see it in women of forty.

The second is a strong practical (intellectual, if you will) interest in the *case*, how it is going on. This is what makes the true Nurse. Otherwise the patients might as well be pieces of furniture, and we the housemaids, unless we see how interesting a thing Nursing is. This is what makes us urge you to begin to observe the very first case you see.

May I say something about this farther on?

The third is the pleasures of administration, which, though a fine word, means only learning to manage a Ward well: to keep it fresh, clean, tidy; to keep up its good order, punctuality; to learn to report your cases with absolute accuracy to the Surgeon or Physician; and to do this you must learn first to report them to the Sister: and all that is contained in the one word—Ward-management; to keep wine lists, diet lists, washing lists—that is Sister's work—and to do all the things no less important which constitute Nurse's work.

But it would take a whole book for me to count up these; and I am going back to the first thing that we were saying: how shallow a thing is Hospital life—which is, or ought to be, the most inspiring—without deep religious purpose! For, as years go on, we shall have others to train; and find that the springs of religion are dried up within ourselves. The patients we shall always have with us while we are Nurses. And we shall find that we have no religion gift or influence with them—no word in season whether for those who are to live, or for those who are to die—no, not even when they are in their last hours, and perhaps no one by but *us* to speak a word to point them to the Eternal Father and Saviour; not even for a poor little dying child, who cries: 'Nursey, tell me, oh, why is it so dark?' Then we may feel painfully about them what we do not at present feel about ourselves. We may wish, both for patients and Probationers, that they had the restraints of the 'fear' of the most Holy God, to enable them to resist temptation. We may regret that our own Probationers seem so worldly and external. And we may perceive too late that the deficiency in their characters began in our own.

For, to all good women, *life* is a prayer; and though we pray in our own rooms, in the Wards and at Church, the end must not be confounded with the means. We are the more bound to watch strictly over ourselves; we have not less but more need of a high standard of duty and of life in our Nursing; we must teach ourselves humility and modesty by becoming more aware of our own weakness and narrowness, and liability to mistake as Nurses and as Christians. Mere worldly success to any nobler, higher mind is not worth having. Do you think AGNES JONES, or some who are now living amongst us, cared much about worldly success? They cared about efficiency, thoroughness. But that is a different thing.

We must condemn many of our own tempers when we calmly review them. We must lament over training opportunities which we have lost—most desire to become better women, better Nurses—*that* we all of us must feel. And then, and not till then, will *life* and *work* among the sick become a prayer.

For prayer is communion or co-operation with God: the expression of a *life* among his poor and sick and erring ones. But when we speak with God, our power of addressing Him, or holding communion with Him, and listening to His still small voice, depends upon our will being one and the same with His. *Is* He our God, as He was Christ's? To Christ He was all, to us He seems sometimes nothing. Can we retire to rest after our busy, anxious day in the Wards, with the feeling: 'Lord, into Thy hands I commend my spirit,' and those of such and such anxious cases; remembering, too, that in the darkness, 'Thou God seest me,' and seest them too? Can we rise in the morning, almost with a feeling of joy that we are spared another day to do Him service with His sick?—

'Awake, my soul, and with the sun,
Thy daily course of duty run.'

Does the thought ever occur to us, in the course of the day, that we will correct that particular fault of mind, or heart, or temper, whether slowness or bustle, or want of accuracy or method, or sharp talking, or tale-bearing or gossipping, or harsh judgments, or want of loyalty to those under whom or among whom we are placed—(oh, how common and how old a fault—as old as Solomon—'He that repeateth a matter, separateth friends'—and how can people trust us unless they know that we are not tale-bearers, who will misrepresent or improperly repeat what is said to us?)—shall we correct this, or any other fault— not with a view to our success in life, or to our own credit, but in order that we may be able to serve our Master better in the service of the sick? Or do we ever seek to carry on the battle against light behavior, against self-indulgence, against evil tempers (the 'world,' the 'flesh,' and the 'devil'), and the temptations that beset us; conscious that in ourselves we are weak, but that there is a strength greater than our own, 'which is perfected in weakness'? Do we think of God as the Eternal, into whose hands our patients, whom we see dying in the Wards, must resign their souls—into whose hands we must resign our own when we depart hence, and ought to resign our own as entirely every morning and night of our lives here; with whom do live the spirits of the just made perfect, and with whom do really live, *ought* really as much to live, our spirits here, and who, in the hour of death, in the hour of life, both for our patients and ourselves, must be our trust and hope? We would not always be thinking of death, for 'we must live before we die,' and life, perhaps, is as difficult as death. Yet the thought of a time when we shall have passed out of the sight and memory of men may also help us to live; may assist us in shaking off the load of tempers, jealousies, prejudices, bitternesses, interests which weight us down, may teach us to rise out of this busy, bustling Hospital world, into the clearer light of God's Kingdom, of which, indeed, this Home is, or might be a part, and certainly and especially this Hospital.

This is the spirit of prayer, the spirit of conversation or communion with God, which leads us in all our Nursing silently to think of Him, and refer it to Him. When we hear in the voice of conscience *His* voice speaking to us; when we are aware that He is the witness of everything we do, and say, and think, and also the source of every good thing in us; and when we feel in our hearts the struggle against some evil temper, then God is fighting *with* us against envy and jealousy, against selfishness and self-indulgence, against lightness, and frivolity, and vanity, for 'our better self against our worse self.'

And when kneeling at prayer or at communion—are there any who have done us good which we would return? or evil which we would forgive? may we not pray to be able to do this in the right way, not from self-glory or love of influence, but from the love of them, and from the love of God?

And thus, too, the friendships which have begun at this School may last through life, and be a help and strength to us. For may we not regard the opportunity given for acquiring friends as one of the uses of this place? and Christian friendship, in uniting us to a friend, as uniting us at the same time to Christ and God? Christ called His disciples friends, adding the reason, 'because He had told them all that He had heard of the Father,' just as women tell their whole mind to their friends.

But we all know that there are dangers and disappointments in friendships, especially in women's friendships, as well as joys and sorrows. A woman may have an honourable desire to know those who are her superiors in education, in the School, or in Nursing. Or she may allow herself to drop into the society of those beneath her, perhaps because she is more at home with them, and is proud or shy with her superiors. And so she gets good or she gets harm out of the companionship of those with whom she lives and nurses. Such as they are, she will be in some degree; she will take from them her manners and style of conversation, though she may be better or worse than they. We do not want to be judges of our fellow-women (for who made thee to differ from another?), but neither can we leave entirely to chance one of the greatest interests of human life.

True friendship is simple, womanly, unreserved; not weak, or silly, or fond, or noisy, or romping, or extravagant, nor yet jealous and selfish, and exacting more than woman's nature can fairly give (for there are other ties which bind women to one another besides friendship); nor, again, intrusive into the secrets of another woman, or curious about her circumstances; rejoicing in the presence of a friend, and not forgetting her in her absence.

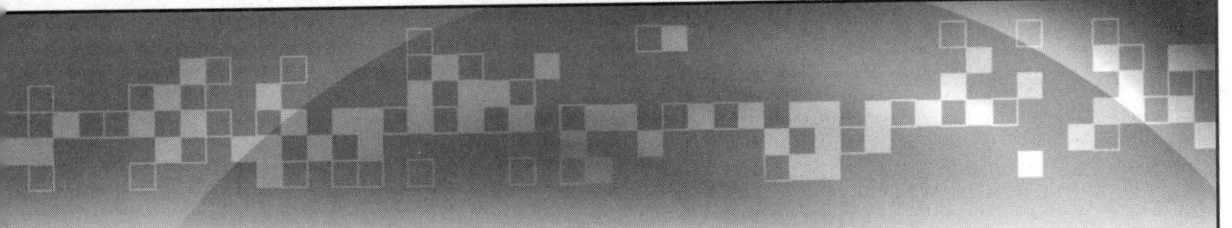

Two Probationers or Nurses going together have not only a twofold, but a fourfold strength, if they learn knowledge or good from one another; if they form the characters of one another; if they support one another in fulfilling the duties and bearing the troubles of a Nursing life, if their friendship thus becomes fellow-service to God in their daily work. They may sometimes rejoice together over the portion of their training which has been accomplished, and take counsel about what remains to be done. They will desire to keep one another up to the mark; not to allow idleness or eccentricity to spoil their time of training.

But some of our youthful friendships are too violent to last: they have in them something of weakness or sentimentalism; the feeling passes away, and we become ashamed of them. Or at some critical time a friend has failed to stand by us, and then it is useless to talk of 'Auld lang syne.' Only still let us remember that there are duties which we owe to the 'extinct' friend (who perhaps on some fanciful ground has parted company from us), that we should never speak against her, or make use of our knowledge about her. For the memory of a friendship is like the memory of a dead friend, not lightly to be spoken of.

And then there is the 'Christian or ideal friendship.' What others regard as the service of the sick, she may recognise as also the service of God; what others do out of compassion for their maimed fellow-creatures, she may do also for the love of Christ. Feeling that God has made her what she is, she may seek to carry on her work in the Hospital as a fellow-worker with God. Remembering that Christ died for her, she may be ready to lay down her life for her patients.

'They walked together in the house of God as friends'—that is, they served God together in doing good to His sick. For if ever a place may be called the 'house of God,' it is a Hospital, if it be what it should be. And in old times it *was* called the 'house' or the 'hotel' of God. The greatest and oldest Central Hospital of Paris, where is the Mother-house of the principal Order of Nursing Sisters, is to this day called the *Hôtel Dieu*, the 'House of God.'

There may be some amongst us who, like St. Paul, are capable of feeling a natural interest in the spiritual welfare of our fellow-Probationers—or, if you like the expression better, in the improvement of their characters—that they may become more such as God intended them to be in this Hospital and Home. For 'Christian friendship is not merely the friendship of equals, but of unequals'—the love of the weak and of those who can make no return, like the love of God towards the unthankful and the evil. It is not a friendship of one or two, but of many. It proceeds upon a different rule: 'Love your enemies.' It is founded upon that charity 'which is not easily offended, which beareth all things believeth all things, hopeth all things, endureth all things.' Such a friendship we may be hardly able to reconcile either with our own character or with common prudence. Yet this is the 'Christian ideal in the Gospel.' And here and there may be found some one who has been inspired to carry out the ideal in practice.

'To live in isolation is to be weak and unhappy—perhaps to be idle and selfish.' There is something not quite right in a woman who shuts up her heart from other women.

This may seem to be telling you what you already know, and bidding you do what you are already doing. Well, then, shall we put the matter another way? Make such friendships as you will look back upon with pleasure in later life, and be loyal and true to your friends, not going from one to another.

'The friends thou hast, and their adoption tried,
Grapple thou to thy soul with hooks of steel;
But do not dull thy palm with entertainment
Of each new hatched, unfledged comrade.'

And, do not expect more of them than friends can give, or weary them with demands for sympathy; and do not let the womanliness of friendship be impaired by any silliness or sentimentalism; or allow hearty and genial good-will to degenerate into vulgarity and noise.

And as was once truly said, friendship, above all perhaps, appears best, as it did in St. Paul in his manner of rebuking those who had erred, 'transferring their faults in a figure to Apollos and to himself.' 'No one knew how to speak the truth in love like him.'

And as has been said of Romans xii.: 'What rule of manners can be better than this chapter?' *E.g.*—'She that giveth, let her do it with simplicity'; that is, let us do our acts of Nursing and kindness as if we did not make much of them, as unto the Lord and not to men. 'Like-minded one towards another'; that is, that we should have the same thoughts and feelings with others, 'rejoicing with them that rejoice, and weeping with them that weep,' going out of ourselves and entering into the thoughts of others.

And have we St. Paul's extraordinary regard for the feelings of others? he was never too busy to think of these: 'If meat make my brother to offend, I will eat no more meat while the world standeth,' he says, though he well knew such scruples were really superstitions. If the spirit of these words could find a way to our women's hearts, we might be able to say, 'See how these Christians (Nurses) love one another!'

Then the courtesy we owe one woman to another: 'for the happiness and the good' of our work and our School is not simply 'made up of great duties and virtues, nor the evil of the opposite.' But both tone and character of our School, introducing light or darkness into the 'Home,' sweetness or bitterness into our intercourse with one another.

And, as to our Wards:—Christ we may be sure did not lose authority, or dignity and refinement, 'even in the company of publicans and harlots,' just as we may observe in the Wards, that there are a few of us whose very refinement makes them do the coarsest and roughest things there with simplicity. A Sister of ours once remarked this of one of her Probationers (who was not a lady in the common sense of the word, but she was the truest gentlewoman in Christ's sense), that she was too refined (most people would have said to do the indelicate work of the Wards, but *she* said) to see indelicacy in doing the nastiest thing; and so did it all well, without thinking of herself, or that men's eyes were upon her. That is real dignity—the dignity which Christ had—on which no man can intrude, yet combined with the greatest gentleness and simplicity of life.

Is there any of us who does not desire to become better? There are faults which we have committed, or feelings which we have entertained towards others, which were not right, or a course of life, frivolous or dressy, in which we have indulged. (Frivolous seems a strange word to apply to Hospital work, where, every day, questions of life or death are decided; and to be frivolous in such work is the more shocking and startling from the contrast. But are there not such frivolities among us? nay, does not high and earnest purpose sometimes decay among us into light vanities and trifling self-indulgences? To be cheerful is a duty; to be frivolous, is it not a sin, most of all in Hospital life?)

One use of prayer is to maintain in us a higher standard, and to prevent our purpose sinking, unawares to us, to our practice, or to the practice of our little world around us.

We desire for a few minutes in each day to live in the more immediate presence of God, in the presence of truth and justice, and holiness and love Then is the time to get rid of our vain self-excuses, and see ourselves as we truly are in the sight of God; and to think of others as they are in the presence of God. Yes, and of ourselves also, that we may free our minds from dislikes and gossips, and jealousies; and learn to devote our gifts wholly to the service of God and man.

II. And let me say a word about self-denial: because, as we all know, there can be no real Nursing without self-denial. We know the story [sic] of the Roman soldier, above 1,400 years ago, who, entering a town in France with his regiment, saw a sick man perishing with cold by the wayside—there were no Hospitals then—and, having nothing else to give, drew his sword, cut his own cloak in half, and wrapped the sick man in half his cloak.

[It is said that a dream visited him, in which he found himself admitted into heaven, and Christ saying, 'Martin hath clothed me with this garment': the dream, of course, being a remembrance of the verse, 'When saw we thee sick or in prison, and came unto thee?' and the answer, 'Inasmuch as ye have done it unto one of the least of these my brethren, ye have done it unto me.' But whether the story of the dream be true or not] this Roman soldier, converted to Christianity, became afterwards one of the greatest bishops of the early ages, Martin of Tours.

We are not called upon to feed our patients with our own dinners, or to dress them with our own clothes. But we can learn Sick Cookery for our Patients, which, one is sorry to think, is, though so important, often so much neglected. But we can give up spending our money in foolish dressy ways, and thus—merely to make ourselves ridiculous in the eyes of better people than ourselves—squandering what we ought to lay by for ourselves or our families.

We may rightly think that our charity is not the better for this; though, if we had to part with what really cost us something for others, we fancy we should be much more cheerful and good tempered.

But, however, we have *not*. So we are the more bound to exercise our cheerfulness and good temper, as it only costs us that, towards our patients and one another. We are comfortable, and cannot make ourselves uncomfortable on purpose.

On one of the severest winter days in the late war between France and Germany, an immense detachment, many thousands, of wretched French prisoners, were passing through the poorest streets of one of the largest and poorest German towns on the way to their prisoners' camp. Every door in this poor 'East End' opened; not one remained closed; and out of every door came a poor German woman, carrying in her hand the dinner or supper she was cooking for herself, her husband, or children; often all she had in the house was in her hands. And this she crammed into the hands of the most sickly-looking prisoner as he passed by,—often into his mouth, as he sank down exhausted in the muddy street. And the good-natured German escort, whose business it was to bring these poor French to their prison, turned away their heads, and let the women have their way, though it was late, and they were weary too. Before the prisoners had been the first hour in their prison, six had lain down in the straw and died. But how many lives had been saved that night by the timely food of these good women, giving all they had, not of their abundance, but of their poverty, God only knows, not we.

This was told by an Englishman who was by and saw it; one of our own 'Aid Committee.'

And a lady at another large German station, which almost all the prisoners' trains passed through, went every night during all that long, long dreadful winter, and for the whole night, to feed, and warm, and comfort and often to receive the last dying words of the miserable French prisoners, as in open trucks, some frozen to the bottom, some arriving only as the dead, others to die in the station, all half-clad and starving (some had been nine days and nights in these open trucks—many had been twenty-four hours without food), she came to receive and nurse the sick, as these long, terrible trainsfull dragged their slow length into the station. Night after night she kneeled on its pavement, supporting the dying heads, receiving their last messages to their mothers; pouring wine or hot milk down the throats of the sick; dressing the frost-bitten limbs; and, thank God, saving many. Many were carried to the prisoners' hospital in the town, of whom about two-thirds recovered. Every bit of linen she had went in this way. She herself contracted incurable ill-health during these fearful nights. But thousands were saved by her means.

She is my friend. She came and saw me here after this; and it is from her lips I heard the story. Small-pox and typhus raged among the prisoners, most of whom were quite boys. Many were wounded; half were frost-bitten. Sometimes they would snatch at all she brought; but sometimes they would turn away their dying heads from the tempting hot wine, and gasp out, 'Thank you, madam; give it to *him*, who wants it more than I.' Or, '*I'm* past help; love to mother.'

We have not to give of our own to *our* sick. But shall we the less give them our all—that is, all our hearts and minds? and reasonable service?

Suppose we dedicated this 'School' to Him, to the Divine Charity and Love which said, 'Inasmuch as ye do it unto one of the least of these my brethren' (and He calls all our patients—all of us, His brothers and sisters) 'ye do it unto me'—or, what a 'Kingdom of Heaven' this might be! Then, indeed, the dream of Martin of Tours, the soldier and Missionary-Bishop, would have come true!

III. May I take this opportunity of saying what I think really very much concerns us? First of all, that you have, or might have, directly and indirectly, a great deal to do with maintaining a supply of good candidates to this School. You know whether you have been happy here or not; you know whether you have had opportunities given you here of training and self-improvement. Many, very many of our old Matrons and Nurses have told me that their time as Probationers with us was 'the happiest time of their lives.' It *might* be so with all, though perhaps all do not think so now.

It is in your power to assist the School most materially in obtaining fresh and worthy recruits. There is hardly one of you who has not friends or acquaintances of her own. *You* ought to advertise us. [We ought not to have to put one advertisement in the newspapers.] If you think this is a worthy life, why do you not bring others to it? I tried to do my part. When Agnes Jones died, though my heart was breaking, I put an article in 'Good Words,' such as I knew she would have wished, in all but the mention of herself; and for years her dear memory brought aspirants to the work in our Schools, or others' Schools.

The object: To reform the Nursing of all the Hospitals and Workhouse Infirmaries in the world, and to establish District Nursing among the sick poor at home, too, as at Liverpool—is this not an object most worthy of the co-operation of all civilized people?

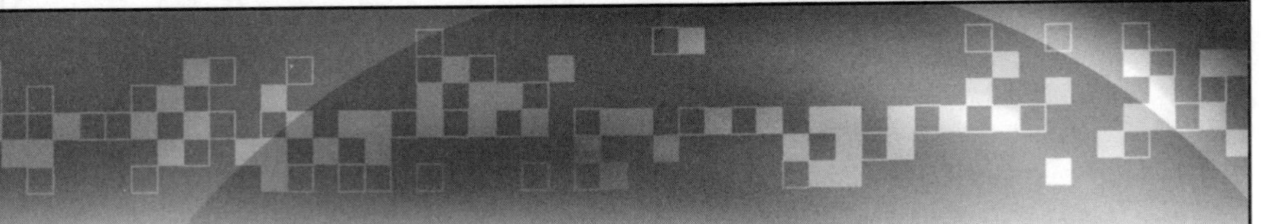

Every one of you can be a missionary in this work, every one can be the reverse.

Every nurse, as also every man and woman, is a Missionary—not in a Hospital ward only, but in all places—for good or for evil. It is not what we say, what we do, or what we appear, that has influence on others, but what we *are*.

Let that be the word for each of us.

In the last ten years, thank God, numerous Training Schools for Nurses have grown up, resolved to unite in putting a stop to such a thing as drunken, immoral, and inefficient Nursing. But all make the same complaint: while the outcry of 'employment for women' continues, why does not this most womanly employment for all good women become more sought after?

I hope to hear that my old friends in St. Thomas' have each done their part; and I feel quite sure that if it is once placed before them, as a thing they ought to do, they will be found in the front.

You who are assembled in this room, and who are each connected with some circle, directly or indirectly, may do a good work for the civilization of the Workhouses and Hospitals of the world. If you inform yourselves on the subject, and if you set yourselves to work to deal with it, as we do with any other great evil that tortures helpless people, you will be able to act directly upon your friends outside, and ultimately get up an amount of public opinion among women capable of becoming Nurses, which will be of the greatest possible aid to our efforts in improving Hospital and Workhouse Nursing. Every one can help—*every one*—better than if she were a 'newspaper,' better than if she were a 'public meeting.' I believe that within a few years you can make it a thing that will be a disgrace to any Hospital or even Workhouse to be suspected of bad Nursing, or to any district (in towns, at any rate) not to have a good District Nurse to nurse the sick poor at home.

If you wish St. Thomas' to lead the opinion of our country upon Hospital Nursing, we must, first of all, be the best Hospital Nurses ourselves; secondly, we must bring the best fresh blood into our Training Schools. And so you may do an essential service to that common cause which we say we are bent upon promoting. I think that in this way you might do a great deal of good.

Those who have made the right use of all the training that came in their way in this School, if they would write to their own homes for the information of their friends outside, an immense help on its way could be given to the work we have all so much at heart. And I look upon it as a certainty that you will each be able, in one way or another, whether purposely or almost unconsciously, to take a great part in reforming the Hospital and Workhouse Nursing systems of our country, perhaps of our colonies and dependencies, and perhaps of the world.

IV. May I pay ourselves even the least little compliment, as to our being a little less conceited than last year? Were we not as conceited in 1872 as it was possible to be? You shall tell. Are we, in 1873, rather less so? And, without having any one particularly in my head—for what I am going to ask is in fact a truism—is not our conceit always in exact proportion to our ignorance? For those who really know something know how little it is.

We are not even so humble as the self-satisfied student in the play, where he is comically made to come in to a philosopher, sinking under the thought of how incomplete is all human knowledge; and the conceited youth says: '*Much* it is true I

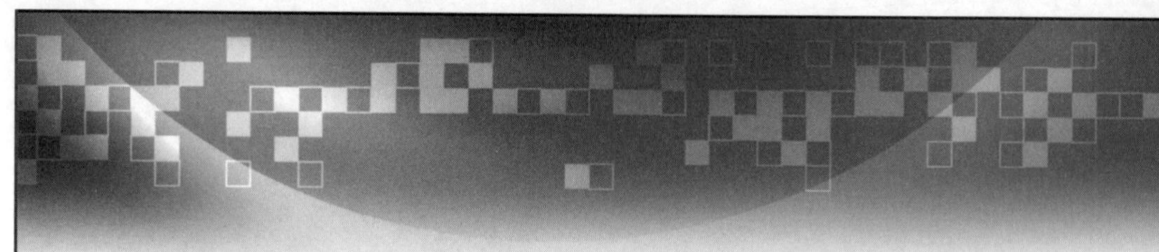

know, but I would fain know all.' We can all laugh at that; but am I wrong in thinking that some of us suppose they do 'know *all*'?

Would that this could be a 'secret' among us! But, unfortunately, is not our name 'up' and 'abroad' for conceit? And has it not even been said ('tell it not in Gath'): 'And these conceited "Nightingale" women scarcely knew how to read and write?'

Now let no one look to see our blushes. But shall we not get rid of this which makes us ridiculous as fast as we can?

But enough of this joke; let us be serious, remembering that the greatest trust which is committed to any woman of us all is, *herself*; and that she is living in the presence of God as well as of her fellow-women.

To know whether we know our Nursing business or not is a great result of training; and to think that we know it when we do *not* is as great a proof of want of training.

Every woman of us all—but above all every one of us Nurses—should be on our guard against the silent growth of any bad habit, such as carelessness, noisiness, untidiness, impatience, petty failures in cheerfulness or kindliness, inaccuracy or want of observation, or not doing things thoroughly, or want of the most exquisite cleanliness and neatness, so essential to the recovery of the sick, or want of punctuality, or want of order, or of trustworthiness in carrying out orders to the smallest detail, or in putting off things, or letting ourselves get into a state of excitement.

The world, more especially the Hospital world, is in such a hurry, is moving so fast, that it is too easy to slide into bad habits before we are aware. And it is easier still to let our year's training slip away without forming any real plan of training ourselves. For, after all, all that any training is to do for us is: to teach us how to train ourselves, how to observe for ourselves, how to think out things for ourselves. Don't let us allow the first week, the second week, the third week to pass by—I will not say in idleness, but in bustle. Begin, for instance, at once making notes of your cases. From the first moment you see a case, you can observe it. Nay, it is one of the first things a Nurse is strictly called upon to do: to observe her sick. Mr. CROFT has taught you how to take notes; and you have now, every one of you, two leisure times a week to work up your notes.

But give but one quarter of an hour *a day* to jot down, even in words which no one can understand but yourself, the progress or change of two or three individual cases, not to forget or confuse them. You can then write them out at your two leisure times. To those who have not much education, I am sure that our kind Home Sister, or the Special Probationer in the same Ward, or nearest in any way, will give help. The race is not always to the swift, nor the battle to the strong; and 'line upon line'— *one* line every day—in the steady, observing, humble Nurse has often won the race over the smarter 'genius' in what constitutes real Nursing. But few of us women seriously think of improving our own mind or character *every day*. And this is fatal to our improving in Nursing. We do not calculate the future by our experience of the past. What right have we to expect that, if we have not improved during the last six months, we shall during the next six? Then, we do not allow for the changes which circumstances—the being put on Staff duty, when we certainly shall not have more time, but less, for improving ourselves, or times of life—the growing older or more feeble in health—make in us. We believe that we shall always have the same powers or opportunities for learning our business which we now have. Our time of training slips away in this unimproving manner. And when a woman begins to see how many things might have been better in her, she is too old to change, or it is too late, too late. And she confesses to herself, or oftener she does not confess:

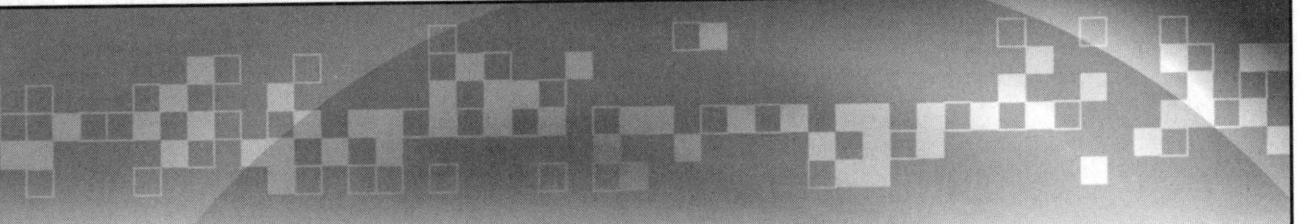

'How all her life she had been in the wrong.'

We are all of us, as we believe, passing into an unknown world, of which this is only a part. We have been here a year, or part of a year. What are we making of our own lives? Are we where we were a year ago? Or are we fitter for that work of afterlife which we have undertaken? Better prepared and equipped for the service of God, and man and child, as Nurses? Do we feel in ourselves that we are gradually becoming more fitted to run the race that is set before us? Do our faults, and weaknesses, and vanities, tend to diminish? Or are we still listless, inefficient, slow, bustling, conceited, unkind, hard judges of others, instead of helping them where we can? There is no greater softener of hard judgments than is the trying to help the person whom we so judge, as I can tell from my own experience; and in this you will tell me whether we have been deficient to each other. There is a true story told of Captain Marryat, when a boy; that he jumped overboard to save an older mid-shipman who had made the boy's life a misery to him by his filthy cruelties. And the boy Marryat wrote home to his mother: 'that he loved this midshipman how—and wasn't it lucky that his life was saved—even better than his own darling mother.'

Do we keep before our minds constantly the sense of our duty here, of our duty to others—Nurses, Sisters, Matron—as well as to ourselves, our fellow Probationers, and our Home Sister, and to the whole School of which we are members? You will tell me whether our duty to our patients is here the only thing, or almost the only thing thought of, and not also our duty to one another, our Matron and School, and whether this is right.

If we thought of this more, if we were more anxious about this, more anxious about following the example of Christ, than about the opinion of our 'world' ['we are the "world," which we often seem to think includes every one but *us*'], we might hope to attain that quiet mind and self-control, which is the 'liberty' spoken of by St. Paul, and might learn how truly to use and enjoy both our fellow Probationers, and this Home and our School.

But few comparatively have the power of disengaging themselves, even in thought, from those about them. They take the view of their own set. If it is the fashion to conceal, they conceal; if to carry tales, they carry tales.

Above all, don't let it be the fashion among us to drag down the level of 'training' to the lowest point compatible with our own credit, but to be always pressing forward to the highest. Every one may help to set the standard, not by levelling it to common ignorance, but by raising it to common intelligence. Every one may help to knit us together; every one in her own circle may do much toward raising it; may raise conversation above the level of mere gossip—and, oh, what a hot-bed of gossip may not a Hospital or 'Home' become if *no* one will do this!—may banish ignoble talk about persons; may refuse to listen to scandals; may seek to bring our Nurses together. There are a few who never allow themselves to speak against others, and exercise such a kind of authority as to prevent others being spoken against in their hearing.

These are the 'peacemakers' of whom Christ speaks. These are they who keep a Home or Institution together, and seem more than any others in this our little world to bear the image of Christ until His coming again.

The 'peacemaker' may have an eye to doing her fellow Probationers good, but she will hardly let them find this out, partly because she shrinks from placing herself above them, conscious as she is of her own defects, and also because she knows that influence must find a way to the hearts of women unperceived. She will feel a womanly affection for them, showing itself on the greater occasions of life in real services to them, of which she studies to conceal the obligation—seen also in daily trifles, the pleasant look, the kindly word, the encouraging answer, the attention to little things, the readiness to listen as well as speak, the absence of lightness or gossip, the little services in the Wards to one another.

If there was more of this in our School, it would begin to wear a different face; for when we find fault with our School, we are really finding fault with ourselves; and when *we* improve, our School improves.

These remarks may have no particular reference to any one here present; for neither can I tell what is passing in your minds, nor can you tell what is passing in mine, but God only.

Do we ever do things because they are right, without regard to our own credit? When we ask ourselves only: 'What is right?' or (which is the same question), 'What is the will of God,' then we are truly entering His 'kingdom.' We are no longer grovelling among the opinions of men and women. We can see God in all things, and all things in God—the Eternal Father shining through the accidents of our lives, which sometimes shake us more, though less conspicuous, than the accidents we see brought in to our Surgical Wards—the accidents of the characters of those under whom and among whom we are placed, and of our own inner life.

Our minds become stronger supported by a power unseen, and our motives freer from vanity and littleness, not with eye-service as men and women pleasers, but as seeing the Lord.

One of the greatest missionaries that ever was, wrote more than 300 years ago to his pupils and fellow-missionaries:—

'Self-knowledge'—(the knowledge by which we see ourselves in God)—'self-knowledge is the nurse of confidence in God. It is from distrust of ourselves that confidence in God is born. This will be the way for us to gain that true interior lowliness of mind which, in all places, and especially here '[and is not Nursing a sort of mission?],' is far more necessary than you think. I warn you also not to let the good opinion which men have of you be too much of a pleasure to you, unless perhaps in order that you may be the more ashamed of yourselves on that account. It is that which leads people to neglect themselves, and this negligence, in many cases, upsets, *as by a kind of trick*, all that lowliness of which I speak, and puts conceit and arrogance in its place. And thus so many do not see for a long time how much they have lost, and gradually lose all care for piety, and all tranquillity of mind, and thus are always troubled and anxious, finding no comfort either from without or within themselves.'

'Come unto me, all ye that labour and are heavy laden,' says our Lord, 'and I will give you rest.' But He adds immediately, *who* are those to whom He will give this 'rest' or quietness of mind—namely to those who, like Himself, are 'meek and lowly of heart.'

These words may seem in a Hospital life 'like dreams.' But they are not dreams if we take them for the spirit of our School and the rule of our Nursing. 'To practise them, to feel them, to make them our own,' this is not far from the 'kingdom of Heaven' in a Hospital.

Pray for me, as I do for you, that 'piety' and a 'quiet mind'—but these always and only in the strenuous effort to *press forwards*—may be ours.

FLORENCE NIGHTINGALE.

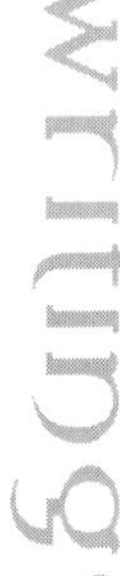

1874

NOTE.— This Address was read by Sir HARRY VERNEY, the Chairman of the Council of the Nightingale Fund, to the Probationer-Nurses in the School at St. Thomas' Hospital, on the 23rd July 1874.

ADDRESS
FROM: FLORENCE NIGHTINGALE
TO THE:
PROBATIONER-NURSES IN THE 'NIGHTINGALE FUND' SCHOOL, AT ST. THOMAS' HOSPITAL, AND THE NURSES WHO WERE FORMERLY TRAINED THERE.
23RD JULY, 1874.
Printed for Private Use.

July 23*rd*, 1874.

ANOTHER YEAR has passed over us, my dear friends. There have been many changes among us. We have each of us tasted somewhat more of the discipline of life: to some of us it may have been very bitter, to others, let us hope, not so; by all, let us trust, it has been put to heroic uses.

'Heroic?' I think I hear you say; 'can there be much of "heroic" in washing porringers and making beds?'

I once heard a man (he is dead now) giving a lesson to some poor orphan girls in an Orphan Asylum. Few things, I think, ever struck me so much, or them. It was on the 'heroic virtues.' It went into the smallest particulars of thrift, of duty, of love and kindness; and he ended by asking them how they thought such small people as themselves could manage to practise those great virtues. A child of seven put up its little nib and chirped out: 'Please, my lord, we might pick up pins when we don't like to.' That showed she understood his lesson.

His lesson was not exactly fitted to us, but we may all fit it to ourselves.

'This night, if we are inclined to make a noise on the stairs, or to linger in each other's rooms, shall we go quietly to bed, alone with God?' Is there such loud laughing and boisterous talking in the day-time, going upstairs to your rooms, that it disturbs any one who is ill, or prevents those who have been on night duty from getting any sleep?

Some of you yourselves have told me that you could get better day sleep in the Night Nurses' Dormitory than in your own 'Home.'

Is that doing what you would be done by—loving your neighbour as yourselves, as our Master told us?

Do you think it is we who invent the duty 'Quiet and orderly,' or is it He?

If our uniform dress is not what we like, shall we think of our Lord, whose very garments were divided by the soldiers?

[But I always think how much more becoming is our uniform than any other dress I see.]

If there is anything at table that we don't like, shall we take it thankfully, remembering Who had to ask a poor woman for a drink of water?

Shall we take the utmost pains to be perfectly regular and punctual to all our hours—going into the wards, coming out of the wards, at meals, &c.? and if we are

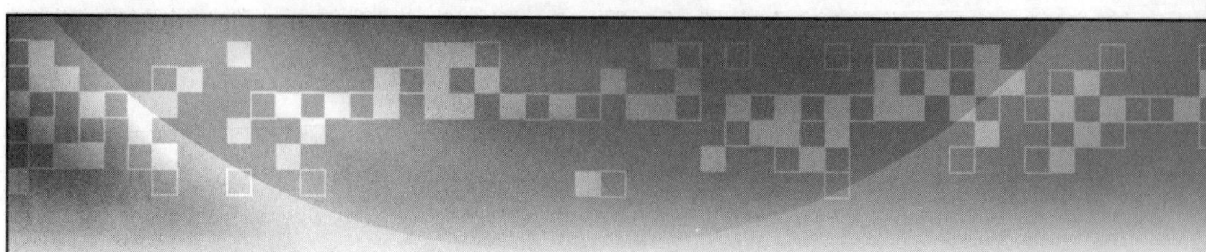

unavoidably prevent, making an apology to the Home Sister, remembering what has been written about those who are in authority over us? Or do we think a few minutes of no consequence in coming from or going to the wards?

Do we carefully observe our Rules?

If we *are* what is printed at the top of our Duties, viz.:—

Trustworthy,

Punctual,

Quiet and orderly,

Cleanly and neat,

Patient, cheerful, and kindly,

we scarcely need any other lesson but what explains these to us. *Trustworthy:* that is, faithful:

Trustworthy when we have no one by to urge or to order us. 'Her lips were never opened but to speak the truth.' Can that be said of us?

Trustworthy, in keeping our soul in our hands, never excited, but always ready to lift it up to God; unstained by the smallest flirtation, innocent of the smallest offence, even in thought.

Trustworthy, in doing our work as faithfully as if our superiors were always near us.

Trustworthy, in never prying into one another's concerns, but ever acting behind another's back as one would to her face.

Trustworthy, in avoiding every word that could injure, in the smallest degree, our patients or our companions, who are our neighbours, remembering how St. Peter says that God made us *all* 'stewards of grace one to another.'

How can we be 'stewards of grace' to one another?

By giving the 'grace' of our good example to all around us.

And how can we become 'untrustworthy stewards' to one another?

By showing ourselves lax in our habits, irregular in our ways, not doing as we should do if our superiors were by. '*Cripple leads the way.*' Shall the better follow the worse?

It has happened to me to hear some of you say—perhaps it has happened to us all—'Indeed, I only did what I saw done.'

How glorious it would be if 'only doing what we saw done 'always led us right!

A master of a great public school once said that he could trust his whole school, because he could trust every single boy in it.

Oh, could God but say that He can trust this Home and Hospital, because He can trust every woman in it!

Let us try this—every woman to work as though success depended on herself.

Do you know that, in this great Indian Famine, every Englishman has worked as if success depended on himself? And in saving a population as large as that of England from death by starvation, do you not think that we have achieved the greatest victory we ever won in India?

Suppose we work thus for this Home and Hospital.

Oh, my dear friends, how terrible it will be to any of us, some day, to hear another say, that she only did what she saw us do, if that was on the 'road that leadeth to destruction'!

Or, taking it another way, how delightful—how delightful to have set another on her journey to heaven by our good example; how terrible to have delayed another on her journey to heaven by our bad example!

There is an old story—nearly six hundred years old—when a ploughboy said to a truly great man, whose name is known in history, that he 'advised' him 'always to live in such a way that those who had a good opinion of him might never be disappointed.'

The great man thanked him for his advice, and—kept it.

If our School has a good name, do we live so that people 'may never be disappointed' in its Nurses?

Obedient: not wilful: not to have such a sturdy will of our own. Common sense tells us that no training can do us any good if we are always seeking our own way. I know that some have really sought in dedication to God to give up their own wills to His. For if you enter this Training-School, is that not in effect a promise to Him to give up your own way for that way which you are taught?

Let us not question so much. You *must* know that things have been thought over and arranged for your benefit. You are not bound to think us always right: perhaps you can't. But are *you* more likely to be right? And, at all events, you know you *are* right, if you choose to enter our ways, to submit yours to them.

In a foreign Training-School, I once heard a most excellent pastor, who was visiting there, say to a nurse: 'Are you *dis*couraged?—say, rather, you are *dis*obedient: they always mean the same thing.' And I thought how right he was. And, what is more, the Nurse thought so too: and she was not 'discouraged' ever after, because she gave up being 'disobedient.'

The 'every one for herself' ought to have no footing here: and these strong wills of ours God will teach—is we do not let Him teach us here, He will teach us by some sterner discipline hereafter—teach to bend first to the will of God, and then to the reasonable and lawful wills of those among whom our lot is cast.

I often say for myself, and I have no doubt you do, that line of the hymn:

'Tell me, Thou yet wilt chide, Thou canst not spare,
O Lord, Thy chastening rod.'

Let Him reduce us to His discipline before it is too late.

If we 'kick against the pricks,' we can only pray that He will give us more 'pricks,' till we cease to 'kick.' And it is a proof of His fatherly love, and that He has not given us up, if He does.

For myself, I can say that I have never known what it was, since I can remember anything, not to have 'prickly' discipline: more than any one knew of: and I hope I have not 'kicked.'

To return to *Trustworthiness:*

Most of you, on leaving the Home, go first on night duty. Now there is nothing like night duty for trying our trustworthiness.

A year hence, you will tell me whether you have felt any temptation not to be quite honest in reporting cases the next morning to your sister or nurse—that is, to say you have observed when you have not observed; to slur over things in your report which, for aught you know, may be of consequence to the patient; to slur over things in your work because there is no one watching you: no one but God.

It has indeed been known that the night nurse has stayed in the kitchen to talk; but we may trust such things will not happen again.

And, for all, let us *all* say this word for ourselves: everything gets toppled over, if we don't make it a matter of conscience: a matter of reckoning between ourselves and our God.

That is the only safeguard of real *trustworthiness*.

If we treat it as a mere matter of business, of success in our career in life, never shall we give anything but eye-service; never shall we be really trustworthy.

Orderly: Let us never waste anything, even pins or paper, as some do, by beginning letters or resolutions, or 'cases,' which they never take the trouble to finish.

Cheerful and Patient: Let us never wish for more than is necessary, and be cheerful when what we should like is sometimes denied us, as it may be some day; or when people are unkind, or we are disregarded by those we love: remembering Him whose attendants at His death were mocking soldiers. I assure you, my friends, that if we can practise those 'duties' faithfully, we are practising the 'heroic virtues' *Patient, cheerful, and kindly:*

Now, is it being patient, cheerful, and kindly to be so only with those who are so to us? for, as St. Peter tells us, even ungodly people do that. But if we can do good to some one who has done us ill, oh, what a privilege that is! and even God will thank us for it, the Apostle says. Let us be kindest to the impatient and unkindly.

Now let me tell you of two Nurses whom we knew:

One was a lady, with just enough to live upon, who took an old widow to nurse into her house: recommended to her by her minister. One day, she met him and reproached him: Why?—because the old widow was 'too good': '*any* body could nurse *her.*' Presently a grumbling old woman, never contented with anything anybody did, who thought she was never treated well enough, and that she never had 'her due,' was found. And this old woman the lady took into her house and nursed till she died: because, she said, nobody else liked to do anything for her: and *she* did. That was something like kindness: for there is no great kindness in doing good to any one who is grateful and thanks us for it.

But my other story is something much better still:

A poor Nurse, who had been left a widow, with nothing to live upon but her own earnings, inquired for some '*tedious children*' to take care of. As you may suppose, there were no difficulty in finding this article ('tedious' orphans). And from that day, for 20 years, she never had less than two, three, or four orphans with her, and sometimes five, whom she brought up as her own, training them for service. She taught them something better: She taught them that they had 'nothing but their character to depend upon': 'I tell them,' she said, 'it was all I had myself': 'God helps girls that watch over themselves.' 'If a girl isn't made to feel this early, it's hard afterwards to make her feel it.' These girls, so brought up, turned out much better than those brought up in most large Union schools, for asylums are not like homes. Of the children whom Nurse took in, one was a girl of such bad habits and such a mischief-maker that no one else could manager her. But Nurse did.

One was a boy of 14, just out of prison for bad ways (for she soon found she could not refuse boys), whom she took, reclaimed, and who became as good a boy as can be. These are only two specimens. They called her 'Mother.' And God, she used to say, gave them to her as her own. You will ask how she supported them. The larger number of them she supported herself by taking in washing, by charing one day a week, and, by and bye, by taking in journeymen as lodgers. Now and then a lady would pay for an orphan. Once she took in a sailor's five motherless children for 5*s*. a week from the father: but she has taken in apprentices as lodgers, whose own fathers could not afford to keep them for their wages.

All this time she washed for a poor sick Irish woman, who never gave her any thanks but that the clothes were not well washed, nor was anything done as it ought to be done.' Yet she took in this woman's child of two years old as her own, till the father came back, when he gave up drink and claimed it.

Every Friday she gave her earnings to some poor women, who bought goods with the money, which they sold again in the market on Saturday, and returned her money to her on Saturday night.

She said she never lost a penny by this; and it kept several old women going.

She must have been a capital manager, you will say. Well, till she took in lodgers, she lived in a cellar which she painted with her own hands, and kept as clean as a new pin. [Afterwards she let her cellar for 2*s*. a week, though she might have got 2*s*. 6*d*. or 3*s*. a week for it, because, she said, 'the poor should not be hard on one another.'] Milk she never tasted: meat seldom: and then she always stewed, never roasted it. She lived on potatoes, and potato pie was the luxury of herself and children.

On Sundays she filled her pot of four gallons and made broth: sometimes for six or eight poor old women besides her own family, as she called her orphans [*these* must be satisfied with what she provided, little or much]. She never let them touch what was sent her for her patients. Sometimes good things were sent her, which she always gave to sick neighbours; yet she has been accused of keeping for herself nice things sent to her care for others. She never owed a penny, for all her charity.

If this Nurse has not practised the 'heroic virtues,' who has?

[I mentioned this Nurse merely as an instance of one who had literally fulfilled the precept to 'do good' to them that 'despitefully use you': to be 'patient, cheerful, and kindly.' There is no time to tell you how she was left a widow with two infants and a blind and insane mother, whom she kept till doctors compelled her to put her mother into a lunatic asylum; how one of her sons was a sickly cripple, whom she nursed till he died, working by day and sitting up with him at night for years; how the other boy was insane, and ran away; how, to ease her broken mother's heart, she returned to sick nursing (chiefly among the poor): nursed through two choleras, till her health broke down. And, by way of taking care of herself, then took up the 'tedious 'orphan system [she felt, she said, as if she were doing something then for her 'own dear boy'], which she never ceased; how, as soon as she lived in a poor house of four rooms and an attic, she has had as many as ten carpenters' men of a night, who had nowhere but the public-house to go to, to whom she gave a good fire, borrowed a newspaper for them, and made one read aloud; they brought her sixpence a week, and she laid it all out in supper for them and cooked it. She gave the only good pair of shoes she had to one of these, because 'he must go to work decent.'

She was a famous sick cook, often carrying home fish-bones, to stew them for the sick, who seldom thanked her; and the remains of damsons and currants, to boil over again as a drink for fever patients: who sometimes accused her of keeping back things sent for them.

'How much more the Lord has borne from me,' she used to say.

And of children she used to say: 'We never can train up a child in the way it should go till we take it in our arms, as Jesus did, and feel: "Of such is the kingdom of heaven," and that there is a "heavenly principle" (a "little angel," I think she said) in each child to be trained up in it.'

She said she had learnt this from the master in a factory where she had once nursed. [How little he knew that he had been one means of forming this heroic Nurse.]

1. And now I have a word for the Ladies; and a word for the Nurse-Probationers. Which shall come first?

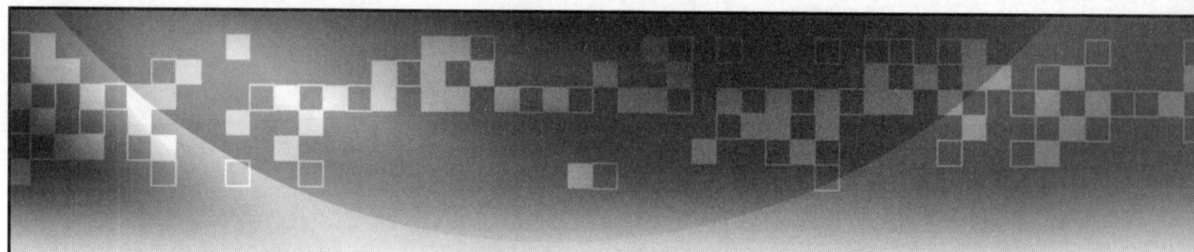

Do the ladies follow up their intellectual privileges? or, are they lazy in their hours of study? Do they cultivate their powers of expression in answering Mr. Croft's examinations?

Ought they not to look upon themselves as future leaders—as those who will have to train others? And bear this in mind during the whole of their year's training, so as to qualify themselves for being so?

It is not just getting through the year anyhow, without being blamed. For the year leaves a stamp on everybody—this is for the *Nurses* as well as the Ladies—and once gone can never be regained.

To the Special Probationers may I say one more word?

Do we look enough into the importance of giving ourselves thoroughly to study *in the hours of study*, of keeping careful *Notes of Lectures*, of keeping notes of all type *cases*, and of cases interesting from not being type cases: so to improve our powers of observation: all essential, *if we are in future to have charge*?

Do we keep in view the importance of helping ourselves to understand these cases by reading at the time *books* where we can find them described, and by listening to the *remarks* made by *Physicians* and Surgeons in going round with their Students? [Take a sly note afterwards, when nobody sees, in order to have a correct remembrance.]

So shall we do everything in our power to become proficients, not only in knowing the symptoms and what is to be done, *but in knowing the* 'REASON WHY' *of* such symptoms, and *why* such and such a thing is done: and so on, till we can some day TRAIN OTHERS *to know the* '*reason why.*'

Many say: 'We have no time; the Ward work gives us no time'

But it is *so easy to degenerate into a mere drudgery about the Wards*, when we have *goodwill* to do it and are fonder of *practical* work than of giving ourselves *the trouble of learning the* '*reason why.*'

Take care, or the Nurses, some of them, will catch you up.

Take ten minutes a day in the Ward to jot down things, and write them out afterwards; come punctually *from* your Ward to have time for doing so.

It is far better to take these ten minutes to write your cases or to jot down your recollections in the Ward than to give the same ten minutes to bustling about.

I am sure that the Sisters would help you to get this time if you asked them: and also to *leave* the Ward punctually.

And do you not think this a religious duty?

Such observations are a religious meditation: for is it not the best part of religion to imitate the benevolence of God to man? And how can you do this—in this your calling especially—if you do not thoroughly understand your calling, and is not every study to do this a religious contemplation?

Without it, *May you not potter and cobble about the patients without ever once learning the reason of what you do, so as to be able to train others?*

[I do not say anything about the 'cards,' for I take it for granted that you can read them easily.]

Our dear Matron, who is always thinking of arranging for us, is going to have a case-paper with printed headings given to you, and to keep this correctly ought to be a mere every-day necessity, and a very easy one, for you.

2. And for the Nurses:

They are placed, perhaps here only, on a footing of equality with educated gentlewomen.

Do they show their appreciation of this by thinking, 'We are as good as they'?—or, by obedience and respect, and trying to profit by the superior education of the gentlewomen?

Both we have known; we have known Nurse-Probationers who took the Ladies 'under their protection' in saving them the harder work, and the Ladies have given them the full return back in helping them in their education.

And we have known—very much the reverse.

Also, do the Nurse-Probationers take advantage of their opportunities—in the excellent classes given them by the Home Sister—in keeping Diaries and some Cases?

Very few of the Nurse-Probationers have taken notes of Mr. Croft's Lectures at all; it is not fair to Mr. Croft to give him people who do not benefit by his instruction.

3. And I have another word to say:

Are there parties in our Home?

Could we but be *not* so tenacious of our own interests, but look at the thing in a larger way!

Is there a great deal of canvassing and misinterpreting Sisters and Matron and other authorities? every little saying and doing of theirs? talking among one another about the superiors? (and then finding we were all wrong when we came to know them better?)

We must all of us know, without being told, that we cannot be trained at all, if in training this will of our own is not kept under; if we think that our superiors want to 'impose upon' us; or that we 'know better' than they do; or that 'there is not much to learn' in this or that way; or if we are indifferent about learning; or if we talk too much among one another of our superiors, and prejudice one another about them. Now I appeal to you whether you have not often found the Sisters not what they were represented?

Do not question so much.

Does not a spirit of criticism go with ignorance? And does not mistake and misjudging always go with uncharitableness?

Are some of you in all the 'opposition of irresponsibility'? Some day, when you are yourselves responsible, you will know what I mean.

Now could not the Ladies help the Nurse-Probationers in this: 1, in never criticising themselves; and 2, in saying a kindly word to check it when it is done?

Let me tell you a true story about this.

In a large college, questions—about things which the students could but imperfectly understand in the conduct of the college—had become too warm. The superintendent went into the hall one morning, and after complimenting the young men on their studies, he said: 'This morning I heard two of the porters, while at their work, take up a Greek book lying on my table; one tried to read it, and the other declared it ought to be help upside down to be read. Neither could agree which *was* upside down, but both thought themselves quite capable of arguing about Greek, though neither could read it. They were just coming to fisticuffs when I sent the two on different errands.'

Not a word was added: the students laughed and retired, but they understood the moral well enough, and from that day there were few questions or disputes about the plans and superiors of the college, or about their own obedience to rules and discipline.

Do let us think of the two porters squabbling whether the Greek book was to be read upside down, when we feel inclined to be questioning about 'things too high for us.'

We are constantly making mistakes in our judgment of our little world.

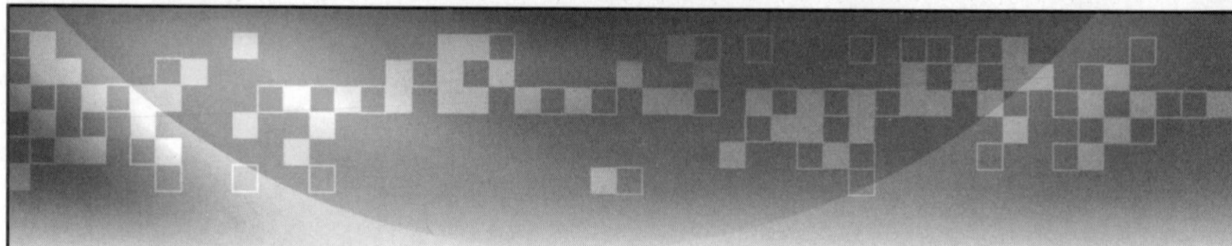

We fancy that we have been harshly treated or misunderstood.

Or we cannot bear our fellow-Probationers to laugh at us.

Believe me, there will come a time when all such troubles will simply seem ridiculous to us, and we shall be unable to imagine how we could ever have been the victims of them. [One of your number told me this herself. She has left St. Thomas' for another post.] Let us not brood or sentimentalise over them.

They should be met in a common-sense way. How much of our time has been spent in grieving over these trifles, how little in the real sorrow for sin, the real struggle for improvement.

4. As for obedience to rules and our superiors: 'True obedience,' said one of the most efficient people who ever lived, 'obeys not only the command, but also the intention,' of those who have a right to command us. Of course, this is a truism: the thing is, *how to do it.* As it is a struggle, it requires a brave and intrepid spirit, which helps us to rise above trifles and look to God, and His leadings for us.

Oh, when death comes, how sorry we shall be to have watched others so much and ourselves so little; to have dug so much in the field of others' consciences and left our own fallow! What should we say of a 'Leopold' Nurse who should try to nurse in 'Edward' Ward, and neglect her own 'Leopold'? Well, that is what we do. Or who should wash her patients' hands and not her own?

It is of ourselves and not of others that we must give an account. Let us look to our own consciences as we do to our own hands, to see if they are dirty.

We take care of our dress, but do we take care of our words?

It is a very good rule to say and do nothing but what we can offer to God.

Now we cannot offer Him backbiting, petty scandal, misrepresentation, flirtation, injustice, bad temper, bad thoughts, jealousy, murmuring, complaining.

Do we ever think that we bear the responsibility of all the harm we do in this way?

Look at that busybody who fidgets, gossips, makes a bustle, always wanting to domineer, always thinking of herself, as if she wanted to tell the sun to get out of her way and let her light the world in its place, as the proverb says.

And when we might do all our actions and say all our words as unto God!

So many imperfections; so many thoughts of self-love.

So many selfish satisfactions that we mix with our best actions!

And when we might offer them all to God.

What a pity!

5. One word more for the Ladies, or those who will have to train and look after others.

What must she be who is to be a Ward or 'Home' Sister?

We see her in her nobleness and simplicity: being, not seeming: without name or reward in this world: 'clothed' in her 'righteousness' merely, as the Psalms would say, *not* in her dignity: often having no gifts of money, speech, or strength: but never preferring seeming to being.

And if she rises still higher, she will find herself, in some measure, like the Great Example in Isaiah l:iii., bearing the sins and sorrows of others as if they were her own: her counsels often 'despised and rejected,' yet 'opening not her mouth' to be angry: 'led as a lamb to the slaughter.'

She who rules best is she who loves best: and shows her love not by foolish indulgence, but by taking a real interest in those of whom she is in charge—for their own sakes and in their highest interests.

Her firmness must never degenerate into nervous irritability. And for this end let me advise you when you become Sisters, always to take your exercise time out of doors: your monthly day out: and your annual holiday.

Be a judge of the work of others of whom you are in charge, not a detective: your mere detective 'is wonderful at suspicion and discovery,' but is often at fault, foolishly imagining that every one is bad.

She must have been tested in the refiner's fire, as the prophets would say: tried by many tests: and have come out of them stainless—in full command of herself and her principles: never losing her temper.

The Head-Nurse never nurses well till she ceases to command for the sake of commanding: or for her own sake at all: till she nurses only for the sakes of those who are nursed.

This is the highest exercise of self-denial: but without it the ruin of the nursing, of the charge, is sure to come.

Have we ever known such a Nurse?

She must be just: not unjust.

Now justice is the perfect order by which every woman does her own business: and injustice is where every woman is doing another's business.

This is the most obvious of all things: and for that very reason has never been found out.

Injustice is the habit of being a busybody and doing another woman's business, which tries to rule and ought to serve: this is the unjust Nurse.

Prudence is doing your nursing more perfectly: aiming at the perfect in everything: this is the 'seeking God and His righteousness' of the Scriptures.

And must not each of us be a Saviour, rather than a ruler: each in our poor measure? Did the Son of God try to rule?

And she must love truth and not opinion: that is, regard not so much what is thought of her as what really *is*.

Oh, my friends, do not scold at women: they will be of another mind if they are 'gently entreated' and learn to know you. Who can hate a woman who loves them? or be jealous of one who has no jealousy? Who can squabble with one who never squabbles? It is example which converts your patients: your ward-maids: your fellow-Nurses or charges: it is example which converts the world.

And is not the Head-Nurse or Sister there, not that she may do as she likes, but that she should serve all for the common good of all?

She who is bet fitted is often the least inclined to rule: but if the necessity is laid upon her, she takes it up as a message from God. And she must no longer live in her own thoughts: making a heaven or hell of her own. For if she does not make a heaven for others, her charge will soon become something else.

Those who rule must not be those who are desirous to rule.

She must never become excited: and therefore I do impress upon you regularity and punctuality: never to get hurried. Those often get most excited who are least in earnest.

The future Sister, if possible, yet more than the Nurse, must feel that her education continues through her whole life.

She who is fierce with her Nurses, her patients, or her ward-maid, is not truly above them: she is below them: and, although a harsh ward-mistress to her patients or Nurses, has no real superiority over them.

The one worst maxim of all for a future Matron, Sister, or Nurse is 'to do as I like': that *is* disorder, not rule. It is giving power to evil.

We know the busy drones among Nurses.

There is no impudence like that of ignorance.

Each night let us come to a knowledge of ourselves before going to rest: as the Psalm says: 'Commune with your own heart upon your bed, *and be still.*'

Is it possible that we who are alive among the sick and dying can be satisfied not to make *friends* with *God* each night?

The future Sister should be neither mistress nor servant: but the *friend* of every woman under her. But if she is mistress of others when she is not mistress of herself, her jealous, faithless temper grows worse with command [oh, let not this be the case with any of us!]—wanting everything of every-body, yet not knowing how to get it of anybody. Always in fear, confusion, suspicion, and distraction, she becomes more and more faithless, envious, unrighteous: the cause of wretchedness to herself and others.

But she who is the most royal mistress of herself is the only woman fit to be in charge.

For she who has no control over herself, who cannot master her own temper, how can she be placed over others, to control them through the better principle, if she has none or little of her own?

She is to control them, we must suppose, for their good, and not for their hurt.

For this is the whole intention of training, education, supervision, superintendence: to give self-control, to train or nurse up in us a higher principle; and when this is attained, you may go your ways safely into the world.

But she who nurses, and does not nurse up in herself the 'infant Christ,' who should be born again in us every day, is like an empty syringe—it pumps in only wind.

The future Sister must be, not of the governessing, but of the Saviour, turn of mind.

Let her reason with the unjust woman who is not intentionally in error.

She must know how to give good counsel, which will advise what is best under the circumstances; not making a lament, but finding a cure; regarding *that* only as 'bettering' their situation which *makes* them *better*.

She must know and teach 'how to refuse the evil and choose the good,' as Isaiah says. Oh, had all but known this, they would not have brought themselves to the verge of ruin, this School to the verge of dishonour.

She must have an iron sense of truth and right for herself and others, and a golden sense of love and charity for them.

If she becomes a tyrant, she comes to devour her own children: and when she afterwards discovers this, she blames everything and everybody but her own self.

But there is a worse enemy to such a Head-Nurse than chance: and that is *herself.*

When a future Sister unites the power of command with the power of thought and love—when she can raise herself and others above the commonplaces of a common self, without disregarding any of our common feelings—when she can plan and effect any reforms wanted step by step, without trying to precipitate them into a single year or month, neither hasting nor delaying: that is indeed a 'Sister.'

But to enjoy the luxury of fine words, and accompany them with not at all fine actions: this is what is called *cant*. And there is no greater contrast than between the ways of Christ and of Christians, as they call themselves.

The future Sister or Head must not see only a little corner of things, her own petty likes and dislikes; she must 'lift up her eyes to the hills,' as David says. She must know that there is a greater and more real world than her own littlenesses and meannesses.

And she must be not only the friend of her Nurses, but also, in her measure, the angel whose mission is to reconcile her Nurses to themselves, to each other, and to God.

[If I wanted to choose a living example of what all this would be in a 'Home' Sister, I should take the 'Home' Sister whom God has given us; and in this I am sure you will all agree with me. But as nothing would distress her so much as to hear this, we must all bury this dangerous secret in the deepest recesses of our own Bosoms.]

III. Now let us not each of us think how this fits on to her neighbour, but how it fits on to oneself.

Shall I tell you what one of you said to me after I last addressed you?—'Do you think we are missionaries?'

I answer, that you cannot help being missionaries, if you would. There are missionaries for evil as well as for good. Can you help choosing? Must you not decide whether you will be missionaries for good, or whether for evil, among your patients and among yourselves?

1. And, first, among your patients:

Hospital Nurses have charge of their patients in a way that no other woman has charge: in the first place, no other woman is in charge really of grown-up men.

[Oh, how careful she ought to be, especially the Night Nurse, to show them what a true woman can be. The acts of a nurse are keenly scrutinised by both old and young patients; if she is not perfectly pure and upright, depend upon it, they know us.]

Also, a Hospital Nurse is in charge of people in their sick and feeble, anxious and dying hours, when they are singularly alive to impressions. She leaves her stamp upon them, whether she will or no.

And this applies almost more to the Night Nurse than to the Day Nurse.

Lastly, if she have children-patients, she is absolutely in charge of these, who come, perhaps for the first and the last time of their lives, under influence.

So many pass by a child without notice.

A whole life of happiness or wretchedness may turn upon an act of kindness to it—a good example set it.

A poor woman once said of a child of hers under just these circumstances: 'The Sister set its face heavenwards: and it never looked back.' Do we ever set their faces the other way? The child she spoke of when it was dying actually gave its halfpence, which it had saved for something for itself, for another dying child 'who had nobody.' I call *that* practising the 'heroic virtues,' if ever there were such. And that was done under just such an influence as we have been speaking of.

On the other hand, do you know anything in its way more heinous than a Nurse, who to the sick and tiresome child might be like an angel 'to set its face heavenward,' by her sympathy with it, and who, by her own bad habits or bad temper, by her unfairness, by her unkindness or injustice, by her coarseness or want of uprightness, sets it the other way?

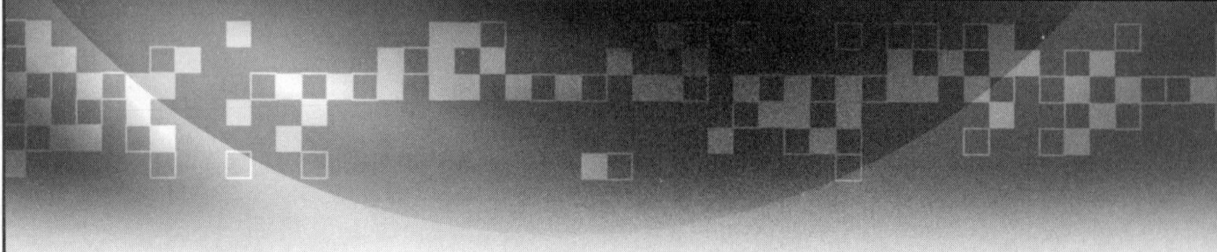

A very good man once said that in each little Hospital patient, he saw not only a soul to be saved, but many other souls that might possibly be committed to this one: for the poor can do so much among one another: do what no others going among them can do. Every child is of the stuff out of which Home Missionaries (or the reverse) may be made—such as God chooses—from the ranks that have furnished His best recruits.

The Apostles were fishermen and workmen.

David Livingstone was a cotton-mill piecer. In each little pauper waif he saw one destined to carry a godly example (or the reverse) where none but they could carry it—into godless and immoral homes.

The Hospital patient may be a missionary to its own class.

The work of a missionary is confined neither to man nor woman: nor to any profession or order of men or women.

I knew a gentleman who, when ill of the disease of which he died, clambered up on a very cold night on the box of his cab, to sit by the cabman who was driving him [perhaps the cabman was a drinker], to talk to him about his duties and advise him about his children: the cabman was a reformed man ever after: he had never entered school or church before, and said he had 'no time.'

You can do this by the bed-side, without going out in the cold or clambering up on a cab.

But if you go out in the corridors to talk to men, are you practising the 'heroic virtues,' even as well as your own patients may be doing in their beds? And how many patients may you have, like the cabman, drinkers or immoral.

We will not repeat here, because we are so fully persuaded of it, that a woman, especially a Nurse, must be a missionary, *not* as a minister or chaplain is, but by the influence of her own character, silent but not unfelt.

It was this, far more than any words, that gave his matchless influence to David Livingstone, whose body—brought upwards of 1,500 miles through pathless deserts by his own negro servants: such a heroic feat as Christians never knew before—was buried this spring in Westminster Abbey.

Some of us knew him: one of our Probationers was with him and his wife, who died in 1862, and Bishop Mackenzie, at their Mission Station in Africa.

He was such a traveller and missionary as we shall never see again perhaps.

He was the son of a cotton-spinning workman: and himself a piecer (as a child) in a cotton-mill; but what he was in influence each of us may be, if we please, in our little sphere. What *he* was *we* may be.

A Nurse *is* like a traveller, from the quantity of people who pass before her in the ever-changing wards.

And she is like a traveller also in this, that, as Livingstone used to say, either the vices or the virtues of civilisation follow the footsteps of the traveller, and he cannot help it; so they do those of the Nurse. And missioning will be, whether she will or no, the background of her nursing, as it is the background of travelling. The traveller may call himself a missionary or not, as he likes. He *is* one, for good or for evil. So is the Nurse.

Livingstone used to say that we fancy a missionary a man with a Bible in his hand and another in his pack. He then went on to say what a real missionary must be in himself to have influence. And he added: 'If I had once been suspected of a single act of want of purity or uprightness, the negroes would never have trusted me again. No, not even the least pure or the least upright of the negroes. And any influence of mine would have been gone for ever.'

What his influence was, even after his death, you know.

2. Then you must be missionaries, whether you will or no, among one another.

We need only think of the friendships that we are made here:

Will you be a missionary of good or of evil to your friend?

Will you be a missionary of indifference, selfishness, lightness of conduct, self-indulgence;

Or a missionary—to her and to your patients—of religious and noble devotion to duty, carried out to the smallest thing?

Will you be a 'hero' in your daily work, like the sick gentleman on the cabman's box, or the dying child giving its hard-saved halfpence to the yet poorer child?

Livingstone always remembered that a poor old Scotchman on his death-bed had said to him:

'Now, lad, make religion the *every-day business* of your life, not a thing of fits and starts; for if you do not, temptation and other things will get the better of you.'

Such a Nurse, one who makes religion the 'every-day business of her life,' *is* a 'Missionary,' even if she never speak a word. One who does not is a missionary for *evil* and not for good, though she may say many words, have many good texts at the end of her tongue, or, as Livingstone would say, a Bible in her hand and a Bible at her back.

Believe me, who have seen a good deal of the world, we may give you an institution to learn in, but it is YOU must furnish the 'heroic' feeling of doing your duty, doing your best, without which no institution is safe, without which Training-Schools are meat without salt. *You* must be our salt, without which civilisation is but corruption, and all churches only dead establishments.

Shall I tell you what one of the most famous clergymen that ever lived said: that, in order to manage people and especially children well, it was necessary to speak more of them to God than of God to them.

If a famous preacher said that, how much more must a woman?

Another learned clergyman, who was also the best translator of the bible (in a foreign language), said: Prayer rather than speech must be relied upon for the reform of any little irregularities: for only through prayer could the proper moment for speech become known.

If a great leader of mankind said that, how much more should a Nurse?

I must end: and what I say now I had better have said: and nothing else.

What are we without God?

Nothing.

Father: glorify Thy name.

How is His name glorified?

We are His glory, when we follow His ways.

Then we are something.

What is the Christian religion?

To be like Christ.

And what is it to be like Christ?

To be High Church, Low Church, Dissenter, or orthodox?

Oh, no. It is: to live for God and have God for our object.

1875

ADDRESS
FROM: FLORENCE NIGHTINGALE
TO THE:
PROBATIONER-NURSES IN THE 'NIGHTINGALE FUND' SCHOOL, AT ST. THOMAS' HOSPITAL, AND THE NURSES WHO WERE FORMERLY TRAINED THERE.
26TH MAY, 1875.
Printed for Private Use only.

LONDON: *May* 26, 1875.
MY DEAR FRIENDS,

This year my letter to you must needs be short, for I am not able to write much. But good words are always short. The best words that ever were spoken—Christ's words—were the shortest. Would that ours were always the echo of His!

First, then:

What is our one thing needful? To have high principles at the bottom of all. Without this, without having laid our foundation, there is small use in building up our details. That is as if you were to try to nurse without eyes or hands. We know who said, If your foundation is laid in shifting sand, you may build your house, but it will tumble down. But if you build it on solid ground, this is what is called being *rooted and grounded in Christ.*

In the great persecutions which there were in France, under Louis XIV, 200 years ago—not only of the Protestants, who came over here and settled in Spitalfields, but of all who held the higher and more spiritual religion—a noble woman who has left her impress on the Christian Church, and who herself endured two hard imprisonments for conscience' sake, would receive no Probationer into her Institution (which was, like ours, for works of Nursing and for the poor) till the Probationer had well considered whether she were really rooted and grounded in God Himself, and not in the mere habit of obeying rule and doing her work; whether she could do without the supports of the example and fellowship of a large and friendly community, the sympathy and praise of fellow-workers—all good things in themselves, but which will not carry us through a life like Christ's. And I doubt whether any woman whom God is forming for Himself is not at some time or other of her life tried and tested in this lonely path.

A French Princess, who did well consider, and who was received into the said Institution on these conditions, has left us in writing her experience. And well she showed *where* she was 'rooted and grounded' through ten after-years of prison and persecution.

We have not to endure these things. Our lot is cast in gentler times.

But I will tell you an old woman's experience—that I can never remember a time, and that I do not know a work, which so requires to be rooted and grounded in God as ours.

You remember the question in the hymn, 'Am I His, or am I not?' IF *I am*, this is what is called our 'hidden life with Christ in God.' We all have a 'hidden life' in ourselves, besides our outward working life. If our hidden life is filled with chatter and fancies, our outward working life will be the fruits of it.

'By their *fruits* ye shall know them,' Christ says. Christ knows the good Nurse. It is not the good talker whom Christ knows as the good Nurse.

If our hidden life *is* 'with Christ in God,' by its fruits too it will be known.

What is it to live 'with Christ in God'? It is to live in Christ's spirit: forgiving any injuries, real or fancied, from our fellow-workers, from those above us as well as from those below,—alas! how small our injuries are that we should talk of forgiving!—thirsting after righteousness—righteousness, *i.e.*, doing completely one's duty towards all with whom we have to do, towards God above as well as towards our fellow-nurses, our patients, our matron, home sister, and instructors; fain to be holy as God is holy, perfect as our Father in Heaven is perfect in our hospital and training school; caring for nothing more than God's will in this His training; careful for our sick and fellow-Nurses more than for ourselves; active, like Christ, in our work; like Christ, meek and lowly in heart in our Wards and 'Home'; peacemakers among our companions, which includes the never repeating anything which may do mischief,—placing our spirits in the Father's charge. ('I am the Almighty's charge,' says the hymn.) *This* is to live a life with Christ in God.

You may have heard of Mr. Wilberforce. He it was who, after a long life of unremitting activity, varied only with disappointment, carried the Abolition of the Slave Trade, one of England's greatest titles to the gratitude of nations. Slavery, as Livingstone said, is the open sore of the world. [Mr. Clarkson and my grandfather were two of his fellow-workers.] Some one asked how Mr. Wilberforce did this, and a man I knew answered, 'Because his life was hid with Christ in God.'

Never was there a truer word spoken. And if we, when the time comes for us to be in charge of Wards, are enabled to 'abolish' anything wrong in them, it can only be in the same way, by our life being hid with Christ in God. And no man or woman will do great things for God, or even small, whose 'hidden life' is employed in self-complacency, or in thinking over petty slights, or of what other people are thinking of her.

We have three judges—our God, our neighbour, and ourselves. Our own judgment of ourselves is, perhaps, generally too favourable; our neighbour's judgment of us too unfavourable, except in the case of close friends, who may sometimes spoil each other. Shall we always remember to seek *God's* judgment of us, knowing this, that it will some day find us, whether we seek it or not? *He* knows who is *His* nurse, and who is not.

This is laying the 'foundation'; *this* is the 'hidden life with Christ in God' for us Nurses.

'Keeping up to the mark,' as St. Paul says, and nothing else *will* keep us up to the mark in Nursing.

'Neglect nothing; the most trivial action may be performed to ourselves, or performed to God.' What a pity that so many actions should be wasted by us Nurses in our Wards and in our 'Home,' when we might always be doing common things uncommonly well!

Small things *are* of consequence—small things are of *no* consequence; we say this often to ourselves and to each other.

And both these sayings are true.

Every brick is of consequence, every dab of mortar, that it may be as good as possible in building up your house.

A chain is no stronger than its weakest link: therefore every link is of consequence. And there can be no 'small' thing in *Nursing*.

How often we have seen a Nurse's life wrecked, in its usefulness, by some apparently small fault!

Perhaps this is to say that there can be no small things in the nursing service of God. But in the service of ourselves, oh! how small the things are!—of no consequence indeed—how small they will appear to us all some day!

For what does it profit a Nurse if she gain the whole world to praise her, and lose her own soul in conceit?

What does it profit if the judgment of the whole world is for us Nurses, and God's is against us?

It is a real danger, in works like these, when all men praise us. We must then see if we are 'rooted and grounded in Christ Himself,' to nurse as *He* would have us nurse, as *He* was in God, to do *His* Saviour-work.

Am I His, or am I not?

It is a real danger, too, if in works like these we do not uphold the credit of our School.

That is *not* bearing fruit.

Can we hope, may we hope that, at least, some day, Christ may say even to our Training School, as He did once to His first followers, 'Ye are the salt of the earth'? But oh! if we may hope this, let us never forget for one moment the terrible conclusion of that verse.

If we can, in the faintest sense, be called 'the salt' of God's nursing world, let us watch, watch, watch, that we may never lose our 'savour.' One woman, as we well know, may be honoured by God to be 'the salt' to purify a whole Ward. One woman may have lost her 'savour,' and a Ward be left without its 'salt,' and untold harm done.

2. And now I must say this. You seek this work yourselves. I hope that some, if not all, feel *called* to it by God. That is the only true safety, to feel that God really requires it of you, and that His Spirit has pointed out this as the path in which you individually are called to enter and work out your usefulness.

All, indeed, cannot be so fortunate as, after consideration, to be able to hold such a strong belief.

Nor do I say that we must wait for it to take up a life's work.

But a few very plain words I must say to all.

You seek this work yourselves—we do not seek you. When you have been admitted, will you not remember, instead of trying to remodel the work, or reform the organisation, or teach your teachers, that you come here to be taught?

We must say, plainly, that we would rather not have a woman at all than have one who will not thoroughly and cordially work into the general system which we, not without much consideration and experience, have adopted. You live together (yet with all means of privacy), you have all meals in common, and the general life and energy of us all would be damaged by any one discordant, conceited body.

Let us try that it may please God every year to put it into the head of some twenty, or thirty, or forty more women of the right sort—people who will feel the wants of the work, and work with us—to join it.

Some of you will have to train others. All will have a charge of Patients before we meet again. May I speak of two great temptations in this life—1, to self-esteem; 2, to a domineering temper—because you (often, not always) find obedience ready, and people like being obeyed?

How unlike Christ, who said that He came as a servant among those He came to teach! And is not this coming as a servant what alone gives us unquestioned authority?

If every one can see that nothing is ordered from a selfish motive, for any advantage to oneself, nothing forbidden except for some very good reason; can see that

we seek nothing for ourselves, that we are quite free from any desire to be admired, to be thought much of, from any love of commanding for the sake of being obeyed—is not that the secret of having authority?

I must add, however, that some of our best and dearest Probationers, now Hospital Sisters, find it their greatest cross to have to command, and are, perhaps, all the better commanders for that. There is no greater fallacy than this, that those can command who cannot obey.

3. We ought to be very much obliged to our kind Medical Instructor for the pains he has taken with us, and to show this by our careful attention. Without this there can be no improvement. We remain not only ill-informed as to our Ward duties, unobservant of our Cases; but we become incapable of learning afterwards (for we must be *always* learning in Nursing), and unfitted for doing our future work thoroughly and creditably.

There is a time for all things—a time to be trained, and a time to use our training.

And if we have thrown away the year we have here, we can hardly recover it.

Besides, what a share it is to come here, as Probationers, at considerable cost (to others, most of us), and then not to make our improvement the chief business of our lives, so that at the end of our year we go away not much better but rather worse than we came!

We are not here to teach, but to learn.

What account can we give of such a waste of time and opportunities, of the best gifts of God, to ourselves and to Him?

'For God requireth that which is past.'

If, when I was young, there had been such opportunities of training for Hospital work as you have, how eagerly I should have made the most of them!

Some of us here will have one day to train others. Such must feel,—'If we are not fit to answer written question, to take notes of Cases and of Lectures, to learn so as to be able one day to give to others what we have learnt ourselves, we are not fit to be Training Matrons, or even Training Nurses or "Sisters."'

Therefore, 'whatsoever thy hand findeth to do, do it with all thy might': be earnest in work, be earnest also even in such things as taking exercise and proper holiday. I say this particularly to future Matrons and 'Sisters,' for there should be something of seriousness in keeping our *bodies** too up to the mark.

Life is short, as preachers often tell us: that is, each stage of it is apt to come to an end, before the work which belongs to it is finished.

Let us

'Act that each to-morrow
Find us farther than to-day.'

Let us be earnest in work;—above all, because we believe this life to be the beginning of another, into which we carry with us what we have been and done here; because we are working together with God—remember the Parting Command—and He is upholding us in our work—remember the Parting Promise; because, when the hour of death approaches, we should wish to think (like Christ), that we have completed life: that we have finished the work which was given us to do: that we have not lost one of those, Patients or Nurses, who were entrusted to us.

* Do you remember the words of one of the greatest poets of the Middle Ages?
'The soul,
Which o'er the body keeps a holy ward,
Placed there by God, yielding alone to Him
The trust He gave.'

4. What was the Parting Command?

What was the Parting Promise?

We Nurses have just kept Ascension Day and Whit-Sunday.

Shall we Nurses not remember the Parting Command on Ascension Day—to preach the Gospel to every Creature?

And the Parting Promise: 'And lo I am with you alway even unto the end of the world.'

That Command and that Promise were given, not to the Apostles or Disciples only, but to each and every one of us Nurses: to each to herself in her own Ward or Home.

Without the Promise the Command could not be obeyed.

Without we obey the Command the Promise will not be fulfilled.

Christ tells us what He means by the Command.

He tells us, over and over again: It is by ourselves, *by what we are in ourselves*, that we are 'to preach the Gospel.'

Not what we say, but what we do, is the Preacher.

Not saying 'Lord, Lord,' for how many ungodly things are done and said in the name of God! but 'keeping His commandments,' this it is which 'preaches' Him: it is the bearing much 'fruit,' not the saying many words. God's Spirit leads us rather to be silent than to speak—to do good works rather than to say fine things or to write them.

Over and over again, and especially in His first and last discourses, He insists upon this.

He takes the sweet little child and places it in our midst: it was as if He had said, 'Ah! that is the best preacher of you all.'

And those who have followed Him best have felt this most.

The most successful preacher the world has probably seen since St. Paul's time said, some 300 years ago, it was by *showing an example*, not by delivering a discourse, that the Apostle's work was really done, that the Gospel was really preached.

And well did he show his own belief in this truth. For when all was ready for his mission to convert China to Christianity, and the plague broke out where he was, he stayed and nursed the plague.

We can every one of us here present, though our teaching may not be much, by our *lives* 'preach a continual sermon, that all who see may understand.' [These words were found in the last letter, left unfinished, of a native convert of the 'greatest missionary of modern times,' Bishop Patteson, who was martyred in the South Seal Islands, in September 1871, and this convert with him. Oh, how he puts us to shame!]

I have sometimes told histories of how a silent life, like this, of a Nurse in a Hospital or Infirmary Ward, has converted many, especially children. Last year I told of a Nurse who spent her after- life in taking poor children from the streets, nearly all of whom turned out well under her charge. I will now tell you a terrible history—I wish it were an uncommon one—of the reverse. A poor little girl was turned out of a Workhouse Ward, cured: no voice had there spoken words of kindness to her: no good example had been set her: no care, no training had been given her. She went in innocent: she came out corrupt. No 'salt' was in that Ward to purify it. She, and I believe one, or, it may be, two of her sisters, had twenty sons and daughters, of whom seventeen lived to grow up. Of these seventeen, it appears, from police records, that nine committed crimes, for which they underwent terms of imprisonment averaging five-and-a-half years each, some more, some less: and all the other eight were repeatedly in Gaol, in a Penitentiary, or in a Workhouse!

Can one wonder? And do we ever think of the consequences of neglecting one little child?

It has happened to me—I daresay it has happened to every one of us—to be told by a Child- Patient, one who has been taught to say its prayers, that it 'was afraid' to kneel down and 'say its prayers' before a whole ward-full of people. Do we encourage and take care of such a little child? Shall we, when we have Wards under our own charge, take care that the Ward is kept so that none at proper times shall be 'afraid' to kneel down and say their prayers? Do we reflect on the immense responsibility of a Nurse towards her helpless Sick, who depend upon her almost entirely for quiet, and thought, and order? Do we think how common* are such consequences as I have been telling of, if these things are not cared for? Do we think that, as was once said, we are to no one as 'rude' as we are to God?

---

* It is simply because no attention is given in following up such cases, not because such cases do not happen that we do not know them. They are well known to those who take the trouble to enquire. I will relate one. There were at the close of last year (1874) 623 people, of one family, so to speak, of whom 201 were criminals: of the other 422, a number were prostitutes, a greater number drunkards, a very large number (nearly the whole) in Idiot or Lunatic Asylums, or in the Workhouse. All these 623 sprang from one poor woman, named M_____. What was this terrible likeness in guilt?—Eighty-five years ago she was a poor little sick pauper child, who never received one word of kindness or one mark of care, or had one good example set her. The gentleman who told me this frightful story, and had himself traced it, calculated that at least £23,000 was the cost to the country of this one neglected little child. But the cost in wretchedness,—the evil she has done to thousands of innocent people, the degradation and misery of 623 people, that one child unrescued, has thus cause: —has thus caused: —who can calculate it? And to whom does this miserably memorable history speak home as it does to us Hospital and Infirmary Nurses?

I believe that one of our St. Thomas' Sisters, who is just leaving us after years of good work, is going to set up a 'Home' for Sick Children, where, under her, they will be cared for in *all* ways. I am sure that we shall all bid her 'God speed.'

And I know that many of those who have gone out from among us, and who are now Hospital Sisters or Nurses—they would not like me to mention their names—do care for their Patients, Children and all, in *all* ways. Thank God for it!

When a Patient, especially a child, sees you acting in all things as if in the presence of God—and none are so quick to observe it—then the names he or she heard at the Chaplain's or the Sister's or the Night Nurse's lips become names of real things and real Persons. There *is* a God, a Father; there *is* a Christ, a Comforter; there *is* a Spirit of Goodness, of Holiness; there *is* another World, to such an one.

When a Patient, especially a Child, sees us acting as if there were *no* God, then there but too often becomes no God to him: —then words become to such a child mere words. And remember, that when such a Nurse,—'salt' which has lost its 'savour,'—speaks to her Patients of God, she puts *a hindrance* in their way to keep them FROM God, instead of helping them *to* God. She had better not speak to them at all.

It is a terrible thought—I speak for myself—that we may *prevent* people from believing in God, instead of bringing them to 'believe in God the Father Almighty.'

5. What is it, 'setting an example'? showing an example—*of what*? *Who* is *our* example, that we are to set Christ is our example, our pattern: this we all know and say. And when this was once said—a very common word—before a very uncommon man, he said: 'When you have your picture taken, the painter does not try to make it rather like, or not very unlike. It is not a good picture if it is not *exactly* like.' Do we try to be *exactly* like Christ? If we do not, 'are we His, or are we not'? Could it be said of each one of us: 'That Nurse *is* (or is trying to be) exactly what Christ would have been in her place'?

Yet this is what every Nurse has to aim at. Aim lower: and you cannot say then, 'Christ is my example.' Aim as high: and, after this life, 'we shall be satisfied when we awake in His likeness.'

6. But this aim cannot be carried out, it cannot even be entertained, without the Parting Promise.

The Parting Promise was fulfilled to the Disciples then days afterwards, on Whit-Sunday, when the Holy Spirit was given them—that is, when Christ came as He promised, and was with them.

Christ comes to each Nurse of us all: and stands at our little room-door and knocks.

Do we let Him in?

The Holy Spirit comes no more with outward show, but comes with no less inward power, to each Ward and to each Nurse of us all, who is trying to do her Nursing and her Ward work *in God*, to live her hidden Nurse's life with Christ in God.

When your Patient asks you for a drink, you do not give him a stone. And shall not our Heavenly Father much more give His Spirit to each one of us, His nurses [*Are* we *His* nurses?] when she asks Him?

What is meant by the Spirit descending upon *us* Nurses, as it did on the first Whitsuntide? Is it not to put us in a state to nurse Him [He has really told us that nursing our Patients is nursing Him], by making our heart and our will His? God asks the *heart*—that is, that we should consecrate *all* our self to Him, *within* as well as without, *within* even more than without, in doing the Nursing work He has given each one of us here to do.

It is not to have the spirit of love, of courtesy, of justice, of right, of gentleness, of meekness, in our Training School; the spirit of truth, of integrity, of energy and activity, of purity, which He *is*, in our Hospital? (This it is to worship God in spirit and in truth. And we need not wait to go into a church, or even to kneel down at prayer, for *this* worship.) Is it not to feel that we desire really nothing for ourselves in our Nursing life, present and future, but only this, 'Thy will be done,' as we say in our daily prayer? Is it not to trust Him, that *His will* is really the best for each one of us? How much there is in those two words, *His will*—the will of Almighty Wisdom and Goodness: which always *knows* what is best for each one of us Nurses, which always *wills* what is best, which always *can* do what it wills for our best!

Is it not to feel that the care and thought of ourselves is lost in the thought of God and the care of our Patients and fellow-Nurses and Ward-Maids?

Is it not to feel that we are never so happy as when we are working *with Him* and *for them?* And we Nurses can *always* do this, if we will.

Is not this what Christ meant when He said, 'The kingdom of heaven is within you'? 'The kingdom of heaven' consists not in much speaking, but in doing—not in a sermon, but in a heart. 'The kingdom of heaven' can *always* be in a Nurse's blessed work, and even in her worries. Is not this what the Apostle meant when he told us to 'rejoice in the Lord'?—that is, to rejoice, whether Matrons, or 'Sisters,' or Nurses, or Night Nurses, in the service of God—which, with us, means good Nursing of the Sick, good fellowship and high example as relates to our fellow-workers—to rejoice in the right, whoever does it; to rejoice in the truth, whoever has it; to rejoice in every good word and work, whoever's it is; to rejoice, in one work, in what God rejoices in.

Let us thank God that some special aids to our spiritual life have been given us lately, for which I know many of us *are* thankful, and some of us have been able to keep this Whitsuntide as we never did before.

7. One little word more about our Training School. Training 'consists in teaching people to bear responsibilities, and laying the responsibilities on them as they are able to bear them,' as Bishop Patteson said of Education. The year which we spend here is generally the most important, as it may be the happiest, of our lives.

Here we find many different characters. Here we meet on a common stage, before we part company again to our several posts. If there are any rich among us, they are not esteemed for their riches. And the poor woman, the friendless, the lonely woman, receives a generous welcome. Everyone who has any activity or sense of duty may qualify herself for a future useful life. Every- one may receive situations without any reference, except to individual capacity, and to a kind of capacity which it is within the power of the most humble and unfriended to work out. Everyone who has any natural kindness or courtesy in her, and who is not too much wrapped up in herself, may make pleasant friends. False pride or over-sensitiveness do us much harm.

But although we know how many and serious faults we have, ought we not also to be able to find here some virtues which do not equally flourish in the larger world?—such as disinterested devotion to the calling we have chosen, and to which we can here fully give ourselves up, and without anxiety; warmhearted interest in each other, for no one of us stands here in any other's way; freedom from jealousy and meanness; a generous self-denial in nursing our charges, and a generous sympathy with other Nurses; above all, an interest in our work, and an earnestness in taking the means given us to improve ourselves in what is to be so useful to others.

And this is also the surest sign of our improvement in it.

This is what St. Paul calls: 'Not slothful in business, fervent in spirit, serving the Lord.'

Always, however, we must be above our work and our worries, keeping our souls free in that 'hidden life' above of which it has been spoken.

And two or three of us perhaps may be so 'rooted' in that 'life' that God blesses their endeavour—an endeavour which all of us ought to make—to do the true Apostolic work in our Hospital: that is, to set the higher standard of morals, temper, and manners in our 'Home'; to inspire, by our energy in our work, energy in others; by our sympathy and power of feeling with others, to be centres of kindliness and goodwill in our Ward; to feel, though many of us are young, that we owe a duty to our Training School, and that we do not meet together, during this year of training, solely for our own profit or pleasure.

This is Christ's real 'Apostolic Church' in a Training School. Let us pray for all who come—let us pray for all who go: for those who have had their year's training, for those who have it yet before them.

Above all, let us pray that God will send real workers into this immense 'field' of Nursing, made more immense this year by the opening out of London *District* Nursing at the bedside of the sick poor at home. A woman who takes the sentimental view of Nursing (which she calls 'ministering,' as if she were an angel), is, of course, worse than useless; a woman possessed with the idea that she is making a sacrifice will never do; and a woman who thinks any kind of Nursing work 'beneath a Nurse' will simply be in the way. But if the right woman is moved by God to come to us, what a welcome we will give her, and how happy she will soon be in a work, the many blessings of which none can know as we know them, though we know the worries too! [Good Bishop Patteson used to talk to his assistants something in this way; would we were like him!]

Nurses' work means downright work, in a cheery, happy, hopeful, friendly spirit. An earnest, bright, cheerful woman, without the notion of 'making sacrifices,' &c., perpetually occurring to her mind, is the real Nurse. Soldiers are sent anywhere, and leave home and country for years; *they* think nothing of it, because they go 'on duty.' Shall *we* have less self-denial than they, and think less of 'duty' than these men? A woman with a healthy, active tone of mind, plenty of work in her, and some enthusiasm, who makes the best of everything, and, above all, does not think herself better than other people because she is a 'Nightingale Nurse,' that is the woman we want.

[Must I tell you again, what I have had to tell you before, that we have a great name in the world for—conceit?]

I suppose, of course, that sound religious principle is at the bottom of her.

Now, if there be any young persons really in earnest whom any of you could wish to see engaged in this work, if you know of any such, and feel justified in writing to them, you will be aiding materially in this work, if you will put it in their power to propose themselves as Candidates.

8. But, when we meet again, our dear 'Home Sister' will have left us, returning to do a work in her own country, which is also ours, and carrying some of us here present with her, and all our hearts.

Let us thank God for having lent her to us; for having enabled her, under our dear Matron, to help to make this 'Home' a place of moral, religious, and practical training—a place of real training of character, habits, intelligence—a place of acquiring knowledge, technical and theoretical, of our art of Nursing—a place something like what a 'Training Home' ought to be.

Some homes are, as we know, places of training in disorder, dirt, discomfort, and ungodliness; some, of training in *nothing*.

She helped to give the 'mothering' care, and moral and religious helps, which you care for, I know, as they serve.

Let us pray for her present work.

And we have our dear Matron left us, who has appointed us another 'Home Sister,' who will in nowise let the work of God fall off here.

My every-day thought is—How will God provide for the introduction of real Christianity among all of us Nurses, and among our Patients?—my every-day prayer (and I know that the prayer of many of you is the same), that He will give us the means and show us how to use them, and give us the people. We ask you to pray for us, who have to arrange for you, as we pray for you, who have to nurse the Patients; and I know you do. The very vastness of the work raises one's thoughts to God, as the only One by whom it can be done. That is the solid comfort: *HE knows.* He loves us all and our Patients infinitely more than we can. He is, we trust, sending us to them; He will bless honest endeavours to do His work among them. Without *this* belief and support, it seems to me, when we look at the greatness of the work, and how far, far we fall short of it, instead of being conceited, we should not have courage to work at all.

And when we say the words in the Communion Service—'Therefore with angels and arch-angels'—and do we think, when we say them, whether we are fit company for angels?—it may not be fanciful to believe that 'angels and archangels,' to whom all must seem so different, may see God's light breaking over the Nursing Service, though perhaps in our time it may not attain the perfect day; only we must work on—and bring no hindrances to that light.

And that not one of us may bring hindrances to that light, believe me, let us pray daily.

I have been longer than I intended or hoped, and will only say one more word.

May we each and all of us Nurses be faithful to the end; remembering this, that no one Nurse stands alone! May we not say, in the words of the Prophet, that it is 'The Lord' who 'hath gathered' us Nurses 'together out of the lands'? Should not, therefore, all this Training School be so melted into one heart and mind, that we may with *one* heart and mind act and nurse and sing together our praise and thanksgiving, blessing and gratitude, for mercies, every one of which seems to belong to the whole School—['It is because we do not *praise* as we proceed,' said a good and great man, 'that our progress is so slow']—since every member alike belongs to the body of which it is a part, and every Nurse alike belongs to the Mother School of which she is a part, and to the Almighty Father who has sent her here, and since to Him alone we each and all of us Nurses owe everything we have and are?

FLORENCE NIGHTINGALE.

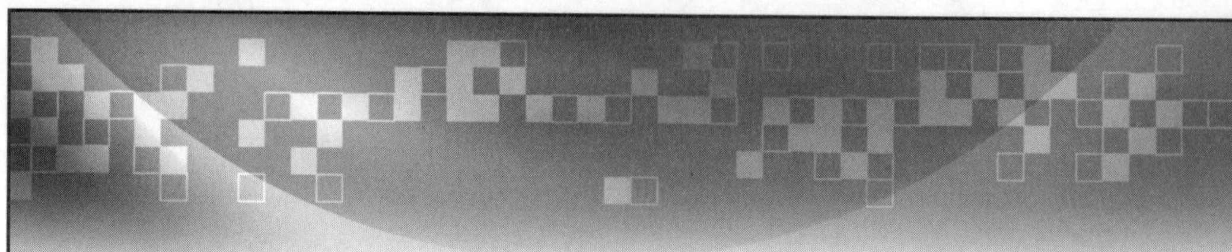

1876

ADDRESS
FROM: FLORENCE NIGHTINGALE
TO THE: PROBATIONER-NURSES IN THE 'NIGHTINGALE FUND' SCHOOL, AT ST. THOMAS' HOSPITAL, AND THE NURSES WHO WERE FORMERLY TRAINED THERE.
28TH APRIL, 1876.
Printed for Private Use only.

April 28, 1876.

MY DEAR FRIENDS,

Again another year has brought us together to rejoice at our successes, and, if to grieve over some disappointments, to try together to find out—what is it? that may have brought them about, and to correct it.

God seems to have given His favour to the manner in which you have been working.

Thanks to you, each and all of you, for the pains you have taken to carry out the work. I hope you feel how great have been the pains bestowed upon you. I hope you feel (what is the truth) that your interests and comfort are as near the hearts of your Trainers as are those of the Patients, whom to nurse well you are being trained; and as those of the patients are, I well know, near *your* hearts.

If you can say 'yes' to this, say it to-night to God. Say to Him a word of gratitude for Matron, for 'Home Sister's' care, for our Ward Sisters,—not omitting our kind Instructor.

You are not 'grumblers' at all: you do try to justify the great care given you—the confidence placed in you, and, after you have left this 'Home,' the freedom of action you enjoy—by that *intelligent* obedience to rules and orders, to render which is alone worthy of the name of 'Trained Nurse' of God's soldier; and we shall be poor soldiers indeed, if we don't *train* ourselves for the battle.

But if discipline is ever looked upon as interference, then freedom has become lawlessness, and we are no 'Trained Nurses' at all.

The trained Englishwoman is the first Nurse in the world: *if*—IF she knows how to unite this intelligent obedience to commands with thoughtful and godly command of herself; and the one cannot exist without the other.

'The greatest evils in life,' said one of the world's highest statesmen, 'have had their rise from something which was thought of too little importance to attend to'? How we Nurses can echo that!

'Immense, incalculable misery' is due to 'the immoral'—he calls 'thoughtlessness' 'immoral'—'thoughtlessness' of women about little things: this is what our training is to counteract in us. Think nothing too small to be attended to in this way. Think everything too small of personal trouble or sensitiveness to be cared for in another way.

It is not knowledge only: it is practice we want. We only *know* a thing if we can *do* it. [There is a famous Italian proverb which says: 'so much'—and no more—'each knows as she *does*.'] You have been most attentive to your Classes: how much benefit is to be derived from them, you know: we need not tell you: they are invaluable. Our

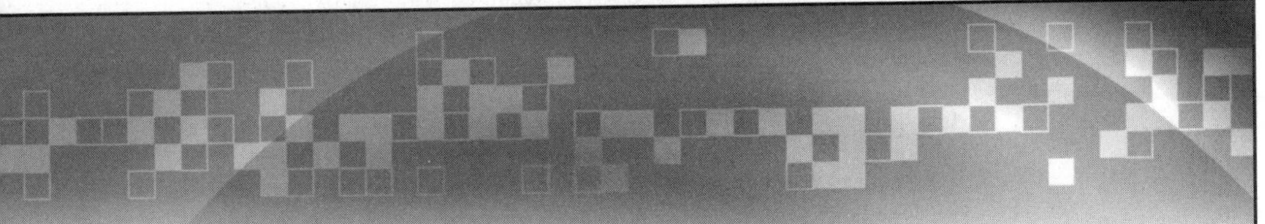

Matron, our 'Home Sister,' our Medical Instructor, have all done their parts by us nobly. We will do our parts by them.

What we did last year we may look upon not as a matter of conceit, but of encouragement. We must not fail this year, and we'll not fail. We'll keep up to the mark: nay more, we will press on to a higher mark. For our 'calling' is a high one (the 'little things,' remember: a high excellence in little things). And we must answer to the call ever more and more strenuously and ever more and more humbly too.

By and bye I have a few words to say about the 'little things.'

Now I say, we live together: let us live for each other's comfort; we are all working together: grasp the idea of this as a larger work than our own little pet hobbies, which are very narrow: our own little personal wishes, feelings, piques, or tempers. This is not individual work: a real Nurse sinks self. Remember we are not so many small selves, but members of a community.

'Little children, love one another.' To love, that is, to help one another, to strive together, to act together, to work for the same end, to bring to perfection the sisterly feeling of fellow-workers, without which nothing great is done, nothing good lasts. Might not St. John have been thinking of us Nurses in our Training Schools when he said that?

May God be with us all and we be *one* in Him and in His *work*.

God speed us all.
Amen in our hearts.

I.

1. These are some of the little things we need to attend to:

To be a Nurse *is* to be a Nurse: not to be a Nurse only when we are put to the work we like. If we can't work when we are put to the work we don't like—and Patients can't always be fitted to Nurses—that is behaving like a spoilt child, like a naughty girl: not like a Nurse. If we can do the work we don't like from the higher motive till we do like it: that is one test of being a real Nurse. A Nurse is not one who can only do what she does like, and can't do what she does not like. For the Patients want according to their wants, and not according to the Nurse's likes or dislikes. If you wish to be trained or exercised in those parts of the work you don't so much like and know you don't do so well, that is wishing to be a real Nurse.

If you wish to be trained or exercised only in that which you like and know you do well, it is needless to say that what you want is not to be a Trained Nurse but to do what you like.

If you want to do what you like and what you do well, it is for your own sake, for your own self-satisfaction, for conceit, in short, that you do it: that you come here—not for the sake of Nursing or of Training.

If you want to do what you like and what you do well for the sake of being praised by others, then you nurse for your own vanity, not for the sake of Nursing. But if you wish to be trained to do *all* Nursing well, even what you do not like—trained to perfection in little things—that is Nursing for the sake of Nursing: for the sake of God and of your neighbour. And remember, in little things as in great, No Cross, no Crown.

Nursing is said, most truly said, to be a high calling, an honourable calling. But what does the honour lie in? In working hard during your training to learn and to do all things perfectly.

The honour does not lie in putting on Nursing like your uniform, your dress: though dishonour often lies in being neat in your uniform within doors and dressy in your finery out of doors. Dishonour always lies in inconsistency.

Honour lies in loving perfection, consistency, and in working hard for it: in being ready to work patiently: to say not 'How clever I am! but I am not yet worthy': but Nursing is worthy; and I will live to deserve and work to deserve to be called a Trained Nurse.

2. What you are in the 'Home' will surely influence you elsewhere and everywhere. Here are two of the plain practical little things necessary to produce good Nurses, the want of attention to which produces some of the 'greatest evils in life:' quietness, cleanliness. (*a*) Quietness in moving about the 'Home'; in arranging your rooms, in not *slamming* every door after you; no noisy talking on the stairs and in the lobbies—forgetting at times some unfortunate Night Nurse in bed. But, if you are Nurses, Nurses ought to be going about quietly, whether Night Nurses are asleep or not. For a Sick Ward ought to be as quiet as a Sick Room; and a Sick Room, I need not say, ought to be the quietest place in God's Kingdom. Quietness in dress, especially being *consistent* in this matter when off duty and going out. And oh! let the Lady Probationers realise how important their example is in these things, so little and so great! If you are Nurses, Nurses ought not to be dressy, whether in or out of their uniform.

Do you remember that Christ holds up the wild flowers as our example in dress? Why? He says: God 'clothes' the field flowers. How does He clothe them?

First: their 'clothes 'are exactly suitable for the kind of place they are in and the kind of work they have to do. So should ours be.

Second: field flowers are never double: double flowers change their useful stamens for showy petals, and so have no seeds. These double flowers are like the useless appendages now worn on the dress, and very much in your way. Wild flowers have purpose in all their beauty. So ought dress to have;—nothing purposeless about it.

Third: the colours of the wild flower are perfect in harmony, and not many of them.

Fourth: there is not a speck on the freshness with which flowers come out of the dirty earth.

Even when our clothes are getting rather old we may imitate the flower: for we may make them look as fresh as a daisy.

Whatsoever we do, whether we eat or drink *or dress*, let us do all to the glory of God. But above all remember, 'be not anxious what ye shall put on': which is the real meaning of 'Take no thought.'

This is not my own idea: it was in a Bible lesson, never to be forgotten. And I knew a Nurse who dressed so nicely and quietly after she had heard this Bible lesson that you would think of her as a model. And alas! I have known, oh how many! whose dress was their snare.

Oh, my dear Nurses, whether gentlewomen or not, don't let people say of you that you are like 'Girls of the Period': let them say that you are like 'field flowers,' and welcome.

(*b*) Cleanliness in person and in our rooms, thinking nothing too small to be attended to in this respect.

And if these things are important in the 'Home,' think how important they are in the Wards, where cleanliness and fresh air not so much give life as *are* the very life of the Patients—and there can be no pure air without cleanliness; where the smallest carelessness may turn the scale from life to death: where Disinfectants, as one of your own Surgeons has said, are but a 'mystic rite.' Cleanliness is the only real Disinfectant. Remember that Typhoid Fever is distinctly a filth disease; that Consumption is distinctly the product of breathing foul air, especially at night; that in surgical cases, Erysipelas and Pyæmia are simply a poisoning of the blood—generally thro' some want of cleanliness or other. And do not speak of these, as little things, which determine the most momentous issues of life and death. I knew a Probationer who when washing a poor man's ulcerated leg, actually wiped it on his sheet, and excused herself by saying she had always seen it done so in another place. The least carelessness in not washing your hands between one bad case and another, and many another carelessness which it is plain I cannot mention here—it would not be nice, tho' it is much less nice to do it; [but I think of writing a short article on this very thing: Carelessnesses in cleanliness about Patients: their persons, utensils, bandages, towels, discharges, secretions,—all that which more especially falls to the duty of the Nurse and not of the Hospital;] the least carelessness, I say, in these things, which every Nurse can be careful or careless in, may cost a life: aye, may cost your own, or at least a finger. We have all seen poisoned fingers.

3. I read with more interest than if they were novels your case papers. Some are meagre, especially in the 'history.' Some are good. Please remember that, besides your own instruction, you can give me some too, by making these most interesting cases as interesting as possible, by making them full and accurate and entering the full history. If the history of every case were recorded, especially of Typhoid Fever, which is, as we said, a filth disease, it is impossible to over-estimate the body of valuable information which would thus be got together, and which might go far, in the hands of Officers of Health and by recent laws, to prevent disease altogether. The District Nurses are most useful in this respect.

When we obey all God's laws as to cleanliness, fresh air, pure water, good habits, good dwellings, good drains, food and drink, work and exercise, health is the result: when we disobey, sickness. 110,000 lives are needlessly sacrificed every year in this kingdom by our disobedience, and 220,000 people are needlessly sick all the year round. And why? Because we will not know, will not obey God's simple Health-laws.

No epidemic can resist thorough cleanliness and fresh air.

4. You must not think of admiration, of conceit; you must think only of excellence: that is, if you wish to be a real Nurse. If we don't we had better not be here. Don't let us put on any disguises: one must be a Nurse or nothing, if one chooses to be here at all.

The first thing is to be sure to serve God by helping every fellow-servant of God, and also many who are not servants of God at all—helping them, not by your words but by your acts, to become fellow- servants; then to build up, by learning to do every little thing to perfection, the real Nurse in ourselves.

You say, perhaps, or rather think: 'I don't do as I am bid, because I know better how to do it than the person who bids me.' Let me tell you this: the best nursing powers that ever constituted a genius of a Nurse afterwards are at first little or nothing more than the power of receiving training—a great capacity for obeying discipline.

If you can't be trained, if you can't obey the impulse and guidance of the training hand in the minutest particular in 'little things,' it's no use: you are no Nurse: you never will be: you are only a potterer in your own way.

Sir Harry Verney, your Chairman, who cares very much about you all, my brother-in-law, has had a frightful accident from his horse falling and rolling over him. Tho' by no means recovered, he is, we are thankful to say, out of danger. His two little grand-daughters,

Ellen, aged 3, and Lettice, a baby, prayed for grandpapa. And then Ellen knelt, and Lettice stood at their mama's knee with her chubby hands clasped, and her serious blue eyes. Ellen looked fixedly at her, and began her prayers with 'Pray God, bless baby's handies.' It was so touching—the four baby hands—one does so long to dedicate all our Nurses' hands to all pure and lovely and earnest work. The dirtiest work may be pure and lovely: done for God and our neighbour; or rather there is *no* dirty work done in that way. And the little voice full of real love for her sister, tho' not understanding her own words! Oh, let us, who do understand our own words, all be sisters! and pray for and help one another's hands!

5. Is there any Nurse here who is a Pharisee? This seems a very cruel and unjust question.

We think of the Pharisees, when we read the terrible denunciation of them by our Master, as a small, peculiar, antiquated sect of 2,000 years ago. Are they not rather the least peculiar, the most widely-spread people of every time? A conceited Nurse who says, "How much cleverer, how much better I am than other people': is she not a Pharisee? A Nurse who nurses well, to be seen of men, or for the love of power or praise, however hard she works—the Pharisees worked very hard—but without love or humility in her heart, or with more ambition and love of success than love of God or her neighbour, is she not a Pharisee? I am sure I often ask myself, sadly enough, Am I a Pharisee? in this sense: Am I, or am I not, doing this with a single eye to God's work, to serving Him and my neighbour, even tho' my 'neighbour' is as hostile to me as the Jew was to the Samaritan,—or am I doing it because I identify my selfish self with the work, and in so doing serve myself and not God? If so, then I am a Pharisee.

It is good to love our Training School and our body, and to wish to keep up its credit. We are bound to do so. That is helping God's work in the world. We are bound to try to be the 'salt of the world' in nursing; but if we are conceited, seeking *ourselves* in this, then we are not 'salt' but Pharisees.

I may be a Pharisee even in writing this to you, if I do it only for the love of our own credit, and not for the love of you and to serve God.

We should have zeal for God's sake and His work's sake: but some seem to have zeal for zeal's sake only.

Zeal does not make a Christian Nurse—tho' Christ was the most zealous mediciner that ever was— (He says: 'The zeal of a God's house hath eaten me up')—if it is zeal for our own credit and glory, and not for God's; zeal for our own work, and not for God's work; zeal for our own good and our own success, and not for our Patients' good; or for our Patients' good only to procure our own. Zeal by itself does not make a good Nurse: it makes a Pharisee. Christ is so strong upon this point of not being conceited, of not nursing to show what 'fine fellows' we are as Nurses, that He actually says 'it is conceited of us to let one of our hands know what the other does.' What will He say if He sees one of us doing all her work to let not only her other hand but other people know she does it? Yet all our best work which looks so well *may* be done from this motive.

And let me tell you a little secret. One of our Superintendents at a distance says that she finds she must not boast so much about St. Thomas'. Nor must you. People have heard too much about it. I dare say you remember the fine old Greek statesman who was banished because people were tired of hearing him called 'The Just.' Don't let people get tired of hearing you call St. Thomas 'The Just' when you are away from us. We shall not at all complain of your proving it 'The Just' by your training and conduct.

I read lately in a well-known medical journal, speaking of the 'Nightingale Nurses,' that the day is quite gone by when a novel would give a caricature of a Nurse as a 'Mrs. Gamp'—a drinking, brutal, ignorant, coarse old woman. The 'Nightingale Nurse,' it said, would be in a novel—What do you think?—an active, useful, clever Nurse. These are the parts I approve of; but what else do you think?

Ah, there's the rub. You see what our name is 'up' for in the world. That's what I should like to be left out. This is what a friendly critic says of us, and we may be very sure that unfriendly critics say much worse. Do we deserve what they say of us? that is the question. Let us not have each one of us to say 'Yes 'in our own hearts. Christ made no light matter of conceit.

Keep the usefulness, and let the conceit go.

6. And may I here say a few words of counsel to those who may be called upon to be Night Nurses? One of these asked me with tears to pray for her: I do pray for all of you, our dear Night Nurses. In my restless nights my thoughts turn to you incessantly by the bed-sides of restless and suffering Patients, and I pray God that He will make, thro' you, thro' your patience, your skill, your hope, faith and charity, every Ward into a Church, and teach us how to *be* the Gospel is the only way to 'preach the Gospel,' which Christ tells us is the duty of every one of us 'unto the end of the world'—every woman and Nurse of us all—and how a collection of any people trying to live like Christ is a Church. Did you ever think how Christ was a Nurse, and stood by the bed, and with his own hands nursed and 'did for' the sufferers? But, to return to those who may be called upon to be Night Nurses:

Do not abuse the liberty given you on emerging from the 'Home,' where you are cared for as if you were our children. Keep to regular hours by day for your meals, your sleep, your exercise. If you do not, you will never be able to do and stand the night work perfectly; if you do there is no reason why night nursing may not be as healthy as day. [I used to be very fond of the night when I was a Night Nurse. I know what it is: but then I had my day work to do besides. You have not.] Do not turn dressy in your going out by day. It is vulgar: it is mean to burst out into freedom in this way. There are circumstances of peculiar temptation when, after the restraints and motherly care of the 'Home,' you, the young ones, are put suddenly into circumstances of peculiar liberty. Is it not the time to act, like Daniel?

You ask me to pray for you. I give you the watchword:

Dare to be a Daniel,
Dare to stand alone,
Dare to have a purpose firm,
Dare to make it known.

Let us repeat this together every night.

Daniel went thro' the hungry lions' den, because he would not deny God: he would not do what God told him not. You have not to go thro' lions, but you may have to be laughed at: you may find many temptations not to stand to your rule of life. You will say, perhaps, that your little sins are very different from denying God. Yes, and so is what you have to fear and to endure very different from what Daniel had to fear and to endure. He had to fear being eaten by savage wild beats: you the not comrade-ing together. But as God delivered Daniel out of the lions' den, so He will deliver you. If you stand by Him, He will stand by you:

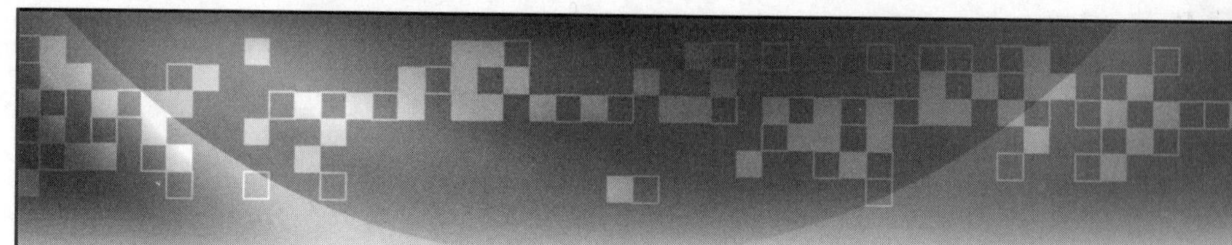

Standing by a purpose true,
Heeding God's command:
Honour them, the faithful few,
All hail to Daniel's band!

All hail to Daniel's band, the Night Nurses of St. Thomas', the Night Nurses from the 'Home.' Oh, may God have this to say to you at the Last Day! Let 'the Judge, the Righteous Judge,' have to call us not 'the Pharisees,' but Daniel's band!

This is what I pray for you, for me, for all of us.

But what is it to be a Daniel's band? What is 'God's command' to Night Nurses?

It is—is it not?—not to slur over any duty—not the very least of all our duties—as Night Nurse: to be able to give a full, accurate, and minute account of each Patient the next morning: to be strictly reserved in your manner with gentlemen ['Thou, God, seest me': No one else]—to be honest and true. You don't know how well the Patients know you: how accurately they judge you. You can do them no good unless they see that you *live* what you say.

It is: not to go out showily dressed, and not to keep irregular hours with others in the day time.

Dare to have a purpose firm,
Dare to make it known.

Watch—watch. Christ seems to have had a special word for Night Nurses: 'I say unto you, watch.' And He says: 'Lo, I am with you always,' when no one else is by.

And He divides us all, at this moment, into the 'wise virgins' and the 'foolish virgins.' Oh, let Him not find any 'foolish virgins' among our Night Nurses! Each Night Nurse has to stand alone in her Ward.

Dare to stand alone.

Let our Master be able to say some day that every one of the patients has been the better, not only in body but in spirit—whether going to life or to death—for having been nursed by each one of you.

II.

But one is gone: perhaps the dearest of all—Nurse Martha Rice.

I was the last to see her in England. She was so pleased to be going to Miss Machin at Montreal.

She said it was no sacrifice, except the leaving her parents. She almost wished it had been, that she might have had something to give to God.

Now she *has* had something to give to God: her life.

'So young, so happy: all so happy together, when in their room they were always sitting round the table, so cheerful, reading their Bible together. She walked round the garden so happy that last night.

So pure and fresh: there was something of the sweet savour of holiness about her. I could tell you of souls upon whom she made a great impression: all unknowing: simply by being herself.

A noble sort of girl: sound and holy in mind and heart: living with God. It is scarcely respectful to say how I liked her, now she is an angel in heaven: like a child to Miss Machin, who was like a mother to her: loved and nursed her day and night.

'So dear and bright a creature,' 'liked and respected by every one in the Hospital,' 'and, as a Nurse, hardly too much can be said in her favour.' 'To the Doctors, Patients, and Superintendent, she was simply invaluable.' 'The contrast between these Nurses and the best of others is to be keenly felt daily': 'doing bravely': 'perfectly obedient and pleasant to their Superintendent.'

Was Martha conceited with all this? She was one of the simplest, humblest Christian women I have ever known. All noble souls are simple, natural, and humble. Let us be like her, and, like her, not conceited with it all. She was too brave to be conceited: too brave not to be humble. *She* had trained herself for the battle.

'With a nice, genial, respectful manner, which never left her, great firmness in duty, and steadiness that rendered her above suspicion': 'happy and interested in her charge.'

More above all petty calculations about self, all paltry wranglings, than almost any. How different for us, for her, had it not been so: could we not have mourned her, as we do. The others of the small Montreal staff who miss her so terribly will like to hear how we feel this. They were all with her when she died: Miss Machin sat up with her every night, and either she or Miss Blower never left her, day or night, during the last nine days of her illness. She died of typhoid fever: peritonitis the last three weeks; but, as she had survived so long, they hoped against hope up to Easter Day.

About seven days before her death, during her delirium, she said: 'The Lord has two wills: His will be done.' It is when we do not know what God's will is to be, that it is the hardest to will what He wills.

Strange to say, on Good Friday, tho' she was so delirious that there was difficulty in keeping her in bed, and she did not know what day it was, Christ on the Cross was her theme all the day long. 'Christ died on the Cross for me: and I want to go and die for Him.' She had indeed lived for Him. Then on Easter Day, she said to Miss Blower: 'I am happy, so happy: we are both happy, so very happy.' She said she was going to hear the 8th Psalm. Shall we remember Martha's favourite psalm? She spoke often about St. Thomas'.

She died the day after Easter Day. The change came at seven in the evening, and she lived till five o'clock the next morning, conscious to the last, repeating sentences, and answering by looks when she could speak no more. Her Saviour, whom she had so loved and followed in her life, was with her thro' the Valley of the Shadow of Death, and she felt Him there. She was happy. 'My best love,' she said, 'tell them it is all for the best, and I am not sorry I came out.'

Her parents have given her up nobly, though with bleeding hearts, with true submission to our Father's will: they *are* satisfied it is 'all for the best.'

All the Montreal Hospital shared our sorrow. The Doctors were full of kindness in their medical attendance. Mr. Redpath, who is a principal Director, and Mrs. Redpath were like a real father and mother to our people. Martha's death-bed and coffin were strewed with flowers.

Public and private prayers were offered up for her at Montreal during her illness. Who can say that they were not answered?

She spoke of dying: but without fear. We prayed that God would spare the child to us: but He had need of her.

Our Father arranged her going out: for she went, if ever woman did, with a single eye, to please Him and to do her duty to the work and her Superintendent. 'Is it well with the child?' 'It is well.' Let us who feel her loss so deeply in the work not grudge her to God.

As one of you yourselves said: 'she died like a good soldier of Jesus Christ, well to the front.' Would any one of us wish it otherwise for her? Would any one of us wish a better lot for herself?

There is but one feeling among us all about her: that she lived as a noble Christian girl, and that she has been permitted to die nobly: in the post of honour, as a soldier thinks it glorious to die: in the midst of our work, so surely do we Nurses think it glorious to die.

But to be like her we must have a mind like hers: 'enduring, patient, firm, and meek.' I know that she sought of God the mind of Jesus Christ. 'Active, like His; like His, resigned'; copying His pattern: ready to 'endure hardness.'

We give her joy: it is our loss, not hers. She is gone to our Lord and her Lord. Made ripe so soon for her and our Father's house,—our tears are her joy. She is in another room of our Father's house. She bids us now give thanks for her. Think of that Easter morn when she rose again. She had indeed 'Another morn than ours'—that 17th of April!

III.

LASTLY:— 'Quit ye like men,' says St. Paul.

What does this mean? To fight on bravely, and humbly, because ye are men, and not Gods. To make progress all your lives: to go on and not to stop: Never. No turning back. No halting. No surrender.

Quit ye like women, he would have said to us Nurses. And what does this mean? Does it not mean much the same thing?—always to press on: no turning back, no giving in: always trying to make Nursing something better and better than it is every year; always like women, not like school-boys, in our quietness everywhere: 'in quietness and in confidence' possessing our strength: always like women, not like jays in borrowed plumes, in our dress: always, like women, quitting ourselves with the Patients, so that every one of them shall be the better, mind as well as body, for having been nursed by us. Trusting happily in God: 'There is a Providence over us,' one would say; 'If I am to have this' (something, or some post one wants), '[I shall have it; if I am not to have it, I shall not have it. What is there to be anxious about?' This is a plain saying, but who of us acts up to it?]

No shrinking from work we don't like, like spoilt children: no selfish tempers about who is thought the most of, but 'in honour preferring one another': no petty wranglings, so shameful before God, among women: remember the family at Bethany—(the book chosen by one of you in going to Montreal)—so may we be all one with each other: in Sisterly love: whether we are on this side the Atlantic or the other: on this or the other side the Tweed: and one with our Matron and Sisters: and one with our Great Master. And may this Home be like the Home of Bethany: one in the fellowship of our Father—*He* calls us *fellow*-workers—and of His Son, our brother: He calls us Sisters: let us be His true Sisters: His Martha and Mary: whom He loved to stay with.

Hold the fort, for I am coming:
Jesus signals still:
Wave the answer back to heaven,
By Thy grace I will.

In a Nurse's career there is no time to fold the hands: it is only the cowardly and the conceited who do that. On, on: there is a hill to climb: there is also a 'Valley of Humiliation' to pass through before we cross the river—before we are welcomed home.

If Bunyan wrote a 'Pilgrim's Progress,' let us write—not in a book, but in our lives—a Nurse's Progress: for a Nurse is, beyond all others, a pilgrim.

On, on: till we can say the course is run: the goal is won: we have got home!

FLORENCE NIGHTINGALE.

1878

(Private)
New Year's Day 1878.~
Letter from Miss Nightingale

New Year's Day 1878. 7 a.m.

My very dear Matron, dear 'Home' Sister.
Dear friends & fellow Nurses all.

I give you joy this blessed New Year of your charge & joy to all who are in your charge. May our New Years be many, "happy & glorious." May your 'shadows never be less.'

Dear comrades let this be really a New Year, a Year of deliverances from all our faults & mistakes: [and, if you know me, you would know that I need deliverance perhaps more than any one of you, perhaps more than all of you put together: But I don't mean to give in: I mean to reform, please God Almighty, yet: sick old woman as I am: then the promise may be made good even to me that I may be able even "to glory in my infirmities"—the almost incredible promise that Christ, that God Himself will "work in us."] Let this be a year of pulling our Patients through—a year of work such as angels might envy: a year of blessings:
for the sick, of blessings for their Nurses—
the "acceptable year of the Lord"—for us all.

Dear Probationers: tho', as I hope you know, you are always with me & always present in my thoughts: I have not thanked you yet for your very kind 'round robin' to me of last May: Thank you again & again, both you who are still with us & you who have already entered on your appointed work to run the (Nursing) race which has been set before you.

All hail to that promise,—dear, we may believe to God,—to strive each & all to keep up & to raise the standard of this Training-School & of Nursing in general, wherever you are.

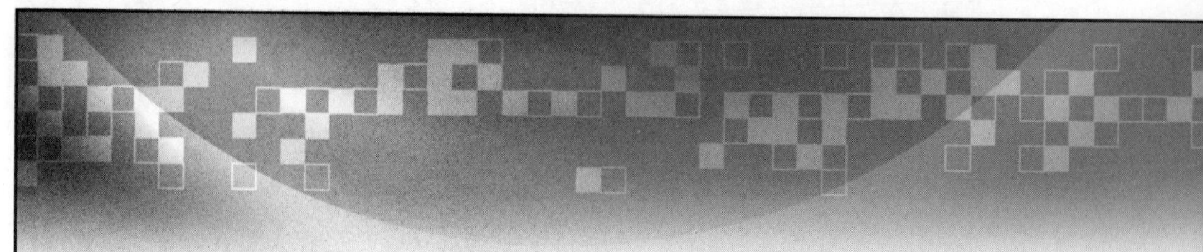

Now hail to the Conqueror,
O praise to the Lord.
Our life is His Spirit,
Our strength is His word.
So only can He "work in us."

And plenty of Case papers this year, please, plenty of proofs that you are interested in your Patients.

And oh remember, please, that each one of those Patients is a 'temple of God.' Let us not shame Him in His temple: that each one of those "little ones" has an angel which 'beholds the face of our Father in heaven.' Let no bad news of us & our doings with each be brought to our Father. He has given every one of us a post: let Him find every one of us in it: true to every one of His Creatures, as He is Himself true to Him.

<u>Every one of us</u>: pray God we remember that! God does not look at us in masses: He looks at each least little woman as if she were the only one in the world.

Wycliffe, the great Reformer, said that all (Training) systems, all forms, all rules & Regulations the whole outward & established Institution & System in short [which some of us, it is whispered, throw in the teeth of some others of us: but I don't believe it.] was good only in as far as each person was good herself or himself. It was worth nothing, without. Without, all fell to the ground [Wycliffe need not have come to tell us this. Yet there are many in the world who have not learnt it yet.]

I knew a woman who said (& who did it too): "Be heroic" in your <u>every day's</u> work: your <u>every</u> day's prayers & resolutions. If you can't work up to them quite all at once, at least you can get a little nearer & nearer every day.

We talk of 'rules.' <u>This</u> was <u>her</u> 'rule.'

It was the rule of her life.

And if a heroine is one who does great things for the sake of others—[no conceit, all humility in it: if she thinks herself a heroine, she is none] & if any woman may be a heroine in small things & in daily life—just as much or almost more than in great things & on grand occasions, surely any Nurse, who has to do every day & to do & to do for others, any Nurse may be a heroine.

God expects each one of us Nurses to be "a heroine" that is, to do <u>& be</u> her very best in herself—in her common work with others, her common work in the 'Home,' her common work in the Hospital, saving Patients' strength & health & perhaps lives:— her common work with the others—Wardmaids & all, in doing <u>their</u> best. Then, if she does her very best, intending & striving to make it better & better every day, till God raises it to the perfect work, we well may say: that Nurse is a hero in her daily work.

And let us each New Year 'take stock' as it were of ourselves: Always bring your Nursing to the bar of your own conscience, rather more when Head Nurse, & Doctors are not by to judge it: rather more when you are Head Nurses yourselves: I in my old age do this: do it all your lives: do it with all your might; today, tomorrow & every Year, if you would be good Nurses—A good Nurse will <u>test</u> her Nursing & learn something to the last day of her Nursing life.

Let us each New Year 'take stock' of our own selves in this way too: "am I keeping up to the motives that led me to choose this work? or do I look upon it merely as a thing to be got through? Do I still think it a work to which I was called by God Himself? And am I daily pressing forward more & more to do the daily task <u>for the good of others</u> not

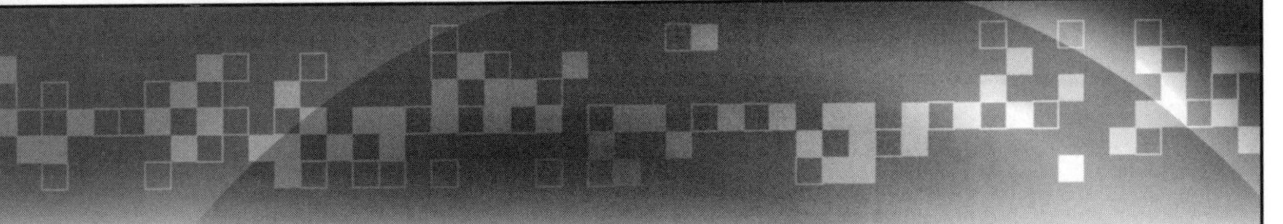

for habit, self or self's glory—not merely because others are doing it & we must do it, like creatures in harness.

"Be not like dumb driven cattle:

Be a hero in the strife."

Always remembering that we are forwarding the work when we do it for the work's sake, for others' sake, for God's sake. As sharers in a common work, helping one another.—And hindering the work when we do it each for her own little sake, like a 'dog in the manger,' or hanging together in little selfish 'parties.'

To do one's day's work as a part of God's great plan: to be about one's own & one's Father's business—I give you joy that as Nurses we can always be about our 'Father's business' in our own.—what can any one do more? what ought any one to do less?

Stick together & to your Matron & to your Home Sister like a bundle of faggots: you know the fable.

No pains will be spared to make the Trained Nurses of Britain worthy;

You spare no pains to answer to the pains.

Wish well to every other Trained & Training Nurse in the world. O what a good thing is friendly rivalry!

If you stand still, I should wish that every other School should pass you: not that every other School should stand still to let you go ahead.

But stick together like a bundle of faggots. And to do this I will tell you a rule in a Society or Company I know: [do you know what that word comes from? it comes from the old Roman custom of a 'company' of soldiers under one Commander. And what were those soldiers not able to do? They would hold a post till the last man of them had died at it—each man forgetting himself, each man standing by the others, no man saying 'oh this is hard.—

These were the men who conquered the world. And not alone among the Romans were such men to be found. Who shall say so? We have our own men, of whom it was written:

"Forward the Light Brigade:

O the brave charge they made!" And I say: Forward the Light Brigade of St. Thomas'. God will back you if you look to Him, against any "charge" of any day. He loves a brave woman, a magnanimous heart.]

I will tell you the rule of the Company or Society I spoke of:

Each to read to herself once a week the verses about 'Charity' in the famous Chapter of Corinthians, and 3 or 4 times a day each just to think to herself: "Am I doing like 'Charity'?— if not, I am a tinkling cymbal rather than a Nurse."

Now, dear comrades, will you make a bargain with me: I will do this till next New Year, (if I live so long; for I am very ill) if you will.

I will send you the Chapter illuminated, if I may.

In past days, the most that was done for a Nurse was to expect from her:—obedience: she was just told what had to be done & ordered to go & do it. Now the utmost pains are taken to show her why it has to be done: & how it is to be done [Ought it not to be much easier now to have the spirit of obedience?]

This is what is called Training. Training which is given her & experience which she must give herself every day of her life—(not the experience which practises the blunders of our predecessors—) & which her training shows her how to give herself, go to make the good Nurse.

But what must we say of the trained Nurse who is not obedient & tries to teach the Doctors? Let your experience cast its light before so as to give light to the path you have

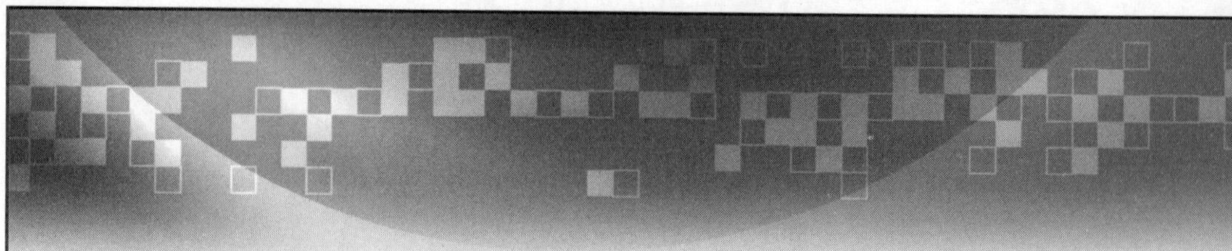

to tread now: & not only to the path behind, which as St. Paul says we must leave behind. That is a melancholy sort of experience.

And don't use your 'training' like an Irish 'shillelagh,' to cudgel other people with. That is no 'training,' is it?

Will you excuse an old, old Hospital Nurse like me who lived before training was so much as thought of for telling the most dangerous flaws in Trained Nurses when they enter upon their appointed places?

"Be watchful, be vigilant,
Danger may be
At an hour when all seemeth
securest to thee.
One is: complaining—as if nothing were good enough for us.
The other: conceit."

Complain? what business have we to complain? is that brave? is that making a 'brave charge'? It is so cowardly to complain. 'Who complains, sins' is a proverb.

Harry the Fifth, before he fought & won the battle of Agincourt with but a handful of half starved men, bade any man who thought it 'hard' & did not want to rough it: to go home.

"His passport shall be made
And crowns of convoy put into his purse."
"I would not die in that man's company,
Who fears his fellowship to die with me."
I would not nurse in that one's company
Who fears her fellowship to nurse with me-

Trained Nurses talk sometimes about being Pioneers: & yet the first trouble or trial we have, or the first discomfort, or the first check to our vanity, we say "O this is not what I was used to," or, "this is not what I expected." [Are we not afraid that God may one day say: this is not what He expected of us.] Or: we never did so: this is not my place. Or: this is "putting upon" me. Or: this is what I don't like—

Call these women Pioneers: they are not fit to be the baggage-guard—are they?

Their talk is all rant & cant: & we are only sounding brass, & we talk it.

Conceit: is that brave?—did we ever know a really brave man conceited? Any conceit is the result not of training but of want of capacity for being trained. And when a Trained Nurse is conceited, she shows herself untrained.

A really great man who lived long, long ago, one of the first of Trainers both of Missionaries & of Nurses: [his Nurses still number some 20,000. I have worked with them myself.] used to say to his Trainers: 'You will not win them by saying fine things': [and I add. you will not win them by saying hard things:] 'perhaps they know more than we do.'

[yes, there may be many Nurses, not of us, who know more than we do:]

[or perhaps we can tell them nothing that they have not heard or read before a hundred terms.' but it is what they *see* that trains them.

O dear Nurses all, by all means let us mind what we say—but still more let us mind what we do: let other Nurses only 'see' in us what they had better do themselves, & never what they had better avoid. What we wish them to do let them see us do. Let our Patients, so sharp to see, only see in us, alike in Nurses & Probationers, what will do them good to see. Show that you have 'been with Jesus' every day, don't be afraid either of seeming 'unlearned & ignorant' [I feel every day of my life, tho' perhaps I number as many years of experience as you do of life: how ignorant & unlearned I am]. Do you remember what it says in Acts about Peter's & John's wonderful influence—& all because of this that, tho' they were "unlearned & ignorant," people could see that they "had been with Jesus"?

[The best trained Nurse is "unlearned & ignorant."]

Show then that you have "been with Jesus" every morning & night.

There is a great temptation in a community of Probationers to be in a hurry [God is never in a hurry:] to scratch the ground & not dig deep: to do surface-work: like sticking in cut flowers, instead of growing flowers & fruit too from the seed or root. Strike your roots deep, rather than spread your branches too far.

Be every day more & more real, honest, thorough Nurses in your Nursing work—O fie to a careless Nurse, when life or death depends upon it.

And I will whisper in your ears a little secret: how uncommonly glad I should have been to have had our Home Sister's classes in my young days!

We are on our trial, dear friends: I can tell you that: we are on our trial again after 17 years—whether we win or not depends upon you. Trial is the only thing to prove if we are worth anything. I hail it: Let us take care not to be left behind—But, if we deserve it I for one shall say I am glad we are left behind.

And now. Forward the Light Brigade of St. Thomas': all over the country. (not heavy in hand with complaints & conceit & self-seeking: that we won't be). And don't let us be like the chorus at the play which cries 'Forward, forward,' every two minutes: & never stirs a step.

May we all be able to say at the next New Year, may God be able to say at our First New Year in His eternity: O the brave charge was made!

May we all be soldiers of God, able to 'endure hardness' & to give to others softness!

Your affectionate servant
(and Mother I fain would be)
Florence Nightingale

The Survivors of the Light Brigade in the Charge of Balaclava have lately sent me their names bound in a book.

May all our names be found written in God's book as His own faithful Nurses.

F.N.

1879

Letter from Florence Nightingale to the Probationer-Nurses in the 'Nightingale Fund' School, at St. Thomas' Hospital.
Easter, 1879.
For private use only.
To the Probationers of the Nightingale Home.
Easter Eve, 1879, 6 A.M.

My dear Friends,

I am always thinking of you, and as my Easter greeting, I could not help copying for you part of a letter which one of my brother-in-law's family had from Col. Degacher (commanding one battalion of the 24th Regiment in Natal), giving the names of men whom he recommended for the Victoria Cross, when defending the Commissariat Stores at Rorke's Drift. [His brother, Capt. Degacher, was killed at Isandula.] He says:—

"Private John Williams was posted, together with Private Joseph Williams and Private William Harrison (1/24th Regiment), in a further ward of the Hospital. They held it for more than an hour—so long as they had a round of ammunition left, when, as communication was for the time cut off, the Zulus were enabled to advance, and burst open the door. A hand to hand conflict then ensued, during which Private Joseph Williams and two of the Patients were dragged out and assegaied [killed with a short spear or dagger].

"Whilst the Zulus were occupied with the slaughter of these unfortunate men, a lull took place, which enabled Private John Williams (who with two of the Patients were by this time the *only men left alive* in the ward) to succeed in knocking a hole in the partition and taking the two Patients with him into the next ward, where he found Private Henry Hook.

These two men together, one man working whilst the other fought and held the enemy at bay with his bayonet, broke through three more partitions, and were thus enabled to bring eight Patients through a small window into the inner line of defence.

In another ward facing the hill, William Jones and Private Robert Jones had been placed; they defended their post to the last, and until six out of seven Patients it contained had been removed. The seventh, Sergeant Maxfield, 2/24th Regiment, was delirious from fever, and although they had previously dressed him, they were unable to induce him to move; and when Private Robert Jones returned to endeavour to carry him off, he found him being stabbed on his bed by the Zulus.

Corporal Wm. Allen and Fd. Hitch, 2/24th Regiment, must also be mentioned. It was chiefly due to their courageous conduct that communication with the Hospital was kept up at all—holding together, at all costs, a most dangerous post, raked in reverse by the enemy's fire from the hill. They were both severely wounded, but their determined conduct enabled the Patients to be withdrawn from the Hospital. And when incapacitated from their wounds from fighting themselves, they continued, as soon as their wounds were dressed, to serve out ammunition to their comrades throughout the night."

These men who were defending the house at Rorke's Drift were 120 of his (Col. Degacher's) men, against 5,000 Zulus, and they fought from 3 p.m. of January 22nd, to 5 a.m. of the 23rd. *There* is a Night Nurse's night's work for you. "When shall such heroes live again?"—In every Nurse of us all. Every Nurse may at all costs serve her Patients as these brave heroic men did at the risk and the cost of their own lives.

Three cheers for these bravest of Night Nurses of Rorke's Drift, who regarded not themselves, not their ease, nor even their lives; who regarded duty and discipline; who stood to the last by God and their neighbour; who saved their post and their Patients. And may we Nurses all be like them, and fight through the night for our Patients' lives—fight through every night and day.

Do you see what a high feeling of comradeship does for these men? Many a soldier loses his life in the field by going back to help a drowning or a wounded comrade, who might have saved it. O, let us Nurses all be *comrades;* stick to the honour of our flag and our corps, and help each other to the best success, for the sake of Him who died, as at this time, to save us all!

And let us remember that petty selfishnesses and meannesses and self-indulgences hinder our honour as good soldiers of Jesus Christ and of the Unseen God, who sees all these little things when no one else does!

What makes us endure to the end?—Discipline. Do you think these men could thus have fought at a desperate post through the livelong night if they had not been trained to obedience to orders, and to acting as a corps, yet each man doing his own duty to the fullest extent—rather than every man going his own way, thinking of his own likings, and caring for himself?

How *Great* may be men and women, "little lower than the angels," and also how *little!*

Humility—to think our own life worth nothing except as serving in a corps, God's nursing corps, unflinching obedience, steadiness and endurance in carrying out His work—that is true discipline, that is true greatness, and may God give it to us Nurses, and make us His own Nurses.

And let us not think that these things can be done in a day or a night. No, they are the result of no rough-and-ready method. The most important part of those efforts was to be found in the patient labour of years. These great tasks are not to be accomplished suddenly by raw fellows in a night; it is when discipline and training have become a kind of second nature to us that they can be accomplished every day and every night. The raw Native levies ran away, determining our fall at Isandula. The well-trained English soldiers, led by their Officers and their Non-commissioned Officers, stuck to their posts.

Every feeling, every thought we have, stamps a character upon us, especially in our year of training, and in the next year or two.

The most unruly boys, weak in themselves—for unruliness is weakness—when they have to submit, it brings out all the good points in their characters. These boys, so easily led astray, they put themselves under the severest discipline, and after training sometimes come out the best of us all. The qualities which, when let alone, run to seed, and do themselves and others nothing but harm, under proper discipline make fine fellows of them.

And what is it to obey? To obey means to do what we are told, and to do it at once. With the nurse as with the soldier—whether we have been accustomed to it or not, whether we think it right or not, is not the question—prompt obedience is the question. We are not in control, but under control. Prompt obedience is the first thing; the rest is traditional nonsense. But mind who we go to for our orders. Go to headquarters. True discipline is to uphold authority, and not to mind trouble. We come into the work to do the work.

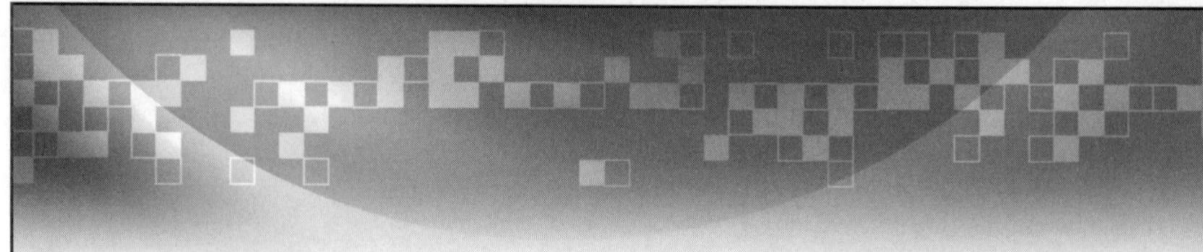

"Was there a man dismay'd?
Not tho' the soldier knew
Some one bad blunder'd:
Theirs not to reason why
Theirs not to make reply:
Theirs but to do and die:
So in the Valley of death
Stood the Eight Hundred—at Isandula.

We Nurses *are* taught the 'reason why,' as soldiers cannot be, of much of what we have to do. But it would be making a poor use of this 'reason why' if we were to turn round in any part of our training and say, or *not* say but *feel*—We know better than you.

Would we be of less use than the Elephant?—the Elephant who could kill a hundred men, but who alike pushes the Artillery train with his head when the horses cannot move it, AND who minds the children and carefully nurses them, and who threads a needle with his trunk. Why? Because he has been taught to *obey*. He would be of no use—but to destroy,—unless he had learnt that.

Sometimes he has a strong will, and it is not easy for him to get his lesson perfect. We can feel for him. We know a little about it ourselves. But he does learn in time to go our way and not his own,—to carry a heavy load, which of course he would rather not do, to turn to whichever side we wish, and to stop when we want him to stop.

So God teaches each one of us in time to go His way and not our own. And one of the best things I can wish each one of us is that we may learn the Elephant's lesson, that is to obey, in good time and not too late.

Pray for me, my dear friends, that I may learn it, even in my old age.

FLORENCE NIGHTINGALE

1881

6th May, 1881.
Letter from Florence Nightengale
London May 6, 1881

My very dear friends,

Now once more "God speed' to you all; my very best greetings & thanks to you all, all:—to our beginners good courage,—to our dear old workers peace, fresh courage too, perseverance: for to persevere to the end is as difficult & needs a yet better energy than to begin new work.

To be a good Nurse one must be a good woman, here we shall all agree. It is the old, old story But some of us are new to the start.

What is it to be "like a woman"? "Like a woman"—"a very woman" is sometimes said as a word of contempt: sometimes as a word of tender admiration.

What makes a good woman is the better or higher or holier nature: quietness – gentleness – patience – endurance – forbearance.

Forbearance with her patients – her fellow workers – her superiors – her equals. We need above all to remember that we come to learn, to be taught. Hence we come to

obey. No one ever was able to govern who was not able to obey. No one ever was able to teach who was not able to learn. The best scholars make the best teachers—those who obey best the best rulers

We all have to obey as well as to command all our lives.

Who does it best?

As a mark of contempt for a woman is it not said, she can't obey?—She will have her own way? As a mark of respect—she always knows how to obey? how to give up her own way. You are here to be trained for Nurses—attendants on the wants of the sick—helpers, in carrying out Doctors' orders (not Medical Students). Though Theory is very useful when carried out by practice, Theory without practice is ruinous to Nurses.

Then a good woman should be thorough. Thoroughness in a Nurse is a matter of life & death to the Patient. Or, rather, without it she is no Nurse.—Especially thoroughness in the unseen work. Do that well & the other will be done well too. Be as careful in the cleansing of the used poultice basin as in your attendance at an antiseptic dressing Don't care most about what meets the eye & gains attention. "How do you know you have grace?" – said a Minister to a housemaid. "Because I clean under the mats;" was the excellent reply. If a housemaid said that how much more should A Nurse, all whose vessels mean Patients.

Now what does "like a woman" mean when it is said in contempt? does it not mean what is petty, little selfishnesses, small meannesses: envy: jealousy: foolish talking: unkind gossip: love of praise.

Now, while we try to be "like women" in the noble sense of the word, let us fight as bravely against all such womanly weaknesses. Let us be anxious to do well, not for selfish praise but to honour & advance the cause, the work we have taken up. Let us value our training not as it makes us cleverer or superior to others, but inasmuch as it enables us to be more useful & helpful to our fellow creatures, the sick who most want our help. Let it be our ambition to be thorough good women, good Nurses—And never let us be ashamed of the name of "nurse."

This to our beginners, I had almost said. But those who have finished their year's training will be the first to tell us they are only beginners; they have just learnt how to learn & how to teach. When they are put into the responsibility of Nurse or 'Sister,' then they know how to learn & how to teach something every day, & year, which, without their thorough training, they would not know. This is what they tell me.

Then their battle cry is:

"Be not weary in well doing'

We will not forget that once we were ignorant tiresome Probationers – we will not laugh at the mistakes of beginners, but it shall be our pride to help all who come under our influence to be better women, more thorough Nurses.' What is influence? the most mighty, the most unseen engine we know. The influence of one year or two in the work, over one month or two in the work, is more mighty, altho' narrow, than the influence of statesmen or sovereigns. The influence of a good woman & thorough Nurse with all the raw Probationers who come under her care is untold. This it is—the using such influence, for good or for bad, which either raises or lowers the tone of the Hospital.

We all see how much easier it is to sink to the level of the low, than to rise to the level of the high—but dear friends all, we know how soldiers were taught to fight in the old times against desperate odds: standing shoulder to shoulder & back to back. Let us each & all, realizing the importance of our influence on others – stand shoulder to shoulder & not alone, in the good cause. But let us be quiet. What is it that is said about the leaven?—Women's influence ever has been & ever should be quiet & gentle in its working like the leaven—never noisy or self asserting

Let us seek all of us rather to be good than clever Nurses.

Now I am sure we will all give a grateful cheer to our Matron & to our Home Sister & our Medical Instructors.

God bless you all, my dear, dear friends And I hope to see you all, one by one, this year.

FLORENCE NIGHTINGALE

1883

From Florence Nightingale to the Probationers – Nurses in the "Nightingale Fund" Training School at St. Thomas' Hospital, and to the Nurses who were formerly trained there.
23rd May, 1883.

My very dear friends,

Here is my love with all my heart. I hope to make the acquaintance of every one of you. And that will be better even than being one of you to day in body. I am with you in spirit. That is nothing new. That is always, always – the old, old story.

And it is the old, old question too: Are we all of us on our mettle in our life's work? Joy to us if we are. If not, there can only be disappointment.

To those of us in earnest in our desire to be thorough workers – thorough women – thorough Nurses [and no woman can be a Good Nurse unless she is a good woman]. We say watch & persevere to do well your appointed work to fill thoroughly your present place: don't give in to the prevailing spirit of the day—hurry, bustle, change.

1. To those of us who are half hearted—[I do not know any – but there may be such] we say pause; either turn over a new leaf—or give up the work altogether—for if we remain half hearted [& no one can do the work, unless she put her whole heart in it.], we are taking up the room of better women, better workers. The eyes of England & perhaps of a still farther & larger world are upon us to pick out our inconsistencies & short-comings. Many sneering remarks are made unworthy of notice But (let this old woman whisper, just between ourselves: I have got my profit all my life out of sneering remarks): is there not some foundation for the epithets, 'conceited Nightingales,' &c &c &c?

2. What is training? We can't put into you what is not there. We want to bring out what is there. Training is enabling you to use the means you have in yourselves. Training is drawing out what you know yourselves. Learn your work thoroughly in your year of training. Store it up & practise it in your brain, eyes & hands, so that you may always know where to find it, & these—brain, eyes & hands—may always be your ready servants. But don't depend on – don't stop at your year's training.

If you don't go on, you will fall back. Aim higher. In the second year & the third year & all your lives, you will have to train yourselves on the foundation you have had in your first. And—you will find, if you are a true Nurse, you have only just begun.

But when you have put your hand to the plough, don't look back.

3. We here below cannot judge the motives which bring you into the work. Let us all have the benefit of the opinion that some high resolve or pure motive actuated us. But how when we become Nurses do we keep that high resolve, that pure motive ever in view? are we proud to be Nurses? to be called Nurse?—not simply to take pride in dressings & work which will bring us notice & praise? Remember, the Nurse is wanted most by the most helpless & often most disagreeable cases—in one sense there is no credit in nursing pleasant patients.

And don't despise what some of you call 'housemaid's work.' If you thought of its extreme importance, you would not mind doing it. As you know, without thorough housemaid's work, everything in the Ward or sick room becomes permeated with organic matter.

The greatest compliment I ever thought I, as a Hospital Nurse, received was: that I was put to clean & "do" the Special Ward, with the severest Medical or Surgical case which I was nursing, every day: because I did it thoroughly & without disturbing the Patient That was the first Hospital I ever served in. [I think I could give lessons in Hospital housemaid's work now.]

We Nurses should remember—to help our suffering fellow creatures in our calling – not to amuse ourselves. Let us make our 'calling' 'sure.' Sisters, Nurses, Probationers shall we start afresh? Shall we all renew—as we every morning need to do—our resolve? As a friend, a Nurse, abroad, said to me: one must be converted not once but every day. Shall it be our aim to be more thorough workers, more thorough women, more thorough Nurses every day, till we become most thorough, & so live down any spiteful sneers & epithets?

4. One word more: Year by year our numbers increase. We are becoming a large band. See that we are banded together by mutual good will: and remember the conduct of each member reflects credit or discredit on the whole. We cannot isolate ourselves if we would.

Thank God there are numerous other Training Schools now in existence. Let us give them the right hand of fellowship. Wherever we see thorough work, let us feel those are our Sisters. Let us run the race where all may win: rejoicing in their successes, as our own, & mourning their failures, wherever they are, as our own. We are all one Nurse. But see that we fall not off. We must fight the good fight steadily, with all our heart & all our mind & all our strength Or they may beat us. And that they will do if we do not hold to our colours to be true workers, true women, true Nurses.

5. We are volunteers; Don't let us forget that. We have chosen our path. Don't let us be worse soldiers in God's army, than those who are enlisted or compulsory conscripts.

For the first time for 25 years I went out last winter to see the return of a Regiment on foot from Egypt.

[And we have Nurses too who volunteered for Egypt & two of them still are there, working hard. They all worked hard & well.]

Any body might have been proud of these men's appearance—shabby skeletons they were—campaigning uniform worn out but well cleaned—not spruce or smart or showy: but alert, silent, steady in discipline.

And not a man of them all, I am sure, but thought he had nothing to be proud of in what he had done, tho' we might well be proud of them.

Now, we don't say: Volunteers take example by this. Assuredly we will be their true comrades in faithfulness to reality & duty. It is the same spirit: the spirit of the nation. Let us stick to it. The great Duke of Wellington said: 'all for duty, & nothing for reward.' So may all we volunteers & Nurses, tho' different in many things, be fellows in duty so may we raise the standard, higher & higher, of thoroughness. (& with thoroughness always goes humility) – of steady, patient, silent, cheerful work. So may we all be on the alert – Always on our mettle. Let us be always in the van of wise & noiseless high training & progress.

God bless you all.
Florence Nightingale
May 23/83

1886

From Florence Nightingale to the Probationer–Nurses in the Nightingale Fund School at St. Thomas's Hospital
New Year's Day, 1886.
(*FOR PRIVATE USE ONLY.*)

MY DEAR FRIENDS,

My first New Year's thoughts are for you all—for dear Matron, Home Sister, Ward Sisters, Nurses, all, Day and Night, all, all. My first prayers are: may the highest blessings be poured upon your New Year. A Happy New Year to you all. And if we really give ourselves to our work in a high and humble spirit, remembering whose "business" it is that we are upon, a Happy New Year will be ours. We thank you all, all, for the progress made. But progress is only a step to more progress, or it may well be going backward instead of forward.

What is giving ourselves to our work? It is when duty, intelligence, humanity, religion (or the tie to God), are all embarked with us in our work. How happy are we Nurses that we can always have this, if we please, in OUR work. *Then* we are always on the winning side. These are our helmet and our breast-plate.

I can remember a famous Teacher of Medicine once saying to his students: [What he said may be turned even better to the use of us Nurses.] I cannot tell it you half as well as in his own words. So here they are, as well as I can remember:—

After saying that "our" business must be with the diseased body, he goes on: "This body must be our study and our continual care,—our active, willing, earnest care. Nothing must make us shrink from it. In its weakness and infirmities, in the dishonours of its corruption, we must still value it, still stay by it, to mark its hunger and thirst, its sleeping and waking, its heat and its cold, to hear its complaints, to register its groans.

"And is it possible to feel an interest in all this? Ay, indeed it is, a greater, far greater interest than even painter or sculptor took in the form and beauties of its health."

Then he asks, "Whence comes this interest? At first, perhaps, it seldom comes naturally."

And he goes on to urge the scientific aspect and interest, winding up with, "But does the interest of nursing the sick stop here?" and pressing the "moral motive" of "humanity," the spiritual motive of "religion," till he concludes, "Why, then, indeed happy is he whose mind, whose moral nature, and whose spiritual being are all harmoniously engaged in the daily business of his life; with whom the same act has become his own happiness, a dispensation of mercy to his fellow creatures, and a worship of God."

The man who taught this is dead. But his life lives after him. As he spoke and taught, so he lived and died.

Does it not seem as if this were spoken precisely for us Nurses?

And, first, we can apply his words to Nurses' care of Patients. Our interest in their weakness and infirmities, our observation of their symptoms and pains, of what they eat and how much they eat, feeding the helpless ones, never leaving their food on the locker and taking it away untasted, giving the drink of milk or of water when wanted; marking the quality of their sleep, of their several functions; attending to their warmth, their hot bottles, their fresh air, their cleanliness, carefully washing, when ordered, between blankets; never weary of changing those who want changing; listening to their complaints, and caring for all the thousand-and-one petty details which *are* important, which often are *vital*, and which make up the good Nurse; saying the word in season, scrupulous as to the cleanliness of Ward—its freedom from dust—of utensils, and Ward Offices. For this, the *sanitary* care of Patients makes the difference as to whether "Hospital" does them good or harm.

And never let this interest flag, however hurried and busy we may be.

Our teacher says to his students that this interest seldom perhaps comes naturally. Perhaps not with students. I think it *does* with Nurses. But it must always be reinforced with the feeling of duty, for Patients often are tiresome and we are tired.

Then comes, too, the intelligent interest in the symptoms and varieties of disease, called, rather grandly, the "spirit of science."

And still we ask, Does the interest of nursing the sick stop here?

No, indeed; if we deserve the name of women, a thousand times, No.

"Humanity" is our "moral motive," more even than it is that of men.

As one nursing a tedious case once wrote: "Don't let us Nurses look at Patients as merely 'cases.' Let us look at what we can do for them."

[She had been shocked at twice hearing Nurses say of their Patients, 'she didn't care for the "case."']

Here comes in our "humanity," our devotion to our fellow creatures.

And, first and last, last and first, comes "religion."

What is religion? Some have the religion of ourselves; some of praise—what people will think of us; some of fear—what they will say of us; some of making our way in the world, &c. Whatever is the motive power is the religion. None of these motives are absolutely bad. Our work *ought* to be worthy to command its pay.

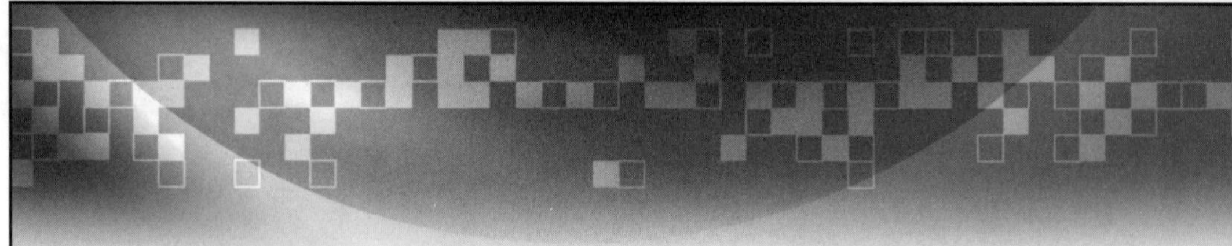

But true religion is *life* in its highest form. True religion is to do all that we are doing to the best of our power. Will God say of *us*, religion was their life? not merely crying Lord, Lord, but inspiring what we do and how we do it, inspiring the *daily business* of our lives.

In *our* work we can be always "worshipping" God, without turning aside a hair's breadth from our daily business.

Like the cabin boy on board the man-of-war the whole night before the battle. When he was kept incessantly on his feet, running, fetching, carrying, he was "alone with" his God for an hour "in the crown of his cap," as he told the mate, who said that during the battle there was not an experienced old tar cooler or readier for everything than he.

That is a very good thought we say, always to be worshipping God in our daily work. Such worship is always acceptable to Him.

But do we live it as well as think it?

Do we each of us, as we think and speak it, do each of us live it? and when we come to die, like the Teacher, shall we die it?

This is my New Year's prayer for you, that such may be your "happiness," such your "mercy," such your "worship." And do you pray for me, for I am grievously wanting, that, in this New Year, I may find "happiness," "mercy," "worship," in my work.

And here I must implore you to remember that God commands us Nurses to keep a sensible but not selfish care of our own bodies. For how can we serve our Patients well, or glorify God in our work, when half-hearted, weary, and dull, as is so often brought on by lack of proper care of the wants of our bodies, fresh air, regularity in going to bed and getting up, taking proper and sufficient food to nourish us, for in a few months you will all be out of this Home. And this caution is needed most by those out of the Home.

And to all who have ever been in this Home I am sure we send a greeting.

You all of you know the precautions against finger poisoning, against breathing "corruption." Try yourselves—you *know* it all—whether you *do* it.

2. A man whom we can scarcely even now mention without tears, a hero who fell at the post of duty, fell with his falling Khartoum, after sustaining a siege of eleven months, unparalleled—in history, a saint whose first anniversary in heaven is on the 26th of this month—General Gordon—said of himself, how he prayed daily that he himself might be "humbled, these poor people blessed and comforted, and God glorified."

And don't think that this sounds dismal. Happiness does not mean self-satisfaction. Always an element of true happiness must be humility, especially in us Nurses. Do you remember how in "Pilgrim's Progress" the "valley of humiliation" is so "soft and green"? The valley of humiliation *is* the valley of happiness. It leads us to the Almighty Father, our strength. Our greatest hero, Gordon, explained that *why* he wished to be "humbled," was that then he felt the "indwelling God" more. How true that is!

Don't you remember how "humility scoops away the barren sand of our self-conceit, that so our foundation may rest solidly upon the Rock."

"Of humility there are many steps. Lay the first solidly, and God will lead thee onward." "The first step is to know seriously, truly, sincerely, thine own nothingness."

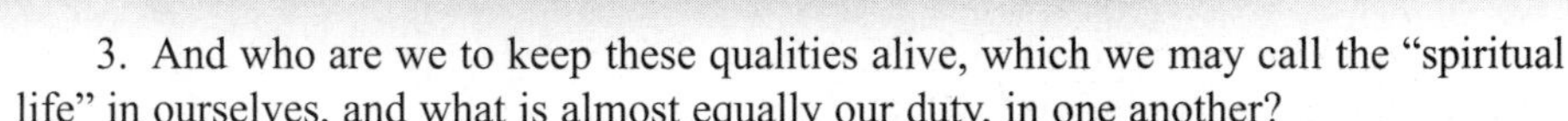

3. And who are we to keep these qualities alive, which we may call the "spiritual life" in ourselves, and what is almost equally our duty, in one another?

By using all opportunities of getting a fresh supply from God, by private prayer, by praying together. As we work for one cause, let us pray together for the welfare of that cause.

On New Year's Day I always think of Christ's parting promise and parting command. The parting command was "to teach all things whatsoever He has commanded" us, each one of us to each other; the parting promise to be with us Himself, with each one of us *always* "to the end of the world."

What a promise!

Let us, then, pray together for the welfare of the cause, striving to fulfil Christ's last command "to teach all things whatsoever He commands"—in the strength of His promise "to be with each of us."

And how are we to "teach," every one of us? How are we to teach the poor Patients, and ourselves, and each other? Not by preaching; by example, by *being* it *ourselves.*

How is every thing spiritual best taught?

We often wonder why it is so much easier to teach what is not good than what is good. Why, but because we teach by *being* it. Nobody *preaches* what is not good. But we teach it, alas! but too successfully by *being* it.

It has often been remarked that an alley in London, a court, an institution, a household, always tends towards the worst instead of towards the best members of it.

But to return, We cannot train others in anything whatsoever without knowing how to do it ourselves.

How much less can we teach goodness, unselfishness, which is the essence of goodness, except by *being* it ourselves!

We may be—we *are*—an example of what is good, or of what is not good, to the Patients every time we pass a bed.

But you will say that Probationers are not so liable to hurt the Patients morally as each other. They impress their "morale" or tone on each other, and so raise or lower that of the School. Still more this is the case when you have left the School, and are in positions of some authority. Staff Nurses, Sisters, please remember that then you can and do help the cause or—do it infinite harm.

I remember when the Commander-in-Chief, the Duke of Cambridge, on inspecting the cadets at Woolwich, was congratulating and thanking them that latterly they had been following the example of the wise cadets, and not of the foolish ones. And the seniors, he said, must set a good example to their juniors. And he ended by saying, "And if they are tempted to be foolish by one mischievous and foolish fellow, they must keep him in his place, and sit upon him." The cadets laughed and cheered. "Yes," he said, "SIT UPON HIM, RATHER THAN LET HIM SIT UPON YOU." That was a far better way of doing it. The fashion had changed, and foolishness, which was a very bad fashion, had gone out, to be, he hoped, no more revived.

And we, too. Shall we, for "wise cadets," put the "wise virgins"? May we say, we have good fashions now, thanks to those who set them; a fashion is always set by somebody—a fashion of obedience, of willingness, or order and discipline, and teachableness. And *we* may be those who set the fashion. As a woman, who founded Institutions some hundred years ago, said "*You* may all be 'founders,' each one 'founds' the fashion of her time."

Our seniors set an example of this, of thoroughness to their juniors, and let the New Year set us a better fashion still.

To sum up: we teach unconsciously that which we are, whether this be good, indifferent, bad. We do not teach what we preach, but what we are.

4. Let the lessons, the training in each item of Ward nursing and Ward work, be ever more and more a very serious business in this New Year. Let the lessons in Class and at Lecture be more and more a very serious business, as serious—as what shall I say?—as any Royal Prince's at Berlin, as serious as our Princess Royal gives them "at a Court which, we are told, is itself a First-class in one vast National School—a Court where no Prince is suffered to be idle"—where the Examinations of Princes are as hard as those of any man being examined for his profession on which he is to live.

Every Prince in Prussia must learn a trade. Let us learn our trade, our practice of Nursing, like Princes.

5. Did you hear of the young naval officer who was appointed by Lord Wolseley to guide the troops in that dark night of Tel-el-Kebir in Egypt, by the light of the stars, to the enemy. He led them to the right spot straight as an arrow; the action began: he was the first to fall, mortally wounded.

The moment the battle was won, back galloped Lord Wolseley to see him once more. What were the dying man's first words? "General," he said, "didn't I lead them straight?"

He lived to be carried on board the Hospital ship where two of our Sisters were Nurses, but not to reach England—not to see again his young wife waiting for him at Portsmouth—not to see his little child born after his death.

But he had "led them straight." May we be able to "go and do likewise!"

If we are to act straightly, and lead others straight, we must be prepared to go wherever, and do whatever our superior officer bids us, and, also, we must stick to our posts.

If we are to act straightly and lead others straight, we must learn each detail of Ward work and of Ward order and cleanliness, with as much thoroughness and conscience we must attend to each rule and regulation, and never evade any, with as much honour and truth, as if we were of an army being led not to defeat but to victory, as indeed we are.

The life and death, the recovery or invaliding of Patients, depend generally not on any great and isolated act, but on the unremitting and thorough performance of every minute's practical duty.

I began my "Notes on Hospitals" with "the first thing in a Hospital is that it should do the Patients no harm." The first thing for a Probationer is that she should do the Patients no harm. She will always be in danger of doing them harm, noticed or unnoticed, if she is not thorough and perfect in every detail of Ward work, of order and cleanliness, and down to the temperature of a hot water bottle (or "up," which you please) or of a poultice. The smallest thing is important to a Patient, to that most delicate instrument, the human body. We are justly horrified at a mistake in giving medicine or stimulant. We are not perhaps so horrified as we should be at mistakes in fresh air, feeding helpless Patients, cleanliness, warmth, order, and all the rest of what we are taught are the Nursing helps to Nature and the Physician and Surgeon.

It is straightness that is so much wanted: straightness of purpose, work, conduct.

I have said nearly these same words before. But let us *do*. Let each of us at the close of every day of this New Year be able humbly to ask of OUR "Great Commander,"—and to lead straight, we must go straight ourselves—did I lead them straight? Did I go straight, and lead straight, in my day's work?

God bless you all.
FLORENCE NIGHTINGALE

1888

To the Probationer Nurses in the "Nightingale Fund" Training School at St Thomas' Hospital, from Florence Nightingale
16th May 1888

London May 16, 1888

My dear friends,

Here, one year more, is my very best love & heart felt 'good speed' to the work.

To each and to all I wish the very highest success in the widest meaning of the word, in the life's work you have chosen. And I am more sorry than for any thing else that my illness, more than usually serious, has let me know personally so little of you, except through our dear Matron & dear Home Sister.

You are going steadily & devotedly on in preparing yourselves for future work.

Accept my heartiest sympathy & thanks.

We hear much of "Associations" now. It is impossible indeed to live in isolation: we are dependent upon others for the supply of all our wants, and others upon us.

Every Hospital is an "Association" in itself. <u>We</u> of this School are an Association in the deepest sense, regulated—at least we strive towards it—on high & generous principles; through organization working at once for our own & our fellow-Nurses' success. For, to make progress possible, we must make this inter-dependence a source of good: not a means of standing still.

All Association is organised "inter-dependence," as a young lady said to me the other day. 'It is impossible to over-estimate the advantages that may result from Association, not only because by it the faculties of individuals are called forth, & their desires & hopes strengthened thro' contact with others, and because the qualities of some supply those that are lacking in others – but on account of the irresistible moral force that can be exerted by numbers united in one common aim', <u>provided</u> – a great 'provided' – that each individual acts up to her highest, to what there is best & deepest in her. There is no magic in the word 'Association', but there is a secret, a mighty call in it, <u>if</u> we will but listen to the 'still small voice' in it, calling upon <u>each</u> of us to do our best.

It calls upon our dear heads. And they answer to calls upon each of us.

We must never forget that the '<u>Individual</u>' makes the Association. What the Association <u>is</u> depends upon each of its members. A Nurses' Association can never be substitute for the individual Nurse. It is she who must, each in her measure, give life to the Association, while the Association helps <u>her</u>.

We have our dear heads. Thank God for them! Let us each one of us be a living member, according to her several ability. It is the individual that signifies – rather than the law or the rule.

Has not every one who has experience of the world been struck by this: you may have the most admirable circumstances & organizations & examinations & certificates—yet, if the individual allows herself to sink to a lower level, it is all but a tinkling 'cymbal' for her. It is how the circumstances are worked that signifies. Circumstances are opportunities.

Rules may become a dead letter. It is the spirit of them that 'giveth life.' So is the individual, inside, that counts – the level she is upon which tells. The rest is only the outward shell or envelope. She must become a 'rule of 'thought' to herself thro' the Ruler.

And on the other hand, it strikes you often, as a great man has said: if the individual finds herself afterwards in less admirable circumstances, but keeps her high level, and rises to a higher & a higher level still – if she makes of her difficulties, her opportunities – steps to ascend – she commands her circumstances; she is capable of the best Nursing work & spirit – capable of the best influence over her Patients. It is, again, what the individual Nurse is and can do during her living training & living work that signifies – not what she is certified for, like a steam-boiler which is certified to stand so much pressure of work.

She may have gone through a first-rate course – plenty of examinations. And we may find nothing inside. It may be the difference between a Nurse nursing, and a Nurse reading a book on Nursing. Unless it bear fruit, it is all gilding & veneering; the reality is not there, growing, growing every year. Every Nurse must grow. No Nurse can stand still, she must go forward, or she will go backward, every year.

And how can a Certificate or public Register show this? Rather, she ought to have a moral 'Clinical' Thermometer in herself. Our stature does not grow every year, after we are 'grown up.' Neither does it grow down. It is otherwise with our moral stature & our Nursing stature. We grow down, if we don't grow up, every year.

At the present time, when there are so many Associations, when periodicals & publicity are so much the fashion, when there is such a dragging of every thing before the public, there is some danger of our forgetting that any true Nursing work must be quiet work – an individual work. Any thing else is contrary to the whole realness of the work. Where am I, the individual, in my inmost soul? What am I, the inner woman, called 'I'? – That is the question.

This 'I' must be quiet yet quick – quick without hurry—gentle without slowness—discreet without self-importance. "In quietness & in confidence must be her strength."

I must be trustworthy, to carry out directions intelligently & perfectly; unseen as well as seen; unto the Lord" as well as unto men; no mere eye service.

[How can this be if she is a mere Association-Nurse, & not an individual Nurse?]

I must have moral influence over my Patients. And I can only have this by being what I appear – especially now that everybody is educated so that Patients become my keen critics & judges. My Patients are watching me. They know what my profession, my calling is: to devote myself to the good of the sick. They are asking themselves: does that Nurse act up to her profession?

This is no supposition. It is a fact. It is a call to us, to each individual Nurse, to act up to her profession.

We hear a good deal now-a-days about Nursing being made a "profession." Rather, it is not the question for me: am I living up to my "profession"?

But I must not crave for the Patient to be always recognizing my services. On the contrary: the best service I can give is that the Patient shall scarcely be aware of any – shall recognize my presence most by recognizing that he has no wants.

[Shakespeare tells me that to be 'nurse like' is to be to the Patient
'So kind, so duteous, diligent
'So tender over his occasions, true,
'So feat.']

I must be thorough – a work, not a word – a Nurse, not a book, not an answer, not a certificate, not a mechanism, – a mere piece of a mechanism or Association.

At the same time, in as far as Associations really give help & pledges for progress – are not mere crutches, stereotypes for standing still – let us bid them 'Godspeed' with our whole hearts.

2. We all know what 'Parasites' are – plants or animals which live upon others & don't work for their own food — & so degenerate. For the work to get food is quite as necessary as the food itself for healthy active life & development.

Now, there is a danger in the air of becoming Parasites in Nursing (& also Midwifery) – of our becoming Nurses (& Midwives) by deputy – a danger now when there is so great an inclination to make School & College education, all sorts of Sciences & Arts, even Nursing & Midwifery, a book-and-examination business – a profession, in the low, not the high sense of the word.

And the danger is that we shall be content to let the book & the theory & words do for us what one of the most religious of men says that we let the going-to-Church & the clergyman do for us, if we have the Parasite tendency – & that even the better the service & the better the sermon & the theory & the teaching, the more danger there is that we may let it do instead of the learning & the practice He says that we may become satisfied to be prayed for instead of praying – to have our work for Christ – done by a paid deputy – to be fed by a deputy who gives us our supply for a week – to substitute for thought what is meant as a stimulus to thought & practice. This is the parasite of the pew, he says, (as the literary parasite thinks he knows every thing because he has a "good library.") He enjoys his weekly, perhaps his daily worship, while character & life, will & practice are not only not making progress but are actually deteriorating.

Do you remember Tennyson's farmer who says of the clergyman
"I 'eerd 'um a bummin' away
ower my 'head,
"An' I thowt a said what a owt
to 'a said an' I coom'd away"

We laugh at that. But is the Parasite much better than that?

Now the Ambulance Classes, the Registration, the Certificates; of Nursing & of Nurses (& of Midwifery), especially any which may demand the minimum of practice – which may substitute for personal progress in active proficiency mere literary or word progress – instead of making it the material for growth in correct knowledge & practice – all such like things may tend this way.

It is not the certificate which makes the Nurse or the Midwife. It may un-make her. The danger is lest she let the certificate be instead of herself, instead of her own never ceasing going-up-higher as a woman and a Nurse.

This is the 'Day' of Examinations – in the turn that Education,—Elementary, the Higher Education, Professional Education,—seems taking. And it is a great step which has substituted this for what used to be called "interest." Only let us never allow it to encroach upon what cannot be tested by Examinations. Only let the 'Day' of Practice, the development of each individual's thought & practice, character & dutifulness,—which are what our classes & our lectures & our examinations & our training are such powerful means for enabling us to work out – & for enabling us to 'take stock' of ourselves—let the practice keep up with the materials given us for growth & for correct knowledge – with the 'Day of Examination' – in the Nurse's life, which is above all a moral & practical life – a life not of show but of faithful action.

3. But above all, dear comrades, let each one of us each individual of us, not only bid 'God speed' in her heart to this, our own School (or Association – call it so if you will) – but strive to 'speed' it with all the best that is in her, even as your 'Association' & its dear heads strive to speed each one of you.

Let each one of us take the abundant & excellent food for the mind which is offered us, in our training, our classes, our lectures, our Examinations & reading – not as 'Parasites,' no – none of you will ever do that – but as bright & vigorous fellow workers: working out the better way every day to the end of life.

Once more my heartiest sympathy, my dearest love to each & to all of you from your ever faithful old comrade.

FLORENCE NIGHTINGALE

1897

To the Nurses and Probationers trained under the "Nightingale Fund."
LONDON, June, 1897.

DEAR NURSES AND PROBATIONERS,

My thanks to you all. God bless you all every one. And what does His blessing mean to us nurses?

Does it not mean that, as nursing has to do with life and death (the greatest gifts of God), with the body which is the "temple" of the Holy Spirit, all our "works" in it must "begin, continue and end" in Him to His "honour above all things"?

If God has given us this calling (nursing to His honour), He has put His honour into our hands. If we let it go down, we are dishonouring Him; we are making it a mere matter of silver and pence.

II. (1) A good nurse must be a good woman. A good woman is one who gives the best of a woman—intellectual, moral, practical to her patients, under the orders of a doctor.

Would you offer less than your best to God?

(2) What should be the characteristics of the good woman? Discipline. The highest discipline is when every woman on the hospital staff works as one, "as members of one body." Loyalty to one's corps and one's chiefs.

Peace and goodwill to all. Love and humility, for without humility there can be no real love or good will, but much ill will.

Kindness.

I must add good habits, and I may almost add joyfulness in one's work. Are not these some of the characteristics of the good woman?

Nursing should not be a sacrifice, but one of the highest delights of life.

(3) Nurse Harvey (the probationer we have lost) was one of these. Her life was in her work. She took as a "handsome present" every new thing that was taught her, and all her cry during her too short illness was, "Won't Matron let me go back to the ward to-morrow?"

Some may think that her last words ought to have been about looking forward to the next world. Surely God would accept her looking forward to His work in this world as the best preparation for death. Is not life the only preparation for death?

But I have another death to tell you of—that of one whom perhaps few of you will remember as I do. She was Night Superintendent at St. Thomas'. She had all the elements of a great teacher, the experience that a night superintendent must have, all the elements of a great leader, like a captain going before his men in war—the war against disease—all the elements of a great mother. She trained the night nurses every night. If anyone did not know what to do, as not seldom was the case, she could tell them and show them with her own hands and out of her own experience. They looked to her. She never failed them. She kept up their tone, kept up their spirits, she mothered them.

She left us to take military service, and for years she was the head of the typhoid wards in one station. The position of a head nurse over orderlies is difficult, because it is not defined. But she was better than a "Regulation." She taught them nursing, cleanliness, hygiene. She taught many of them to live better lives. If they complained that promotion was given not to nursing, but to clerks' work, she would say, "Then practise your figures and your writing, you've plenty of time, and you will be promoted too."

I saw her here only two months before her death on her way out to take her turn on foreign service, and thought she would survive me thirty years. She died almost suddenly, and when the sad news came her orderlies were grief-stricken and wept like little children.

I have yet another to tell you of, who has just now died after a painful illness. She was our first Sister Victoria (Children's Ward)—the one who, if she did but hold up her finger, the little patients stopped crying. That is, perhaps an unusual power, born of unusual love. But cannot we try to imitate her? If you knew what a difference it makes when a kindly nurse has to go down the Ward to the door, if, as she passes, she nods to one child, smiles to another, says a cheerful word to a third (it was a nurse told me this, who did it), you would not pass the children as if they were so many mummies. Children often cry because they feel so desolate. You may say; then we want as many nurses as we have children. Yes, but if there are some dear five or six year old patients, it leavens the whole mass. Such from the cradle to the grave is our influence over one another. Some one said that the strongest influence we know is that exercised by a child of five taking care of a little one of three.

Sister Victoria, as she will ever be to me, sent me a message, as she lay dying, that she had ever been faithful to the nursing work, had always done what she could. And it was true. Never was there a sick person, rich or poor, within her reach that she did not do for, as no one else could. She was not the most unselfish person you ever knew; she had no self.

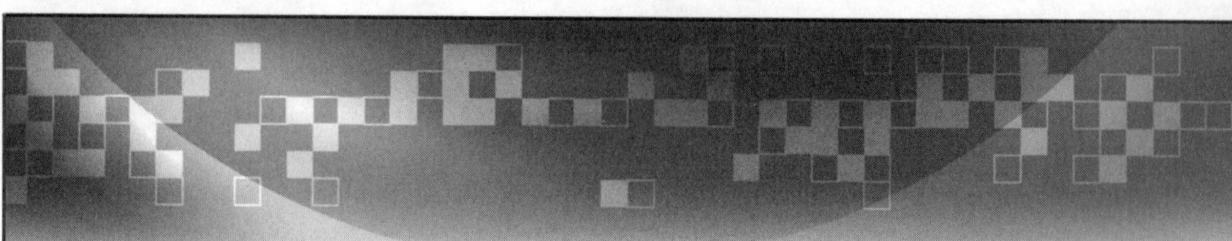

III. The extension of District Nursing has been so great, that of Private Nursing has been so enormous, that some words must be given to each, besides to our particular subject—Hospital and Workhouse Infirmary Nursing.

A thing was said to me the other day, which, though it related only or chiefly to Private Nursing, should give us cause for practical thought—even painful thought. It was this:

"Nursing has been invented, now it has to be reformed."

It is true that we are the fashion, but what does fashion mean? It means decay.

IV. Let me note here in passing. Every year we know more of the great secrets of Nursing. One is the Aseptic. [Now I am doing exactly what we ought to be told not to do—i.e. never use a Latin (or a Latin-Greek) word where you can use an English word.] But we have been eminently taught this Aseptic by our Doctors and Surgeons in their Operating Theatres. We have to carry it out in our Nursing.

Septic means blood poisoning; Antiseptic means using certain substances supposed to counteract blood-poisoning. Aseptic means doing away with everything that can possibly produce blood-poisoning. Aseptic means absolute cleanliness.

A great Doctor, a friend of mine, says, "Call it germs, bacillus or dirt, the treatment is the same—that is, cleanliness."

Never let Doctors have to say of us what they have said of some Nurses:

"She knows as many words as I do: but she does not know how to make a patient comfortable."

V. Hospital Nursing

(1) And first let me whisper a thing which probably you are all of you aware of.

Primary Education has made our patients, especially our new patients, much sharper than they were, in observing us and of course in criticising us. "Is the Sister worthy of her calling?" "Will the Probationer get her uniform?" And (but I hope this is never heard now) "Probationer does not come when I call her to ask for a drink" (or something).

(2) Nursing is in general made up of little things; little things they are called, but they culminate in matters of life or death.

Here is an old Hymn:

Teach me, my God and King,
  In all things Thee to see;
And what I do in any thing,
  To do it as to Thee.
The housemaid (but, say, the nurse—especially the nurse) with this clause
  Makes drudgery divine
Who sweeps a room, as for this cause
  Makes that and the action fine.

(3) Children require the most observing and best nursing because they cannot tell you what they feel, and, what is more, a fretful complaining child is by no means always the most suffering. Still, you must not neglect fretfulness.

Love for *children* is a necessity in a children's ward. There are two aspects in which a children's ward presents itself. One is that there is much dirty work which there is not in adult wards—it is by no means an angel's ward—and much noise, which, however, a skilful, loving nurse can much diminish. If she can stop the elder children from crying, the babies will often stop. But there are some causes for crying which ought to be prevented, and can be prevented, and are not always. They must be either "those dear little souls" or "those tiresome dirty things."

One likes to see in a Victoria Probationer's diary "My three babies"—"changed my seven children." And often one does hear this.

The other aspect is the ready response of children to real feeling. A little boy was heard to say to the children nearest to him: "Bobby"—that was the child in the bed opposite to him— "is dead; sister has carried him into the corridor." She had washed and dressed the little corpse first as if it had been alive—"And do you know, God was waiting in the corridor to carry him to Heaven." How different this, from what he might have heard elsewhere—that Bobby was gone into the black pit. The little witness to Bobby's resurrection died soon after him.

We had a little boy in hospital in an adult ward of men about six years old. He was an incurable spine case. When he came in, he literally could not speak without an oath. The sister did not scold him, but by degrees, after placing his bed between those of two young men she could depend upon, she taught him his little prayers and his little hymns. And he would call out " Sister, I have not said my prayers," and put his arms round her neck and pray. And with the tail of her eye she would see one of the young men crying and putting his head under the bed-clothes. Perhaps he was thinking of the time when he, too, said his prayers at his mother's knee.

This child became the little missionary—the salt of the ward. No one said a word or sang a song he ought not to hear. The dressers were so fond of him they carried him about.

He was never goody, never preached like the children in little good books, he was always a little elf, but a conscience developed itself, and when, after two years, the Hospital could keep him no longer, and he was put with some "Sisters," he would not ask for the sweets given at Christmas. That was a glorious self-sacrifice. After two more years there he died.

A little boy of three, who was crying with pain after an operation, stopped himself from crying with, "God has pain, but He does not cry." (The child's own words.)

(4) There are some advantages, I think, in putting children above infancy, and old enough to feed themselves, in an adult ward. There they cheer the other patients, who are delighted to take some care of them, and are happier themselves, and it is more like home.

In well-nursed workhouse infirmaries, the children sometimes say of the Sisters' words, "it is the first 'good words' we ever heard." And one little girl whom her bad parents were going to take out, was heard praying behind her cot that she might not forget the good "words" she had heard.

Speaking generally, children, and even adults, in hospitals and in workhouse infirmaries remind one of the parable about bringing in from the highways and hedges those who were to share the Lord's hospitality, while we, who have been invited from our childhood, we do not come.

VI. Workhouse (Union) Infirmaries.

It is extremely likely that as the population of London increases (it has almost doubled in my time) and the populations of other great towns increase and almost overflow the hospitals, hospital cases will more and more be sent to these new infirmaries. Happily, we may now look up to many of them, and to the training they give, and the revolution they, in their improved nursing, have effected.

How we ought to thank the pioneers, those who have begun, and those who have thus far carried out this great reform in the nursing. All hail to them!

I do not mean that there is not still a great deal more to be done, both in town and country, especially in the country, where the solitary trained nurse has not even the rank of a school-mistress.

I will not go back to the time when, in the old workhouses, the favourite Sabbath amusement of the sick male wards was to shy their tin plates and cups at each other across the ward, and then send for the police and give each other into custody.

In many an infirmary the policeman might have almost been called the night nurse.

All that disappeared at once with the educated and trained nurse. She became the powerful policeman. She is the salt of the wards.

But let me allude to certain advantages which the modern workhouse infirmary has over the hospitals. There is such a " drive " in the hospitals now. Operation cases are got out as quickly as possible to make room for other operation cases.

There is more time to do good to an infirmary case.

It is true there are many infirm cases for whom at first sight it would seem that little can be done, except to treat them as idiot children. But this is a mistake. A clever kind-hearted nurse addresses an old woman, who perhaps has not spoken for months, and been a most troublesome patient (she has looked in the register for the old woman's occupation).

"Oh, you were an orange-woman, weren't you?—How much did you sell an orange for? A penny. Yes; and I daresay you gave a penniless boy an orange. Bad for trade, but very good for the penniless boy." The old woman looks up delighted. The nurse has got a hold upon her. "Oh, you know all about me," says the old woman, and one murmured, "Perhaps the Queen knows about me."

So much for intelligent loving-kindness.

It is said that the training in a large well-nursed workhouse infirmary is as good for a district nurse as in a hospital, because the cases are more like what she will have to see.

A poor woman, left a widow at twenty-three, with five of her husband's children by a former wife to bring up, opened a little shop, worked like a slave till she was forty, got out all the children as apprentices or in little places, then at forty she collapsed in consumption.

She was put into a workhouse infirmary, which she had much dreaded. She lived a happy four months there, and died there. She said, constantly, "I always prayed that I might have some time for thought before I died. And now I have had it in this beautiful place. Why, it is like heaven."

VII. District Nursing.

This is (or may be) the "Star of Bethlehem," the crown of good nursing, the modern civilizer of the poor, or it may be a very poor thing indeed.

Which it will be depends almost entirely on the character of the woman, for the excellence of the nursing may be the same in two opposite characters.

It is multifarious in its powers and opportunities, for it is not only in the nursing of the patient, but in the nursing of the room, the teaching of the family or neighbour how to help nurse, the teaching of how to keep in health as well as how to carry out the doctor's orders for the cure of disease, and the influence gained is not by preaching, but by what we *are*. Yes, even to influence over drunkenness.

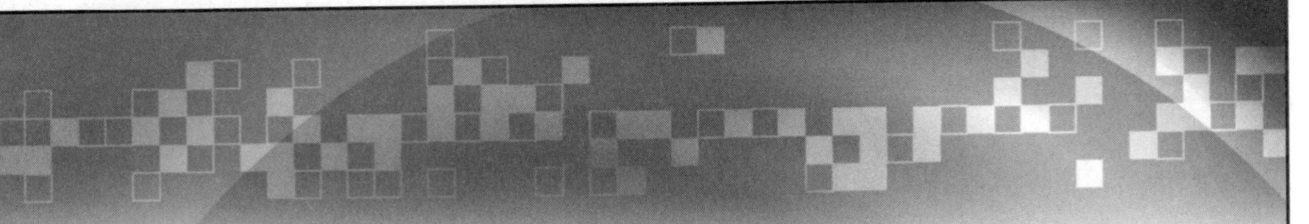

A drunken man or woman will not let himself or herself be seen twice in that state by the nurse, although she has not said a word.

One nurse (the nursing is the same, say) will come in with a cheerful face and sympathetic voice—not put on—the real outcome of her character; the whole family welcomes her as a friend; the patient, who has been longing for her to come, cheers up.

She has been a ray of sunshine in the lives of all.

Another nurse (the nursing is the same) brings no cheerfulness to hope with her; she performs her duty like a machine, and goes out again as she came in, like a machine, not particularly acceptable; for, although she may have conscientiously carried out the doctor's orders, she has left no sunshine behind her. The most experienced of district nurses said: "All depends on the first hour; if the district nurse says, 'I hope to find all cleared up and cleaned up under the bed before I come again,' they want her never to come again." It is quite easy for nurse the first to manage it pleasantly, doing it herself once, *after* she has made friends.

Moreover, nurse the second has not called out the kindness of the poor as the first nurse has.

The kindness of the poor to one another is some- thing beautiful.

A district nurse, in London, was called in to a child two months old, apparently dying of bronchitis, in one of those tenements so common in London, many stories high, with one room on each side the stair, and a family in each room.

In the room, with the two months' old child—of course illegitimate—were the mother, aunt, and grandmother, all drunk. The child was in an indescribable state of filth and vermin.

Seeing how the land lay, the nurse ran up stairs, and in the first room, at which she knocked, the woman gave her a clean little nightgown; in the second another woman gave her a clean bit of blanket to wrap the child in; from the third a woman came with a handful of chips and a handful of coal to light the fire in the child's room, but a fourth came with the handsomest present of all, a kettle full of hot water to wash the baby in; a fifth ran out to buy a ha'porth of milk for it, and would not have the ha'penny back.

When the poor see a nurse who can be trusted, who knows her business, and to whom drink is impossible, there is nothing that they will not do for each other through her.

But beware of the district nurse becoming an almsgiver.

VIII. Private Nurses.

And to these, God's honour is as much, perhaps more, entrusted than to any other branch of Nurses, to be maintained, perhaps, with more difficulty.

For, except those Private Nurses who are attached to the Hospitals where they were trained, or to adequately supervised homes, they have no home, no supervision, no anything to keep up the tone of their high calling.

But they have God.

If they knew how any touch of vulgarity, foolish jesting, loud laughter, gossip about their patients, weakens their own character, destroys the influence not only of themselves but of the body to which they are supposed to belong, whether they do or not, they would pause and ask themselves, "Am I supporting God's honour? Am I even supporting the Nurse's honour?"

Then the Private Patient is so much in the power of the Nurse. Is her kindness, consideration, gentleness, courtesy, refinement, what the Patient has a right to expect? Or is she caring for being waited on more than for waiting on her Patient?

The Private Nurse, like every other, must have proper sleep, time for proper meals, and, if possible, some fresh air every day. But it is for her to take care to provide fresh air for her patient's room, and that both by day and night.

Private Nurses are sometimes spoilt, sometimes put upon. In this respect the Private Nurse is worse off than the Hospital or the District Nurse.

Let her not allow spoiling to spoil her, and let her learn from being put upon not to put upon others.

Private Nurses must even more than all others work under Doctors; otherwise they are quacks; and what are we to say to a nurse who deliberately determines, "Doctor has ordered so and so, but I shan't give it"?

If it is something which she knows or fancies she knows by experience disagrees with the patient, let her respectfully explain to the Doctor. There are very few doctors who will not listen to a nurse who talks gently and cautiously, like a woman who knows what she is about.

A Hospital Doctor constantly desires the Sister to report to him upon this or that. That is because he knows she knows what she is about.

IX. (1) MATERNITY NURSING is one of the great needs, but it is extremely difficult to organise satisfactorily. It must include teaching the mothers

the feeding,
washing,
clothing of infants and children.

Maternity leaflets, though excellent, are of little use. Teaching by practice is of great use.

As to feeding, the extraordinary error is common that milk is not a food, but only a drink, and the equally extraordinary one that the toothless child may have meat and solid food. "It has everything that we have," is the constant answer you receive.

We had a beautiful little boy of seven months old (would that it were the only case), in hospital. It was very ill, but entirely recovered under treatment and a milk diet, and was discharged. The mother fetched it away under special instructions from both Sister and "Resident" about its diet.

In four days she came back, "Child's dead." You may imagine the horror felt. "Yes," she said, "and I gave him a good meal an hour before he died."

"What?" "Steak, bacon, beer."

Who killed that child?

(2) A great change has taken place in my time about milk. People in the country who used to drink their milk at home now send it all to the great towns to sell. It is said that the effect is seen in our national constitutions, and that indigestion in children under two years is seldom or never cured.

An inspector of infant schools is said to have reported that he had examined many hundreds of infant throats, and scarcely found one perfectly healthy.

(3) With regard to cleanliness, mother and child equally suffer from the want of strict cleanliness. The mother is left not properly washed for days after her delivery,

and afterwards, and in their daily life, want of privacy prevents these most hard-worked mothers from washing.

The infant's eyes suffer from not being cleaned at birth and afterwards. It is lamentable how many cases in blind asylums are blind from birth.

(4) Many of the district nurses take a few maternity cases, visiting them twice a day, once before they go to their other cases, and then, if they return to their "home" for dinner, changing their clothes, &c., and taking the maternity case again before their other cases. But this requires the utmost caution.

This, the neglect of mothers and infants after child-birth, is a national matter of importance.

CONCLUSION.

(1) There is no doubt that this is a critical time for nursing.

Will you have women, or will you have words? What nurse best?

There is a curious old legend that the nineteenth century is to be the age for women, and has it not been so? Shall the twentieth century be the age for words? God forbid.

But words we must have, you will say.

Undoubtedly, and the greatest discoverers have generally given a large portion of their time for putting their discoveries into words which are intelligible to the common people like you and me.

Mrs. Somerville was an astronomer famous for this, and I remember when I was quite a girl hearing my mother complimenting her on her "genius." "Genius, my dear," said Mrs. Somerville, "there is no such thing. There is industry and regularity. I write every morning of my life from 7 to 11. I allow nothing to interrupt me. From 11, I see the scientific men who wish to see me."

There appears to be some danger of our being suffocated with words, of our thinking that we can learn nursing in six ambulance classes. This is now so common a superstition—I can't call it anything else—that circulars announcing such classes reach me continually. Nursing takes a whole life to learn. We must make progress in it every year. It takes five years, not of words, but of practice, to make a ward sister.

There seems some danger that the twentieth century will be an age not of facts, but of enthusiasms without facts.

(2) Let us run in another current. The patient is to us a threefold interest; the intellectual interest as a case, which requires the closest observation of facts, to be explained by the lecture and the clinical teaching—the moral interest, as a fellow-creature to whom we must do, while under our care, either moral good or moral harm—the technical interest, whereby we learn what to do for the patient, and how to do it, under the orders of the doctor.

Let us try to fulfil our obligations to our patients in God's strength (not our own) in all these ways.

(3) It has been recorded that the three principles which represent the deepest wants of human nature, both in the East and West, are the principles

of discipline,
of religion,
of contentment,

this last not meaning that we are to be stationary, but just the reverse. It means that our education is to fit us for our business in life—not to be merely ornamental or clerkly—

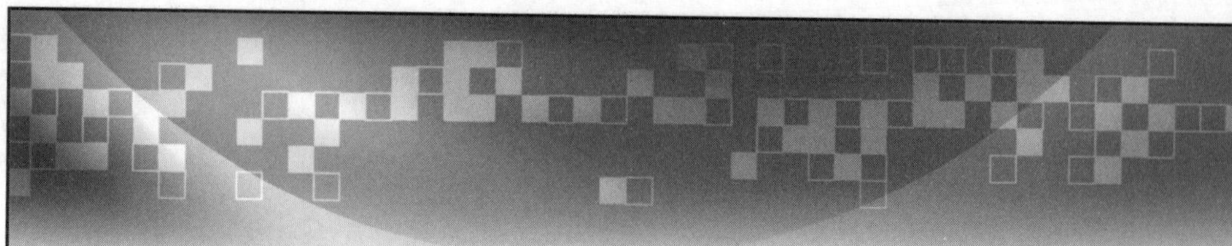

that we are to make progress with the calling we have chosen, and not with registers, uniforms, or the outward forms.

(4) Nursing is not an adventure, as some have now supposed:

"When fools rush in where angels fear to tread."

It is a very serious, delightful thing, *like life*, requiring training, experience, devotion not by fits and starts, patience, a power of accumulating, instead of losing—all these things.

(5) We are still only on the threshold of training. Till every mother knows how to *feed*, clothe, wash her children, especially under two years of age, so as to secure them the best chance of health; till every sick poor person can have a share of a trained district nurse; till every private nurse has some organisation, some principle of life, a higher idea of what a private nurse should be; till there is no longer any danger of *words* taking place of women, we are not far beyond the threshold of training.

I pray that we may know the times and the seasons, and be true to our calling.

God help us all.

F. N.

1900

May 28, 1900

My dear children

You have called me your Mother–chief, it is an honour to me—& a great honour, to call you my children.

Always keep up the honour of this honourable profession. I thank you—may I say our Heavenly Father thanks you for what you do!

"Lift high the royal banner"

"It shall not suffer loss"

the royal banner of Nursing. It should gain through every one of you. It has gained through you immensely.

The old Romans were in some respects I think superior to us. But they had no idea of being good to the sick and weak That came in with Christianity. Christ was the author of our profession. We honour Christ when we are good Nurses. We dishonour Him when we are bad or careless Nurses. We dishonour Him when we do not do our best to relieve suffering—even in the meanest creature.

Kindness to sick man, woman & child came in with Christ. They used to be left on the banks of the great rivers to starve or drown themselves. Lepers were kept apart. The nation did not try to avert or to cure leprosy. There have been lepers in England. Now it is a thing almost if not quite unknown.

There have been great, I may say, discoveries in Nursing: A very remarkable Doctor, a great friend of mine, now dead, introduced new ideas about Consumption, which might then be called the curse of England. His own wife was what is called "consumptive" i.e. she had tubercular disease in her lungs. He said to her: "now you have to choose: either you must spend the next 6 months in your room. Or you must garden every day": [they had a wretched little garden at the end of a street] "you must

dig – get your feet wet every day." She chose the latter – became the hardiest of women & lived to be old.

The change in the treatment of Pneumonia—disease of the lungs—is complete. I myself saw a Doctor take up a child sufferer—which seemed as if it could hardly breathe—carry it to the window, open the window at the top, & hold it up there. The nurse positively yelled with horror. He only said: "When my Patient can breathe but little air, I like that little good." The child recovered & lived to old age.

Nursing is become a profession. Trained Nursing no longer an object but a fact. But, oh, if home Nursing could become an every day fact here in this big city of London, the biggest in the world, in an island the smallest inhabited island in the world. But here in London in feeding – a most important branch of it

– [I]f you ask a mother who has perhaps brought you a sick child to "look at": "What have you given it to eat?" she answers triumphantly, "O, it has the same as we have"(!). Yes, often including the gin. And a city where milk, & good milk, is now easier to get than in the country. For all farmers send their milk to London or the great cities.

A sick child has been sent to Hospital (and recovered). You ask what it had: 'O, they gave it 'nothing – nothing'—It is true they gave it nothing but milk—Milk is 'nothing.' Milk the most nourishing of all things. Sick men have recovered & lived upon milk. "My soul doth magnify the Lord: & my spirit hath rejoiced in God my Saviour."

The 19th Century (there was a tradition) was to be the century of Woman. How true that legendary prophecy has been! Woman was the home drudge. Now she is the teacher. Let her not forfeit it by being arrogant—the "Equal with men." She does not forfeit it by being the help "meet."

Now, will you let me try to thank you, tho' words cannot express my thankfulness, for all your kind thoughts, for your beautiful Books & basket of flowers & kind wishes, all.

God bless you all and me your mother chief as you are good enough to call me,
My dear children
Florence Nightingale

To
All our Nurses

Florence Nightingale's 1893 Essay: Sick-Nursing and Health-Nursing

This section contains the text of Florence Nightingale's last major publication, the 1893 essay "Sick-Nursing and Health-Nursing" (Burdett-Coutts, 1893). Representing as it does the culmination of Nightingale's career, it reflects the broad scope of her nursing practice from the perspective of over 40 years of experience, study, research, and analysis. Encompassing her vision for the future of both nursing and health promotion, the premise of this piece was that these topics were significant to everyone because they encompassed a whole world of human need and suffering.

Nightingale wrote this essay upon invitation as part of a formal Royal British Commission contribution to the 1893 Chicago World's Fair, also called the Columbian Exposition. For the first time, such an event featured women's contributions to humankind with specific exhibits and meetings. Chapter 2 is devoted to the first historical study of this important document.

In addition, the first Pentimento of Chapter 8 (page 168) details how this work was virtually forgotten, largely due to a controversy that arose from one feature of the essay: Nightingale's firm stance against the registration of nurses. At the 1893 Exposition, an international nursing congress was convened for the first time in history. As events unfolded, the issue of nursing registration became the key focus of discussion, and the vital, and ultimately far-seeing, content of the essay, in effect, faded from sight. It is only in the context of both this event and this entire essay that Nightingale's position on this topic can be fully understood.

Sick-Nursing and Health-Nursing

By Florence Nightingale

I. A new art and a new science has been created since and within the last forty years. And with it a new profession—so they say; we say, *calling*. One would think this had been created or discovered for some new want or local want. Not so. The want is nearly as old as the world, nearly as large as the world, as pressing as life or death. It is that of sickness. And the art is that of *nursing the sick*. Please mark—nursing the *sick; not* nursing sickness. We will call the art nursing proper. This is generally practised by women under scientific heads—physicians and surgeons. This is one of the distinctions between nursing proper and medicine, though a very famous and successful physician did say, when asked how he treated pneumonia, "I do not treat pneumonia, I treat the person who has pneumonia." This is the reason why nursing proper can only be taught by the patient's bedside, and in the sick room or ward. Neither can it be taught by lectures or by books, though these are valuable accessories, if used as such; otherwise, what is in the book stays in the book.

II. But since God did not mean mothers to be always accompanied by doctors, there is a want older still and larger still. And a new science has also been created to meet it, *but not* the accompanying art, as far as households are concerned, families, schools, workshops; though it is an art which concerns every family in the world, which can only be taught from the home in the home.

This, is the art of health, which every mother, girl, mistress, teacher, child's nurse, every woman ought practically to learn. But she is supposed to know it all by instinct, like a bird. Call it *health nursing* or *general nursing*—what you please. Upon womankind the national health, as far as the household goes, depends. *She* must recognize the laws of life, the laws of health, as the nurse proper must recognize the laws of sickness, the causes of sickness, the symptoms of the disease, or the symptoms, it may be, not of the disease, but of the nursing, bad or good.

It is the want of the art of health, then, of the cultivation of health, which has only lately been discovered; and great organizations have been made to meet it, and a whole literature created. We have medical officers of health; immense sanitary works. We have not nurses, "missioners" of health-at-home.

How to bring these great medical officers to bear on the families, the homes and households, and habits of the people, rich as well as poor, has not been discovered, although family comes before Acts of Parliament. One would think "family" had no health to look after. And woman, the great mistress of family life, by whom everybody is born, has not been practically instructed at all. Everything has come before health. We are not to look after health, but after sickness. Well, we are to be convinced of *error* before we are convinced of *right*; the discovery of sin comes before the discovery of righteousness, we are told on the highest authority.

Though everybody *must* be born, there is probably no knowledge more neglected than this, nor more important for the great mass of woman, viz., how to feed, wash and clothe the baby, and how to secure the utmost cleanliness for mother and infant. Midwives were informed that many lady doctors consider that they have "nothing to do with the baby," and that they should "lose caste with the men doctors" if they attempted it. One would have thought that the ladies "lost caste" with themselves for *not* doing it, and that it was the very reason why we wished for the "lady doctors," for them to assume these cares which touch the very health of everybody from the beginning. But I have known the most admirable exceptions to this most cruel rule.

I know of no systematic teaching for the ordinary midwife or the ordinary mother, how to keep the baby in health, certainly the most important function to make a healthy nation. The human baby is not an invalid, but it is the most tender form of animal life. This is only one, but a supremely important instance of the want of health-nursing.

III. As the discovery of error comes before that of right, both in order and in fact, we will take first: (*a*) Sickness, nursing the sick; training needful; (*b*) Health, nursing the well at home; practical teaching needful. We will then refer (IV) to some dangers to which nurses are subject; (V) the benefit of combination; and (VI) our hopes for the future.

What is sickness? Sickness or disease is nature's way of getting rid of the effects of conditions which have interfered with health. It is nature's attempt to cure. We have to help her. Diseases are, practically speaking, adjectives, not noun substantives. What is health? Health is not only to be well, but to be able to use well every power we have. What is nursing? Both kinds of nursing are to put us in the best possible conditions for nature to restore or to preserve health—to prevent or to cure disease or injury. Upon nursing proper, under scientific heads, physicians or surgeons must depend partly, perhaps mainly, whether nature succeeds or fails in her attempts to cure by sickness. Nursing proper is therefore to help the patient suffering from disease to live—just as health nursing is to keep or put the constitution of the healthy child or human being in such a state as to have no disease.

What is training? Training is to teach the nurse to help the patient to live. Nursing the sick is an art, and an art requiring an organized, practical and scientific training; for nursing is the skilled servant of medicine, surgery and hygiene. A good nurse of twenty years ago had not to do the twentieth part of what she is required by her physician or surgeon to do now; and so, after the year's training, she must be still training under instruction in her first and even second year's hospital service. The physician prescribes for supplying the vital force, but the nurse supplies it. Training is to teach the nurse how God makes health, and how He makes disease. Training is to teach a nurse to know her business, that is, to observe exactly in such stupendous issues as life and death, health and disease. Training has to make her, not servile, but loyal to medical orders and authorities. True loyalty to orders cannot be without the independent sense or energy of responsibility, which alone secures real trustworthiness. Training is to teach the nurse how to handle the agencies within our control which restore health and life, in strict, intelligent obedience to the physician's or surgeon's power and knowledge; how to keep the health mechanism prescribed to her in gear. Training must show her how the effects on life of nursing may be calculated with nice precision, such care or carelessness, such a sick rate, such a duration of case, such a death-rate.

What is discipline? Discipline is the essence of moral training. The best lady trainer of probationer nurses I know says, "It is education, instruction, training—all that, in fact, goes to the full development of our faculties, moral, physical, and spiritual, not only for this life, but looking on this life as the training ground for the future and higher

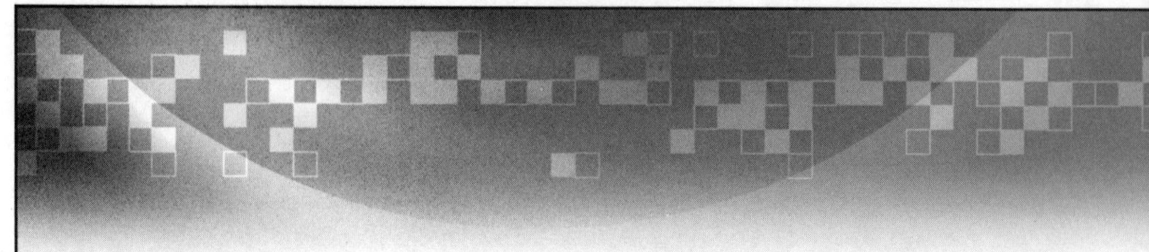

life. Then discipline embraces order, method; and as we gain some knowledge of the laws of nature ('God's laws'), we not only see order, method, a place for everything, each its own work, but we find no waste of material or force or space; we find, too, no hurry, and we learn to have patience with our circumstances and ourselves; and so, as we go on learning, we become more disciplined, more content to work where we are placed, more anxious to fill our appointed work than to see the result thereof. And so God, no doubt, gives us the required patience and steadfastness to continue in our 'blessed drudgery,' which is the discipline He sees best for most of us."

What makes a good training school for nurses? The most favourable conditions for the administration of the hospital are:

First. A good lay administration with a chief executive officer, a civilian (be he called treasurer or permanent chairman of committee), with power delegated to him by the committee, who gives his time. This is the main thing. With a consulting committee, meeting regularly, of business men, taking the opinions of the medical officers. The medical officers on the committee must be only consulting medical officers, not executive. If the latter, they have often to judge in their own case, which is fatal. Doctors are not necessarily administrators (the executive), any more than the executive are necessarily doctors. Vest the charge of financial matters and general supervision, and the whole administration of the hospital or infirmary, in the board or committee acting through the permanent chairman or other officer who is responsible to that board or committee.

Secondly. A strong body of medical officers, visiting and resident, and a medical school.

Thirdly. The government of hospitals, in the point of view of the real responsibility for the conduct and discipline of the nurses, being thrown upon the matron (superintendent of nurses), who is herself a trained nurse, and the real head of all the female staff of the hospital. Vest the whole responsibility for nursing, internal management, for discipline and training of nurses in this one female head of the nursing staff, whatever called. She should be herself responsible directly to the constituted hospital authorities, and all her nurses and servants should, in the performance of their duties, be responsible in matters of conduct and discipline, to her only. No good ever comes of the constituted authorities placing themselves in the office which they have sanctioned her occupying. No good ever comes of any one interfering between the head of the nursing establishment and her nurses. It is fatal to discipline. Without such discipline, the main object of the whole hospital organization, viz. To carry out effectively the orders of the physicians and surgeons with regard to the treatment of the patients, will not be attained.

Having then, as a basis, a well organized hospital, we require as further conditions:

(I) A special organization for the purpose of training, that is, where systematic technical training is given in the wards to the probationers; where it is the business of the ward "sisters" to train them, to keep records of their progress, to take "stock" of them; where the probationers are not set down in the wards to "pick up" as they can.

(2) A good "home" for the probationers in the hospital where they learn more discipline—for technical training is only half the battle, perhaps less than half—where the probationers are steadily "mothered" by a "home" sister (class mistress).

(3) Staff of training school. (*a*) A trained matron over all, who is not only a housekeeper, but distinctly the head and superintendent of the nursing. (*b*) A "home"

sister (assistant superintendent)—making the "home" a real home to the probationers, giving them classes, disciplining their life. (*c*) Ward sisters (head nurses of wards) who have been trained in the school—to a certain degree permanent, that is, not constantly changing. For they are the key to the whole situation, matron influencing through them nurses (day and night), probationers, ward-maids, patients. For, after all, the hospital is for the good of the patients, not for the good of the nurses. And the patients are not there to teach probationers upon. Rather, probationers had better not be there at all, unless they understand that they are there for the patients, and not for themselves.

There should be an *entente cordiale* between matron, assistant matrons, "home" sister, and whatever other female head there is, with frequent informal meetings, exchanging information, or there can be no unity in training.

Nursing proper means, besides giving the medicines and stimulants prescribed, or the surgical appliances, the proper use of fresh air (ventilation), light, warmth, cleanliness, quiet, and the proper choosing and giving of diet, all at the least expense of vital power to the sick. And so health-at-home nursing means exactly the same proper use of the same natural elements, with as much life-giving power as possible to the healthy.

We have awakened, though still far from the mark, to the need of training or teaching for nursing proper. But while a large part of so-called civilization has been advancing in direct opposition to the laws of health, while uncivilized persons, the women, in whose hands rests the health of babies, household health, still persevere in thinking health something that grows of itself (as Topsy said, "God made me so long, and I grow'd the rest myself"), while we don't take the same care of human health as we do of that of our plants, which, we know very well, perish in the rooms, dark and close, to which we too often confine human beings, especially in their sleeping rooms and workshops.

The life duration of babies is the most "delicate test" of health conditions. What is the proportion of the whole population of cities or country which dies before it is five years old? We have tons of printed knowledge on the subject of hygiene and sanitation. The causes of enormous child mortality are perfectly well known; they are chiefly, want of cleanliness, want of fresh air, careless dieting and clothing, want of whitewashing, dirty feather-beds and bedding—in one word, want of household care of health. The remedies are just as well known; but how much of this knowledge has been brought into the homes and households and habits of the people, poor or even rich? Infection, germs, and the like are now held responsible as carriers of disease. "Mystic rites," such as disinfection and antiseptics, take the place of sanitary measures and hygiene.

The true criterion of ventilation, for instance, is to step out of the bedroom or sick-room in the morning into the open air. If on returning to it you feel the least sensation of closeness, the ventilation has not been enough, and that room has been unfit for either sick or well to sleep in. Here is the natural test provided for the evil.

The laws of God—the laws of life—are always conditional, always inexorable. But neither mothers, nor school-mistresses, nor nurses of children are practically taught how to work within those laws, which God has assigned to the relations of our bodies with the world in which He has put them. In other words, we do not study, we do not practise the laws which make these bodies, into which He has put our minds, healthy or unhealthy organs of those minds; we do not practise how to give our children healthy existences.

It would be utterly unfair to lay all the fault upon us women, none upon the buildings, drains, water-supply. There are millions of cottages, more of town dwellings, even of the rich, where it is utterly impossible to have fresh air.

As for the workshops, work-people should remember that health is their only capital, and they should come to an understanding among themselves not only to have the means, but to use the means to secure pure air in their places of work, which is one of the prime agents of health. This would be worth a "Trades Union," almost worth a strike.

And the crowded National or Board School—in it how many children's epidemics have their origin! And the great school dormitories! Scarlet fever and measles would be no more ascribed to "current contagion," or to "something being much about this year," but to its right cause; nor would "plague and pestilence" be said to be "in God's hands," when, so far as we know, He has put them into their own.

The chief "epidemic" that reigns this year is "folly." You must form public opinion. The generality of officials will only do what you make them. *You*, the public, must make them do what you want. But while public opinion, or the voice of the people, is somewhat awake to the building and drainage question, it is not at all awake to teaching mothers and girls practical hygiene. Where, then, is the remedy for this ignorance?

Health in the home can only be learnt from the home and in the home. Some eminent medical officers, referring to ambulance lectures, nursing lectures, and fashionable hygienic lectures of the day, have expressed the opinion that we do no more than play with our subject when we "sprinkle" lectures over the community, as that kind of teaching is not instruction, and can never be education; that as medicine and surgery can, like nursing, only be properly taught and properly learnt in the sick-room and by the patient's side, so sanitation can only be properly taught and properly learned in the home and house. Some attempts have been made practically to realize this, to which subsequent reference will be made.

Wise men tell us that it is expecting too much to suppose that we shall do any real good by giving a course of lectures on selected subjects in medicine, anatomy, physiology, and other such cognate subjects, all "watered down" to suit the public palate, which is really the sort of thing one tries to do in that kind of lectures.

It is surely not enough to say, "The people are much interested in the lecture." The point is, Did they practise the lecture in their own homes afterwards? did they really apply themselves to household health and the means of improving it? Is anything better worth practising for mothers than the health of their families?

The work we are speaking of has nothing to do with nursing disease, but with maintaining health by removing the things which disturb it, which have been summed up in the population in general as "dirt, drink, diet, damp, draughts, drains."

But, in fact, the people do not believe in sanitation as affecting health, as preventing disease. They think it is a "fad" of the doctors and rich people. They believe in catching cold and infection, catching complaints from each other, but not from foul earth, bad air, or impure water. May not some remedy be found for these evils by directing the attention of the public to the training of health-nurses, as has already been done with regard to the training of sick-nurses?

The scheme before referred to for health-at-home nursing has arisen in connection with the newly-constituted administration of counties in England, by which the local authority of the county (County Council) has been invested by Act of Parliament with extended sources of income applicable to the teaching of nursing and sanitary knowledge, in addition to the powers which they already possessed for sanitary inspection and the prevention of infectious diseases. This scheme is framed for rural districts, but the general principles are also applicable to urban populations, though, where great numbers are massed together, a fresh set of difficulties must be met, and different treatment be necessary.

The scheme contemplates the training of ladies, so-called health missioners, so as to qualify them to give instruction to village mothers in: (I) The sanitary condition of the person, clothes and bedding, and house. (II) The management of health of adults, women before and after confinement, infants and children. The teaching by the health missioners would be given by lectures in the villages, followed by personal instruction by way of conversation with the mothers in their own homes, and would be directed to: (I) The condition of the homes themselves in a sanitary point of view; (II) the essential principles of keeping the body in health, with reference to the skin, the circulation, and the digestion; and (III) instruction as to what to do in cases of emergency or accident before the doctor comes, and with reference to the management of infants and children.

In the addendum to this paper will be found a scheme for training health-at-home missioners, a syllabus of lectures given by the medical officer to the health missioners, and a syllabus of health lectures given by the health missioners to village mothers.

IV. Dangers. After only a generation of nursing arise the dangers: (I) Fashion on the one side, and its consequent want of earnestness. (II) Mere money-getting on the other. Woman does not live by wages alone. (III) Making nursing a profession, and not a calling.

What is it to feel a *calling* for anything? Is it not to do our work in it to satisfy the high idea of what is the right, the best, and not because we shall be found out if we don't do it? This is the "enthusiasm" which every one, from a shoemaker to a sculptor, must have in order to follow his "calling" properly. Now, the nurse has to do not with shoes or with marble, but with living human beings.

How, then, to keep up the high tone of a calling, to "make your calling and election sure"? By fostering that bond of sympathy (*esprit de corps*) which community of aims and of action in good work induces. A common nursing home in the hospital for hospital nurses and for probationer nurses; a common home for private nurses during intervals of engagements, whether attached to a hospital, or separate; a home for district nurses (wherever possible), where four or five can live together; all homes under loving, trained, moral, and religious, as well as technical superintendence, such as to keep up the tone of the inmates with constant supply of all material wants and constant sympathy. Man cannot live by bread alone, still less woman. Wages is not the only question, but high home-helps.

The want of these is more especially felt among private nurses. The development in recent years of trained private nursing, *i.e.* of nursing one sick or injured person at a time at home, is astonishing. But not less astonishing the want of knowledge of what training is, and, indeed, of what woman is. The danger is that the private nurse may become an irresponsible nomad. She has no home. There can be no *esprit de corps* if the "corps" is an indistinguishable mass of hundreds, perhaps thousands, of women unknown to her, except, perhaps, by a name in a register. All community of feeling and higher tone absents itself. And too often the only aim left is to force up wages. Absence of the nursing home is almost fatal to keeping up to the mark. Night nurses even in hospitals, and even district nurses (another branch of trained nursing of the sick poor without almsgiving, which has developed recently), and above all, private nurses, deteriorate if they have no *esprit de corps*, no common home under wise and loving supervision for intervals between engagements. What they can get in holidays, in comforts, in money, these good women say themselves, is an increasing danger to many. In private nursing the nurse is sometimes spoilt, sometimes "put upon," sometimes both.

In the last few years, private trained nursing, district trained nursing, have, as has been said, gained immeasurably in importance, and with it how to train, how to govern (in the sense of keeping up to training), must gain also immeasurably in importance, must constitute almost a new starting-point. Nursing may cease to be a calling in any better sense than millinery is. To have a life of freedom, with an interesting employment, for a few years—to do as little as you can and amuse yourself as much as you can, is possibly a danger pressing on.

(4). There is another danger, perhaps the greatest of all. It is also a danger which grows day by day. It is this: as literary education and colleges for women to teach literary work start and multiply and improve, some, even of the very best women, believe that everything can be taught by book and lecture, and tested by examination—that memory is the great step to excellence.

Can you teach horticulture or agriculture by books, *e.g.* describing the different manures, artificial and natural, and their purposes? The being able to know every clod, and adapt the appropriate manure to it, is the real thing. Could you teach painting by giving *e.g.* Fuseli's Lectures? Fuseli himself said, when asked how he mixed his colours, "With brains, sir"—that is, practise guided by brains. But you have another, a quite other sort of a thing to do with nursing; for you have to do with living bodies and living minds, and feelings of both body and mind.

It is said that you give examinations and certificates to plumbers, engineers, etc. But it is impossible to compare nurses with plumbers, or carpenters, or engineers, or even with gardeners. The main, the tremendous difference is that nurses have to do with these living bodies and no less living minds; for the life is not vegetable life, nor mere animal life, but it is human life—with living, that is, conscious forces, not electric or gravitation forces, but human forces. If you examine at all, you must examine all day long, current examination, current supervision, as to what the nurse is doing with this double, this damaged life entrusted to her.

The physician or surgeon gives his orders, generally his conditional orders, perhaps once or twice a day, perhaps not even that. The nurse has to carry them out, with intelligence of conditions, every minute of the twenty-four hours.

The nurse must have method, self-sacrifice, watchful activity, love of the work, devotion to duty (that is, the service of the good) the courage, the coolness of the soldier, the tenderness of the mother, the absence of the prig (that is, never thinking that she has attained perfection or that there is nothing better). She must have a three-fold interest in her work—an intellectual interest in the case, a (much higher) hearty interest in the patient, a technical (practical) interest in the patient's care and cure. She must not look upon patients as made for nurses, but upon nurses as made for patients.

There may also now—I only say *may*—with all this dependence on literary lore in nurse training, be a real danger of being satisfied with diagnosis, or with looking too much at the pathology of the case, without cultivating the resource or intelligence of the thousand and one means of mitigation, even where there is no cure.

And never, never let the nurse forget that she must look for the fault of the nursing as much as for the fault of the disease, in the symptoms of the patient.

(5). Forty or fifty years ago a hospital was looked upon as a box to hold patients in. The first question never was, will the hospital do them no harm? Enormous strides have had to be made to build and arrange hospitals so as to do the patients no sanitary or insanitary harm. Now there is danger of a hospital being looked upon as a box to train nurses in. Enormous strides must be made not to do them harm, to give them something that can really be called an "all-around" training.

Can it be possible that a testimonial or certificate of three years' so-called training or service from a hospital—*any* hospital with a certain number of beds—can be accepted as sufficient to certify a nurse for a place in a public register? As well might we not take a certificate from any garden of a certain number of acres, that plants are certified valuable if they have been three years in the garden.

(6). Another danger—that is, stereotyping, not progressing. "No system can endure that does not march." Are we walking to the future or to the past? Are we progressing or are we stereotyping? We remember that we have scarcely crossed the threshold of uncivilized civilization in nursing; there is still so much to do. Don't let us stereotype mediocrity.

To sum up the dangers:

i. On one side, fashion, and want of earnestness, not making it a life, but a mere interest consequent on this.

ii. On the other side, mere money-getting; yet man does not live by bread alone, still less woman.

iii. Making it a profession, and not a calling. Not making your "calling and election sure"; wanting, especially with private nurses, the community of feeling of a common nursing home,* pressing towards the "mark of your high calling," keeping up the moral tone.

iv. Above all, danger of making it book-learning and lectures—not an apprenticeship, a workshop practise.

v. Thinking that any hospital with a certain number of beds may be a box to train nurses in, regardless of the conditions essential to a sound hospital organization, especially the responsibility of the female head for the conduct and discipline of the nurses.

vi. Imminent danger of stereotyping instead of progressing. "No system can endure that does not march." Objects of registration not capable of being gained by a public register. Who is to guarantee our guarantors? Who is to make the inquiries? You might as well register mothers as nurses. A good nurse must be a good woman.

---

*In the United States it is probable that private nurses are of higher education than in England. On the other hand, they have the doubtful dignity of graduates.

V. The health of the unity is the health of the community. Unless you have the health of the unity there is no community health.

Competition, or each man for himself, and the devil against us all, may be necessary, we are told, but it is the enemy of health. Combination is the antidote—combined interests, recreation, combination to secure the best air, the best food, and all that makes life useful, healthy and happy. There is no such thing as independence. As far as we are successful, our success lies in combination.

The Chicago Exhibition is a great combination from all parts of the world to prove the dependence of man on man.

What a lesson in combination the United States have taught to the whole world, and are teaching!

In all departments of life there is no apprenticeship except in the workshop. No theories, no book-learning can ever dispense with this or be useful for anything, except as a stepping-stone. And rather more, than for anything else, is this true for health. Book-learning is useful only to render the practical health of the health-workshop intelligent, so that every stroke of work done there should be felt to be an illustration of what has been learned elsewhere—a driving home, by an experience not to be forgotten, what has been gained by knowledge too easily forgotten.

Look for the ideal, but put it into the actual. "Not by vague exhortations, but by striving to turn beliefs into energies that would work in all the details" of health. The superstitions of centuries, the bad habits of generations, cannot be cured by lectures, book, or examination.

VI. May our hopes be that, as every year the technical qualifications constituting a skillful and observing nurse meet with more demands on her from the physicians and surgeons, progress may be made year by year, and that not only in technical things, but in the qualifications which constitute a good and trustworthy woman, without which she cannot be a good nurse. Examination papers, examinations, public registration, graduation, from little or no test of these qualifications. The least educated governess, who may not be a good nurse at all, may, and probably will, come off best in examination papers, while the best nurse may come off worst. May we hope that the nurse may understand more and more of the moral and material government of the world by the Supreme Moral Governor—higher, better, holier than her "own acts," that government which enwraps her round, and by which her own acts must be led, with which her own acts must agree in their due proportion, in order that this, the highest hope of all, may be hers; raising her above, *i.e.*, putting beneath her, dangers, fashions, mere money-getting, solitary money-getting, but availing herself of the high helps that may be given her by the sympathy and support of good "homes"; raising her above intrusive personal mortifications, pride in her own proficiency (she may have a just pride in her own doctors and training-school), sham, and clap-trap; raising her to the highest "grade" of all—to be a fellow-worker with the Supreme Good, with God! That she may be a "graduate" in this, how high! That she may be a "graduate" in words, not realities, how low!

We are only on the threshold of nursing.

In the future, which I shall not see, for I am old, may a better way be opened! May the methods by which every infant, every human being, will have the best chance of

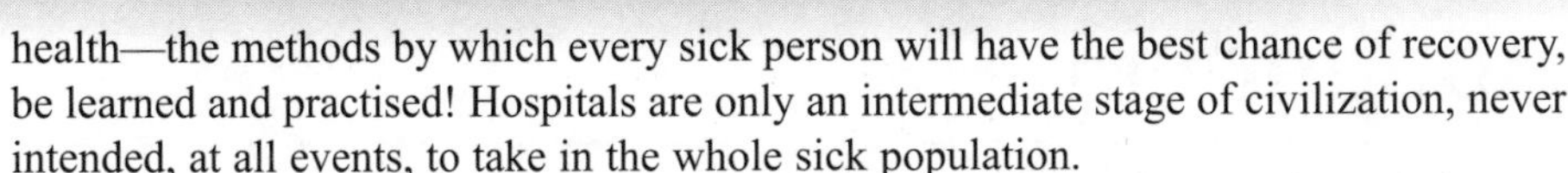

health—the methods by which every sick person will have the best chance of recovery, be learned and practised! Hospitals are only an intermediate stage of civilization, never intended, at all events, to take in the whole sick population.

May we hope that the day will come when every mother will become a health nurse, when every poor sick person will have the opportunity of a share in a district sick-nurse at home! But it will not be out of a register; the nurse will not be a stereotyped one. We find a trace of nursing here, another there; we find nothing like a nation, or race, or class who know how to provide the elementary conditions demanded for the recovery of their sick, whose mothers know how to bring up their infants for health.

May we hope that, when we are all dead and gone, leaders will arise who have been personally experienced in the hard, practical work, the difficulties and the joys of organizing nursing reforms, and who will lead far beyond anything we have done! May we hope that every nurse will be an atom in the hierarchy of the ministers of the Highest! But then she must be in her place in the hierarchy, not alone, not an atom in the indistinguishable mass of the thousands of nurses. High hopes, which will not be deceived!

Addendum.

District Nursing.

It is necessary to say a word about district nursing, with its dangers like private nursing, and its danger of almsgiving.

District nurses nurse the sick poor by visiting them in their own homes, not giving their whole time to one case, not residing in the house. They supply skilled nursing without almsgiving, which is incompatible with the duties of a skilled nurse, and which too often pauperizes the patient or the patient's family. They work under the doctor, who, however, rarely comes more than once a day, if so often. The district nurse must be clinical clerk, and keep notes for him, and dresser as well as nurse. She must, besides, nurse the room—often in towns, the family's only room—that is, put it in good nursing order as to ventilation, cleanliness, cheerfulness for recovery; teach the family, the neighbour, or the eldest child to keep it so; report sanitary defects to the proper authority. If the patient is the wage-earner, and the case is not essentially one for the hospital, she often thus prevents the whole family from being broken up, and saves them from the workhouse. If essentially a case for the hospital, she promotes its going there.

Though the district nurse gives nothing herself, she knows, or ought to know, all the local agencies by whom indispensable wants may be supplied, and who are able to exercise a proper discrimination as to the actual needs.

Having few or no hospital appliances at her disposal, she must be ingenious in improvising them.

She must, in fact, be even more accomplished and responsible than a nurse in a hospital.

She may take, perhaps, eight cases a day, but must never mix up infectious or midwifery nursing with others.

She must always have the supervision of a trained superior. She should, whenever possible, live in a nursing home with other district nurses, under a trained superintendent, not in a lodging by herself, providing for herself, and so wasting her powers and deteriorating. This is, of course, difficult to manage in the country, and especially in a sparsely populated country, *e.g.* like Scotland. Still approximations may be made; *e.g.*, periodical inspection may take the place of continuous supervision. She also should be a health missioner as well as a sick nurse.

Health Nurse Training.

The scheme for health-at-home training and teaching to health missioners may be summarized as follows:

1. A rural medical officer of health selected by the proper local authority for his fitness and experience.
2. Lectures to be given by the rural officer of health to ladies desirous of becoming health missioners, and others. This course, not less than fifteen lectures, to include elementary physiology, that is, an explanation of the organs

of the body, how each affects the health of the body, and how each can be kept in order,—a summary in fact, of the science of hygiene, framed to give the scientific basis on which popular familiar village teaching is to be founded.

3. Further instruction by the lecturer to those who wish to qualify themselves as health missioners, both by oral instruction and papers.
4. Instruction by the medical officer to those who attend the classes, by taking them into the villages to visit the cottages, and showing them what to observe and how to visit.
5. Selection by the medical officer of a certain number of candidates as qualified to be examined for health missioners. These qualifications are—good character, good health, personal fitness for teaching, and tact in making herself acceptable to the village mothers.
6. Examination of the candidates by an independent examiner appointed by the local authority; one who is familiar with the conditions of rural and village life, who then, in conjunction with the medical officer, recommends the candidates who have satisfied them both to the local authority, and the latter appoints as many as are required.
7. The health missioners are appointed to districts consisting each of a number of small villages grouped with a larger one, or the market town. Over these there is a district committee, which is represented on the local authority. Each village has a local committee, represented on the district committee. The local committee makes arrangements for the lectures by the health missioner, and makes the necessary arrangements for receiving her.
8. The health missioner works under the supervision of the medical officer of health, who as often as possible introduces her to the village in the first instance, and he makes it his business to inquire into the practical results of her work.
9. The lectures are delivered in simple, homely language. The lecturer aims at making friends with the women, and by afterwards visiting them at their own homes, endeavours practically to exemplify in their houses the teaching of the lectures.
10. After a health missioner has become settled in a district she will then be able to receive a probationer, who, while attending the medical officer's lectures and classes, will find time to accompany the health missioner in her round of visiting.

Syllabus of Lectures to Health Missioners.

I. Sanitary condition of the (1) Person; (2) Clothes and Bedding; (3) House.

II. Management of Health of (1) Adults; (2) Women before and after Confinements; (3) Infants and Children.

I. Sanitary condition of:

(1) *Person.* Care of the whole body; cleanliness of the skin; hair and hair-brushes; teeth and tooth-brushes; simplest appliances sufficient, with knowledge; large vessels and much water not indispensable for daily cleansing (though in some cases a bath and much scrubbing with soap are absolutely necessary); advantages of friction of the skin; the body the main source of defilement of the air, and the most essential thing to keep clean.

(2) *Clothes and bedding.* Clothes to be warm, light, and loose, no pressure anywhere; danger of wearing dirty clothes next to the skin; re-absorption of poison cast out by the body; danger of wearing the same underclothing night and day; importance of airing clothes and bedding; hanging out non-washing clothes in sunshine; infection stored up in old clothes and bedding; danger of using damp sheets and damp underlinen; bed reform; feather beds should be picked, and the tick washed every year.

(3) *House.* How to choose a healthy dwelling—aspects, situations, not to be in a hole; fogs in valleys; good foundations; value of sunshine and wind; look after water and air and all that poisons them; you must swallow the air in your house; fresh air will do, even with poor food (well cooked), but the best food will not make up for the absence of fresh air. What sanitary authorities to appeal to in the country about drains, water, sewage, privies, etc., plumbing, traps, what shows a trap to be unsafe; best disinfectants—cleanliness, clean hands, fresh air.

Ventilation in bedrooms; poisonous air in close bedrooms at night; bad smells as danger signals; danger of overcrowding sleeping rooms; danger of dust, dirt and damp; how to make the beds; how to clean the floors, walls, bedroom crockery, kitchen pots and pans; foul floors a source of danger; bricks porous; interstices between boards may become filled with decaying matter; dangerous to sluice with much water, wipe with a damp cloth, and rub with a dry one; clean wall papers, not put up over old dirty ones; merits of whitewash; effect of direct sunlight; danger of uninhabited rooms; the genteel parlour, chilling to the bone, kept for company; danger of dirty milk pans and jugs, kitchen tables, chopping blocks, etc.; water, hard and soft—see that it is water, not water plus sewage; that milk is milk—not milk plus water, plus sewage.

II. Management of Health of:

(1) *Adults*. Diet; influence of sex, age, climate, occupation, variety; animal food, vegetable food; milk, butter, cheese eggs, etc.; effects of insufficient food, of unwholesome food, food insufficiently cooked; danger of diseased meat, of decaying fish, meat, fruit, and of unripe fruit and vegetables; spread of disease through milk; chills, constipation, diarrhoea, indigestion, ruptures, rheumatism, gathered fingers, etc.

(2) *Women before and after Confinements*. Diet, fresh air, cheerfulness; danger of blood-poisoning by lying-in on dirty feather beds.

(3) *Infants and Children.* Nursing, weaning, hand-feeding; regular intervals between feeding; flatulence, thrush, convulsions, bronchitis, croup; simple hints to mothers about healthy conditions for children; cleanliness; food; what to give to prevent constipation or diarrhoea; danger of giving children alcohol or narcotics; danger of a heavy head covering to a child while bones of skull still open; deadliness of soothing syrups; how to recognize the symptoms of coming illness in body and mind—fever, hip disease, curvature of the spine, indigestion, sleeplessness, drowsiness, headache, peevishness, etc. *What to do till the Doctor comes.*—If clothes catch fire, or for burns, scalds, bites, cuts, stings, injuries to the head; swallowing fruit-stones, pennies, pins, etc. *After the Doctor has left.*—How to take care of convalescents; how to feed; danger of chills; overwork at school, etc.

Syllabus of Health Lectures given by the Health Missioners to Village Mothers.

I. Our Homes.
  1. The Bedroom.
  2. The Kitchen and Parlour.
  3. The Back Yard and Garden.

II. Ourselves.
  4. The skin, and how to keep the body clean—washing.
  5. The circulation, and how to keep the body warm—clothes.
  6. The digestion, and how to nourish the body—food.

III. Extra Lectures.
  7. What to do till the doctor comes, and after the doctor has left.
  8. Management of Infants and Children.

Lecture I.—The Bedroom.

(*a*). *Introductory.*—Busy life of cottage mothers; why they should come to classes; preventable illnesses; the mothers should ask questions, and help the lecturers by relating their own experiences; proposed plan of the lecturers.

(*b*). *Bedroom.*—What we want to get into a bedroom; what we want to get out of a bedroom; sunshine—its effect on health; fresh air—difference between clean air and foul air; an unaired bedroom is a box of bad air; ventilation near the ceiling; fireplace—no chimney boards.

(*c*). *Furniture of Bedroom.*—The bed and bedding; walls; carpets; airing of room during the day; cleansing of bedroom crockery; danger of unemptied slops; how to get rid of dust—washing of floors; vermin; damp; lumber; fresh air and sunshine in the bedroom by day promote sleep by night.

Lecture II.—The Kitchen and Parlour.

Kitchen.—Danger from refuse of food; grease in all the rough parts of kitchen table and chopping block—crumbs and scraps in interstices of floor—remains of sour milk in saucepans, jugs; all refuse poisons the air, spoils fresh food, and attracts vermin, rats, beetles, etc.; bricks porous; dangerous to sluice with too much water; water for cooking, whence obtained—often water plus sewage; milk easily injured—often milk plus water plus sewage; how to clean kitchen table, crockery, pots and pans; how to keep milk cool; danger of dirty sink.

Parlour.—Danger of uninhabited rooms without sunlight and fresh air; genteel parlour chilling to the bone; clean papers not to be put over dirty ones; tea-leaves for sweeping carpets.

Lecture III.—The Back Yard and Garden.

Back Yard.—Where are slops emptied? slops to be poured slowly down a drain, not hastily thrown down to make a pool around the drain; gratings of drain to be kept clean, and passage free; soil around the house kept pure, that pure air may come in at the window; danger of throwing bedroom slops out of window; no puddles allowed to stand around walls; privy refuse to be got into the soil as soon as possible; danger of cesspools; well and pump; wells are upright drains, so soil around them should be pure; bad smells danger-signals; pigsties, moss-litter to absorb liquid manure cheap and profitable; danger from pools of liquid manure making the whole soil foul.

Lecture IV.—The Skin, and how to keep the Body clean.

The Skin.—Simple account of functions of skin: as a covering to the body; beauty dependent on healthy state of skin; use of the skin as throwing out waste matter; dangers of a choked skin; how and when to wash; care of whole body; teeth—sad suffering by their neglect; hair and hair-brushes; large vessels and much water not indispensable for daily cleansing; advantages of a bath; friction of the skin; not babies only, but men and women require daily washing; the body the source of defilement of the air.

Lecture V.—The Circulation, and how to keep the Body warm.

Clothes.—Simple account of how the heart and lungs act; clothes to be warm and loose, no pressure; test for tight-lacing if measurement round the waist is more with the clothes off than when stays are worn; danger of dirty clothes next the skin—re-absorption of poison; danger of wearing the same clothes day and night; best materials for clothing; why flannel is so valuable; danger of sitting in wet clothes and boots; too little air causes more chills than too much; the body not easily chilled when warm and well clothed.

Lecture VI.—The Digestion, and how to nourish the Body.

Food.—Simple account to how food is digested and turned into blood—worst food (well cooked) and fresh air better than best without fresh air; diet, not medicine, ensures health; uses of animal and of vegetable food; danger of all ill-cooked and half-cooked food; nourishing value of vegetables and whole-meal bread; danger of too little food and too much at the wrong times; dangers of uncooked meat, especially pork, diseased meat, decaying fish, unripe and overripe fruit, and stewed tea; vital importance of cooked fruit for children, stewed apples and pears, damsons, blackberries; value of milk as food; influence of diet upon constipation, diarrhoea, indigestion, convulsions in children; small changes of diet promote appetite and health.

Lecture VII.—What to do till the Doctor comes, and after the Doctor has left.

Small Treatment.—Grave danger of being one's own doctor, of taking quack medicines, or a medicine which has cured some one else in quite a different case; liquid food only to be given till the doctor comes; danger-signals of illness, and how to recognize them, hourly dangers of ruptures if not completely supported by trusses; what to do if clothes catch fire; and for burns, scalds, bites, cuts, stings, injuries to the head and to the eye, swallowing fruit-stones, pins; etc.; simple rules to avoid infection. *After the Doctor has left.* How to take care of convalescents; how to feed; when to keep rooms dark, and when to admit plenty of light; danger of chills.

Lecture VIII.—Management of Infants and Children.

Infants and Children.—Nursing, weaning, hand-feeding, regular intervals between feeding; flatulence, thrush, convulsions, bronchitis, croup; simple hints to mothers about healthy conditions for children; baths; diet; how to prevent constipation and diarrhoea; what to do in sudden attacks of convulsions and croup; deadly danger of giving soothing syrups or alcohol; headache often caused by bad eyesight; symptoms of overwork at school—headache, worry, talking in the sleep danger to babies, and to little children of any violence, jerks, and sudden movements, loud voices, slaps, box on the ear; good effects upon the health of gentleness, firmness, and cheerfulness; no child can be well who is not bright and merry, and brought up in fresh air and sunshine, surrounded by love—the sunshine of the soul.

Pilgrimage to Scutari

Barbara M. Dossey

On a cool evening in early November 1995, I arrived in Istanbul. I was finally going to explore the area where Florence Nightingale had arrived on November 4, 1854, as part of my historical research (B. Dossey, 2000). My thoughts were focused on what it would feel like to walk down the great halls of the Selimiye Barracks, which became know as the Barrack Hospital. Built between 1794 and 1799, the hospital was turned over to the British by the Turkish authorities during the Crimean War, 1854–1856.

Traveling from the airport by cab, we passed primitive roads and small, shacklike wooden houses. Along the roads from the outskirts into Istanbul proper, streetlights shed a yellow glow onto this sprawling, modern, yet otherworldly city.

As we drove along a four-lane highway, we passed signs advertising cell phones and computers, and I thought of how different it was for Florence Nightingale to arrive here over 140 years earlier. In her first note home to her family, after an arduous two-week trip starting in London to Paris and a voyage from Marseille (*Image 1*) on the steamship *Vectis*, she wrote:

> … staggering on deck to look at the plains of Troy, the tomb of Achilles, the mouths of the Scamander, the little harbor of Tenedos, between which and the mainshore our *Vectis,* with steward's cabins and galley torn away, blustering, creaking, shrieking, storming, rushed on her way. It was in a dense mist that the ghosts of the Trojans answered my cordial hail, through which the old Gods, nevertheless, peered down from the hill of Ida upon their old plain. My enthusiasm for the heroes though was undiminished by wind and wave. We ... reached Constantinople* this morn in a thick and heavy rain, through which the Sophia, Sulieman, the Seven Towers, the walls, and the Golden Horn looked like a bad daguerreotype washed out. (Nightingale, 1854, in Goldie, 1987, p. 33.)
> (**Note: The city's name was changed to Istanbul in 1930; its ancient name was Byzantium.*)

Istanbul is unique in that it literally rests on two continents, Europe and Asia, and is cleaved by the Bosphorus Strait (*Image 2*). We arrived at our hotel, situated on the European side; before settling into our room we rushed out onto the tenth-floor balcony to see what the night sky and the Strait might reveal. The hotel was right next to the water, and we could hear the mournful foghorns of passing freighters and see their blinking signals, but we could see little else, save for a faint amber light in the hotel courtyard.

The next morning I awoke and again went out onto the balcony. The bright sunshine sparkling off the azure, white-capped Bosphorus and the busy waterway with huge freighters, barges, fishing boats, and ferries scurrying about and just barely missing one another was a sight to behold. On both sides of the strait were houses and buildings of cement, brick, and wood painted in every color of the rainbow. People were bustling off to work, crossing streets clogged with traffic and on sidewalks lined with palaces and mosques, many dating back two millennia.

It was a bright sunny day in the mid-fifties. From the balcony, I could see about four miles on a diagonal line, across the Bosporus and onto the Asian side of the city, where the sprawling Selimiye Barracks sat. It was huge, as I had thought it would be, and I followed the sunlight off its long white walls and red tile roof until I found the northwest tower, where Nightingale had lived. "There it is! There it is!" I called out to my sleeping (not for long) husband, who knew exactly what I was talking about because it was the last thing I had mumbled before falling off to sleep the night before. As much as I wanted to walk the corridors of the Barracks immediately, we decided to wait a few days and become completely rested after our 24 hours of travel from Santa Fe via Dallas and London to Istanbul.

By noon we were about to set off sightseeing. The weather had changed dramatically. It was now overcast and a light snow was falling. We decided that we would hire a cab to take us to some of the most famous sites in old Istanbul. The oldest part of the city is situated on Seraglio Point, and its most famous landmark is the Hagia Sophia, an 800-year-old structure that for most of its life was the largest covered space in the world. At its apex, its dome is as high as a 15-story building. Next to it is the Blue Mosque, named for its beautiful cobalt-blue tiles; across the square is the splendid Topkapi Palace, built by Sultan Mehmet II after he conquered Constantinople in 1453.

But of course the minute we paid our driver and got out of the cab, all I wanted to do was look at the Selimiye Barracks from this new perspective. I thought of Nightingale and her troop of 38 nurses anchored off Seraglio Point, "waiting for our fate whether with our heterogeneous mass, we should prefer." Looking north, I saw the Golden Horn, which she had written looked "like a bad daguerreotype washed out." Here three waterways converged, the Golden Horn, the Bosphorus, and the Sea of Marmora; they are the busiest, most exciting waterways I've ever seen.

As we made our way toward the Topkapi Palace, we passed modern department stores, sitting right next to small shops made of wood or stone or simply tin sheets braced together —each proprietor sitting cross-legged on carpets by the entrance. Right on the street merchants were selling food, leather goods, and books. Many local Turkish people in western dress headed to 10- and 15-story-high office buildings; many men and women dressed in farm-style dress and traditional turbans and caftans and some women in veils were headed off to the local markets. And, of course, tourists in casual dress tried to take in every sight. But as if all these people were not enough to absorb, my mind's eye settled on the soldiers in uniform 140 years ago and waterways filled with steamships and the sultan's elaborate caiques, the gondola-like rowing boats once used for transport from one shore to the other.

We walked up the long walkway, lined by stately, 50-foot-tall deciduous trees, to the Topkapi Palace, which stands on the highest point of the tip of the peninsula, exactly where the ancient acropolis had been. Dusted with snow, the Moorish-style buildings were breathtakingly beautiful. It is truly a feast for the eyes with its magnificent treasures: elaborate gold- and silver-embroidered satin and velvet robes and dresses worn by the emperors and their entourage; their crown jewels—two uncut emeralds,

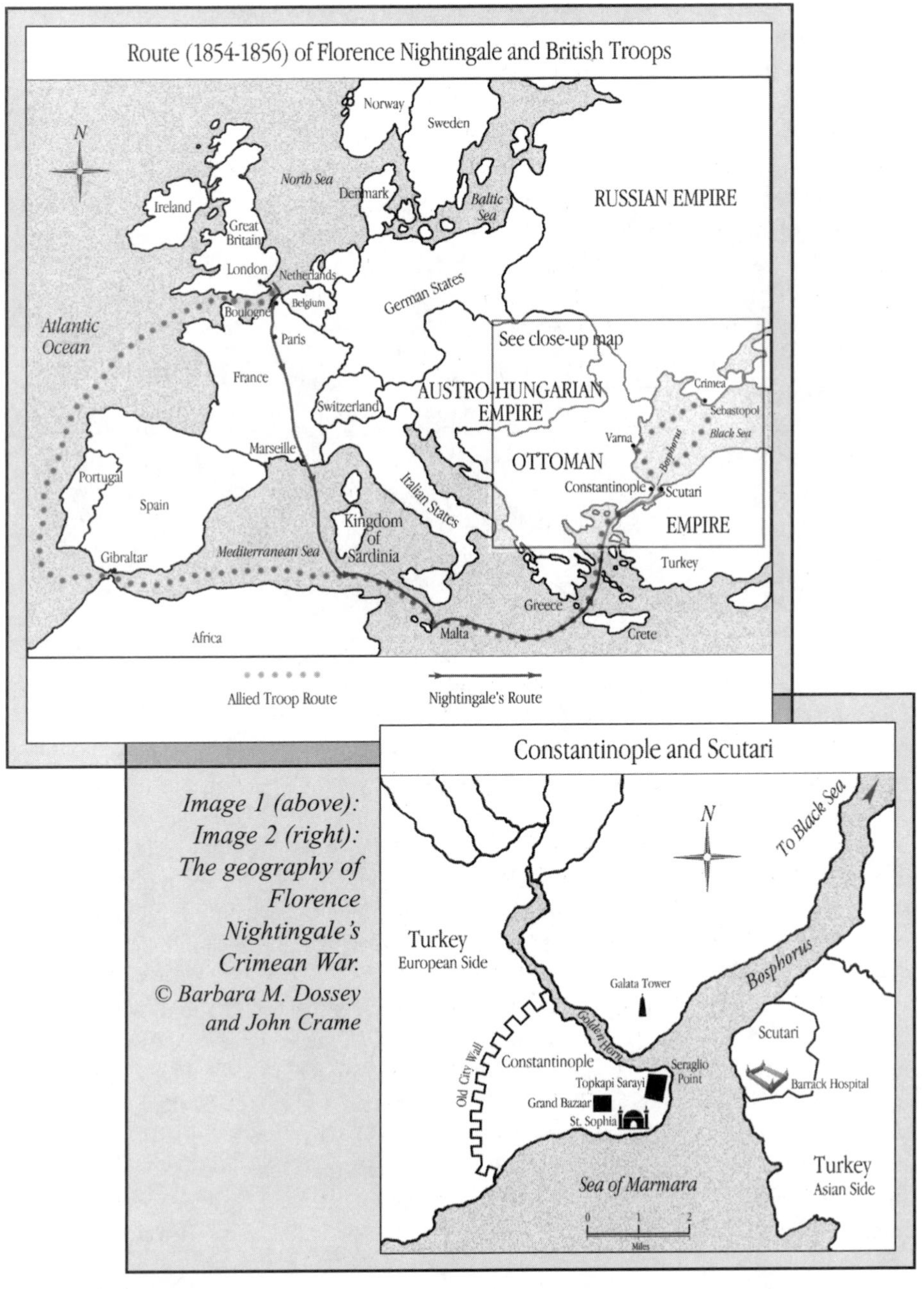

Image 1 (above): Image 2 (right): The geography of Florence Nightingale's Crimean War. © Barbara M. Dossey and John Crame

Image 3: Selimiye Barracks, Üsküdar, Turkey (formerly Scutari, now part of greater Istanbul). Currently the Selimiye Barracks serves as the Turkish First Army Headquarters. © Barbara M. Dossey.

eight pounds each, the dazzling emerald dagger seen in the movie *Topkapi,* the 84-carat Spoonmaker's diamond.

With each room revealing more and more jewels and relics of Ottoman splendor, I nevertheless found myself making beelines to the window, peering out to take in yet another view of the Barrack Hospital across the water (*Image 3, above*), Nightingale's work and legacy filling my mind. I was struck by the contrast of the opulent residence and lifestyle of the sultan during the Crimean War, and just a mile and a quarter across the Bosporus was the Barrack Hospital where Nightingale, a wealthy English lady, had entered the barren, filthy corridors, which she described shortly after her arrival as "Dante's Inferno."

Over the next few days we wandered through the streets of Istanbul, which reflect a myriad of cultures—Turkish, Russian, European, Chinese, Japanese, American, and more. The city is immense, and it is easy to get lost. One of the many delights of traveling with Larry is that he always has his compass and is an excellent map reader, with his frequent "trust me, we need to go this way" when we'd come to yet another maze of nameless streets going off at all angles. The streets gave me a personal feeling for the meaning of "Byzantine." We walked across the Galata Bridge, now lined with men and boys fishing, eventually coming to the ancient Galata Tower, where we

climbed some stairs and then took an elevator to the top. From there we could see a panorama of wooden houses, mosques, and commercial buildings that seemed a motionless fleet moored on these historic waterways.

As we continued to walk the streets, it was easy to imagine the Crimean period Nightingale knew. Istanbul, although a modern city of over nine million people, still vibrates with ancient energies. Alongside modern cars, buses, trucks, and motor scooters are caravans of donkeys, horse-drawn wagons, and farmers herding sheep and carrying chickens. The men carried baskets full of gorgeous red tomatoes, green peppers, yellow and green squash, asma kabah (a vegetable several feet long), nuts, fruits, spices, and herbs—mint, scallions, parsley, dill, curry, coriander, cinnamon, and nutmeg. And the place to buy all these is the Grand Bazaar, located just behind Topkapi Palace.

Guidebooks cannot possibly convey what awaits here, and, amazingly, no sounds from inside the covered structure seep out. The bazaar is an immense stone structure, and the walls are five feet thick. Shoulder to shoulder with hundreds of people, we passed through the entrance, a wide, wooden archway. Despite the throng of people, there was an unexpected politeness about the crowd, and on several occasions a push from a person was quickly followed by a nod of apology. Once inside, it seemed our five senses went into overdrive: spices and herbs sprinkled on meat, sausage, falafel, fish, and bread created aromas that were at once sweet and pungent. Bright colors, fabrics, carpets, cushions, pillows, brocades, silks, and jewelry were everywhere. Rug dealers and their helpers moved in and out of shops quickly, carrying, literally, hundreds of pounds of carpets on their heads and shoulders. It was by far the grandest, most majestic, and most outrageous bazaar we had ever seen.

The bazaar goes on for miles. Rounding each corner there would be another maze of streets, narrow alleys and shops with products stacked, hanging, and piled to the ceiling. In each direction, as far as you can see, hundreds of merchants and vendors hawked their goods shouting and gesturing to us all at once to enter their shops and stalls—Miss, Mrs., Mr., Monsieur, Signore, Caballero, Senorita. Once inside, they'd quickly decide whether you were a good candidate for tea at the back of the shop, where, it just so happened, more expensive carpets and jewels were stored in locked chests. Some merchants sat cross-legged on their gorgeous carpets, while others lured us into their shops with their intriguing black marble eyes and friendly smiles and gestures. We had tea in one shop; thick, fragrant, Turkish coffee in the next. And of course, we knew never to accept the first price offered to us, and, much to our surprise, enjoyed the bargaining for a few rugs and beads we just happened to take home!

It seemed there was nothing that could not be found in this labyrinth of arcades, streets, cubicles, and stalls. I found myself looking for the socks, shirts, flannels, plates, knives, forks, spoons, scrubbing brushes, towels, soap, and lanterns that Nightingale's assistants had been sent to find. All were there! All of my senses were wildly overstimulated, and I felt dizzy and stunned with open-mouthed wonder, laughing and shaking my head at the cacophony of sounds and activities. That evening before falling asleep I read my husband several of the long letters that Nightingale wrote during November and December 1854 at the Barrack Hospital, which were fascinating to him.

Image 4: Painting of the Barrack Hospital at Scutari, Nightingale's headquarters during the Crimean War. The "Sister's" tower is in the rear, near the mosque. ©Florence Nightingale Museum

Image 5: Exterior of Selimiye Barracks, Üsküdar, Turkey.
© Barbara M. Dossey

After a few days of sightseeing and with some afternoon naps, we were now rested and ready to venture to the Selimiye Barracks (as seen in 1854, *Image 4*). The Barracks (*Image 5*) is in the large suburb of Üsküdar, located on the Asian shore. Today, the Barracks serves as the Turkish First Army Headquarters and is a training facility; tall chain-link fences mounted with barbed wire for security surround it. Two of the sides have huge, barren cement parking lots with miles of parking places, with tanks and trucks sitting ready for military maneuvers.

By taxi once again, we crossed a large, modern bridge to Üsküdar on the Asian side. Üsküdar is a smaller-scale Istanbul, with many covered bazaars, mosques, and palaces. I compared our travel in a comfortable, heated taxi to that of Nightingale, who had arrived at the Barrack Hospital on a cold, wet day in an uncomfortable open caique. Weaving our way through the narrow streets crowded with traffic and pedestrians oblivious to the moving cars was a challenge. Several times we had to stop, once to let a farmer with his donkey-drawn wagon pass, and another time to allow a man carrying a caged rooster and a teenage boy coaxing his three goats along to cross. And finally, after a 45-minute ride, we stopped on a high hill near the Barracks, so that we might see the entire, gigantic structure.

Continuing along to the entrance, we saw the ancient mosque that sits adjacent to the northwest tower. Loudspeakers located on the serefiye (the galleries high on the minarets) were calling worshippers to prayer. Before modern times muezzins would climb to the top of the minarets to give vocal call to prayer five times a day. The call's haunting monotone almost demands that you stop and listen as the echoing sounds resonate throughout the city and seem to vibrate into every cell of your body. They echo for miles and can even penetrate a closed, modern hotel room. There is no doubt that Nightingale heard the call to prayer from the Barrack Hospital.

Tears filled my eyes as I thought about Nightingale's own call to be of service in her teens, her conviction of religious tolerance, and the core of her spiritual philosophy: that the universe is the embodiment of a transcendent God, and that all human beings can experience the underlying divinity of themselves and the world by a shift in consciousness. Although she emphasized Christian values and studied the medieval Christian mystics, Christian mysticism, and Eastern spiritual traditions, she argued "you must go to Mahometanism, to Buddhism, to the East, to the Sufis & Fakirs, to Pantheism, for the right growth of mysticism" (Nightingale, 1853, in Calabria & Macrea, 1994, p. xiii). I stood on the curb for a few moments, needing to be still and silent within myself before entering the building because I felt shaky with excitement. My dear husband noticed and simply smiled and waited, knowing how much this visit meant to me.

Entering the Selimiye Barracks we went through a security gate where three military guards inspected my purse and our briefcases. We were asked a few simple questions and had to show our passports and state the reason for our visit. On stepping into the main entrance, I shivered with excitement.

Although the Barrack Hospital tower, where Nightingale lived, is open to the public at different hours, I had called ahead so that I might meet an officer in the Turkish Army Protocol Department that could answer some specific questions I had. A male officer greeted us and introduced himself to us in English, then led us down the main hallway toward the northwest tower. When we reached the end of the main corridor, I looked to my left and saw another of the great hallways. Before entering the large room that joins the northwest tower, I looked back down this immense corridor behind me (in 1854, as shown in *Image 6*) and was speechless, for here was one of the wide, empty corridors where Nightingale had worked (*Image 7*). These corridors are now painted white and have glossy, waxed tile floors with an occasional institutional-type heater cabinet, a few plants, and medals and certificates hanging on the walls.

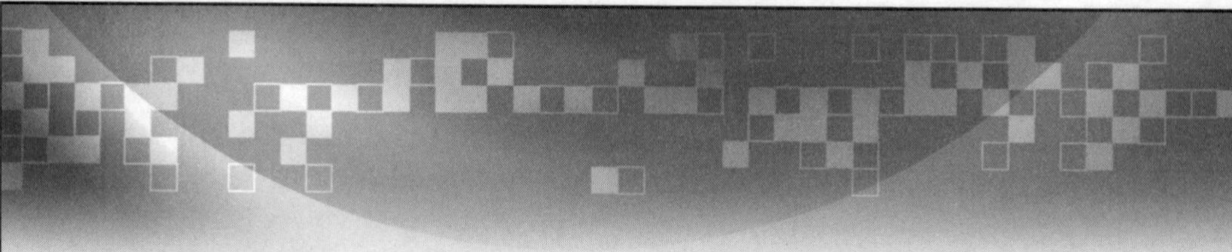

But that's not what I saw. I started walking down this empty corridor instead of heading toward the northwest tower and saw Florence Nightingale as she carried her lantern down this great hall; her shadow was cast on the wall, and was experienced by the wounded soldiers as a healing presence. I started reciting one of the most famous known poems of the American poet Henry Wadsworth Longfellow, "Santa Filomena," that fixed the image of Nightingale and her lamp firmly in the public mind (published in November 1857 in the first issue of the *Atlantic Monthly*):

> … The wounded from the battle-plain
> In dreary hospitals of pain,
> The cheerless corridors,
> The cold and stony floors.
>
> Lo! In that house of misery
> A lady with a lamp I see
> Pass through the glimmering gloom,
> And flit from room to room
>
> And slow, as in a dream of bliss,
> The speechless sufferer turns to kiss
> Her shadow, as it falls
> Upon the darkening walls. …

I saw her as she stopped at bed after bed to tend the sick and wounded soldiers — young men lying prostrate on their beds, suffering from battle wounds, high fevers, dysentery, typhoid, and typhus. I heard the soldiers moaning, crying in pain, and calling for help. I smelled their foul, infected wounds, and the stench of blocked sewage. I saw soldiers salute her when she passed, and I heard her as she talked to the soldiers and cheered them with her calm voice, her warm smile, and her gentle touch saying, "Never be ashamed of your wounds, my friend." I couldn't get enough of this corridor, and I walked a long way down the center of this empty corridor. As I turned around, Larry lovingly smiled at me, knowing that in my mind I was walking where Nightingale had walked.

We next walked from the corridor into an empty room that was part of Nightingale's and the nurses' living space, and I was seeing in my mind Nightingale's own floor-plan sketch from her letters (*Image 8*). At the back was a narrow wooden staircase leading to the first-floor room, at the back of which was a staircase leading up to another small room to the top of the tower. We climbed the staircase and entered Nightingale's sitting room, smaller than I had imagined. Within the small northwest tower was a collection of a few of her letters, pictures, and newspaper clippings hanging on the wall, but the first thing that caught my attention was a Turkish lantern (*Image 9*) like the one she used on her night rounds sitting on a marble-top side table!—It was thrilling—then to slowly walk and take in the other period treasures such as a table and chairs with a Turkish urn (*Image 10*), and writing desk with an old oil lamp and inkwell (*Image 11*). As I looked at the inkwell, I imagined Nightingale writing her voluminous letters, making her notes and lists, meeting with the doctors, nurses, orderlies, and numerous others, and watching her pet turtle, Jimmy, as he crawled along the tiles. (In 1954, one hundred years after the start of the Crimean War, the Turkish Nurses'

Image 6: Hallway of the Barrack Hospital, showing some of the "four miles of beds" that were hastily assembled to make room for the thousands of casualties from the Crimea.
© Florence Nightingale Museum

Image 7: One of the long halls within the Selimiye Barracks tower, where Florence Nightingale and her nurses cared for wounded soldiers during the Crimean War.
© Barbara M. Dossey

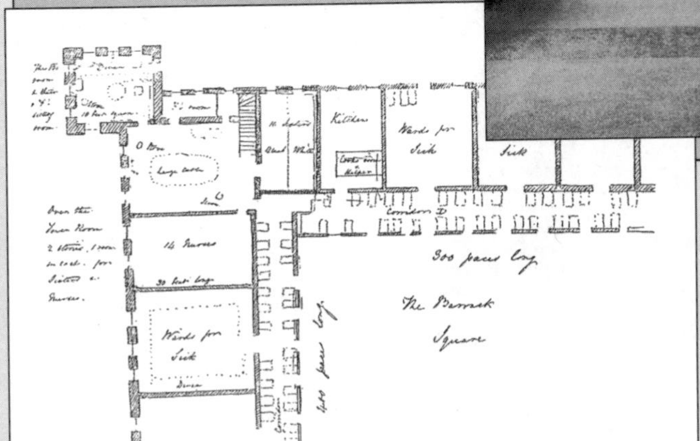

Image 8: Nightingale's hand-drawn floor plan of the nurses' tower at the Barrack Hospital.
© Florence Nightingale Museum

Image 9: A Crimean lantern and furniture displayed in the Florence Nightingale Museum in a tower within the Selimiye Barracks.
© Barbara M. Dossey

Image 10: Table and chairs, and 19th-century Turkish posts displayed in the Florence Nightingale Museum in a tower within the Selimiye Barracks.
© Barbara M. Dossey

Image 11: Desk, chair, and oil lamp displayed in the Florence Nightingale Museum in a tower within the Selimiye Barracks.
© Barbara M. Dossey

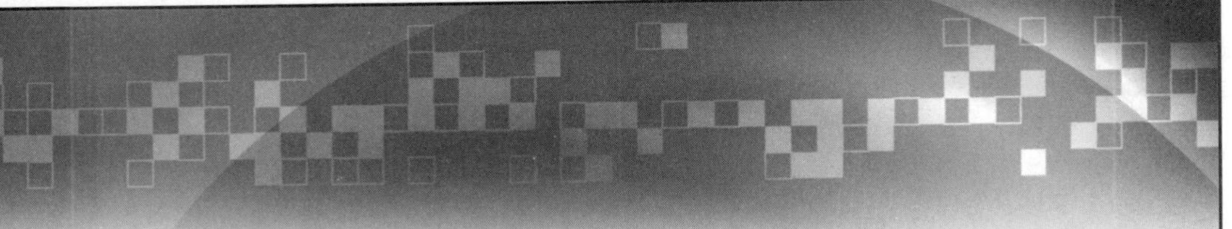

Association, with the cooperation of the Turkish First Army, organized this Florence Nightingale Museum in the northwest tower.)

I opened the window and leaned slightly out to take a photograph of the southwest tower (*Image 12*), a sight Nightingale had often seen. Again I felt overwhelmed with immense gratitude for her visionary, spiritual work, and was thinking of her volumes of letters, memos, and meetings that came from this little tower and that changed the course of medical and nursing history throughout the world. I felt deeply grateful to be involved in my chosen work of nursing.

During my research, I had often imagined what it would have been like to work with Nightingale during the Crimean War. Standing here in the Barrack Hospital, I could almost hear her, giving properly enunciated directions to my imagined colleagues and me. I compared the abysmal working conditions of the Barrack Hospital to my various nursing experiences—to the modern, pristine, critical care units staffed with superbly competent colleagues working with the latest technology, to state-of-the-art universities and hospitals where I have taught the "art and science" of nursing. I thought back to my days with the Texas Air National Guard Air Force Reserve, setting up the field hospital to maintain our readiness in case our unit was sent to Vietnam and to my experience in leading nursing organizations where we continue to evolve the profession of nursing, and create strategies in how we can carry forth Nightingale's message and work. To think that the foundation of modern nursing started here, where I stood, in the midst of previous human agony and primitive conditions!

Leaving the Barrack Hospital, the bright shining sun was out and the blue sky above was welcome after the overcast sky when we had begun our visit. We next took a 10-minute drive, weaving our way once again through the streets of Üsküdar, arriving

Image 12: The view from the Selimiye Barracks tower where Florence Nightingale and her nurses lived during the Crimean War.
© Barbara M. Dossey

at the gates of the Haydarpasa Cemetery where the dead of the Crimean War and two world wars are buried.

Anticipating that there would be thousands of grave markers, I had brought with me a copy of an 1856 lithograph (*Image 13*) of the British military cemetery in Scutari, showing two specific grave markers in the foreground with a Turkish gravedigger kneeling on his prayer rug, the Barrack Hospital in the background, and the Bosphorus on the left. The first was a five-foot-high white marble marker, elaborately carved; the second a four-foot elongated, three-tiered white marble marker with a large ornate cross on it. Entering the cemetery was a bit overwhelming at first. It was very crowded and there were thousands of markers everywhere. There were no people here except us, and as I looked around the beautifully terraced landscape filled with deciduous and evergreen trees, 40 to 60 feet tall, I steadied myself and then knew that we could find the Crimean markers. I was looking, for my mind's eye was back in 1854–1856, to the open fields and Turkish gravediggers burying the dead British soldiers.

We strolled a while, looking for grave markers dating back to the Crimean War years—without success. Then we saw an older Turkish gentleman cleaning a newer area of the grounds some distance away. When he saw us coming toward him he bowed, and we smiled. He spoke no English, so I showed him my lithograph, but he did not recognize anything in it. Today, with the modern, tall buildings in the sprawling city of Üsküdar between the cemetery and the Selimiye Barracks, it was a very hard to gain the perspective during 1854–1856.

I was persistent and wrote the numbers "1856," on the margin of this picture and pointed to the grave markers and the Selimiye Barracks in the background. He scratched his head, and after a few moments he gestured that he understood and motioned for us to follow him. We walked a short distance to a tall hedge and found ourselves on a narrow dirt path. In the distance and in the opposite direction from the Bosporus, I saw a large, solitary granite obelisk standing alone and I knew immediately that it was the obelisk (*Image 14*) that Nightingale had requested to be built; it fit precisely her description and design. We were now closer to identifying the two grave markers in the picture.

Very few graves date from 1854 to 1856, because many of the men and women, the wives and lovers of the soldiers who had accompanied them to war, who died from cholera and fevers, were all buried quickly to decrease the spread of infection. Haunted by the more than 5,000 dead, Nightingale firmly believed that they needed their own monument. She had recorded in letters her walks through the cemetery that was between the Barrack Hospital and the General Hospital, another facility for wounded and sick British soldiers. As we walked a little further through the fallen leaves off the tree-lined path, I felt I was walking where Nightingale had walked many times, and it seemed sacred. I felt the spirit of Nightingale with me as I recalled a letter that she wrote to her family in which she talked about having the spirit of her deceased pet owl, Athena, with her:

Image 13: An 1856 lithograph of the British military cemetery in Scutari, with a Turkish gravedigger kneeling on his prayer rug, and the Barrack Hospital in the background.
©Florence Nightingale Museum

Image 14: Walking up the path to the Scutari Cemetery, now contained within the Haydarpasa Cemetery, Üsküdar, Turkey.
© Barbara M. Dossey

"I saw Athena last night. She came to see me. I was walking home late from the Gen'l Hospt'l round the cliff, my favorite way, & looking, I really believe for the first time, at the view - the sea glassy calm & of the purest sapphire blue - the sky dark deep blue - one solitary bright star rising above Constantinople - our whole fleet standing with sails idly spread to catch the breeze which was none - including a large fleet of Sardinians carrying up Sardinian troops - the domes & minarets of Constantinople sharply standing out against the bright gold of the sunset - the transparent opal of the distant hills, (a color one never sees but in the East) which stretch below Olympus always snowy & on the other side the Sea of Marmora when Athena came along the cliff quite to my feet, rose upon her tiptoes, bowed several times, made her long melancholy cry, & fled away - like the shade of Ajax. I assure you my tears followed her." (Vicinus & Nergaard, 1989, p. 110–111)
(*Note: Ajax, the strongest of the Greek warriors of the Trojan War, killed himself when Achilles' armor was given to Odysseus.*)

Image 15: Crimean British Soldiers Memorial, Haydarpasa Cemetery, Üsküdar, Turkey; erected in 1957 after Florence Nightingale requested permission from Queen Victoria to begin the design and secure the site with the British Secretary of Foreign Affairs and the Turkish Sultan.
© Barbara M. Dossey

Image 16: Florence Nightingale was responsible for the details of the massive granite memorial for the British officers and men who died in the Crimean War.
© Barbara M. Dossey

This walk was one of the few where she could be in solitude and contemplate her work of service for God and the soldiers. And when she heard the muezzins sound the call to prayer and watched the gravediggers stopping to kneel and pray, she undoubtedly said her own prayers.

As we walked toward the monument, I thought about a letter Queen Victoria had written to Sidney Herbert, Secretary at War. The queen had asked if she personally might do anything to assist Nightingale. As I walked up to the monument, I again was struck by how Nightingale could focus on an idea and act on it quickly. After receiving word from Herbert that the queen wished to help her, Nightingale replied within days that she would like an obelisk erected as a memorial to the dead and that it should be placed in a lovely spot overlooking the Sea of Marmora. Not long after, the British government was in correspondence with Sultan Aldulmecid, and the sultan granted approval for the British military cemetery at Scutari on March 5, 1855. Three days later, Nightingale wrote to her sister:

...Please put yourself at once in communication, dear Pop [Parthenope], with the Chaplain-General Gleig, to get us working drawings for our Public Monument & Private Chapel in the British burial ground now to be enclosed on the cliff looking over Sea of Marmora—.... I should like "Wingless Victory" for Chapel—one single solitary column for monument to greet first our ships coming up the Sea of Marmora. It is such a position—high o'er the cliffs... Five thousand & odd brave hearts sleep there—three thousand, alas! dead in Jan. & Feb. alone—here. But what of that? they are not there —But, for once, even I wish to keep their remembrance on earth—for we have been the Thermopylae* of this desperate struggle, when Raglan & cold & famine have been the Persians, our own destroyers —We have endured in brave Grecian silence... We have folded our mantles about our faces & died in silence without complaining... (Vicinus & Nergaard, 1989, p. 112)

(*Note: Thermopylae is in ancient Greece; a mountain pass in Locris, near an inlet of the Aegean Sea; scene of a battle in 480 BCE in which the Persians under Xerxes destroyed a Spartan army under Leonidas.*)

And here I was, standing in front of this obelisk erected in 1857, a year after the Crimean War had ended (*Image 15, Image 16*). The plaque had the name of the Italian designer Baron Marochetti and an epitaph by the great English historian and statesman, 1st Baron Thomas Babington Macaulay of Rothley:

> To the memory of the British soldiers and sailors, who during the years 1854 and 1855 died far from their country in defense of the liberties of Europe, this monument is erected by the gratitude of Queen Victoria and her people 1857.

And below that:

> To Florence Nightingale Whose Work Near This Cemetery A Century Ago Relieved Much Human Suffering And Laid The Foundation For The Nursing Profession, 1854–1954.
>
> This Tablet Cast in the Coronation Year of Her Majesty Queen Elizabeth II, Has Been Raised By The British Community In Turkey in Her Memory.

According to the plaque on the obelisk, shortly after it was erected, families of the deceased soldiers began requesting that individual grave markers be placed nearby. Although I had found the monument to the more than 5,000 soldiers and others, I still wanted to identify the individual markers in the lithograph that I carried. I was thinking about Nightingale's philosophy and how she saw each and every soldier as a human being to be treated individually, and this underlying philosophy is the cornerstone of holistic nursing.

I again pointed to the two distinct monuments for the Turkish gentleman, but he kindly gestured with a shrug of his shoulders and upturned hands that he did not know the location of others. But, wishing to help us, he picked up a fallen tree branch and began to sweep leaves from very small, simple, flat grave markers, many of which had no engraving left from years of harsh weather. There are hundreds of old grave markers, some standing and some flat, in this area that covers several acres. How I wanted to identify the grave markers in the drawing! Since we couldn't see the Selimiye Barracks over the tall buildings of the modern Üsküdar, I walked in a straight line from the monument, about one long city block, as far as I could to the edge of the cemetery and placed myself in the position at the cliff edge where the Turkish workers were praying in my 1854 picture. I peered through the 40-foot-high hedge and looked straight down the steep cliffs from the edge of the cemetery, about one-fourth mile, and saw old houses and buildings. They were clinging to the steep cliffs that drop further down to a train station and neighboring freighter docks situated at the junction of the Bosporus Strait and the Sea of Marmora. Next, I turned in the direction of the Selimiye Barracks. Before long I recognized the grave markers I'd been searching for, and screamed with joy (*Image 17*). The raised carvings are still on the markers, but the words have all disappeared from the years of harsh weather. I also wanted to find some of the smaller flat grave markers that the soldiers' families were responsible for placing here. Very quickly I did find 50 or so that were weathered, and only a few have remaining letters that are visible (*Image 18*):

> Major C.S. Glazebrook, 49th Reg. on Foot, Died at Scutari, The 18th December 1854, of Wounds Received Before Sebastopol, on the 17th Nov. 1854.

Nightingale's wisdom, humanitarianism, and compassion still ring true and are timeless, and can guide us. And we can ask ourselves, will an epoch of awakening to healing, leadership, and global action arrive, as so many people today hope, or will the illiteracy, poverty, religious intolerance, spiritual cynicism, and materialism of our age continue? Will we learn to live in harmony with nature and in unity with one another, as Nightingale encouraged us?

The burning flame of light represents healing. What kind of pattern will nurses and others cast in the dark shadows of health care? What light will we shed? This human quality of light is at the core of the human spirit. Sometimes human suffering is experienced as the "dark night of the soul" as expressed in the great spiritual mystic literature. Yet, with stillness and reflection, clarity often emerges, and we find our inner strengths to weave new patterns in our tapestry of healing. Each person can use her or his own light to return to the ultimate experience of unity and connection with all that is. Each nurse is a touchstone for patients, their family and friends, and colleagues.

As I looked around the huge cemetery and thought about our visit to the nearby Selimiye Barracks, I was filled with a profound sense of peace and joy. I thought about the work of Florence Nightingale—mystic, visionary, and healer—and reflected on her profound life's work that has had and will continue to have implications for generations upon generations. And driving out of the cemetery, I recalled Nightingale's words, which came forth from her last great 1893 paper, "Sick-Nursing and Health-Nursing," and had captured me for a long time:

> In the future which I shall not see, for I am old, may a better way be opened! May the methods by which every infant, every human being will have the best chance at health—the methods by which every sick person will have the best chance at recovery, be learned and practiced. Hospitals are only an intermediate stage of civilization, never intended, at all events, to take in the whole sick population.
>
> May we hope that when we are all dead and gone, leaders will arise who have been personally experienced in the hard, practical work, the difficulties and the joys of organizing nursing reforms, and who will lead far beyond anything we have done! May we hope that every nurse will be an atom in the hierarchy of ministers of the Highest! But then she [or he] must be in the hierarchy, not alone, not an atom in the indistinguishable mass of thousands of nurses. High hopes, which will not be deceived! (Nightingale, 1893, p. 199)

Image 17: Crimean grave markers photographed in 1995.
© Barbara Dossey

Image 18: A grave marker from the Crimean War, Haydarpasa Cemetery, Üsküdar, Turkey.
© Barbara Dossey

(*Note: The author thanks Nancy Ramsey for her excellent suggestions on this essay.*)

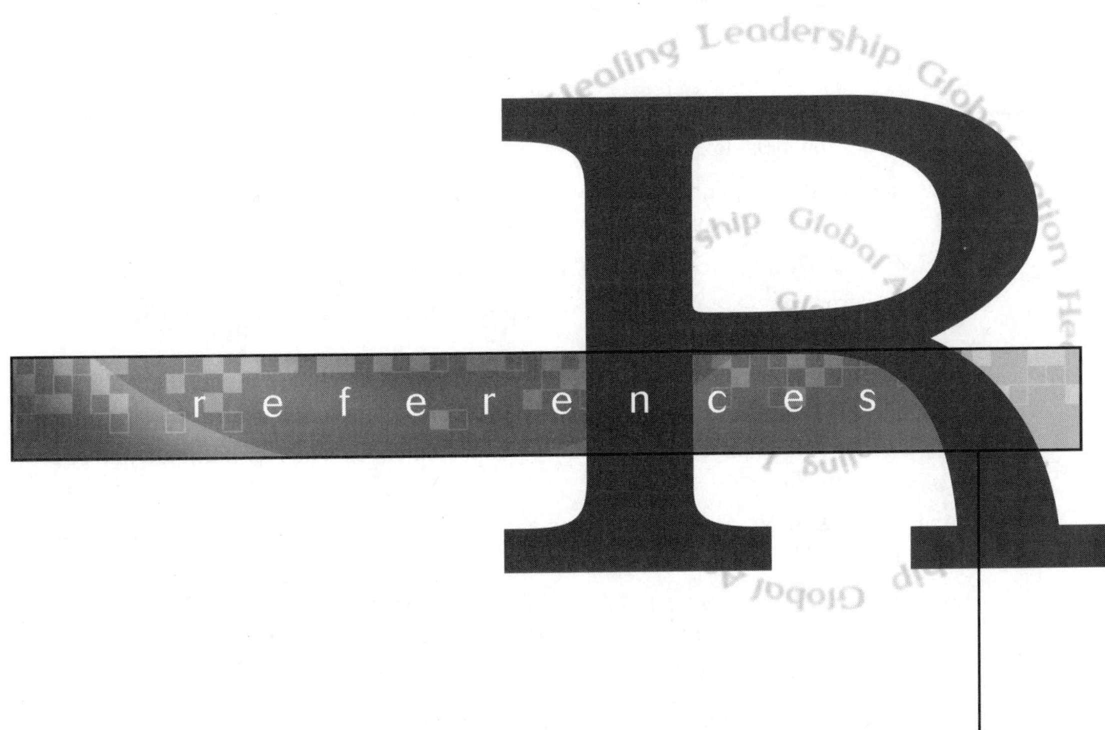

Abel-Smith, B. 1960. *A history of the nursing profession*. London: Heinemann.

Achterberg, J. 1991. *Woman as healer.* Boston: Shambhala Press.

Aiken, L. H., S. P. Clarke, & D. M. Sloane. 2000. Hospital restructuring: Does it adversely affect care and outcomes? *Journal of Nursing Administration* 30(10): 457–465.

Aiken, L. H., S. P. Clarke, D. M. Sloane, J. Sochalski, & J. H. Sibler. 2002. The Aiken Study: Hospital nurse staffing and patient mortality, nurse burnout, and job dissatisfaction. *Journal of the American Medical Association* 266(6): 1987–1993.

Aiken, L., S. P. Clarke, D. M. Sloane, J. Sochalski, & J. Silber. 2002. Hospital nurse staffing and patient mortality, nurse burnout, and job dissatisfaction. *Journal of the American Medical Association* 288(16): 1987–1993.

Ajami, F. 2001. 9/11 and after: The sentry's solitude. *Foreign Affairs* 80(6): 2–16.

Alligood, M., & A. Tomey. 2002. Significance of theory for nursing as a discipline and a profession, in *Nursing theorists and their work.* 5th ed. Edited by A. Tomey & M. Alligood. St. Louis: Mosby.

Altick, R. 1973. *Victorian people and ideas*. New York: W.W. Norton and Co.

American Historical Association. 2003. Statement on Standards of Professional Conduct. [online] http://www.historians.org/pubs/Free/ProfessionalStandards.htm

American Holistic Nurses Association (AHNA). 2002. *AHNA standards of holistic nursing practice*. Flagstaff, AZ: AHNA.

———. 2003a. *AHNA standards of advanced holistic nursing practice for graduate prepared nurses*. Flagstaff, AZ: AHNA.

———. 2003b. *Annual commemorative moment for Florence Nightingale and nursing* [online].http://www.ahna.org/events/fnight.html.

American Nurses Association. 2003. *Nursing's social policy statement* (2nd ed.). Washington, D.C.: nursesbooks.org.

———. 2004. *Nursing: Scope and standards of practice*. Washington, D.C.: nursesbooks.org.

ANAnova. 2002. Nurses most trusted profession—Politicians the least. *ANAnova News Service* [online]. http://www.ananova.com/news/story/sm_520488.html?menu=news.surveys.

Anselmo, J. 2001. Creating a healthy work environment in the midst of organizational change [online]. http://www.nursingvision.org/pages/initi.html#Anchor-Creating-47857.

Ardern, P. 2002. *When matron ruled.* London: Robert Hale.

Ashley, J. 1977. *Hospitals, paternalism and the role of the nurse.* New York: Teachers College Press.

Associated Press. 2003, May 3. Ailment of nurse Nightingale is diagnosed (by Dr. Kathy Wisner, Professor, Department of Psychiatry, University of Pittsburgh Medical Center, at a conference at the University of Maryland School of Medicine, Baltimore, Maryland. *New York Times.*

Astin, J. A., & A. W. Astin. 2002. An integral approach to medicine. *Alternative Therapies* 8(1): 70–75.

Asubel, K. 2004. The Coming of Age of Ecological Medicine. In Asubel, K (ed). *Ecological Medicine: Healing the Earth, Healing Ourselves*. San Francisco: Sierra Club Books.

Attewell, A. 1998a. Florence Nightingale 1820–1910. *Prospects* 28:153–166.

———. 1998b. Florence Nightingale's relevance to nurses. *Journal of Holistic Nursing* 16(2): 281–291.

Baker, C. 1997. *Development of an assessment tool for adult insomnia for advanced practice nurses.* Unpublished Master's Scholarly Project. East Lansing: Michigan State University.

Baly, M. E. 1986. *Florence Nightingale and the nursing legacy: Building the foundations of modern nursing & midwifery.* Beckenham, UK: Croom Helm.

———. 1997. *Florence Nightingale and the nursing legacy: Building the foundations of modern nursing & midwifery.* 2nd ed. London: Whurr. (The 1998 American printing is available from Bainbridge Books.)

———. 1995. *Nursing and social change.* 3rd ed. New York: Routledge.

Bang, B. 1996. The etiology of epizootic abortion. *Journal of Comprehensive Pathology Therapies* 19: 91.

Barker, A. M. 1991. An emerging leadership paradigm: Transformational leadership. *Nursing and Health Care* 12(4): 204–207.

———. 1992. *Transformational nursing leadership: A vision for the future*. New York: National League For Nursing Press.

Barlow, M. 2002. *Profit is not the cure: A citizen's guide to saving Medicare.* Toronto: McClelland & Stewart, Ltd.

Baum, F. 2003. *The new public health.* 2nd ed. New York: Oxford University Press.

Baye, J. In Press. *Nursing in Canada with the integral framework* (in press).

Barnum, B. 2003. *Spirituality in nursing: From traditional to new age*. 2nd ed. New York: Springer.

Beck, D. M. 1996a, June 4. In the context of Habitat II: Revisiting Florence Nightingale at Scutari. Keynote address presented at the International Tribute To Florence Nightingale, United Nations Human Settlements Summit, Scutari, Istanbul.

———. 1996b, June 4. *The flame of Florence Nightingale's legacy.* Keynote address presented at the International Tribute To Florence Nightingale at Scutari, United Nations Human Settlements Summit, Scutari, Istanbul.

———. 1998. The flame of Florence Nightingale's legacy. *Journal of Holistic Nursing* 16(2): 105–106.

———. 2001, August 12. *The flame of Florence Nightingale's legacy.* Prayer recited at the First Inaugural Commemorative Service for Florence Nightingale and Nursing, Washington National Cathedral, Washington, D. C.

———. 2002. *Florence Nightingale's 1893 "Sick-Nursing and Health Nursing:" Weaving a tapestry of positive health determinants for personal, community and global wellness.* Ph.D. Diss. Ann Arbor, MI: UMI Dissertation Services

Beck, D. M, & J. Wright. 1996. *The Art and science of wellness*. Ottawa: The Wellness Foundation, Canada.

Benetar, S. R. 1998. Global disparities in health and human rights: A critical commentary. *American Journal of Public Health* 88(2): 295–300.

Benner, P. 1984. *From novice to expert: Excellence and power in clinical nursing practice*. Menlo Park, CA: Addison-Wesley.

Benner, P., P. Hooper-Kyriakidis, & D. Stannard. 1999. *Clinical wisdom and interventions in critical care: A thinking-in-action approach*. Philadelphia: W.B. Saunders.

Benner, P., & J. Wrubel. 1989. *The primacy of caring: Stress and coping in health and illness*. Menlo Park, CA: Addison-Wesley.

Benson, A., & S. Latter. 1998. Implementing health promotion nursing: The integration of interpersonal skills and health promotion. *Journal of Advanced Nursing* 27:107.

Berry, T. 1999. *The great work: Our way into the future.* New York: Bell Tower.

Birnbach, N. 1986. The development of organized nursing and the Pan-American Exposition at Buffalo in 1901: Doing historical research, in *Nursing research: A qualitative perspective* (pp. 372–390). Edited by P. L. Munhall & C. J. Oiler. Norwalk, CT: Appleton-Century-Crofts.

Britton, B. 2003. Children's peace quilt [online]. http://www.florencenightingale2010.net/PeaceQuilt.html.

Brook, J. J. 1990. Some thoughts and reflections on the life of Florence Nightingale from a twentieth century perspective. Cited in *Florence Nightingale and her era: A collections of new scholarship* (pp. 23–39). Edited by V. L. Bullough, B. Bullough, and M. P. Stanton. New York: Garland.

Brooks, R. 2001, July 8. Nightingale's nursing 'helped kill soldiers.' *The London Times* pp. 1–14.

Bruce, D. 1888. The micrococcus of Malta Fever. *Practitioner* 40: 241.

Brundtland, G. H. 2001. Response from Dr. Gro Harlem Brundtland. *Health Promotion International* 16(1): 5.

Brunton, L. 1911. Preface to *Reproduction of a printed report originally submitted to the Bucks. County Council in the year 1892, containing letters from Miss Florence Nightingale on health visiting in rural districts*. London: PS King.

Buerhaus, P. I., & D. O. Staiger. 1999. Trouble in the nurse-labor market? Recent trends and future outlook. *Health Affairs* 18(1): 214–222.

Buhler-Wilkerson, K. 1983. False dawn: The rise and decline of public health nursing in America, 1900–1930, in *Nursing history: New perspectives, new possibilities* (pp. 89–106). Edited by E. C. Lagemann. New York: Teachers' College Press.

———. 1985. Public health nursing: In sickness or in health? *American Journal of Public Health* 75(10): 1155–1161.

———. 1993. Bringing care to the people: Lillian Wald's legacy to public health nursing. *American Journal of Public Health* 83(12): 1778–1786.

Burdett-Coutts, A. 1893. *Women's mission: A series of congress papers of the philanthropic work of women by eminent writers.* London, UK: Sampson, Low, Marston and Co., Ltd. (American edition also available from New York: Charles Scribner's Sons.)

Buresh, B., & S. Gordon. 2000. *From silence to voice: What nurses know and must communicate to the public.* Ottawa: Canadian Nurses Association.

Burkhardt, M. A. 1998. Awakening spirit and purpose. *Journal of Holistic Nursing* 16(2): 165–167.

Burns, J. 1978. *Leadership.* New York: Harper & Row.

Calabria, M. D. 1997. *Florence Nightingale in Egypt and Greece: Her diary and "visions."* Albany: State University of New York Press.

Calabria, M. D., & J. A. Macrae, eds. 1994. *Suggestions for thought by Florence Nightingale: Selections and commentaries*. Philadelphia: University of Pennsylvania Press.

Carper, B. A. 1978. Fundamental patterns of knowing in nursing. *Advances in Nursing Science* 1:11–19.

Carrell, J. 2003. *The speckled monster: A historical tale of battling smallpox.* New York: Dutton.

Carty, R. M. 2002. The changing face of nursing. *Journal of Professional Nursing* 18(3): 117.

Centers for Disease Control and Prevention (CDC). 2003. Preparing for the return of SARS: Are we ready? [online]. http://www.phppo.cdc.gov/PHTN/webcast/sars-return/.

Charter, D. 2001, April 11. Clean-up campaign names worst wards. *London Times* pp. 10–11.

Chinn, P. L. 2002. Living in a post-September 11 world. *Advances in Nursing Science* 24(3): v.

Chinn, P., & J. Watson, J. 1994. *Art and aesthetics in nursing*. New York: National League for Nursing Press.

Chinn, P., & M. K. Kramer. 1999. *Theory and nursing: Integrated knowledge development.* 5th ed. St. Louis, MO: Mosby.

Cohen, I. B. 1984. Florence Nightingale. *Scientific American* 250(3): 128–137.

Cohen, J. J. 2003. Women in medicine: Much progress, much work to do. *Association of American of Colleges Reporter* [online]. http://www.aamc.org/newsroom/reporter/dec01/word.htm.

Cook, E. T. 1913. *The life of Florence Nightingale.* 2 vols. London: Macmillan.

Cope, Z. 1958. *Florence Nightingale and the doctors.* London: Museum Press.

Crosby, B. C. 1999. *Leadership for global citizenship: Building transnational community.* Thousand Oaks, CA: Sage.

Davies, C. 1983. Professionalising strategies as time and culture-bound: American and British nursing, circa 1893, in *Nursing history: New perspectives, new possibilities* (pp. 47–63). Edited by E. C. Lagemann. New York: Teacher's College Press.

———. 1992. Gender, history and management style in nursing: Towards a theoretical synthesis. In *Gender and bureaucracy,* edited by A. Witz & M Savage. (Sociological Review Monograph.) Oxford: Blackwell.

de Kadt, E. 1982. Ideology, social policy, health, and health services: A field of complex interactions. *Social Science and Medicine* 16:741–752.

Dennis, K. E., & P. A. Prescott. 1985. Florence Nightingale: Yesterday, today and tomorrow. *Advances in Nursing Science* January: 66–81.

Denzin, L. M. 1989. *Interpretive biography*. Newbury Park, CA: Sage.

Dickinson-Hazard, N. 2002. Looking for that 10-second sound bite. *Reflections on Nursing Leadership: Honor Society of Sigma Theta Tau International*. 3rd quarter, pp. 10–16.

Disch, J. 2002. The nursing shortage is a symptom. *Journal of Professional Nursing* 18(2): 62.

Dock, L. 1912. *A history of nursing*. Vol. III. New York: Putnam.

Dolan, J. A. 1968. *History of nursing*. Philadelphia: W. B. Saunders.

Dossey, B. M., ed. 1997. *American Holistic Nurses Association core curriculum for holistic nursing*. Gaithersburg, MD: Aspen.

———., ed. 1998a. Florence Nightingale and her legacy for holistic nursing [special issue]. *Journal of Holistic Nursing* 16(2): 101–294.

———. 1998b. Florence Nightingale: Her personality type. *Journal of Holistic Nursing* 16(2): 202–222.

———. 1998c. Florence Nightingale: A nineteenth-century mystic. *Journal of Holistic Nursing* 16(2): 111–164.

———. 1998d. Florence Nightingale's Crimean fever and chronic illness. *Journal of Holistic Nursing* 16(2): 168–196.

———. 2000a. *Florence Nightingale: Mystic, visionary, healer.* Philadelphis, PA: Lippincott, Williams, & Wilkins.

———. 2000b, November 8. *Florence Nightingale.* Keynote address presented at the "Courage to Care" Remembrance Week Celebrations, Canadian National Press Club, Ottawa.

———. 2001, August 12. Florence Nightingale, mystic, visionary, healer. Keynote address presented at the National Cathedral, Washington D. C. [online]. http://www.dosseydossey.com/barbara/florenceLecture.asp.

———. 2002. *Letters from a Mystic: Florence Nightingale's legacy for postmodern nursing.* Ph.D. Diss. Cincinnati, OH: The Union Institute.

———. In press. *Integral nursing: A Theory for practice, education, and research.*

Dossey, B.M., L. Keegan, & C. E. Guzzetta. 2005a. *Holistic nursing: A handbook for practice.* 4th ed. Sudbury, MA: Jones and Bartlett.

———. 2005b. Holistic nursing practice, in Dossey, Keegan, & Guzzetta, 2005a.

———. 2005c. *Holistic nursing* (30 interactive web modules). Based on Dossey, Keegan, & Guzzetta 2005a.

Dossey, L. 1993. *Healing words: The power of prayer and the practice of medicine*. San Francisco: HarperSanFrancisco.

———. 1999. *Reinventing medicine: Beyond mind–body to a new era of healing*. San Francisco: HarperSanFrancisco.

———. 2003. Samueli Conference On Definitions and Standards in Healing Research. Working definitions and terms, in Definitions and standards of healing research, edited by W. B. Jonas & R. A. Chez. Supplement to *Alternative Therapies in Health and Medicine* 9(3): A11.

———. 2004. Think globally, act non-locally: Consciousness beyond space and time. In Asubel, K (ed). *Ecological medicine: Healing the earth, healing ourselves*. San Francisco: Sierra Club Books.

———. 2005. *The Extraordinary healing power of ordinary things*. New York: Bell Tower/Random House.

Duhl, L. J. 1996, June 4. Florence Nightingale and the Healthy Cities movement. Keynote address presented at the International Tribute to Florence Nightingale, United Nations Human Settlements Summit, Scutari, Istanbul.

———. 2000. A short history and some acknowledgments. *Public Health Reports* 115:116–117.

Eddy, M. B. G. 1881. *Science and health with key to the Scriptures.* 3rd ed. Vol. 1. Boston: E. J. Foster Eddy. (For online access to the latest edition, see also http://www.marybakereddylibrary.org.)

———. 1895. *Science and health with key to the Scriptures.*

Elkind, D. 1998. *Ties that stress: The new family imbalance.* Cambridge, MA: Harvard University Press.

Erickson, G. P. 1996. To pauperize or empower: Public health nursing at the turn of the 20th and 21st centuries. *Public Health Nursing* 13(3): 163–169.

Evans, A. C. 1934. Chronic brucellosis. *Journal of the American Medical Association* 103: 665–667.

Fagin, C. M. 2001. *When care becomes a burden.* New York: Milbank Memorial Fund.

Fawcett, J. 1984: The metaparadigm of nursing: Present status and future refinements. Image: The Journal of Nursing Scholarship (16):84–87.

Fawcett, J., J. Watson, B. Neuman, & P. H. Walker. 2001. On nursing theories and evidence. *Journal of Nursing Scholarship* 36(2): 115–119.

Fenn, E. 2001. *Pox Americana: The great smallpox epidemic of 1775–82.* New York: Hill and Wang.

Fenton, M.V. & Morris, D.L. 2003. The integration of holistic nursing practices and complementary and alternative modalities into curricula of schools of nursing. *Alternative Therapies in Health and Medicine* 9(4): 62–67.

Ference, H. 1998. Lead at Lea. *Notes on nursing science* 1:118.

Fitzpatrick, M. L. 1986. A historical study of nursing organization: Doing historical research. In *Nursing research: A qualitative perspective* (pp. 195–225). Edited by P. L. Munhall & C. J. Oiler. Norwalk, CT: Appleton-Century-Crofts.

Flinders, C. L. 1993. *Enduring grace.* San Francisco: Harper San Francisco.

Flinn, J. L. 1893. *The best things to see at the World's Fair.* Chicago: Columbian Guide Co.

Florence Nightingale Foundation. 2003. The Florence Nightingale Commemoration Service [online]. http://www.florence-nightingale-foundation.org.uk.

Florence Nightingale International Foundation. 1934. Pamphlet. London: Smith and Ebbs.

Flynn, B. C. 1997. Partnerships in healthy cities and communities: A social commitment for advanced practice nurses. *Advanced Practice Nursing Quarterly* 2(4): 1–6.

Freshwater, D. 2000. Crosscurrents: Against cultural narration in nursing. *Journal of Advanced Nursing* 32(2): 481–484.

———. 2004. Tools for developing clinical leadership. *Leadership* 30(2): 20–22.

Frisch, N. C. 2005. Nursing theories, in Dossey, Keegan, & Guzzetta 2005a.

Frisch, N. C., B. M. Dossey, C. E. Guzzetta, & J. A. Quinn. 2000. *American Holistic Nurses Association standards of holistic nursing practice*. Gaithersburg, MD: Aspen.

Gandhi, M. K. 1994. No. 80, Florence Nightingale, in *The collected works of Mahatma Gandhi*, Vol. 5, 1905–1906 (pp. 61–62). New Delhi: Publications Division, Ministry of Information & Broadcasting, Government of India. (Errata: Printed as September 9, 1905, in vol. 5, but actually published September 9, 1915.)

Garrett, L. 1994. *The coming plague: Newly emerging diseases in a world out of balance.* New York: Farrar, Straus and Giroux.

Gaydos, H. L. 1999. *Illuminated lives: Co-created portraits of contemporary women healers*. PhD Diss. Cincinnati: The Union Institute University.

———. 2005. The art of nursing and the human health experience, in Dossey, Keegan, & Guzzetta 2005.

Gazella, K. 2003. The Martin Luther King Symposium: Be the change you wish to see in the world. *The University of Michigan Record Online*. http://www.umich.edu/~urecord/0203/Jan13_03/40.shtml.

Gelinas, A. 1949. Preface. In *Nursing of the sick: 1893*. Edited by I. Hampton Robb. New York: McGraw-Hill.

Gibbon, J. M., & M. S. Matthewson. 1947. *Three centuries of Canadian nursing*. Toronto: MacMillan.

Gillies, P. 1998. Effectiveness of alliances and partnerships for health promotion. *HealthPromotion International* 13(2): 99–120.

Goldie, S. M. 1987. ed. *"I have done my duty": Florence Nightingale in the Crimean War, 1854–58*. Iowa City: University of Iowa Press. (Reissued in 1997 as *Florence Nightingale: Letters from the Crimea, 1854–1856*. Manchester, UK: Mandolin.)

Griffon, D. P. 1995. Crowning the edifice: Ethel Fenwick and state registration. In J. E. Lynaugh, ed., special issue, *Nursing History Review* 3:201–212.

Hawkins, D. R. 2002. *Power vs. force: The hidden determinants of human behavior*. Carlsbad, CA: Hay House.

Hayes, S. 1983 *An investigation of the relationship between the recumbent position and the second stage of labor*. Unpublished Master's Thesis. East Lansing: Michigan State University.

Healing HealthCare Systems. 2004. Healing HealthCare Systems: Creating environments that heal. http:www.healinghealth.com.

Henderson, J. 1996. So what was Beijing like? *Oxfam Community Aid Abroad* [online]. http://www.caa.org.au/horizons/h15/nalini.html.

Henry, J. & Henry L. 2004. *The soul of the caring nurse: Stories and resources for revitalizing professional passion*. Washington, D.C.: nursesbooks.org.

Hertzman, C. 1996. What's been said and what's been hid: Population health, global consumption and the role of national health data. In *Health and Social Organizations*. Edited by D. Blane, E. Brunner, & R. Williamson. London: Routledge.

Hughes, M. L. 1897. *Mediterranean, Malta or undulant fever*. London: Macmillan and Company.

Hume, L. P., & K. M. Offen. 1981. Introduction to Part III: The adult woman: Work, in *Victorian Women: A documentary account of women's lives in nineteenth century England, France, and the United States* (pp. 272–291), edited by E. O. Hellerstein, L. P. Hume, & K. M. Offen. Stanford, CA: Stanford University Press.

Illich, I. 1976. *Medical nemesis: The expropriation of health*. New York: Pantheon.

Illustrated London News, 1856. Saturday, August 30. Miss Nightingale's carriage at the seat of war.

International Council of Nurses (ICN). 2000a. Nurses, physicians and pharmacists create a global alliance. *International Nursing Review* 47:130.

———. 2000b. Nursing numbers: Fractions, figures and percentages tell a story [online]. Geneva. http://www.icn.ch/indpr4.pdf.

Jeans, M. E. 2000, October 4. *Health first!* Keynote address presented at the Courage to Care Millennium Celebration, Ottawa, ON. [online]. http://www.florencenightingale2010.net/CouragetoCare.html.

Johns, J. 2004. Becoming a transformational leader through reflection. *Leadership* 30(2): 24-26.

Jonas, W. B., & R. A. Chez. 2003. The role of definitions and standards in healing research. Supplement to *Alternative Therapies in Health and Medicine* 9(3): A1–A104.

Jowett, B. 1867/1913. Letter to Florence Nightingale, quoted in Cook, 1913.

Jung, C. G. 1971. Psychological types. Vol. 6 of *The collected works of C. G. Jung.* Bollingen Series XX. Princeton, NJ: Princeton University Press.

Kalnins, I. 1999. Sowing the seeds of public health nursing: 1920–39. *International Nursing Review* 46(2): 47–51.

Katz, F. E. 1969. Nurses. In *The semi-professions and their organizations* (pp. 54–77). Edited by A. Etzioni. New York: The Free Press.

Kavanagh, G. 1990. *History curatorship*. Leicester: Leicester University Press.

Keith, J. M. 1989. Florence Nightingale: Statistician and consultant epidemiologist. *International Nursing Review* 35(5): 147–149.

Kerlinger, F. 1986. *Foundations of behavioral research.* 3rd ed. New York: Holt, Rinehart & Winston.

Kibrick, E., D. M. Beck, & M. A. Burkhardt. 2003. *The power of words: Linking mind–body research to educational interventions aimed at helping to address the nursing shortage.* Science of Whole Person Healing Conference Proceedings. Lincoln, NE: iUniverse Publishers.

Kickbusch, I. S. 1997. Think health: What makes the difference? *Health Promotion International* 12(4): 265–272.

———. 1999. Good planets are hard to find, in *Health Ecology. Health, culture and human-environment interaction*. Edited by Honari. M. & Boleyn. T. Great Britian. Routledge.

———. 2000. The development of international health policies: Accountability intact? *Social Science and Medicine* 51(6): 979–989.

———. 2001a. Health literacy: Addressing the health and education divide. *Health Promotion International* 16(3): 289–297.

———. 2001b. Mexico and beyond. *Health Promotion International* 16(1): 1.

Kickbusch, I. S., & J. Quick. 1998. Partnerships for health in the 21st century. *World Health Statistics Quarterly* 51(1): 68–74.

Kimball, B., & E. O'Neil. 2002. *Health care's human crisis: The American nursing shortage.* Health Workforce Solutions for the Robert Wood Johnson Foundation [online]. http://www.rwjf.org/newsEvents/nursing_report.pdf

King, I.M. 1995. The theory of goal attainment. In M.A. Frey & C.L. Seiloff (Eds.). *Advancing King's systems framework and theory of nursing.* (pp. 23–33). Thousand Oaks, CA: Sage.

King, A. E. V. 2000. The global perspective: Outcomes of Beijing+5, gender equality, development and peace. *WomenWatch* [online]. http://www.un.org/womenwatch/confer/documents/04Dec2000_AK.htm.

Kingma, M. 2001. *The emerging global nursing shortage.* Geneva: International Council of Nurses.

Kleffel, D. K. 1991. Rethinking the environment as a domain of nursing knowledge. *Advances in Nursing Science* 14(1): 40–51.

Klein, E. 2004. Missing Something in Your Career. *Leadership* 30(1), 41-42.

Knutson, L. (2005) Exploring integrative medicine and the healing environment: The story of a large urban acute care hospital, in Dossey. Keegan, & Guzzetta, 2005a.

Koerner, J. 2001. Nightingale II: Nursing in the new millennium, in *The nursing profession: Tomorrow and beyond* (pp. 17–27). Edited by N. L. Chaska. Thousand Oaks, CA: Sage.

Koerner, J.E. 2003. *Mother, Heal Thy Self.* Santa Rosa, CA: Crestpoint Press.

Kozier, B., G. Erb, & R. Olverieri. 1991. *Fundamentals of nursing: Concepts, process and practice.* 4th ed. Menlo Park, CA: Addison-Wesley.

Krietzer, M.J. and Disch, J. 2002. Leading the way: The Gillette Nursing Summit on Integrated Health and Healing. *Alternative Therapies* 9(1), 1A–10A.

Lachman, B. 1993. *The journal of Hildegard of Bingen*. New York: Bell Tower.

Laffrey, S., & G. Page. 1989. Primary health care in public health nursing. *Journal of Advanced Nursing* 13:1044–1050.

The Lancet. 1897, July 17. The Victorian era exhibition at Earl's Court. 2:161–162.

Lang, N.M., & Jennings, B.M.(2002). Nurses and nursing in the health care quality policy arena. *Journal of Professional Nursing,* 18, 60,112.

Lerer, L. B., A. D. Lopez, T. Kjellstrom, & D. Yach. 1998. "Health for All": Analyzing health status and determinants. *World Health Statistics Quarterly* 51(1): 7–20.

Lerner, M. 2004. Personal Healing and Planetary Healing, in *Ecological Medicine: Healing the Earth, Healing Ourselves*. Edited by Asubel, K. San Francisco: Sierra Club Books.

Levine, B. H. 1991. *Your body believes every word you say.* Lower Lake, CA: Aslan Publishing.

Levine, M. 1995. The rhetoric of nursing theory. *Image: Journal of Nursing Scholarship,* 27(1): 11–14.

Lewis, S. 2000, November 12. *Health as a bridge to peace.* Keynote address presented at the 7th annual Canadian Conference for International Health, National Capital Region, Hull, Quebec.

Lindeke L. L., & D. E. Block. 1998. Maintaining professional integrity in the midst of interdisciplinary collaboration. *Nursing Outlook* 46:213–218.

Lindsey, E., & G. Hartwick. 1996. Health promoting nursing practice: The demise of the nursing process? *Journal of Advanced Nursing* 23:106–112.

Maben, J., & J. Macleod-Clark. 1995. Health promotion: A concept analysis. *Journal of Advanced Nursing* 22:1158–1165.

Macleod-Clark, J. 1993. From sick nursing to health nursing: Evolution or revolution? In *Research in health promotion and nursing.* Edited by J. Wilson-Barnett & J. Macleod-Clark. Basingstoke, Hampshire: Macmillan.

Macrae, J.A.1995. Nightingale's spiritual philosophy and its significance for modern nursing. *Image: Journal of Nursing Scholarship* 27(1): 8–10.

———. 2001. *Nursing as a spiritual practice: A contemporary application of Florence Nightingale's views*. New York: Springer.

Mahler, H. 1983. "Health for All" by the year 2000: The countdown has begun. *Bulletin of the Pan American Health Organization* 17(4): 193–197.

Malloch, K., & T. Porter-O'Grady. 1999. Partnership economics: Nursing's challenge in a quantum age. *Nursing Economics* 17(6): 298–307.

Marston, J. A. 1863. Report on fever (Malta). In Vol. 3 of *Army Medical Department Reports* (pp. 486–521). London: HMSO. Cited in D. A. B. Young. Florence Nightingale's fever. *British Medical Journal* 311:1697–1700.

Maslach, C., & S. E. Jackson. 1986. *The Maslach burnout inventory manual.* 2nd ed. Palo Alto, CA: Consulting Psychologists.

Mason, D. J. 2001. Tales of leadership, heroism, and courage. *American Journal of Nursing* 101(11): 7.

Mawhinney, J. 2001, March 16. Illuminating the many sides of the lady with the lamp. *Toronto Star* p. F1.

Maxwell, J. 1998. *The 21 irrefutable laws of leadership.* Nashville, TN: Thomas Nelson Publishers.

Mayou, R. 2003. Everyone is responsible to everyone for everything [online]. Geneva: International Red Cross and Red Crescent Museum. http://www.micr.ch/e/director_e.html

McAndrews, R. M. 1999. Thinking at intersection. *Network* 16(1): 43.

McBeath, W. H. 1991. "Health for All": A public health vision. *American Journal of Public Health* 81(12): 1560–1565.

McDonald, L. 1994. *The women founders of the social sciences*. Ottawa, Canada: Carleton University Press.

McDonald, L. 1998. Florence Nightingale: Passionate statistician. *Journal of Holistic Nursing* 16(2): 267–277.

———., ed. 2000, February. Florence Nightingale and the foundations of public health care, as seen through her collected works. *Collected works of Florence Nightingale* [online]. http://www.sociology.uoguelph.ca/fnightingale/fnightingale.htm

———. 2002a. Florence Nightingale: An introduction to her life and family. Vol. 1 of *The collected works of Florence Nightingale*. Waterloo, Ontario: Wilfrid Laurier University Press.

———. 2002b. Florence Nightingale's spiritual journey: Biblical annotations, sermons, and journal notes. Vol. 2 of *The collected works of Florence Nightingale*. Waterloo, Ontario: Wilfrid Laurier University Press.

———. 2002c. Florence Nightingale's theology: Essays, letters, and journal notes. Vol. 3 of *The collected works of Florence Nightingale*. Waterloo, Ontario: Wilfrid Laurier University Press.

———. 2003. Florence Nightingale on mysticism and Eastern religion. Vol. 4 of *The collected works of Florence Nightingale*. Waterloo, Ontario: Wilfrid Laurier University Press.

McEwen, M. 2002. Philosophy, science and nursing, in *Theoretical basis for nursing* (pp. 3–22). Edited by M. McEwen & E. Wills. Philadelphia: Lippincott Williams & Wilkins,.

McGann, S. 1994. *The battle of the nurses*. London: Scutari Press.

McKivergin, M. 2005. Nurse as an instrument of healing, in Dossey, Keegan, & Guzzetta, 2005a.

Medicins Sans Frontieres (MSF). 2003. MSF tackles malaria outbreak in Indonesia [online]. http://www.msf.org/countries/.

Merriam, C. 1969. *American political ideas: Studies in the development of American political thought 1865–1917.* New York: Augustus M. Kelley, Publishers.

Messias, D. K. H. 2001. Globalization, nursing and "Health for All." *Journal of Nursing Scholarship* 33(1): 9–11.

Mittlemark, M. B., M. Akerman, D. Gillis, K. Kosa, M. O'Neil, D. Piette, H. Restrepo, I. Rootman, H. Sann, J. Springett, N. Wallerstein, M. F. Westphal, & M. Wise. 2001. Mexico conference on health promotion: Open letter to WHO Director General, Dr. Gro Harlem Bruntland. *Health Promotion International* 16(1): 3.

Monteiro, L. A. 1985. Florence Nightingale on public health nursing. *American Journal of Public Health* 75(2): 181–186.

———. 1991. Florence Nightingale on public health nursing, in *Readings in community health nursing*. Edited by B. W. Spradley. Philadelphia: Lippincott.

Moore, N. 2005. About St. Charles: Why and how a healing philosophy became integrated into the hospital's strategic initiative, in Dossey, Keegan, & Guzzetta, 2005a.

Moore, T. 2004. Dark night of the soul. A guide to finding your way through life's ordeals. New York: Gotham Books.

Morgan, H. A. 1892. *The historical World's Columbian Exposition*. St. Louis: Pacific Publishing Co.

Muff, J. 1988. Altruism, socialism and nightingalism: The compassion traps, in *Socialization, sexism, and stereotyping: Women's issues in nursing* (pp. 234–247). Edited by J. Muff. St. Louis: C. V. Mosby.

Munhall, P. L. 1993. Unknowing: Toward another pattern of knowing in nursing. *Nursing Outlook* 41:125–129.

Mustard, J. F., & J. W. Frank. 1998. The determinants of population health: A critical assessment [online]. http://www.founders.net; use search.

Myers, I. B., & P. B. Myers. 1980. *Gifts differing*. Palo Alto, CA: Consulting Psychologists Press.

National Council for Research on Women. 1996. Turning words into action: Women take the world stage. *Issues Quarterly* 2(1): 2–45.

Naylor, M. D., & K. Buhler-Wilkerson. 1999, May/June. Creating community-based care for the new millennium. *Nursing Outlook* 47(3): 120–127.

Needleman, J., P. Buerhaus, S. Matke, M. Stewart, & K. Zelevinsky. 2002. Nurse-staffing levels and the quality of care in hospitals. *New England Journal of Medicine* 346(22): 1715–1722.

Neuman, B. M. (Ed.). (1995). *The Neuman systems model* (3rd ed.). Norwalk, CT: Appleton & Lange.

Neuman, M. A. 2002. The pattern that connects. *Advances in Nursing Science* 24(3): 1–7.

Newman, M.A. 1986. *Health as expanding consciousness*. St. Louis: C.V. Mosby. (The second edition was published in 1994: Sudbury MA: NLN Press / Jones and Bartlett).

Nicoll, L. 1997. *Perspectives on nursing theory*. 3rd ed. Philadelphia: Lippincott.

Nicholson, G. W. L. 1975. *Canada's nursing sisters*. Toronto: Samuel Stevens Hakkert.

Nieswiadomy, R. 1993. *Foundations of nursing research*. Norwalk, CT: Appleton & Lange.

Nightingale, F. 1853. Private note. March 2, 1853. Cited in Calabria & Macrae, 1994).

———. 1853–4. *Florence Nightingale at Harley Street: Her reports to the governors of her nursing home 1853–4*. London: J.M. Dent & Sons Ltd.

———. 1854. Florence Nightingale to the Nightingales, November 4, 1854. London: Wellcome Institute Library. Cited in Goldie, 1987.

———. 1856, July 18. Letter to Jerry Barrett. London Metropolitan Archives: Florence Nightingale Museum collection, H1/ST/NC3/SU.193.

———. 1858. Subsidiary notes as to the introduction of female nursing into military hospitals. In Seymer 1954.

———. 1859. *Notes on hospitals*. London: John W. Parker and Son.

———. 1860a. *Notes on nursing: What it is, and what it is not*. London: Harrison and Sons.

———. 1860b. *Suggestions for thought to the searchers after truth among the artizans of England*. 3 vols. London: George E. Eyre and William Spottiswoode.

———1860c. Revised and enlarged. *Notes on nursing: What it is, and what it is not.* London: Harrison and Sons.

———. 1863. *Notes on hospitals.* 3rd ed. London: Longmans.

———. 1867. Letter to Mary Jones. Greater London Metropolitan Archives (Formerly Greater London Record Office [GLRO]) H1/ST/NCI/67(25).

———. 1868, June-8. Una and the lion. *Good Words* p. 362.

———. 1869, March. A note on pauperism. *Fraser's Magazine*, pp. 281–291.

———. 1871. *Introductory notes to lying-in institutions.* London: Longmans, Green and Co.

———. c. 1872a. *Notes from devotional authors of the Middle Ages: Collected, chosen, and freely translated by Florence Nightingale.* London: BL Add. Mss. 45841:ff 1–87. (Unpublished mansucript.)

———. 1872b. *Address from Miss Nightingale to the probationer-nurses in the 'Nightingale Fund' at St. Thomas' Hospital, and the nurses who were formerly trained there*. London: Spottiswoode.

———. 1873a. *Address from Miss Nightingale to the probationer-nurses in the Nightingale Fund school at St. Thomas's Hospital, and the nurses who were formerly trained there.* London: Spottiswoode.

———. 1873b, July. A subnote of interrogation: What will be our religion in 1999? *Fraser's Magazine* pp. 25–36.

———. 1874a. *Address from Miss Nightingale to the probationer-nurses in the Nightingale fund school at St. Thomas's Hospital, and the nurses who were formerly trained there.* London: Spottiswoode

———. 1874b, August. Irrigation and means of transit in India. *The Illustrated London News.*

———. 1875. *Address from Miss Nightingale to the probationer-nurses in the 'Nightingale Fund' at St. Thomas's Hospital, and the nurses who were formerly trained there.* London: Spottiswoode.

———. 1876. *Address from Miss Nightingale to the probationer-nurses in the 'Nightingale Fund' at St. Thomas's Hospital, and the nurses who were formerly trained there.* London: Spottiswoode.

———. 1878. *New Year's Day 1878. Letter from Miss Nightingale*. (Privately printed.)

———. 1879a. *Letter from Florence Nightingale to the probationer-nurses in the 'Nightingale Fund' at St. Thomas's Hospital, Easter 1879*. London: Spottiswoode.

———. 1879b, July. A missionary health officer in India. *Good Words,* pp. 492–496.

———. 1879c, August. A missionary health officer in India. *Good Words,* pp. 565–571.

———. 1879d, September. A missionary health officer in India. *Good Words,* pp. 635–640.

———. 1881. *Letter from Florence Nightingale.* London: Spottiswoode.

———. 1882. Nursing the sick in Quain's dictionary of medicine, in *Selected writings of Florence Nightingale.* Edited by L. Seymer. New York: The Macmillan Company.

———. 1883. *From Florence Nightingale to the probationer-nurses in the 'Nightingale Fund' at St. Thomas's Hospital, and the nurses who were formerly trained there.* London: Spottiswoode.

———. 1886. *To the probationer-nurses in the 'Nightingale Fund School at St. Thomas's Hospital.* London: Blades, East and Blades.

———. 1888. *To the probationer-nurses in the Nightingale Fund School at St. Thomas' Hospital from Florence Nightingale 16th May 1888*. London: Blades, East and Blades.

———. 1893. Sick-nursing and health-nursing. In Burdett-Coutts, 1893 (pp. 184–205).

———. 1894a. Health teaching in towns and villages, in Seymer, 1954 (pp. 378–396).

———. 1894b. Private note. British Library Additional Manuscripts. 45844f232.

———. 1897a. *To the nurses and probationers trained under the 'Nightingale Fund'*. London: Blades, East and Blades.

———. 1897b, March. Letter to unidentified correspondent, quoted in *The life of Florence Nightingale.* 2 Vols. Edited by E. T. Cook. London: Macmillan.

———. 1897c, March 10. Letter to Edmund Verney, quoted in McDonald, L., ed. 2001.

———. 1900. *Letter. May 28, 1900.* Privately printed.

Norris, T., & M. Pittman. 2000. The Healthy Communities movement and the Coalition for Healthier Cities and Communities. *Public Health Reports* 115:118–124.

Novak, J. C. 1991. The social mandate and historical basis for nursing's role in health promotion, in *Perspectives in family and community health* (pp. 9–16). Edited by K. A. Saucier. St. Louis: Mosby.

Nuland, S. B. 2003. *The doctors' plague: Germs, childbed fever, and the strange story of Ignac Semmelweis.* New York: Norton.

Nursing Record and Hospital Review. 1893, June 1. The Chicago exhibition. 10:271–275.

Nursing Record and Hospital Review. 1897, May 29. The Victorian era exhibition. 18:443.

Nutbeam, D. 1998. Evaluating health promotion: Progress, problems and solutions. *Health Promotion International* 13(1): 27–44.

Nutbeam, D., & I. S. Kickbusch. 2000. Advancing health literacy: A global challenge for the 21st century. *Health Promotion International* 15(3): 183–184.

Nutting, A. 1929, July 3. Letter to Nina Gage.

———. 1946, 15 May. *Notes on a possible International Memorial to Florence Nightingale.* Florence Nightingale International Foundation. Unpublished typescript.

O'Brien, R., A. M. Goetz, J. A. Scholte, & M. Williams. 2000. *Contesting global governance: Multilateral economic institutions and global social movements.* Cambridge, UK: Cambridge University Press.

Orem, D. E. 1995. *Nursing: Concepts of practice.* St. Louis: Mosby-Year Book.

Owens, R. G. 1987. *Organizational behavior in education.* 3rd ed. Englewood Cliffs, NJ: Prentice-Hall.

PACT. 2002. WORTH: A women's empowerment program [online]. http://www.pactworld.org/initiatives/worth.

Pesut, D. J. 2001. Spiral dynamics: Leadership insights. *Nursing Outlook* 49:70.

Pickering, G. 1974. *Creative malady.* London: Allen and Unwin.

Porter, R. 1987. *Disease, medicine and society in England: 1550–1850.* Basingstoke: Macmillan Education Ltd.

Porter-O'Grady, T. 1999. Leading in the quantum world. *Surgical Services Management* 5(8): 14–19.

———. 2000. Visions for the 21st century: New horizons, new health care. *Nursing Administration Quarterly* 25(1): 30–38.

Pratt, M. B. 1999. Where the lenses overlap. *Network* 16(1): 49.

Porter-O'Grady, T. & K. Malloch. 2003. *Quantum leadership: A textbook of new leadership.* Sudbury, MA: Jones and Bartlett.

Pringle, D. M., & D. J. Roe. 1992. Voluntary community agencies; VON Canada as an example, in *Canadian nursing faces the future.* Edited by A. J. Baugart. Toronto: Mosby.

Pryor, E. B. 1988. *Clara Barton, professional angel.* Philadelphia: University of Pennsylvania Press.

Quinn, J. F. 2002. Revisioning the nursing shortage: A call to caring and healing the healthcare system. *Frontiers of Health Services Management* 19(2): 3–21.

Quinn, J. F., M. Smith, C. Rittenbaugh, K. Swanson, & J. Watson. 2003. Research guidelines for assessing the impact of the healing relationship in clinical nursing, in *Definitions and Standards of Healing Research*, edited by W. B. Jonas & R. A. Chez. Supplement to *Alternative Therapies in Health and Medicine* 9(3): A65–A79.

Quinn, V., & Prest, J., eds. 1987. *Dear Miss Nightingale: A selection of Benjamin Jowett's letters to Florence Nightingale (1860–1893).* Oxford, UK: Clarendon.

Rafael, A. R. F. 1998. Nurses who run with wolves: The power and caring dialectic revisited. *Advances in Nursing Science* 21(1): 29–41.

Rafael, A. R. F. 1999. The politics of health promotion: Influences on public health promoting nursing practice in Ontario, Canada from Nightingale to the nineties. *Advances in Nursing Science*, 22(1): 23–39.

Raffensperger, C., and Tickner, J. 1999. *Protecting Public Health and the Environment: Implementing the Precautionary Principle.* Washington, D.C.: Island Press.

Raffensperger. C. 2004. The Precautionary Principle: Golden Rule for the New Millennium, in *Ecological Medicine: Healing the Earth, Healing Ourselves*. Edited by Asubel, K. San Francisco: Sierra Club Books.

Ratzan, S. C. 2001. Health literacy: Communication for the public good. *Health Promotion International* 16(2): 201–214.

Reed, P. G. 2000. Nursing reformation: Historical reflections and philosophic foundations. *Nursing Science Quarterly* 13(2): 129–136.

Remen, R. N. 1996, Spring. In service of life. *Noetic Science Review* 24–25.

Reverby, S. 1979. The search for the hospital yardstick: Nursing and the rationalization of hospital work, in *Health care in America: Essays in social history* (pp. 206–225). Edited by S. Reverby & D. Rosner. Philadelphia: Temple University Press.

———. 1987. A caring dilemma: Womanhood and nursing in historical perspective. *Nursing Research* 36(1): 5–11.

———. 1993. From Lillian Wald to Hillary Rodham Clinton: What will happen to public health nursing? *American Journal of Public Health* 83(12): 1662–1663.

Ritchie, M. A., M. Minsek, & D. W. Conner. 1995. Roles and approaches of nongovernmental organizations in health development. *World Health Forum* 16:35–41.

Rivard, N. 2002. Message from the president. *Airline Ambassadors* [online]. http://www.airlineamb.org/letter.php.

Robertson, A., & M. Minkler. 1994. New health promotion movement: A critical examination. *Health Education Quarterly* 21(3): 295–312.

Robinson, S., & Y. Hill. 1995. Miracles take a little longer: Project 2000 and the health promoting nurse. *International Journal of Nursing Studies* 32(6): 568–579.

Rogers, M. E. 1990. Nursing: Science of unitary, irreducible human beings. In E. A. M. Barrett (ed.), *Visions of Roger's science-based nursing* (pp. 5–11). New York: National League for Nursing.

Rogge, M. M. 1986. Nursing and politics: A forgotten legacy. *Nursing Research* 36(1): 26–30.

Roy, C. 1992. Vigor, variables and vision: Commentary on Florence Nightingale, in *Notes on nursing: What it is and what it is not* (pp. 63–71), commemorative ed., by F. Nightingale. Philadelphia: Lippincott.

Roy, C., & Andrews, A. A. (1999). *The Roy adaptation model* (2nd ed.). Norwalk, CT: Appleton and Lange.

Rush, K. L. 1997. Health promotion ideology and nursing education. *Journal of Advanced Nursing* 25:1292–1298.

Saumarez-Smith, C. 2001. *Miss Florence Nightingale at Embley* (sketch), by Sir George Scharf. The National Portrait Gallery: unpublished script of the Annual Arts Lecture at St. Thomas' Hospital.

Selanders, L. C. 1992. *An analysis of the utilization of power by Florence Nightingale 1856–1872.* Ph.D. Diss. Kalamazoo: Western Michigan University. UMI# 9310445.

———. 1993. *Florence Nightingale: An environmental adaptation theory*. Thousand Oaks, CA: Sage.

———. 1998a. The power of environmental adaptation: Florence Nightingale's original theory for nursing practice. *Journal of Holistic Nursing* 16(2): 247–263.

———. 1998a. The power of environmental adaptation: Florence Nightingale's original theory. *Journal of Holistic Nursing* 16(2): 262–266.

———. 1998b. Florence Nightingale: The evolution and social impact of feminist values in nursing. *Journal of Holistic Nursing* 16:227–243.

———. 2001, Fall. Florence Nightingale and the transvisionary leadership paradigm. *Nursing Leadership Forum* 6(1): 12–16.

Seymer, L. R., ed. 1954. *Selected works of Florence Nightingale.* New York: Macmillan.

Silva, M. C., J. M. Sorrell, & C. D. Sorrell. 1995. From Carper's patterns of knowing to ways of being: An ontological philosophical shift in nursing. *Advances in Nursing Science* 17:1–5.

Simpson, D. 1977. Florence Nightingale by her god-daughter. *Nursing Times* 73(5): 50–51.

Skretkowicz, V. 1996. *Florence Nightingale's "Notes on Nursing."* London, UK: Bailliere Tindall.

Small, H. 1998. *Florence Nightingale: Avenging angel.* London: Constable.

Smith, F. B. 1982. *Florence Nightingale: Reputation and power.* New York: St. Martin's Press.

Smith, H. 1986. *The religions of man*. Philadelphia: Harper and Row.

Smith, H. 1994. *The illustrated world's religions: A guide to our wisdom traditions.* San Francisco: HarperSanFrancisco.

Spellbring, A. M. 1991. Nursing's role in health promotion: An overview. *Nursing Clinics of North America* 25(4): 805–814.

Spink, W. W. 1956. *The nature of brucellosis.* Minneapolis: University of Minnesota Press.

———. 1972. Brucellosis. In *Harrison's principles of internal medicine* (pp. 819–821), 6th ed. Edited by M. M. Wintrobe. New York: McGraw-Hill.

Starfield, B. 2000. Is US Health Really the Best in the World? *Journal of the American Medical Association* 284 (4): 483-485.

Stern, L. 2001, August 27. There she is, your ideal. *Newsweek* pp. 60–61.

Stewart, I. 1948. Introduction, in *Nursing of the sick,* by I. Hampton. New York: McGraw-Hill.

———. 1949. Introduction, in *Nursing of the sick: 1893.* Edited by I. Hampton Robb. New York: McGraw-Hill.

Sullivan, E. 2002. In a woman's world. *Reflections on Nursing Leadership. Honor Society of Sigma Theta Tau International* 3rd quarter, pp. 10–16.

Swearingen, T. 2000. Why I went to jail to protect my daughter from toxic polluters, in *Ecological Medicine: Healing the Earth, Healing Ourselves*. Edited by Asubel, K. San Francisco: Sierra Club Books.

Terris, M. 1994. Determinants of health: A progressive political platform. *Journal of Public Health Policy* 15(1): 5–17.

Thomas À Kempis. 1890. *Imitation of Christ*. London: Thomas Nelson and Sons. (Original work published in 1427.)

Thompson, J. T. 2002. The WHO Global Advisory Group on Nursing and Midwifery. *Journal of Nursing Scholarship* 34(2): 111–113. 2nd Quarter.

Thornton, S. N.D. The bust of Florence Nightingale. Unpublished paper.

Toffler, A. 1980. *The third wave*. New York: William Morrow and Company.

Torres, G. 1985. The place of concepts and theories within nursing, in *Nursing theories: The base for professional nursing practice.* Edited by J. George. Englewood Cliffs, NJ: Prentice-Hall.

Tresoli, C. P., & the Pew and Fetzer Task Force Health Professions Commission. 1994. *Relationship-centered care*. San Francisco: Pew Health Professions Commission.

Trujillo, I. Z., A. N. Zavala, J. C. Caceres, & C. Z. Miranda. 1994. Brucellosis. *Infectious Disease Clinics of North America* 21:225–241.

Underhill, E. (1925). *Mystics of the church*. Cambridge: James Clarke & Co., Ltd.

Underhill, E. 1911/1961. *Mysticism: A study in the nature and development of man's spiritual consciousness*.

———. 1915/1943. *Practical mysticism.* New York: E.P. Dutton and Co. Inc.

United Nations Integrated Regional Information Networks. 2003. United Nations agencies urge one-week ceasefire for health campaign [online]. http://allafrica.com/stories/200308010042.html.

U. S. Department of Health and Human Services. 2002. HIV/AIDS statistics. http://www.niaid.nih.gov/factsheets/aidsstat.htm.

Vallée, G. 2003. Florence Nightingale on mysticism and eastern religion, in *The collected works of Florence Nightingale* (Volume 4). Edited by McDonald, L. Waterloo, Ontario, Canada: Wilfrid Laurier University Press.

van der Peet, R. 1995. *The Nightingale model of nursing.* Edinburgh: Campion Press.

Veith, S. 1990. The recluse: A retrospective health history of Florence Nightingale. In *Florence Nightingale and her era: A collection of new scholarship* (pp. 75–89), edited by V. L. Bullough, B. Bullough, & M. P. Stanton. New York: Garland.

Vicinus, M., ed. 1972. *Suffer and be still: Women in the Victorian age* Bloomington: Indiana University Press.

———. ed. 1977. *A widening sphere: Changing roles of Victorian women*. Bloomington: Indiana University Press.

Vicinus, M., & B. Nergaard. 1989. *Ever yours, Florence Nightingale*. London: Virago Press.

Victorian Order of Nurses (VON). 1996. *A century of caring: 1897–1997: The history of the Victorian Order of Nurses for Canada.* Ottawa: Author.

Vincent, R. 1939. Personal letter to Miss M. Adelaide Nutting [online]. http://www.countryjoe.com/nightingale/vincent.htm.

Vonderheid, S. C., & N. Al-Gasseer. World Health Organization and global health policy. *Journal of Nursing Scholarship* 34(2): 109–110.

Wade, G. 1999. Professional nurse autonomy: Concept analysis and application to nursing education. *Journal of Advanced Nursing* 30:310–317.

Wakefield, M. K. 2001. What becomes visible when it disappears? Answer: The essential role of nurses in the health care system. *Nursing Economics* 19(4): 188–191.

Walker, L., & K. Avant. 1995. *Strategies for theory construction in nursing.* Norwalk, CT: Appleton & Lange.

Walker, L., & K. Avant. 1988. *Strategies for theory construction in nursing.* 2nd ed. Norwalk, CT: Appleton & Lange.

Wallerstein, N. 1992. Powerlessness, empowerment and health: Implications for health promotion programs. *American Journal of Health Promotion* 6(3), 197–205.

of Health Promotion 6(3), 197–205.

Ward, K. 2002. A vision for tomorrow: Transformational nursing leaders. *Nursing Outlook* 50 (3): 121–126.

Watson, J. 1992. Notes on nursing: Guidelines for caring then and now, in *Notes on nursing: What it is and what it is not* (pp. 80–85), commemorative ed., by F. Nightingale. Philadelphia: Lippincott.

———. 1988. *Nursing: Human science and human caring.* New York: National League for Nursing Press.

———. 1998. Florence Nightingale and the enduring legacy of transpersonal human caring. *Journal of Holistic Nursing* 16(2): 292–294.

———. 1999. *Postmodern nursing and beyond.* Edinburgh: Churchill Livingston.

Webb, V. 2002. *Florence Nightingale: Radical theologian.* St. Louis: Chalice Press.

Weingart, R.M., Wilson. R.W., Gibberd, R.W., & Harrison, B. 2000. Epidemiology and Medical Error. British Medical Journal 320: 774-775.

Wellness Foundation. 2002. Florence Nightingale National Cathedral events [online]. http://www.FlorenceNightingale2010.net/1WashingtonCath.html.

White, J. 1995. Patterns of knowing: Review, critique, and update. *Advances in Nursing Science* 17:73 –76.

White Ribbon Alliance. 2001. International activities of the White Ribbon Alliance for Safe Motherhood [online]. http://www.whiteribbonalliance.org/internationalactivities.php.

Widerquist, J. G. 1992. The spirituality of Florence Nightingale. *Nursing Research* 41(1): 49–55.

Williams, J. 1999. The international campaign to ban landmines: A model for disarmament initiatives? [online]. http://www.nobel.se/peace/articles/williams/index.html.

Wolfer, J. 1993. Aspects of reality and ways of knowing in nursing: In search of an integrating paradigm. *Journal of Nursing Scholarship* 25:141 –145.

Woodham-Smith, C. 1950. *Florence Nightingale.* London: Constable.

———. 1953. *Florence Nightingale: 1820–1910.* New York: Atheneum.

Woodman L. A. 2000. Business and complexity: The phenomenon of lock-in in business in light of complexity theory. *Network* 16(2): 158–167.

World Health Organization (WHO). 1978. *Declaration of Alma-Ata* [online]. http://www.who.int/hpr/archive/docs/almaata.html.

———. 1986. *Ottawa charter for health promotion* [online]. http://www.who.int/hpr/archive/docs/ottawa.html.

———. 1997. *Jakarta Declaration on health promotion in the 21st century* [online]. http://http://www.who.int/hpr/archive/docs/jakarta/english.html.

———. 1998. WHO estimates of health personnel: Physicians, nurses, midwives, dentists and pharmacists [online]. http://www3.who.int/whosis/health_personnel/health_personnel.

World Health Organization (WHO) Joint FAO/WHO Expert Committee on Brucellosis. 1986. Sixth report. *WHO Technical Report Series*. Geneva: World Health Organization.

Wright, J. 1995, October. *The Earth is our capital*. Paper presented at the World Bank Symposium on Environment, Health and Sustainable Development, Washington, D. C.

Young, D. A. B. 1995. Florence Nightingale's fever. *British Medical Journal* 311:1697–1700.

Young, E. J. 1994. An overview of human brucellosis. *Clinical Infectious Disease* 21:283–290.

Yukl, G. A. 1989. *Leadership in organizations*. Englewood Cliffs, NJ: Prentice-Hall.

Zammit, T. 1905. A preliminary note on the examination of the blood of goats suffering from Mediterranean fever. Part IV of *Reports of Royal Society of London* by the Mediterranean Fever Commission. London: Harrison's and Sons.

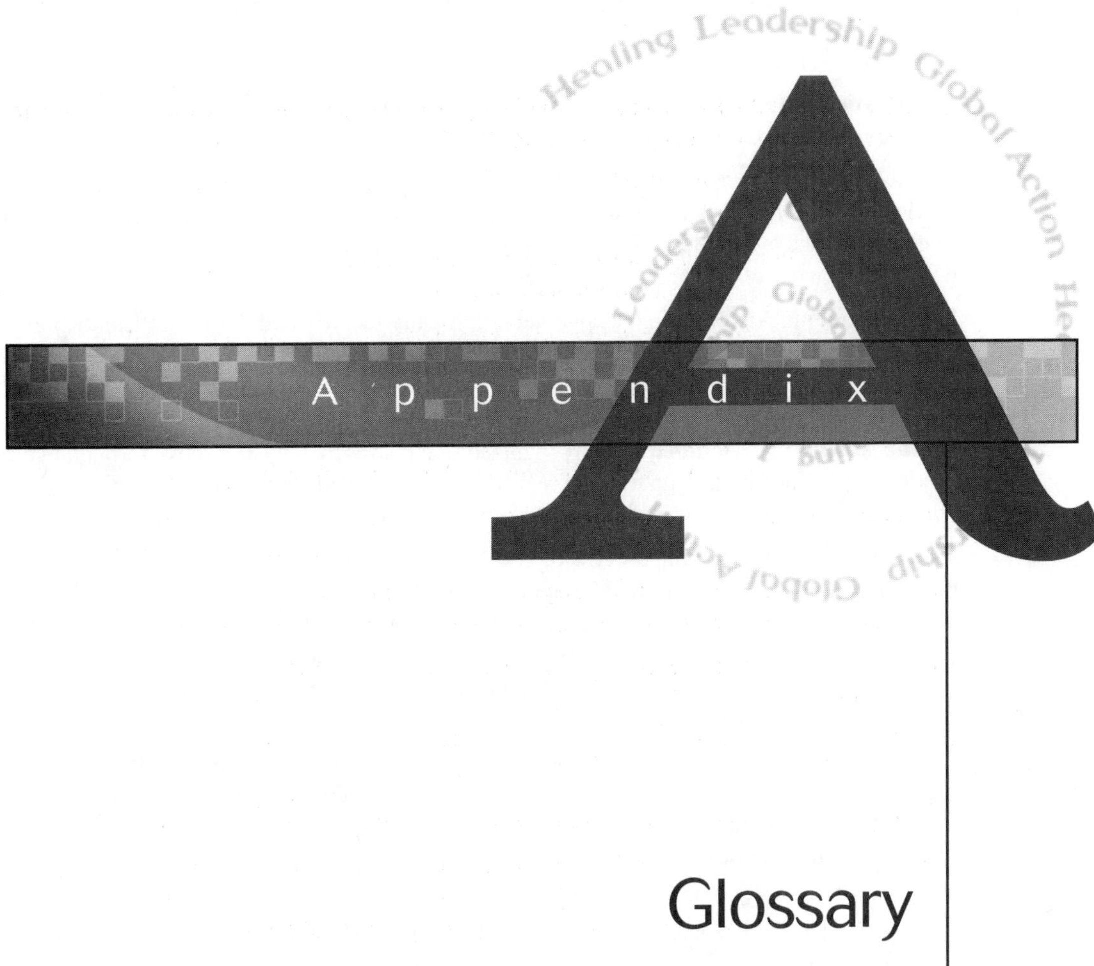

Appendix A

Glossary

For this book, the following glossary of terms applies.

Aesthetic knowing. The combination of knowledge, experience, instinct, and intuition that connects the nurse with a patient in order to explore the meaning of a situation about the human experiences of life, health, illness, and death. Such a combination calls forth resources and inner strengths from the nurse to be a facilitator in the healing process.

Awakening. The first phase of a mystic's spiritual development; it involves a conversion of the experience of the ego-oriented self to that of a higher Self, which leads to an awareness or consciousness of a divine reality within.

Empirical knowing. Explaining and structuring of empiric phenomena to create a formal expression, replication, and validation of scientific knowledge and scientific competence in nursing practice, education, and research.

Epiphanies. Those interactional moments and experiences that leave marks on an individual's lived experience; these are considered existential events where the fundamental structure of one's life is forever changed.

Ethical knowing. Valuing and clarifying situations to create formal behaviors, expressions, and dimensions of both morality and ethics intersecting with legally prescribed duties.

Foundational philosopher. One who is able to identify the concepts, assumptions and outcomes of a profession that are so basic to that profession that they are assumed always to have existed.

Healing. The process of bringing together aspects of oneself—body-mind-spirit—at deeper levels of inner knowing, leading towards integration and balance, with each aspect having equal importance and value. This process can lead to more complex levels of personal understanding and meaning; it may be synchronous, but not necessarily synonymous, with curing.

Illumination. The third phase of a mystic's spiritual development; the self detaches from ego attachment and enjoys a sense of the Divine presence, but not union with it; a state in which the mystic draws strength and peace from this new level of consciousness.

Interpretive biography. The creation of literary, narrative accounts, and representations of lived experiences with the telling and inscribing of experiences that includes the researcher within the context of the interpretive process.

Meta-paradigm. A group of concepts that specifically identify and define a phenomenon.

Mysticism. A way of life; an individual's direct experience of God.

Mystic. A person who has, to a greater or lesser degree, a direct experience of God.

Mystic spiritual development. The recognized five phases that mystics move through in their lifetime: (1) awakening, (2) purgation, (3) illumination, (4) surrender, and (5) union, each of which are also defined in this glossary.

Personal knowing. Dynamic process of becoming whole and self-aware of valued wholeness through reflection, synthesis of perceptions, and being with self or another in authentic, therapeutic presence; this allows for engaged interactions where personal knowing of the nurse and the patient/client emerge; may create an "A-ha!" experience; includes the experience of being with "unknowing," the not-knowing or understanding of events, situations, dreams, or the experience and perceptions of another.

Practical mystic. One whose direct experience of God and the Divine reveals the presence of the divine everywhere, whose sense of spirituality and action, of being and doing, are so integrated as to be impossible to distinguish, and whose engaged activity derives much of its power from that mystical experience.

Purgation. The second phase of a mystic's spiritual development that involves great pain and effort where the self becomes increasingly aware of the Divine beauty, and realizes by contrast its own imperfection.

Social action. The mystic's call to personal action is an element in the pattern of full mystic spiritual development; this "call to action" is not an externally imposed task but an inner compulsion; love is the motivating force for the mystic's work in the world.

Spirituality. The unifying force of a person; the essence of being that permeates all of life and is manifested in one's knowing, doing, and being; the interconnectedness with self, others, nature, and God/Life Force/Absolute/Transcendent.

Stories. Any series of connecting events that are written with the intention of convey truths and exemplars of how to live a life of truth and purpose.

Surrender. The fourth phase of a mystic's spiritual development; the journey of undergoing a deepening commitment to dissociate from personal satisfaction. Also called the "dark night of the soul" or the "great desolation," personal happiness must now be abandoned, and the service to God moves to a deeper level.

Tenet. Any basic principle, doctrine, or belief that is held as true, generally by a group or profession.

Transformational leadership. The mutual interaction of followers and leaders for the satisfaction of mutual goals and establishment of long-term outcomes.

Transvisionary leadership. A blend of transactional and transformational leadership, in which the leader (i) desires to create mutual, permanent change, but cultural constraint or knowledge deficit prohibits mutuality as a process; and (ii) requires to have an active vision of the outcome of the developing area or profession. Such an outcome has not been previously achieved or is commonly considered to be impossible under current circumstances.

Union. The fifth phase of a mystic's spiritual development; union with the Absolute is the ultimate goal of the mystic's quest.

Interpretive Biography: An Overview

Barbara M. Dossey

Approaching the Interpretive Biographical Approach

An interpretive biography centers on the studied use and collection of the documents, stories, accounts, narratives, and written manuscripts of personal life, as well as the documents that describe turning-point moments in individuals' lives (Denzin, 1989). In interpretive biography, one is writing not only about a person, but also about the researcher within the context of the process of interpretive biography. For reasons that will become clear, I used this approach in my assessment of Florence Nightingale's 13 letters to her nurses from 1872 through 1900 (also referred to as formal addresses as in this appendix and in Chapter 2).

During these years, Florence Nightingale was in the surrender and union phase of her mystic spiritual development. (See both Pentimentos in Chapter 2.) Specific epiphanies and events that I also explored were her work and writings on mysticism and the lives of medieval mystics—*Notes from Devotional Authors of the Middle Ages* (Nightingale, 1872a) and the *Imitation of Christ* by Thomas À Kempis (1890); her *Notes on Nursing* (Nightingale, 1860a, 1860c); and her three-volume work *Suggestions for Thought* (Nightingale, 1860b). Nightingale's motivations for writing these 13 formal letters and the patterns that emerged were determined through my systematic examination of these works. Additional primary and secondary sources related to Nightingale's mystic spiritual development and her tenets for contemporary nursing and beyond were also used (B. Dossey, 2000, 2002).

Interpretive biography is the result of creating narrative accounts and representations of lived experiences with the telling and inscribing of experiences. The challenges include understanding how lives are to be studied and finding the meaning and purpose in the lived experiences. The researcher using interpretive biography must identify the historical, political, economic, sociological, cultural, educational, structural, religious, and public health forces, issues, and influences on the lives of the individuals studied.

The Interpretive Biographical Process

This form of biographical writing challenges the traditional approaches; it asks that the biographer be cognizant of how studies are both read and written. In interpretive biography, then, biographers must include their own biases and values, and bring themselves into the process; this is reflected in the writer's work, and must be stated as such in this genre. Given the central assumptions of biography, Denzin (1989) advances these five procedural steps:

1. The investigator begins with an objective set of experiences in the subject's life, noting life courses, *stages,* and *experiences*. The stages may be childhood, adolescence, early adulthood, or old age written as a chronology, or as experiences such as education, marriage, and employment.
2. The researcher gathers concrete, contextual biographical materials using interviewing (e.g., the subject materials of life experiences in the form of a story or narrative). Thus, a focus is on gathering *stories*.
3. These stories are organized around themes that indicate pivotal events (or *epiphanies*) in an individual's life.
4. The researcher explores the *meaning of these stories*, providing explanations and searching for multiple meanings.
5. The researcher also searches for larger structures to explain the meanings, such as social interactions in groups, cultural issues, ideologies, and *historical context*, and provides an interpretation for the life experiences of the individual, or a cross-interpretation if several individuals are studied.

Thus, interpretive biography is challenging for the following reasons:

- The researcher needs to collect extensive information from and about the subject of the biography.
- The investigator needs to have a clear and comprehensive understanding of historical and contextual material to position the subject within the larger trends in that person's society and culture.
- It takes a keen eye to determine the particular stories, slant, or angle that "works" in writing a biography and to uncover the "figure under the carpet" that explains the multilayered context of a life.
- Writers using an interpretive approach need to be able to bring themselves into the narrative and acknowledge their standpoint.

Experiences and Stories

In interpretive biography, the researcher studies collected documents and narratives to trace evidence of the personal experiences or "self-stories" contained within these documents. In this case, Nightingale's 13 formal letters to her nurses are complex documents—documents that weave in her own life stories and circumstances—that are analyzed in Chapter 2. (The complete collection of these letters is included in this book, beginning on page 203.) I also engaged my ability to probe, capture, and make sense of problematic passages that seemed unrelated to the previous paragraphs or section header, or her use of bullets, dashes, and unusual sentence structure and punctuation such as short dashes, underlined words, extra commas, semicolons, and colons.

Stories always exist in multiple versions, with various beginnings and endings. They are focused and grounded in a cultural context. Stories change over time, and a story told one way may appear in a different form with a different ending in another circumstance. Ideological forces always shape stories, as they place pressure on individuals to establish their individuality in the stories that they construct. In these formal letters Nightingale not only told stories, but she also placed stories upon stories and stories within stories. She also wrote her own self-narrative within these documents. She pours out her inner self to herself, and to her nurses who were in training or those nurses who had already graduated and were present at the formal reading of each letter. Her words of kindness, passion, worry, fear, and guidance from the Divine are apparent in each letter.

Epiphanies

Epiphanies are those interactional moments and experiences that leave marks on an individual's lived experience. They are existential events where the fundamental structure of one's life is forever changed. They may take the form such as an encounter with another, or about a crisis. Denzin (1989) identifies four types of epiphanies: (1) a major event, (2) a representative event, (3) a minor epiphany, and (4) the reliving of an experience.

The first type of epiphany, a major event, is one that touches the core or fabric of an individual's life. The second type of epiphany, the representative or cumulative event, is one that signifies reactions or eruptions to experiences that have been going on for a long period of time. The third type, a minor epiphany, is experienced in a problematic moment in a person's life or relationship. The fourth type, the reliving of an experience, is what gives meaning to one or all of the other types of epiphanies.

For Nightingale, her major epiphany was hearing the voice of God at age 16, and then trying to find ways to be of service in her work and life. She struggled into her mid-twenties before she realized that her work would be nursing. The first Pentimento in Chapter 2 examined her awakening on February 7, 1837, her Call from God. The other Pentimento in Chapter 2, and those in Chapters 3 and 4, explore other driving events, epiphanies, and forces in her work; for example, the influences of writings of the medieval mystics, or when her family and friends urged her to give up her passion for nursing, and not work so continuously.

Cultural Context of Representing Lives

The intent of an interpretive biography is to uncover the social, economic, cultural, structural, and historical factors and forces that shape, change, and distort lived experiences of an individual. In uncovering new meaning, the subjectivity must not be romanticized, but the researcher must keep a focus on the individual being studied and what structures shaped her or his lived experience. A person's life story is never developed in a vacuum or in isolation. It is worked out through a larger culture and historical context of people, events, and crises.

For Nightingale, her 90-year and three-month life (1820–1910) spanned an age that followed the turbulent times of the 18th century and the Industrial Revolution. Her time included much of the 19th century and its Victorian era (1837–1901), in which political, social, cultural, educational, religious, medical, nursing, media, public health, business, and other societal structures and rules were being developed throughout the British Empire and, indeed, the entire Western world. Nightingale even lived 10 years into the 20th century, a critical transitional decade. The chaotic, dynamic, and complex interactions of England's involvement throughout the British Empire had a huge impact on the world.

Nightingale was a major change agent and leader in many of these areas starting with her appointment as the first nurse superintendent of Female Nurses in the British army in Turkey and later in the Crimea during the Crimean War (1854–1856). This was followed by her return to England, her meeting with Queen Victoria, and her writing several thousand-page documents and preparing of the witnesses for the Royal Commissions on the investigation of the problem during the Crimean War. Next came her participation in the reorganizing of the British Army Medical Department, the creation of the first Army Medical School, and the educating of five viceroys to India on the health of the army in India from 1857 to 1890. All of this paralleled her work with the Nightingale School from 1860 to 1900, and other areas of nursing and social reform (as detailed in Table 1-2 on page 12). Her influence can be traced in the 14,000 letters that she wrote; her vision for a healthy world can be found in her books, booklets, monographs, pamphlets, letters, meetings, and correspondence with the most famous politicians, kings, queens, princes, princesses, presidents, and other prominent people of that time throughout the world.

In effect, Nightingale left her legacy for us to unravel and to reweave new meaning for today's turbulent times. Her stories are a continuation of all those other stories that came before. Her legacy and stories have come into our lifetime; our task is to revisit her work and to find new meaning for contemporary nursing that can have a positive impact on not only the nursing profession but other health professionals, and for health and healing throughout the world.

Applying the Interpretive Biographical Method to Nightingale's 13 Letters

The researcher enters into an interpretive circle and must be faithful to the subject, both apart from and within the research. Such was my journey during all phases of the analysis of Nightingale's 13 formal letters. I also was aware of the ethical considerations of historical research. I followed sections of the *American Historical Association Statement on Standards of Professional Conduct* (American Historical Association, 1998). This research did not involve the study of personal or clinical aspects of living individuals; therefore, no informed consent was required.

Biographies are narrative expressions of a person's life experiences that shape how lives are told and written in nine areas. The following nine areas show how the interpretive process creates and shapes how stories are told and written (Denzin, 1989):

1. *The existence of other/s* — The "existence of other," for Florence Nightingale, was always God, who helped shape her vision of healing, life mission, and purpose. God's laws and principles in nature were a constant for her. She believed that human beings must understand God's laws in nature in order to maintain health. She wrote in the first-person voice about her relationship with God.
2. *Gender and class* — In Nightingale's life, gender and class were central issues. Patriarchy dominated the time in which she lived, and Nightingale had to overcome male biases and values as a wealthy, upper-class Victorian woman. Her family expected her to never work, and to marry into wealth and high society. Yet on two occasions she refused serious proposals for marriage in order to serve God. Nightingale broke the glass ceiling and functioned in a man's world at a time when only one other woman, Queen Victoria, was doing so at the level in which Nightingale was engaged.
3. *Family observations* — Family gave depth to Nightingale's life. She had to fight her family to find her chosen work. In particular, her mother and older sister were always conscious of the proper Victorian, upper-class way of being and doing. For Nightingale, this was unbearable. Finally, when she was in her late teens, she learned to be comfortable in a man's world through her home education taught by her father, who had a classical Cambridge education, as well as through lengthy dialogues with him about all of the conventions of the day. Both of her parents came from a Unitarian background: 19th-century Unitarians rejected both the divinity of Christ and the Trinity (Father, Son, and Holy Spirit). They used human reason and

conscience rather than the literal interpretation of the Bible to set their course. Other major doctrines that they questioned were sin, atonement, the last judgment, and eternal damnation. Nightingale's grandfather, William Smith, was a prominent Unitarian in the Parliament who secured civil and legal rights for non-Anglican Protestants, Catholics, and Jews. In 1813, he convinced Parliament to pass the Unitarian Toleration Act that made denying the divinity of Christ no longer a crime. (Although Nightingale was raised in the Anglican Church because her mother felt it was socially more acceptable, Nightingale held firm to many Unitarian beliefs.)

4. *Starting points* — A biographical text always has a starting point. This means that the biographical genre begins with and includes the knowledge that lives have beginnings in families. Thus, a biographical text most often begins with a family history.
5. *Knowing authors and observers* — This aspect of interpretive biography presumes that the "outside" observer is deeply engaged in the process. As a scholar, I was faithful to this description during all phases of the study.
6. *Objective life markers* — Objective life markers are critical points about the person being studied that create a real world that can be mapped, charted, and given meaning. For Nightingale, one of the first objective markers was her awakening, the first phase of mystic spiritual development. She recorded hearing the voice of God on February 7, 1837. This was the first significant call from God, which was followed by three more during her life. She wrote about these events in diaries throughout her lifetime. These are just a few markers that gave coherence to her life and were the driving force in her mystic spiritual development.
7. *Real persons and real lives* —The person's life is told through stories that reveal the character of the person, and human emotions such as love, hate, anger, despair, and caring concern for others and society. This is the "real" subject of the biographical method.
8. *Turning-point experiences* — Many of Nightingale's turning-point experiences flowed out of her early learning and interactions with her father and other leading thinkers of the day, such as politicians and theologians. As she grew older, she had lengthy conversations with the Broad Church members, a group of liberal Anglicans who stressed the ethical dimensions of Christianity. This group believed that universal spiritual truths had been given to humanity throughout history. The Broad Church differed from the Anglican Church on many theological issues and held to their belief in freedom of inquiry. She had a 30-year spiritual relationship with one of the leading Broad Church members, Benjamin Jowett, the Master at Balliol College at Oxford and a Greek scholar, who gave her the sacraments on a regular basis. They exchanged letters and conversations on the topic of religion and spirituality until his death in 1893. Nightingale's belief was that "unless you make a life which shall be the manifestation of your religion, it does not much signify what you believe" (Macrae, 2001).
9. *Truthful statements* — Characterizing a statement as "truthful"(and as distinguished from fictional statements) suggests that facts about a person's life are factually correct, that is "truth-like." However, as the picture of a "real" person is being told or written, it is important to remember that the "real person may alter the facts"; for example, as Nightingale records her story, or as the storyteller or researcher records her story, the focus may be on certain parts to make the story more interesting. It is also important to remember that the person writing a biography writes himself or herself into the life of the subject about whom he or she is writing. This is also true of the reader who reads a biographical text; the text is read through the person's life.

Interpretive Format

An interpretive work may take one of three forms (Denzin, 1989):

- The first is from the subject's point of view without interpretation by the researcher.
- The second format is subject-produced forms that rely upon the subject's perspective and are often written by the subject. These are then used for psychological, sociological, or anthropological interpretive purposes.
- The third approach is to weave the subject's life into and through the researcher's interpretations of that life, with the intent to make sense of the life; however, it is not for sociological or anthropological purposes.

This study used the third approach. My process was to establish some of the ways that Nightingale gave meaning and coherence to the period of her life from 1872 to 1900, and to determine the place that her 13 formal letters to her nurses had in this period and their relevance for contemporary nursing. These written narratives are part of the coherence that she left behind for today and beyond. The structure and underlying complexities within these letters were uncovered as I attempted to interpret Nightingale's meanings by reading these documents and placing them within the context of her lived experience and the circumstances that she faced in these years. It is the unraveling process whereby the researcher finds the relationship of the individual to the works being studied. It is to discover meaning within the documents that give meaning to a situation and to pivotal events in the person's lived experience.

Approach and Setting for Reading Primary Documents

After my previous research on the life of Florence Nightingale (B. Dossey, 2000), I was very aware of her health challenges with her chronic illness during these years (see the Pentimento on this subject on page 90), as well as the political, societal, public health, medical, nursing, educational, and Indian reform issues in which she was engaged. I was aware of Nightingale's role in developing the first secular nursing school, the politics of the Nightingale school, the key leaders who found bright women to enter the nursing profession, her various projects resulting in lengthy papers including applied statistics, and her laying the foundation for collaboration with other schools of nursing, all of which enhanced my understanding of her letters.

Several other experiences were always present with me while reading and rereading these letters. From my Nightingale archival photograph collection and many visits to the Florence Nightingale Museum in London, I was aware of what she looked like during these years. I knew the physical layout of her sitting room and bedroom, and I had seen many of her personal possessions. I also had a recording of her voice that I had listened to many times: on June 30, 1890, 12 years after Thomas Edison invented his phonograph, his assistant in London, Colonel George Gouraud, made a 41-second recording of Nightingale's voice at her home on South Street. I also had clear and accurate pictures in my mind of other settings; specific faces of nurses in their uniforms; and other individuals, situations, and scenes that she described in her letters. I also knew that these letters were read aloud by Sir Harry Verney to all the nurses in training, or those who had graduated from the Nightingale School. I imagined hearing him bringing greetings from Nightingale, and being among these nurses in their lovely, starched uniforms to hear her words.

After 1872, when Nightingale began to meet with her nurses one at a time, she is said to have talked with her hands to tell stories and to gain information from her nurses. Letters and biographies indicate that when she greeted a person, Nightingale would often extend her hands outward, draw the person near, and kiss the person's forehead. I have often imagined what it would be like to meet Nightingale after hearing the reading of a letter, and then to have her ask my opinion about some of the concepts.

Steps in Analysis of Primary Documents

Prior to reading copies of these 13 formal letters, I was aware that the letters contained some of Nightingale's thoughts on spirituality. I had no other preconceived ideas of what I would find. For this analysis, over a three-week period, I first read the letters slowly, in a quiet, meditative place within my home, with moving lips, in the same way that words and letters were always read by followers of medieval mystics (Lachman, 1993). On this first reading of the letters I did not take notes or mark on any of the study documents. It was merely a reflection period. It was important that I become centered and be fully present with my intention for reading these archival documents in their proper context: a mystic writing to her followers. Reading her words carefully and clearly allowed me to be brought into the present moment. It was like the pure sound of a ringing bell, or a beam of bright light shining to let her wisdom and message of universal truth and God/Life Force/Absolute/Transcendent resonate within me. I must say there were several passages where I was surprised when I read her words, "And I will whisper in your ears a little secret. …" It was as if she was speaking these words, and I was deeply touched.

After the initial reading of all the letters, the next step was to read each letter three times, at three different readings. This was done over a three-month period so that I could keep enough psychological and intellectual distance from the documents. As I immersed myself in reading Nightingale's 13 letters, I spiraled down to the essence of the message contained within them.

These documents were both typeset and handwritten; they varied in length from 4 to 19 pages. The typeset letters were on 8" by 11" paper in a font similar to Times, and the text was set in font size 10 with references in font sizes 8 and 9. Two handwritten letters were on 8" by 11" paper, and two letters were on 7" by 10" paper. The handwritten letters show Nightingale's characteristic, flowing script in a staccato, rhythmic fashion that galloped across the pages, with many exclamation marks, quotes, bullets, underlines, and specific concepts, key points, and marginal notes underlined.

Before reading each letter, I first reflected on Nightingale's nursing and social reform (again, see Table 1-2 on page 12) and the major events in her life during that year, to establish a context for her examples and her focus for each letter. I was highlighting and making notes, so the first reading took one to three hours for each of the handwritten and shorter letters, and four to six hours to read the longer letters. On the second reading, the time was two hours on the shorter letters and three to four hours on the longer letters. The third reading took one to two hours for each letter.

At each reading I used a different highlighter color to signify key words, ideas, insights, and concepts. I also used a lined legal pad divided into three columns to determine what new thoughts, words, and concepts might emerge at each first reading. I made notes in my journal at each reading. I also reflected on the meanings of stories, metaphors, symbols, images, parables, representations, accounts, situations, people, and events about which Nightingale wrote.

There were significant additions from the first to the second reading, and minimal additions between the second and third reading. Each reading allowed me to revise, delete, or add additional reflections, ideas, or words as I took into consideration the other events that were moving in parallel to her nursing and social reform and other work. It also enhanced my intuition and creativity, as well as my rational and analytical response to the letters. After the third reading, I began a thoughtful study of all the words, concepts, insights, and reflections from these three rounds. My conclusions from this interpretive biographical study can be found at the end of Chapter 2.

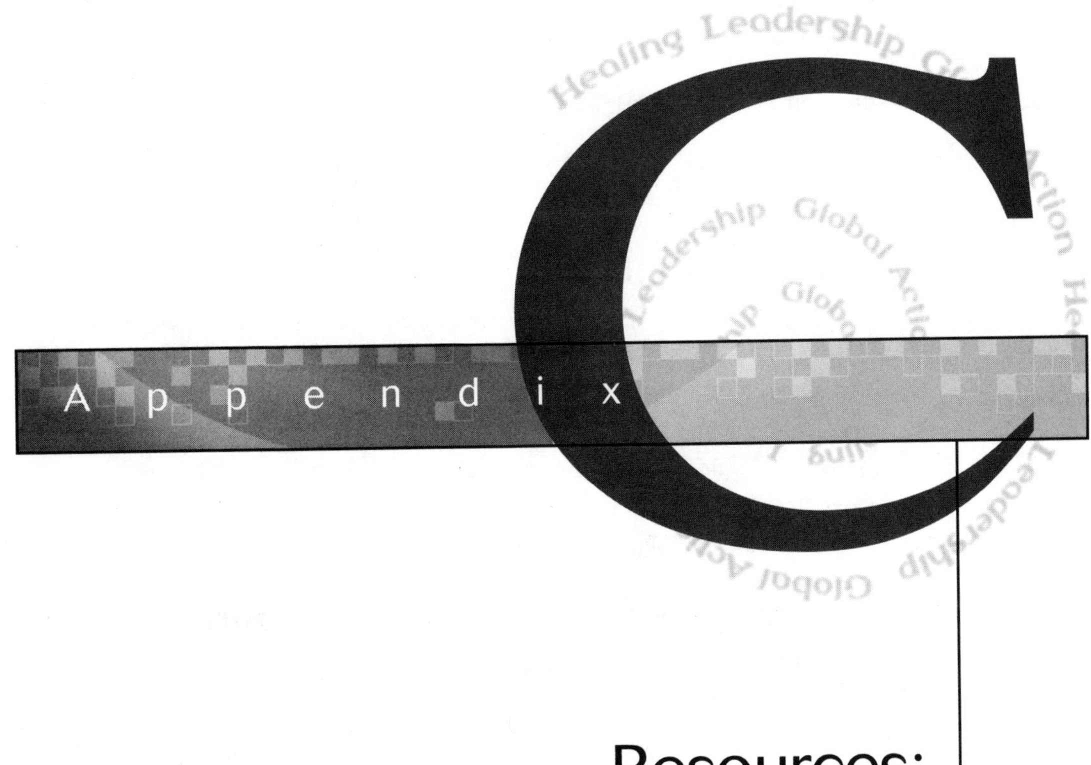

Appendix C

Resources: Florence Nightingale Today and Tomorrow

We hope that many of our readers have become as excited and motivated by discovering (or rediscovering) Florence Nightingale as we the authors find ourselves at the end of writing this book. If so, we hope you will find these resources help you to further your journey into the heart of nursing and health care.

The Florence Nightingale Museum

The Florence Nightingale Museum conserves and displays a unique collection of Florence Nightingale's personal possessions, artifacts connected with her nursing and humanitarian work in the Crimean War, and nursing material from the Nightingale Training School from 1860.

The museum is at St. Thomas' Hospital in central London, on the south bank of the River Thames. Although the buildings are new, this is the historical location of the nurse training school that was established by Florence Nightingale.

Over a quarter of a million people have visited the museum since it opened in 1989, and its displays have won several awards. An international focus for all nurses with an interest in their professional heritage, it is an active educational center with programs for young and old alike. The museum's Resource Center enables researchers to access the museum's collections, and the expert staff members provide advice and guidance on the many other collections of Nightingale material scattered around the world.

The conservational and educational objectives of the museum are overseen by 10 volunteer trustees: they are planning for expansion of a new Florence Nightingale Museum, guided by a vision that will communicate to a wider public the many remarkable achievements of Florence Nightingale. What she accomplished remains remarkably fresh and relevant to today's world; her writings on health promotion, caring for the sick, and hospital planning and management alone can enrich the thinking of nurses who share her goals of helping people live healthier lives.

Florence Nightingale Museum
Gassiot House
St. Thomas' Hospital
2 Lambeth Palace Road
London SE1 7EW
United Kingdom

Telephone: +44 20 7620 0374
Fax: +44 20 7928 1760
E-mail: info@florence-nightingale.co.uk

For full details on the museum, see the web site:
www.florence-nightingale.co.uk

The Collected Works of Florence Nightingale

The *Collected Works of Florence Nightingale* will make available for the first time all the available surviving writings of Florence Nightingale.

Sixteen printed volumes are scheduled, including Nightingale's major published books, articles, and pamphlets (many long out of print), and a vast amount of heretofore unpublished correspondence and notes. Extensive databases, notably a chronology and an index of names, and the original, unedited, transcriptions will also be published in electronic form. This will permit convenient access to scholars interested not only in Nightingale but in other major figures of her time.

Original material has been obtained from some 200 archives and private collections worldwide. There is much new material in all the areas of her life and work: four volumes on religion, two on her family and early travels; two each on India, war, and nursing; and one each on society and politics, public health care, women, and hospital reform. The volumes show Nightingale's careful methodology, high standards of scholarship, and linguistic abilities. They reveal as well her ability to draw on a wide range of expertise to formulate reform plans and an astute use of the political process to achieve them.

Not only is much of the material new, that is, not previously known to scholars, there is much to upset standard interpretations of Nightingale's life and work. Much of the published work on Nightingale has been based only on secondary sources or, at best, a limited viewing of the vast amount of original sources that exist but are not easily accessible.

Four of the volumes deal with health care, beginning with Volume 6, *On Public Health Care*, two on nursing, and one on hospital reform (these three to be published later in the series).

On Public Health Care reports Nightingale's considerable accomplishments in the development of a public healthcare system based on health promotion and disease prevention. It follows directly from her understanding of social science and broader social reform activities related in *Society and Politics. On Public Health Care* includes a critical edition of *Notes on Nursing for the Labouring Classes*, papers on mortality in aboriginal schools and hospitals, her "Sick Nursing and Health Nursing," given at the Chicago Exposition in 1893, and later short papers on rural health.

On Public Health Care also includes much unknown material on Nightingale's signal contribution of bringing professional nursing into the dreaded workhouse infirmaries. It publishes letters and notes on a wide range of issues from specific diseases to germ theory, and relates some of her own extensive work as a nurse practitioner, organizing referrals to doctors, and providing related care. Here Nightingale's opposition to germ theory is evident, as is her considerable expertise as a practitioner dealing effectively with infectious diseases.

The series is published by Wilfrid Laurier University Press, a Canadian academic press. All volumes are peer reviewed. Volumes presently available are:

Volume 1 Florence Nightingale: An Introduction to Her Life and Family, 2001

Volume 2 Florence Nightingale's Spiritual Journey: Biblical Annotations, Sermons and Journal Notes, 2002

Volume 3 Florence Nightingale's Theology: Essays, Letters and Journal Notes, 2002

Volume 4 Florence Nightingale on Mysticism and Eastern Religions, 2003

Volume 5 Florence Nightingale on Society and Politics, Philosophy, Science, Education and Literature, 2003

Volume 6 Florence Nightingale on Public Health Care, 2004

Still in preparation are these:

Volume 7 Florence Nightingale's European Travels, 2005

Volume 8 Florence Nightingale on Women, Medicine, Midwifery and Prostitution

Volume 9 Florence Nightingale's Suggestions for Thought

Volume 10/11 Florence Nightingale and the Foundation of Professional Nursing

Volume 12/13 Florence Nightingale and Public Health Care in India

Volume 14 Florence Nightingale: the Crimean War and War Office Reform

Volume 15 Florence Nightingale on War and Militarism

Volume 16 Florence Nightingale and Hospital Reform

The series editor and project director is Lynn McDonald, Professor of Sociology at the University of Guelph, Ontario. She has a PhD from the London School of Economics and has published extensively on sociological theory and women theorists. McDonald has herself been a public health advocate. As a Member of the Canadian Parliament she succeeded in getting the Non-smokers' Health Act adopted in 1988 as a private member's bill. It not only made Parliamentary history but it made Canada a leader in the "tobacco wars." A well-known women's advocate, McDonald was president of the largest women's organization in Canada and was the first "Ms." in the House of Commons.

For information on the project see the website:
www.sociology.uoguelph.ca/fnightingale
For orders in the United States and Canada contact Wilfrid Laurier University Press
Fax: (519) 725-1399
Email: press@wlu.ca
Website: www.wlupress.wlu.ca

For orders in the UK and elsewhere contact:
Wilfrid Laurier University Press
c/o Gazelle Book Services Ltd.
White Cross Mills, High Town
Lancaster LA1 4XS, UK
Tel: 00 44 (O)1524 68765
Fax: 00 44 (0)1524 63232
Email: orders@gazellebooks.co.uk

Essential Books for the Nightingale Scholar

While the Collected Works project noted above will eventually publish all of Nightingale's writings, the following books are those that readers inclined to a serious study of this eminent Victorian life should read. While those with an astrisk are out of print, they are still worth tracking down.

Baly, M. (1995). *Nursing and social change.* 3rd edition. New York: Routledge.

Baly, M. (1998). *Florence Nightingale and the nursing legacy: Building the foundations of modern nursing and midwifery*. 2nd edition. Philadelphia: Trans-Atlantic Books. (This same title was published in the UK in 1997 by Whurr.)

Bishop, W., & S. Goldie (1962). *A bio-bibliography of Florence Nightingale.* London: Dawsons of Pall Mall.*

Calabria, M., & J. Macrae (eds.). (1994). *Suggestions for thought by Florence Nightingale: Suggestions and commentaries.* Philadelphia: University of Pennsylvania Press.

Cook, E. (1913). *The Life of Florence Nightingale.* (Vols. I and II). London: Macmillan and Co., Limited.*

Dossey, B. (2000). *Florence Nightingale: Mystic, visionary, healer*. Philadelphia, PA: Lippincott, Williams, & Wilkins.

Gill, G. (2004). *Nightingales: The extraordinary upbringing and curious life of Miss Florence Nightingale*. New York: Ballentine Books.

Goldie, S. (ed.). (1987). *"I have done my duty": Florence Nightingale in the Crimean War 1854–56.* Manchester: Manchester University Press.

Herbert, R. (1981). *Florence Nightingale: Saint, reformer or rebel?* Malabar, FL: Robert F. Krieger Publishing.

Nightingale, F. (1859). *Notes on hospitals.* London: John W. Parker.

Nightingale, F. (1860). *Notes on nursing: What it is and what it is not*. London: Harrison.

Sattin, A. (ed.). (1987.) *Letters from Egypt: A Journey on the Nile 1849–1850 by Florence Nightingale.* New York: Grove Press.

Seymer, L. (ed.). (1954). *Selected writings of Florence Nightingale*. New York: The Macmillan Co.*

Skretkowicz, V. (1996). *Florence Nightingale's Notes on Nursing.* London: Baillere Tindall.

Small, H. (1998). *Florence Nightngale: Avenging angel*. London: Constable.

O'Malley, I. (1932). *Florence Nightingale 1820–1856: A study of her life down to the end of the Crimean War.* London: Thornton Butterworth, Ltd.*

Vicinus, M., & B. Nergaard (1990). *Ever yours, Florence Nightingale: Selected letters.* Cambridge, MA: Harvard University Press.

Woodham-Smith, C. (1951). *Florence Nightingale: A biography*. New York: McGraw-Hill.*

Nursing Theory—The website of the library of the Cardinal Stritch University offers an annotated nursing theory bibliography that covers the work of the major nurse theoreticians, many of whom are mentioned in Chapter 5, "Leading Through Theory." Titled "Models and Theories of Nursing," it is available in two forms:

- An extensive HTML file: http://library.stritch.edu/nursingtheroies/nursingtheories.htm
- A PDF document of the same material and hot links as the HTML file: http://library.stritch.edu/pdfs/NursingTheory.pdf

Global Action Internet Resources

In addition to two key international nursing sites that have useful global health action information—the **International Council of Nurses** at **www.icn.ch** and Sigma Theta Tau's **Nursing Knowledge International** at **www.nursingknowledge.org/Portal/main.aspx**—the following sites have been selected to assist readers in gaining a sense of programs that are actively and effectively serving global health with a civil society, global citizenship approach.

Rotary International is a global network of community volunteers. It is a worldwide organization of business and professional leaders that provides humanitarian service—focusing on health, literacy, and education—and encourages high ethical standards in all vocations, helping to build goodwill and peace in the world. Approximately 1.2 million Rotarians belong to more than 31,000 Rotary clubs located in 166 countries. **www.rotary.org/index.html**

Global Health educator, advocate and consultant **Ilona Kickbusch** has an excellent website that covers many key interrelated issues. **www.ilonakickbusch.com/home/index.shtml**

Healthlink Worldwide works to improve the health and well-being of disadvantaged and vulnerable communities in developing countries, working with partners in Africa, Asia, Latin America, and the Middle East. Partnerships seek to strengthen the local provision, use, and impact of health communication and to support advocacy initiatives to increase local participation and inclusion. **www.healthlink.org.uk/**

People's Health Movement objectives include: to hear the unheard; to reinforce the principle of health as a broad cross-cutting issue; to formulate a People's Health Charter; and to share and increase knowledge, skills, motivation, and advocacy for change. **www.phmovement.org/**

Global Health Watch mobilizes civil society around the world with an alternative (to WHO) World Health Report. A platform for the strengthening of advocacy and campaigns to promote equitable health for all. **www.ghwatch.org/**

International Women's Health Coalition works to generate health and population policies, programs, and funding that promote and protect the rights and health of girls and women worldwide, particularly in Africa, Asia, and Latin America. **www.iwhc.org/**

The International Federation of Red Cross and Red Crescent Societies is the world's largest humanitarian organization. Founded in 1919, the International Federation comprises 181 member Red Cross and Red Crescent societies, including the American Red Cross. The Red Crescent is used in place of the Red Cross in many Islamic countries. The Federation's mission is to improve the lives of vulnerable people by mobilizing the power of humanity through providing assistance without discrimination as to nationality, race, religious beliefs, class, or political opinions. **www.ifrc/org/**

The following two websites have provide excellent link listings for Canadian health and global health sites of all kinds:

- Canadian Society for International Health. **www.csih.org/links.html**
- Website for Women's Health.
  www-unix.umbc.edu/~korenman/wmst/links_hlth.html

The new **Nightingale Initiative for Global Health (NIGH),** developed by the authors of this book (see below for details), seeks to enlist and enable nurses and other healthcare workers and educators to work together toward the adoption of a universal plan of action declaring a healthy world as the priority global goal. **www.FlorenceNightingale2010.net**

The Nightingale Initiative for Global Health (NIGH)

This section was written by the NIGH board of directors effective September 2004.

Vision

The Nightingale Initiative for Global Health (NIGH) envisions a healthy world for all peoples.

Mission

NIGH seeks to achieve a healthy world by:

- Enabling peoples of the United Nations, as citizens of its Member States, to work together in a worldwide campaign for health as the top global priority;
- Enlisting nurses and other healthcare workers and educators to work together effectively in mobilizing public opinion to this purpose; and
- Encouraging individual initiative and cooperative action toward these ends by highlighting the life of Florence Nightingale and the lives other nurses and healthcare workers—past and present—who have devoted themselves to building a healthy world.

Goals

- To build a grassroots movement among nurses, healthcare workers, educators, and other global citizens—from every country and community—who will work together to inform, educate, and mobilize public opinion throughout the world toward the adoption of health as the universal priority of the United Nations and its Member States;
- To use communications, media, and promotional tools for advocacy to these ends;
- To identify, share, and actively encourage approaches that work to create a healthy world; and
- To contribute positive solutions to the worldwide nursing shortage.

Initial Strategies

To create real projects from the above vision, mission, and goals, we are developing and implementing several initial interrelated strategies. These include:

- Preparing for:
  - two United Nations General Assembly Resolutions to be voted upon in 2007,
  - the United Nations International Year of the Nurse in 2010, and
  - the United Nations Decade for a Healthy World, 2010–2020;
- Empowering nurses around the world as leaders of a grassroots global campaign to circulate "The Nightingale Declaration for Our Healthy World" as a universal Signature Campaign to be organized for early 2007. (The draft text of the Declaration is included below.)
- Convening key NIGH consultations in the United States, Canada, and Europe, including London, Geneva, Copenhagen, Oslo, and Helsinki, with potential collaborators from Asia, Africa, the South Pacific, Central and South America, and the Middle East, as well as those from the U.S. and Canada;
- Establishing sites and contact persons for the initial network of regional NIGH Communities around the world, creating related NIGH Resources Files and identifying contacts and themes for each File;

- Designing, publishing, and circulating a print tabloid to establish an ongoing global circulation to highlight major world health issues, key aspects of the NIGH plans, and news of exemplary "local best practices that create a healthy world";
- Preparing to convene the first international conference of NIGH, as early as late 2005, proposed site, Nairobi, Kenya:
  - to focus on global health issues in the African context,
  - to specifically enable nursing students from around the world to return with communication skills in print and broadcast media, public speaking, networking, and promotional advocacy as well as group leadership; and
  - to establish worldwide video-conferencing capacity;
- Developing and implementing plans for related educational and media programs in a variety of formats, including on-site workshops and a major Internet presence; and
- Participating in key conferences between 2004 and 2009.

Staying Connected and Updated about NIGH

The NIGH idea was birthed by communities through discussions among the four authors of this book and their colleagues with extensive experience in nursing education, in international media and development fields, as well as in business, education, and medicine. While the above range of experience is a good way to birth such an idea, we are also clear that the only way NIGH can successfully grow—at any level of this vision—is with the enthusiastic participation of many people with many talents, across the globe. From the very beginning of these endeavors, we are encouraging the start-up of NIGH throughout the world as soon as initial point persons who wish to join this project can be identified.

Wherever you are in the world, we welcome you to join these endeavors. To discuss the possibilities, please call us, leave a voice-mail message detailing your name, phone number, and the best times to reach you, and we will call you to discuss the possibilities. As of October 2004, our start-up office phone numbers are: in Canada (613) 990-1114 at Global Forum and NIGH International, and in the United States (703) 892-6665 at NIGH (USA). To begin the launch of this project, these two initial organizations have been formed, NIGH (International), based in Ottawa, Canada, and NIGH (USA), based in Washington, D.C.

To obtain regular updates regarding the progress of the NIGH and to contact us by email, check our website at www.FlorenceNightingale2010.net. If you wish to be on our print mailing list, let us know by sending us a postcard with your name and full mailing address to:

NIGH International at the Global Forum
347 Croil Street
Ottawa, Ontario, Canada, K1V 1J4.

These above addresses and numbers will be updated from time to time, and we will be adding additional contact information and phone numbers as new NIGH Communities are established around the world. Be sure to check our website for current information.

Nightingale: The Declaration for Our Healthy World

The following is NIGH's draft The Nightingale Declaration for Our Healthy World, which is being developed to be circulated and signed by millions of nurses, healthcare professionals, and other caregivers around the world in 2007, and in advance of the proposed United Nations General Assembly Resolutions for an International Year of the Nurse in 2010 and a United Nations Decade for a Healthy World, 2010–2020.

We, the nurses, health workers, and caregivers of the world, as peoples of the United Nations and citizens of its Member States, hereby dedicate ourselves to the accomplishment of a healthy world by the year 2020.

We declare our willingness to unite in a program of action, sharing information and solutions to resolve problems and improve conditions—locally, nationally, and globally—in order to achieve health for all humanity.

We further resolve to adopt personal practices and to implement public policies in our communities and nations, making this goal for the year 2020 achievable and inevitable, beginning today in our own lives, in the life of our nations, and in the world at large.

Practical Mysticism

The term *practical mysticism* refers to the experience of a mystic—someone whose direct experience of God and the divine reveals the presence of the divine everywhere—whose sense of spirituality and action are so mutual and integrated as to be impossible to distinguish the two. Not only is the practical mystic a contemplative who is engaged in the "outer" (sociopolitical) world, but one who whose engaged activity derives much of its power from that mystical experience. The term takes much of its meaning from the title of a 1915 book by scholar Evelyn Underhill, *Practical Mysticism*, in which she examines the Western mystical tradition. (In this book, the author refers to Florence Nightingale as "one of the most balanced contemplatives of the 19th century.")

While self-educated in theology and spirituality, Underhill also combined a deep appreciation of the various paths to God, a scholar's drive to unearth the roots of all religious traditions, and a remarkable ability to communicate with a wide range of readers. Her appeal also lies in the fact that she lived, by all accounts, a "modern" life very much like our own. After her death in 1941, *The Times of London* noted Underhill's "insight into the meaning both of the culture and the individual groping of the soul, that was unmatched by any professional teacher of her day." Her classic work, *Mysticism,* has remained in print since its first edition in 1911. Thus, learning more about Evelyn Underhill is a good way to better understand the Christian expressions of the timeless ways of practical mysticism.

One way to get quickly oriented to this remarkable woman is the website of the Evelyn Underhill Society: www.evelynunderhill.org/. Even though there is no sign of new content since early 2003, all that is there is active, comprising an excellent and comprehensive overview of her life and work. In the context of this book, two articles (in the section Articles on the Life and Work of Evelyn Underhill) are particularly relevant:

- Grace Adolphsen Brame (1990). Evelyn Underhill and the Mastery of Time
- Dana Greene (1987). Adhering to God: The Message of Evelyn Underhill for Our Time

The opening line of the Greene article particularly resonates with this book: "Biography has power to move, inspire, and provoke. It provides a model of personal integration, and in times like our own when the sense of the world's complexity and the loss of shared meaning cripple us, the individual attempt to make sense of life has great appeal."

A site written and maintained by an individual (Robert Woodward) contains online copies of many of Underhill's writings: http://homepages.ihug.co.nz/~dcandmkw/spirit/uhill.htm.

Another site that might help readers is the Spiritual Experience section of the website of the Council on Spiritual Practices (www.csp.org/experience/), which reflects extra-Christian perspectives on this concept. Under Writings on that page, readers will find three of the included articles to be especially relevant to the topics in this book:

- The two 1999 pieces by Wayne Teasdale: The Interspiritual Age: Practical Mysticism for the Third Millennium, and Mysticism as the Crossing of Ultimate Boundaries.
- David Steindl-Rast's 1989 essay, The Mystical Core of Organized Religion: A Theological Reflection.

Other more contemporary (and extra-Christian) senses of the term certainly exist. Some have characterized the Vietnamese-born monk Thich Nhat Hanh, the leading figure in the Engaged Buddhism movement, as a practical mystic, and others likewise identify His Holiness the Dalai Lama and other Tibetan Buddhists.

Other Resources

Each nurse is challenged to go light her or his own world, and collectively we become the "return of the Nightingales," those who will bring caring healing, leadership, and global action to the Earth. These two songs below, each sung or spoken by a nurse, are inspiring.

- Go Light Your World, recorded by Dee Jones
  www.cdbaby.com/deejones

- Return of the Nightingale™: A Tribute to Nurses
  Recorded by Jill L. Schumacher. Music, lyrics, and vocals by Jill Schumacher
  Spoken words by Meredith A. McCord
  www.returnofthenightingale.com
  Email: nursehealer@returnofthenightingale.com

To celebrate the passion of nursing, see the Florence Nightingale Silver Commemorative Coin.

www.returnofthenightingale.com
Email: nursehealer@returnofthenightingale.com

nurseradio.org

This nonprofit Internet radio station is dedicated to supporting the voices of and for contemporary nursing, providing in-depth interviews with nurse leaders and nurse healers. This programming is supported by members of the American Holistic Nurses Association, other nursing and healthcare organizations, and nurses across the United States. This programming is available worldwide, year-round, 24 hours daily, via streaming audio.

http://nurseradio.org/nurseradio/

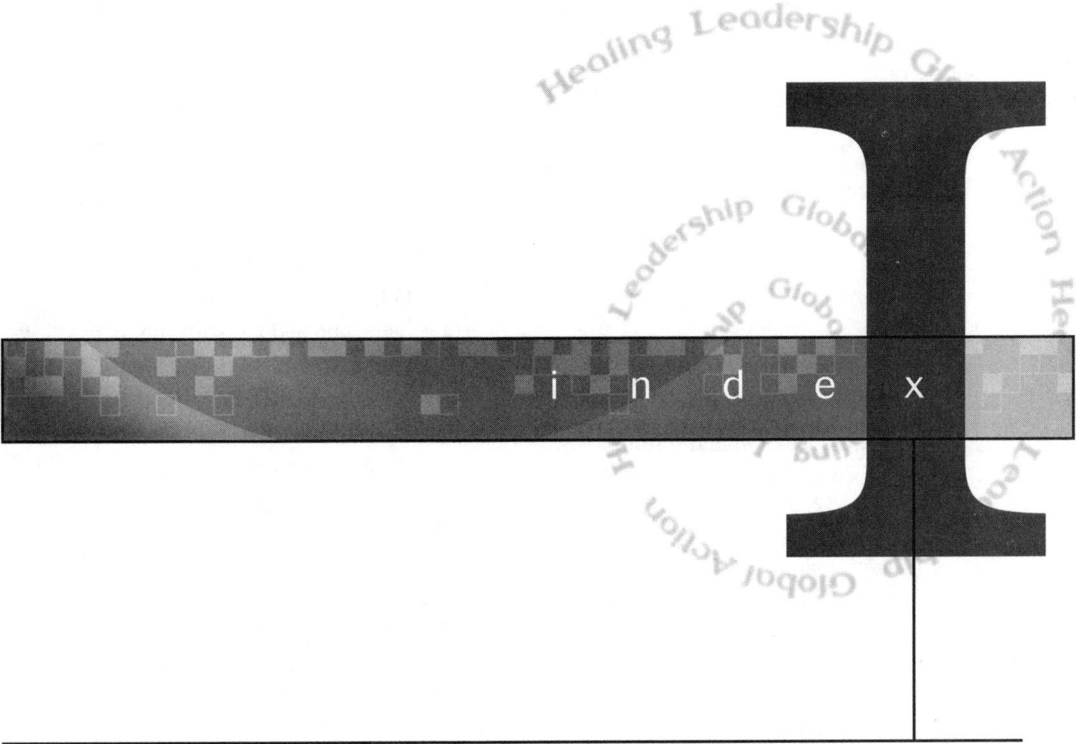

Index

A

B

C

D

M

N

P